M000222642

King, Governance, and Law in Ancient India

King, Governance, and Law in Ancient India

Kauṭilya's Arthaśāstra

A New Annotated Translation by

PATRICK OLIVELLE

OXFORD
UNIVERSITY PRESS

OXFORD
UNIVERSITY PRESS

Oxford University Press is a department of the University of Oxford.
It furthers the University's objective of excellence in research, scholarship,
and education by publishing worldwide.

Oxford New York
Auckland Cape Town Dar es Salaam Hong Kong Karachi
Kuala Lumpur Madrid Melbourne Mexico City Nairobi
New Delhi Shanghai Taipei Toronto

With offices in
Argentina Austria Brazil Chile Czech Republic France Greece
Guatemala Hungary Italy Japan Poland Portugal Singapore
South Korea Switzerland Thailand Turkey Ukraine Vietnam

Published in the United States of America by
Oxford University Press
198 Madison Avenue, New York, NY 10016

First issued as an Oxford University Press paperback, 2016

Library of Congress Cataloging-in-Publication Data
Kautalya.
[Arthasastra. English]
King, governance, and law in ancient India : Kautilya's Arthasastra : a new annotated translation / by Patrick Olivelle.
p. cm.
Includes bibliographical references.
ISBN 978–0–19–989182–5 (hardcover); 978–0–19–064412–3 (paperback)
1. Political science—India—History—Early works to 1800. 2. State, The—Early works to 1800. 3. Kings and rulers (Hindu law)—Early works to 1800. 4. India—Politics and government—To 997—Early works to 1800. 5. India—Social conditions—Early works to 1800.
I. Olivelle, Patrick. II. Title.
JA84.I4.K3813 2013
351.01—dc23
2012018348

ISBN 978–0–19–064412–3

For Keya

ketakyai śubhasundaryai mātāmahakulaśriyai |
putrikāputrikāyai me pustakam arpitaṃ mayā ||

Contents

Preface

THERE ARE MANY things that I would never have undertaken if I had only known how difficult they would turn out to be! Translating the *Arthaśāstra* can be counted among them. It was a little over five years ago in a moment of foolishness that I embarked on this project, motivated partly by the fact that one of my students, Mark McClish, was doing his dissertation on the *Arthaśāstra*. Now, five years later and much wiser, I present this translation to my colleagues and readers, deeply conscious of its shortcomings. For this, I beg forgiveness of that great master of intrigue and political wisdom, Kauṭilya; this translation clearly cannot measure up to his masterpiece.

It would have been far worse if not for the help and wisdom of several friends and colleagues. First and foremost, my heartfelt thanks go to Professors Albrecht Wezler and Hartmut Scharfe, who patiently and generously read through my entire translation and notes, and offered judicious criticism and prudent suggestions for improvement. They put their vast knowledge of ancient India and the *Arthaśāstra* at my disposal. I also thank Professor Gyula Wojtilla for help with the sections on agriculture. Our height is always measured by the shoulders upon which we ride, and it is a pleasure to acknowledge my debt to the numerous scholars who have worked on the *Arthaśāstra* over the past century. I can name only a few here: first, the pioneers in the field, R. Shamasastry, Julius Jolly, Gaṇapati Śastri, and J. J. Meyer. Harihara Sastri is an unsung hero in Arthaśāstric scholarship; his edition of the most significant commentary and insightful introductions were of enormous help. R. P. Kangle, with his critical edition, translation, and study, set a firm foundation for future scholarship. Finally, the works of Hartmut Scharfe, Thomas Trautmann, Dieter Schlingloff, and my former student Mark McClish are models of scholarship. Sometimes, those who spend countless hours preparing electronic versions of Sanskrit texts remain unacknowledged. I want to especially thank Muneo Tokunaga of the University of Kyoto; his electronic version of the *Arthaśāstra* was always by my side and proved invaluable as I searched for words within the text.

Many others, both institutions and individuals, helped to get me to the finish line. A visiting fellowship from Wolfson College, Oxford, provided early support, as did the financial assistance of the Jacob and Frances Sanger Mossiker Chair in the Humanities at the University of Texas at Austin. My colleagues Joel Brereton, Oliver Freiberger, Martha Selby, and Cynthia Talbot were constant sounding boards, ever ready to answer obscure questions and provide valuable comments on the introduction. Wendy Doniger used an early draft of the translation in her class and offered criticisms and new insights. Madhav Deshpande was always there to explain points of grammar. My student Amy Hyne proofread the entire manuscript and prepared the words for the appendices and index. I want to thank in a special way Cynthia Read of Oxford University Press for her sustained assistance and friendship over a period of two decades and for taking on generously this overly long book, and Molly Morrison who patiently and efficiently oversaw the complex production process. My wife Suman was a helpful partner in this, as in all my other scholarly ventures. As this translation was struggling to be born, we were blessed with the birth of our granddaughter Keya—the Monsoon Flower—who has occupied much of our time since then. To her and her future, this book is fondly dedicated.

Patrick Olivelle
Austin, Texas

Abbreviations

AitBr	*Aitareya Brāhmaṇa*
ĀpDh	*Āpastamba Dharmasūtra*
ĀpŚr	*Āpastamba Śrautasūtra*
AŚ	*Kauṭilya's Arthaśāstra*
AV	*Atharva Veda Saṃhitā*
BauŚr	*Baudhāyana Śrautasūtra*
BDh	*Baudhāyana Dharmasūtra*
B-R	*Böhtlingh and Roth, Sanskrit-Wörterbuch*
BṛSm	*Bṛhaspati Smṛti*
EDS	*Encyclopaedic Dictionary of Sanskrit on Historical Principles*
GDh	*Gautama Dharmasūtra*
JAOS	*Journal of the American Oriental Society*
Kangle	*Kangle, R. P., 1969, 1972*
KātŚr	*Kātyāyana Śrautasūtra*
KSm	*Kātyāyana Smṛti*
MBh	*Mahābhārata*
MDh	*Mānava Dharmaśāstra*
Meyer	*Meyer, J., 1926*
M-W	*Monier Monier-Williams, Sanskrit-English Dictionary*
NSm	*Nārada Smṛti*
Rām	*Rāmāyaṇa*
ŚB	*Śatapatha Brāhmaṇa*
TS	*Taittirīya Saṃhitā*
VaDh	*Vasiṣṭha Dharmasūtra*
ViDh	*Vaiṣṇava Dharmaśāstra*
WZKSA	*Wiener Zeitschrift für die Kunde Südasiens*
YDh	*Yājñavalkya Dharmaśāstra*
ZDMG	*Zeitschrift der Deutschen Morganländischen Gesselschaft*

Note to the Translation

THIS WAS THE most difficult translation project I have ever undertaken. Even after a century of modern scholarship on the *AŚ*, parts of the text are still opaque. Sometimes one is fortunate, as when I had the benefit of Scholingloff's (1969) work on fort construction; without it much of *AŚ* 2.3 would remain unintelligible. After spending five years on this translation, I can appreciate the poet Daṇḍin's comment that it is not possible to understand this treatise without first acquiring knowledge of the entire range of scholarship.[1] In this note I want to alert the reader to some of the translational difficulties I encountered and some of the translational choices I made.

As has been my practice, I have not placed English words in the translation within parentheses except in the rarest of cases. The two languages are grammatically and syntactically different. Some things that are understood implicitly in Sanskrit need to be stated explicitly in English. This is especially true when Sanskrit simply uses a verb in the third person without any indication as to the subject. It is impossible to leave the subject out in English, and simply using the pronoun "he" is not helpful. Whenever needed, therefore, I have supplied the missing noun based on the context. I have attempted to be accurate, but not literal.

All names of flora and fauna were left untranslated, unless they refer to well-known species, such as mango, coconut, crows, peacocks, and myna birds. Sanskrit names are explained in appendix 1. Likewise, all measurements of weight, length, and distance are left in the original Sanskrit. The reason for this choice is that, most frequently, the numbers attached to measurements have connotations that are lost when converting them into grams or meters, much like when someone says she walked a mile, but the connotation is lost when one translates it as having walked 1.609 kilometers. I have given the conversion tables for weights and measures in appendix 2.

1 Daśakumāracarita (ed. Kale), 191.

Money is generally given in Paṇas. In most cases, Sanskrit will give the term Paṇa after the number—for example, 32 Paṇas. I noted the curious practice of Kauṭilya that he added the term Paṇa to all numbers below 100; in the case of numbers 100 and above, he omitted Paṇa, which was apparently understood. This system is not invariable, as in 4.2.14, where 92 is listed without Paṇa. Examples of this practice can be found in 2.25.2; 2.36.32; 3.10.5; 3.17.9–10; 4.1.52; 4.2.16, 21; 4.9.9; 4.10.6; 4.11.2, 4; and 4.12.24. Clearly, the translation would be confusing if I had followed this practice. Hence, I have included Paṇa with all numbers.

I have attempted to be consistent in translating specialized or technical terms in Sanskrit. To help the reader identify the original Sanskrit behind my translation, I give below the Sanskrit equivalents. One problem with Kangle's translation is the inconsistency in rendering technical terms into English. As much as possible, I have tried to use a single English term for each technical term of the *AŚ*.

First, I deal with the names of government and military officials. The term *amātya* has been translated as "minister"; clearly, we are not talking here about cabinet ministers in a modern state. This term generically refers to any high official of the state. Table 0.1 is a list of the major officials of the state bureaucracy with Sanskrit equivalents.

The network of spies and secret agents was large, and there is a vast number of technical terms used for various specialized agents. The poverty of the English language in this regard was brought home to me as

Table 0.1

accounts officer *kāraṇika*	director of factories *kārmāntika*
administrator *praśāstṛ*	frontier commander *antapāla*
chaplain *purohita*	head of palace guard *antarviṃśaka*
chief gate guard *dauvārika*	high official *mahāmātra*
chief of the armed forces *senāpati*	junior officer *upayukta*
chief officer *mukhya*	magistrate *pradeṣṭṛ*
city manager *nāgarika*	military commander *daṇḍacārin*
city overseer *pauravyāvahārika*	minister *amātya*
collector *samāhartṛ*	regent *śūnyapāla*
commander *nāyaka*	revenue officer *gopa*
counselor *mantrin*	superintendent *adhyakṣa*
council of counselors *mantripariṣad*	treasurer *saṃnidhātṛ*
crown prince *yuvarāja*	works officer *kārmika*

I struggled to come up with different words for each Sanskrit term. The word *-vyañjana* is often used as the second member of a compound. When so used, the term means that an agent is posing as a member of society indicated by the first term; for example, *gṛhapativyañjana* is an agent working undercover as a householder. I have omitted these from table 0.2 below.

Another area of specialized vocabulary is foreign relations. Different kinds of kings and polities are given technical names in table 0.3.

Another group of specialized terms relates to the various kinds of ascetics and holy people, who were a special target of spy agencies (see table 0.4). It is interesting to note that *bhikṣukī*, a female mendicant, is used only in the context of spying; she is not referred to simply as a holy woman.

There are also technical terms with reference to bookkeeping and the numerous taxes, duties, fees, penalties, and fines bringing revenue to the treasury (see table 0.5).

My translation is broadly based on the text as constituted by Kangle (1969), but there are several problems with Kangle's edition that I want to address here. Given the paucity of manuscripts, the translator is faced

Table 0.2

apostate recluse *udāsthita*	female mendicant agent *bhikṣukī*
assassin *tīkṣṇa*	informant *cāra*
clandestine operative *gūḍhapuruṣa*	poisoner *rasada*
covert agent *yogapuruṣa*	secret agent *sattrin*
crafty student *kāpaṭika*	spy *apasarpa*
double agent *ubhayavetana*	

Table 0.3

backer (of rear ally) *āsāra*	neutral *udāsīna*
circle *maṇḍala*	rear ally *ākranda*
confederacy *saṅgha*	rear enemy *pārṣṇigrāha*
constituent element *prakṛti*	seeker after conquest *vijigīṣu*
intermediate king *madhyama*	tribal chief *āṭavika*
neighboring ruler *sāmanta*	vulnerable king *yātavya*

Table 0.4

ascetic *tāpasa,yati, liṅgin*	religious order *pāṣaṇḍa*
forest hermit *vānaprastha*	member of religious order *pāṣaṇḍin*
holy theurgist *siddha*	renouncer *pravrajita*
matted-haired ascetic *jaṭila*	shaven-headed ascetic *muṇḍa*
mendicant *bhikṣu(ka)*	thaumaturgic ascetic *siddhatāpasa*
recluse *tapasvin*	wandering ascetic *parivrājaka*

Table 0.5

balance	*nīvī*	income	*aya*
compensation	*pratipāta*	investment	*prakṣepa*
compensatory tax	*vaidharaṇa*	loss	*kṣaya*
customs duty	*śulka*	penalty	*atyaya*
escort charge	*ātivāhika*	profit	*udaya*
exemption	*parihāra*	road toll	*vartanī*
expenditure	*vyaya*	royal gift	*paṇyāgāra*
fee for sex	*bhoga*	share	*bhāga*
fine	*daṇḍa*	surcharge	*vyājī*
fixed rent	*prakraya*	tax	*kara*
gratuity	*aupānayika*	tribute	*bali*

with evidently corrupt readings found in all of them. Presenting conjectural readings in such cases is inevitable without the discovery of new manuscripts. Frequently, Kangle claims that, in such cases, his conjecture is based on the reading of the Malayalam commentary. But as Scharfe (1993, 7) has pointed out, what Kangle often takes to be the reading of this commentary is simply the text attached to the published version of it, a text that simply gives the version published by Gaṇapati Śāstri: "What Kangle offers in his critical apparatus as the readings of the Malayalam commentary are, therefore, nothing but the text of the Trivandrum edition of the Arthaśāstra." Even though Kangle had access to Harihara Sastri's edition of the commentaries *Jayamaṅgalā* and *Cāṇakyaṭīkā*, it is unfortunate that he does not make use of the excellent suggestions for textual emendations

Table 0.6

1.15.20	1.15.41	2.1.9	2.4.20–21	2.5.2	2.5.16
2.11.32	2.11.72	2.12.17	2.13.41	2.15.17	2.15.35
2.15.43	2.19.34–35	2.24.10	2.24.32	2.28.5	2.28.26
2.29.41	2.30.36	2.31.1	2.32.8–9	2.36.35	2.36.46
3.1.2	3.1.34–35	3.3.10	3.3.17–18	3.5.36	3.7.36
3.8.3	3.8.5	3.8.6	3.8.26	3.11.16–17	3.12.2
3.13.6	3.15.18	3.16.7	4.1.30	4.2.13–23	4.2.25
4.4.6	4.4.9	4.6.2	4.7.11	4.8.12	4.12.16
5.1.21	5.2.24	5.2.43	5.2.57	5.2.64	5.3.1
5.4.8	7.4.1	7.8.27	7.9.43	7.12.8	8.2.7
11.1.42	13.4.4	13.4.20–22	14.1.35		

offered by this most perceptive reader of the *Arthaśāstra*. I have made a series of textual emendations in connection with this translation, and they are defended in the respective notes. Table 0.6 is a cumulative list of all such emendations.

The headings given in the translation are my own and not found in the manuscripts, except the headings of Books and Topics.

Outline of the *Arthaśāstra*

Book One: On the Subject of Training

Book Two: On the Activities of Superintendents

Book Three: On Justices

Book Four: Eradication of Thorns

Book Five: On Secret Conduct

Book Six: Basis of the Circle

Book Seven: On the Sixfold Strategy

Book Eight: On the Subject of Calamities

Book Nine: Activity of a King Preparing to March into Battle

Book Ten: On War

Book Eleven: Conduct toward Confederacies

Book Twelve: On the Weaker King

Book Thirteen: Means of Capturing a Fort

Book Fourteen: On Esoteric Practices

Book Fifteen: Organization of a Scientific Treatise

King, Governance, and Law
in Ancient India

Introduction

THE STORY OF the discovery of Kauṭilya's *Arthaśāstra* reads like a thriller, one of the few exciting, Indiana Jones-like moments in the rather drab history of ancient Indian scholarship. Jolly's (1923, 1) assessment, echoing that of F. W. Thomas,[1] of this work made 90 years ago still rings true: "The recently discovered Arthaśāstra of Kauṭilya, *alias* Cāṇakya or Viṣṇugupta, is perhaps the most precious work in the whole range of Sanskrit literature." The existence of such a text was known from various direct and indirect references to it in the extant literature.[2] But a manuscript of the work had not turned up—until sometime before 1905, when a pandit from Tanjore, whose name is unfortunately not known, handed a complete manuscript of the text written in Grantha script to Dr. R. Shamasastry, the chief librarian at the Mysore Government Oriental Library. The enormous difficulty of understanding and interpreting this text can be assessed by the fact that nothing like it had ever been seen before. All the modern Sanskrit dictionaries had been published before its discovery, and the vocabulary of the *Arthaśāstra* presented and continues to present great challenges to any translator. Notwithstanding, Shamasastry began to publish translations of sections from it in the journals *Indian Antiquary* and *Mysore Review* between 1905 and 1909. He published the *editio princeps* of the Sanskrit text in 1909 and the entire translation as a book in 1915 (Shamasastry 1909, 1915).

Thus began the modern history of *Arthaśāstra* scholarship. Although this scholarship owes much to the pioneering work of Shamasastry, more text-critical work had to await the discovery of further manuscripts and commentaries and the preparation of better and more critical editions. The new edition prepared by Jolly and Schmidt (1923–1924) was a substantial improvement over that of Shamasastry; it also contained the commentary *Nayacandrikā* by Mādhavayajvan, the first, albeit incomplete, commentary to be published. The editors used a Devanāgarī manuscript, which was thought to have been copied from a Grantha manuscript from Madras. Kangle, however, has demonstrated that the transcript was probably made from a Malayalam manuscript now in the Oriental Manuscript Library in Trivandrum. Using this original manuscript and making use of quite an old Malayalam commentary, T. Gaṇapati Śāstrī published a new edition along with his own commentary called *Śrīmūla* in 1924–1925. Soon thereafter, Meyer (1926) produced a German translation with copious notes, suggested emendations, and comments.

In the meantime, four medieval commentaries on the *AŚ*, all of them also fragmentary, were published.[3] The text of the *AŚ* did not undergo significant improvement until 1960 when R. P. Kangle published his critical edition of the *Arthaśāstra* (a second edition was produced in 1969) based on all the manuscript and commentarial evidence available at that time. Besides the six commentaries, Kangle had the fortune of using a fragmentary Devanāgarī manuscript discovered in Gujarat (Jina Vijaya 1959), the only known northern manuscript of the text. Kangle also published an English translation (1963) with copious notes based on his critical edition, as well as a study (1965). In spite of deficiencies and inaccuracies that I have pointed out in the endnotes, these works of Kangle set a new and firmer foundation for all subsequent *Arthaśāstric* scholarship.

One question that may be asked relates to the need for a fresh translation of the *Arthaśāstra*. Over half a century has passed since Kangle's translation, and numerous groundbreaking studies on this text have since appeared, including those by Trautmann (1971), Scharfe (1968, 1993),[4] Schlingloff (1965, 1967, 1969), and McClish (2009). Given the uniqueness and centrality of the *Arthaśāstra* for the study of governance, society, and material culture in ancient India, a fresh translation with copious notes taking into account the latest advances in Kauṭilya studies seemed to me a desirable goal to pursue.

The first four sections of this introduction deal with textual issues, focusing especially on the compositional history, date, and authorship of the *AŚ*. The fifth investigates the content of the *Arthaśāstra* under three broad headings: how a king should govern, enhance economic activities, and foster relations with neighboring states in such a way as to enhance his own power and wealth. In the final section, I deal with the reception and later history of the *AŚ*.

1. Structure and Style

In this section I discuss the received text, that is, the text of the *Arthaśāstra* as we have it in the manuscript tradition. It is clear even to those who maintain its unitary authorship that some redactoral activity must have intervened between the "original" and the received text. I will deal with these issues of higher criticism in the next section.

Looking first at the formal structure, the treatise has three overlapping divisions: 15 books (*adhikaraṇa*),[5] 150 chapters (*adhyāya*), and 180 topics (*prakaraṇa*).[6] The book and chapter divisions appear to be closely linked, the one presupposing the other. Each book is subdivided into chapters. The topic division, on the other hand, stands apart from the other two divisions, and I will argue below that these multiple divisions correspond to the compositional history of the treatise.

Each book has a title and deals with a broad subject, even though frequently not all the material covered quite corresponds to the subject given in the title. Book 15 stands apart from the rest of the treatise. It is short with a single chapter containing 73 sentences, and it does not deal with statecraft at all. Its purpose is to show how the treatise is well crafted and has all the 32 organizational elements (*yukti*) of a perfect scientific treatise (*tantra*).[7] The same can be said of chapter 1 of book 1; it is merely a table of contents for the entire treatise according to book and topic, chapter divisions being ignored. Even though it is given a chapter number, it does not constitute a topic; the topic enumeration begins with chapter 2.

Each book is divided into chapters adding up to a total of 150, which is ten times the number of books. This correspondence, as we will see in the next section, was probably not accidental. It is unclear whether the numbering of chapters ran consecutively through the entire text or started anew in each book. Editions give two numbers: one corresponding to the chapter number within a specific book (a practice I have followed in this translation) and another counting from the very beginning. It is unclear how closely this practice follows the evidence of the manuscripts. The chapter division of the treatise is somewhat artificial and does not always correspond to a particular subject matter; indeed, chapters do not have titles and take on the titles of the respective topics. Although over half the time (85), chapters and topics coincide, not infrequently a chapter may contain more than one topic, or a topic may spill over into two or more chapters.[8] This is not uncommon in other Sanskrit texts of the period; the *adhyāya* (literally, reading or lesson) appears to have been devised for the convenience of students and readers, covering a section of the text that could be read or taught in one sitting. I will return to the issues relating to these divisions in the next section within the context of the compositional history of the treatise.

A striking feature of the chapter division is that, even though the treatise is primarily composed in prose, every chapter concludes with one or more verses, the transition to verse signaling the conclusion of a chapter, much like the change of meter signaling the end of a section in the epics and in later epic poetry (*kāvya*). Most frequently (in 101 cases), chapters end with a single verse (McClish 2009, 49). Less frequently, they end in two verses (in 23), in three verses (in 7), or in four or more verses (in 19). Indeed, these end verses add up to 303, or 80 percent of the total number of verses (378) in the *Arthaśāstra* (McClish 2009, 107). Each chapter, at least in the extant manuscripts and editions, ends with a colophon giving the respective number of the book and the chapter, as well as the title of the book and the topic(s) contained within the chapter.

The third division, topics, appears to be unrelated to either of the other two divisions and to stand alone as a thematic division of the entire treatise. The numbering of the 180 topics runs consecutively through the text without regard to book and chapter divisions. I will deal with the redactoral history that may have given rise to these three divisions in the next section, and which of these three divisions may have been original and which were superimposed. The number 180, however, was probably not accidental: The number 18 was significant or even sacred in ancient India, with the *Mahābhārata* having 18 *parvans* and the *Bhagavad Gītā* consisting of 18 chapters.

The 14 books that constitute the substance of the treatise vary enormously in size: The largest is book 2 with 36 chapters and a total of 1,285 sentences.[9] The next largest is book 7 with 18 chapters and 684 sentences, while the shortest are book 11 with just one chapter and 56 sentences, and book 6 with two chapters and 58 sentences. Thus, the book divisions of the treatise are uneven with respect to overall length and the number of chapters contained in each. The entire *Arthaśāstra* in Kangle's edition has 5,392 sentences[10] and, if we eliminate the very first chapter and the last book, both of which fall outside the treatise proper, it contains 5,300 sentences.

The *Arthaśāstra* appears to be divided into two parts. Even though the text itself does not allude to or demarcate this division, there is sufficient evidence within the text itself to show that this division was part of an intentional editorial plan and that the author used distinctly different sources in composing the two parts. The first contains books 1–5 and deals with the king and the internal administration of a kingdom. The second contains books 6–14 and deals with foreign relations, policies toward neighboring polities, and warfare. As I will demonstrate in the next section, these two parts also differ from each other in their vocabularies and classificatory systems, pointing to at least two different textual sources used by the author. Later texts call the first *tantra* and the second *āvāpa*.[11] The first part has 3,137 sentences constituting about 60 percent of the text, and the second part has 2,163 sentences constituting about 40 percent of the text. Table I.1 contains a synopsis of the sentences in each book of the two parts.

The literary genre of the *AŚ* is what has been called the *sūtra* or aphoristic style (Renou 1963) commonly used in composing scholarly texts in ancient India (Kangle 1965, 37). Although brevity of expression is regarded as a hallmark of this genre, many texts falling within it are written in normal Sanskrit prose with grammatically and syntactically complete sentences. The algebraic brevity of Pāṇini's grammar or texts such as the *Mīmāṃsā Sūtra* and the *Vedānta Sūtra* is not the norm but rather

Table I.1

Part One: *Tantra*	**Part Two:** *Āvāpa*
Book 1: 481 (minus Ch. 1)	Book 6: 58
Book 2: 1,285	Book 7: 684
Book 3: 699	Book 8: 235
Book 4: 418	Book 9: 340
Book 5: 254	Book 10: 221
Total = 3,137	Book 11: 56
	Book 12: 166
	Book 13: 216
	Book 14: 187
	Total = 2,164

Book 1, Chapter 1 = 19
Book 15 = 73
Grand Total = 5,392

the exception. The sentences of the *AŚ*, like those of the Dharmasūtras, are for the most part complete and readily understood, even though occasionally they may imply (*anuvṛtti*) words from previous sentences. The difficulties are created more by the specialized vocabulary often unknown from other Sanskrit works and by the specialized areas of knowledge, such as fort construction and techniques of goldsmiths, that may have been known to his original audience but that are often a closed book to modern readers.[12]

2. *Compositional History*

With regard to the compositional history of the *AŚ*, there are two separate issues to consider. The first is whether the author created a fresh text ex novo, or made use of existing material in his composition. The second is whether the received *AŚ* is the result of emendations and redactions of the author's original work.

The first issue is not controversial. The *AŚ* itself states at the very beginning (1.1.1): "This singular Treatise on Success (Arthaśāstra) has been composed for the most part by drawing together the Treatises on Success (Arthaśāstras) composed by former teachers for gaining and administering the earth."[13] Even though it is not certain that this statement goes back to the author himself or is part of a later redaction, it is clear that the tradition conceived of the *AŚ* as the distillation of earlier works on the subject. Apparently the distillation was so good that it eclipsed the earlier works to such an extent that they have disappeared from the manuscript tradition. Many names of earlier or rival traditions (Bārhaspatyas, Auśanasas, Mānavas, Pārāśaras, and Āmbhīyas, or simply "teachers" or "some"), as well as specific teachers of statecraft (Bhāradvāja, Viśālākṣa, Piśuna, Kauṇapadanta, Vātavyādhi, and Bāhudantīputra), are listed. It is unclear how much trust we can put on the historicity of these traditions and individuals. Scholars have viewed at least some of these names, such as Vātavyādhi, as fictitious (Scharfe 1993, 9 and below). The *Mahābhārata* presents a mythological history of the original composition of a work on statecraft by the creator Brahmā himself, consisting of ten thousand chapters, that was repeatedly abridged, until the final two editions were created by Bṛhaspati and Uśanas.[14] These two appear to have some historical grounding, because the second-century C.E. Buddhist author Aśvaghoṣa, in his *Buddhacarita* (1.46), says that Bṛhaspati and Śukra (another name for Uśanas) were able to produce works on kings (*rājaśāstra*) that their predecessors could not.

It is not simply these problematic ascriptions of some opinions to various authorities that argue for the author's use of pre-existing material in his composition. Especially in book 2, we have discussions of specific areas of expert knowledge, perhaps handed down orally, ranging from architecture and town planning to metallurgy, agriculture, and animal husbandry. As Schlingloff (1967, 1969) has amply demonstrated, the *AŚ* description of the building of forts and fortifications is shown to be remarkably accurate when compared to the extant archeological evidence. If we can extrapolate from this to the accuracy of the accounts in other areas of expert knowledge, then it is certain that these sections must have been taken from expert textual or oral traditions within those areas. The technical terminology employed in them also argues for such borrowings. Indeed, one of the most remarkable and unique features of the *AŚ* is that it has preserved for posterity the expert traditions of architects, masons, farmers, metal workers, jewelers, and the like, traditions that for the most part must have been handed down orally from fathers to sons and from teachers to apprentices. Indeed, as we will see, an independent treatise called *Adhyakṣapracāra* (now the title of book 2) existed before the *AŚ*, and continued to exist even after its incorporation into the *AŚ*. It also appears that, in 4.8.24, Kauṭilya refers to a work on methods of torture called *Kharapaṭṭa*, from which he expects his reader to gather further information on this topic.

The second issue, namely whether the received *AŚ* is the result of emendations and redactions of the author's original work, has divided the scholarly community. Even those who espouse the singular authorship of the *AŚ*, however, concede that there are numerous individual passages within it that are clearly extraneous and are the result of either interpolations or marginal glosses that have found their way into the text proper. Kangle (1965, 26), for example, acknowledges: "The possibility that the passage 1.1.18–19 was added to the text by a later hand would lead one to suppose that there may be other similar additions made to the text in later times. And it cannot be denied that a few such additions or interpolations can be traced in the text as it has come down to us." The issue that divides scholars, however, is whether one or more major redactions have intervened between the author's original and the received text. I agree with those who posit precisely such editorial interventions.

Within the compass of an introduction, it is not possible to survey the variety of scholarly opinion over the past century on the composition of the *AŚ*.[15] I will here attempt to present as clearly as I can my own hypothesis[16] regarding the compositional history of the *AŚ*, first in outline and then in detail.

After its initial composition, the received *AŚ* was subjected to one major redaction and perhaps to several minor revisions. The initial composition I will call the "Kauṭilya Recension." It is with this recension that the history of the *AŚ* proper begins; the sources used by the author should be considered as belonging to the prehistory of the *AŚ*. I will argue (1) that a historical person named Kauṭilya was responsible for this recension; (2) that this recension contained substantially the received text; and (3) that it did not contain any of the three divisions into which the received text has been segmented (book, chapter, and topic), even though it probably had a topic division that was different from the one in the received text and on which the latter was based. It is unclear what the title of this Kauṭilya Recension was, but the likely candidate is "Daṇḍanīti," literally the administration of punishment but more broadly the exercise of governance.

The major redaction of this original composition I will call the "Śāstric Redaction." This redaction was carried out by a scholar well versed in Dharmaśāstras. He carried out the division of the *AŚ* into 15 books and 150 chapters; and he also probably tweaked the original topic division into a new format, following more or less the pattern of the chapters and creating 180 topics. He was also responsible for the verses that signal the conclusion of chapters and perhaps also for other changes that brought the *AŚ* more into line with the mainstream of Brāhmaṇical social ideology expressed most prominently in the Dharmaśāstras. He added the first chapter containing the table of contents and the last book that establishes the *AŚ* as a formally true and perfect *śāstra*, scientific treatise, containing all the required attributes of one, as well as other books, chapters, and smaller segments (McClish 2009), some of which I will identify below. Finally, it was this redactor who put the stamp of Kauṭilya authorship of the *AŚ* directly into the text itself by (1) inserting colophons at the end of each chapter and book that explicitly ascribe the text to Kauṭilya; (2) inserting all or most of the dialogues in which Kauṭilya opposes the views of other experts on statecraft; and (3) inserting the very first sentence of the text (1.1.1) and the verse at the end of 2.10 that deal with the composition and authorship of the *AŚ*.[17] This redaction created an *Arthaśāstra* out of a Daṇḍanīti.

Kauṭilya Recension

The *AŚ* as it has come down to us, then, is the result of a substantive redaction; its original shape was markedly different. The two issues I want to address here are the content and characteristic features of the original recension, and how that recension was composed. To a large degree, the isolation of the original recension is intrinsically connected with the features of the Śāstric Redaction. Some of the arguments for the delineation of the original recension, therefore, will be presented below when I deal with that redaction.

Once we accept that the division into chapters (*adhyāya*) was a later redactoral imposition, it becomes clear that the verses that mark the conclusion of each chapter must also derive from this redaction.[18] The same hand is responsible for the table of contents given in the first chapter (1.1), which does not have a topic (*prakaraṇa*) assigned to it, and the last book (15), which gives the enumeration of *tantrayuktis* or the organizational elements of a scientific treatise (Trautmann 1961, 75) and presupposes the finished *AŚ*. I will argue further that the division of the *AŚ* into books (*adhikaraṇa*) must also go back to the same redactor; both the division into chapters and the table of contents presuppose such a division (Scharfe 1993, 41).

The original recension, in all likelihood, had a single division into topics, although this topic division was different from the one in the received text. There is some doubt as to whether these topics were simply a smooth sequence of subjects dealt with by the author or whether there was a clear segmentation with topic headings and perhaps numbers. I think that it is probable that there was a formal division into topics with titles, especially because that may have been the reason for the redactor to maintain and possibly expand this division and to integrate it, somewhat clumsily, into the chapter division. Further, the very first sentences of many topics, especially in the exemplary book 2, serve as introductions, often reiterating the very words of the topic headings.[19] So, as we examine the content and structure of the original recension, we must look at the text with fresh eyes, leaving out of consideration all the book and chapter divisions.

McClish (2009) has also identified several books that were added by the śāstric redactor, as well as several chapters within original books. I will only enumerate the major sections here briefly and offer a more detailed examination in the next section. The books that were added by this redactor are 5, 8, 11, 12, 14, and 15. Thus, the Kauṭilya Recension consisted of the material presented in books 1–4, 6–7, 9–10, and 13 of the received text, even though, as we will see, some sections of these books were also recast by the redactor.

If we ignore the book and chapter divisions and the redactoral additions noted above, a logical structure of the text emerges, making it likely that the substance of the received *AŚ* goes back to what I have called the Kauṭilya Recension. This original structure of the text is both simple and elegant, and the clue to it is provided in topic 96 (6.1 of the received text) that stands at the center of the treatise dividing the two sections on internal administration (*tantra*) and external affairs (*āvāpa*) and provides a link between the two. The theory of the state enunciated there gives seven basic elements or constituents (*prakṛti*) of a kingdom: king, minister, countryside, fort, treasury, army, and ally (*AŚ* 6.1.1). This division becomes the blueprint for structuring the text. The first five are the organizing principles of the first half: king in topics 1–3, ministers (under which term is encompassed all upper-level administrators and counselors, as well as clandestine operatives) in topics 5–8,[20] countryside in topics 19–20, fort in topics 21–22, and treasury in topics 23–53, with further discussions on the protection and governance of the countryside and fort (topics 54–84). The last two—army and ally (under which is also included the enemy, *AŚ* 6.1.12–14)—underlie the organization of the second half dealing with foreign relations, diplomacy, and warfare. Both halves have extraneous material given as appendices at the end of each (books 5 and 14) that derive from the śāstric redactor. It is at these two seams that major additional material was incorporated.

This structure in many ways parallels the one presented by Bhikṣu Prabhāmati in his commentary *Cāṇakyaṭīkā*, the only commentator, as far as I know, who discusses the overall structure of the *AŚ* and is by far the most perspicacious of all the commentators. In his introductory comments on book 2, he says that in book 1 the author shows that the king has acquired the ability to carry out his tasks because of the teaching on a king's training contained in it (1.2–21). The rest of the treatise is devoted to the ways in which these tasks are to be carried out along with his ministers. These tasks are twofold, depending on whether they are carried out in one's own territory (*svamaṇḍala*) or in enemy territory (*paramaṇḍala*); the first is treated in books 2–5, and the second in books 6–14. Then he introduces the concept of *yogakṣema*,[21] enterprise and security: The king has to acquire property and wealth through enterprise and then provide security for what he has gained. Bhikṣu Prabhāmati sees book 2 as dealing with enterprise through the activities of various department heads:

> Thus, through the instruction in training, the competence of the king to carry out his tasks has been taught. Now, he has to carry out those tasks together with his ministers and the like. These tasks are of two kinds depending on whether they pertain to one's own territory or to the territory of the enemy. Of these, the tasks pertaining to one's own territory are dealt with first, because they are internal and are the cause of others. These tasks are also of two kinds following the distinction between enterprise and security. Of these, given that security presupposes enterprise, (the Book) "On the Activities of Superintendents" that focuses on the latter is dealt with.[22]

Bhikṣu Prabhāmati returns to the issue of the compositional structure in his introductory remarks on book 3. He says that, after discussing enterprise in book 2, Kauṭilya turns to the discussion of security in books 3, 4, and 5:

> After explaining enterprise in the extensive Book [2] "On the Activities of Superintendents," he devotes the three Books [3–5]: "On Justices," "Eradication of Thorns," and "On Secret Conduct" to the discussion of security.[23]

The next issue to consider is how Kauṭilya put together his treatise. I have already noted that he used several sources, probably both oral and written, in composing his work.[24] The statistical analysis done by Trautmann (1971) also confirms that especially the relatively long books 2, 3, and 7 were authored by different individuals. Looking at the complex structure and diverse vocabularies within the *AŚ*, one can agree with Trautmann (1971, 75) when he points out that "no single author working from scratch would be likely to create such anomaly." For the first half, we can isolate a text called *adhyakṣapracāra* ("Activities of Superintendents"), which is the title of book 2 in the extant *AŚ*, a text that was integrated into the *AŚ*. This text probably existed as a separate document even after the composition of the *AŚ*. It is referred to in the *Kāmasūtra* (1.2.10) and by Medhātithi in his commentary on the *MDh* (7.61; 7.81).[25] It is possible that this source of the *AŚ* may have included topics broader than simply the *adhyakṣas*, because Medhātithi's citation deals with counselors (*mantrin*).

Trautmann (1971, 174) is correct in his assessment that "the forebear of Book 2 was a work entitled *Adhayakṣapracāra* dealing with ministers as well as overseers, and that parts of it have contributed to *Arthaśāstra* Book I, and parts were lost through abridgment."

Trautmann (1971) has shown that the author of book 3 of the received text was probably different from the author of book 2. It may well be that Kauṭilya took the material in book 3, and possibly also book 4, from a different source dealing with transactions, dispute resolution, and security.

It is likely that the anchor of the second half of the *AŚ*, namely book 7 of the received text (Trautmann 1971, 119), also goes back to a different pre-existing source. In fact, we have a very distinct vocabulary in the second half of the *AŚ*. Key concepts of this section, such as *prakṛti* (in the sense of a constituent of the kingdom),[26] *maṇḍala* (in the meaning of circle of kings),[27] *vijigīṣu* (seeker after conquest), and *ṣāḍguṇya* (sixfold strategy), that play a pivotal role in this half are completely absent in the first half. Even if one were to argue that their absence can be accounted for because of the difference in content and focus of the two halves, there are other more common terms that are distinct in the two halves. One is the term for a mine. In the first half, the dominant term is *ākara* (2.12), even though we see the use of *khani* occasionally. The *khanyadhyakṣa* (superintendent of *khani*, 2.12.27), however, is distinct from the *ākarādhyakṣa* (superintendent of *ākara;* 2.12.1), and *khani* appears to have become more or less restricted to underwater mining for shells, pearls, and coral. In the second half, however, *ākara* is never used, while *khani* is used a total of 11 times (Olivelle 2012a). The superintendents of horses (*aśvādhyakṣa;* 2.30.1), of chariots (*rathādhyakṣa;* 2.33.1), and of foot soldiers (*pattyadhyakṣa;* 2.33.7) are important officials mentioned in the first half; they are all lacking in the second half devoted to warfare, where we should have expected to find them. Even though there is scholarly disagreement on this point, one may also draw attention to the fact that, in the first half of the text, *mantripurohita* is given as a single office (at the very least the distinction is not made explicitly, 1.9 n.; 1.12.6 n.) while in the second half, *mantrin* (counselor) and *purohita* (chaplain) are separated, often the compound being given in the dual (7.15.27 n.).

Beyond these specific differences, there is also a stark contrast with regard to the style of presentation. For the most part, the first half of the treatise presents material in a straightforward manner, with instructions and injunctions using verbs in the optative. The first half, even though it contains some theoretical material, is primarily a book of instructions to state officials. Even though it contains instructions to officials, especially to military officials, the second half of the treatise is dominated by academic and theoretical considerations, very similar to Brāhmaṇical texts of later times. It belongs to what is called the śāstric genre. Classifications abound, along with commentaries on the classifications: There are four of this and six of that. Then there are the rhetorical questions: Is this better or that? Is this worse or that? The second half looks very much like a textbook for use in school.

Even though the two halves appear to be derived from different sources, Kauṭilya has woven them together to form a distinct whole. I think he has selected his sources and placed them in a logical sequence in such a way that the organization of the text bears his stamp. He has also provided introductory material to the two halves: the statement on the systems of knowledge and the training of the king (topics 1–3) to the first half, and the concept of circle and constituents of topics 96–97 to the second, with the latter providing, as already noted, a key to the organization of the whole treatise.

It is also clear that Kauṭilya has edited the entire text closely and with a heavy hand. We see this most explicitly in the numerous cross-references to different parts of the text. These include references in earlier sections to later parts and references in later parts to earlier sections. Most of these are within the first half dealing with internal administration (books 1–5), although there are a few references in the first half to sections in the second half on external affairs, and vice versa.[28] It is noteworthy that there is no reference within passages of the Kauṭilya Recension to passages we have identified as belonging to the Śāstric Redaction.

Even more significant are the nearly identical phrases and lists found throughout the treatise; these probably come from Kauṭilya's editorial activities. I can give here only a few examples. See, for instance, the expression *kāmādir utsekaḥ* (indiscretions such as a love affair) at 1.15.11 and 9.7.1, and the parallel *mantrapūrvāḥ sarvārambhāḥ* (counsel precedes all undertakings, 1.15.2) and *kośapūrvāḥ sarvārambhāḥ* (the treasury precedes all undertakings, 2.8.1). We have a long and identical list of entertainers at 1.12.9 and 2.1.34: *naṭa-nartaka-gāyana-vādaka-vāgjīvana-kuśīlava* (actors, dancers, singers, musicians, bards, and performers); and at 7.17.34 we have the same list with the addition of *plavaka* (rope dancer) and *saubhika* (dramatic storytellers), and at 2.27.25 with those two plus a third, *cāraṇa* (wandering troubadour). See also the long compound *aṭavyantapālapurarāṣṭramukhyaiḥ* (with tribal chiefs, commanders of the frontier, and the city and provincial chiefs) at 1.16.7 and 2.16.21. Such examples can be multiplied.

An issue that relates to the Kauṭilya Recension is what, if any, title this original treatise of Kauṭilya had. The title *Arthaśāstra* is found only in the colophons, in three verses (5.6.47; 7.10.38; 7.18.42), in 1.1.2 and 15.1.1–2, all of which are clearly part of the Śāstric Redaction, and in 1.5.14, which also belongs to that redaction. It is fair to assume, therefore, that the redactor has introduced this title; the word *arthaśāstra* does not occur in any part of the text belonging to the Kauṭilya Recension. I think the evidence supports the view that the original title of the text was probably *Daṇḍanīti*. When Kauṭilya discusses the four systems of knowledge, he calls his own system *daṇḍanīti* and goes on to explain the meaning of the two words and of the compound (1.2.1, 4, 6, 11; 1.4.3). He says that the king should learn *daṇḍanīti* from the scholars and practitioners, and that the chaplain should be versed in it (1.5.8; 1.9.9). Even Kāmandaki, who called his own work *Nītisāra*, says that Viṣṇugupta, that is Kauṭilya, extracted the nectar of *Nītiśāstra* from the ocean of *Arthaśāstras* (1.6), pointing again to *nīti* as part of the original title. Likewise, Daṇḍin in his *Daśakumāracarita* (ed. Kale, p. 191) speaks of the *Daṇḍanīti* composed by Cāṇakya. It appears then that not only was the original title *Daṇḍanīti*, but this title also survived even after the Śāstric Redaction, which entitled it *Arthaśāstra*.

One final issue relating to the original *AŚ* is whether it was composed in prose or in verse. Arguments for a metrical original of the *AŚ* have been put forward by both Indian and Western scholars from the very beginning of *AŚ* scholarship. Trautmann's (1968) study has clearly demonstrated the untenability of this position. More recently, Scharfe (1993, 42–66) has subjected the verses as they relate to the prose that immediately precedes them to a close examination and shown that often the prose appears to presuppose the verses. Scharfe's claim is specific and restricted to the prose sentences surrounding the verses and does not extend to the prose text as a whole.[29]

Śāstric Redaction

The Kauṭilya Recension must have gained some popularity and authority at least by the time of Manu (mid-second century C.E.), who, as we will see, used the Kauṭilya Recension. Some time after Manu, a scholar well versed in both the Dharmaśāstric and the Arthaśāstric traditions attempted to transform the Kauṭilya text into a true scientific treatise (*śāstra*) compatible with the major principles of Dharmaśāstra.

The isolation of the Kauṭilya Recension, outlined in the preceding section, implicitly involved an examination of the textual and structural interventions of the śāstric redactor. Here I want to deal with the contours of the Śāstric Redaction more explicitly and in greater detail. I will deal first with the new structure the redactor gave to the text, and second with the additions, revisions, and rewriting he carried out to produce the *AŚ* as we have it.

With reference to the structure, as I have noted earlier, there is a consensus that the chapter (*adhyāya*) division of the text and the chapter-ending verses were imposed on it at a later date by the redactor. To the same redactor must be attributed the first chapter consisting of a table of contents and the last book (15), which is a scholarly reflection on the entire text. I think Trautmann (1971, 75) has summarized the position well:

> [T]here is excellent reason to regard the division into chapters, the terminal verses, the entirety of *Arthaśāstra* 1.1 with its table of contents and its enumeration of book, chapter, topic and *śloka* totals and, since it refers to the first chapter, Book 15 (*Tantrayukti*), as the work of a later, tidying and organizing hand, reworking a text already divided by books and topics, and already possessing an adequate introduction in *Arthaśāstra* 1.2.

Taking this as the basis, I want to explore what other emendations and additions may have been done by this redactor. First, from an organizational point of view, I think that the division of the text into 15 books (*adhikaraṇa*) also goes back to the redactor; in this I depart from Trautmann's assessment. First, book 15 is clearly the work of the redactor. Thus, if the original had the book division, it would have contained at most 14 books. I will further argue, following McClish (2009), that several books (5, 8, 11–12, 14) belong to this redaction. Second, the titles of some of the books do not correspond to the subjects covered in them. Book 1 is entitled "On the Subject of Training," even though only the first three topics deal with this subject; the rest deal with the appointment of ministers, the creation of a spy network, and matters relating to the personal security of the king. Book 2 is entitled "On the Activities of Superintendents," and yet its first topics have nothing to do with superintendents. Book 4 is entitled "Eradication of Thorns" (*kantakaśodhana*), yet its first three chapters have nothing to do with this subject. The redactor has simply added the initial sentence at 4.1.1 to introduce this subject in an artificial manner. Book 5 is entitled

"On Secret Conduct" (*yogavṛttam*), yet it contains material having nothing to do with this subject, such as a salary list, the conduct of a dependent, and royal succession. Evidently, the title of this book came from the subject matter of its very first chapter, which deals with the infliction of secret punishment. The title of book 12, "On the Weaker King" (*ābalīyasam*), is derived simply from the very first words of its first chapter set within a dialogue, which, as we will see, belong to the Śāstric Redaction. It is easier to see how the book division was introduced in order to facilitate the chapter division, given that chapter numbering probably began anew at each book, than to assume that the book division was original to the Kauṭilya Recension. The topics, which form the basic division of that recension, are numbered sequentially through the entire text and are independent of the books. In other words, the chapter division demands the book division, but the topic division does not. The artificiality of the book division also indicates that it was imposed on pre-existing material.

The manner in which the redactor introduced book divisions can be detected in books 3 and 4. Both books begin with parallel sentences that link the substance of the books to their respective titles:

> *dharmasthās trayas trayo 'mātyāḥ … vyāvahārikān arthān kuryuḥ* | (3.1.1)
>
> *pradeṣṭāras trayas trayo 'mātyāḥ kaṇṭakaśodhanaṃ kuryuḥ* | (4.1.1)
>
> Justices of ministerial rank in groups of three should conduct trials … of lawsuits arising from transactions.
>
> Magistrates of ministerial rank in groups of three should carry out the eradication of thorns.

These introductory sentences have transformed these books into discussions of the judiciary and the eradication of thorns. When we proceed beyond these statements, however, we see little to justify the statements or the titles of the books.

The content of book 3 deals with transactions (*vyavahāra*) that have legal ramifications; but the book itself is not about the judiciary, court procedures, or the conduct of lawsuits.[30] This subject comes up in topic 58 about writing down the plaint, at the end of chapter 1. If we exclude this passage, there is a logical continuity between topic 57 on valid and invalid transactions and topic 59 on marriage, given that marriage is the essential precondition of any transaction. The only other place that deals with judicial procedure is the section on witnesses, which comes at the very end of topic 63 on debts (3.11.28–50). The placement of this discussion is quite suspicious; it was probably prompted by the fact that in most other texts on legal procedure, the subject of witnesses is taken up within the context of the nonpayment of debts.[31] In these texts, however, the nonpayment of debts is the very first topic. The treatment of witnesses within the discussion of debt becomes anomalous in the *AŚ* because, there, this subject is dealt with after the long discussion of marriage and inheritance covering chapters 1 to 10 of book 3. It appears that this section on witnesses within the discussion of the nonpayment of debts was taken from a Dharmaśāstric source and introduced here, perhaps by the śāstric redactor.

Further, the Justice does not appear in the main portion of the book with any judicial functions. He appears at 3.4.35 (his permission is required for a woman to remarry); at 3.12.14 (his permission is needed to sell a pledge when the man who made the pledge is missing); and at 3.12.10, 12 (when a stolen article is discovered, the owner gets the Justice to confiscate it). He appears at the very end of the book in a section called "miscellaneous" (3.20.22), where he is asked to personally look into the affairs of gods, ascetics, and the like. His final appearance, this time in a judicial capacity, is in the concluding verse (3.20.24), which ties it to the opening sentence and provides a conclusion to the entire book. Clearly, the first sentence and last verse have converted the section into a legal text, perhaps under the influence of Dharmaśāstric texts on the topic.[32]

In book 4 also, after the initial statement, we have three topics (76–78) that have nothing to do with the title of the book, the eradication of thorns, that is, the suppression of criminal activities. When finally this subject is introduced in topic 79, it is the Collector who is supposed to work at eradicating thorns. We hardly hear about Magistrates in the rest of the book. They appear twice (4.4.8 and 4.9.18) along with Justices as the object of punishment by the Collector for malfeasance. Once, they appear in a compound along with the Collector (4.9.1) as officials who should investigate superintendents. Magistrates are evidently minor officials working under the Collector, as explicitly stated at 2.35.7. The other two times that they appear singly are in verses (4.6.20; 4.10.18). Nothing within this book indicates that the provisions given there were intended for the Magistrates. With a book number, title, and an introductory sentence, the redactor has converted a set of miscellaneous topics into a separate book on the eradication of thorns.

Turning now to the additions and revisions by the redactor, it is probable that books 5 and 14 were added by him as appendices to the two sections of the treatise. Their titles also parallel each other: Book 5 contains the term *yoga*, which has the connotation of secret conduct, while book 14 is *aupaniṣadikam*, dealing with esoteric knowledge and practices. Further, McClish (2009) has singled out books 8, 11, and 12 as redactoral insertions, and I can only briefly mention a couple of key reasons in his long argument. Books 11 and 12, dealing with confederacies and a weaker king, appear as an excursus that disrupts the description of the preparation for war (book 9), conduct of the war (book 10), and the finale of the military campaign, which is the capture of the enemy fort (book 13). The position of book 8 is more problematic. It stands between the central book 7 and book 9 that begins the discussion of war, and it consists almost entirely of dialogues, which would place it within the Śāstric Redaction. It picks up the style of some passages in book 7, asking which of two things is better. As I will note below, it is likely that the brief non-dialogue portions of this book were taken from some other source and then expanded into a full book by the addition of multiple dialogues.

Besides the insertion of several books, the Śāstric Redaction, I believe, was also responsible for several revisions that expanded the text, often in directions that favored Dharmaśāstric ideology, especially the supremacy of the Brāhmaṇical community within the ideology of the *varṇa* (social class) system, what McClish (2009) has called "Brāhmaṇical exceptionalism." A good example of this is the very first topic on the systems of knowledge. This single topic is spread over three chapters (2–4). The original of this topic consisted of brief *sūtra*-type statements regarding the four systems of knowledge. The redactor expanded them into long commentaries (*bhāṣya*) enabling him to create several new chapters out of them. Here are the succinct statements, which flow seamlessly and are interconnected:

> *anvīkṣikī trayī varttā daṇḍanītiś ceti vidyāḥ* || 1.2.1
>
> *sāṃkhyaṃ yogo lokāyataṃ cety ānvīkṣikī* || 1.2.10
>
> *sāmargyajurvedās trayas trayī* || 1.3.1
>
> *kṛṣipāśupālye vāṇijyā ca vārttā* || 1.4.1
>
> *ānvīkṣikītrayīvārttānāṃ yogakṣemasādhano daṇḍaḥ tasya nītir daṇḍanītiḥ* || 1.4.3
>
> Critical inquiry, the Triple, economics, and government—these are the knowledge systems.
>
> Sāṃkhya, Yoga, Lokāyata—these constitute critical inquiry.

> The three Vedas—Sāma, Ṛg, and Yajur—constitute the Triple.
>
> Agriculture and animal husbandry, along with trade, constitute economics.
>
> What provides enterprise and security to critical inquiry, the Triple, and economics is punishment (*daṇḍa*); its administration (*nīti*) is government (*daṇḍa-nīti*).

The succinct statement on the systems of knowledge and the definition of government has been expanded by the redactor to give a Dharmaśāstric stamp on the text. See, for example, the expansion of the Triple to the four Vedas, the supplementary sciences, and the *dharma* pertaining to the social classes (*varṇa*) and the orders of life (*āśrama*). Here we also have the specific duties (*svadharma*) of each social class, including the requirement that Śūdras serve the upper classes. These ideas are absent in the rest of the document.

As McClish (2009, 173) has pointed out, this succinct enumeration of the systems of knowledge has a nice parallel in topic 98 (7.1) where the six foreign policy strategies are enumerated:

> *saṃdhivigrahāsanayānasaṃśrayadvaidhībhāvāḥ ṣāḍguṇyam* || 7.1.2

Into this simple enumeration of the sixfold strategy has been introduced a dialogue containing an invented dispute (7.1.2–5).[33] After this interruption, the text continues with the definitions of the six strategies, much like the definitions of the four systems of knowledge in topic 1.

> *tatra paṇabandhaḥ saṃdhiḥ* ||
>
> *apakāro vigrahaḥ* ||
>
> *upekṣaṇam āsanam* ||
>
> *abhyuccayo yānam* ||
>
> *parārpaṇaṃ saṃśrayaḥ* ||
>
> *saṃdhivigrahopādānaṃ dvaidhībhāvaḥ* ||
>
> *iti ṣaḍguṇāḥ* || 7.1.6–12
>
> The sixfold strategy consists of peace pact, initiating hostilities, remaining stationary, marching into battle, seeking refuge, and double stratagem.[34]
>
> Of these, peace pact is a negotiated agreement;

Initiating hostilities is harmful action;

Remaining stationary is awaiting patiently;

Marching into battle is strength;

Seeking shelter is surrendering to another;

Double stratagem is pursuing a peace pact and initiating hostilities at the same time.

These are the six strategies.

A principle that we can extrapolate from the examination of topic 1 and apply to the rest of the text is that when a single topic is spread over several chapters, we can suspect that the text may have been expanded by the redactor. We see such expansions especially at topic 59 (spread over 3.2–4), topic 60 (spread over 3.5–7), topic 61 (spread over 3.8–10), and topic 116 (spread over 7.9–12). We should expect to find additional material from the hand of the redactor at these points.

There are also places where two statements are syntactically connected, but this connection is obscured by intervening redactoral commentary. In 8.3, for example, we have a straightforward enumeration of vices, an enumeration that is made disjointed by several intervening dialogues between Kauṭilya and other authorities. Thus, at 8.3.4, we have the statement about vices (*vyasana*):

kopajas trivargaḥ kāmajaś caturvargaḥ ||

There is a set of three that stem from wrath, and a set of four that stem from pleasure.

Then follows a long dialogue, after which the original thread is continued (8.3.23):

vākpāruṣyam arthadūṣaṇaṃ daṇḍapāruṣyam iti …

Verbal abuse, injury to property, and physical assault …

This is again interrupted by a dialogue about the relative seriousness of these three, after which the initial sentence is completed (8.3.37):

iti kopajas trivargaḥ ||

constitute the triple set stemming from wrath.

Note the insertion of *iti* (the Sanskrit term that indicates the closure of a list) here, because the *iti* at the end of the first half of the sentence has now been separated from the rest of the sentence. The second *iti* was necessitated only because of the intervening insertion. After this there follows immediately the enumeration of the four vices stemming from pleasure (8.3.38), an enumeration that parallels the previous statement:

> *kāmajas tu mr̥gayā dyūtaṃ striyaḥ pānam iti caturvargaḥ* ||
>
> The fourfold set stemming from pleasure, however, consists of hunting, gambling, women, and drinking.

Three significant points arise from this. First, the redactor expanded the brief *sūtra*-like text by commentarial interventions, in the current case through a dialogue that sought to assess the relative seriousness of the vices. Second, if these inserted dialogues are removed, the remaining text would be too short to constitute a chapter. Thus we see that the expansion of the original brief statement may have been carried out in order to create a text sufficiently long to be made into a chapter. We see this clearly in 8.4, where the initial statement of the four kinds of divine afflictions is expanded into an entire chapter by appended dialogues. Third, this kind of expansion through the insertion of dialogues makes all the Kauṭilya dialogues in the text suspect, requiring closer examination of them in relation to their immediate contexts. A final interesting point to note is that, as McClish (2009) has pointed out, the entire book 8, composed almost entirely of dialogues, may well be an insertion by the redactor. If this is so, then it appears that he used a source containing these brief statements but expanded them to fit the needs of his composition.[35] Alternatively, although less likely, this brief enumeration of vices may have constituted a topic in the Kauṭilya Recension itself, coming at the end of the discussion on strategies in book 7.

There is good reason to believe that most, if not all, of the Kauṭilya dialogues belong to the Śāstric Redaction. The artificiality of these dialogues has been noted by scholars.[36] A close examination of the dialogues confirms this and leads us to believe that these dialogues were added at a later time to the pre-existing text. There are altogether 75 such dialogues, with three additional statements that simply ascribe a view to Kauṭilya.[37] The dialogues themselves can be divided into three groups: The first presents views of one or more of four schools: Mānavas, Bārhaspatyas, Auśanasas, and Pārāśaras.[38] The second gives opinions of one or more of seven individual authorities: Bhāradvāja, Viśālākṣa, Pārāśara, Piśuna, Kauṇapadanta, Vātavyādhi, and Bāhudantīputra.[39] The third gives opinions of authorities that are collectively referred to as teachers (*ācāryāḥ*).[40]

One noteworthy feature is that the schools appear only in the first half of the treatise, specifically in books 1, 2, and 3. Generally, the order is Mānavas, Bārhaspatyas, and Auśanasas,[41] while in the only place (2.7.11–15) where four are listed, the Pārāśaras occupy the second position. The views ascribed to these schools always involve numbers: for example, Mānavas prescribing 12 ministers, the Bārhapatyas 16, and the Auśanasas 20 (1.15.47–50). No numbers are involved when individual authors are cited, yet the artificiality of the views ascribed to them is apparent. They are all cited in the same order, and often each contradicts the opinion given by the preceding author. The opinions ascribed generically to teachers are the most numerous, accounting for 50 of the 75 dialogues. It is difficult to say whether these dialogues represent historical controversies, but at least some of them probably do. For example at 3.7.1–3, Kauṭilya takes a middle position between the two opposing views about the man to whom a son belongs: his biological father or the legal husband of his mother. This controversy is found in most Dharmaśāstras and probably represents two schools of thought. Other statements ascribed to teachers appear to be mere foils to present the view of Kauṭilya.[42]

The mechanical and formalistic way in which the putative opinions of others are cited in the *AŚ* stands in sharp contrast to the Dharmasūtras, where the passages giving contrasting opinions of others are organically connected to the rest of the text (Olivelle 2010, 38). It is clear, then, that someone introduced these dialogues into the pre-existing text. The questions are who, and why?

Even though it is possible that Kauṭilya himself is responsible for at least some of them, the far more likely scenario is that the person responsible for them is the śāstric redactor. It is much less likely that Kauṭilya would have inserted such extraneous material that disrupted and disfigured his own elegant composition. Further, as McClish (2009) has pointed out, a few times the dialogues either spill into (1.8.29) or are carried out entirely within the concluding verses, showing their relationship to the Śāstric Redaction.

The reasons for the introduction of these dialogues are unclear and may have been multiple; for example, some chapters would disappear if the dialogues are removed. But one reason may have been the redactor's desire to establish Kauṭilya not only as the author of the text, which he did with the colophons and some of his verses, but also as someone standing in a long line of Arthaśāstric authorities, someone who has surpassed them all when he composed his *Arthaśāstra*. In a sense, then, it was this redactor who invented the Kauṭilya tradition as the preeminent school of political science and thereby made the *AŚ* the preeminent treatise on political science.

I have already discussed the redactoral additions to 1.2–4 that expanded a single brief topic into three chapters. Redactoral intervention is also evident in 1.8, which consists entirely of a dialogue. The section on edicts (2.10), which is probably very old as it contains the term *varga* unknown from other sources (see 2.10.21 n.), nevertheless has been identified by McClish (2009) as belonging to the later redaction. Here I am a bit cautious, because the directives about writing edicts are addressed to the scribe (*lekhaka*), who is a high official of ministerial rank. So the entire discussion may fall under the activities of superintendents. Yet the concluding verse, returning again to authorship of the *AŚ*, is unique, and this chapter also contains 12 verses in the body of the text, which is quite unusual. Finally, we see that three topics (59–61) have been spread over nine chapters (3.2–10), which, as I noted earlier, is a good sign of a redactoral intervention. It is not quite clear, however, which of these chapters or sections of chapters are the work of the redactor. But several topics common in the Dharmaśāstras appear here: the eight forms of marriage (3.2.2–13); the length of time the wives of various social classes must wait for their absent husbands (3.4.24–36); levirate (3.4.37–41); division of property according to the social class of the mother (3.6); and classification of sons and mixed castes (3.7). The very prominence of the *varṇa* system in them makes these sections suspect. Sometimes, clues to later insertions are found in the terminology. Thus 2.4.6, with its reference to the four *varṇas,* is probably a later insertion, and this is demonstrated by the use of *rājaniveśa* for the king's residence. This term is never used elsewhere in the *AŚ*, where *niveśa* is regularly used with only the meaning of settling the land with people (see 2.1), and the term for the king's residence is *antaḥpura.*

Although the separation of the Kauṭilya Recension from the Śāstric Redaction is not easy or clear, there is one external check that offers some assistance and assurance. It appears that Manu, in composing chapters 7–9 of his treatise, used the Kauṭilya Recension.[43] Time and again, as McClish has shown (2009, 203–209; 2012), Manu fails to refer to the redactoral additions we have identified in the *AŚ*. In listing the four systems of knowledge (*MDh* 7.43), Manu adds a fifth, knowledge of the self, but omits all the additional material from the redaction (*AŚ* 1.2–4). He also omits all of books 5, 8, 11, 12, and 14; we see a transition from book 7 to 9 (at *MDh* 7.162–187), ignoring book 8, and from book 10 to 13 (*MDh* 7.194–197), ignoring books 11 and 12. A significant clue is found in Manu's description of the grounds for litigation (*vyavahārapadas*), which concludes with gambling. Manu, first of all, does not deal with gambling as a matter for litigation; he merely instructs the king to suppress this practice in his kingdom. If Manu was so hostile toward gambling, why did he include it as one of the *vyavahārapadas*? It appears that Manu was forced to deal with this subject even though he disliked it, probably because, at the end of various matters subject to dispute, the *AŚ* lists gambling to be carried out under the direction of the Superintendent of Gambling; Manu placed this as the last *vyavahārapada*. After gambling, as topic 75, it was probably the redactor who inserted a section on miscellaneous matters called *prakīrṇaka*. Possibly he found such a discussion in the legal texts he consulted. But Manu does not have a ground for litigation called *prakīrṇaka*, probably because he did not find this discussion in the copy of the *AŚ* he had, which was the Kauṭilya Recension prior to its Śāstric Redaction. When we look at the Dharmaśāstras of Yājñavalkya and Nārada, on the other hand, we find precisely such a ground for litigation called *prakīrṇaka*. These later authors presumably had before them the Śāstric Redaction of the *AŚ*.

Although it is not possible to deal with this issue adequately within the compass of an introduction, it must be noted that the full expression of Brāhmaṇical ideology and exceptionalism that are the hallmarks of the Dharmaśāstras is found mostly in the Śāstric Redaction.[44] Prose passages expressing this ideology are found frequently at the end of chapters just before the concluding verses. It appears, therefore, that these final prose passages were added by the same redactor responsible for the verses.[45] I can give here only a few examples: At 2.12.32–33, we have an exception to the state monopoly over salt manufacture in the case of hermits and learned Brāhmaṇas; at 2.24.30, where those learned in the Vedas may take flowers and fruits; at 3.1.37, where Brāhmaṇas are an exception to the rule that fines may be paid off through manual labor; at 4.8.27–28, where Brāhmaṇas are exempt from torture; at 13.4.62, which deals with social classes (*varṇa*) and order of life (*āśrama*). Sometimes, such exceptions are given at the end of a sentence containing a prescription, indicating that the exception was possibly added later.[46]

Even though the text that has come down to us is substantially the Śāstric Redaction, there is no doubt that revisions, errors, additions, and perhaps even subtractions have occurred over the many centuries of transmission by scribes. I have recorded in the notes numerous places where improvements to the text can be made through higher criticism and given a cumulative list of such places in the note to the translation. However, for the task of an editor engaged in lower criticism, we do not have much to go on: just two complete manuscripts, one partial one, and a few commentaries removed from the original by many centuries. As an example of scribal errors and interpolations, we can take 4.11.21, which reads: "He should tear out the tongue of anyone who reviles the king or reveals his secret counsel, who spreads pernicious news reports, or licks a Brāhmaṇa's cooking utensils." Even Meyer and Kangle think that the phrase about licking a Brāhmaṇa's cooking utensils is an interpolation or a commentarial gloss that found its way into the text. Many similar intrusions into the text are noted by Kangle.[47] Unfortunately, given the paucity of manuscript material, it is difficult to isolate such interpolations and errors.

3. *Date*

Given its compositional history outlined above, the very question regarding *the date* or *the author* of the *AŚ* becomes moot. We have to instead seek *dates* and *authors* in the plural[48] for the three major phases of its composition: the sources used by Kauṭilya, the original Kauṭilya composition, and the subsequent Śāstric Redaction.

Sources of Kauṭilya

My procedure is to move forward from the possible dates for the sources of Kauṭilya, because most of the data we have for dating the text derive from these sources. Given the later association between the *AŚ* and Cāṇakya, who is regarded as the prime minister of Candragupta Maurya, there has been a trend from the inception of *Arthaśāstra* scholarship to date the text to the Maurya period. The latest and the most sustained arguments in favor of such a date are offered by Kangle (1965, 106): "We may, therefore, conclude that there is no convincing reason why this work should not be regarded as the work of Kauṭilya, who helped Candragupta to come to power in Magadha." Relying on this dating, scholars in a variety of fields, ranging from history to political science and economics, have used data from the *AŚ* to reconstruct Mauryan society and polity. This dating of the *AŚ* has been refuted by numerous scholars, and I will not engage in a sustained argument against the Maurya dating here.[49] It suffices to say that these arguments based on linguistic and cultural data should put to rest once and for all the Maurya origin of the *AŚ*.

To these arguments, I want to add just one derived from the work of Schlingloff (1967). The *AŚ* (2.3.8–9) forbids the use of wood in defensive fortifications of cities because of the obvious danger posed by fire. Yet, the fortifications excavated at Pāṭaliputra, the capital of the Maurya empire, are made of wood.[50] It is impossible for the prime minister of Candragupta to have tolerated such defenses if he was the same person who authored the *AŚ*. Clearly, the defenses in older cities were made of wood, as the use of *sāla* (a kind of tree) as a common term for defensive walls in later literature including the *AŚ* (2.4.16 n.) indicates. At some point, however, stone and brick became the norm, as at Kauśambhī (Schlingloff 1967, 48f; 1969, 13). The data on the construction of forts in the *AŚ* (2.3), therefore, must come from a period later than the Maurya. The arguments I present below on the likely place of composition of the *AŚ* also precludes its authorship by Cāṇakya.

Can we, however, narrow the time period when these sources of Kauṭilya may have been composed? The best data for this purpose come from book 2, which contains information on material culture, especially luxury goods. Trautmann (1971, 174–187) and Scharfe (1993, 275–293) have used several pieces of such data to assess the age of the *AŚ*, although in my argument these assessments pertain rather to the sources of the *AŚ*. Of these, I think the most compelling is the listing of coral (*pravāla*)[51] among luxury goods, an argument first put forward by Sylvain Lévi.[52] First, the term is integral to the text; it is found not just in book 2, where it is a precious item for entry into the royal treasury, but also in book 5 and, importantly, in book 7 dealing with foreign policy. So, in a sense, this term may provide a clue to the dating of not just the sources of book 2, but also all the source material used by Kauṭilya.

Now, coral of sufficiently good quality for making jewelry or ornaments is not found in the seas around the Indian subcontinent. Further, *AŚ* 2.11.42 gives two types of coral: *ālakandakam* and *vaivarṇikam*. It is certain that the first refers to Alexandria in Egypt.[53] Indeed, the reading of the commentator Bhikṣu Prabhāmati in his *Cāṇakyaṭīkā* is *alatsādrakam*, which he explains as *alatsāndradeśabhavam*, "originating in the country Alatsāndra." The other kind of coral, *vaivarṇika*,[54] also probably refers to a place of origin. Bhaṭṭasvāmin in his commentary *Pratipadapañcikā* says that this coral originates in a coastal region of *yavanadvīpa* (Greek island or country), which probably refers to some area of the Mediterranean. Pliny,[55] writing in the second half of the first century C.E,, bears witness to the extent to which Indians prized Mediterranean coral (Trautmann 1971, 178). That coral was an import is also suggested by the term *pravāla*, which is absent in the vocabulary of early Sanskrit texts, including that of the second-century B.C.E. grammarian Patañjali. The term itself was probably coined when the precious substance was first introduced into India through maritime trade.

The central question with regard to the dating of the text is when such commerce involving sea trade began to flourish between the Mediterranean and Indian ports. Recent studies by several scholars and archeological finds in southern Indian ports have pushed back the date for the commencement of sea trade to the late second century B.C.E., even though it is likely that the full flourishing of such trade did not happen until several decades later, that is, in the first century B.C.E.[56] The recent work of De Romanis (2000) posits four phases in the export of Mediterranean coral to the east, including India and China. He dates the second phase, including sea trade between Egypt and India, to the first century B.C.E. Clearly, by the time Pliny wrote, around 78 C.E., this trade had been flourishing for quite some time. So we shall not be far wrong in assuming that the earliest date, the *terminus post quem*, for the sources of Kauṭilya was the middle of the first century B.C.E.[57]

The upper limit, *terminum ante quem*, is provided by the position of gold within the *AŚ*. Gold (*suvarṇa*) is central to the economic prosperity of a kingdom, and Kauṭilya devotes several chapters (2.12.–14) to discussing goldsmiths and the government officials overseeing mines and the gold industry. Yet, the discussion of the production of coins (*AŚ* 2.12.24) mentions only silver and copper coins, and the term *hiraṇya* is uniformly used to refer to such coins. Although *suvarṇa* is mentioned as a particular weight (*AŚ* 2.14.3), a gold coin is never mentioned in the *AŚ*. All fines are given in Paṇas, which are assumed to be silver coins (Gupta 1960, 1969). This is in sharp contrast to the law book of Manu, which assesses several fines in gold coins called Suvarṇa (see Olivelle 2005, 24–25). The indigenous production of gold coins was introduced into India by the Kushana ruler Vima Kadphises, whose rule extended from the end of the first to the beginning of the second century C.E. It is thus quite likely that Kauṭilya's sources were composed prior to the end of the first century C.E. We may not be too far off if we assign these sources to a period between the middle of the first century B.C.E. and the middle of the first century C.E.

This dating is also supported by the prominent place accorded to the political formation known as *saṅgha*, confederacy, in the *AŚ* (see book 11). These polities were numerous and powerful in the second half of the first millennium B.C.E. Apart from the Buddhist literature, they are mentioned in the second-century B.C.E. grammarian Patañjali's commentary on Pāṇini's grammar. The very term *saṅgha* is conspicuous by its absence in the two epics, *Mahābhārata* and *Rāmāyaṇa*, and in the Dharmaśāstra of Manu. The prominence given to *saṅgha* in the *AŚ* argues for a date for the sources of Kauṭilya earlier than the epics.

Although it impossible to say when particular sections of Kauṭilya's source material were composed, it is theoretically possible that some may reach close to or into the Maurya period. The reason for this is that early Dharmasūtras, for example that of Āpastamba (2.25–29), which can be dated to a period before Patañjali (i.e., third or early second century B.C.E.; Olivelle 2012b), have discussions about the king and his fort, taxes, crime and punishment, and the judicial process. So, the presumption must be that texts dealing with such subjects were probably extant during the third and second centuries B.C.E. Some, therefore, have argued that a "core" or some sources of the *AŚ* may go back to the Maurya period, but such an argument is meaningless unless one can point with some confidence to such a core. Reflections and even compositions relating to kingship, governance, and statecraft may well have taken place during that distant period and may well be represented within the sources of Kauṭilya. This theoretical possibility, however, does not permit us to assign particular sections of the *AŚ* or particular information derived from them to the Maurya period or to use them to make historical reconstructions of that period.

The Kauṭilya Recension

The date of Kauṭilya's sources permits us to establish the lower limit of the Kauṭilya Recension. Given that some time must have elapsed between the composition of these source materials, especially the rather long and self-contained *adhyakṣapracāra*, and their use by Kauṭilya, I think we can put the lower limit, *terminus post quem*, at the middle of the first century C.E.

We have two major authors who date to the second century C.E. at the latest: the author of the law book of Manu and the Buddhist poet

Aśvaghoṣa. There is little doubt that Manu used the *AŚ* extensively in composing chapters 7–9 dealing with the king, governance, and legal procedure. This has been demonstrated repeatedly, and I will take it as established. Johnston (1929) has shown, likewise, the probable influence, especially in the technical vocabulary, of the *AŚ* on the works of Aśvaghoṣa, especially the *Saundarananda*. We are safe, I think, in taking the first half of the second century C.E. as the upper limit of the Kauṭilya Recension. The absence of gold coins also argues for a date close to or before 100 C.E.; if Kauṭilya was familar with gold coins, one would assume that he would have mentioned them in the context of the manufacture of coins.

Given that the composition of the *AŚ* proper begins with this recension, we can conclude with some confidence that Kauṭilya composed his treatise sometime between 50 and 125 C.E..[58]

The Śāstric Redaction

In dating the Śāstric Redaction of the *AŚ*, I begin with the assumption, spelled out above and demonstrated by McClish (2009, 203–09), that Manu used the Kauṭilya Recension and was unaware of the emendations carried out by the śāstric redactor. I have dated Manu to the middle of the second century C.E. (Olivelle 2005, 18–25). So the lower limit, the *terminus post quem*, for the Śāstric Redaction is the second half of the second century C.E.: for simplicity's sake, let us say 175 C.E.

In fixing the upper limit, the *terminus ante quem*, we are assisted by several texts broadly falling within the Gupta era, probably in the fourth–fifth centuries C.E.: Vātsyāyana's *Kāmasūtra*, Viśākhadatta's *Mudrārākṣasa*, and the works of Kālidāsa.[59]

It has been pointed out repeatedly that the structure of the *Kāmasūtra* imitates the *AŚ*. What must be noted, however, is that this structure is the one imposed by the redactor, with the threefold division into books, chapters, and topics. Indeed, the openings of the two texts parallel each other almost verbatim (see table I.2).[60]

This opening Chapter of the *AŚ* and the threefold division, as I have demonstrated above, are part of the Śāstric Redaction. Vātsyāyana, therefore, had before him the *AŚ* more or less as we have it.

The case of Viśākhadatta's drama *Mudrārākṣasa* is a bit more complicated. It is set during the time when Candragupta Maurya overthrew the Nanda king. The main architect of this event, according to Viśākhadatta,

Table I.2

Kāmasūtra (1.1.14–15)	Arthaśāstra (1.1.1–2)
... *kāmasūtram idaṃ praṇītam* / *tasyāyaṃ prakaraṇādhikaraṇasamuddeśaḥ* / ... this Kāmasūtra has been composed. The following is the list of its topics and books.	... *idam arthaśāstraṃ kṛtam* / *tasyāyaṃ prakaraṇādhikaraṇasamuddeśaḥ* / ... this Arthaśāstra has been made. The following is the list of its topics and books.

was Candragupta's prime minister, Cāṇakya, and he is the main character of the play. The *Arthaśāstra* is not directly quoted or mentioned, but Cāṇakya is introduced in a verse (I.7) as *kauṭilyaḥ kuṭilamatiḥ*, "Kauṭilya, namely, a man with a crafty mind."[61] Here Viśākhadatta presents the name Kauṭilya not as a lineage name (*gotra*) but as an epithet or nickname based on his famously crafty mind, which was able to overpower enemies with the strength of his intellect (see also 3.11). The net that he weaves in the play to capture Rākṣasa, the last prime minister of the Nandas, and to bring him into the service of Candragupta is a display of this intellect. Viśākhadatta uses technical terms from the *AŚ*, such as *tīkṣṇa* (assassin) and *kṛtya* (seducible person). In the prose after 3.19, he refers to the composers of *Arthaśāstras* in the plural (*arthaśāstrakārāḥ*), or it could be simply a majestic plural for Cāṇakya. Given that the ascription of the *AŚ* to Cāṇakya, as I will show, happens under the Guptas, we may be safe in assuming that Viśākhadatta had before him the Śāstric Redaction of the *AŚ*.

Numerous studies have shown that Kālidāsa was well acquainted with the *AŚ*.[62] The issue I am interested in relates to the recension of the text Kālidāsa used. The study by Rāgavan (1951) shows clearly that Kālidāsa's *AŚ* contained sections that certainly belonged to the Śāstric Redaction. For example, in the drama *Mālavikāgnimitra* (5.14), Kālidāsa talks about the advantages of a dual reign (*dvairājya*), echoing the opinion of Kauṭilya given in a dialogue at *AŚ* 8.2.7. The virtues and evils of hunting given in *Śakuntalā* (2.5) and the merits of the hunt in *Raghuvaṃśa* (9.49) parallel the discussion in *AŚ* 8.3.39–46. Other parallels to the Śāstric Redaction in the *Raghuvaṃśa* are 4.35 to *AŚ* 12.1; 19.48 to *AŚ* 8.3.7; 19.52 to *AŚ* 5.6.2; and 19.55–57 to *AŚ* 5.6.34.

If we allow at least a few decades for this new edition of the *AŚ* to reach a wide audience and to gain renown, then we can place the upper limit, the *terminus ante quem*, of the Śāstric Redaction at around 300 C.E., or perhaps a bit earlier. Thus, we should not be too far off the mark in dating the redaction to 175–300 C.E..

4. *Authorship*

Just as with the dates, with regard to authorship we also have to speak in the plural; the *AŚ* as we have it has multiple authors corresponding to the three phases of its composition. Beyond that, we should also inquire about the early history of its reception, especially the ascription of the *AŚ* to Cāṇakya and to Viṣṇugupta.

The first phase has many authors, that is, the authors of the sources used by Kauṭilya. Their names are unknown, but they probably belonged to the tradition of scholarship in various areas of governance and politics, as well as expert traditions in areas of material culture, such as architecture, metallurgy, and agriculture. These are probably the so-called "Arthaśāstras" that Kauṭilya says in the opening verse (1.1.1) he consulted in composing his own treatise.

The name of the historical person who composed what I have called the "Kauṭilya Recension" is not altogether certain. The text itself, as we have seen, ascribes the composition to Kauṭilya or Kauṭalya (Jolly 1927), a discrepancy in spelling/pronunciation that I will discuss presently. I want to argue that this was the real name of the actual author who composed the initial recension of the *AŚ*. My argument is based precisely on the fact that the eponymous ascriptions of many of the śāstric compositions of the time, for example, the ascriptions of Dharmaśāstras to Manu, Yājñavalkya, Viṣṇu, or Nārada, follow a definite pattern: The eponymous authors are celebrated figures in the ancient literature, either a god or a seer. Consider the authors of texts on kings or government listed in the epic *Mahābhārata* (12.59), Bṛhaspati and Uśanas, two well-known Vedic seers. Ascribing the authorship of a text to revered figures of the past confers prestige and authority. So, it is most likely that, if someone wanted to ascribe a work to an eponymous author, he could have found a better candidate than Kauṭilya or Kauṭalya! This name is quite unknown to early literature, although it appears occasionally in later literature and inscriptions as an obscure *gotra* name.[63] It seems prudent, therefore, to take the declaration of the text itself at face value: Kauṭilya was indeed the author's name.

Manuscripts of the *AŚ*, commentators, and references in other ancient Sanskrit texts present two forms of the name: Kauṭalya (with *ṭa*) and

Kauṭilya (with *ṭi*). There has been a long scholarly debate regarding which form is the original. Given the long and detailed analysis by Kangle (1965, 109–113), it is unnecessary to rehearse here the arguments for both positions. I am not convinced that either set of arguments proves to be conclusive. Here I want to comment briefly on some aspects of this issue that have not received attention.

First, even though much ink has been spilt over the past one hundred years on this issue, in the preceding thousand years and more, apart from Viśākhadatta's reference to Kauṭilya as crafty-minded (*kuṭilamati*), where *kuṭila* is intended explicitly by the author, not a single Sanskrit author has thought this issue significant enough to comment. Different authors use the one or the other form, but they never make an issue of it. To use a bit of slang, for them it was "no big deal." There may have simply been two ways of pronouncing the same name, as it so often happens, perhaps due to regional or dialectical variations, or perhaps through influences of the speakers' own mother tongues. It is very clear that whichever way it is pronounced, it is a lineage (*gotra*) name. Viśākhadatta's attempt is at most a popular or didactic etymology. As Burrow (1968, 24) notes, the Vṛddhi derivation of a masculine noun or adjective from an adjective (*kuṭila*) is grammatically impossible; in this case *kauṭilyam* in the neuter would simply mean crookedness. This makes it certain that even with the pronunciation Kauṭilya, it is a *gotra* name, and that Viśākhadatta could not have invented this form of the name for his literary purpose, because such a derivation was grammatically impossible. What he did was to make a punning etymology of a well-established name.

Viśākhadatta's pun may have had some unintended consequences. In the earliest available sources for the name of the author of the *AŚ*, only Viśākhadatta's work used all three names: Cāṇakya, Kauṭilya, and Viṣṇugupta. Others completely omit Kauṭilya/Kauṭalya and either give Cāṇakya (*Pañcatantra*), Viṣṇugupta (Kāmandaka's *Nītisāra*), or both of these (Daṇḍin's *Daśakumāracarita*). Why didn't these authors mention Kauṭilya, and was this omission intentional? Scholars have not addressed or even noted the issue of this silence. I think this silence may have been intentional. The reason is that authors who revere the *AŚ* no longer refer to its author by the name Kauṭilya, because, thanks to Viśākhadatta, it may have taken on a pejorative connotation. On the other hand, those authors who had a negative view of this work or of its author gladly use this specific form of his name: Kauṭilya. These are Bāṇa in his *Kādambarī* and three Purāṇas, *Viṣṇu* (4.24.6–7), *Vāyu* (37.324–25), and *Matsya* (227.22).

The fourth-century C.E. Buddhist author Āryasūra also uses the pun on the name Kauṭilya as crooked (Johnston 1929, 84). Bāṇa excoriated the *Arthaśāstra,*[64] and the Purāṇas mention Kauṭilya in the context of his helping Candragupta overthrow the Nandas. These Purāṇas view the Mauryas as Śūdras and illegitimate kings. Interestingly, it is only these Purāṇas that use the name Kauṭilya for the prime minister of Candragupta rather than the more common Cāṇakya.

When we move to the early middle ages, however, we see no trace of such a controversy. The two forms are used by different authors without comment. We have two inscriptions, one using Kauṭilya (Nidhanpur plate of Bhāskaravarman, seventh century C.E.) and the other using Kauṭalya (Vastupāla's inscription of 1234 C.E.). Two of the three independent *AŚ* manuscripts have Kauṭalya, and one has Kauṭilya. Three commentaries use Kauṭalya, while two use Kauṭilya.[65]

For pragmatic as well as substantive reasons, I have chosen to adopt the form Kauṭilya. Most people today recognize this form more readily. Our oldest source, the *Mudrārākṣasa,* incontrovertibly used the form Kauṭilya. Given that for most other sources we do not have strong manuscript traditions, it is impossible to determine what the form may have originally been. Finally, there is a contemporary community of Śukla-yajurvedīya Mādhyandina Brāhmaṇas in Maharashtra with the *gotra* name Kauṭilya, with this pronunciation.[66]

Many scholars, especially those like Kangle who date the *AŚ* to the time of Candragupta Maurya, argue for the identity of Kauṭilya and Cāṇakya, the other name by which the author of the *AŚ* is known in the tradition. The counter argument to this, articulated well and in detail by Trautmann (1971, 1–67), is that the connection between the two is not made until texts dating to or after the Gupta period. After an exhaustive examination of all the sources of what he calls the *Cāṇakya-Candragupta-Kathā* (Pāli, Jain, Kashmiri, and *Mudrārākṣasa* versions, as well as Greek accounts), Trautmann comes to the conclusion that all these sources provide "sufficient grounds to believe that Cāṇakya is as historical a figure as Nanda or Candragupta.... To doubt Cāṇakya's existence places a greater strain on the imagination: some other origin for the stories of him would have to be found." None of the earlier sources recording the narrative of Cāṇakya, however, mentions either Kauṭilya or Cāṇakya's authorship of the *AŚ*. Identifying the historical figure linked to the first Maurya emperor with Kauṭilya, the author of the *AŚ*, did not happen until the rise of the next major empire in north India, the

Gupta, which also arose in the same geographical region as the Maurya and probably occupied the same capital, Pāṭaliputra.

I want to argue that this linkage happened some time after the production of the Śāstric Redaction of the *AŚ*. If, indeed, this redactor knew the identity of Kauṭilya and Cāṇakya, or if he wanted to invent such a connection and a link to the Maurya dynasty, it would have been an easy matter to include Cāṇakya's name somewhere within the text itself or in the colophons. The name Cāṇakya, however, is completely absent from the text. It is reasonable to assume that this linkage happened after the *AŚ* took its final form. This is done for the first time and without the explicit use of the name Cāṇakya in a verse placed at the very end of the *AŚ* (15.1.73), raising doubts regarding its authenticity, that is, whether it was part of the original Śāstric Redaction. This verse identifies the author as the man who overthrew the Nandas.

Such associations, especially as powerful a historical association of a text on political science with one of the most powerful political operatives of ancient India linked closely to the most powerful Indian empire, do not happen by accident; some political motive must have driven some individuals to establish this association. I want to propose the hypothesis that the identity of Cāṇakya with Kauṭilya was forged during the Gupta rule as one way of connecting the new dynasty to the fabled Maurya empire as its legitimate successor. The recent book by Michael Willis (2009) has shown how the Gupta court attempted to symbolically connect itself to the Maurya empire, whose territory and capital city it now occupied. The very name Candragupta assumed by its first major emperor and his grandson and the last name "Gupta" of the dynasty connect this dynasty to Candragupta, the founder of the Maurya empire. Samudragupta, the son of Candragupta I, inscribed his famous eulogy on Aśoka's Allahabad pillar alongside Aśoka's own edict. We see this connection more explicitly in the drama *Mudrārākṣasa*, in which the founding of the Maurya dynasty is narrated. Composed perhaps under Candragupta II (so Trautmann 1971, 41) or in the fifth–sixth century C.E., the wordplay and allusions to the two Candraguptas would have been obvious to the contemporary audience.[67]

Within this symbolic connection between the two dynasties, we can see how the renowned minister and architect of the Maurya dynasty could have been presented as the author of the major treatise on political science that had already gained fame before the Gupta period, especially if, as seems likely, Cāṇakya also had a reputation for political acumen. Cāṇakya now becomes identified with Kauṭilya: two names for the same person. It may not be too far-fetched to see how another major treatise on law and kingship produced during the Gupta period came to be ascribed to another renowned theologian connected with the other fabled king from northeastern India, Janaka: This is the Dharmaśāstra of Yājñavalkya. It has been noted repeatedly that the text of Yājñavalkya follows the *AŚ* very closely; many of its verses are simply versifications of Kauṭilya's prose. Bronkhorst (2011) has drawn attention also to the Brāhmaṇical interest in presenting Brāhmaṇas as the counselors and power brokers for the royalty during the early centuries of the Common Era. What better way to exemplify this role than to present Cāṇakya, the archetypal Brāhmaṇa counselor and politician, as the author of the basic textbook on how to run a kingdom.

The third name associated with the author of the *AŚ* is Viṣṇugupta. The identification of Viṣṇugupta with the author of the *AŚ* is found in a verse tucked in at the very end of the *AŚ*, after the colophon of book 15. Even Kangle agrees that this verse is a later addition to the text with the intention of ascribing the authorship of the *AŚ* to Viṣṇugupta:

> Noticing the many errors committed by commentators on treatises, Viṣṇugupta himself composed both the aphoristic text (*sūtra*) and the commentary (*bhāṣya*).

Burrow (1968, 28–29) has argued against dismissing this verse and presented evidence from Kṣīrasvāmin's commentary on the lexicon *Amarakośa* for the possible existence of a commentary composed by Kauṭilya himself, an issue I address below. Kāmandaki also, in the opening stanzas of his *Nītisāra* (1.2–6), ascribes the authorship of the *AŚ* to Viṣṇugupta, without mentioning either Cāṇakya or Kauṭilya.

Viṣṇugupta is identified with both Cāṇakya and Kauṭilya in Viśākhadatta's *Mudrārākṣasa* (1.23–24; 5.22; 7.8–9). We find the identification of Cāṇakya and Viṣṇugupta, without any mention of Kauṭilya, in Daṇḍin's *Daśakumāracarita* (ch. 8, ed. Kale, p. 191), where it is said that the *AŚ* was composed by Viṣṇugupta for the sake of the Maurya, whereas elsewhere he ascribes the authorship to Cāṇakya (ch. 8, ed. Kale, p. 191).

Several questions arise with regard to the rise of this new name. The long history of the Cāṇakya narrative that Burrow (1968) and Trautmann (1971) have analyzed in detail contains no mention of the name Viṣṇugupta, apart from its use by Viśākhadatta in his political drama *Mudrārākṣasa*.

Thus, it does not make much sense to argue, as Kane (1962, 75, III: 166–167) does, that Viṣṇugupta was the personal name, while Cāṇakya was the *gotra* name. Given that the literature, apart from the *Mudrārākṣasa*, identifies Viṣṇugupta as the author of the *AŚ*, I think Burrow (1968, 28) may be right in considering this to have been the personal name of the man whose *gotra* name was Kauṭilya.

We may also need to pay attention to other factors during the fourth–sixth centuries C.E., such as the Vaiṣṇava orientation of the Gupta dynasty with its deep connection to the boar incarnation (*varāha*), a topic discussed in detail by Willis (2009). The name Viṣṇugupta makes him onomastically connected to Candragupta; the possible Brāhmaṇical heritage of the Guptas has been discussed by Willis (2009). We see the connection to Viṣṇu as boar in the verse added at the end of the *AŚ* (15.1.73) I have noted above. The Sanskrit reads:

> *yena śāstraṃ ca śastraṃ ca nandarājagatā ca bhūḥ |*
> *amarṣeṇoddhṛtāny āśu tena śāstram idaṃ kṛtam ||*
>
> The man who out of indignation quickly rescued the treatise (*śāstra*) and the weapon (*śastra*), as also the land that had fallen into the hands of the Nandas, it is he who composed this treatise.

Clearly, we have a nice wordplay here, but note the expression *nandarājagatā ca bhūḥ*, which recalls the earth that had been taken into the depths of the ocean by demons, in this case the Nanda kings. Note also the verb *uddhṛtāni*, which directly refers to the raising up of the earth by Cāṇakya, just as Viṣṇu as boar had done earlier.[68]

The relationship of Viṣṇugupta to Kāmandaki, the author of the *Nītisāra*, has been debated for over half a century. Ojha's (1952) thesis that Viṣṇugupta was both the final redactor of the *AŚ* and the teacher of Kāmandaki has been renewed by Willis (2009). This is based on the eulogy of Viṣṇugupta at the beginning of the *Nītisāra* (1.2–6) and on the reference in the body of the text (2.6) to the "view of my teacher" (*no gurudarśanam*), which is an allusion to *AŚ* 1.2.8 affirming that, according to Kauṭilya, there are indeed four systems of knowledge. As Scharfe (1993, 3) has pointed out, the sense of *guru* here is, in all likelihood, a revered teacher of a tradition that Kāmandaki follows, as opposed to the views of other authorities listed in this same passage. Given that Kāmandaki clearly states that Viṣṇugupta overthrew the Nandas, if Viṣṇugupta were to be his teacher, we would have the impossible anachronism of Kāmandaki placing himself several hundred years before his time. As Kangle (1965, 105) observes, texts are frequently ascribed to famous people of old, but never is a person known to someone placed in the distant past. Willis (2009, 62) further places Kāmandaki during the time of Candragupta II because of the use of *deva* in the initial verse of his work. This is too slender a piece of evidence on which to base such a significant conclusion, in spite of some inscriptional references to this king as *deva* or *devagupta*. I think Willis's (2009, 62) estimate that the *AŚ* was composed 30 or 40 years before Candragupta II is untenable. The very vocabulary of the *Nītisāra*, which outwardly follows the *AŚ*, shows a great distance in time between the two. To take just one example, the entire diplomatic and military strategy of Kauṭilya, as I will show below, is based on "outwitting" one's opponent, and the technical term used for this throughout the *AŚ* is *atisaṃdhi* and its verbal equivalents. This term is completely absent in the *Nītisāra*.[69]

A final issue relating to authorship is geography: Where was the *Arthaśāstra* composed? Given the complexity of its composition and the multiplicity of authorship, it is difficult to pinpoint a single location. However, a clue is found in *AŚ* 2.20.37 and 41 (also 1.19.7), where it is said that the shadow of a sundial disappears at midday during Āṣāḍha (June–July) and that the day and night are equal during Caitra (March–April) and Āśvayuja (September–October). Willis (2009, 23–25) has shown that this can happen only along the Tropic of Cancer. This would include a wide swath of northern India from present-day Gujarat, through Madhya Pradesh and Jharkhand, to Bengal. This area would be to the south of the ancient capital of Pāṭaliputra and major cities such as Allahabad and Vārānasī, but it would include such ancient sites such as Vidiśā and Ujjain. We can narrow this geography further if we follow Burrow (1968, 29–30) in taking Avanti and Aśmaka broadly as the regions that Kauṭilya was most familiar with and for which he gives the annual rainfall with precision at *AŚ* 2.24.5. This region encompasses today's Gujarat and northern Maharashtra. Burrow also concludes that the term *grāmakūṭa* (*AŚ* 4.4.9) for a village official or headman indicates that he was a native of this region and refers to the related term *gāvḍā* in Marathi. Further, as we have seen, the *gotra* name Kauṭilya is still extant in Maharashtra (Kangle 1965, 112). This location, close to important seaports along the

Gujarat coast, such as Sopara, also explains Kauṭilya's familiarity with sea trade (2.28.1–13).

5. *Reading the Arthaśāstra*

The *Arthaśāstra* is a unique and complex text that poses challenges to both the translator (see note to the translation) and the reader. The cultural, religious, legal, economic, and political areas it covers are vast, and with respect to some of them, the *AŚ* is either the only or the oldest available document. It deals with its subject matter at a meta-level, never entering the real and historical world of actual states and kingdoms. In this it is vastly different from its European counterpart, Machiavelli's *The Prince,* to which it has often been compared. Machiavelli is firmly anchored in 15th-century European, especially Italian, principalities. Kauṭilya's world is ideal-typical, abstracted from contact with history. His book is intended for all ages, and in this he participates in the normal custom of Brāhmaṇical writers of scientific treatises, who attempt to impart a timeless character to their work.

Yet, Kauṭilya's work is deeply rooted in the social, economic, and political realities of his time. His work is addressed to kings who want to be successful and to ministers whose own success is inextricably bound to their ability to make their kings succeed. It is, therefore, helpful to the readers, I think, to bring to the surface some of the basic presuppositions of the *AŚ*.

The king to whom the *AŚ* is addressed is an absolute monarch; all authority in areas of governance, law, economic activities, foreign relations, and the conduct of war rests with him. Although this was theoretically true, in reality, a king had to negotiate numerous centers of power both within his kingdom and in neighboring regions occupied by other kings (enemies, allies, and neutrals), as well as by tribal groups. The need to resort to subterfuge and assassinations to get rid of powerful men in his kingdom exemplifies this reality; the king often could not openly kill a powerful individual. Then there is the ideology of the king as protector and father of the people. One influential theory of kingship says that the legitimacy of taxation is dependent on the king providing protection to the subjects. There were also intangible areas of importance to the king: nobility, generosity, majesty, and especially the pursuit of fame. So, even though the king of Kauṭilya was an absolute monarch, he was not a despot or tyrant. Kauṭilya's cunning strategies have to negotiate these competing goals and expectations.

Given the requirement of completeness in a scientific treatise, Kauṭilya has adopted the strategy of considering his king as creating a kingdom ex novo, even though the text itself assumes that a king generally succeeds to the kingdom of his father or conquers an existing kingdom through warfare. In either case, the main structures of the state—fortresses, towns, villages, agricultural land, governmental apparatus, and the like—would already be in place. Kauṭilya, however, ignores this and proceeds to deal with each and every aspect of constructing a kingdom from the bottom up.

Among the many areas of importance for the proper running of a kingdom, I have selected three for comment here, in the hope that they will provide a key to entering the world of Kauṭilya: governance, economy, and foreign affairs.

A preliminary issue that must be addressed, however, is how much of what the *AŚ* has to say about society and material culture reflects historical reality and how much is an idealized portrayal—what should be rather than what is. Even though we see occasionally the śāstric proclivity to put everything into neat categories, the *AŚ* on the whole gives us valuable data on ancient Indian society, especially its material culture. First, Kauṭilya was writing for his contemporaries, and he would have been laughed out of court if he made obvious errors with regard to such subjects as building forts, agriculture, metals, precious stones, arrangement of armed forces, and the like, in which expert traditions already existed. One area where we can actually check the *AŚ* information against archeological remains is the information on fort-building. Here we find amazing correspondence that has been analyzed by Schlingloff who concludes: "Wherever we can confront the text with the results from excavations, they illuminate the difficult passages often in a surprisingly simple manner" (Schlingloff 1967, 77). If the data on construction correspond so well to what can be gathered from archeological excavations of ancient cities, we can, I believe, extrapolate from this to other areas of material culture on which the *AŚ* provides valuable, and often the only existing, data. We find, for example, one of the earliest cooking recipes (2.15.47–49). We are told how houses were sold or auctioned (3.9.3), and that rooms of homes were often rented out (3.8.24). We are told that inquests were held when there was a sudden and unexplained death and that autopsies were carried out on the bodies (4.7).

Governance

Given that, in an absolute monarchy, there is no clear distinction between king and government, between the wealth and property of the king and that of the state, and between governance and the enhancement of revenue to the state, the structures of government and state bureaucracy cannot be neatly separated from the economic activities of the state. The king did not merely rule; he also made money. It is as if the U.S. Departments of Agriculture and Commerce were responsible for both operating farms and factories and extracting taxes from farmers, industrialists, and businessmen. The situation is closer to the way the British East India Company ran parts of India than to that of a modern state. So, the state apparatus I will discuss below is also part of the economic infrastructure of the state.

Even though all power rests with the king, he cannot govern a complex kingdom all by himself. The *AŚ*, therefore, instructs the king to construct a bureaucracy that would carry out his various responsibilities. Unfortunately, Kauṭilya does not lay out clearly or in detail the structure of the government bureaucracy. Instead, he appears to assume that his audience already has a pretty good idea of that bureaucracy; his aim is to show how each of these bureaucrats should function. To complicate matters further, given that there may be a gap of a century or more between different parts of the text, these parts often give different or even contradictory information about the bureaucracy.

The governance structure recommended by the *AŚ* for domestic affairs appears to have four interlocking layers. I will describe the bureaucracy that deals with foreign affairs and the military later, even though officials at the upper levels of government, such as the counselors, were engaged in both. The term *amātya*, minister,[70] is applied to various kinds of the high-ranking officials in the kingdom. Kauṭilya speaks of the exemplary or ideal qualities of a minister (1.9.1), and the highest-ranking ministers are expected to possess all these qualities. Individuals not possessing all of them are appointed to lesser offices.

The most important ministers comprise the king's innermost circle of advisors called *mantrin*, counselors, within which his Chaplain (*purohita*) occupies a central position. The counselors do not have specific tasks to carry out, but the king is always expected to consult them before initiating any task. "All undertakings presuppose counsel," says Kauṭilya (1.15.2): Think before you act! In book 7, we encounter in textualized form the kinds of deliberations that counselors may have engaged in: Is this better or that? Is this more serious or that? Should one attack this enemy or that?

Another category of official without specific duties is the *mahāmātra,* a term I have translated as "high official." This term is already encountered in the Aśokan inscriptions. It is used sometimes in the *AŚ* as a generic designation of senior officers (1.10.7; 1.13.1; 4.6.2). At other times, it appears to refer to specific individuals with personal wealth and status within the kingdom. They review the annual accounts presented by superintendents (2.7.24), for example, and they participate in the process of succession at the death of the king (5.6.34).

Two officers of the highest rank and central to the state administration are the Collector (*samāhartr̥*) and the City Manager (*nāgarika*). The former is responsible for the territory (*janapada*) outside the capital city, while the latter functions like a mayor within the capital city. Both are responsible for internal security in their respective jurisdictions, and they are assisted by numerous mid-level officials. The Collector, much like his namesake during the British Raj, is also responsible for collecting revenue from the countryside, especially taxes on agricultural produce. On the security side, the Collector is assisted by a group of Magistrates (*pradeṣṭr̥*), whose activities include the suppression of criminal activities and the investigation of crimes, sudden deaths, and the like (see Book book 4). Officers under the City Manager include the Revenue Officer (*gopa*) and County Supervisor (*sthānika,* see 2.36).

An important group of officials called *dharmastha,* a term I have translated as Justice, was in charge of dispute resolution. The entire book 3 is devoted to this topic and to their duties (see above p. 16). They also probably worked under the Collector and, perhaps, under the City Manager, and paralleled the institution of Magistrate. In fact, jails attached to each officer are mentioned together at 2.5.5. The role of the Justices, however, was much broader than dispute resolution and functioning as judges in courts of law. They resided in population centers and were entrusted with broad authority regarding the proper observance of duties and laws, and their permission was needed for a variety of activities (see above p. 17).

The largest number of government officials listed in the *AŚ* consists of what we would today call department or agency heads. These are called the *adhyakṣas,* or superintendents. Their duties are narrowly defined, and most of these officials oversee the state's economic infrastructure so vital for its survival. Indeed, Kauṭilya says that the king himself should learn about economics (*vārttā*) from such superintendents (1.5.8). Thirty-five superintendents are either discussed in detail or referred to in passing, overseeing elephant forests (2.2.6–16), bureau of official records (2.7), treasury (2.11), mines (2.12), metals (2.12.23), the mint (2.12.24), coins (2.12.25), pit mines (2.12.27), salt (2.12.28), gold (2.13), the storehouse (2.15), commodities (2.16), forest produce (2.17), the armory (2.18), standardization (2.19), weights and measures (2.20), customs (2.21), yarn (2.23), agriculture (2.24), liquor (2.25), abattoirs (2.26), courtesans (2.27), shipping (2.28), ports (2.28.7), cattle (2.29), horses (2.30), elephants (2.31), chariots (2.33), infantry (2.33.7), passes (2.34.1), pasture land (2.34.5), gambling (3.20), the marketplace (4.2), prisons (4.9.23), and temples (5.2.38). Another important official discussed along with superintendents is the royal scribe (2.10), although he is not called a superintendent. He is responsible for drafting royal correspondence, especially those with foreign powers. Another senior official central to the state economy is the treasurer (*saṃnidhātṛ*, 2.5). The Collector is the high official tasked with overseeing the superintendents and testing their integrity (2.35.13).

The smallest administrative unit of the state was a village, and there was a parallel leadership structure for human settlements. Each village had a headman or elder (3.4.9; 3.10.16, 18). Kauṭilya recommends creating administrative centers encompassing several villages: a revenue collection center (*saṃgrahaṇa*) for ten villages, a county seat (*kārvaṭika*) for 200 villages, a district municipality (*droṇamukha*) for 400 villages, and a provincial capital (*sthānīya*) for 800 villages (2.1.4). We hear of revenue officers looking after five or ten villages (2.35.2); each officer was expected to draw up a census of fields, households, and other income-producing units within his jurisdiction.

What I have listed above is the open and visible apparatus of government. But an equally important element of the state was what we would today call the secret service, that is, the various spies and secret agents under the control of either the king himself or senior officials such as the Collector. The drama *Mudrārākṣasa* of Viśākhadatta provides a colorful glimpse into this secret world of espionage and sting operations envisaged by Kauṭilya. Spies and secret agents are spread across the entire treatise, and it is difficult to get an accurate picture of the entire secret service apparatus. In 1.11–12, however, Kauṭilya presents as close to a structure of the secret service as we get. The secret service is divided into clandestine establishments and mobile agents. The establishments are staffed by five kinds of agents: crafty students, apostate recluses, and agents working undercover as householders, merchants, or ascetics. These are described in 1.11.1–20. There are four kinds of mobile agents (1.12), who spread incognito throughout the kingdom: secret agents, assassins, poisoners, and female wandering ascetics.[71] Given the need for secrecy, the agents would normally adopt various roles and guises, appearing as householders, ascetics, doctors, astrologers, thieves, cooks, and the like. The term used to indicate this outward personality is *vyañjana,* literally meaning appearance. Some of these agents were actually members of these professions recruited into the secret service; others simply assumed these roles. The secret service was used internally to spy on the population, to test the integrity of government officials, and to get rid of troublesome people who were too powerful to be dealt with openly. It was used externally, like many spy agencies of modern states, to spy on neighboring kingdoms and to destabilize them by fomenting dissent and carrying out assassinations.

We have a detailed list of the salaries paid to various government officials at 5.3, even though, as I have already noted, this section of the text probably belongs to the Śāstric Redaction. Yet, it gives us insight into both the scale of such remunerations and the disparity in the wages of officials at different levels in the hierarchy.

Economy

Right at the beginning of his treatise Kauṭilya advises the king to learn *vārttā,* roughly economics, from his superintendents (1.5.8), thus placing the knowledge of economics at the heart of a king's education.[72] It is, of course, a truism to say that any state is ultimately an economic unit, and unless its economy can keep the people fed, clothed, and housed, the state will ultimately collapse. The Indian state envisaged by Kauṭilya, the absolute monarchy, is in a double sense an economic entity; the ultimate aim of a monarchy is to enhance the power and wealth of the king. One of the central meanings of the very term *artha* is wealth. Kauṭilya, therefore, pays close attention to the ways in which the royal treasury could be filled and to the various streams of revenue.

The Kauṭilyan state had what we would call today a mixed economy. Broadly speaking, there were three areas of economic activity: (1) agriculture, animal husbandry, and forest produce; (2) mining and manufacturing; and (3) trade. Agents of the king participated in all three areas, either as royal monopolies or, more frequently, side by side with private enterprise. Royal statutes and functionaries regulated private economic activities, both to create an advantage to state enterprises and to ensure an orderly and well-regulated environment for business. As we saw, numerous areas of economic activity were under the jurisdiction of a superintendent (*adhyakṣa*), who was responsible both for state enterprises and for regulating private economic activities in his area.

Central to the economy was, of course, agricultural land. The state intervened proactively to make sure that arable land was cultivated by relocating people, sometimes forcibly, to newly opened agricultural land, by providing tools, seeds, and funding, and by granting tax exemptions. The old theory of Oriental despotism, according to which the king owned all the land, has been shown to be false and fraudulent (Gopal 1961; Trautmann 201, 119–125). Kauṭilya makes a clear distinction between private agricultural land and state land, which bears the technical name *sītā*. Produce from privately held land is taxed at the rate of one-sixth. The superintendent of agriculture (*AŚ* 2.24) is responsible for cultivating state land and for getting the produce to the state warehouses. Land unsuitable for cultivation was reserved for pasture. It appears that there were royal herds under the superintendent of cattle (*AŚ* 2.29), as well as private herds, generally cattle, goats, and sheep. The state had an interest in the meat trade, with the superintendent of abattoirs overseeing the butchering of animals and the sale of meat. Kauṭilya assumes that a kingdom will also have forests, and he envisages three kinds of forest preserves set apart for state purposes. These are elephant forests (*hastivana*), where wild elephant herds are maintained and protected for capture for military and state use; produce forests (*dravyavana*), from which timber and other forest products are extracted; and game reserves for the royal hunt. All these forest preserves are royal monopolies with officials and guards to maintain and protect them, even though forest tribes (*aṭavī*) appear to have occupied some of the forest areas. This, once again, is an ideal-typical geography of a kingdom, given that Kauṭilya aims at addressing all possible eventualities. It is clear, for example, that not all ancient kingdoms of India included the natural habitats of elephants.

Mines were a royal monopoly, even though mines that required a lot of work and expenditure could be leased out to private individuals (2.12.22). Mines produced a wide variety of metals, including gold and silver, as well as precious stones. As I have already noted (see above p. 12), there are two terms for mines: *ākara* and *khani,* the first indicating a rich distribution of the precious substances and the second indicating digging into the ground (Olivelle 2012a). Associated with mines are factories for refining the metals and for turning out consumer and luxury goods. The state took a great deal of interest in these workplaces, especially those connected with gold and silver. There was a general suspicion in ancient India that goldsmiths and silversmiths were inherently dishonest, and Kauṭilya discusses in detail how superintendents could discover when craftsmen substituted base metals for silver and gold (2.14). The state appears to not have had a direct hand in other areas of manufacture; there is, for example, no mention of pottery, wood craftsmanship, and the building trade (Trautmann 2012, 146). The exception is clothes. The superintendent of yarn (*sūtrādhyakṣa)* was responsible for producing yarn from raw cotton, wool, and silk and for the manufacture of finished products. Poor women and widows were generally recruited for this work, which was a cottage industry and could be carried out in their own homes. However, it is likely that private industry worked side by side with state enterprises in producing local cloth, which was supplemented by luxury imports, such as silk from China (2.11.114).

Trade, both internal and foreign, was one of the most lucrative of economic activities. The state had to balance the promotion of private enterprise in trade and its exploitation as a major source of revenue through various kinds of taxes, fees, and duties. The state also had a trading arm and operated side by side with private traders. The single most important element in promoting trade was security along trade routes. No trader would take his wares to a kingdom where highway robbers could easily waylay him. The state, however, was equally interested in benefiting from a thriving trade, and numerous officials headed by the Superintendent of Customs (2.21–22) kept tabs on all traders, especially those bringing goods from foreign lands. There was an inherent suspicion that traders are generally corrupt (4.2). Traders had to obtain a pass from officers guarding the frontiers, at which time their packages were sealed. Assessments included road tolls, escort charges, ferry charges, and the like (2.16.18). Spies were employed to find out whether the declarations of goods made by the traders were accurate. Then, at the gate to the fortified city, the caravans had to stop at the customs house and pay the duties, indicating that trans-regional trade was carried out mainly between cities. Sometimes, traders traveled by boats along rivers and waterways, as well as by sea. This kind of commercial activity was overseen by the superintendents of shipping (2.28) and ports (2.28.7). Here also, Kauṭilya is attempting to be complete; not all kingdoms would have the seaports envisioned by him (2.28.11). Trade did not take place in completely free-market conditions. State officials fixed the prices of goods sold by traders, taking into account their expenses and favoring goods brought from foreign lands (2.16). The aim was to maintain price stability and to eliminate price gouging and wide fluctuations in prices. So, when there was a glut of a particular commodity, the officers would restrict its sale to one location, thus artificially raising the price (4.2.33).

There were also other minor sources of revenue. The state, for example, had a monopoly on salt (2.12.28–34) and liquor (2.25). The state also had an interest in brothels, providing prostitutes and courtesans with an initial investment to set up their businesses (2.27), although it is likely that private enterprise also had a hand in this industry.

State finances were under the control of the treasurer (2.5). There was also a bureau of official records in which books with meticulous records of receipts and expenses were kept. Writing and recordkeeping were widespread, and all the superintendents were expected to keep record books, which were brought to the central records office of the treasury once a year (2.7).

A final source of state revenue was the multitude of fines and penalties collected by judges and state functionaries. The *AŚ* is careful to point out the amount of the fines for specific offenses and, when compared to the remunerations enumerated in the salary list (5.3), which give us some idea of the earning capacity of the population, many of the fines appear rather exorbitant. A fine is assessed upon conviction of a crime and bears the technical term *daṇḍa*. Penalties, with the technical term *atyaya*, on the other hand, are imposed when officials or people working for the government violate rules. The *AŚ* discussions of both these indicate that they must have been substantial sources of revenue to the state.

Foreign Affairs

Except for the periods when the Maurya, the Gupta, and other regional empires ruled, the usual ancient Indian kingdom covered a relatively small territory. The result was that small states were butting against each other, and they had to deal with each other as either enemies or allies. The ancient Indian trade also was trans-regional and crossed state boundaries. The *maṇḍala* or circle theory of kingdoms espoused by Kauṭilya in book 6 also presents the scenario of numerous small states dealing with each other diplomatically and attempting to outwit each other. Foreign policy, therefore, occupies a central position in Kauṭilya's work. The entire second half of the treatise, books 6–14, is devoted to this topic.

Kauṭilya's attitude to foreign policy is based on the king as *vijigīṣu,* seeker after conquest, the pivotal concept in Kauṭilya's ideology of kingship. The whole point of being a king was to expand his territory and treasury by conquest. But, of course, all the neighboring kings were operating under the same assumption. Foreign policy, therefore, was of paramount importance to the king; if he failed in it, he may well lose his kingdom and even his life.

Although counsel (*mantra*) was important for all state affairs, it was of paramount importance when dealing with foreign powers. The group of counselors (*mantrin*) headed by the chaplain did double duty in advising the king on both domestic matters and foreign affairs. There was, however, a bureaucracy that specialized in dealing with other states. With reference to diplomacy, the most significant official was the envoy (*dūta*). Kauṭilya speaks of three levels of envoys: The highest, the plenipotentiary, has the broadest authority to negotiate with foreign governments, and he is expected to possess all the qualities of a minister. The mid-level envoys are given circumscribed and specific missions, while the low-level envoys merely carry royal edicts and messages.

Internal security was another important consideration, because kings were constantly attempting to undermine and destabilize neighboring states by infiltrating secret agents, assassins, and spies. Given normal trade relations and the mobility of wandering ascetics, this was a difficult task. Border guards headed by the frontier commander, often residing in a fort and assisted by friendly forest tribes, were responsible for border security to prevent infiltration of enemy operatives. On the other hand, Kauṭilya recommends a robust secret service with a wide variety of covert operations directed against neighboring states.

Finally, there was the military organization headed by the chief of armed forces (*senāpati*). Books 9 and 10 deal extensively with the various kinds of military forces and their deployments. In general, an army was supposed to have four kinds of regiments: infantry, cavalry, chariot corps, and elephant corps. The kinds of troops one would deploy in an actual military conflict would, of course, depend on the terrain where the fighting was to take place and the kinds of troops deployed by the enemy.

It was too expensive to maintain a large standing army. Therefore, Kauṭilya recommends a small army consisting mostly of hereditary soldiers called *maula,* belonging to the heartland of the kingdom. These are the best and most loyal of troops. Other troops could be mobilized when a war was imminent. Kauṭilya at one place points to four kinds of troops besides the hereditary (7.8.27). The first consists of hired troops or mercenaries (*bhṛta*). Then there are corporate troops (*śreṇi*), who were probably men belonging to martial castes or guilds. They would offer their services to the highest bidder. The third consists of troops provided by an ally, and the fourth of those provided by a tribal chief (*āṭavika*). To this we should add troops provided by an enemy with whom the king may be temporarily allied, probably when he is attacking their common enemy.

In crafting his foreign policy, Kauṭilya presents a theory of the foreign powers with which his ideal-typical king would have to contend. True to his desire to present abstract rather than historical realities, he enunciates the theory of *maṇḍala*, the circle of kingdoms.[73] A king is surrounded in a circle by other states, and because they have common boundaries with him, they are his natural enemies. Around these enemy kingdoms is a second circle of kingdoms. Because they abut the territories of enemy kings of the first circle, they become his natural allies: My enemy's enemy is my friend. Those forming the third outer circle would, by the same logic, be the enemies of his allies, and thus his own enemies—and so on. That this theoretical construct is artificial is obvious, but it also highlights the truism that you are most in conflict with your immediate neighbors. Here also, this theory, as also the central concept of the king as *vijigīṣu* (seeker after conquest), was probably developed by the author(s) of the sources Kauṭilya used for the second half of his treatise; the very terms *maṇḍala* and *vijigīṣu* are absent in the first half. The only two kings Kauṭilya considers outside the *maṇḍala* theory of ally and enemy are the *madhyama*, who is an intermediate king located between two enemies, and the *udāsīna*, a powerful king who remains, or can afford to remain, neutral.

There is another neighbor of the king that Kauṭilya frequently mentions but who falls outside the *maṇḍala* scheme, and that is the *āṭavika*, or tribal chief. Kauṭilya assumes that his ideal kingdom has forests where forest tribes live with their own social and military organizations. They are often viewed as bandits who can pose a serious threat and who are not easily subjugated. Kauṭilya attempts to co-opt these marginal social groups in a variety of ways, including their incorporation into the military.

There is also a non-monarchical state envisaged by Kauṭilya. The *saṅgha* are the confederacies where power is shared by leaders of clans. These confederacies, often erroneously termed republics (Jayaswal 1924), appear to have been common in the second half of the first millennium B.C.E. They are referred to frequently in the Buddhist literature, and they gave their name to the Buddhist monastic order, the *saṅgha*. Kauṭilya is aware of both the strengths and the weaknesses of confederacies. His political philosophy, however, is wedded to the monarchy, and he devotes the whole of book 11 to discussing how best to sow dissension within and thus subjugate confederacies.

Kauṭilya presents a second classification of foreign powers. While the *maṇḍala* theory is a more abstract conception of states and foreign relations, this classification pertains directly to the context of an actual military expedition. Although attacks against such a military formation could come from the flanks, the theory principally takes into account attacks from the front and the rear. According to the *maṇḍala* theory, the king immediately to the rear is the enemy of the king on the march and the ally of the enemy in the front against whom he is marching. This rear enemy is given the colorful epithet *pārṣṇigrāha,* the one grabbing at the heels. Likewise, the king immediately to the rear of the enemy against whom he is marching, that is, the enemy's *pārṣṇigrāha,* is his own ally. Behind the *pārṣṇigrāha* is an ally of the king on the march on whom the latter can call if the *pārṣṇigrāha* attacks him from the rear. This ally has the technical name *ākranda,* one to whom he can cry for help. The *ākranda* can attack the *pārṣṇigrāha* from the latter's rear, forcing him to turn around and face his attacker. But behind the *ākranda* would be an ally of the *pārṣṇigrāha* whom the latter can call for help—and so it can go on and on! This is also a highly abstract and theoretical construct of what could happen when a king begins his march. Yet, a king has to be aware of these possibilities and take precautions against them.

Although military might is important, Kauṭilya recognizes that it is a double-edged sword: One can lose a war as easily as one can win. War is inherently unpredictable. War is also expensive. So he recommends a variety of other strategies that are several steps removed from actual warfare and that can further the king's goals more effectively and less expensively.

One set of strategies called *upāya* (2.10.47) has four elements: conciliation (*sāma*), gifts (*dāna*), dissension (*bheda*), and military force (*daṇḍa*).[74] The second set of strategies containing six elements is called simply *ṣāḍguṇya* (sixfold strategy): peace pact (*saṃdhi*), initiating hostilities (*vigraha*),[75] remaining stationary (*āsana*), marching into battle (*yāna*), seeking refuge (*saṃśraya*), and double stratagem (*dvaidhībhāva;* 7.1.1–19). The four *upāyas* are discussed throughout the *AŚ*, including the first half (books 1–5), whereas the *ṣāḍguṇya* is confined mostly to books 6 and 7.

It appears that the former was a more general, widespread, and perhaps older, formulation of major foreign policy strategies, whereas the latter was a more sophisticated and nuanced strategy developed by the author of the sources Kauṭilya used in crafting the second half of his treatise. Further, the *upāyas* appear to be concerned principally with policies toward other kings and states, whereas the *ṣāḍguṇya* is focused on strategies that a king himself would use vis-à-vis his opponents. Although both lists contain the option of resorting to military force, the other components of these strategies are directed at achieving the desired objectives without war.

The central strategy that runs through all of Kauṭilya's foreign policy is captured in the word *atisaṃdhāna* and its nominal (*atisaṃdhi*) and verbal equivalents (*atisaṃdhatte, atisaṃdhīyate*). There is an obvious connection between this term and *saṃdhi* as a peace pact. The origin of the term is probably located in precisely such a peace pact, which is used not to ensure peace but to outmaneuver and outwit the opponent. I have thus translated this term as outwitting (Olivelle 2011). At every step, Kauṭilya wants his king to pay attention to the larger picture and to use the tools at hand—whether it is negotiating a peace pact or initiating a state of hostilities, or even going on a military expedition with allied troops—in order to outwit and ultimately defeat the opponent. Much of book 7 is given to the ways in which the strategy of outwitting an opponent can be used in diverse situations. This proverb highlights the centrality of good policy in foreign affairs:

> An arrow unleashed by an archer may kill a single man or not kill anyone; but a strategy unleashed by a wise man kills even those still in the womb. (10.6.51)

When everything fails, the king must resort to military force to attain his objective, namely the conquest of adjoining lands. Books 9, 10, and 13 are devoted to war: mobilization, military preparation, marching, and capturing the fort. I will leave out the intricate details of the march, the various military formations, the foraging raids to obtain food for the soldiers, the ambushes, and other military tactics. The ideal-typical battle is waged in an open field with the two armies arrayed facing each other, although battles in less ideal terrain, such as forests, marshes, and water, are also discussed. Besides open and formal warfare, there are various kinds of special operations aimed at weakening the enemy, including surprise night attacks, burning of crops, and poisoning water supplies. When everything is said and done, the enemy can always escape into his fortress and barricade himself there. The whole of book 13 is devoted to how one can capture a fort, first by trickery—inciting the people within the fort to sedition, drawing the enemy out of the fort by various tricks, destroying its food and water supply, and the like—then by laying siege, and finally by taking it by storm.

The discussion of foreign policy and war culminates, as does the entire treatise, with instructions regarding the conduct of the victor and how a newly conquered territory should be pacified and its people induced to shift their loyalty to the new ruler (13.5). The incorporation of conquered territories into one's own kingdom always poses challenges and dangers. Kauṭilya does not envisage a centrally controlled large empire. He instructs the victor to act magnanimously with the leaders and the people of the conquered land and to adopt their habits, dress, language, and conduct.

6. Reception of the Arthaśāstra

There were no journalists, journals, or book reviews in northern India in the third–fifth centuries C.E., but it appears that Kauṭilya's *Arthaśāstra,* much like Manu's *Dharmaśāstra,* was a big hit, taking the place by storm. In discussing the date and authorship of the *AŚ*, I have dealt with many of the sources during this period that show the strong impact of Kauṭilya: Manu himself and his successors Yājñavalkya and Nārada, Vātsyāyana's *Kāmasūtra,* the literary corpus of Kālidāsa, Viśākhadatta's *Mudrārākṣasa,* Kāmandaki's *Nītisāra,* the literary works of Daṇḍin, the story tradition (*kathā*) represented by the *Pañcatantra* and its Kashmiri predecessor the *Tantrākhyāyikyā,* and last but not least, Bhāruci, the earliest commentator on Manu. The very identification of Cāṇakya as the author of the *AŚ*, thus giving it an illustrious pedigree going back to the foundation of the Maurya empire, and its likely close association with the Gupta court show the popularity and influence of this text during the early and mid-centuries of the Common Era.

Contrast this with the fact that, at most, two manuscripts of the entire text have survived, both derived from a manuscript in one isolated corner of the subcontinent, Kerala, along with a single fragment from northern India. Not a single commentary on the entire text has survived. We are thus left wondering what happened to make such a popular text nearly disappear from the manuscript tradition. It is not just the manuscript tradition from which the *AŚ* disappeared; major scholars from about the ninth century C.E. appear to have ignored or been ignorant of it. This transition from the seventh–eighth centuries C.E. to the ninth–tenth centuries is an interesting phenomenon that the available evidence does not permit us to explain. As Derrett (1965) and, even more convincingly, Trautmann (1971, 132–168) have shown, Medhātithi in his commentary on Manu derives much of his material on the *AŚ* not directly, but rather from the citations of his predecessor, Bhāruci, who also commented on Manu. Now, even if we do not accept Derrett's (1975, I: 10) very early dating of 600–650 C.E. for Bhāruci, he clearly falls at least in the eighth century C.E. The consensus among most scholars is that Medhātithi belongs to the ninth or, at most, the very early tenth century. Trautmann has shown that Schlingloff's (1965) claim that Medhātithi had access to both Bhāruci and another Arthaśāstric source different from Kauṭilya's work is untenable. If we are not to ascribe pure laziness to Medhātithi, we must recognize that he did not have direct access to this great work, which he cites with the help of Bhāruci. Even by the time of Bhāruci, however, *Arthaśāstra* scholarship was on the wane. Bhāruci, for example, who had access to a copy of the *AŚ* and was conversant with its principles, was ignorant of the precise meaning of technical terms such as *deśa* for a legal document, a term that is found in Manu's citation of the *AŚ* (*MDh* 8.552–53).[76]

We also have another well-known author to support this claim. Daṇḍin was an illustrious poet and wrote the most famous book on poetics, the *Kāvyādarśa*. After an exhaustive examination of previous scholarship and available evidence, Bronner (2012, 76) concludes that "Daṇḍin's active career took place around 680–720 C.E. under auspices of Narasiṃhavarman II Rājasiṃha in Kāñcī." This timeframe roughly corresponds to the probable date of Bhāruci. As I have already noted, Daṇḍin, in his *Daśakumāracarita,* repeatedly refers to and cites from the *AŚ*, ascribing its authorship to Viṣṇugupta and noting its extent as 6,000 *ślokas*. So, toward the end of the seventh and the beginning of the eighth century, Daṇḍin, writing in the southeastern corner of India, was familiar with the *AŚ*, but Medhātithi could not find a copy of it just a century or so later.

This picture is confirmed when we look at the medieval literature. Even erudite scholars such as Vijñāneśvara, the 12th century commentator on Yājñavalkya, the later writers of legal digests (*dharmanibandha*), and most of the commentators of Manu do not appear to have been familiar with the *AŚ* or its technical vocabulary. Let me offer a single, telling example. Manu uses the verb *pravāsayet* with the technical meaning it has in the *AŚ*, namely to execute; it appears to have been some kind of euphemism much like our "get rid of." At *MDh* 8.123, we have two verbs *pravāsayet* and *vivāsayet.* Most commentators do not know what to make of these two and what difference, if any, there is between them. Only Bhāruci and Nandana correctly interpret that the first means to execute and the second to send into exile. Medhātithi gives first the meaning of exile for *pravāsayet* and then appears to follow Bhāruci in saying that the term may also refer to execution, as pointed out in the *Arthaśāstra* (see Olivelle 2005, 311). This is interesting in that there is some reason to believe that Bhāruci, just as Nandana, belonged to southern India (Derrett 1975, I: 27–34). This may indicate that the *AŚ* continued to have a stronger presence in southern India than in the north from a comparatively early date. It should also be noted that of the five extant medieval commentaries on the *AŚ*, all but the *Nītinirṇīti* of Yogghama are from the south, where Kauṭilya's text continued to be copied and studied at least among some pandits long after it had ceased to exist by and large in the north.

After a hiatus of close to a millennium, Kauṭilya's *Arthaśāstra* was rediscovered and published in south India. More attention to and study of this unique and invaluable text has been made in the last hundred years than in the previous thousand. My hope is that this translation will spur further engagement with Kauṭilya's masterpiece among cultural and political historians not only of India but also of the world.

Notes

1. *Cambridge History of India* (Cambridge, UK: Cambridge University Press), I: 467.
2. As Jolly (1923, 5–6) indicates, several European scholars, including Aufrecht, Zachariae, and Hillebrandt, had collected fragments of Kauṭilya's work.
3. The Malayalam commentary *Bhāṣāvyākhyāna* (1930–60); *Jayamaṅgalā* and *Cāṇakyaṭīkā* of Bhikṣu Prabhamati (Harihara Sastri 1958, 1956–71, 2011), *Nītinirṇīti* by Yogghama (Jina Vijaya Muni 1959), and *Pratipadapañcikā* by Bhaṭṭasvāmin (Jayaswal 1925–26).
4. Even though Scharfe's first study and Trautmann's work appeared before the second edition of Kangle's (1972) translation, he appears to have been unaware of either and has not taken them into account.
5. The term *adhikaraṇa* to refer to a text division is found also in the *Mīmāṃsā Sūtra* and the *Vedānta Sūtra*, but in them this division refers to the smallest subsection dealing with individual topics (paralleling the *prakaraṇa* of the *AŚ*). The only other ancient Indian text that follows the *AŚ* model is Vātsyāyana's *Kāmasūtra*, a text that is modeled after the *AŚ* in numerous ways (Jolly 1914, 351–354).

6. See the outline of the *Arthaśāstra* (above, pp. xix–xxvii) for these divisions and the subject matter covered within each.
7. Discussions of *tantrayuktis* are also found in two medical treatises from the first half of the first millennium C.E., the *Caraka Saṃhitā* and the *Suśruta Saṃhitā.*
8. For a detailed list of these cases, see Scharfe 1993, 16–23, where he also deals with the relation between the two systems of division in great detail.
9. I use the term "sentence" to refer to discrete units of the treatise, which for the most part constitute syntactic units. Most are in prose, although some are verses. For practical reasons, I take Kangle's numbering as the basis for sentence division. Sometimes these syntactic units are called *sūtras,* and I will discuss below issues relating to this genre.
10. At *AŚ* 1.1.18, the extent of the entire text is given as 6,000 *ślokas*, that is, the prose equivalent of verses containing 32 syllables each. This is confirmed by the *Daśakumāracarita* (ed. Kale, 191), which gives the same number. The received *AŚ* contains the equivalent of about 4,800 *ślokas.* For this problem and solutions offered by scholars, see Kangle 1965, 21–25.
11. *Daśakumāracarita* (ed. Kale, 194); *Śiśupālavadha* 2.88; here Mallinātha comments: *tantrāvāpau svapararāṣṭracintanam*—"*tantra* and *āvāpa* means reflection on one's own and the enemy's kingdom."
12. Edgerton (1928, 293) calls the style of the *AŚ* "crabbed and difficult." For the difficulties in the vocabulary, see Kangle 1965, 38–39; Scharfe 1993, 78–101; Know 1945, 52–65.
13. Tradition also remembers this feature. Kāmandaki in his *Nītisāra* (1.6) says that the author of *AŚ* drew out the nectar of *Nītiśāstra* from the ocean of *Arthaśāstra* (see also note 68 below).
14. For a detailed discussion of these early traditions of statecraft, see Kangle 1995, 5–10, 42–53.
15. For extended discussions of scholarly opinion and arguments, see McClish 2009; Scharfe 1993; Trautmann 1971.
16. Although the views expressed here are my own, I owe much of them to my colleagues Thomas Trautmann and Mark McClish, who have expressed their own views in their publications (Trautmann 1971, 2012; McClish 2009, 2011). I must acknowledge that my argument here is based principally on that of McClish in his 2009 dissertation, and I refer the reader to it for a more complete discussion of the reasons supporting the hypothesis of two recensions.
17. I will deal later with the final verse of book 15 that connects the *AŚ* with the destruction of the Nanda dynasty.
18. This point has been made repeatedly; see Renou 1961, 185–86; Trautmann 1971, 75; McClish 2009, 104. Regarding the chapter division itself, Scharfe (1993, 35) concludes: "The chapter divisions must now appear rather arbitrary in the observations just made; they even appear unnecessary, since the

topics are so well marked in the text itself." The vocabulary of the verses also indicates their lateness. For example, we see the use of *dama* for a fine (3.9.36; 4.9.28); the term is never used in the body of the text, although it is common in later Dharmaśāstras (see *MDh* 8.59, 108, 191, 192 etc.). The verses also espouse more strongly the Brāhmaṇical ideology of society and Brāhmaṇical privileges. See also 1.10.16–20 (and my note there) where the verses contradict and reject the views expressed in the preceding prose.

19. See, for example, topics 19, 21, 23, 31–56.

20. It is unclear whether topics 9–18 belonged to the Kauṭilya Recension or to the Śāstric Redaction.

21. The concept of *yogakṣema*, which goes back to the Vedic period when the trek (*yoga*) in search of new pasture or booty was followed by camping for a period of rest (*kṣema*), is central to the *AŚ* (see 6.2.1 n.) It is first introduced at 1.4.3, and is often invoked: 1.5.2; 1.7.1; 1.13.7; 6.2.1, 11; 7.10.10; etc.

22. *evaṃ vinayopadeśāt rājñaḥ kāryānuṣṭhānayogyatā pratipāditā | idānīm amātyādibhiḥ saha tena kāryāṇy anuṣṭheyāni | tāni ca svaparamaṇḍalāśrayabhedād dvividhāni | tatra antaraṅgatvād anyeṣāñ ca kāraṇatvāt svamaṇḍalāśritāny ucyante | tāny api yogakṣemabhedād dvividhāni | tatra yogapūrvakatvāt kṣemasyeti tadabhiprāyako 'dhyakṣapracāra ucyate |*

23. *adhyakṣādhikaraṇena prapañcavatā yogam abhidhāya kṣemāya dharmasthīyakaṇṭakaśodhanayogavṛttāni trīṇy adhikaraṇāny ucyante |* Unfortunately, the extant manuscript of Bhikṣu Prabhamati's commentary ends after the first chapter of book 3, and we do not know how he presented the structure of books 6–14 that constitute the second half of the treatise.

24. In the notes to the translation I have drawn attention to passages that appear to have been brought into the text without much thought to consistency. Sometimes, what is said in these passages goes against statements elsewhere in the *AŚ*. See, for example, 2.7.22 n.; 2.9 n.

25. For a discussion, see Trautmann 1971, 166–68, 173–74. Trautmann also deals with Schlingloff's (1965) arguments for an earlier or a different *AŚ* than that of Kauṭilya, based on citations in Medhātithi. Kane (1962–75, III: 143) cites two inscriptions that refer to officials "mentioned in the *adhyakṣapracāra*" (*adhyakṣapracārokta*), although it is unclear whether the reference here is to a separate treatise by that name or to the second book of the extant *AŚ*.

26. The term occurs in the first half in its usual meaning of subjects of a kingdom. The only place where this technical meaning is present is at 5.6.28, a book that was added by the redactor. The technical meaning of *prakṛti* is viewed by the author of book 15 (*tantrakyukti*) as Kauṭilya's own and is not acknowledge by other authors (15.1.51–52).

27. Interestingly, the compound *rājamaṇḍala* at 2.27.28 simply means the king's coffers or exchequer, and not the circle of kings.

28. Scharfe (1993, 9–10) has collected these cross-references, to which I have added some missed by him: 1.12.17 → 4.4.3; 2.13.28 → 2.19; 2.15.12 → 2.24; 2.15.50 → 2.30 and 31; 2.28.6 → 2.12.27; 2.33.1 → 2.30; 3.2.22 → 3.4.37–42; 3.10.4 → 2.4.3–5; 3.10.18 → 4.13.3–4; 3.12.1 → 3.11.11–24; 3.16.1 → 3.11; 4.3.4 → three passages: 2.36.15–20, 1.20.4–9, and 2.5.6; 4.4.1 → 2.35; 4.8.16 → 3.12.38–50; 4.9.8 → 2.5.16–20; 5.1.3 → three passages: 1.12, 1.13, and 13.1; 5.6.15 → 5.1; 5.6.17 → 9.3–7; 5.6.22 → 9.3–7; 6.1.7 → 1.9.1; 6.1.9 → 2.3; 7.4.1 → 7.1.8f and 7.2.3; 7.11.39 → 7.13; 7.14.11 → 9.5.9, 12, 20; 8.3.56 → 1.20.14–17; 9.1.41 → 7.4; 12.2.8 → 11.1 and 13.2; 12.2.10 → 1.21; 12.5.12 → 7.15.9–12; 13.3.50 → 4.4.3.
29. This was reiterated by Scharfe in a personal communication to me.
30. For a detailed analysis of the differing roles of Dharmastha in the *AŚ* and Prāḍvivāka in the Dharmaśāstras, and for a discussion of book 3 of the *AŚ*, see Olivelle 2012c.
31. This is true in the case of the *MDh* 8.62–123 and *ViDh* 7–9 (here dealing with both documents and witnesses). In the *YDh* (2.68–83) and *NSm* (1.115–217), witnesses and documentary proof come after debt, pledges, and deposits, perhaps because all of them share the characteristic of something given to another.
32. It should also be noted that the *dharmastha* (Justice) is not listed in the salary list in 5.3.
33. I deal below with the artificial way in which most, if not all, Kauṭilya dialogues have been constructed, showing that these are not representations of historical scholarly disputes but stories invented by the redactor.
34. Here I ignore the introduction of the dialogue that ascribes this statement to the teachers and inserts an alternative list proposed by Vātavyādhi.
35. We find a similarly artificial insertion of a dialogue at 7.4.8–12; see McClish 2009, 160–161. An enumeration of vices stemming from pleasure and wrath is also given in the *MDh* 7.45–48.
36. See Scharfe 1993, 9, for the artificiality of the name Vātavyādhi, a humorous name meaning one suffering from the "wind-disease," perhaps rheumatism.
37. 1.7.6; 1.10.17; 13.4.5. The second, 1.10.17, is within a chapter-concluding verse, making it likely that this ascription belongs to the Śāstric Redaction.
38. These schools are mentioned in five dialogues: 1.2.2–8 (three schools); 1.15.47–50 (three schools); 2.7.11–15 (four schools); 3.11.44–49 (three schools); 3.17.3–5 (two schools). A fifth school called Āmbhīya is given alone at 1.17.28–33, although, appearing within a dialogue containing views of individual authors, Āmbhīya, like Pārāśara, may refer to an individual author.
39. 1.8.1–28 (seven names); 1.15.13–41 (four); 1.17.4–27 (six); 4.6.23–52 (one); 8.1.5–59 (six); 8.3.8–61 (six); 12.1.1–9 (two). At 7.1.2–5, we have teachers

and Vātavyādhi. His view, given at 8.3.56, refers to an earlier passage at 1.20.14–17, which is not by him but belongs to the current *AŚ*.

40. 1.4.5–14; 2.9.10–12; 3.4.9–10; 3.5.23–25; 3.7.1–3 (here we have also the opinion of "others": *anye*); 3.14.6–9; 3.17.17–18; 3.17.19–21; 3.20.3–7; 7.1.30–31; 7.4.8–12; 7.5.3–8; 7.5.12–15; 7.6.30–31; 7.9.9–32 (with seven separate dialogues); 7.10.12–15; 7.11.13–16; 7.11.37–38; 7.12.9–24 (with four separate dialogues); 7.13.29–33; 7.15.13–20; 7.17.3–5; 8.2.5–24 (with four separate dialogues); 8.4.2–43 (with 12 separate dialogues); 9.1.2–9; 9.1.10–15; 9.1.26–33 (here we have also two opinions of "some": *eke*); 9.1.42–44; 9.2.21–24. At 3.17.6–14, we have teachers and Bārhaspatyas; at 8.1.5–18, teachers and Bhāradvāja; and at 7.1.2–5, teachers and Vātavyādhi.
41. Once, in 3.11.44–49, the Auśanasas occupy the first position, followed by Mānavas and Bārhaspatyas.
42. See 7.1.2 given above. McClish (2009, 163) has listed other places where a normal text has been transformed into a dialogue.
43. For correspondences between the *AŚ* and the *MDh*, see Kangle 1964b and Olivelle 2004a.
44. For an extensive discussion of this subject, see McClish 2009, 213–312.
45. Note the comments of Scharfe (1993, 42–66) that indicate the dependence of the final prose passages within a chapter on the concluding verses.
46. See, for example, 3.11.20, 31; 3.19.8–10; 4.11.12, 21.
47. See, for example, 1.5.14; 1.15.39, 55–57; 2.4.6 (n.); 2.13.5; 3.1.37; 3.5.1; 3.7.29, 38–39; 3.9.26; 3.12.2; 5.1.10; 10.2.5–8.
48. A point already made by Trautmann (1971, 174): "It being shown that the *Arthaśāstra* has not one author but several, it follows that it is to be referred to not one date but to as many dates as it has authors." I depart from Trautmann, however, when he takes these dates to be bound up with the dates of the books. As I have tried to show above, the division into books (*adhikaraṇa*) itself was probably the work of the śāstric redactor. Instead, in looking at the sources, we have to ignore the current book division.
49. See, for example, Trautmann 1971; Scharfe 1993; McClish 2009. Scharfe (1993, 66) has also argued that the "use of *vacana* 'grammatical number' affirms that the tractate was composed not only after Pāṇini but also after Kātyāyana," that is, after the third century B.C.E.
50. Kangle's (1965, 69–70) counter-arguments are, at least to me, unconvincing. Historical reconstructions are always beset with uncertainty. We must, however, accept the more plausible, rather than the mere possible.
51. The term *pravāla* is found nine times in the *AŚ* spread across three books: 2.6.4; 2.11.35, 42; 2.12.27; 2.13.59; 2.14.43; 2.22.5; 5.2.17; 7.12.14.
52. Lévi 1936. For further discussion, see Trautmann 1971, 177–78. For a general discussion of the relations with countries outside the Indian subcontinent contained in the *AŚ*, see Scharfe 1993, 275–293.

53. In the 13th Major Rock Edit of Aśoka, Alexandria is rendered variously as *alikyaṣudale, alikasudaro,* and *alikasudare.* It should be noted that in the long argument in defense of a Maurya date for the *AŚ*, Kangle does not refer to the issue of coral.
54. De Romanis (2000, 211) takes *vaivarṇika* to be descriptive of the coral: lacking color. But I think this is mistaken, and the commentators are correct in taking this also to be related to the place of origin.
55. *Natural History* 32: 11. Pliny says that so much of the Mediterranean coral was exported to India during his time that it had become rare in the country of its origin.
56. Arguments for a later date are given by Trautmann (1971, 177f). An earlier date is suggested by Begley 1991, Will 1991, Salles 2007.
57. I do not deal here with other evidence for dating, such as the use of *cīna* for China, the silk trade, the term *pārasamudra* for Sri Lanka, and the term *suruṅgā* for a tunnel, all of which have been dealt with adequately by Trautmann (1971, 174f). Trautmann has argued that the term *Palaisimoundou* for Sri Lanka "was current in the Greco-Roman world from the second quarter of the first century A.D. and was obsolete by the middle of the second." However, it is difficult to conclude that the same time span can be extrapolated to the Indian context; one can assume that the term may have been current in India for some time before it was picked up by the Roman traders.
58. This is broadly in agreement with the date proposed by Scharfe (1993, 278): "[T]he text in its present form dates from the first century B.C. at the earliest, and more likely from the first century A.D." The difference is that, according to my argument, this date applies to the Kauṭalya Recension and its sources, while the final redaction that gave us "the text in its present form" dates to a period a century or two later.
59. I have refrained from adding the earliest form of the *Pañcatantra,* which was probably the Kashmiri *Tantrākhyāyikā,* given the uncertainty of its date. This text of animal stories presents itself as a work on political science. It is indebted to the *AŚ* and in the opening stanzas pays homage to the ancient teachers of the science, among them Cāṇakya. A version of the *Pañcatantra* was translated into Pahlavi around 550 C.E., but this translation does not include the opening section (*kathāmukha*). It is only in this introduction that mention is made of Cāṇakya.
60. For other parallels between the two texts, see Shamasastry 1961, xi–xii.
61. As I will show below, the compound *kuṭilamatiḥ* is not an adjective describing Kauṭilya, but a grammatical gloss giving the meaning of the term *kauṭilya,* known as a Vṛddhi derivative in Sanskrit grammar.
62. Aruṇagirinātha (c. 1300 C.E.), the south Indian commentator of Kālidāsa's *Raghuvaṃśa,* says: "[M]ost of the work of 180 Topics that the sage

Viṣṇugupta composed from the ocean of Arthaśāstra is illustrated here" (see Harihara Sastri 2011, 60). See also Shah 1919–1920; Ayyar 1924; Raghavan 1951.

63. For details, see Kane 1962–1975, III: 196–197; Kangle 1965, 109–113. Taking the name as a *gotra* makes it likely that Kauṭilya was a Brāhmaṇa, and internal evidence in the text also makes this very probable.

64. Commenting on cruel kings, it says they take as their authority "the dreadful treatise of Kauṭilya which contains advice mostly of a very cruel nature." Kale's translation in his edition, 151 (Sanskrit text on 179).

65. Kauṭalya is used in the manuscripts M1 and D; by commentators: Malayalam, Bhikṣu Prabhāmati, and Yogghama; and the inscription of Vāstupāla, the minister of Vāghelā King Vīradhavala, dated 1234 C.E. The form Kauṭilya is used in manuscript G1; by commentators Mādhavayajvan and Bhaṭṭasvāmin; and by other medieval authors and texts: Jayamaṅgalā commentary on the *Nītisāra*, Kṣīrasvāmin's commentary on the *Amarakośa*, Mallinātha; Bhoja's *Nāmamālā*, and the *Vaijayantīkośa*.

66. This group of Kulkarṇi Brāhmaṇas appears to be located in the Maharashtrian town of Pathri. See *Akhila Mahārāṣṭrātīla Śuklayajurvedīya Mādhyaṃdina Brāhmaṇāṃcī Gotrāvali*. Saṃpādaka Viśvanātha Tryaṃbak Śeṭe. Second ed., Pune: Yājñavalkya Āśrama, 1941, 33. I thank Madhav Deshpande for this reference.

67. Willis (2009, 35, 63) has noted the connection of some of the play's symbolism to Udayagiri, which was an important cultural and religious center of the Guptas. For the use of Sanskrit to project political power within a Sanskrit cosmopolis, see Pollock 2006.

68. This image is found also in Kāmandakī's *Nītisāra* (1.6), where Viṣṇugupta is said to have raised up (*uddadhre*) the nectar of the *nītiśāstra* out of the ocean of *arthaśāstra*.

69. For the presence of this term in Kālidāsa, see Raghavan 1951, 105. The term is also used in the *Kāmasūtra*, 6.3.46; 6.4.16; 6.6.17. Willis (2009, 63) claims that "[a]s is well known, the *Arthaśāstra* speaks of 'Candragupta Maurya.'" This is clearly not the case; the name does not occur in the *AŚ* at all, and the only reference to the Maurya times is in the interpolated verse 15.1.73, which speaks of the Nandas.

70. Even though I use "minister" to translate this term, it does not refer to cabinet ministers in the modern sense of the term, but to high officials, including agency heads, performing diverse functions.

71. I have given the various designations of these secret agents in the note to the translation.

72. See Trautmann's (2012) just-published excellent overview of the economic activities in the *AŚ*.

73. See Scharfe 1993, 103–124 for a discussion and helpful diagrams.

74. We find these strategies listed together or separately at *AŚ* 1.13.25; 2.10.47; 7.14.11; 7.16.3–7; 9.3.6; 9.5.20; 9.6.57–61; 9.7.68; 11.1.3; 12.1.18. They also play a prominent role in the *MDh* 7.108–09, 200.
75. For the meaning and significance of peace pact (*saṃdhi*) and initiating hostilities (*vigraha*), see Olivelle 2011.
76. See Olivelle 2004a. It is noteworthy that many of these technical terms are absent in Kāmandakī's *Nītisāra*.

Translation

Book One

On the Subject of Training

Chapter 1: Enumeration of Topics and Books

OṂ Homage to Śukra and Bṛhaspati!

[1]This singular Treatise on Success has been composed for the most part by drawing together the Treatises on Success composed by former teachers for gaining and administering the earth. [2]The following is the list of its topics and books.

[3]Enumeration of Knowledge Systems; Association with Elders; Mastery over the Senses; Establishment of Ministers; Establishment of the Counselor-Chaplain; Ascertaining the Ministers' Integrity and their Lack of Integrity through Secret Tests; Establishment of Clandestine Operatives; Regimen of Secret Agents; Guarding Seducible and Non-Seducible Factions within One's Own Territory; Winning over Seducible and Non-Seducible Factions in an Enemy's Territory; Subject of Counsel; Employment of Envoys; Surveillance of Princes; Actions of a Prince in Disfavor; Actions Regarding a Prince in Disfavor; Regimen of the King; Regimen of the Residence; Personal Protection of the King—these constitute Book One: "On the Subject of Training."

[4]Settlement of the Countryside; "Covering the Crevices on the Land"; Construction of Forts; Layout of a Fort; Treasurer's Management of Storage Facilities; Organization of Revenue Collection by the Collector; Subject of Accounts in the Bureau of Official Records; Recovery of Revenue Embezzled by Officials; Inspection of Officers; Topic of Decrees; Examination of Precious Stones to be Received into the Treasury; Setting up Mines and Factories; Superintendent of Gold in the Workshop; Operations of the Chief Goldsmith in the Market Street; Superintendent of the Storehouse; Superintendent of Commodities;

Superintendent of Forest Produce; Superintendent of the Armory; Standardization of Balances and Measures; Measures of Space and Time; Superintendent of Customs; Superintendent of Yarn; Superintendent of Agriculture; Superintendent of Liquor; Superintendent of Abattoirs; Superintendent of Courtesans; Superintendent of Shipping; Superintendent of Cattle; Superintendent of Horses; Superintendent of Elephants; Superintendent of Chariots; Superintendent of the Infantry; Activities of the Chief of the Armed Forces; Superintendent of Passes; Superintendent of Pasture Land; Activities of the Collector; Secret Agents Working Undercover as Householders, Traders, and Ascetics; Regimen of the City Manager—these constitute Book Two: "On the Activities of Superintendents."

5 Enunciation of Transactions; Writing Down the Grounds for Litigation; Matters Relating to Marriage; Partitioning of Inheritance; On Immovable Property; Non-Observance of Conventions; Non-Payment of Debts; On Deposits; Rules Governing Slaves and Laborers; Partnerships; Cancellation of Sale or Purchase; Non-Delivery of Gifts; Sale by a Non-Owner; Relation between Owner and his Property; Forcible Seizure; Verbal Assault; Physical Assault; Gambling and Betting; Miscellaneous—these constitute Book Three: "On Justices."

6 Surveillance of Artisans; Surveillance of Traders; Remedial Measures against Disasters; Surveillance of People with Secret Income; Disclosing Criminals Using Agents Working Undercover as Thaumaturgic Ascetics; Arrest on Account of Suspicion, Articles, or Activities; Investigation into a Person Who Has Died Suddenly; Investigation through Interrogation and Torture; Surveillance of All Agencies; Reparation in Lieu of Cutting Individual Limbs; Rules on the Clean and the Vivid Forms of Capital Punishment; Deflowering of Virgins; Punishments for Transgressions—these constitute Book Four: "Eradication of Thorns."

7 On the Infliction of Punishment; Stocking the Treasury; On Remuneration for Officials; On the Conduct Appropriate for Dependents; On Sanctioned Conduct; Transition of Regime; Continuity of Sovereignty—these constitute Book Five: "On Secret Conduct."

8 The Exemplary Qualities of the Constituent Elements; On Rest and Exertion—these constitute Book Six: "Basis of the Circle."

9 Enumeration of the Sixfold Strategy; Decisions during Decline, Stability, and Prosperity; Conduct when Seeking Refuge; Adherence to Strategic Measures on the Part of Equal, Weaker, and Stronger Kings; Peace Pacts by Weaker Kings; Remaining Stationary after Initiating Hostilities;

Remaining Stationary after Entering into a Peace Pact; Marching into Battle after Initiating Hostilities; Marching into Battle after Entering into a Peace Pact; Marching Forth into Battle after Forming a Partnership; Reflections on Attacking a Vulnerable Ruler and an Enemy; Causes of the Impoverishment, Greed, and Disaffection among the Subjects; Discussion of Consociates; Concerning the Marching into Battle after Concluding a Pact; Peace Pacts with and without Stipulations, and Those Made with Deserters; Peace Pact and Attack Linked to Double Stratagem; Proper Behavior on the Part of a Vulnerable Ruler; The Kinds of Allies Deserving Assistance; Peace Pacts for Allies, Money, Land, and Projects; Reflections on the Attacker from the Rear; Augmenting Weakened Power; Reasons for Barricading Oneself after Initiating Hostilities on a Strong King; Behavior Proper for a King Surrendering with his Troops; Behavior Proper for a King Enforcing a Surrender with Troops; Making a Peace Pact; Liberating a Hostage; Conduct toward the Intermediate King; Conduct toward the Neutral King; Conduct toward the Circle—these constitute Book Seven: "On the Sixfold Strategy."

[10]Set of Calamities Affecting the Constituent Elements; Reflection on Calamities Affecting the King and his Reign; Set of Human Vices; Set of Afflictions; Set of Hindrances; Set of Factors Blocking Revenue to the Treasury; Set of Calamities Affecting the Army; Set of Calamities Affecting the Allies—these constitute Book Eight: "On the Subject of Calamities."

[11]Ascertaining the Relative Strengths and Weaknesses with Respect to Power, Place, and Time; Proper Times for Military Expeditions; Proper Times for Deploying Troops; Relative Values of Equipping for War; Deployment Of Counterforces; Reflection on the Revolt in the Rear; Countermeasures against Revolts by Constituent Elements in Outlying Regions and in the Interior; Discussion of Losses, Expenses, and Gains; Dangers from the Outlying Regions and from the Interior; Dangers Associated with Traitors and Foes; Dangers Associated with Advantage, Disadvantage, and Uncertainty; Overcoming These Dangers through Various Means—these constitute Book Nine: "Activity of a King Preparing to March into Battle."

[12]Setting up the Military Camp; Marching into Battle from the Military Camp; Guarding at a Time of Calamity to the Army and of a Surprise Attack; Kinds of Covert Military Operations; Rousing One's Own Troops; Deployment of One's Troops against Enemy Troops; Terrain Suitable for Fighting; Respective Tasks for Infantry, Cavalry, Chariot Corps, and Elephant Corps; Arrangement of Battle Formations in the Wings, Flanks, and Breast according to the Total Troop Strength; Arrangement of Strong and Weak Troops; Methods of Fighting for Infantry, Cavalry, Chariot Corps,

and Elephant Corps; Arraying the Battle Formations of Staff, Snake, Circle, and Non-Compact; Deployment of Counter Formations against Them—these constitute Book Ten: "On War."

[13]Ways of Fomenting Dissent; Secret Punishments—this constitutes Book Eleven: "Conduct toward Confederacies."

[14]Work of an Envoy; War of Wits; Assassination of Army Chiefs; Stirring up the Circle; Secret Deployment of Weapons, Fire, and Poison; Destroying Supplies, Reinforcements, and Foraging Raids; Outwitting through Trickery; Outwitting through Military Force; Victory of a Lone King—these constitute Book Twelve: "On the Weaker King."

[15]Enticing to Sedition; Drawing out by Trickery; Deployment of Spies; Task of Laying Siege; Taking by Storm; Pacifying the Territory Gained—these constitute Book Thirteen: "Means of Capturing a Fort."

[16]Secret Means of Killing Enemy Troops; Deception; Countermeasures against Harm to One's Own Troops—these constitute Book Fourteen: "On Esoteric Practices."

[17]Organizational Elements of a Scientific Treatise—this constitutes Book Fifteen: "Organization of a Scientific Treatise."

[18]Contents of the treatise: 15 books, 180 topics, 150 chapters, and 6,000 verses.

> [19]The treatise composed by Kauṭilya is easy to learn and comprehend, precise in doctrine, meaning, and wording, and free of prolixity.

THAT CONCLUDES THE FIRST CHAPTER: "ENUMERATION OF TOPICS AND BOOKS" OF THE FIRST BOOK: "ON THE SUBJECT OF TRAINING" OF KAUṬILYA'S *ARTHAŚĀSTRA*.

Chapter 2

Topic 1: Enumeration of Knowledge Systems

[1]Critical inquiry, the Triple, economics, and government—these are the knowledge systems.*

[2]"The Triple, economics, and government," the Mānavas assert,* [3]"for critical inquiry is simply a special subdivision of the Triple." [4]"Economics and government," the Bārhaspatyas maintain, [5]"for the Triple is merely a cloak for a person conversant with how the world operates." [6]"Government is the only knowledge system," the Auśanasas contend, [7]"for the pursuit

of all the knowledge systems* is dependent on it." [8]"Four, indeed, are the knowledge systems," affirms Kauṭilya.

[9]With them one comes to know (*vid*) Law and Success—this fact gives the name to and reveals the essence of the knowledge systems (*vidyā*).*

Topic 1a: Enunciation of Critical Inquiry

[10]Sāṃkhya, Yoga, Lokāyata*—these constitute critical inquiry.* [11]It benefits the people by critically inquiring through logical reasoning into the Triple to determine what is Law and what is contrary to Law, into economics to determine what is Success and what is contrary to Success, into government to determine what is good policy and what is bad policy, and about the relative strength and weakness of these knowledge systems. It keeps their minds steadfast in times of adversity and prosperity. And it makes them skillful in thinking, speaking, and acting.

> [12]Critical inquiry is always considered the lamp for all knowledge systems, the right strategy for all activities, and the basis for all Laws.*

THAT CONCLUDES THE SECOND CHAPTER: "ENUNCIATION OF CRITICAL INQUIRY" WITHIN THE "ENUMERATION OF KNOWLEDGE SYSTEMS" OF THE FIRST BOOK: "ON THE SUBJECT OF TRAINING."

Chapter 3

Topic 1b: Enunciation of the Triple

[1]The three Vedas—Sāma, Ṛg, and Yajur—constitute the Triple; [2]and the Atharva Veda* and Itihāsa Veda* are the Vedas. [3]Phonetics, ritual, grammar, etymology, metrics, and astronomy—these are the limbs.*

[4]This Law laid down in the Triple Veda is of benefit because it enunciates the Laws specific to the four social classes and the four orders of life.

[5]The specific Law of a Brāhmaṇa consists of studying, teaching, offering sacrifices, officiating at sacrifices, giving gifts, and receiving gifts. [6]That of a Kṣatriya consists of studying, offering sacrifices, giving gifts, obtaining a livelihood through the use of weapons, and protecting creatures. [7]That of a Vaiśya consists of studying, offering sacrifices, giving gifts, agriculture, animal husbandry, and trade. [8]That of a Śūdra consists of the obedient service of twice-born people, economic activities,* and the occupations of artisan and performer.

[9]The specific Law of a householder consists of obtaining his livelihood in accordance with the Law specific to him, establishing matrimonial relations with persons of equal class but of different lineages, having sexual relations with his wife during her season,* venerating* gods, ancestors, and guests, generosity toward servants,* and eating what is left over.* [10]That of a Vedic student consists of Vedic recitation, tending the fire, ablution, the practice of subsisting on almsfood, and living until death with his teacher—or, in his absence, with his teacher's son or with a fellow student. [11]That of a forest hermit consists of celibacy, sleeping on the ground, wearing matted hair and antelope skin, offering the daily fire sacrifice, bathing, venerating gods, ancestors, and guests, and eating forest produce. [12]That of a wandering ascetic consists of mastery of the senses, abstaining from ritual activities,* living without possessions, abandoning attachments, practicing mendicancy, residing in the wilderness but not in a single place, and purifying himself externally and internally.

[13]Non-injury, truthfulness, purification, lack of malice, compassion, and forbearance—these are common to all.

[14]The Law specific to someone leads him to heaven and to eternal bliss. [15]When it is violated, people are destroyed through the intermixture.*

> [16]Therefore, the king should not permit people to violate the Law specific to each of them, for when they adhere to the Law specific to each they rejoice here and in the hereafter.
>
> [17]When among a people, the bounds (3.9.2 n.) of the Ārya way of life are firmly fixed and the social classes and orders of life are firmly established, and when they are protected by the Triple, they prosper and do not perish.

THAT CONCLUDES THE THIRD CHAPTER: "ENUNCIATION OF THE TRIPLE" WITHIN THE "ENUMERATION OF KNOWLEDGE SYSTEMS" OF THE FIRST BOOK: "ON THE SUBJECT OF TRAINING."

Chapter 4

Topic 1c: Enunciation of Economics

[1]Agriculture and animal husbandry, along with trade, constitute economics. It is of benefit because it provides grain, livestock, money, forest produce, and labor. [2]By means of that, he brings under his power his own circle and his enemy's circle using the treasury and the army.*

Topic 1d: Enunciation of Government

[3]What provides enterprise and security (6.2.1 n.) to critical inquiry, the Triple, and economics is punishment (*daṇḍa*); its administration (*nīti*) is government (*daṇḍa-nīti*). Government seeks to acquire what has not been acquired, to safeguard what has been acquired, to augment what has been safeguarded, and to bestow what has been augmented on worthy recipients.* [4]On it depends the proper operation of the world.

[5]"Seeking the proper operation of the world, therefore, he should always stand ready to impose punishment;* [6]for there is nothing like punishment for bringing creatures under his power"—so state the teachers.*

[7]"No," says Kauṭilya; [8]"for one who punishes severely terrifies the people, [9]and one who punishes lightly is treated with contempt, [10]whereas one who dispenses appropriate punishment is treated with respect. [11]For punishment, when it is dispensed after the proper ascertainment of facts, makes his subjects embrace Law, Success, and Pleasure.* [12]When it is dispensed improperly, whether in passion or anger or through contempt, it incites even forest hermits and wandering ascetics to revolt; how much more, then, the householders! [13]When one fails to dispense it, on the other hand, it gives rise to the law of the fish*—[14]for in the absence of the dispenser of punishment, a weak man is devoured by a stronger man, [15]and, protected by him, he prevails."*

> [16]People belonging to the four social classes and orders of life, when they are governed by the king through punishment, become devoted to the Law and activities specific to them and follow their respective paths.

THAT CONCLUDES THE FOURTH CHAPTER: "ENUNCIATION OF ECONOMICS" AND "ENUNCIATION OF GOVERNMENT" WITHIN THE "ENUMERATION OF KNOWLEDGE SYSTEMS" OF THE FIRST BOOK: "ON THE SUBJECT OF TRAINING."

Chapter 5

Topic 2: Association with Elders

[1]Punishment, therefore, is the foundation of the three knowledge systems.* [2]Punishment, when it has training* as its foundation, provides enterprise and security (6.2.1 n.) to living beings.

[3]Training is both acquired and innate, [4]for an activity can train only a suitable subject, not an unsuitable one. [5]A knowledge system can train only someone whose intellect is endowed with these qualities: desire to

learn, attentive listening, grasping, retention, comprehension, reasoning, rejection, and devotion to truth;* and not anyone else.

[6]Training and drilling in the knowledge systems, however, depend on the authority of the teachers of each respective knowledge system.

[7]Once the rite of tonsure* has been completed, he should apply himself to writing and arithmetic. [8]Once the rite of initiation has been completed, he should learn the Triple and critical inquiry from experts, economics from the superintendents, and government from scholars and practitioners.

[9]He should remain chaste, moreover, until he is 16 years old. [10]After that, his hair cutting* rite should be performed, as also his marriage.

[11]He should, moreover, always associate with people accomplished in knowledge in order to become accomplished in his training, because that is the foundation of training.

[12]During the first part of the day, he should undergo training in the knowledge systems pertaining to elephants, horses, chariots, and weapons, [13]and during the later part in studying Lore (*itihāsa;* 1.5.13 n.). [14]Lore consists of Purāṇas, Reports (*itivṛtta*), Narratives (*ākhyāyikā*), Illustrations (*udāharaṇa*), Treatises on Law (*dharmaśāstra*), and Treatises on Success (*arthaśāstra*).* [15]During the rest of the day and night, he should learn new materials and commit to memory what he has already learnt, as well as study repeatedly materials he has not learnt. [16]For studying produces a keen intellect, a keen intellect produces disciplined performance, and disciplined performance produces the exemplary qualities of the self;* such is the capacity of the knowledge systems.

> [17]For a king who is trained in the knowledge systems and devoted to the training of his subjects enjoys the earth without a rival, being devoted to the welfare of all beings.

THAT CONCLUDES THE FIFTH CHAPTER: "ASSOCIATION WITH ELDERS" OF THE FIRST BOOK: "ON THE SUBJECT OF TRAINING."

Chapter 6

Topic 3: Mastery over the Senses

Topic 3a: Giving Up the Set of Six Enemies

[1]Mastery over the senses results from training in the knowledge systems and is to be accomplished by giving up passion, anger, greed, pride,

conceit, and excitement. [2]Mastery over the senses consists of the senses—ear, skin, eye, tongue, and nose—not wandering inappropriately among sounds, touches, visible forms, tastes, and smells; or rather, putting into practice what the treatise prescribes. [3]For this entire treatise boils down to the mastery over the senses. [4]A king who behaves contrary to it and has no control over his senses will perish immediately, even though he may rule the four ends of the earth.

[5]The Bhoja king named Dāṇḍakya,* for example, who violated the young daughter of a Brāhmaṇa through passion, was destroyed along with his kinsmen and kingdom; so also Karāla* of Videha; [6]Janamejaya* assailing Brāhmaṇas out of anger, as also Tālajaṅgha* assailing the Bhṛgus; [7]Aila* extorting money from the four social classes out of greed, as also Ajabindu* of the Sauvīras; [8]Rāvaṇa* not returning the wife of another out of pride, as also Duryodhana* not returning a portion of the kingdom; [9]Dambhodbhava* treating people with contempt out of conceit, as also Arjuna* of the Haihayas; [10]Vātāpi* assailing Agastya through excitement, as also the Vṛṣṇi confederacy* assailing Dvaipāyana.

> [11]These and many other kings, addicted to the set of six enemies (1.6.1) and not having mastered their senses, came to ruin along with their kinsmen and kingdoms.
> [12]Having abandoned the set of six enemies, Jāmadagnya,* who had mastered his senses, as well as Ambarīṣa,* the son of Nabhāga, enjoyed the earth for a long time.

THAT CONCLUDES THE SIXTH CHAPTER: "GIVING UP THE SET OF SIX ENEMIES" WITHIN "MASTERY OVER THE SENSES" OF THE FIRST BOOK: "ON THE SUBJECT OF TRAINING."

Chapter 7

Topic 3b: Conduct of a Royal Seer

[1]Therefore, he should gain mastery over the senses by abandoning the set of six enemies, gain a keen intellect by association with elders, gain a keen eye through information provided by spies, gain enterprise and security (6.2.1 n.) by energetic activity, enforce the Law specific to each by providing guidance on duties, provide training by giving instruction in the knowledge systems, gain the love of his people by linking them to Success, and provide them a livelihood by doing what is beneficial.*

[2]Having thus brought his senses under control, he should shun the wives and property of others and refrain from causing injury, as also from sloth, frivolity, falsehood, wearing lavish clothes, associating with pernicious individuals, and transactions that go against Law or Success.

[3]He should pursue Pleasure without transgressing Law or Success; he should not deprive himself of enjoyments. [4]Or, he should pursue the Triple Set equally, each intimately linked to the others. [5]For, among Law, Success, and Pleasure, when one is pursued excessively, it harms itself as well as the other two.*

[6]"Success alone is paramount," says Kauṭilya, [7]"for Success is the foundation of Law and Pleasure."

[8]He should designate teachers or ministers to set the proper bounds (3.9.2 n.), individuals who would keep him away from harmful situations or, when he wastes his time away in private,* prod him using the goad of the sundial and the water clock.*

> [9]The king's office can be carried out only with associates; one wheel does not move.* Therefore, he should appoint mentors and listen to their views.

THAT CONCLUDES THE SEVENTH CHAPTER: "CONDUCT OF A ROYAL SEER" WITHIN "MASTERY OVER THE SENSES" OF THE FIRST BOOK: "ON THE SUBJECT OF TRAINING."

Chapter 8

Topic 4: Establishment of Ministers*

[1]"He should appoint his fellow students as ministers,* because their integrity and competence is known to him," states Bhāradvāja; [2]"for he can have confidence in them."

[3]"No," says Viśālākṣa; [4]"because they have played with him, they will treat him with disrespect. [5]He should appoint as ministers individuals who share the same mindset as he with respect to secret matters, because they have the same good and evil propensities as he. [6]Because they fear that he knows their vulnerabilities, they will not work against him."

[7]"This drawback is mutual,"* says Pārāśara; [8]"because he fears that they too know his vulnerabilities, he will put up with what they do or omit to do.

> [9]"A king will come under the power of as many people as he reveals a secret to, becoming powerless because of that act.

[10]"He should appoint as ministers those who have supported him during calamities that threatened his life, because they have demonstrated their loyalty."

[11]"No," says Piśuna; [12]"that is devotion and not the quality of intelligence. [13]He should appoint as ministers those who, when they have been employed in tasks whose income has been calculated, would realize the projected amount or even more, because they have demonstrated their quality."

[14]"No," says Kauṇapadanta; [15]"for they do not possess other qualities of a minister. [16]He should appoint as ministers those who have come down from his father and grandfather, because he has witnessed their achievements. [17]For they will not abandon him even when he behaves improperly, because of their 'common smell.'* [18]This is seen even among nonhuman beings, [19]for cows, disregarding a cattle herd without a common smell, reside only among those with a common smell."

[20]"No," says Vātavyādhi; [21]"for they will bring under their grip all his affairs and act like lords themselves. [22]Therefore, he should appoint as ministers new individuals well versed in governmental affairs. [23]Now, new individuals consider the dispenser of punishment as occupying the place of Yama and will not work against him."

[24]"No," says Bāhudantīputra; [25]"one who knows the science but has no practical experience will become confounded when confronted with practical tasks. [26]Therefore, he should appoint as ministers individuals who are endowed with high birth, intellect, integrity, bravery, and loyalty, because quality has to be paramount."

[27]"All that is appropriate," says Kauṭilya; [28]"for the capability of an individual is measured by his capability to carry out undertakings." [29]In accordance with their capabilities, moreover,

> he should allocate ministerial ranks, as also the place, time, and activity, and then appoint all these as ministers, but not as counselors.

THAT CONCLUDES THE EIGHTH CHAPTER: "ESTABLISHMENT OF MINISTERS" OF THE FIRST BOOK: "ON THE SUBJECT OF TRAINING."

Chapter 9

Topic 5: Establishment of the Counselor-Chaplain*

[1]Native of the country; of noble birth; easy to manage; trained in the crafts; insightful; intelligent; with a keen memory; skilled; articulate; bold; quick-witted; possessing energy and might; able to endure hardships; honest; friendly; firmly loyal; endowed with character, strength, health, and spirit; free of obstinacy and fickleness; amiable; and not a fomenter of enmities—these are the exemplary qualities of a minister.* [2]Someone who lacks one-quarter of these qualities is mid-ranked, and someone who lacks one-half of them is low-ranked.

[3]Of these qualities, one should investigate the country of origin, nobility of birth, and ease of management through reliable close acquaintances of his; training in the crafts and insight into the treatises through experts in the same branches of knowledge; intellect, resolution, and skill from the way he carries out undertakings; articulateness, boldness, and presence of mind from the way he engages in conversations; energy, forcefulness, and ability to endure hardships from the way he handles adversity; honesty, friendliness, and firm loyalty from the way he interacts with others; character, strength, health, and spirit, as also lack of obstinacy and fickleness, from those who live with him; and amiability and the non-fomenting of enmities by direct observation.

[4]For a king's affairs are directly observed, unobserved, or inferred. [5]The observed is something a man sees himself. [6]The unobserved is what is reported by someone else. [7]The inferred is the surmising of what has not yet been done with respect to tasks through what has already been done.

[8]Because tasks are numerous and have to be carried out at the same time and in different places, he should employ ministers to carry out what he cannot directly observe for fear that the proper time and place may pass by.

That concludes the appointment* of ministers.

[9]He should appoint as Chaplain a man who comes from a very distinguished family and has an equally distinguished character, who is thoroughly trained in the Veda together with the limbs (1.3.3 n.), in divine omens, and in government, and who could counteract divine and human adversities through Atharvan* means. [10]He should follow* him as a pupil his teacher, a son his father, and a servant his master.

> [11]Royal power (*kṣatra*) set ablaze by the Brāhmaṇa, consecrated
> by mantras consisting of the counsel (*mantra*) of the counselor

(*mantrin*), and protected by the weapon (*śastra*) consisting of following the treatise (*śāstra*) conquers without ever being conquered.*

THAT CONCLUDES THE NINTH CHAPTER: "ESTABLISHMENT OF THE COUNSELOR-CHAPLAIN" OF THE FIRST BOOK: "ON THE SUBJECT OF TRAINING."

Chapter 10

Topic 6: Ascertaining the Ministers' Integrity and their Lack of Integrity through Secret Tests

[1]In cooperation with the Counselor-Chaplain,* after installing the ministers in regular departments, he should test their integrity with secret tests.

[2]The Chaplain becomes indignant at being appointed to officiate at a sacrifice of a person at whose sacrifice one is forbidden to officiate or to teach such a person. The king should then dismiss him.* [3]He* should send secret agents to instigate each minister individually under oath: "This king is unrighteous. Come on! Let us install in his place* some other righteous person—a pretender from his family, a prince in disfavor, a member of the royal household, the man who is the sole support* of the kingdom, a neighboring lord, a forest chieftain, or a man who has risen to power.* Everyone likes this idea. What about you?" [4]If he rebuffs it, he is a man of integrity. That is the secret test relating to righteousness.*

[5]The Chief of the Armed Forces, dismissed because of the support he has given to bad people, should send secret agents to instigate each minister individually with tempting monetary rewards to bring about the downfall of the king: "Everyone likes this idea. What about you?" [6]If he rebuffs it, he is a man of integrity. That is the secret test relating to money.*

[7]A female wandering ascetic who has won the confidence of and is received with honor in the royal residence should instigate each high official individually: "The chief queen is in love with you and has made arrangements to meet with you. You will also receive a lot of money." [8]If he rebuffs it, he is a man of integrity. That is the secret test relating to lust.*

[9]On the occasion of a festivity, one minister should invite all the ministers. [10]Alarmed at that, the king should imprison them. [11]A crafty student (1.11.2) who had already been imprisoned there should instigate each minister individually who has been robbed of money and honor: "This king's conduct is evil. Come on! Let us kill him and install someone else. Everyone likes this idea. What about you?" [12]If he rebuffs it, he is a man of integrity. This is the secret test relating to fear.

[13]Among these, individuals whose integrity has been proven through the secret test relating to righteousness (*dharma*) should be appointed to positions as Justices* and in the Eradication of Thorns;* individuals whose integrity has been proven through the secret test relating to money, to positions with the Collector* and in the storage facilities of the Treasurer;* individuals whose integrity has been proven through the secret test relating to lust, to guarding the outer and inner compounds;* and individuals whose integrity has been proven through the secret test relating to fear, to tasks close to the person of the king. [14]Individuals whose integrity has been proven through all the tests should be appointed as counselors. [15]He should employ individuals proven to lack integrity through every test in pit mines,* in produce forests, in elephant forests, and in factories.

> [16]"He should appoint individuals whose integrity has been proven through the secret test relating to the Triple Set and fear as ministers in tasks appropriate to each in accordance with their integrity," so have the teachers ordained.*
> [17]"The king, however, should never make himself or his queen the target in order to test the integrity of ministers," that is the view of Kauṭilya.*
> [18]He should never corrupt a person who is not corrupt, like water with poison; for it may well be that a remedy may not be found for a person who has been corrupted.*
> [19]Once the mind is tainted by the four kinds of secret tests, moreover, it will not cease until it has reached its goal, abiding in the firm resolve of spirited men.
> [20]Therefore, making an outsider the target of the four kinds of undertakings, the king should test the ministers' integrity or lack thereof through the medium of secret agents.*

THAT CONCLUDES THE TENTH CHAPTER: "ASCERTAINING THE MINISTERS' INTEGRITY AND THEIR LACK OF INTEGRITY THROUGH SECRET TESTS" OF THE FIRST BOOK: "ON THE SUBJECT OF TRAINING."

Chapter 11

Topic 7: Establishment of Clandestine Operatives

Topic 7a: Establishment of Clandestine Establishments

[1]With the body of ministers, whose integrity has been proven by secret tests, in place, he* should commission clandestine operatives: crafty

students,* apostate recluses,* and agents working undercover* as householders, merchants, or ascetics, as well as secret agents, assassins, poisoners, and female mendicant agents.*

[2]The crafty student is a pupil who is bold and knows the vulnerabilities of others. [3]After instigating him with money and honors, the Counselor should tell him: "Taking the king and me as your authority, report immediately anything untoward you may observe in anyone."

[4]An apostate recluse is someone who has reverted from renunciation and who is endowed with intellect and integrity. [5]In a place assigned to him for some economic activity* and supplied with plenty of money and apprentices, he should have the work carried out. [6]From the profits of his work, moreover, he should provide food, clothing, and shelter to all renouncers. [7]And he should instigate those who are looking for a livelihood: "Wearing this same outfit, you should work for the benefit of the king and come here at the time for rations and wages." [8]All renouncers, furthermore, should similarly instigate their respective groups.

[9]An agent working undercover as a householder is an agriculturalist endowed with intellect and integrity whose means of livelihood has been depleted. [10]In a place assigned to him for agriculture ...—the rest is the same as above.

[11]An agent working undercover as a merchant is a trader endowed with intellect and integrity whose means of livelihood has been depleted. [12]In a place assigned to him for his trade ...—the rest is the same as above.

[13]An agent working undercover as an ascetic is a shaven-headed or a matted-haired ascetic looking for a livelihood. [14]Living in the vicinity of a city with a lot of shaven-headed or matted-haired apprentices, he should eat a piece of vegetable or a handful of barley once a month or once in two months openly, while eating all the food he wants in secret. [15]And apprentices of agents working undercover as merchants should eulogize him for performing secret rites for prosperity, [16]while his own pupils should announce: "He is a thaumaturgic ascetic, able to secure prosperity." [17]And to those who come to him with the expectation of prosperity, he should point out incidents that have occurred in their families through the interpretation of limbs* and by means of signs made by his pupils, incidents such as a small gain, a fire, danger from thieves, the execution of a traitor, a gratuity, and knowledge of things happening in a foreign country, and proclaim: "This will happen either today or tomorrow;" or "The king will do this." [18]Clandestine operatives and secret agents should bring that about.* [19]He should inform those endowed with spirit, intellect, and eloquence about an impending boon from the king or association with the

Counselor.* [20]And the Counselor should arrange for their livelihood and work.

[21]He should pacify with money and honors those who have turned hostile due to a good reason, and with silent punishment* those who are hostile without a reason, as also those who do what is inimical to the king.

> [22]Revered by the king with money and honors, they should discover the integrity of those who work for the king. Thus have been described the five clandestine establishments.*

THAT CONCLUDES THE ELEVENTH CHAPTER: "ESTABLISHMENT OF CLANDESTINE ESTABLISHMENTS" WITHIN "ESTABLISHMENT OF CLANDESTINE OPERATIVES" OF THE FIRST BOOK: "ON THE SUBJECT OF TRAINING."

Chapter 12

Topic 7b: Establishment of Mobile Agents

[1]Secret agents are those members of a corps who have to be necessarily maintained* when they study the interpretation of signs,* the interpretation of limbs (1.11.17 n.), magical lore, creating illusions,* Law of hermitages,* interpretation of omens, and interpretation of the interstices of a circle,* or when they study the science of association.*

[2]Assassins are brave individuals from the countryside who, brushing aside personal safety, would do battle with an elephant or a vicious animal for the sake of money.

[3]Poisoners are those who have no feelings toward their relatives, and who are cruel and lazy.

[4]A female wanderer is one who is looking for a livelihood, who is poor, a widow, bold, and a Brāhmaṇa woman, and who is treated respectfully in the royal residence; she should visit the homes of high officials.* [5]Her case explains that of shaven-headed ascetics who are Śūdra women.

These are the mobile agents.*

Topic 8: Regimen of Secret Agents

[6]The king should employ them*—according to devotion* and capabilities and with credible disguises in terms of region, attire, craft, language, and birth—to spy on these: Counselor-Chaplain, Chief of the Armed Forces, Crown Prince, Chief Gate Guard, Head of the Palace Guard, Administrator, Collector, Treasurer, Magistrate, Commander, City Overseer, Director of

Factories, Council of Counselors, Superintendent, Army Commander, Commander of the Fort, Frontier Commander, and Tribal Chief.*

[7]Assassins, employed as keepers of umbrellas, pitchers, fans, shoes, seats, vehicles, and mounts, should find out their out-door activities. [8]Secret agents should report that to the clandestine establishments.

[9]Poisoners* employed as chefs, cooks,* bath attendants, masseurs, preparers of beds, barbers, valets, and water servers, or disguised as* hunchbacks, dwarfs, Kirātas,* dumb, deaf, mentally retarded, or blind, or as actors, dancers, singers, musicians, bards, and performers—as also women—should find out their indoor activities. [10]Female mendicant agents should report that to the clandestine establishments.

[11]The apprentices of clandestine establishments should communicate the secret information gathered by spies through signs and written messages.* [12]Neither they nor the clandestine establishments should know each other.

[13]If female mendicant agents are forbidden access, a series of people coming to the door in the guise of mother or father, female artisan, performer, or slave should carry outside the information gathered by spies through songs, recitations, written messages hidden within musical instruments, or signs. [14]Alternatively, they should get away during a long illness or a nervous breakdown, or after setting fire or giving poison.

[15]When three report the same thing, it should be trusted. [16]When they fail constantly, their removal is through silent punishment (1.11.21 n.).

[17]Spies mentioned in the Eradication of Thorns (4.4.3) should live with the enemies receiving wages from them to obtain secret information, without associating with each other. [18]These are the double agents.

> [19]He should appoint double agents after taking their wives and children into custody, and he should find out such agents deployed by his enemies. He should ascertain the integrity of his double agents using agents of the same type.*
>
> [20]In this manner, he should spread out spies among his enemy, his ally, the intermediate king, and the neutral king (6.2.13–22), as well as among their 18 high officials.*
>
> [21]The spies placed within their homes should be hunchbacks, dwarfs, eunuchs, women skilled in the crafts, dumb individuals, and persons from various barbarian groups.
>
> [22]The clandestine establishments in the forts should consist of traders; in the outskirts of the forts, of thaumaturgic ascetics;

in the provinces, of agriculturalists and apostate ascetics; and in frontiers of the provinces, of herdsmen.

[23]In forests he should appoint forest dwellers—recluses, forest tribals, and the like—a series of informants who are quick and intent on learning news about the enemies.

[24]Similar individuals deployed by the enemy should be discovered—whatever kinds are deployed by using similar kinds (1.12.19 n.), and carriers of secret information and clandestine operatives in clandestine establishments by using people who are unrecognizable as clandestine operatives.*

[25]He should settle at the frontiers prominent officials who cannot be seduced in order to discover spies deployed by the enemy, officials who are shown to be acting for reasons connected with seducible factions.*

THAT CONCLUDES THE TWELFTH CHAPTER: "ESTABLISHMENT OF MOBILE AGENTS" WITHIN "ESTABLISHMENT OF SECRET AGENTS" AND "REGIMEN OF SECRET AGENTS" OF THE FIRST BOOK: "ON THE SUBJECT OF TRAINING."

Chapter 13

Topic 9: Guarding Seducible and Non-Seducible Factions within One's Own Territory

[1]Once he has deployed spies on the high officials (1.12.6 n.), he should deploy spies on the inhabitants of the cities and the countryside.

[2]Secret agents wrangling with each other should engage in debates at sacred fords, assemblies, congregations, and gatherings of people: [3]"We hear that this king is endowed with all virtues. But we don't see any virtue in this man who oppresses the inhabitants of the cities and the countryside with fines and taxes." [4]The other should rebut him, as also the people there who would applaud it: [5]"Oppressed by the law of the fish (1.13.5 n.), people made Manu,* the son of Vivasvat, king. [6]They allocated to him as his share one-sixth of the grain and one-tenth of the merchandise, as also money.* [7]Subsisting on that, kings provide security to the subjects. [8]Those who do not pay fines and taxes take on the sins of kings, while kings who do not provide security take on the sins of their subjects. [9]Even forest dwellers, therefore, present one-sixth of their gleanings, with the thought: 'This is the share of him who provides us protection.' [10]The position of Indra and Yama—it

is this that is occupied by kings, but with their wrath and grace visibly manifest.* [11]Divine punishment itself strikes those who treat them with disrespect.[12]Therefore, kings should not be treated with disrespect." [13]In this way he* should restrain the common people; [14]and they* should discover rumors.

[15]With regard to people who live on its* grain, animals, and money, who help him with these in times of prosperity and adversity, who suppress a rebellious relative or province, or who repel an enemy or a tribal chief—agents working undercover as shaven-headed and matted-haired ascetics should find out whether they are satisfied or dissatisfied. [16]He should regale those who are satisfied with additional money and honors [17]and placate those who are dissatisfied with gifts and conciliatory words so as to make them satisfied. [18]Alternatively, he should divide the latter from each other, as well as from neighboring rulers, tribal chiefs, pretenders from his family, and princes in disfavor. [19]If they are still dissatisfied, he should make them the object of hatred in the countryside by appointing them to enforcing the payment of fines and taxes. [20]When they have become the object of hatred, he should subdue them through silent punishment (1.11.21 n.) or a revolt in the countryside. [21]Alternatively, he should station them in factories attached to mines (1.18.8 n.) after taking their sons and wives into custody for fear that they might become susceptible to instigation by his enemies (see 5.3.4).

[22]Those who are angry, greedy, frightened, or proud, however, are people who are open to seduction by enemies. [23]Diviners, soothsayers, and astrologers, working undercover, should find out their contacts with each other and with enemies or tribal chiefs. [24]He should regale those who are satisfied with money and honors [25]and subdue those who are dissatisfied through conciliation, gifts, sowing dissension, or military force.*

> [26]In this manner a prudent king should guard both seducible and non-seducible individuals living within his territory, whether they are eminent persons or common people, from being instigated to sedition by his enemies.

THAT CONCLUDES THE THIRTEENTH CHAPTER: "GUARDING SEDUCIBLE AND NON-SEDUCIBLE FACTIONS WITHIN ONE'S OWN TERRITORY" OF THE FIRST BOOK: "ON THE SUBJECT OF TRAINING."

Chapter 14

Topic 10: Winning over Seducible and Non-Seducible Factions in an Enemy's Territory

[1]We have explained how seducible and non-seducible factions may be won over within one's own territory; we have yet to describe how it is carried out in an enemy's territory.

[2]The set* of angry people is as follows: someone who is cheated out of things he had been promised; between two people who carry out a craft or a service equally well, the one who is slighted; someone disgraced on account of a king's favorite; someone who is defeated after being challenged; someone who is incensed at being exiled; someone who did not get the job after incurring expenses; someone who is prevented from carrying out the Law specific to him or from receiving his inheritance; someone stripped of honors or office; someone held back by members of the royal family; someone whose wife has been forcibly molested; someone put in prison;* someone who has been fined after losing a lawsuit; someone who has been restrained from engaging in wrongful conduct; someone whose entire property has been confiscated; someone who has been harassed in prison; and someone whose relative has been executed.

[3]The set* of frightened people is as follows: someone who has hurt another;* someone who has committed a wrong; someone whose sinful acts have been disclosed; someone who is alarmed at a punishment meted out for a similar crime; someone who has seized land; someone who has surrendered with his troops;* a head of any department who has suddenly become wealthy; someone who expects a pretender from the royal family to succeed; someone detested by the king; and someone who hates the king.

[4]The set* of greedy people is as follows: someone who has become destitute; someone whose property has been taken by another; a miser; someone who has fallen on hard times; and someone who has entered into ill-considered business transactions.

[5]The set* of proud people is as follows: someone who thinks highly of himself; someone desirous of honors; someone rankled by the respect paid to an enemy; someone who has been demoted; someone with a bad temper; someone who is violent; and someone dissatisfied with his compensation.

[6]Among these, he should incite to sedition each individual belonging to a seducible faction through one of the agents working undercover as shaven-headed or matted-haired ascetics to whom he may be devoted.

[7]He should get the set of angry people incited in this manner: "As an elephant blinded by intoxication* and controlled by an intoxicated man crushes whatever it encounters, so this king, blind because he lacks the eyesight provided by the science,* has set out to exterminate the inhabitants of cities and the countryside. It is possible to liquidate him by instigating a rival elephant. Display your indignation!"

[8]He should get the set of frightened people incited in this manner: "As a snake lying in wait discharges its poison at anything that poses a threat, so this king has become suspicious that you may cause him harm. Go elsewhere before he directs the poison of his wrath at you."

[9]He should get the set of greedy people incited in this manner: "As a cow of those who hunt with dogs is milked for the dogs and not for Brāhmaṇas, so this king is being milked for those lacking spirit, intellect, and eloquence,* and not for those endowed with qualities of the self (6.1.6). That king over there appreciates persons of quality. Go there."

[10]He should get the set of proud people incited in this manner: "As a Caṇḍāla's well is fit to be made use of* only by Caṇḍālas and not by others, so this king is vile and is fit to be made use of* only by vile people and not by Āryas like you. That king over there appreciates persons of quality. Go there."

> [11]When they have agreed to this, saying, "Yes," and have allied themselves to him under negotiated terms, he should employ them* in his own activities according to their abilities, along with spies attached to them.
>
> [12]He should win over those who are seducible in the enemy territories through conciliation and gifts and those who are not seducible through sowing dissension and by military force (1.13.25 n.), while pointing out the failings of his enemies.

THAT CONCLUDES THE FOURTEENTH CHAPTER: "WINNING OVER SEDUCIBLE AND NON-SEDUCIBLE FACTIONS IN AN ENEMY'S TERRITORY" OF THE FIRST BOOK: "ON THE SUBJECT OF TRAINING."

Chapter 15

Topic 11: Subject of Counsel

[1]After winning over the factions in his own realm and in those of his enemies,* he should focus his attention on initiating his undertakings.

[2]The initiation of all undertakings presupposes counsel (cf. 2.8.1). [3]The place where it is conducted should be enclosed, a place from which it is impossible to overhear conversations and into which even birds cannot peek; [4]for we hear of counsel being divulged by parrots and myna birds, as also by dogs and other animals. [5]Therefore, no unauthorized person should go near the place of counsel.

[6]He should exterminate anyone who divulges counsel. [7]Now, counsel is divulged by the gestures and bearing of envoys, ministers, and the lord. [8]Gesture is acting in a non-normal way. [9]Bearing is putting on an expression. [10]All that* should be kept concealed, and the officers appointed should be kept under surveillance until the time when the undertaking is completed. [11]For their blathering through carelessness or when they are drunk or asleep, or their indiscretions such as a love affair, or else someone who has remained hidden or who has been treated with disrespect, may divulge counsel. [12]Therefore, he should safeguard counsel.

[13]"The divulging of counsel is truly detrimental to the enterprise and security (6.2.1 n.) of the king and of the officers appointed by him. [14]Therefore, he should take counsel alone and in secret," states Bhāradvāja; [15]"for even counselors have their own counselors, and these too have others. [16]This series of counselors will divulge counsel.

> [17]"Therefore, let others not know any action that he plans to undertake. Only those undertaking that action should know when it has commenced or when it has in fact been completed."

[18]"Counsel can never be carried out successfully by a single individual," says Viśālākṣa; [19]"for a king's affairs are directly observed, unobserved, or inferred.* [20]Finding out what is unknown, bringing certainty to what is known, reinforcing what is certain,* removing doubt in matters with alternative possibilities, and finding out the rest when something is only partially perceived—all this can be successfully carried out only with the aid of counselors. [21]Therefore, he should take counsel with individuals of mature intellect.

> [22]"Let him not treat anyone with disrespect. Let him listen to the views of everyone. A learned man should take advantage of a significant statement made even by a child."*

[23]"All that pertains to the apprehension of counsel and not to the safeguarding of counsel," says Pārāśara. [24]"When he wants to initiate an undertaking, he should ask the counselors about an undertaking analogous to

it: 'Were this undertaking to have been like this—or—If this undertaking were to be like this, then how should it be carried out?' [25]He should do as they say. [26]In this manner, counsel is both obtained and kept concealed."

[27]"No," says Piśuna; [28]"for when counselors are questioned about a hypothetical matter, whether it has taken place or not, they will speak without much care or will disclose it. [29]That is a defect. [30]Therefore, he should take counsel with regard to particular activities only with those who have been approved for those activities; [31]for, when he takes counsel with these, he secures success in counsel and its protection as well."

[32]"No," says Kauṭilya; [33]"for that would create instability.* [34]He should take counsel with three or four counselors, [35]for if he takes counsel with just one, he would not reach a firm decision when things are going badly.* [36]A single counselor, moreover, will act as he pleases without constraint. [37]When he takes counsel with two, the two, if they conspire, will constrain him and, if they bicker, will destroy him. [38]It is difficult for this to happen when there are three or four—[39]if this does happen, it will be a catastrophe.* [40]If they are more than that it becomes difficult to reach a decision on any issue or to safeguard counsel. [41]Under the pressure of place, time, and undertaking, however, he may, as far as possible, take counsel with even one or two."*

[42]Counsel has five components:* strategy for initiating the undertakings, men and material of exemplary quality (1.9.1 n.), allocation of place and time, precautions against failure, and bringing the undertaking to a successful conclusion.

[43]He should question the counselors individually and collectively. [44]He should find out their diverse views along with the reasons behind their views. [45]Once he has settled on a project, he should not waste time.* [46]Let him not take counsel for too long a time or with partisans of those whom he may harm.

[47]"He should constitute a council of counselors consisting of 12 ministers," state the Mānavas. [48]"Sixteen," say the Bārhaspatyas. [49]"Twenty," say the Auśanasas. [50]"According to ability,"* says Kauṭilya. [51]For they should ponder over the king's own party and that of his enemy. [52]With regard to activities, they should initiate what has been left undone, complete what has been initiated, enhance what has been completed, and bring the commission to an exemplary conclusion (1.9.1 n.).

[53]He should examine his undertakings with those nearby, [54]and consult with those far away through the transmittal of letters.

[55]Indra's council of counselors consists of 1,000 seers. [56]That is his eye. [57]Therefore, this two-eyed individual is called thousand-eyed.*

[58]With regard to an urgent* undertaking, he should summon the counselors and the council of counselors* and confer with them. [59]In that regard, he should follow what the majority advise, or* rather what would bring the undertaking to a successful conclusion.

[60]And as he carries out the undertaking—

> He must not let the enemies discover his secret, but discover any weakness of the enemy; and he should hide anything of his that may be exposed, like a tortoise its limbs.*
> [61]For, as none but a Vedic scholar deserves to eat a funeral offering made by virtuous people, so none but a person who has mastered the science ought to listen to counsel.*

That concludes the Fifteenth Chapter: "Subject of Counsel" of the First Book: "On the Subject of Training."

Chapter 16

Topic 12: Employment of Envoys

[1]Once counsel has been taken, the employment of envoys takes place.

[2]One who has all the exemplary qualities of a minister (1.9.1) is an envoy with a broad mission. [3]One who lacks one-quarter of those qualities is an envoy with a limited mission. [4]One who lacks one-half of those qualities is an envoy who delivers royal decrees.

[5]He should set out after making proper arrangements for vehicles, mounts, and the retinue of assistants.* [6]He should travel rehearsing in this manner: "The royal decree should be communicated to the enemy in this manner. He will make this sort of a reply. This will be the response to that. In this manner, he should be outwitted." [7]As he travels, moreover, he should keep in close touch with tribal chiefs, commanders of the frontier, and the city and provincial chiefs. [8]He should be on the lookout for areas suitable to station the army, to engage in combat, to locate reserve troops, and to make a retreat for both himself and the enemy. [9]He should obtain information about the extent of the forts and the provinces, as well as the strength, sources of income, defenses, and the vulnerable points.

[10]When permission is granted, he should enter the enemy's dwelling [11]and deliver the royal decree exactly as instructed, even if he perceives a danger to his life.

[12]He should interpret these as signs that the enemy is pleased: cordiality in his speech, face, and gaze; complimenting the envoy's speech; asking what he would like; showing an interest in talking about his good qualities;* offering a seat close by; treating him hospitably; recalling pleasant times; and placing confidence in him; and the inverse of these as signs that he is displeased.

[13]He should tell the enemy: "Kings—both you and others—speak through the mouths of envoys. [14]Therefore, even when weapons are raised, envoys say exactly what they were instructed to say. [15]Even the lowest-born among them are exempt from being killed; how much more, then, the Brāhmaṇas. [16]This is the statement* of someone else. [16]This is the Law with respect to an envoy."

[18]If he is prevented from leaving, he should live there without feeling elated by the deference shown to him. [19]Among enemies, he should not consider himself to be powerful. [20]He should put up with offensive words patiently, [21]avoid women and drink, [22]and sleep alone; [23]for one sees that inner thoughts are revealed when someone is asleep or intoxicated.

[24]He should obtain information about the instigation of seducible parties, the deployment of clandestine operatives against non-seducible parties, the affection and disaffection toward their master, and the vulnerable points among the constituents of the kingdom* through agents working undercover as ascetics and merchants or their apprentices, or through agents working undercover as physicians and members of religious orders or double agents. [25]If it is impossible to establish communication with them,* he should obtain the information gathered by spies through the blathering of beggars, drunkards, lunatics, and those asleep, or by way of drawings, writings, and signs displayed in holy places and temples. [26]Acting on the information received, he should employ instigation.

[27]When asked by the enemy, moreover, he should not divulge the extent of the constituents of his own kingdom (1.16.24 n.). [28]He should say, "Your Lordship knows everything!" or something that would bring his undertaking to a successful conclusion.

[29]If he is detained while his undertaking has not been brought to a successful conclusion, he should ponder in this manner: "Is he detaining me because he sees an imminent calamity befalling my master? Or because he wants to take countermeasures against a calamity affecting him? Or because he wants to rouse up our rear enemy* or his backer, to stir up a revolt within our realm, or to incite a tribal chief? Or because he wants to

obstruct our ally in front* or the rear ally*? Or because he wants to take countermeasures with respect to a conflict with him initiated by another enemy of his, or against an internal revolt of his own, or against a tribal chief of his? Or because he wants to impede the time for military action for which my master has prepared so well? Or because he wants to store up crops, merchandise, and forest produce, to carry out work on the fort, or to raise troops? Or because he is awaiting the proper place and time for operations of his own army? Or because of disdain or oversight? Or because he intends to continue his close relationship with us?" [30]After he has ascertained, he should either remain or flee. [31]Or else, he should take into consideration a desirable objective.

[32]After delivering a disagreeable royal decree, he should flee even if he is not given leave for fear of imprisonment or execution; otherwise he may be put under confinement.

> [33–34]Sending messages, protecting the terms of peace pacts, projecting prowess, wooing allies, inciting sedition, causing dissension among allies, deploying clandestine operatives and troops, kidnapping relatives and precious stones, gathering intelligence through espionage, displaying prowess, freeing hostages, and employing secret measures—these are the activities of an envoy.
> [35]He should get all this done by his envoys and keep the envoys of his enemy under surveillance by means of counter-envoys and spies, and through open and secret guards.

THAT CONCLUDES THE SIXTEENTH CHAPTER: "EMPLOYMENT OF ENVOYS" OF THE FIRST BOOK: "ON THE SUBJECT OF TRAINING."

Chapter 17

Topic 13: Surveillance of Princes

[1]The king can protect the kingdom only when he is protected from those close to him and from enemies, but first of all from his wives and sons. [2]We will explain the surveillance of wives in "Regimen for the Residence" (1.20).

[3]With respect to the surveillance of sons,* however—

[4]"From their very birth, he should maintain surveillance of princes, [5]for princes and crabs share the same nature; they eat their progenitors. [6]Before love toward them has been kindled in the father, it is best to subject them to silent punishment (1.11.21 n.)," so states Bhāradvāja.

[7]"That is cruel; it involves the killing of the innocent and the eradication of the Kṣatriya race," says Viśālākṣa. [8]"Therefore, it is best to confine them in one location."

[9]"That is like the danger posed by a snake," says Pārāśara; [10]"for the prince, realizing, 'My father is confining me because he is afraid of my prowess,' will get him into his clutches. [11]Therefore, it is best to make him reside in the fort of the Frontier Commander."

[12]"That is like the danger posed by a ram," says Piśuna; [13]"for, realizing that this is precisely the means of his return, he will ally himself with the Frontier Commander. [14]Therefore, it is best to make him reside outside his territory in the fort of a neighboring lord."

[15]"That puts him in the position of a calf," says Kauṇapadanta; [16]"for as one milks the cow with the aid of the calf,* so the neighboring lord will milk his father. [17]Therefore, it is best to make him reside with his mother's kinsmen."

[18]"That puts him in the position of a banner," says Vātavyādhi; [19]"for, by means of that banner, his mother's kinsmen will make demands, in the same way as Aditi-Kauśikas.* [20]Therefore, he should let him loose amidst vulgar pleasures; [21]for sons enslaved by pleasures will not turn hostile against their father."

[22]"That is a living death," says Kauṭilya; [23]"for, like a piece of wood eaten by worms, the royal family with undisciplined sons will fall apart the moment it is attacked. [24]Therefore, when the chief queen is in her season (1.3.9 n.) the officiating priests should offer an oblation of milk-rice to Indra and Bṛhaspati. [25]When she has become pregnant, a pediatrician should make arrangements for the nurture of the fetus and for the delivery. [26]When she has delivered, the Chaplain should perform the rite of passage* for the son. [27]When he is capable, specialists should train him."

[28]"One of the secret agents, moreover, should entice him with hunting, gambling, liquor, and women, saying, 'Attack your father and seize the kingdom.' [29]Another secret agent should dissuade him," so state the Āmbhīyas.

[30]"To awaken one who is not awake is greatly detrimental," says Kauṭilya; [31]"for a fresh object* absorbs anything smeared on it. [32]In like manner, a prince, whose mind is fresh, will accept anything he is told as if it were the teaching of a treatise. [33]Therefore, one should teach him what accords with Law and Success, never anything that is contrary to Law and Success."*

[34]The secret agents,* on the contrary, should guard him, saying, "We are yours." [35]If he sets his mind on other people's wives out of youthful insolence,

they should make him recoil by introducing him at night in deserted houses to squalid women posing as Ārya ladies. [36]If he takes a fancy for liquor, they should make him recoil by administering a doctored drink. [37]If he takes a fancy for gambling, they should make him recoil with the help of crafty student agents (1.11.1 n.). [38]If he takes a fancy for hunting, they should frighten him through agents posing as bandits. [39]If he sets his mind on attacking his father, they should gain his trust by saying, "Yes," and then thwart him, saying, "It's not right for you to attack* the king. If you fail, you will be killed. If you succeed, you will be heading to hell, there will be fury, and the people will smash you like a clod."* [40]They should inform on him if he is disaffected.

[41]If he is an only son who is dear to him, the king should imprison him. [42]If he has many sons, the king should banish him to the frontier or to another region* where he would not become a son, a bargaining chip, or an embryo.*

[43]A son who possesses the exemplary qualities of the self (6.1.6) he should appoint as the Chief of the Armed Forces or as the Crown Prince.

[44]One who has a keen intellect, one whose intellect needs to be prodded, and one who has an evil intellect: These are the three varieties of sons. [45]The one with a keen intellect, when he is being taught, understands and follows Law and Success. [46]The one whose intellect needs to be prodded understands but does not follow. [47]The one with an evil intellect constantly pursues evil and detests Law and Success.

[48]If the latter is his only son, the king should try to get him to have a son, [49]or get a "female-son"* to bear sons. [50]If the king is suffering from an illness or is old, he should get a son fathered on his field* through one of the following: mother's kinsman,* member of the royal family, a virtuous neighboring lord. [51]Never should he, however, install an only son who is undisciplined over the kingdom.

> [52]If there are many, confinement in one place—the father should do what is beneficial to his sons. Except in a time of adversity, conferring sovereignty on the eldest is deemed praiseworthy.
> [53]Alternatively, sovereignty should reside in the family, for a family confederacy is difficult to conquer, and it endures on earth forever without facing the risk from a calamity befalling the king.

THAT CONCLUDES THE SEVENTEENTH CHAPTER: "SURVEILLANCE OF PRINCES" OF THE FIRST BOOK: "ON THE SUBJECT OF TRAINING."

Chapter 18

Topic 14: Actions of a Prince in Disfavor

[1]A disciplined prince who finds it difficult to maintain himself should obey his father when he is appointed to an unbefitting task, unless it endangers his life, provokes the people to revolt against him, or involves a sin that would cause him to fall from caste.

[2]If he is appointed to a felicitous task, he should request an official to supervise his work. [3]Supervised by that official, further, he should carry out the directive with great distinction, [4]and have the standard profit from the enterprise, as well as any gratuities obtained, delivered to his father.

[5]If the father is still displeased and shows affection to another son or wife, he should request leave to repair to the wilderness. [6]Or, if he fears imprisonment or death, he should take refuge with a neighboring lord of upright conduct who is righteous and truthful, who does not break his word, and who always receives and honors those who come to him for help. [7]Having gathered the finest treasure and troops (1.9.1 n.) while living there, he should establish marriage relations with eminent warriors, make alliances with tribal chiefs, and win over seducible factions.

[8]If he has to operate alone, he should gain a living from factories connected with gold-smelting, coloring gems,* making gold and silver articles, and mines.* [9]Or else, he should secretly steal the property of religious orders, of temples—except what is meant for use by Vedic scholars—and of wealthy widows, after gaining their trust; or he should rob caravans and boats, after tricking the men with a coma-inducing drink. [10]Or, he should employ the secret method of capturing an enemy settlement.* [11]Or, he should set to work by winning over the people on his mother's side (1.17.50 n.). [12]Or, changing his appearance by taking on the guise of an artisan, craftsman, performer, physician, bard, or a member of a religious order, and accompanied by accomplices in the same disguises, he should enter through some vulnerable points, attack the king with weapons or poison, and announce: "I am prince N. N.! This kingdom should be enjoyed jointly; it is not proper for a single person to enjoy it. I will reward all those who desire to support me with double the rations and wages."

That concludes the actions of a prince in disfavor.

Topic 15: Actions Regarding a Prince in Disfavor

[13]Sons of high-ranking officials acting as spies should conciliate him and bring him back; or his mother, if she is in good terms with him, should do the same.

[14]If the king has given up on him, clandestine operatives should kill him with a weapon or poison. [15]If the king has not given up on him, getting him addicted to women of similar character, to drink, or to hunting, they should apprehend him at night and bring him back.

> [16]Once he has come, moreover, the king should appease him with the offer of the kingdom, saying, "After me (all this is yours)." He should then confine him in one location. If he has many sons, however, he should have him executed.

THAT CONCLUDES THE EIGHTEENTH CHAPTER: "ACTIONS OF A PRINCE IN DISFAVOR" AND "ACTIONS REGARDING A PRINCE IN DISFAVOR" OF THE FIRST BOOK: "ON THE SUBJECT OF TRAINING."

Chapter 19

Topic 16: Regimen of the King

[1]When the king is energetic, people in his service, in turn, become energetic; [2]and when he is lethargic, they, in turn, become lethargic. [3]They, moreover, consume his enterprises, [4]and he will be outwitted by his enemies. [5]Therefore, he should make himself energetic.

[6]Using a water clock, he should divide the day and the night into eight parts, or using the shadow of a sundial (1.7.8 n.). [7]A shadow of three Pauruṣas, one Pauruṣa, eight Aṅgulas,* and midday when the shadow disappears—these are the four earlier eighth parts of a day. [8]These also explain the later parts.

[9]Of these, during the first eighth part of the day, he should listen to reports on defensive arrangements and on income and expenditure. [10]During the second, he should try cases* brought by inhabitants of the cities and the countryside. [11]During the third, he should bathe, take his meal, and engage in Vedic recitation. [12]During the fourth, he should attend to monetary receipts and to the superintendents.* [13]During the fifth, he should consult with his council of counselors by dispatching letters and find out the secret intelligence carried by his informants. [14]During the sixth, he should engage in recreational activities of his choice or in taking

counsel. [15]During the seventh, he should inspect elephants, horses, chariots, and troops (2.33.9 n.). [16]During the eighth, he should ponder over military strategies together with the Chief of the Armed Forces. [17]At the end of the day, he should perform the twilight worship.

[18]During the first part of the night, he should meet with clandestine operatives. [19]During the second, he should bathe, take his meal, and engage in Vedic recitation. [20]During the third, he should retire to the sound of music and sleep during the fourth and fifth. [21]During the sixth, he should wake up to the sound of music and reflect on the treatise* and on activities that need to be carried out. [22]During the seventh, he should attend to counsel and dispatch clandestine operatives. [23]During the eighth, he should receive the blessings of the Officiating Priest, Teacher, and Chaplain, and meet with his physician, chef, and astrologer. [24]After circumambulating clockwise a cow with a calf and a bull, he should go to the assembly hall.

[25]Alternatively, he should divide the day and night into segments according to his individual capacity and attend to his duties.

[26]Having come to the assembly hall, he should permit free access to those who have come to plead their cases.* [27]For when people find it difficult to see the king, those surrounding him make him do what ought not to be done and not do what ought to be done. [28]As a result, the people will revolt against him, or he will fall into the clutches of his enemy. [29]Therefore, he should try the cases—those relating to gods,* hermitages, members of religious orders, Vedic scholars, farm animals, and holy places; those relating to children, the elderly, the sick, those in distress, and the helpless; and those relating to women—in that order, or according to the gravity of the case or its urgency.

> [30]He should hear every urgent case and not delay it; a postponed case becomes difficult or even impossible to settle.
>
> [31]He should try cases pertaining to gods (1.19.29 n.) and recluses within the fire hall and in the company of his Chaplain and Teacher, and after getting up from his seat and paying his respects.
>
> [32]He should try lawsuits of recluses and experts in magical lore not by himself but along with scholars of the triple Veda, because such persons may be provoked to anger.
>
> [33]For a king, the vow is energetic activity, the sacrifice is pursuing his undertakings, the sacrificial fee is impartiality in conduct, and the sacrificial consecration is his royal consecration.

[34]A king's happiness lies in the happiness of his subjects, and his welfare in the welfare of his subjects; a king's welfare consists not in what pleases him but in what pleases his subjects.

[35]Therefore, a king, being always energetic, should pursue Success; the foundation of Success is energetic activity, and that of non-Success is the opposite.

[36]In the absence of energetic activity, the destruction of what has been achieved and of what is yet to be achieved is certain. Through energetic activity, one gains the reward and obtains abundant Success.

THAT CONCLUDES THE NINETEENTH CHAPTER: "REGIMEN OF THE KING" OF THE FIRST BOOK: "ON THE SUBJECT OF TRAINING."

Chapter 20

Topic 17: Regimen of the Residence

[1]On land recommended as a building site,* he should get a royal residence constructed with palisade, moat, and gates, and provided with many courtyards.*

[2]He should get the living quarters constructed following the plan for the treasury—either a labyrinthine building containing passages within false walls with the living quarters at its center; or an underground chamber (2.5.2) equipped with a door concealed by an adjacent wooden statue of a sanctuary deity and with passages through several underground tunnels, and above it the mansion; or else living quarters with a stairway inside a false wall and a hollow pillar providing entrance and exit—as well as a floor connected to a mechanical device that would drop it down* as a safeguard against a calamity or for a time of calamity.* [3]Or he may design it differently from this for fear of fellow students.*

[4]When a fire produced by churning human bones is taken around the royal residence three times counterclockwise, no other fire will burn it and no other fire will flare up there; this happens also when it is daubed with ash produced by lightning and with water from hail mixed with earth.*

[5]Snakes or poisons are powerless in a place protected by Jīvantī, Śvetā, Muṣkaka, Puṣpa, and Vandākā and by the aerial root of an Aśvattha tree* growing on a drumstick tree* (14.4.12). [6]Releasing peacocks, mongooses, and spotted deer exterminates snakes. [7]Parrots, myna birds, and Bhṛṅgarāja-drongo cry out when they suspect the presence of a snake or

poison. [8]In the presence of poison, a Krauñca-crane becomes agitated, a Jīvaṃjīvaka-pheasant faints, a Mattakokila-cuckoo dies, and the eyes of Cakora-partridge turn red.

[9]In this manner, he should take countermeasures against fire, poison, and snakes.

[10]In an area of the courtyard at the back should be the women's quarters, maternity room, infirmary, and a yard with trees and water.* [11]Outside* is the residence for young girls and princes. [12]In the front are the dressing room, the counsel chamber, the assembly hall, and the offices for the supervisors of the princes. [13]In the areas between the courtyards should be stationed the palace guard.

[14]Going to the inner chamber, he should meet with the queen after she has been inspected and cleared by elderly women. [15]For Bhadrasena was killed by his brother hiding in the queen's chamber, and Kārūṣa by his son hiding under his mother's bed.* [16]The king of Kāśi was killed by his queen with puffed grain mixed with poison disguised as honey; Vairantya with an anklet smeared with poison; Sauvīra with a girdle jewel smeared with poison; and Jālūtha with a mirror smeared with poison. And the queen killed Vidūratha by hiding a weapon in her braids.* [17]Therefore, he should avoid these situations.

[18]He should prohibit interaction* with shaven-headed and matted-haired ascetics, and charlatans,* as well as with female slaves coming from outside. [19]Members of their families should not be permitted to see them, except in the maternity room and the infirmary. [20]Prostitutes, after they have cleansed their bodies by bathing and rubbing and changed their clothes and jewelry, may be permitted to visit them. [21]Men at least 80 years old and women at least 50 years old, appearing as mothers and fathers, and elderly eunuch stewards should find out the honesty and dishonesty of the inmates of the harem and make them devoted to what is beneficial to the lord.

> [22]All should reside in their own quarters and not visit the quarters of others; and no one living within should interact with anyone outside.
> [23]Further, every article coming in or going out should be inspected and its entry and exit recorded; and the transportation to its destination should be under seal.

THAT CONCLUDES THE TWENTIETH CHAPTER: "REGIMEN OF THE RESIDENCE" OF THE FIRST BOOK: "ON THE SUBJECT OF TRAINING."

Chapter 21

Topic 18: Personal Protection of the King

[1]When he rises from bed, he should be escorted by teams of female guards armed with bows; in the second courtyard, by eunuch stewards wearing robes and turbans; in the third, by hunchbacks, dwarfs, and Kirātas (1.12.9 n.); in the fourth, by counselors and relatives and by the gate guards armed with spears.

[2]He should place close to him individuals who have served his father and grandfather, who are bound to him by close relationships, and who are trained, loyal, and men of accomplishment, but never individuals who are from another country and have not been granted wealth and honors, and not even individuals from his own country who have been taken into service after they had been slighted. [3]Troops of the palace guard should protect the king and the royal residence.

[4]The chef should get all the cooking carried out in a secure location, tasting it frequently. [5]The king should eat it in the same manner,* after first making an offering to fire and birds.*

[6]The signs of food mixed with poison are the blue color of the flame and smoke of the fire and its crackling sound, as also the death of birds. [7]The signs of articles mixed with poison are the following: in the case of boiled rice—steam the color of a peacock's neck, frigidity, quick discoloration as if stale, presence of water, and not being moist; in the case of curries—becoming dry quickly, bubbling continuously, having a dirty appearance, frothing, curdling, and the destruction of smell, texture, and taste;* in the case of liquids—appearance of a hue more faint or more pronounced, and appearance of upward streaks at the edges of the froth; in the case of juice—a blue streak in the middle; in the case of milk—a reddish streak in the middle; in the case of liquor and water—a black streak in the middle; in the case of curd—a dark streak in the middle; in the case of honey—a white streak in the middle; in the case of wet substances—becoming quickly withered, becoming overcooked, and a bluish dark color while boiling; in the case of dry substances—crumbling quickly and discoloration; in the case of hard and soft substances—softness in the former and hardness in the latter, as also the death of small creatures in their vicinity; in the case of bedsheets and covers—appearance of dark circles and the crumbling of the thread, wool, and hair; in the case of articles made of metal and gems—appearing soiled with muddy dirt, and the destruction of the smoothness, pigment, weight, potency, color, and texture.

[8]The signs of a poisoner, on the other hand, are as follows: dry and dark look on the face, stuttering speech, excessive perspiration and yawning, trembling, stumbling, looking around while speaking, agitation while working, and not remaining in his place.

[9]Therefore, experts in the cure of poisons and physicians should remain close to him. [10]The physician should take the medicine, whose purity has been tested by tasting, from the pharmacy, have it tasted by the cook, the pounder, and himself, and then present it to the king. [11]The discussion of medicine explains also the handling of drink and water.

[12]Barbers and valets, with clean clothes and hands after a bath, should take the implements in a sealed container from the hands of the chief of the palace guard and wait on him. [13]Female slaves of proven integrity should perform the work of bath attendants, masseurs, preparers of beds, launderers, and garland-makers, or artisans should do so under their supervision. [14]They should give him garments and garlands after touching their own eyes with them, and bath oils, rubbing powders, perfumes, and bathing lotions after applying them on their own chests and arms. [15]This explains also the handling of anything that has been received from someone else.

[16]Performers should entertain him without employing performances involving weapons, fire, or poison. [17]Their musical instruments should remain within the palace, as also the ornaments of their horses, carriages, and elephants.

[18]He should ride a carriage or a mount under the control of a trusted officer and a boat captained by a trusted boatman. [19]He should not get into a boat tied to another boat or buffeted by a strong wind. [20]Troops should stand by at the water's edge.

[21]He should enter a body of water that has been cleared by fishermen, [22]and visit a park that has been cleared by snake catchers. [23]He should go to a game forest for practice on moving targets after fowlers and those who hunt with dogs have cleared it of dangers posed by thieves, vicious animals, and enemies.

[24]He should meet a thaumaturgic ascetic attended by trustworthy armed guards, and an envoy from a neighboring lord in the company of the council of counselors. [25]Dressed in full military attire and riding on a horse or an elephant, he should inspect his troops dressed in full military attire.

[26]When he goes out or comes in, he should travel along the royal highway guarded on both sides, from which armed men, renouncers, and

cripples have been removed by guards armed with weapons and batons. [27]He should not lunge into crowds. [28]He should attend an excursion, fair, feast, or festivity only when they are supervised by squad commanders.

> [29]As the king keeps others under surveillance through covert agents, so, possessing the exemplary qualities of the self (1.5.16 n.), he should protect himself from the dangers posed by others.

THAT CONCLUDES THE TWENTY-FIRST CHAPTER: "PERSONAL PROTECTION OF THE KING" OF THE FIRST BOOK: "ON THE SUBJECT OF TRAINING."

THAT CONCLUDES THE FIRST BOOK: "ON THE SUBJECT OF TRAINING" OF KAUṬILYA'S *ARTHAŚĀSTRA*.

Book Two

On the Activities of Superintendents

Chapter 1

Topic 19: Settlement of the Countryside

[1]He should settle the countryside—whether it has been settled before or has never been settled—by forcing people out* of enemy territories or by transferring people from overpopulated areas of his own territory.

[2]He should settle villages with mostly Śūdra agriculturalists (see 6.1.8), each village consisting of a minimum of 100 families* and a maximum of 500 families,* with boundaries extending one or two Krośas, and affording mutual protection. [3]He should make the junctures of their boundaries demarcated by a river, a hill, a forest, a band of pebbles, a cave, a dike, a Śamī tree, a Śālmalī tree, or a milk tree.*

[4]In the middle of an 800-village unit, he should establish a provincial capital, in the middle of a 400-village unit, a district municipality, in the middle of a 200-village unit, a county seat, and a collection center for each collection of ten villages.*

[5]At the frontiers, he should construct the forts of the Frontier Commanders as gateways into the countryside and under the control of the Frontier Commanders. [6]Areas between them should be guarded by trappers, tribals, mountaineers, Caṇḍālas,* and forest dwellers.

[7]He should present Brāhmaṇa land grants* exempt from fines and taxes to the officiating priest, teacher, Chaplain, and Vedic scholars, gifts that are inherited by heirs of equal competence. To superintendents, accountants, and the like, as also to revenue officers, county supervisors, elephant trainers, physicians, horse trainers, and couriers, he should present gifts that cannot be sold or mortgaged.

[8]He should give cultivated* land to taxpayers for as long as they live, [9]and uncultivated* lands, made exempt from taxes,* to those who would cultivate them. [10]He should seize lands from those who do not cultivate them and give them to others. [11]Alternatively, village servants* or traders should cultivate them; [12]or else, those who have not cultivated them should compensate the losses.*

[13]He should assist them with grain, farm animals, and money. [14]They should return those later at their convenience. [15]He should grant them the kinds of favors and exemptions* that would enhance the revenue to the treasury and avoid those that would cause a decrease in revenue to the treasury; [16]for a king with a depleted treasury devours the very inhabitants of the cities and the countryside. [17]At the time of settlement or when the people actually arrive, he should grant them exemptions. [18]Like a father, he should assist those whose exemptions have come to an end.

[19]He should set up the operations (2.7.3 n.) of factories attached to mines (1.18.8 n.), produce forests, elephant forests, herd stations, and trade routes, as well as water routes, land routes, and ports.

[20]He should get reservoirs constructed, reservoirs that are fed either with naturally occurring water or with water channeled from elsewhere;* [21]or he should render assistance to others constructing them by giving land, routes,* trees, and implements, as also to those constructing holy places and parks. [22]When someone quits a joint project to build a reservoir, his workmen and bullocks should carry out the work; [23]and he has to pay his share of the expenses, but he will not receive a share of the returns.* [24]The ownership of fish, water fowl, and commercial vegetables* in the reservoirs belongs to the king.

[25]The king should enforce discipline on slaves, persons given as pledges, and relatives, when they fail to obey. [26]The king should, moreover, provide for children, old people, those fallen into misfortune, and the helpless,* as also for women who have not borne children and the sons of women who have borne children.

[27]The elders of a village should make the property of minors increase in value until they reach the legal age,* as also the property of a temple. [28]When a person who has the capacity does not provide for his children, wives, mother, father, brothers who are minors, or unmarried and widowed sisters, he should be fined 12 Paṇas, unless they have fallen from their caste, except the mother.*

[29]For a man who renounces without providing for his sons and wives, the punishment is the lowest seizure fine;* so also for anyone who induces

a woman to renounce. [30]A man who has lost his potency* may renounce after seeking the permission from the Justices.* [31]Otherwise, he should be detained.

[32]He should not let the following settle in his countryside: any kind of renouncer other than forest hermits, any association other than one consisting of kinsmen,* and any group governed by conventions other than one created for a joint task.* [33]No parks,* moreover, or buildings for recreational activities should be permitted there; [34]and actors, dancers, singers, musicians, bards, and performers shall not cause any hindrance to work. [35]When villages do not provide shelter* and men are intent on cultivation, they create increases in treasure,* labor, goods, grains, and juices.

> [36]The king should grant an exemption (2.1.15 n.) to a region devastated by an enemy king or a tribal chief, or beleaguered by sickness or famine, and ban expensive sports.
>
> [37]He should safeguard agriculture when it is stressed by the hardships of fines, forced labor, and taxes, and animal herds when they are harassed by thieves, vicious animals, poison, and crocodiles, as well as by sickness.
>
> [38]He should keep trade routes clear when they are oppressed by his favorites, works officers, robbers, and Frontier Commanders, or worn out by herds of farm animals.
>
> [39]In this manner the king should protect produce forests, elephant forests, reservoirs, and mines established in the past and also set up new ones.

THAT CONCLUDES THE FIRST CHAPTER: "SETTLEMENT OF THE COUNTRYSIDE" OF THE SECOND BOOK: "ON THE ACTIVITIES OF SUPERINTENDENTS."

Chapter 2

Topic 20: "Covering the Crevices on the Land"*

[1]On land unsuitable for cultivation, he should allot pastures for farm animals. [2]He should allot wild tracts to recluses for Vedic study and Soma sacrifice, tracts with a maximum area of one Goruta and where all mobile and immobile creatures have been granted immunity from harm.

[3]He should get an animal reserve of the same extent established for the king's relaxation—a reserve with a single gate, protected by a moat, and containing shrubs and bushes bearing tasty fruit, trees without thorns,

shallow ponds, tame deer and other game, vicious animals with their claws and fangs removed, and male and female elephants and elephant cubs for use in the hunt. [4]At its border or as dictated by the lay of the land, he should get another animal reserve established where all the animals are treated as guests.*

[5]He should also establish a forest for each product classified as forest produce,* as well as factories attached to the produce forests and foresters* living in the produce forests.

[6]At the frontier, he should establish an elephant forest guarded by foresters. [7]The Superintendent of Elephant Forests* should protect elephant forests located near hills, rivers, lakes, or marshy land, with the help of elephant-forest wardens, keeping the boundaries, entrances, and exits under surveillance. [8]They should put to death anyone who kills an elephant. [9]Anyone who brings the two tusks of an elephant that has died naturally shall receive a reward of four and a quarter Paṇas.

[10]The elephant-forest wardens, assisted by elephant keepers, foot chainers, border guards, foresters, and attendants—their body odors masked by rubbing elephant urine and dung, camouflaged with branches of Bhallātakī-tree, and moving about with five or seven female elephants acting as lures—should find out the size of the elephant herds by means of clues provided by where they sleep, their footprints and dung, and the damage they have done to river banks. [11]They should keep a written record of elephants—those moving in herds, those roaming alone, those driven from a herd, and the leaders of herds, as well as those that are vicious or in rut, the cubs, and those released from captivity.

[12]They should capture elephants that, in the judgment of elephant trainers, have excellent marks and demeanor. [13]A king's victory is led by elephants, [14]for elephants, with their enormous bodies and lethal onslaughts, can crush an enemy's troops, battle arrays, forts, and military camps.

> [15]Among elephants, those born in Kaliṅga and Aṅgara are the best; those born in the east, Cedi, and Karūṣa, and those from the Daśārṇas and Aparāntas are considered middling.
> [16]Those from Surāṣṭra and Pañcanada are said to be the worst. The courage, speed, and energy of all are increased with training.

THAT CONCLUDES THE SECOND CHAPTER: "COVERING THE CREVICES ON THE LAND" OF THE SECOND BOOK: "ON THE ACTIVITIES OF SUPERINTENDENTS."

Chapter 3

Topic 21: Construction of Forts*

[1]At each of the four directions along the frontiers of the countryside, he should have a fort built providing an advantage in battle and natural protection: a water fort—an island in the middle of water or a high ground encircled by water courses; a hill fort—a rocky outcrop or a cave; a desert fort—land without water and shrubbery or a salt flat; and a forest fort—a marshy swamp or a thicket of shrubs.* [2]Of these, the river and hill forts are locations for the defenders of the countryside, while the desert and forest forts are locations for forest tribals* or a place of retreat in a time of adversity.

[3]In the center of the countryside, he should construct a provincial capital as a revenue collection center on land recommended as a building site (1.20.1 n.) at the confluence of rivers or on the bank of a lake—either a natural pond or a reservoir—that never dries up. It should be round, rectangular, or square, or as required by the lay of the land, with water flowing clockwise,* and function as a market town* served by a land route and a water route.

[4]Around it,* he should get three moats* constructed at distances of one Daṇḍa from each other. Each should be 14, 12, and ten Daṇḍas* wide, respectively. The depth of each is three-quarters or one-half its width; the bottom width of each is one-third its width at the surface, or their bottoms should be square.* They should be revetted with stone or their sides should be lined with stone or brick. They should be fed either by natural springs or by channeled water, and they should be provided with means of drainage and stocked with lotuses and crocodiles.*

[5]At a distance of four Daṇḍas from the moat,* he should get a rampart constructed using the earth that has been dug out. It should be six Daṇḍas high, well contained,* and twice as wide as that. It should be vaulted with a flat top or pot-bellied,* and it should be compacted using elephants and bulls and covered with thorny shrubs and poisonous creepers. [6]With the remainder of the dirt, he should have the cavities in the building sites or the royal residence filled.*

[7]On top of the rampart, he should get a wall constructed whose height is twice the width. It should be built with bricks to a height of more than 12 Hastas—either an odd or an even number—up to a maximum of 24 Hastas. It should have a passageway for chariots and a foundation reinforced with Palmyra trunks,* its top being capped with "drums" and

"monkey heads."* [8]Alternatively, he should have it built of stone, using wide stones stacked together tightly, but never of wood, [9]for fire lurks hidden within it.

[10]He should have towers with rectangular foundations* built at a distance of 30 Daṇḍas from each other.* They should be equipped with dropdown ladders* of the same height. [11]Midway between two towers, he should get a postern gate built, its length one and a half times its width, and having two stories equipped with a hall.* [12]Midway between each tower and postern gate, he should get an embrasure built, large enough for three archers and constructed with tightly fitting planks with shuttered loopholes. [13]In the intervening spaces, he should construct a "god's path" two Hastas wide and four times as long along the side.* [14]He should get routes* constructed one or two Daṇḍas apart, and in an impregnable area, a passageway* and an egress door.*

[15]On the outside,* he should get a clandestine path constructed that is laid with knee-breakers, spike clusters, pits, hidden traps, barbed strips, "snake's backs," "palm leaves," "triple horns," "dog's teeth," bars, "stumblers," "shoes," "frying pans," and waterholes.*

[16]Having made the wall circular by one and a half Daṇḍas on both sides,* he should erect a gate large enough for six beams of a postern gate.* It should be quadrangular in shape, with a minimum of five Daṇḍas, increasing by one Daṇḍa up to a maximum of eight Daṇḍas, and one-sixth or one-eighth more than its length.* [17]The height of the floor is a minimum of 15 Hastas and increasing by one up to a maximum of 18 Hastas. [18]The circumference of a column should be one-sixth of its length; twice that is the section buried in the ground; and the circumference of the capital is one-fourth of its length.

[19]The five sections of the ground floor are a hall, a well, a border room, [20–21]and two platforms facing each other and occupying one-tenth of the area.* In between are two side doors and a hall at half the height of the floor, as also a pillared edifice.* [22]The hall on the top floor covers half the built-up area or extends over one-third of it, with its sides lined with brick, with a staircase on the left spiraling clockwise, and on the other side a staircase with a false wall.

[23]The pinnacle of the arched portal measures two Hastas; [24]the two panels of the door are three-fifths wide;* [25]there are two bars; [26]the threshold* measures one Aratni; [27]the side door (2.3.20–21 n) measures five Hastas; [28]there are four elephant bars;* [29]to facilitate access, there is an "elephant nail"; [30]and the concourse is equal in width to the gate opening

and either consists of a drawbridge or, where there is no water, is built with earth.*

[31]Having prepared an opening equal in extent* to the wall, he should get the "cow fort" constructed, one-third of it resembling the snout of a monitor lizard.* [32]After cutting a pit* in the middle of the wall, he should get the "lotus-pond" gate* constructed; as also the four-halled "princess fort" with one and a half the space in between and equipped with loopholes;* and the two-storied "bald" gate with a bald upper hall.* Alternatively, he should construct them as dictated by the land and the material.

[33]He should get trenches constructed one-third as long as they are wide for the storage of equipment.

> [34–35]In them should be stored stones, spades, axes, arrows, knives, clubs, hammers, cudgels, discuses, mechanical devices, bludgeons, spears prepared by blacksmiths, bamboos with sharpened points, camel necks, incendiary devices, and items listed in the section on forest produce (2.17.4–16).*

THAT CONCLUDES THE THIRD CHAPTER: "CONSTRUCTION OF FORTS" OF THE SECOND BOOK: "ON THE ACTIVITIES OF SUPERINTENDENTS."

Chapter 4

Topic 22: Layout of a Fort

[1]Three royal highways running east and three running north constitute the division* of the area for building sites. [2]It should have 12 gates* and contain suitable places for water canals, drainage ditches,* and clandestine passages.

[3]Streets* should be four Daṇḍas wide.* [4]Royal highways and roads in district municipalities, provincial capitals, provinces, and pasture land, as well as roads in port towns, military encampments, cemeteries, and villages, should be eight Daṇḍas wide. [5]Roads on dikes and in forests should be four Daṇḍas wide; roads for elephants and in fields, two Daṇḍas; roads for carriages, five Aratnis; roads for farm animals, four Aratnis; and roads for small animals and humans, two Aratnis.

[6]The king's dwelling should be on an excellent building site suitable for inhabitation by the four social classes.* [7]In the one-ninth sector to the north of the center of the area for building sites,* he should get the royal residence built according to the prescribed plan and facing either the east or the north.

[8]In its* east-northeast sector* is the dwelling for the teacher and Chaplain and the location for sacrifices and water*—and the counselors should reside there.* In the east-southeast sector are the kitchen, the elephant stables, and the storehouse. [9]Beyond that, in the eastern direction, should be the residences of traders dealing in perfumes, garlands, and juices, and manufacturers of toiletries, as well as Kṣatriyas.

[10]In the south-southeast sector are the warehouse (4.9.6 n.), bureau of official records (2.7.1), and workshops;* and in the south-southwest sector, the storage facility for forest produce and the armory. [11]Beyond that, in the southern direction, should be the residences of the City Manager, grain dealers, Director of Factories,* military officers, traders dealing in cooked food, liquor, and meat, prostitutes, and dancers, as well as Vaiśyas.

[12]In the west-southwest sector are the stables for donkeys and camels and the workshop,* and in the west-northwest sector, the garages for carriages and chariots. [13]Beyond that, in the western direction, should be the residences of workers in wool, yarn, bamboo, leather, armor, weapons, and shields, as well as Śūdras.

[14]In the north-northwest sector are the stores for merchandise and medicines, and in the north-northeast sector, the treasury, as well as cattle and horses. [15]Beyond that, in the northern direction, should be the residences of the deities of the city and deities of the king, and workers in metal and gems, as well as Brāhmaṇas.

[16]In an area along the walls unsuitable as a building site* should be the housing for guilds and foreign traders.

[17]In the middle of the city,* he should have these built: shrines for Aparājita, Apratihata, Jayanta, and Vaijayanta, and abodes for Śiva, Vaiśravaṇa, Aśvins, Śrī, and Madirā.* [18]He should install deities of the building sites according to the location. [19]The presiding deities of the gates are Brahmā, Indra, Yama, and Senāpati.* [20]Outside at a distance of 100 Dhanuṣes from the moat should be built sanctuaries, holy places, groves, and reservoirs, as also in each quarter its respective deity,* or in the north-northeast.

[21]Conveyance to the cemetery is through the southern (gate and the rest) incrementally for each social class.* [22]For violating this, the punishment is the lowest seizure fine (see 2.1.29 n.).

[23]The residences of religious orders* and Caṇḍālas are on the outskirts of the cemetery.

[24]In accordance with the land required for their workshops, he should fix the boundaries of householders. [25]Within those boundaries they may,

with permission, establish flower gardens and fruit orchards, as well as storage facilities for grain and merchandise. [26]In a compound with ten families, there should be a site for a well.

[27]He should have storage facilities constructed for the following goods sufficient to last several years: all kinds of fats, grains, sweeteners, salts, perfumes, medicines, dried vegetables, green fodder, dried meats, hay, wood, metals, hides, charcoal, tendons, poisons, horns, bamboos, barks, strong timber,* weapons, shields, and stones. [28]He should refresh the old with new stock.*

[29]He should station forces made up of the elephant corps, cavalry, chariot corps, and infantry led by separate commands; [30]for forces under separate commands do not succumb to enemy instigation because they fear each other.

[31]The above discussion also explains issues relating to the construction of the forts of the Frontier Commanders.

> [32]He should not permit outsiders who would destroy the realm to remain in the city. He should expel them to the countryside, or make them pay all the taxes.

THAT CONCLUDES THE FOURTH CHAPTER: "LAYOUT OF A FORT" OF THE SECOND BOOK: "ON THE ACTIVITIES OF SUPERINTENDENTS."

Chapter 5

Topic 23: Treasurer's Management of Storage Facilities

[1]The Treasurer* should have a treasury, a depot for merchandise, a storehouse, a storage facility for forest produce, an armory, and a prison constructed.

[2]He should have an underground chamber* constructed by getting a square pit free from water or dampness dug and lining it with large slabs of stone both on the sides and at the bottom. It should have joists of strong timber, be level with the ground with a triple floor of different compositions—a paved floor inlaid with pebbles, a local floor, and a standing floor—and have a single door with a staircase attached to a mechanical device and concealed by a statue of a deity.* [3]Above that, he should have the treasury constructed—it should be sealed off on both sides,* have an entry hall, and be built of brick and surrounded by trenches for the storage of equipment—or a mansion.*

[4]At the border region of the countryside, he should get people condemned to death* to construct a place containing a permanent treasure for a time of adversity.

[5]He should have the following constructed: on the two sides, a depot for merchandise and a storehouse—built with burnt-brick pillars, containing four halls* with a single door and several ground and upper floors, and equipped with escape routes through hollow pillars; in the middle, a storage facility for forest produce with several long halls, and with its walls lined with courtyards;* an armory constructed to the same specifications and equipped with an underground vault; and separately a lockup for the office of the Justices and a jail for tribunals of high officials with separate facilities for men and women, and a prison with well-guarded courtyards to prevent escape.*

[6]In all these, he should have the halls equipped with a ditch, a well, a latrine, a bathroom, defenses against fire and poison, cats and mongooses for protection,* and provisions for the worship of the deity specific to each.* [7]In the storehouse, he should place an urn with a mouth one Aratni in diameter as a rain gauge.*

[8]Guided by a bureau of experts in each commodity,* he* should accept precious stones, articles of high or low value, and forest produce, both new and old. [9]When there is fraud in these transactions, the punishment for both the man who did it and the one who put him up to it is the highest fine (2.1.29 n.) in the case of precious stones, and the middle fine in the case of articles of high value; in the case of articles of low value and forest produce, they should pay compensation and a fine equal to the value.

[10]He should accept money after it has been authenticated by the Examiner of Coins, [11]and cut up any that are counterfeit. [12]The punishment for a man bringing it is the lowest seizure fine (2.1.29 n.).

[13]He should accept grain that is unadulterated, fully developed,* and new. [14]In the opposite case, the fine is twice the value.

[15]The above discussion also explains issues relating to merchandise, forest produce, and weapons.

[16]In all the departments, for the directors, junior officers, and their servants, in the case of thefts of one Paṇa, two Paṇas, four Paṇas, and more than that,* the punishments are the lowest, the middle, and the highest fines (2.5.9 n.), and death, respectively. [17]When a manager of the treasury* pilfers from the treasury, he should be executed. [18]Those who act as their agents* should be assessed half the fine;* [19]if they did it unknowingly, they should be reprimanded.

[20]In the case of breaking and entry, the punishment for thieves is vivid execution (4.9.7; see 4.9.2 n.).

[21]Therefore, the Treasurer, guided by trustworthy subordinates, should attend to the storage facilities.

> [22]He should know the external and internal revenues even after 100 years, so that when he is questioned, he will not vacillate with regard to expenditures, balances, and revenues.

THAT CONCLUDES THE FIFTH CHAPTER: "TREASURER'S MANAGEMENT OF STORAGE FACILITIES" OF THE SECOND BOOK: "ON THE ACTIVITIES OF SUPERINTENDENTS."

Chapter 6

Topic 24: Organization of Revenue Collection by the Collector

[1]The Collector should oversee the following: fort, province, pit mine, irrigation works, forest, herd, and trade route.*

[2]Duties, fines, standardization of weights and measures, city manager, director of the mint, director of passports, liquor, abattoirs, yarn, oil, ghee, sweeteners, goldsmiths, commercial establishments, prostitutes, gambling, building compounds (1.20.1 n.), unions of artisans and craftsmen, temple superintendent, and taxes (2.1.9 n.) at the gates and from outsiders*—these constitute "fort."

[3]Agriculture (2.24.1 n.), share, tribute, tax, trader, river warden, ferry, boat, port, pasture, road toll, land survey, and capture of thieves*—these constitute "province."*

[4]Gold, silver, diamonds, gems, pearls, coral, conchs, metals, salt, and ores in the earth, rocks, and liquids (2.12.1, 2 n.)—these constitute "pit mine" (2.12.27).

[5]Flower gardens, fruit orchards, vegetable plots, wet farm land, and root crops—these constitute "irrigation works."

[6]Forest preserves for game animals, deer, produce, and elephants—these constitute "forest."

[7]Cattle and buffaloes, goats and sheep, donkeys and camels, horses and mules—these constitute "herd."

[8]Land routes and water routes—these constitute "trade route."

[9]These constitute the corpus of revenue.*

[10]Price, share, surcharge, monopoly tax, fixed levy, coinage fee, and penalty*—these are the categories of revenue (2.6.9 n.).

[11]Allocations for the worship of gods and ancestors and for gifts; rites for prosperity; royal residence; kitchen; diplomatic missions; storehouse; armory; depot for merchandise; storage facility for forest produce; factories; labor; procurement of foot soldiers, horses, chariots, and elephants; cattle herds; enclosures for game animals, deer, birds, and vicious animals; and enclosures for firewood and grass—these constitute the corpus of expenditure.

[12]The accounting period* is recorded according to the regnal year, month, fortnight, and day; the third and seventh fortnights of the rainy season, winter, and summer have one day less, while the others have a full number of days;* the intercalary month* is counted separately—these constitute time.

[13]Estimated revenue, established revenue, outstanding revenue, income and expenditure, and balance.*

[14]Canons, procedures (2.7.3 n.), setting out the corpus of revenue, receipts, aggregate of all revenues, and grand total*—these constitute the estimated revenue.

[15]Deliveries to the treasury, levies by the king, and city outlay* constitute deposits; and carryovers from the previous year and payments deferred by royal decree or oral command constitute what may not be rescinded—these constitute established revenue.

[16]Gains from work when completed and unpaid balances of fines constitute the recoverables, and what has been forcibly withheld and what has been expended* constitute what has to be reclaimed—these constitute outstanding revenue, which should include no or few items of high value.

[17]Income consists of the current, the arrears, and the miscellaneous. [18]The current consists of daily receipts. [19]The arrears consist of carryovers from the previous year and what is remitted from someone else's operations.* [20]The miscellaneous* consists of the lost and forgotten, fines on officials, side income,* compensation for loss, gratuities,* property of people involved in riots, property of people without sons (3.5.28), and treasure trove. [21]Balances from demobilization* and from discontinuation of projects interrupted by an illness are return of expenditure. [22]Price increases on merchandise at the time of sale, increment, special weights and measures, surcharge (2.6.10 n.), and price increases due to competition for purchase*—these constitute income.*

[23]Expenditure consists of regular expenses and those arising from regular expenses, and periodic payments* and those arising from periodic payments. [24]The regular consists of daily outlays. [25]The periodic consists of fortnightly, monthly, and annual payments. [26]Expenses derived from these two* are those arising from the regular and those arising from the periodic—these constitute expenditure.

[27]When the grand total has been adjusted for income and expenditure, it is the balance, consisting of both what has been received and what is carried forward.*

> [28]In this way, the wise man should bring in revenue. He should also show an increase in income and a decrease in expenditure and rectify the opposite.

THAT CONCLUDES THE SIXTH CHAPTER: "ORGANIZATION OF REVENUE COLLECTION BY THE COLLECTOR" OF THE SECOND BOOK: "ON THE ACTIVITIES OF SUPERINTENDENTS."

Chapter 7

Topic 25: Subject of Accounts in the Bureau of Official Records*

[1]The Superintendent* should get the bureau of official records with separate rooms constructed facing the east or the north* as a depository for registry books.* [2]In that bureau, he should have the following entered in the registry books:

concerning departments—the totality of their number, procedures (2.7.3 n.), and income;

concerning factories—the extent of the following: gain and loss* of material in the manufacturing process, expenses, additional weight,* surcharge (2.6.10 n.), admixture,* location, wages, and labor;

concerning precious stones, articles of high value, articles of low value, and forest produce*—price, sample,* size, weight, height, depth, and container.

concerning regions, villages, castes, families, and associations—Laws, conventions, customs, and canons;*

concerning those in the king's service—the receipt by them of favors, land, benefits, exemptions, rations, and wages;

concerning the king's wives and sons*—the receipt by them of precious stones and land, and of special allowances and remedial measures during disasters;

concerning allies and enemies—payments and receipts in connection with peace pacts and declarations of war.

[3]From that bureau,* he should deliver in writing to all departments the records of their estimated revenue, established revenue, outstanding revenue, income and expenditure, balance, additional revenue,* procedures,* customs, and canons (2.7.2 n.).

[4]For low-level, mid-level, and high-level activities, he should appoint as superintendent an individual of the same level, but for revenue-producing activities, he should appoint an appropriate individual whom the king could punish without regret.* [5]Any loss relating to the work of such a superintendent should be borne by the sureties who assume co-responsibility (3.11.14–17 n.), those gaining a livelihood from that work, sons, brothers, wives, daughters, and servants.

[6]The work year consists of 354 days and nights.* [7]He should define it as ending on the full-moon day of Āṣāḍha (June–July), whether it is short or full,* [8]and have a bureau of experts oversee the intercalary month.*

[9]He should have their procedures (2.7.3 n.), moreover, overseen by spies.* [10]For, an official may cause a loss of revenue—if he is unacquainted with the procedures (2.7.3 n.), customs, and canons, through ignorance; if he is incapable of enduring the travails of entrepreneurial activity, through laziness; if he is addicted to sensual objects such as sound, through carelessness; if he is scared of agitations or of acting against Law or Success, through fear; with regard to those who come to plead their cases, if he is inclined to favor them, through love, and if he is inclined to hurt them, through anger; if he relies on his learning, wealth, or connection to a royal favorite, through arrogance; and if he inserts discrepancies in weights, measures, estimates,* and accounting, through greed.

[11]"The fine for these is the amount of the loss; it is increased onefold for each subsequent one in the list," say the Mānavas. [12]"In every case, it is eight times," say the Pārāśaras. [13]"Ten times," say the Bārhaspatyas. [14]"Twenty times," say the Auśanasas. [15]"Proportionate to the offense," says Kauṭilya.

[16]They should come in on the full-moon day of Āṣāḍha [June–July] for statements of account.* [17]When they have come with the sealed books and the balances in sealed boxes, he should have them confined in one place,

forbidding them from speaking to one another. [18]After hearing the totals of income, expenditure, and balance, he should have the balance taken away. [19]When, with respect to the balance, the income turns out to be larger than its total given in the inner folio, or when he subtracts an amount from the total of expenditures, he should make the superintendent pay eight times that amount.* [20]In the reverse case, the amount should go back to him.

[21]When they do not come at the proper time or come without the books and the boxes with the balances, the fine is one-tenth the amount due.* [22]When, moreover, the works officer arrives but the accounts officer does not present the corresponding account,* his punishment is the lowest seizure fine (2.1.29 n.); [23]in the reverse case, however, the works officer is assessed double that fine.

[24]All the high officials should unanimously announce those who conformed to the procedures (2.7.3 n.).* [25]Anyone of them who takes a separate stand or who states an untruth should pay the highest fine (2.1.29 n.).*

[26]If someone* does not bring in the daily accounts, he should wait for one month. [27]After one month, he should pay a fine of 200 Paṇas, increased by 200 Paṇas for each additional month. [28]If a small amount of the recorded balance remains outstanding, he should wait for five days.* [29]If he first deposits the amount in the treasury and then brings in the daily accounts after that period, he should investigate the matter by taking into account the Laws, conventions, customs, and canons; by examining the sum total; by scrutinizing the work carried out; and by inference and the use of informants.

[30]He should corroborate* them* by comparing them with the daily, five-day, fortnightly, monthly, four-month, and annual accounts. [31]He should verify the income with reference to the accounting period (2.6.12), place, time, category, source, what is brought forward,* quantity, person making the payment, person having the payment made, recorder, and receiver. [32]He should verify the expenditure with reference to the accounting period, place, time, category, periodic payment,* occasion, articles given, use,* quantity, one who gives the order, one who takes out, one who arranges, and one who receives.* [33]He should verify the balance with reference to the accounting period, place, time, category, what is brought forward,* articles, their characteristics,* quantity, container in which they are deposited, and security guard.

[34]When, in a matter relating to the king, the accounts officer does not present the relevant account (2.7.22 n.) or offers a disclaimer, or else arranges income and expenditure in ways different from the written

orders,* he is assessed the lowest seizure fine (2.1.29 n.). [35]If he writes down an item without any order, in the wrong order, illegibly, or iteratively, he should be fined 12 Paṇas. [36]If he writes down the balance in such a manner, the fine is doubled; [37]if he consumes* it, the fine is made eight-fold; [38]and if he destroys it, the fine is one-fifth of the amount (2.7.21 n.), as well as restitution.* [39]If he lies, he is assessed the fine for theft.* [40]If he acknowledges it afterward, the fine is doubled,* as also when he brings in an item that had been forgotten.

> [41]He should overlook a small offense, he should be pleased with
> even a small amount of revenue, and he should honor with favors
> a superintendent who provides great assistance.

THAT CONCLUDES THE SEVENTH CHAPTER: "SUBJECT OF ACCOUNTS IN THE BUREAU OF OFFICIAL RECORDS" OF THE SECOND BOOK: "ON THE ACTIVITIES OF SUPERINTENDENTS."

Chapter 8

Topic 26: Recovery of Revenue Embezzled by Officials

[1]All undertakings presuppose the treasury (2.8.1; 8.1.23–53). [2]Before anything, therefore, he should attend to the treasury.

[3]The flourishing of procedures,* fostering customs, suppressing thieves, controlling officials, success of crops, abundance of commodities, relief during misfortune, reducing exemptions, and gifts of money—these are the ways to increase the treasury.

[4]Obstruction, lending, trading, cover-up, causing loss, usufruct, substitution, and misappropriation—these are the ways to decrease the treasury.

[5]Obstruction consists of the failure to carry out projects, to harness their profits, or to hand over the profits; [6]the fine for it is one-tenth of the amount (2.7.21 n.). [7]Lending consists of lending on interest articles belonging to the treasury, [8]and trading consists of trading in merchandise; [9]the fine for these is double the profit. [10]When one records the established date as not the due date, or a non-due date as the due date, it is cover-up; [11]the fine for it is one-fifth the amount. [12]When one causes a reduction in the income or an increase in the expenditure that have been fixed, it is causing loss; [13]the fine for it is four times the loss. [14]Using himself or letting others use articles belonging to the king is usufruct; [15]the punishment

for it is execution if precious stones were utilized, the middle seizure fine (2.1.29 n.) if an article of high value was utilized, and if an article of low value or forest produce was utilized, its restitution and an equal amount as a fine. [16]Taking articles belonging to the king and replacing them with other articles is substitution, [17]and it is explained under usufruct.* [18]When one does not hand over accrued income, pay the expenses authorized in writing, or acknowledge a secured balance, it is a misappropriation; [19]the fine for it is 12 times the amount.

[20]Their* methods of embezzlement are 40:*

[21]what was accrued earlier is set down later;*
what was accrued later is set down earlier;
what is to be carried out is not carried out;
what is not to be carried out is carried out;
what has been carried out is presented as not carried out;
what has not been carried out is presented as carried out;
what has been minimally carried out is presented as largely carried out;
what has been largely carried out is presented as minimally carried out;
one thing is carried out but is presented as something else;
what has been carried out using one source of income is presented as carried out using another source.
what should be given* is not given;
what should not be given is given;
not giving* at the proper time;
giving at an improper time;
a small amount given is presented as a large amount;
a large amount given is presented as a small amount;
one thing is given and is presented as something else;
what is given from one source is presented as given from another source;
what has been deposited is presented as not deposited;
what has not been deposited is presented as deposited;
forest produce whose price has not been paid is deposited;
forest produce whose price has been paid is not deposited;
consolidation is presented as dispersion,*
or dispersion as consolidation;
an article of great value is exchanged for one of small value,

or an article of small value for one of great value;
the price is raised,
or lowered;
a year is made discrepant to the months,
or a month is made discrepant to the days;*
discrepancy with regard to sources of income;
discrepancy with regard to categories (2.7.31);
discrepancy with regard to work officers (2.7.22 n.);
discrepancy with regard to performance;
discrepancy with regard to the sum total;
discrepancy with regard to quality;
discrepancy with regard to price;
discrepancy with regard to weight;*
discrepancy with regard to measuring;*
discrepancy with regard to containers (2.7.2, 33)—
these are the methods of embezzlement.

[22]In these cases, he should question individually the junior officer, the storekeeper, the record keeper, the receiver of deliveries, the disburser, the paymaster, the counselor, and the agent (2.5.18 n.). [23]And if they lie, they are subject to the same fine as the officer (2.9). [24]In his area of activity (2.7.3 n.), moreover, he should issue the proclamation: "Those who have been harmed by this official should inform me." [25]To anyone who so informs, he should pay compensation proportionate to the harm done to that person.

[26]If someone offers denials while facing several accusations and is convicted* of even one, he is liable for all. [27]If he admits to some and denies others, he should be questioned with regard to all. [28]In the case of a large theft of money, if he is proven guilty even with regard to a small portion of it, he is liable for all.

[29]When the accusation is proven, an informant,* to whom a guarantee against reprisal has been given, should receive one-sixth of the amount, one-twelfth if he happens to be an employee. [30]If only a small portion of a much larger accusation is proven, he should receive a share of the amount proven. [31]If his accusation is not proven, he should receive a corporal or monetary punishment and not be granted any favors.

> [32]When the accusation has been proven, however, if the informant, instigated by the accused, withdraws the case or makes himself unavailable, he should be executed.*

THAT CONCLUDES THE EIGHTH CHAPTER: "RECOVERY OF REVENUE EMBEZZLED BY OFFICIALS" OF THE SECOND BOOK: "ON THE ACTIVITIES OF SUPERINTENDENTS."

Chapter 9

Topic 27: Inspection of Officers*

[1]All superintendents, endowed with the exemplary qualities of a minister (1.9.1), should be employed in various tasks according to their abilities. [2]And he should have them constantly investigated with respect to their tasks, because men's minds are fickle. [3]For, given that their nature is like that of horses, men become corrupt when employed in tasks. [4]Therefore, he should keep himself informed of the worker, the bureau, the place, the time, the work to be carried out, the investment, and the profit, with respect to those tasks.

[5]They should carry out their tasks according to the instructions, without conspiring or quarreling with each other. [6]If they conspire, they will consume, and if they quarrel, they will destroy.* [7]They should not initiate any undertaking, moreover, without informing their master,* except for remedial measures against disasters.

[8]In cases of negligence on their part, furthermore, he should impose a penalty of twice the daily wages and expenses. [9]Anyone among them who carries out a task according to instructions or in even a superior way, on the other hand, should be awarded status and honors.

[10]"If someone producing a small income has large expenses, he consumes (2.9.6 n.). [11]In the reverse case and when his expenses are in keeping with his income, he does not consume," so state the teachers. [12]"That can be ascertained only through spies," says Kauṭilya.

[13]Someone who causes a loss of revenue consumes the king's assets. [14]If he causes the loss through ignorance and so forth,* he should be forced to pay the right multiple of the amount.* [15]Someone who raises twice the normal revenue consumes the countryside. [16]If he delivers it for the benefit of the king, he should be admonished to desist in the case of a small offense; in the case of a major offense, he should be punished proportionate to the offense.

[17]Someone who presents revenue as expenditure* consumes people's labors. [18]In the case of a theft pertaining to workdays, the price of articles, and the wages of men, he should be punished proportionate to the offense.

[19]Therefore, a person who has been appointed to a particular department by his decree* should report to him the true status of the task and the income and expenses related to it both in detail and in summary form.

[20]He should keep in check anyone who squanders his patrimony, a spendthrift, and a miser.* [21]A man who consumes in improper ways the property of his father and grandfather is a squanderer of patrimony. [22]A man who consumes whatever is produced is a spendthrift. [23]A man who accumulates wealth at the cost of causing deprivation to his dependents and himself is a miser. [24]If he has a retinue,* he should not be subjected to expropriation (2.1.9 n.); in the opposite case, all his property should be confiscated.*

[25]When a miser who has been put in charge of a large source of revenue hoards, deposits, or transmits—that is, hoards in his own house, deposits with people of the city or the countryside, or transmits to an enemy territory—a secret agent should find out his retinue of advisors, friends, dependents, and relatives, as well as the way goods are brought in and sent out. [26]And should one of his men travel about in an enemy territory, the agent should win that man's trust and find out the plan. [27]When that is fully discerned, he should get him* killed under the pretext of finding a decree from the enemy.*

[28]Therefore, his superintendents should carry out their tasks attended by accountants, scribes, examiners of coins, receivers of balances, and higher-ranking supervisors.* [29]Higher-ranking supervisors are those who ride on elephants, horses, and chariots. [30]Their apprentices, endowed with skill and integrity, act as spies on the accountants and others.

[31]He should have each department headed by several individuals with limited tenure.

> [32]Just as it is impossible not to taste honey or poison placed upon the tongue, so it is impossible for an officer in charge of money not to taste the king's money even though the amount is small.
> [33]Just as it is impossible to know when fish, moving about in water, are drinking water, so it is impossible to know when officers, appointed to carry out tasks, are embezzling money.
> [34]Even if it is possible to know the path of birds as they are flying in the air, it is never possible to know the path of officials as they move with concealed designs.
> [35]He should make those who have hoarded hand it over and shuffle them among different tasks, so that they do not consume his wealth or disgorge what they have consumed.

> [36]Those who do not consume his wealth and make it grow in the proper way, however, should be made permanent officeholders, for they are devoted to what is pleasing and beneficial to the king.

THAT CONCLUDES THE NINTH CHAPTER: "INSPECTION OF OFFICERS" OF THE SECOND BOOK: "ON THE ACTIVITIES OF SUPERINTENDENTS."

Chapter 10

Topic 28: Topic of Decrees*

[1]Decrees, they explain, are for decreeing; [2]for kings mostly rely on decrees, because on them are based both peace pacts and declarations of war.

[3]Therefore, a scribe should be a man who is endowed with the exemplary qualities of a minister (1.9.1), knows all the conventions, writes quickly,* has beautiful handwriting, and is able to read written documents. [4]He should listen with single-minded attention to the king's directive and then compose a document characterized by precision of meaning—in the case of the king, with the respectful mention of the country, sovereignty, genealogy, and name; in the case of someone other than the king, with the respectful mention of the country and name.

> [5]Having examined closely the caste, family, position, age, learning, profession, accomplishments, character, place, time, and marriage relationships with respect to the task, he should compose the document appropriate for the individual concerned.

[6]The sequence of points, consistency, completeness, charm, grandeur, and clarity—these are the exemplary qualities of a document. [7]Of these, the sequence of points consists of constructing a proper sequence and placing the main point at the beginning. [8]Consistency consists of stating a subsequent point without contradicting a previous point right up to the conclusion. [9]Completeness consists of the absence of deficiency or excess in points, words, and letters; explicating the points through the use of reasons, citations, and illustrations; and not using tiresome words.* [10]Charm consists of using words with lovely meanings that are easily communicated. [11]Grandeur consists of using words that are not vulgar. [12]Clarity consists of using well-known words.

[13]There are 63 sounds,* beginning with "a." [14]An aggregate of sounds is a word. [15]It is of four kinds: noun, verb, preposition, and particle. [16]Of these, a noun signifies being. [17]A verb form, having no specific gender, expresses action.* [18]Words, beginning with *pra,** when they qualify actions, are prepositions. [19]The indeclinables, beginning with *ca,** are particles. [20]A collection of words, when the meaning is completed, constitutes a sentence.*

[21]A cluster should be made with a minimum of one and a maximum of three words so as not to create an impediment to meaning of the other words.* [22]The word "*iti*"* has the function of concluding a letter, along with "This is the statement of so-and-so."

> [23–24]Insult, acclaim, query, report, petition, refusal, rebuke, prohibition, command, conciliation, assistance, threat, and appeasement: Points made in a document relate to these 13.

[25]Of these, insult consists of pointing out blemishes in someone's birth, body, or actions. [26]Pointing out distinctions in the same areas is acclaim. [27]"How did this happen?" is a query. [28]"Thus" is a report. [29]"Give" is a petition. [30]"I will not give" is a refusal. [31]"This befits you not" is a rebuke. [32]"Do not do this" is a prohibition. [33]"Do this" is a command. [34]"I am the same as you! Whatever wealth I have is yours!" Such soothing words constitute conciliation. [35]Assistance consists of providing help during times of adversity. [36]Threat consists of pointing to the future as full of hazards. [37]Appeasement is threefold: relating to getting something done, relating to a transgression, and relating to a calamity affecting a person and so forth.*

> [38]Documents conveying communications, commands, and gifts; documents conveying exemptions and authorizations; documents conveying news; documents containing replies; and documents applicable everywhere: These are the decrees.
> [39]"So-and-so has reported," "He said this," "If it is true, it should be given," "He has spoken of an excellent deed in the presence of the king"—these are the various kinds of communications laid down.*
> [40]The characteristic of a command document is that it contains a command of the master relating to chastisement and favors, especially with regard to his servants.

> [41]Where respect that is deserved and in accordance with one's merits is noticed, whether it is made during a time of misfortune or in connection with a gift—these are the two kinds of compliments.*
>
> [42]A favor conferred at the command of the king on a caste and on specific cities, and on various villages and regions, experts in these matters point out, is exemption.
>
> [43]The granting of authorization for carrying out tasks and for issuing orders constitutes a document relating to issuance of orders or one that contains authorization.*
>
> [44]With reference to decrees, they point out, there are two kinds of news: various kinds of news relating to acts of god and news relating to humans based on facts.
>
> [45]After perusing a document accurately and then reading it aloud, he should compose a reply exactly according to the words of the king.
>
> [46]Where the king tells the royals and the officers to provide protection and assistance to travelers, it is called a document applicable everywhere, and it should be made known along roads, in the region, and everywhere.

[47]The strategies are conciliation, gifts, dissension, and military force.*

[48]Among these, conciliation is of five kinds: praise of distinctions, reference to relationships, pointing out mutual benefits, revealing what is in store for the future, and placing oneself at the other's disposal. [49]Of these, the praise of distinctions is the mention, praise, and eulogy of his birth, physique, actions, character, learning, wealth, and the like. [50]Reference to relationships is the celebration of their connections through kinship, marriage, study, sacrifice, and lineage, of their affection to each other, and of their common allies.* [51]Pointing out mutual benefits is the celebration of the mutual benefits coming to one's own side and to the other's side. [52]Revealing what is in store for the future consists in generating expectations by saying, "When this is done in this way, we will both obtain this." [53]"I am the same as you! Whatever wealth I have is yours! Use it in your undertakings"—that is putting oneself at the other's disposal.

[54]Gifts consist of rendering assistance with money.

[55]Dissension consists of creating doubts and threatening.

[56]Military force consists of killing, tormenting, and plundering property.

[57]Inelegance, inconsistency, tautology, ungrammatical usage, and disorganization are the defects of a document. [58]Among these, inelegance consists of dark paper* and letters that are unattractive, uneven, and faded.* [59]Inconsistency is when what is stated later does not agree with what was stated earlier. [60]Tautology is when what has already been said is stated again without any differentiation. [61]Ungrammatical usage consists of the use of wrong gender, number, tense, and case. [62]Disorganization is overturning of linguistic excellence by using a cluster where there should be no cluster and not using a cluster where there should be a cluster (2.10.21 n.).

> [63]Having gone through all the treatises and observed actual usage, Kauṭilya has given the rules for composing a decree for the benefit of kings.

THAT CONCLUDES THE TENTH CHAPTER: "TOPIC OF ROYAL DECREES" OF THE SECOND BOOK: "ON THE ACTIVITIES OF SUPERINTENDENTS."

Chapter 11

Topic 29: Examination of Precious Stones To Be Received into the Treasury

[1]The Superintendent of the Treasury should accept articles to be received into the treasury—precious stones, articles of high and low value, or forest produce—guided by a bureau of experts in each commodity (2.5.8 n.).

PEARLS

[2]Pearls come from Tāmraparṇī, Pāṇḍyakavāṭa, Pāśikā, Kulā, Cūrṇī, Mahendra, Kardamā, Srotasī, Hrāda, and Himavat,* [3]and their sources are oysters, conchs, and other diverse creatures.

[4]The following are inferior: those that are shaped like Masūra-lentil, Tripuṭa-lentil,* or a tortoise; those that are semicircular or with a covering; two attached together; those that are cut, rough, spotted, shaped like a gourd, dark, blue, or improperly bored. [5]The following are superior: large, round, with no flat surface, full of luster, white, heavy, smooth, and bored at the proper place.

[6]Śīrṣaka, Upaśīrṣaka, Prakāṇḍaka, Avaghāṭaka, Taralapratibaddha*—these are the types of pearl strings. [7]An Indracchanda has 1,008 pearl strings; [8]a Vijayacchanda has half that number; [9]an Ardhahāra has 64; [10]a Raśmikalāpa has 54; [11]a Guccha has 32; [12]a Nakṣatramālā has 27; [13]an

Ardhaguccha has 24; [14]a Māṇavaka has 20; [15]and an Ardhamāṇavaka has half the latter number. [16]Each of these when it has a gem at the center becomes a Māṇavaka of its type.*

[17]A pure Hāra consists of a single Śīrṣaka. [18]Others follow the same pattern.* [19]An Ardhamāṇavaka has a gem at the center. [20]A Phalakahāra has three Phalakas or five Phalakas.*

[21]A pure Ekāvalī consists of one string. [22]The very same with a gem at the center is a Yaṣṭi; [23]when embellished with gold and gems, a Ratnāvalī; [24]when interspersed with gold, gems, and pearls, an Apavartaka; [25]and when stringed with a gold thread, a Sopānaka [26]or, with a gem in the center, a Maṇi-Sopānaka.

[27]The above discussion also explains the classifications of strings and meshes for the head, hands, feet, and waist.

GEMS

[28]Gems come from Koṭi,* Mālā,* and Pārasamudra.* [29]A ruby may have the color of a red lotus, of a saffron flower,* of a Pārijāta flower, or of the morning sun. [30]A beryl* may have the color of a blue lotus, a Śirīṣa flower,* water,* bamboo,* a parrot's wing, turmeric root,* cow's urine, or cow's fat. [31]A sapphire may have blue streaks, the color of a Kalāya flower, a deep blue color, the radiance of a rose apple, or the luster of a dark cloud, or be a "delighter" or a "flowing-middle."* [32]A clear crystal may have the color of a Mūlāṭī flower,* resemble a cool shower, or be a sunstone.* These are the gems.

[33]These are the qualities of gems: hexagonal, square, or round; with an intense color; with a suitable shape; clear; smooth; heavy; sparkling; gleaming inside; and radiating luster. [34]And these are their defects: dull in color or luster, grainy, pitted in the bloom, broken, improperly bored,* and covered with scratches.

[35]The following are the secondary classes: Vimalaka, Sasyaka, Añjanamūlaka, Pittaka, Sulabhaka, Lohitākṣa, Mṛgāśmaka, Jyotīrasaka, Māleyaka, Ahicchatraka, Kūrpa, Pratikūrpa, Sugandhikūrpa, Kṣīrapaka, Śukticūrṇaka, Śilāpravālaka, Pulaka, and Śukrapulaka.*

[36]The rest are crystalline gems.*

DIAMONDS

[37]Diamonds come from Sabhārāṣṭra, Tajjamārāṣṭra, Kāstīrarāṣṭra, Śrīkaṭana, Maṇimanta, and Indravāna,* [38]and their sources are pit mines, streams, and other diverse sources (see 2.11.3).

[39]These are the colors of diamonds: cat's eye, Śirīṣa flower (2.11.30 n.), cow's urine, cow's fat, clear crystal, Mūlāṭī flower (2.11.32 n.), and any color listed under the colors of gems.*

[40]One that is plump, heavy, resistant to impact, with symmetrical points, able to mark a vessel, spinning like a spindle, and sparkling bright is superior. [41]One with missing tips, without edges, and with a defective side is inferior.

CORAL

[42]Corals come from Alakanda* and Vivarṇa* and are red and lotus-colored;* they should not be eaten by insects or have a bulging center.

SANDALWOOD

[43]Sandalwood from Sātana is red and has an earthy smell; [44]that from Gośīrṣa is dark coppery in color and has a fishy smell; [45]sandal from Hari has the color of a parrot's wing and the smell of a mango; so also that from Tṛṇasā; [46]that from Grāmeru is red or reddish black and has the smell of goat's urine; [47]that from Devasabhā is red and has the smell of a lotus; so also that from Jāpa; [48]that from Joṅga is red or reddish black and is smooth; so also that from Turūpa; [49]that from Mālā is light red; [50]Kucandana is rough, black like aloe, red, or reddish black; [51]that from Kāla mountain is reddish black or saffron-colored (2.11.29 n.); [52]that from Kośāgāra mountain is black or dappled black; [53]that from Śītodakā has the luster of a lotus or is glossy black; [54]that from Nāga mountain is rough or has the color of moss; [55]and that from Śālaka is brown.*

[56]Light, smooth, not dried up, smearing with the unctuousness of ghee, pleasant smelling, penetrating the skin, unobtrusive, unfading, able to bear heat, absorbing heat, and pleasing to the touch—these are the qualities of sandalwood.

ALOE

[57]Aloe from Joṅga* is black, dappled black, or dappled with round spots; [58]that from Doṅga* is dark; [59]and that from Pārasamudra (2.11.28 n.) has a dappled appearance and smells like Uśīra or the Navamālikā flower.

[60]The qualities of aloe are heavy, smooth, pleasant smelling, diffusing fragrance, able to bear fire, not producing thick smoke, evenly fragrant, and able to sustain rubbing.

INCENSE

[61]Tailaparṇika* from Aśokagrāma has the color of flesh and the smell of a lotus; [62]that from Joṅga is reddish yellow in color and has the smell of a blue lotus or cow's urine; [63]that from Grāmeru is smooth and has the smell of cow's urine; [64]that from Suvarṇakuḍya is reddish yellow in color and has the smell of citron; [65]and that from Pūrṇakadvīpa has the smell of a lotus or fresh butter.

[66]Bhadraśriya from beyond Lauhityā has the color of a Jātī flower; [67]that from Antaravatī* has the color of Uśīra; [68]and both have the smell of Kuṣṭha.

[69]Kāleyaka grown in Svarṇabhūmi is smooth and yellow; [70]that from Uttaraparvata is reddish yellow.*

[71]Ability to sustain being turned into lumps, being boiled, and turned into smoke; not losing color; amenable to being combined;* [72]qualities similar to those of sandalwood and aloe—these are their qualities.

That concludes the articles of high value.*

SKINS*

[73]Kāntanāvaka and Praiyaka are skins from Uttaraparvata (2.11.61–70 n.). [74]Kāntanāvaka has the sheen of a peacock's neck; [75]Praiyaka is dappled with blue, yellow, and white stripes and spots; [76]and both are eight Aṅgulas in length.

[77]Bisī and Mahābisī are from Dvādaśagrāma. [78]Bisī is fuzzy-colored, shaggy,* or dappled; [79]Mahābisī is coarse and mostly white; [80]and both are 12 Aṅgulas in length.

[81]Śyāmikā, Kālikā, Kadalī, Candrottarā, and Śākulā are produced in Āroha. [82]Śyāmikā is brown or dappled with spots; [83]Kālikā is brown or has the color of a dove; [84]and both are eight Aṅgulas in length. [85]Kadalī is coarse and a Hasta in length; [86]Candrottarā is the same, but dappled with "moons";* [87]and Śākulā is one-third the size of Kadalī, and it is dappled with circular spots or with natural knots of the skin.

[88]Sāmūra, Cīnasī, and Sāmūlī are from Bāhlava.* [89]Sāmūra is 36 Aṅgulas in size and has the color of collyrium; [90]Cīnasī is reddish black or pale black; [91]and Sāmūlī is wheat-colored.

[92]Sātinā, Nalatūlā, and Vṛttapucchā are from Odra. [93]Sātinā is black; [94]Nalatūlā has the color of Nalatūla;* [95]and Vṛttapucchā is brown.

These are the varieties of skin.

[96]Among skins, those that are soft and smooth and have a lot of fur are the best.

CLOTH

[97]Woolen textiles may be undyed, completely dyed, or partially dyed;* and they may be knitted, dappled by weaving, patchwork, or with cut-off threads.* [98]Blanket, Kaucapaka, Kulamitikā, Saumitikā, horse's saddle cloth, colored blanket, Talicchaka, armor cloth, Paristoma, and Samantabhadraka*—these are the kinds of woolen textiles. [99]Those that are slick and looking wet, and those that are fine and soft are the best.

[100]Those from Nepal are the Bhiṅgisī, which are black and manufactured by combining eight woven strands, and the Apasāraka, which keep off the rain.*

[101]Those made from animal hair are Saṃpuṭikā, Caturaśrikā, Lambarā, Kaṭavānaka, Prāvaraka, and Sattalikā.*

[102]Dukūla* from the Vaṅgas is white and smooth; [103]that from the Puṇḍras is dark and smooth like a gem; [104]that from Suvarṇakuḍya has the color of the sun, is smooth like a gem with a watery weave, a square weave, and a mixed weave.* [105]Among these, there are textiles woven with one, one and a half, two, three, and four yarns.

[106]The above also explains linen from Kāśī and the Puṇḍras.

[107]"Leaf-wool" silk* comes from Magadha, Puṇḍra, and Suvarṇakuḍya. [108]Their sources are the Nāga-vṛkṣa, the Likuca, the Bakula, and the banyan. [109]Silk from the Nāga-vṛkṣa is yellow; [110]that from Likuca is wheat-colored; [111]that from Bakula is white; [112]and the last has the color of new butter. [113]Of these, the silk from Suvarṇakuḍya is the best.

[114]The above also explains Kauśeya silk and Cīna cloth coming from the land of Cīna.*

[115]Cotton textiles from Madhurā, the Aparāntas, the Kaliṅgas, Kāśī, the Vaṅgas, the Vatsas, and the Mahiṣas are the best.

> [116–117]With regard to precious stones other than these, he should be conversant with their sizes, prices, characteristics, varieties, and appearance, as also their proper storage, the manufacture of new ones, the repair of old ones, secret treatments, tools, their use at the proper place and time, and remedies against things that may cause them harm.

THAT CONCLUDES THE ELEVENTH CHAPTER: "EXAMINATION OF PRECIOUS STONES TO BE RECEIVED INTO THE TREASURY" OF THE SECOND BOOK: "ON THE ACTIVITIES OF SUPERINTENDENTS."

Chapter 12

Topic 30: Setting up Mines and Factories

[1]The Superintendent of Mines*—who is either proficient in geometry (2.24.1 n.), metallurgy, smelting, and coloring gems (1.18.8 n.), or assisted by one so proficient, and who is provided with workers skilled at such tasks along with suitable equipment—should inspect abandoned mines revealed by dross, crucibles, coal, and ashes, or new mines with ore-bearing earth, rocks, or liquids that have a strong color, exceptional weight, and acrid smell and taste.*

[2]Gold-bearing liquids* are those that flow in the interior of hollows, caves, valleys, rock cuts, or covert excavations on mountains in recognized regions;* liquids that have the color of rose apple, mango, Palmyra nut, slice of ripe turmeric, jaggery, orpiment, red arsenic, honey, vermilion, white lotus, or feathers of a parrot or peacock; that have water and plants of the same color in the vicinity; and that are viscous, limpid, and heavy. [3]If they spread like oil when thrown in water and soak up mud and dirt, they are capable of infusing copper and silver over a hundredfold.* [4]What is similar to them but with an acrid smell and taste should be identified as bitumen.

[5]Ores from earth and rocks that have a yellow, copper, or coppery-yellow color; that contain blue streaks or have the color of Mudga-bean, Māṣa-bean, or Kṛsara porridge when they are split; that are speckled as if with drops or globs of curd; that have the color of turmeric, myrobalan, a lotus leaf, moss, liver, spleen, or saffron (2.11.29 n.); that contain lines, dots, or svastikas of fine sand when they are split; that have nodules and are lustrous; and that do not split but do produce a lot of foam and smoke when they are heated—they are the ones that are gold ores. When used as an admixture,* they are capable of infusing copper and silver.

[6]Those that have the color of conch, camphor, crystal, fresh butter, a dove, a pigeon, a Vimalaka* gem, or a peacock's neck; or the color of Sasyaka* gem, Gomedaka* gem, jaggery, or raw sugar; or the color of the flowers of Kovidāra, lotus, Pāṭalī, Kalāya, flax, or linseed; those that contain lead or antimony; that smell like raw flesh; that are black with a white sheen, white with a black sheen, or all speckled with lines or dots; that are soft and, when smelted, do not split but produce a lot of foam and smoke—they are the ones that are silver ores.

[7]In the case of all ores, as their weight increases so does their metal content.

[8]Those among them that are impure or with a murky interior will flow in a pure form when they are infused with caustic urine or alkali; or made into lumps using Rājavṛkṣa, banyan, Pīlu, cow's bile or yellow bile, or the urine and dung of a buffalo, donkey, or camel; or when they are combined with an admixture or a paste of the same substances.

[9]The admixture of the bulbous roots of banana and Vajra, along with alkali from barley, Māṣa-bean, sesame, Palāśa, and Pīlu, or with the milk of cows or goats, makes them* soft.

> [10]Even if broken into a hundred thousand pieces, it becomes soft when it is bathed just three times with goat milk mixed with honey, liquorice, sesame oil, ghee, jaggery, and ferment,* along with the Kandalī* plant.

[11]The admixture of cow's teeth and horns arrests the process of softening.*

[12]When ore from rocks or an area of earth is heavy, oily, and soft*—it is copper ore if it is yellow, green, pale red, or blood red; [13]it is lead ore if it is black like a crow, or has the color of a pigeon or yellow bile, or is studded with white lines, and smells like raw flesh; [14]it is tin ore if it is variegated like saline soil or has the color of baked clay; [15]it is iron ore if it is orange,* pale red, or the color of Sinduvāra flower; [16]it is Vaikṛntaka* ore if it is colored like a Kākāṇḍa* or a birch leaf; [17]it is gem* ore if it is clear, smooth, gleaming, sonorous, cool, and with a very intense color.*

[18]He should use the extracts from ores in their respective factories. [19]He should fix a single location for trade in manufactured goods and a penalty* for those who manufacture, sell, or buy them elsewhere.

[20]When a mine worker steals, he should be forced to pay eight times the value, except in the case of gems.* [21]He should employ a thief or someone who lives by mining without permission (2.12.32) in bonded labor, as also anyone who wants to pay off a fine through manual labor.*

[22]When a mine is too onerous because of the expenses or effort required, he should lease it for a share of the proceeds or lease it out for a fixed rent; he should operate by himself one that is easy to manage.

[23]The Superintendent of Metals should establish factories for copper, lead, tin, Vaikṛntaka metal (2.12.16 n.), brass,* steel, bronze, bell metal, and iron, as well as the trade in metal goods.

[24]The Superintendent of the Mint should get silver coins minted containing 25 percent copper along with one Māṣa of one of the following

hardening alloys: iron, tin, lead, and antimony, issuing them in the denominations of one Paṇa, half-Paṇa, quarter-Paṇa, and eighth-Paṇa; as also copper coins containing 25 percent of a strengthening alloy,* issuing them in the denominations of one Māṣaka, half-Māṣaka, one Kākaṇī, and half-Kākaṇī.

[25]The Examiner of Coins should institute the Paṇa currency for purposes of trade and receipt into the treasury, [26]as well as a coinage fee of 8 percent, a surcharge* of 5 percent, an inspection fee* of one-eighth percent, and a penalty (2.6.10 n.) of 25 Paṇas for those who manufacture, buy, or inspect elsewhere.

[27]The Superintendent of Pit Mines (2.12.1 n.) should establish factories for conch shells, diamonds, gems, pearls, corals, and alkali,* as well as the trade in them.

[28]The Superintendent of Salt should collect at appropriate times both the share of salt produced by crystallization and the fixed rent on the lease, as well as the original value, the inspection fee, and the surcharge (2.6.10 n.) from the sale. [29]On imported salt, one should give one-sixth share. [30]Its sale shall take place after the share and levies* have been paid, as well as the 5-percent surcharge, the inspection fee, and the manufacturing fee (2.6.10 n.). [31]The buyer* should pay the duty and a compensatory tax corresponding to the loss accruing to state merchandise. If the buyer purchases at another place, he should also pay a penalty of 600 Paṇas. [32]He should impose the highest fine (2.1.29 n.) on anyone selling adulterated salt, as well as on anyone who makes a living from salt without permission, except forest hermits. [33]Vedic scholars, recluses, and laborers may take salt for use in their food, [34]while all others should pay a duty for any kind of salt and sugar.

> [35–36]In this manner, he should collect from pit mines the original value, the share, the surcharge, the monopoly tax, the penalty, the duty, the compensatory tax, the fine, the inspection fee, and the manufacturing fee (2.6.10 n.), as well as the 12 kinds* of ore and merchandise. In this manner, he should establish the collection under various classes for all kinds of merchandise.
>
> [37]The treasury originates from mines, and the army is born from the treasury; the earth adorned by the treasury is obtained through the treasury and the army.

THAT CONCLUDES THE TWELFTH CHAPTER: "SETTING UP MINES AND FACTORIES" OF THE SECOND BOOK: "ON THE ACTIVITIES OF SUPERINTENDENTS."

Chapter 13

Topic 31: Superintendent of Gold in the Workshop

[1]The Superintendent of Gold should construct a workshop with a single door, a workshop that contains four halls* that are not interconnected for working gold and silver.

[2]In the middle of the market street, he should install the Chief Goldsmith,* who should be an expert craftsman, of noble birth, and trustworthy.

[3]The varieties of gold are as follows: from the Jambū river, from Śatakumbha, from Hāṭaka, from Veṇu, from Śṛṅgaśukti, naturally occurring gold, extracted from liquid ores (2.12.3 n.), and produced in mines. [4]The best kind has the color of lotus filament and is soft, smooth, not sonorous, and radiant; the middling has a reddish yellow color; and the lowest kind is red.

[5]Among the best,* what is pale and white is not fully refined.* [6]He should purify it by using lead, four times the amount still needing refining.* [7]If it becomes brittle with the admixture of lead, he should smelt it with dried cow dung; [8]if it becomes brittle because of its own roughness, he should have it moistened in a mixture of sesame oil and cow dung. [9]If gold produced in a mine becomes brittle with the admixture of lead, he should make leaves by heating and get them pounded on wooden anvils; alternatively, he may have it moistened in a paste made with the bulbous roots of the plantain and Vajra.

[10]The varieties of silver are as follows: produced in Tuttha, from Gauḍa, from Kambu, and from Cakravāla. [11]The best kind is white, smooth, and soft. [12]One that has the opposite characteristics and tends to burst is of poor quality; [13]he should purify it by using one-quarter portion of lead. [14]When a crest appears at the top, and when it is clear and radiant and has the color of curd, it is pure.

[15]One Suvarṇa (2.19.3) of pure gold with the color of turmeric is the standard. [16]Beyond that, by the sequential substitution of one Kākaṇī of copper for an equal amount of the gold up to an upper limit of four (Māṣas) of copper, one obtains 16 standards.*

[17]After first rubbing a piece of gold on the touchstone, he should afterward rub the standard. [18]When it produces a streak of the same color on an area of the touchstone that has no pits or humps, it is properly tested. When it is rubbed too hard or too soft, or dusted with red chalk underneath the fingernails, he should recognize it as deception. [19]When gold is

touched with the tip of the hand smeared with Jāti-vermilion or with iron sulfate infused with cow's urine, it turns white. [20]The coloration on the touchstone that contains filaments and is soft and radiant is the best.

[21]Touchstones from Kaliṅga or Tāpī-stones* that have the hue of Mudga-beans are the best. [22]Ones that produce an even coloration are favorable for both selling and buying. [23]Ones that have the pigmentation of an elephant with a green tinge and produce a heightened coloration favor the seller, [24]while those that are hard, rough, and of uneven color, and do not produce a heightened coloration favor the buyer.

[25]When a slice is slick, of uniform color, smooth, soft, and radiant, that is the best gold. [26]When the glow from heat is even inside and out and has the color of a lotus filament or a Kuraṇḍaka flower, that is the best gold; [27]while a dark or blue color shows that it is not fully refined (2.13.5 n.).

[28]We shall discuss balances and weights in the section on the Superintendent of Standardization (2.19); [29]and in accordance with those instructions, he* should give and receive gold and silver.

[30]No unauthorized person shall approach the workshop, [31]and anyone advancing should be eliminated. [33]Even an authorized person, if he is carrying gold or silver, shall forfeit the same.

[33]Artisans engaged in settings, beadmaking, gilding, and ornamental work,* as well as blowers, bearers, and dust washers, should enter and exit only after their clothes, hands, and private parts have been inspected. [34]All their instruments, moreover, and unfinished projects should remain right there.

[35]He should assign the gold received and the project in the middle of the bureau. [36]In the evening and morning, he should deposit it stamped with the seals of the artisan and his supervisor.*

[37]The kinds of work are setting, stringing, and minor jobs. [38]Setting consists of activities such as laying down the mounting;* [39]and stringing, of activities such as braiding the threads. [40]Minor jobs consist of making solid objects, hollow articles, beads, and the like.

[41]In laying down the mounting, one-fifth is used for the base and one-tenth for the side fastening.* [42]Silver alloyed with one-quarter copper, or gold alloyed with one-quarter silver is factitious; he should guard against this.*

[43]In the work of beadmaking,* he should use three parts* for the encircling border and two parts* for the seat, or four parts* for the seat and three parts* for the encircling border.

[44]In the work of gilding, he should plate a copper article with gold of equal weight. [45]A silver article, whether solid or hollow, he should overlay

with gold half its weight, [46]or cover with gold one-quarter its weight by using sand vermilion in liquid or powder form (see 2.14.17 n.).*

[47]The best ornamental gold* with a fine color that has gone through (a crucible) with an equal amount of lead and that has been turned into leaves by heating and burnished with Sindhu-earth,* becomes the base for blue, yellow, white, green, and parrot-feather colors. [48]A Kākaṇī of iron* is used to add color to one Suvarṇa of gold, iron that has the color of a peacock's neck, that is white when cut, that is sparkling, and that has been made into a powder after heating.

[49]Alternatively, silver that has been well purified*—four times in a crucible with bones, four times in a crucible with an equal amount of lead, four times in a dry crucible, three times in a potsherd, and twice in one with cow dung, thus going through 17 crucibles, and finally burnished with Sindhu-earth. [50]From this, one Kākaṇī at a time up to two Māṣas should be added to one Suvarṇa,* followed by the blending of the coloring material,* which results in white silver.

[51]When three parts of ornamental gold are hardened with 32 parts of white silver, it becomes white red.* [52]This process* gives a yellow color to copper. [53]After burnishing the ornamental gold, he should add one-third part of the coloring;* it becomes yellowish red. [54]Two parts of white silver and one part of ornamental gold produce the color of Mudga-bean; [55]and when smeared with half a part* of black iron, it becomes black. [56]Ornamental gold smeared with covering liquid* takes on the color of a parrot's feather. [57]At the start of this work, he* should obtain the particular touchstone* for those specific colors.

[58]He should, furthermore, understand the processing of iron and copper, [59]and, therefore, the amount subject to depletion incurred in the manufacture of ornaments with diamonds, gems, pearls, and corals, as also the quantity of silver and gold required to manufacture various articles.

> [60–61]Having a uniform color, symmetrical, with beads not sticking to each other, strong, polished well, without alloys,* proportionately segmented, pleasant to wear, decorous, gleaming, with a charming shape, even, and pleasing to the mind and the eye— these are given as the superior attributes of a gold ornament.

THAT CONCLUDES THE THIRTEENTH CHAPTER: "SUPERINTENDENT OF GOLD IN THE WORKSHOP" OF THE SECOND BOOK: "ON THE ACTIVITIES OF SUPERINTENDENTS."

Chapter 14

Topic 32: Operations of the Chief Goldsmith in the Market Street

[1]The Chief Goldsmith should arrange for gold and silver work of people of the city and the countryside to be carried out by workshop owners.*

[2]They should perform any task, moreover, only after stipulating the time it would take and the kind of work involved; the kind of work may be an excuse for leaving the time unstipulated. [3]If the work is done in a different way, the result is the loss of wages and a fine of twice that amount.* [4]If the stipulated time is exceeded, the result is the loss of one-quarter of the wages and a fine of twice that amount.*

[5]In terms of both quality* and quantity, they should return the deposit* in exactly the same condition as they received it. [6]Even after a lapse of time, they* should get it back in exactly the same condition, except for depletion and wear.

[7]He* should be knowledgeable about every detail with respect to the characteristics and the manufacturing processes of gold and gold articles undertaken by workshop owners. [8]In the case of ornamental gold and silver,* depletion of one Kākaṇī per Suvarṇa* should be allowed. [9]One Kākaṇī of iron—twice that in the case of silver*—is inserted to produce color; one-sixth of that is allowed as the depletion.

[10]When there is a reduction in quality amounting to at least one Māṣa in weight,* the punishment is the lowest seizure fine (2.1.29 n.); when there is a reduction in quantity,* the middle fine; and when there is fraud with respect to balances and weights, the highest fine, as also in the case of fraud with respect to a manufactured article.* [11]Anyone getting work done unseen by the Chief Goldsmith or in some other location is fined 12 Paṇas, [12]and one who does that work twice that amount, if there is a valid excuse. [13]If there is no excuse, the former should be brought before the agency for the Eradication of Thorns,* [14]while the man doing the work should be fined 200 Paṇas or his five fingers* should be cut off.

[15]They* should buy balances and weights directly from the Superintendent of Standardization (2.19); [16]otherwise they are fined 12 Paṇas.

[17]Manufacture of solid and hollow objects, plating, overlaying, fastening, and gilding* are the varieties of an artisan's work.

[18]Irregular balance, removal, substitution, sheath, and embedding are the means of pilfering.

[19]The kinds of fraudulent balances are one that bends, one that is perforated, one with a cleft top, one with a secondary neck, one with defective strings, one with faulty scales, one with an excessive swing, and one that is magnetic.*

[20]Two parts of silver and one part of copper is Tripuṭaka. [21]By means of that gold originating from mines is removed;* that is "removal by Tripuṭaka"; [22]when it is done with copper, it is "removal by copper"; when it is done with Vellaka,* it is "removal by Vellaka"; and when it is done with gold containing one-half copper, it is "removal by gold." [23]Fake crucible, stinking dross, "crane's beak," pipette, tongs, water vessel, borax, and that same gold;* these are the means of removal. [24]Alternatively, sand lumps placed there beforehand are taken out of the fireplace in which the crucible has broken.*

[25]Substitution consists of replacing with a silver piece either at the time of the subsequent fastening or at the inspection of gilding leaves, or of sand lumps with sand iron lumps.*

[26]A sheath is either fixed or removable, and it is made when there is a need to plate, overlay, or fasten. [27]A fixed sheath is a lead article overlaid with gold leaf with its interior secured with lac. [28]The very same, when there are layered envelopes, is a removable sheath. [39]Either a compact leaf or a twin leaf is made for those requiring overlaying. [30]The interior of the leaves is made of copper or silver for those requiring fastening. [31]A copper article fastened with gold leaf and polished is "fine-sided." The very same fastened with a twin leaf and polished, as also an article made of a copper-silver alloy, is "outside-quality."* [32]He should detect both these* through the use of heat and the touchstone, or by its not having the proper sound and by scratching. [33]They place the removable sheath in acidic juice of the Badara fruit or in saltwater. That is the sheath.

[34]Within a solid or hollow article, earth mixed with gold or a paste of sand vermilion* when heated becomes deposited.* [35]Or, in an article with a firm base, lac mixed with sand or a paste of red lead when heated becomes deposited. [36]The genuineness of both these is tested by heating or dismantling.* [37]Or, within an article encircled with a metal band, salt, when heated with a firebrand along with caustic gravel,* becomes deposited. [38]Its genuineness is tested by boiling. [39]Or, in an article with a double base, a layer of mica is attached by means of lac. [40]In its case, where the fraud* has been covered up, when it is dipped in water one side sinks; alternatively, it is pierced* with a needle in between the layers. [41]Gems,

silver, or gold constitute the embedding in the case of solid and hollow articles.* [42]Its genuineness is tested by heating or dismantling (2.14.36 n.). That is embedding.

[43]Therefore, he* should acquire a thorough knowledge of the varieties, appearance, quality, quantity, items, and characteristics of articles made with diamonds, gems, pearls, and corals.

[44]In the course of inspecting manufactured articles or of repairing old articles, there are four ways of pilfering: snipping, cutting off, scratching, and rubbing. [45]When they cut out a bead, a string, or a casing under the pretext of detecting a sheath, it is "snipping." [46]Or when they insert a piece of lead into an article with a double base and then cut off a piece from the interior, that is "cutting off."* [47]When they scratch a solid article with a sharp instrument, that is "scratching." [48]When they coat a piece of cloth with the powder of any of these: yellow orpiment, red arsenic, or vermilion, or with the powder of black salt and then rub that cloth on the article, that is "rubbing." [49]By these means, gold and silver articles undergo loss of weight and yet there is no obvious damage done to them.

[50]In the case of plated articles that are broken, cut, or abraded, he should make an inference* by comparing them with similar ones. [51]In the case of overlaid articles, he should make an inference by cutting off as much of it as has been cut off. [52]In the case of articles that have an altered appearance, he should heat them and rub them with water repeatedly.

[53]He should know the following as kinds of fraudulent acts: tossing, weights, fire, wooden anvil, toolbox, receptacle, feather, string, garment, conversation, head, lap, fly, looking at his own body, bellow skin, water pan, and brazier.*

[54]He should know that in the case of silver articles, one that smells like raw flesh or attracts dirt, or is rough, overly hard, or discolored is spurious.

> [55]In this manner, he should inspect both new and old articles, as well as those that have an altered appearance, and impose penalties on them as prescribed.

THAT CONCLUDES THE FOURTEENTH CHAPTER: "OPERATIONS OF THE CHIEF GOLDSMITH IN THE MARKET STREET" OF THE SECOND BOOK: "ON THE ACTIVITIES OF SUPERINTENDENTS."

Chapter 15

Topic 33: Superintendent of the Storehouse

SOURCES OF RECEIPTS

[1]The Superintendent of the Storehouse should acquire a thorough knowledge of agricultural produce, revenue from the provinces, purchase,* barter, requisition, borrowing, labor in lieu of taxes, income from miscellaneous sources, return of expenditure, and supplementary income.

[2]The various kinds of crops brought in by the Superintendent of Agriculture are "agricultural produce" (2.24.1 n.). [3]Subsistence tax,* sixth share,* provisions for the army, tribute, tax, donation, side income, compensation for loss, gratuity,* and income from stores are "revenue from the provinces." [4]Price of grain, disbursements by the treasury, and recovery of outlays are "purchase." [5]When various kinds of crops are exchanged at different prices, it is "barter." [6]Demanding* crops from another person is requisition. [7]The same with the intention of returning it is borrowing. [8]The work of pounding, grinding, crushing, fermenting, and milling* in the case of those who live by these occupations; pressing oil in the case of those who press oil using hand presses or wheel presses; and extracting molasses from sugarcane constitute "labor in lieu of taxes." [9]The lost, the forgotten, and the like constitute "income from miscellaneous sources" (see 2.6.20). [10]Balances from demobilization and from discontinuation of projects interrupted by an illness are return of expenditure (see 2.6.21). [11]Discrepancy in weights and measures,* filling the hand,* the heap,* the surcharge (2.6.10 n.), arrears (2.6.19), and earned income* constitute "supplementary income."

VARIETIES OF PRODUCE

[12]With regard to grains, fats, sweets, and salts—the rules relating to grains we will discuss in the section on the Superintendent of Agriculture (2.24); [13]butter, oil,* lard, and marrow are fats; [14]treacle, jaggery, raw sugar (2.12.6), candied sugar, and sugar constitute the category of sweets; [15]Indus salt, sea salt, Biḍa salt,* saltpeter, borax, and surface salt* constitute the category of salts.

[16]Bee's honey and grape juice are honey. [17]One of the following—sugarcane juice, jaggery, honey, treacle, rose-apple juice, and jack-fruit juice—blended with a decoction of Meṣaśṛṅgī plant and long pepper and kept for one month, six months, or a year, and then either mixed

with Cirbhiṭa* fruit, Urvāruka fruit, sugarcane stalk, mango fruit, and myrobalan or remaining unmixed constitute the category of fermented juices. [18]Tamarind, Karamarda, mango, pomegranate, myrobalan, citron, Kola, jujube, Sauvīraka, Parūṣaka, and the like constitute the category of sour-fruit juices. [19]Curd, sour gruel, and the like constitute the category of sour liquids.

[20]Long pepper, black pepper, ginger, cumin, Indian Gentian, white mustard, coriander, Coraka, Damanaka, marjoram, stalk of the drumstick tree, and the like constitute the category of spices.

[21]Dried fish and meat, bulbous roots,* roots, fruits, vegetables, and the like constitute the category of vegetables.

[22]Of these, he should keep in reserve one-half earmarked for inhabitants of the countryside during a time of adversity and make use of the other half. [23]Further, he should refresh the old with new stock (see 2.4.28).

LOSS AND GAIN IN PROCESSING

[24]He should personally inspect the amount of gain or loss that different kinds of grain undergo when they are pounded, ground, milled, and fried, or when they are soaked, dried, or cooked. [25]In the case of Kodrava-grain and Vrīhi-rice, one-half consists of the kernel; in the case of Śāli-rice, one-half less than the latter; and in the case of Varaka-grain, one-third less.* [26]In the case of panic grain, the kernel consists of one-half, and there is an increase of one-ninth.* [27]Udāraka remains the same; and so do barley and wheat when pounded, and sesame, barley, Mudga-beans, and Māṣa-beans when ground. [28]Wheat increases by one-fifth, as also ground barley. [29]Flour of Kalāya-pea decreases by one-quarter, [30]and that of Mudga-beans and Māṣa-beans decreases by one-eighth. [31]In the case of legumes, one-half consists of the kernel, one-third less than that in the case of Masūra-lentil. [32]Raw flour and Kulmāṣa-grain* increase one and a half times, [33]while barley meal doubles, as do porridge* and cooked flour. [34]When cooked, Kodrava-grain, Varaka-grain, Udāraka-grain, and panic grain increase threefold; Vrīhi-rice increases fourfold; and Śāli-rice increases fivefold. [35]Inferior grains* when soaked double; one-half more than that when sprouted. [36]Fried grain increases by one-fifth, [37]while Kalāya-pea doubles, as also roasted rice and barley.

[38]From flax seed, one-sixth is extracted as oil; [39]and from neem, Kuśāmra,* wood apple, and the like, one-fifth. [40]Oil extracts from sesame, safflower, Madhūka, and Iṅgudī amount to one-quarter.

[41]In the case of cotton and flax, five Palas yield one Pala of yarn.

RATIONS

42From five Droṇas of unhusked Śālī-rice, 12 Āḍhakas of rice kernel serve as feed for young elephants; 11 for vicious elephants; ten for riding elephants; nine for war elephants; eight for foot soldiers; seven for officers; six for queens and for princes; and four for kings.*

43A Prastha of unbroken and fully cleaned rice kernels,* one-quarter that amount of stew, one-sixteenth of the amount of stew in salt, and one-quarter in butter or oil constitute a single daily ration* for an Ārya male; 44one-sixth of stew and half the above quantity of fat for lower-class males; 45one-quarter less for women; 46and one-half for children.

47For 20 Palas of meat, one uses half a Kuḍuba of fat, one Pala of salt, one Pala of sugar, two Dharaṇikas of spices, and half a Prastha of curd. 48This also explains higher quantities.* 49For vegetables, one uses one and a half times as much, and for dried foods, twice as much. The ingredients are the same.

50With regard to elephants and horses, we will discuss the quantity of rations in the section on the respective superintendents (2.30–31). 51For oxen, a Droṇa of Māṣa-beans or barley porridge (2.15.33 n.); the rest is the same as in the diet of horses, 52except for the special provision that oxen are given a Tulā of oilcake from the press or ten Āḍhakas of a grain-bran mixture. 53Twice as much is the ration for buffaloes and camels; 54half a Droṇa for donkeys, spotted deer, and red deer; 55one Āḍhaka for Eṇa deer and Kuraṅga deer; 56half an Āḍhaka for goats, rams, and boars—or twice that much of a grain-bran mixture; 57a Prastha of boiled rice for dogs; 58and half a Prastha for ruddy geese, Krauñca-cranes, and peacocks. 59For other deer, game animals, birds, and vicious animals other than these, he should make an estimate from what they eat during one day.

60He should have coal and chaff taken to metal factories and to sites where walls need to be plastered.* 61He should hand out low-quality grain to slaves, workers, and cooks, and what is left over* to those who deal in cooked rice and flat bread.

62The implements are the following: equipment for weighing and measuring, grinding stones, mortars and pestles, machines for pounding and grinding, scatterers, winnowing baskets, strainers, cane baskets, boxes, and brooms. 63Labor consists of the following: sweepers, watchmen, weighers, measurers, supervisors of measuring, distributors, supervisors of distribution, bookkeepers,* and the group of slaves and workers.

[64]Grain is stored in a high location; tightly woven baskets for sugar; clay and wooden vats for fats; and the floor for salt.*

THAT CONCLUDES THE FIFTEENTH CHAPTER: "SUPERINTENDENT OF THE STOREHOUSE" OF THE SECOND BOOK: "ON THE ACTIVITIES OF SUPERINTENDENTS."

Chapter 16

Topic 34: Superintendent of Commodities

[1]The Superintendent of Commodities should be knowledgeable about the price differentials of high-value and low-value items, as also the popularity and unpopularity, of the different kinds of commodities; whether they have been produced on land or in water; and whether they have been transported by land or by water; as well as about the appropriate times for employing dispersal and consolidation,* and purchase and sale.

[2]He should collect in one place a commodity that is plentiful and then raise its price; [3]and once that price has been established, he should set another price.*

[4]He should assign to one location the transaction in commodities with a royal monopoly that are produced in his own land, but to multiple locations commodities from other lands. [5] He should have both kinds of commodities sold as a favor to his subjects;* [6]and he should forgo even a large profit if it will cause hardship to his subjects. [7]He should not create either a time restriction or the evil of crowds* with respect to essential commodities.

[8]Alternatively, traders may sell commodities with a royal monopoly in multiple locations at fixed prices, [9]and they should pay compensatory tax proportionate to the losses.*

[10]On commodities sold by measure, the surcharge (2.6.10 n.) is one-sixteenth; on commodities sold by weight, one-twentieth; and on commodities sold by the number of pieces, one-eleventh.

[11]He should facilitate the import of commodities from other lands by granting favors. [12]To boat and caravan operators, moreover, he should grant exemptions that would allow them to make a profit, [13]as well as immunity from lawsuits to foreign traders with respect to financial matters, except for those who are members or associates of local corporate bodies.*

[14]Overseers of commodities should deposit the sale price of commodities in one location in a wooden chest covered by a lid with single opening.

[15]They should hand that over to the Superintendent of Commodities during the eighth part of the day, saying, "This much was sold, and this much remains." [16]They should also hand over to him the equipment for weighing and measuring.

[17]So far we have explained trade within one's own territory.

[18]With regard to other territories, however, he should estimate the value and the sale price of the commodities exported and the commodities imported in return, and calculate the net profit after subtracting expenses for duties, road toll, escort charges, payments at security stations and ferries,* rations,* and shares.* [19]If there is no profit, he should calculate whether there is any gain* to be had in exporting goods or in importing commodities in return for exports. [20]Thereafter, with one-quarter consisting of valuable goods,* he should engage in trade by land, taking a safe road. [21]And he should keep in close touch with tribal chiefs, Frontier Commanders, and city and provincial chiefs in order to secure their goodwill. [22]In a time of adversity, he should save the valuable goods for himself. [23]Or, when he has reached his own country,* he should conclude the transaction after clearing all the dues.

[24]Alternatively, when taking a water route, he should acquire a thorough knowledge of the charges for the boats, provisions for the journey, the value and quantity of his own commodities and the commodities received in exchange, the suitable times for the voyage, safeguards against dangers, and the regulations at ports (see 2.28.7).

> [25]On a river route also he should find out the conditions of trade
> from the regulations (at ports) and go to the location from which
> a profit can be made and avoid any loss.

THAT CONCLUDES THE SIXTEENTH CHAPTER: "SUPERINTENDENT OF COMMODITIES" OF THE SECOND BOOK: "ON THE ACTIVITIES OF SUPERINTENDENTS."

Chapter 17

Topic 35: Superintendent of Forest Produce

[1]The Superintendent of Forest Produce should have the guards of the produce forests bring in the forest produce. [2]He should also establish factories

for produce forests, [3]and fix charges and penalties for those cutting down produce forests, except during times of adversity.

[4]The category of forest produce consists of the following:

Teak, Tiniśa, Dhanvana, Arjuna, Madhūka, Tilaka, sal, sissoo, acacia, mimusops, siris, cutch, chir pine, Palmyra palm, Indian copal, flowering murdah, white cutch, Kuśāmra (2.15.39 n.), Priyaka, Dhava, and the like constitute the category of hard woods.

[5]Uṭaja, Cimiya, Cāpa, Veṇu, Vaṃśa, Sātina, Kaṇṭaka, Bhāllūka, and the like constitute the category of reeds.

[6]Vetra, Śīkavallī, Vāśī, Śyāmalatā, Nāgalatā, and the like constitute the category of vines.

[7]Mālatī, Mūrvā, Arka, Śaṇa, Gavedhukā, Atasī, and the like constitute the category of fibrous plants.

[8]Muñja, Balbaja, and the like provide material for ropes.

[9]Leaves* come from Tālī palm, Palmyra palm, and birch.

[10]Flowers come from flame of the forest, safflower, and crocus.*

[11]Bulbous roots, roots, fruits and the like constitute the category of medicinal products.

[12]Poisons such as Kālakūṭa, Vatsanābha, Hālāhala, Meṣaśṛṅga, Mustā, Kuṣṭha, Mahāviṣa, Vellitaka, Gaurārdra, Bālaka, Mārkaṭa, Haimavata, Kāliṅgaka, Dāradaka, Aṅkolasāraka, and Uṣṭraka; snakes and insects; and these same kept in pots—these constitute the category of poisons.

[13]Skin, bones, bile, tendons, eyes, teeth, horns, hooves, and tails are those of monitor lizards, Serakas, leopards, bears, river dolphins,* lions, tigers, elephants, buffaloes, yaks, deer, rhinoceros, wild cattle, and gayals, or of other deer, game animals, birds, and vicious animals.

[14]Metals are iron, copper, steel, bronze, lead, tin, Vaikṛntaka (2.12.16 n.), and brass (2.12.23 n.).

[15]Vessels are made of cane or clay.

[16]Charcoal, husks, and ashes; enclosures for deer, game animals, birds, and vicious animals; and enclosures for firewood and grass.*

> [17]He who lives on forest produce* should construct separate factories, both within and without,* for producing all kinds of wares for securing the livelihood and the protection of the city.

THAT CONCLUDES THE SEVENTEENTH CHAPTER: "SUPERINTENDENT OF FOREST PRODUCE" OF THE SECOND BOOK: "ON THE ACTIVITIES OF SUPERINTENDENTS."

Chapter 18

Topic 36: Superintendent of the Armory

[1]The Superintendent of the Armory should employ artisans and craftsmen with expertise in these to manufacture mechanical devices for use in battle, for the defense of forts, and for assaulting enemy citadels, as well as weapons, armor, and equipment, after he has come to an agreement with them as to the amount of work, the time for completion, the wages, and the final product.* Further, he should store them in places appropriate for each.

[2]He should, moreover, move them around and expose them to sun and wind frequently, [3]and store differently those that may be damaged by heat, moisture, or insects. [4]He should also acquire a thorough knowledge of them according to their class, appearance, characteristics, size, origin, value, and place of storage.

[5]The stationary mechanical devices are Sarvatobhadra, Jāmadagnya, Bahumukha, Viśvāsaghātin, Saṃghāṭī, Yānaka, Parjanyaka, Bāhu, Ūrdhvabāhu, and Ardhabāhu.* [6]The mobile mechanical devices are Pāñcālika, Devadaṇḍa, Sūkarikā, Musalayaṣṭi, Hastivāraka, Tālavṛnta, hammer, mace, Spṛktalā, spade, Āsphāṭima, Utpāṭima, Udghāṭima, Śataghni, trident, and discus.* [7]Weapons with sharp ends, moreover, are: Śakti, Prāsa, Kunta, Hāṭaka, Bhiṇḍipāla, Śūla, Tomara, Varāhakarṇa, Kaṇaya, Karpaṇa, Trāsikā, and the like.

[8]Kārmuka, Kodaṇḍa, and Drūṇa* are the bows, and they are made of Palmyra palm, Cāpa,* wood, and horn. [9]Bow strings are made of Mūrvā, Arka, Śaṇa, Gavedhu, bamboo,* and sinews. [10]Arrows are made of bamboo, Śara, Śalākā, Daṇḍāsana, and Nārāca; [11]their tips, intended to cut, pierce, or pound, are made of iron, bone, or wood.*

[12]Nistriṃśa, Maṇḍalāgra, and Asiyaṣṭi* are the swords, [13]and their hilts are made of rhinoceros and buffalo horns, elephant tusks, wood, and bamboo roots.

[14]Hatchet, ax, Paṭṭasa,* shovel, spade, saw, and Kāṇḍachedana* are the razor weapons.

[15]Stones for mechanical devices, slings, and fists, and millstones are the stone weapons.

[16]Metal coat of mail, metal fabric, metal plate, armor made of fabric, and dense structures made of the skin, hooves, and horns/tusks of the river dolphin (2.17.13 n.), rhinoceros, Dhenuka,* elephant, and cattle are the kinds of armor. [17]Helmet, neck guard, cuirass, corselet, mail, breast

plate, and thigh guard, as well as box, leather shield, Hastikarṇa, Tālamūla, Dhamanikā, Kapāṭa, Kiṭikā, Apratihata, and Balāhakānta* are the protective gear.

[18]The fittings for harnessing elephants, chariots, and horses, and items used to decorate them and to prepare them for battle constitute equipment.

[19]Net of magic and esoteric practices are the kinds of rites.*

[20]And with regard to the factories—

> The Chief of Armaments should know the intention,* accomplishment of the undertaking, application, fraud, profit, loss, and expenditure of the forest produce.

THAT CONCLUDES THE EIGHTEENTH CHAPTER: "SUPERINTENDENT OF THE ARMORY" OF THE SECOND BOOK: "ON THE ACTIVITIES OF SUPERINTENDENTS."

Chapter 19

Topic 37: Standardization of Balances and Measures*

[1]The Superintendent of Standardization should have factories constructed for the manufacture of standard weights and measures (see appendix 2).

BALANCES AND WEIGHTS

[2]Ten Māṣa-beans—or five Guñja-berries—make one gold Māṣaka.* [3]Sixteen of these make one Suvarṇa or one Karṣa. [4]One Pala weighs four Karṣas.

[5]Eighty-eight white mustard seeds make one silver Māṣaka. [6]Sixteen of those—or 20 Śimbā-beans—make one Dharaṇa.

[7]A diamond Dharaṇa weighs 20 rice kernels.

[8]Half-Māṣaka, one-Māṣaka, two-, four-, and eight-Māṣakas, one-Suvarṇa, two-, four-, and eight-Suvarṇas, as well as ten-, 20-, 30-, 40-, and 100-Suvarṇas* (are the standard weights). [9]This explains also the Dharaṇas.

[10]Weights should be made of iron or of stones from Magadha and Mekala, or else of substances that do not increase in weight with water or smearing, or decrease with heating.

[11]He should have ten kinds of balance beams manufactured, beginning with six Aṅgulas and increasing successively by eight Aṅgulas, and

beginning with one Pala of metal and increasing successively by one Pala, with a mechanical device or a sling on both sides.*

[12]He should have the Samavṛttā-balance* made with 35 Palas of metal and with a length of 72 Aṅgulas. [13]After tying a five-Pala ball to it, he should have the level established, [14]and from that point he should get degrees recorded for one Karṣa, in increments of one Karṣa up to one Pala; and then in increments of one Pala up to ten Palas; then for 12 Palas, 15 Palas, and 20 Palas; [15]and then he should have them recorded in increments of ten up to 100. [16]At each fifth marking* he should have it decked with the Nāndī mark.*

[17]He should have the Parimāṇī-balance made with double that amount of metal and with a length of 96 Aṅgulas. [18]On it, beyond the 100th mark, he should get degrees recorded for 20, 50, and 100.*

[19]A Bhāra is 20 Tulās. [20]A Pala is ten Dharaṇikas. [21]The balance for revenue (can weigh up to) 100 such Palas.* [22]Progressively less by five Palas is the balance for trade, the balance for payments, and the balance for palace payments.* [23]Of these, the Pala is progressively less by half a Dharaṇa, the metal of the upper beam is progressively less by two Palas, and the lengths are progressively less by six Aṅgulas.*

[24]In the case of the first two, the additional weight* is five Palas, except for meat, metals, salt, and gems.

[25]A wooden balance is eight Hastas in length, with degrees recorded, provided with weights, and mounted on "peacock's feet."*

[26]Twenty-five Palas of firewood cooks one Prastha of rice. [27]This is exemplary with regard to higher and lower quantities.*

[28]That is the explanation of balances and weights.

MEASURES

[29]Now, a Droṇa used as a measure for revenue holds 200 Palas of Māṣa-beans; while a Droṇa for trade holds 187.5 Palas; a Droṇa for payments, 175 Palas; and a Droṇa for palace payments (2.19.22 n.), 162 Palas. [30]Of these, Āḍhaka, Prastha, and Kuḍuba are each one-quarter less than the preceding.* [31]Sixteen Droṇas make one Khārī; [31]twenty Droṇas make one Kumbha; [33]and ten Kumbhas make one Vaha.

[34–35]He should have measures constructed out of dry hardwood, measures that are even,* with the heap amounting to one-quarter of the measure.* For juice, however, the heap is included within the measure.* [35]The quantity of the heap of liquor, flowers and fruits, chaff and charcoal, and lime is increased twofold.*

PRICES AND INSPECTION

36The price of a Droṇa is one and a quarter Paṇas; of an Āḍhaka, three-quarters of a Paṇa; of a Prastha, six Māṣakas; and of a Kuḍuba, one Māṣaka. 37The price of measures for juice and the following are twice as much (2.19.34–35).

38The price of a weight is 20 Paṇas, 39and the price of a balance is one-third of that.

40He should have the stamping of weights and measures carried out every four months. 41The penalty for an unstamped one is 27 and a quarter Paṇas. 42They should pay to the Superintendent of Standardization a stamping fee of one Kākaṇī every day.

43The heat surcharge* for ghee is one-thirty-second part, and for oil one-sixty-fourth. 44In the case of liquids, the measure-flow* is one-fiftieth part.

45He should have measures constructed with the following capacities: one Kuḍuba, half a Kuḍuba, quarter Kuḍuba, and one-eighth Kuḍuba.*

> 46A Vāraka is viewed as consisting of 84 Kuḍubas in the case of ghee, and 64 in the case of oil; while one-quarter of those two constitutes a Ghaṭikā.

THAT CONCLUDES THE NINETEENTH CHAPTER: "STANDARDIZATION OF BALANCES AND MEASURES" OF THE SECOND BOOK: "ON THE ACTIVITIES OF SUPERINTENDENTS."

Chapter 20

Topic 38: Measures of Space and Time

1The Superintendent of Measures should be knowledgeable about the measures of space and time (see appendix 2).

MEASURES OF SPACE

2Eight Paramāṇus make one Rathacakravipruṣ; 3eight of those make one Likṣā; 4eight of those make one Yūkā; 5eight of those make one Yavamadhya; 6and eight Yavamadhyas make one Aṅgula. 7Alternatively, an Aṅgula is the extent of the middle section of the middle finger of a middle-sized man. 9Four Aṅgulas make one Dhanurgraha; eight Aṅgulas make one Dhanurmuṣṭi; 10twelve Aṅgulas make one Vitasti, as also one

Chāyāpauruṣa;* [11]and 14 Aṅgulas make one Śama, as also one Śala, one Pariraya, and one Pada.

[12]Two Vitastis make one Aratni, that is, a Hasta of Prajāpati—[13]which, together with one Dhanurgraha, is the measure for standardized measurements and for pasture land;* [14]and which, together with one Dhanurmuṣṭi, makes a Kiṣuka or a Kaṃsa. [15]Forty-two Aṅgulas make a saw-Kiṣuka of a carpenter, which is the measure for military camps, forts, and royal properties. [16]Fifty-four Aṅgulas make one Hasta used in produce forests. [17]Eighty-four Aṅgulas make one Vyāma, which is the measure for ropes, and one Pauruṣa used for digging. [18]Four Aratnis make one Daṇḍa, one Dhanuṣ, one Nālikā, and one Pauruṣa for a householder. [19]One hundred and eight Aṅgulas make one Dhanuṣ for measuring roads and city walls, and one Pauruṣa for constructing fire altars.* [20]Six Kaṃsas make one Daṇḍa, which is the measure for gifts to Brāhmaṇas and to guests.*

[21]Ten Daṇḍas make one Rajju; [22]two Rajjus make one Parideśa; [23]three Rajjus make one Nivartana along one side;* [24]and two Daṇḍas more than the latter make a Bāhu.

[25]Two thousand Dhanuṣes make one Goruta, [26]and four Gorutas make one Yojana.

[27]The above are the measures of space.

MEASURES OF TIME

[28]From here on, the measures of time.

[29]Tuṭa, Lava, Nimeṣa, Kāṣṭā, Kalā, Nālikā, Muhūrta, forenoon, afternoon, day, night, fortnight, month, season, Ayana,* year, and Yuga: These are the times.

[30]Two Tuṭas make one Lava; [31]two Lavas, one Nimeṣa; [32]five Nimeṣas, one Kāṣṭā; [33]thirty Kāṣṭās, one Kalā; [34]forty Kalās, one Nālikā—[35]alternatively, a Nālikā is the time taken for one Āḍhaka of water to run through a hole in a pot, a hole that has the diameter of four Māṣakas of gold stretched to a length of four Aṅgulas—; [36]and two Nālikās make one Muhūrta.

[37]During the months of Caitra (March–April) and Āśvayuja (September–October), a day consists of 15 Muhūrtas, as does a night. [38]Thereafter, during the following six months, each increases and then decreases by three Muhūrtas.*

[39]When the shadow is eight Pauruṣas* long, one-eighteenth part of the day has elapsed; when it is six Pauruṣas long, one-fourteenth part;

when it is three Pauruṣas* long, one-eighth part; when it is two Pauruṣas long, one-sixth part; when it is one Pauruṣa long, one-fourth part; when it is eight Aṅgulas long, three-tenths part; when it is four Aṅgulas long, three-eighths part; and when there is no shadow, it is midday. [40]When the day turns around, one should reckon the remainder in the same manner. [41]In the month of Āṣāḍha (June–July), the shadow disappears at midday. [42]Thereafter, the shadow increases by two Aṅgulas a month during the six months beginning with Śrāvaṇa (July–August), and decreases by two Aṅgulas a month during the six months beginning with Māgha (January–February).

[43]Fifteen days and nights make one fortnight; [44]when the moon waxes, it is bright, [45]and when the moon wanes, it is dark. [46]Two fortnights make one month. [47]Thirty days and nights make one work month.* [48]A solar month has one-half day more, [49]while a lunar month has one-half day less. [50]Twenty-seven days and nights make a constellation month, [51]and 32 make a military month. [52]A month for maintaining horses is 35 days and nights, [53]and for maintaining elephants, 40.*

[54]Two months make a season. [55]The months of Śrāvaṇa (July–August) and Prauṣṭhapada (August–September) are the rainy season; [56]Āśvayuja (September–October) and Kārttika (October–November) are autumn; [57]Mārgaśīrṣa (November–December) and Pauṣa (December–January) are winter; [58]Māgha (January–February) and Phālguna (February–March) are the cool season; [59]Caitra (March–April) and Vaiśākha (April–May) are spring; [60]and Jyeṣṭhāmūlīya (May–June) and Āṣāḍha (June–July) are summer.

[61]The Uttarāyaṇa* begins with the cool season, [62]and the Dakṣiṇāyana* begins with the rainy season. [63]Two Ayanas* make one year. [64]Five years make one Yuga.

> [65]The sun subtracts one-sixtieth part of a day. Therefore, in one season, he causes the loss of one day; so also does the moon cause the loss of one day.
> [66]Thus, the two produce one additional month every two and a half years, the first one in the summer and the second one at the end of the five-year cycle.*

THAT CONCLUDES THE TWENTIETH CHAPTER: "MEASURES OF SPACE AND TIME" OF THE SECOND BOOK: "ON THE ACTIVITIES OF SUPERINTENDENTS."

Chapter 21

Topic 39: Superintendent of Customs

[1]The Superintendent of Customs should set up the customs house along with the flag facing the east or the north near the main gate (2.3.31–32).

[2]The customs collectors, four or five in number, should write down with reference to the traders arrived in caravans—who they are, where they are from, how much merchandise they have, and where the identity card or the seal was issued (2.21.26).

[3]The penalty on goods without a seal is twice the amount due. [4]The fine on goods with forged seals is eight times the customs duty. [5]The penalty on goods with broken seals is distraint in the Ghaṭikāsthāna.* [6]When the royal seal has been altered or the name has been changed, he should be made to pay one and a quarter Paṇas for each load.

[7]The traders should announce the quantity and price of a commodity that has reached the foot of the flag: "Who will buy this commodity at this price for this quantity?" [8]After it has been proclaimed aloud three times, he should give it to the bidders.* [9]If there is competition among buyers, the increase in price* along with the customs duty goes to the treasury.

[10]When a man, fearing customs duty, declares a lower quantity or price, the king shall confiscate the amount in excess of that; [11]or, he should pay eight times the customs duty. [12]He should do the same when someone decreases the value of a package containing merchandise by presenting a lower-quality sample, or when someone conceals a package with goods of high value within a package containing goods of low value.

[13]Or, when a man, fearing competing buyers,* increases the price beyond the normal price of a commodity, the king shall confiscate the increase in price or assess twice the customs duty—[14]eight times that much when the Superintendent conceals this.*

[15]Therefore, the sale of commodities should be made by weight, measure, or number, while an estimate should be made in the case of articles of low value and those enjoying special concessions (2.22.8).

[16]For those who evade the foot of the flag and have not paid the customs duties, moreover, the fine is eight times the customs duty. [17]Secret agents deployed on roads and in areas without roads (2.36.13) should find that out.

[18]The following should pass without customs duty: articles for use in a marriage; wedding gifts accompanying a bride; articles meant for gifts; what is received on the occasion of a sacrifice, a religious ceremony, or a birth;

and articles for use in special rituals such as divine worship, tonsure, Vedic initiation, first shave, and consecration for a religious observance.* [19]A person who makes a false statement incurs the fine for theft (2.7.39 n.).

[20]When a trader takes away for export goods on which customs duty has not been paid mixed with goods on which customs duty has been paid, or carries away a second item under a single seal by breaking open a package of merchandise, his punishment is its confiscation plus a fine of an equal amount. [21]One who carries away merchandise from the customs house using cow dung and straw as the standard* should be assessed the highest seizure fine (2.1.29 n.).

[22]Anyone who takes away for export any of the following items that are forbidden to be exported, namely weapons, armor, coats of mail, metals, chariots, gems, grain, and farm animals, is assessed the promulgated fine and the merchandise is confiscated. [23]If any of these items is brought in as an import, it is to be sold outside* duty free.

[24]The Frontier Commander should collect a road levy of one and a quarter Paṇas for a vehicle loaded with goods, one Paṇa for a one-hoofed animal, half a Paṇa each for farm animals, a quarter Paṇa each for small farm animals,* and one Māṣika for a man carrying a load on his shoulder. [25]He should, moreover, pay compensation for anything that is lost or stolen. [26]He should dispatch to the Superintendent* any foreign caravan after examining its goods of high and low value and providing an identity card and a seal.

[27]Alternatively, an agent working undercover as a trader should report to the king the size of a caravan. [38]Using that information, the king should notify the Superintendent of Customs about the extent of the caravan so as to broadcast his omniscience. [29]Then, meeting the caravan, the Superintendent should say: "These are goods of high value and these of low value belonging to these and these other traders. They should not be concealed. This is the might of the king." [30]If anyone conceals a commodity of low value, he is fined eight times the customs duty; if he conceals a commodity of high value, everything is confiscated.

> [31]He should destroy goods that would cause harm to the country,
> as also those that are of no use, while he should make goods of
> high utility duty free, as also rare seeds.

THAT CONCLUDES THE TWENTY-FIRST CHAPTER: "SUPERINTENDENT OF CUSTOMS" OF THE SECOND BOOK: "ON THE ACTIVITIES OF SUPERINTENDENTS."

Chapter 22

Topic 39a: Operation of Customs

[1]What is external and what is internal constitute exchange.* [2]Export duty and import duty constitute customs duty.

[3]On imports the duty is one-fifth of the price.

[4]He should collect one-sixth portion of flowers, fruits, vegetables, roots, bulbous roots, fruits of creepers, seeds, and dried fish and meat.

[5]In the case of conchs, diamonds, gems, pearls, corals, and necklaces, he should get experts in each to make an estimate after he has come to an agreement with them as to the amount of work, the time for completion, the wages, and the final product (2.18.1 n.).

[6]In the case of flax, Dukūla (2.11.102 n.), silk,* armor, yellow orpiment, red arsenic, antimony, vermilion, different kinds of metal, and ore; sandalwood, aloe, spices, ferment (2.12.10 n.), and minor items; skins, ivory, bedspreads, coverlets, and silk cloth; and products of goats and sheep—he should collect one-tenth portion or one-fifteenth portion.

[7]In the case of clothes, four-footed and two-footed creatures, yarn, cotton, perfumes, medicines, wood, bamboo, bark, leather goods, and earthenware; as well as grain, fat, sugar, salt, liquor, cooked food, and the like—he should collect one-twentieth portion or one-twenty-fifth portion.

[8]The customs duty to be collected at the gate is one-fifth portion.* Alternatively, he should fix a concessional rate according to the benefit accruing to the country.

[9]Commodities should not be sold at the place of production.* [10]For taking mineral commodities from pit mines, the penalty* is 600 Paṇas. [11]For taking flowers or fruit from a flower garden or an orchard, the fine is 54 Paṇas. [12]For taking vegetables, roots, and bulbous roots from vegetable plots, the fine is 51 and three-quarter Paṇas; [13]and for taking any kind of crop from fields, 53 Paṇas. [14]The royal-land penalty is one Paṇa and one and a half Paṇas.*

> [15]Therefore, he should fix the customs duty on commodities, both new and old, according to the region, type of commodity, and custom,* as also the penalties according to the offense.

THAT CONCLUDES THE TWENTY-SECOND CHAPTER: "OPERATION OF CUSTOMS" WITHIN "SUPERINTENDENT OF CUSTOMS AND TOLLS" OF THE SECOND BOOK: "ON THE ACTIVITIES OF SUPERINTENDENTS."

Chapter 23

Topic 40: Superintendent of Yarn

[1]The Superintendent* of Yarn should organize trade in yarn, armor, cloth, and rope through experts in each.

[2]He should employ widows, crippled women, spinsters,* female renouncers, and women paying off a fine through manual labor (2.12.21 n.), as well as prostitutes and madams,* old female slaves of the king, and female slaves of gods* whose divine service has ended, to spin yarn from wool, bark fiber, cotton, silk-cotton, hemp, and flax.

[3]After determining whether the yarn is fine, coarse, or middling, as well as whether its quantity is large or small, he should set their wages. [4]After finding out the quantity of yarn, he should regale them with unguents of oil and myrobalan. [5]He should induce them to do the work by giving them gifts and honors on festive days.* [6]When the quantity of yarn decreases, the wages should be decreased proportionate to the value of the material.

[7]He should have the work done by artisans after he has come to an agreement with them as to the amount of work, the time for completion, the wages, and the final product (2.18.1 n.), and he should keep in close touch with them. [8]As he sets up weaving factories for flax, Dukūla (2.11.102 n.), silk, Raṅku-hair, and cotton, he should win their goodwill with perfumes, garlands, and gifts, as well as other kinds of favors. [9]He should initiate the production of various kinds of clothes, spreads, and coverlets; [10]and he should set up factories for armor using specialized artisans and craftsmen.

[11]He should employ secluded women*—women whose husbands have gone away,* widows, crippled women, and spinsters (2.23.2 n.)—who wish to maintain themselves to carry out the work, being considerate by sending his own female slaves.* [12]Or else, if they come to the yarn workshop on their own, he should arrange for the payment of wages in exchange for the wares early in the morning. [13]A lamp should be used only to inspect the yarn. [14]For looking at the face of a woman or for speaking with her on other matters, the penalty is the lowest seizure fine (2.1.29 n.); and for delay in paying the wages, the middle fine, as also for giving wages for work not completed.

[15]When a woman takes the wages but does not carry out the work, he should have a thumb-pinch administered to her,* as also to women who have been accused of squander and theft.*

[16]With regard to wages of workers, moreover, a fine is imposed proportionate to the offense.

[17]He should personally keep in touch with the rope makers and the manufacturers of armor. [18]Further, he should have articles such as straps manufactured.

> [19]He should get ropes made of yarn and bark fibers and straps made of cane and bamboo as harnesses and bindings for carriages and draught animals.

THAT CONCLUDES THE TWENTY-THIRD CHAPTER: "SUPERINTENDENT OF YARN" OF THE SECOND BOOK: "ON THE ACTIVITIES OF SUPERINTENDENTS."

Chapter 24

Topic 41: Superintendent of Agriculture

[1]The Superintendent of Agriculture,* who must be either proficient in agricultural science, geometry,* and plant science, or assisted by experts in these, should collect in the appropriate seasons seed stock from all kinds of grains, flowers, fruits, vegetables, bulbous roots, roots, creepers, flax, and cotton.

[2]He should have them sown by slaves, workers, and men paying off their fines through manual labor (2.12.21 n.) on land that is suitable for each and has been thoroughly plowed several times. [3]He should make sure that they are not hampered* on account of plowing implements, equipment, and oxen; also on account of artisans, as well as smiths, carpenters, hunters,* rope makers, snake catchers, and the like. [4]If there is a loss in the output of their work, the fine is equal to the loss of the output.

[5]The amount of rainfall in dry regions* is 16 Droṇas* and in wet regions,* one and a half times that—regions where sowing is carried out according to the zone. The amount of rainfall in the Aśmaka* region is 13 and a half Droṇas;* in the Avanti* region, 23 Droṇas;* and in the Aparānta* region, as also in the snowy regions, an unlimited amount*—unlimited in terms of time also in lands where sowing is carried out with irrigation.

[6]When one-third of the rain falls in the first and the last month* and two-thirds in the middle two months,* it has the characteristic of an excellent year.* [7]Its* prognostication is done from the position, motion, and

impregnation of Jupiter, from the rise, setting, and movement of Venus, and from the natural and the unnatural appearance of the sun—[8]from the sun, that the seeds will sprout; from Jupiter, that the crops will form stalks; and from Venus, that there will be rain.*

> [9]Three periods in which clouds rain continuously for seven days each; clouds drizzling for 80 days; and clouds along with sunshine for 60 days*—this kind of rain is even and beneficial.
> [10]A place where it rains with wind and sunshine well apportioned and providing three periods for plowing,* there crops flourish for certain.

[11]In accordance with that, he should sow either crops that require a lot of water or grains that require little water. [12]Śāli-rice, Vrīhi-rice, Kodrava-grain, sesame, panic grain, Udāraka, and Varaka are the first to be sowed.* [13]Mudga-bean, Māṣa-bean, and Śaimbya are to be sowed in the middle period.* [14]Safflower, Masūra-lentil, Kulattha, barley, wheat, Kalāya, linseed, and mustard are the last to be sowed.* [15]Alternatively,* seeds are to be sown in accordance with the season.

[16]The land that is left over after sowing may be cultivated by those who sharecrop for half the harvest or by those who subsist on their labor, receiving one-fourth or one-fifth share. [17]They* should give a share of the produce from land that had been uncultivated* as stipulated, except in times of adversity.* [18]They* should give one-fifth share* for water consumption when water is raised by hand operation from their own irrigation works, one-fourth when raised by shoulder operation, and one-third when raised by a mechanical device operated by a water current;* one-fourth when lifted from a river, lake, reservoir, or well.*

[19]He should plant* a wet crop, a winter crop, or a summer crop according to the amount of irrigation water* available. [20]Śāli-rice and so forth (2.24.12) are the best; vegetables are middling; and sugarcane is the worst, [21]for sugarcane plants are beset with many dangers and require a lot of expenditure.* [22]An area where foam strikes the banks is good for fruits growing on creepers; areas near overflows, for long pepper, grapes, and sugarcane; areas near wells, for vegetables and root vegetables; areas near canals, for green herbs; and ridges for plants reaped by cutting, such as herbs for perfume and medicine, Uśīra-grass, Hrībera, and Piṇḍāluka. [23]And in fields suitable for each, he should plant dry-land and wetland herbs.*

[24]Seeds of grains are soaked in dew (at night) and dried in the heat (of the day) for seven days; and seeds of pulses, for three or five days. Cuttings for propagation are smeared at the cuts with honey, ghee, and pig's fat mixed with cow dung; and bulbous roots, with honey and ghee. Stony seeds are smeared with cow dung. In the case of trees, the hole is burnt with cow's bones and cow dung, and the pregnancy longing is carried out at the proper time.* [25]When they have sprouted, moreover, he should douse them with fresh acrid fish* along with the milk of the Snuhi-plant.

> [26]He should bring together cotton seeds and the slough of a snake. Snakes do not remain in a place with this smoke.*

[27]At the first sowing of any kind of seed, however, he should sow the first fistful after immersing it in water containing gold, and also recite this mantra:

> Adoration always to Prajāpati, to Kāśyapa, and to Deva.* May Goddess Sītā* prosper in my seeds and riches.

[28]He should provide rations to those who guard vegetable plots, flower gardens, fruit orchards, and cattle,* and to slaves and workers proportionate to the retinue of their people (1.16.5 n.), as well as a monthly wage of one and a quarter Paṇas. [29]Rations and wages of artisans* should be proportionate to their work.

[30]Vedic scholars and recluses may gather what has broken off—flowers and fruits for use in rituals for gods, and rice and barley for use in the sacrifice of first fruits; and those who live by gleaning* may gather what is at the bottom of heaps.*

> [31]At their proper time, he should have crops and the like brought in as soon as they are harvested. A prudent man should not leave anything in the field, not even a straw.
> [32]From the stacks, he should build high mounds or ridges of a similar kind, making the tops neither too bulky nor too flimsy.*
> [33]He should locate the stacks at the outer edge of the circle* of the threshing floor. Within the threshing floor, the workers should carry water but never any fire.

THAT CONCLUDES THE TWENTY-FOURTH CHAPTER: "SUPERINTENDENT OF AGRICULTURE" OF THE SECOND BOOK: "ON THE ACTIVITIES OF SUPERINTENDENTS."

Chapter 25

Topic 42: Superintendent of Liquor

[1]The Superintendent of Liquor should organize the trade of liquor and ferment (2.12.10 n.) in the fort, countryside, and military camp through traders with expertise in liquor and ferment,* the trade being carried out either in one place or in several locations (2.16.4), or else according to the demands of sale and purchase. [2]He should impose a penalty of 600 Paṇas on those who manufacture, buy, or sell elsewhere.

[3]Liquor may not be taken out of a village or be hoarded because of the following dangers: People commissioned may neglect their work, Āryas may transgress the proper bounds (3.9.2 n.), and assassins (1.12.2) may become emboldened. [4]Alternatively, people known to be upright may take out a small quantity that is clearly marked—one-fourth or one-half of a Kuḍuba, or a full Kuḍuba, or half a Prastha or a full Prastha. [5]Or rather, they should drink in taverns without wandering around.

[6]With the intention of discovering articles that have been stolen after they have been given as a deposit, pledge, or loan, or wrongfully obtained, he should do the following: When he finds some article or money without an owner, he should have the person depositing it arrested in another locality under some pretext, as well as anyone who spends lavishly or spends without having a source of income.*

[7]No one should offer liquor at a non-regulation price or on credit, except for spoilt liquor. [8]He should have that sold in some other place, [9]or give it to slaves and workers as wages, [10]to draught animals as a stimulating drink,* or to pigs as a nutrient.

[11]He should have taverns constructed, taverns that have many rooms, contain separate beds and seats,* advertise drinking,* have perfumes, garlands, and water, and are comfortable in all seasons.

[12]Clandestine operatives placed there should spot both normal and unusual expenditures, as well as any newcomers. [13]They should ascertain the ornaments, clothes, and money of customers when they are intoxicated or asleep. [14]When these are lost, the traders* should pay restitution and a fine of an equal amount. [15]Using their own charming female slaves, however, the traders should find out the disposition of newcomers and local residents bearing the appearance of Āryas as they remain drunk or asleep in secluded sections of the rooms.

[16]With regard to Medaka, Prasannā, Āsava, Ariṣṭa, Maireya, and Madhu*—[17]one Droṇa of water, half an Āḍhaka of rice kernels, and

three Prasthas of ferment (2.12.10 n.) is the mixture for Medaka. [18]Twelve Āḍhakas of flour and either five Prasthas of ferment or the mélange* of its class (see 2.25.27) mixed with the bark and fruit of areca nut is the mixture for Prasannā. [19]One Tulā of wood apple, five Tulās of treacle, and one Prastha of honey is the mixture for Āsava; [20]when this is increased by one-quarter, it is of the highest quality, and when it is decreased by one-quarter, it is of a lower quality. [21]Ariṣṭas are formulated by physicians for each kind of illness. [22]Maireya is an extract from a decoction of Meṣaśṛṅgī bark infused with jaggery and either combined with a mélange of long pepper and black pepper or mixed with the three fruits.* [23]An alternative is that a mélange of the three fruits mixed with jaggery is used in all preparations. [24]Madhu is the juice of grapes. [25]The explanation for its names "Kāpiṣāyana" and "Hārahūraka" is their places of origin.*

[26]One Droṇa of Māṣa-bean pulp, either raw or cooked, and one-third more than that of rice kernels, mixed with one-Karṣa portions of the ingredients beginning with Moraṭā (see 2.25.33) is the composition of the ferment.

[27]For Medaka and Prasannā, the mélange that is mixed consists of five Karṣas each of Pāṭhā, Lodhra, Tejovatī, Elāvāluka, liquorice, Madhurasā, Priyaṅgu, Dāruharidrā, black pepper, and long pepper. [28]Kaṭaśarkarā mixed with a decoction of liquorice, moreover, produces a clear color.

[29]One Karṣa each of cinnamon bark, Citraka, Vilaṅga, and Gajapippalī, and two Karṣas each of Kramuka, liquorice, Mustā, and Lodhra constitute the mélange for Āsava. [30]And one-tenth part of these is the composition of the seed.*

[31]The mixture of Prasannā is used for white Surā-liquor.* [32]Mango Surā-liquor with a high proportion of juice or of seed—or containing the mélange—is great Surā-liquor. [33]Of these kinds of liquor, one Kumbhī fit to be drunk by a king is made clear by one closed fistful* of the following: the powder of burnt Kaṭaśarkarā, infused with a decoction of Moraṭā, Palāśa, Pattūra, Meṣaśṛṅgī, Karañja, and Kṣīravṛkṣa, and mixed with half that quantity of the pulp of Lodhra, Citraka, Vilaṅga, Pāṭhā, Mustā, Kaliṅgayava, Dāruharidrā, Indīvara, Śatapuṣpā, Apāmārga, Saptaparṇa, neem, and Āsphota. [34]And to this five Palas of jaggery should be added to increase its sweetness.

[35]Householders should be permitted to produce white Surā-liquor during festive occasions, and for medicinal purposes Ariṣṭa or other kinds. [36]During festivals, fairs, and excursions, he should grant a Surā-liquor license* for four days. [37]During those days, he should collect

a daily penalty from those who are unauthorized until the end of the festivities.

[38]Women and children should search for ingredients of Surā-liquor and ferment.

[39]Those dealing in commodities not controlled by the king should pay a duty of 5 percent. And with regard to Surakā, Medaka, Ariṣṭa, Madhu, Phalāmla, and Āmlasīdhu—

> [40]after ascertaining a day's sale and the surcharge on measures and on cash, he should fix the compensatory tax (2.12.31) and carry out what is customary.*

THAT CONCLUDES THE TWENTY-FIFTH CHAPTER: "SUPERINTENDENT OF LIQUOR" OF THE SECOND BOOK: "ON THE ACTIVITIES OF SUPERINTENDENTS."

Chapter 26

Topic 43: Superintendent of Abattoirs

[1]The Superintendent of Abattoirs should impose the highest fine (2.1.29 n.) for tying up, killing, or injuring deer, game animals, birds, or fish that are legally protected from harm and that are living in sanctuaries; the middle fine when it is carried out by householders in enclosed areas by the sanctuaries.* [2]For tying up, killing, or injuring fish and birds whose killing is not recognized,* he should impose a penalty of 26 and three-quarter Paṇas, and twice that amount in the case of deer and game animals.

[3]In the case of creatures whose killing is recognized and who are not in preserves (2.6.6), he should collect one-sixth share, as also* an additional one-tenth share in the case of fish and birds and an additional duty* in the case of deer and game animals. [4]In the case of birds and deer that are alive,* he should release one-sixth into sanctuaries.

[5]Sea fish with the appearance of an elephant, horse, man, bull, or donkey, as also such fish from lakes, rivers, reservoirs, or canals; birds for amusement—Krauñca-crane, Utkrośaka, Dātyūha, ruddy geese, Cakravāka-duck, Jīvaṃjīvaka-pheasant, Bhṛṅgarāja-drongo, Cakora-partridge, Mattakokila-cuckoo, peacocks, parrots, and Madadanaśārikā-myna—and also other auspicious creatures, whether birds or wild animals, should be protected from being injured or killed. [6]For violating their protection, one should be assessed the lowest seizure fine (see 2.1.29 n.).

[7]They* shall sell boneless meat of deer and game animals that have been freshly killed. [8]For meat containing bones, they should pay compensation;* [9]and if the weight is short, eight times the amount that is short.

[10]Calves, studs, and milking females of these animals are not to be slaughtered. [11]Anyone slaughtering one of them should be fined 50 Paṇas, as also anyone who slaughters using torture.

[12]They should not sell an animal that is bloated, that is missing its head, feet, or bones,* smells bad, or has died on its own; [13]otherwise, he should be fined 12 Paṇas.

> [14]When game animals, deer, vicious animals, and fish* living in sanctuaries become wicked, they should be killed or bound in a place outside the protected areas.

THAT CONCLUDES THE TWENTY-SIXTH CHAPTER: "SUPERINTENDENT OF ABATTOIRS" OF THE SECOND BOOK: "ON THE ACTIVITIES OF SUPERINTENDENTS."

Chapter 27

Topic 44: Superintendent of Courtesans

[1]The Superintendent of Courtesans should settle a woman coming from a courtesan or a non-courtesan family, and endowed with beauty, youth, and artistic skills, as a courtesan with 1,000 Paṇas, and an alternate courtesan with half the above investment in the establishment.*

[2]When a courtesan has run away* or died, her daughter or sister should run the establishment; or the madam* should assign the alternate courtesan. [3]If these are unavailable, the king should confiscate it.*

[4]According to the eminence in beauty and adornments, he should appoint one to the lowest, the middle, or the highest rank with 1,000 Paṇas so as to add distinction to the parasol, ceremonial water jug, fan, palanquin, seat, and chariot.* [5]When her beauty is gone, he should appoint her as a madam.

[6]The ransom* for a courtesan is 24,000 Paṇas, and for a son of a courtesan, 12,000 Paṇas. [7]From the age of eight, he should carry out the function of a performer for the king.* [8]When a courtesan who is a slave* is no longer able to earn fees for sex, she should work in the storehouse or the kitchen. [9]If she refuses to go there, she should be kept confined and should pay a monthly wage of one and a quarter Paṇas.*

[10]He should keep a record of fees for sex, gifts, income, expenses, and profit* of a courtesan and prohibit activities requiring excessive expenditure.

[11]If she deposits her ornaments* anywhere other than in the hands of her madam, the fine is four and a quarter Paṇas; [12]and if she sells or pawns her belongings,* the fine is 50 and a quarter Paṇas.

In the case of verbal abuse, the fine is 24 Paṇas; in the case of physical abuse, twice that amount; and in the case of cutting off an ear, 50 and a quarter Paṇas plus one and a half Paṇas.* [13]For forcibly taking an unwilling woman or a young girl,* the punishment is the highest fine (see 2.1.29 n.), but the lowest seizure fine if the woman was willing. [14]For a man who confines an unwilling courtesan, or induces her to run away, or ruins her beauty by causing lacerations, the fine is 1,000 Paṇas; [15]or the fine will increase in proportion to the distinction of her position up to twice the amount of her ransom (see 2.27.6). [16]For a man causing the death of a courtesan who has attained high rank,* the fine is three times the amount of her ransom. [17]For killing a madam, a courtesan's daughter, or a female beauty-slave,* the punishment is the highest seizure fine.

[18]In all cases, the primary fine* is for the first offense, twice that for the second offense, three times that for the third offense; for the fourth offense he may do as he pleases.

[19]A courtesan who refuses to go to a man when ordered by the king should be given 1,000 lashes, or imposed a fine of 5,000 Paṇas.

[20]One who, after receiving the sex fee, shows antipathy should be fined twice her fee. [21]In the case of her stealing the sex fee for residency,* she should give eight times the sex fee, except in the case of illness or a defect in the man. [22]If she kills a man, the punishment is being burnt on a pyre or entering water.

[23]A man who steals a courtesan's ornaments, wealth, or her sex fee should be fined eight times that amount.

[24]A courtesan should report her sex fee, profit, and the man.

[25]This also explains what pertains to women of actors, dancers, singers, musicians, bards, performers, rope dancers, dramatic storytellers,* and wandering troubadours—men who pimp their wives—as well as women who live by secret professions (see 4.4). [26]Their musical instruments when brought from outside should be charged a fee of five Paṇas per show.

[27]Prostitutes should pay every month twice their sex fee.*

[28]He should provide a livelihood from the royal coffers to those who instruct courtesans, female slaves, and actresses in the following skills:

singing; playing musical instruments; reciting; dancing; acting; writing; painting; playing the lute, flute, and drum; reading another's mind; preparing perfumes and garlands; conversation; shampooing; and the arts of a courtesan. [29]They should also prepare the sons of courtesans to become leaders among stage actors, as well as among all dancers.

> [30]And their* wives, proficient in various signs and languages, should be employed under the guidance of their relatives against evil-doers to inform on them, to kill them, and to get them to be careless.

THAT CONCLUDES THE TWENTY-SEVENTH CHAPTER: "SUPERINTENDENT OF COURTESANS" OF THE SECOND BOOK: "ON THE ACTIVITIES OF SUPERINTENDENTS."

Chapter 28

Topic 45: Superintendent of Shipping

[1]The Superintendent of Shipping should oversee within provincial capitals (2.3.3) and the like the operations of seafaring vessels and ferries at the mouths of rivers, as also ferries across natural lakes, artificial lakes, and rivers.

[2]Villagers* located along their shores and banks should pay a fixed levy (see 2.6.10 n.). [3]Fishermen should pay one-sixth portion as the boat fee.* [4]Traders should pay a portion as duty prevailing at the port, and those traveling by royal boats, also the charges for the trip. [5]Conch and pearl fishermen should pay the boat fee* or travel in their own boats. [6]What pertains to the superintendent of these, furthermore, has been explained under the Superintendent of Pit Mines.*

[7]The Superintendent of Shipping should uphold the customs of a port recorded by the Superintendent of Ports.*

[8]Like a father, he* should come to the aid of boats battered by gale winds, [9]and charge no customs duty or half the customs duty on commodities damaged by water. [10]He should dispatch these boats, moreover, at times suitable for sailing from the ports, according to their assignments.

[11]He should demand customs duty from boats traveling by sea when they sail within his territory. [12]He should destroy pirate ships, as well as those approaching* from an enemy's territory and those that violate the customs (2.28.7) of the port.

[13]He should deploy large boats controlled by a captain, a navigator, an operator of cutters and ropes,* and a water bailer in large rivers where ferry operations continue during winter and summer, and small boats in small rivers that flow only during the rainy season.

[14]They should be assigned fixed crossing points, moreover, because of the danger that people doing what is inimical to the king may undertake such crossings; [15]and anyone undertaking a crossing at an unauthorized time or crossing place should be assessed the lowest seizure fine (2.1.29 n.). [16]Anyone who undertakes a crossing without authorization even at an authorized time and crossing place should pay a penalty of 26 and three-quarter Paṇas. [17]There is no penalty for fishermen, porters of wood and grass, farmers of flower gardens, fruit orchards, and vegetable gardens, and cowherds; as well as for both an entourage of a recognizable envoy and those occupied with army equipment, when they cross with their own ferries; and for villagers (2.28.2 n.) along the banks who ferry seeds, foodstuffs, and household utensils. [18]Brāhmaṇas, renouncers, children, old people, the sick, those conveying royal edicts, and pregnant women may cross (for free) with passes stamped by the Superintendent of Shipping.

[19]Persons from other territories may enter when they have obtained an entry permit or when vouched for by the caravan. [20]He should have the following arrested: someone abducting another man's wife, daughter, or property; one who is apprehensive, agitated, or hiding behind a package; one who covers (his face) with a load on his head containing a large package; a renouncer with emblems that he has just put on or without any emblem; a sick person whose illness cannot be perceived; one whose bearing has changed because of fear; someone carrying covertly valuable goods, royal edicts, weapons, or an incendiary mixture;* anyone carrying poison; one who has been on the road a long time; and one without a stamped pass.

[21]A small farm animal or a man carrying a load should pay one Māṣaka; a man with a load on his head or his back, a cow, or a horse, two; a camel or a buffalo, four; a light vehicle, five; a cart drawn by bullocks, six; a wagon, seven; and a Bhāra* of commodities, a quarter.* [22]That also explains a Bhāra of wares.* [23]The fare for crossing large rivers is double. [24]Villagers (2.28.2 n.) along the banks should pay a fixed levy in rations and wages.*

[25]At the frontiers, ferrymen should collect custom duties, escort charges, and road tolls; and they should confiscate the packages of anyone leaving with unstamped goods, as well as of anyone who crosses with an excessive load or at an unauthorized time or crossing point.

26When a boat without the requisite crew or equipment or in bad repair capsizes, the Superintendent of Shipping shall be liable* for anything that is lost or destroyed.

> 27A ferry shall operate from the eighth day after the full moon of Āṣāḍha (June–July) until the full moon of Kārttika (October–November). The works officer (2.7.22 n.) should provide the guarantee and each day bring in the daily revenue.*

THAT CONCLUDES THE TWENTY-EIGHTH CHAPTER: "SUPERINTENDENT OF SHIPPING" OF THE SECOND BOOK: "ON THE ACTIVITIES OF SUPERINTENDENTS."

Chapter 29

Topic 46: Superintendent of Cattle

1The Superintendent of Cattle should acquire a thorough knowledge of the following (pertaining to the herd): taking charge for wages, levy and counter-levy, the impaired and discharged,* joining the herd for a share, the full reckoning of the herd, what is lost, what has perished, and the totality of the milk and ghee produced.

2Cowherd, buffaloherd, milker, churner, and hunter—these should each look after 100 milk cows for cash payments; 3for those paid in milk and ghee abuse the calves. That deals with taking charge for wages.

4One man should look after 100 animals equally divided among old cows, milk cows, pregnant cows, cows that have calved for the first time, and heifers. 5Every year he should give eight Vārakas of ghee, one Paṇa per head of cattle, and the skin with the brand.* That deals with levy and counter-levy.*

6Those who look after 100 animals equally divided among sick cows, crippled cows, cows that do not allow someone else to milk them, cows that are difficult to milk, and cows that kill their calves should give a share proportionate to each category. That deals with the impaired and discharged.

7When, out of fear of an enemy king or forest tribes, people have entered their farm animals into the herd, they should give one-tenth portion in accordance with the law for providing protection. That deals with entering the herd for a share.

8Calves, weaned calves, young bulls yet to be broken in, bullocks, and stud bulls constitute male cattle; those pulling yoked carts and wagons, stud buffaloes, buffaloes raised for meat, and those hauling loads on their backs and shoulders constitute male buffaloes; heifers, weaned heifers, those that have calved for the first time, pregnant ones, ones giving milk, those that have not calved, and the barren constitute cows and female buffaloes; their additional* offspring when they are one month and two months old are calves and heifers, respectively. [9]He should brand those that are one or two months old. [10]He should brand an animal that has been with the herd for one or two months. [11]He should keep a written record of any additional* calf born, noting its brand, marks, color, and features between its horns.* That deals with the full reckoning of the herd.

[12]Those that are stolen by thieves, those that have entered another herd, and those that have disappeared constitute what is lost.

[13]Those that have perished in mud, in hazardous terrain, because of sickness or old age, or as a result of water or food;* or those that have been killed by a tree, a river bank, a log, or a rock; or those that have perished because of lightning, a predator, a snake, a crocodile, or a forest fire, constitute what has perished.

[14]They* shall be liable if these happen through negligence.

[15]In this manner, he should keep himself informed about the total number of animals.

[16]Anyone who kills by himself or gets someone to kill, or who steals or gets someone to steal, should be executed. [17]Anyone who switches* the cattle of others by the use of the royal brand should pay the lowest seizure fine (2.1.29 n.) per animal.

[18]When animals are stolen by thieves, a man who recovers them while they are in one's own country should take the animal that had been agreed upon; [19]and one-half of the animals, when he liberates them while they are in another country.*

[20]Cowherds should care for the young, old, and sick animals. [21]They should let the animals graze in areas of the wilderness suitable for different seasons, areas from which fowlers and hunters have eliminated the threat of attacks by thieves, vicious animals, and enemies. [22]To frighten away snakes and vicious animals and to find out what is going on in the pasture, they should tie resonant bells on the timid animals. [23]They should take the animals down to water that is free of mud and crocodiles at a ford that is even and wide, and stand guard over them.

[24]They should report any that have fallen prey to thieves, vicious animals, snakes, or crocodiles, or that have succumbed to sickness or old age; otherwise they must compensate the value of the animal. [25]When

an animal dies through a justifiable cause, they should bring back the branded hide in the case of a cow or buffalo, the mark on the ear in the case of a goat or sheep, the tail and the branded hide in the case of a horse, donkey, or camel—as well as the hair, hide, bladder, bile, tendons, teeth, hooves, horns, and bones. [26]They may sell the meat either fresh or dried.

[27]They should give buttermilk* mixed with water to the dogs and hogs, [28]and bring the hard curd as food for the army. [29]The whey is used to moisten the oilcakes from the oil presses.

[30]One who sells a farm animal should pay a quarter Paṇa per animal.*

[31]They should milk at both times* during the rainy season, autumn, and winter, and at only one time during cool season, spring, and summer. [32]For a man milking at the second time, the punishment is the cutting off of the thumb. [33]For a man who lets the milking time pass, the punishment is the value of the lost output. [34]The above also explains* the times for putting the nose string, for breaking in an animal, and for training in yoking and in going around.

[35]One Droṇa of milk yields one Prastha of ghee in the case of cows; one-fifth more in the case of buffaloes; and one-half more in the case of goats and sheep. [36]Alternatively, churning determines the amount in all cases; [37]for the increase in the milk and ghee depend on the quality of the ground, grass, and water.

[38]For a man who gets* a stud bull of a herd to be knocked down by a stud bull, the punishment is the lowest seizure fine (2.1.29 n.); for getting it killed, the highest fine.

[39]By segregating them according to class,* one should guard groups of ten animals. [40]The place where they rest should be determined depending on the movement of the cattle or the relative strength of the cattle, and according to the capacity to guard them.

[41]He should get the wool collected from goats and the like* every six months.

[42]The above also explains what pertains to herds of horses, donkeys, camels, and hogs.

[43]For bullocks with nose strings and capable of pulling at the pace of a gentle horse, the ration is half a load* of green fodder, twice that much of grass, a Tulā of oilcake from the oil press, ten Āḍhakas of broken grain, five Palas of rock salt, one Kuḍuba of oil for the nose and one Prastha for drink, a Tulā of meat* and an Āḍhaka of curd, a Droṇa of barley or Māṣa-bean porridge (2.15.33 n.); a Droṇa of milk or half an Āḍhaka of liquor,* a Prastha of fat, ten Palas of sugar, and a Pala of ginger as a

stimulating drink (2.25.10 n.)—[44]one-quarter less of these for mules, cows, and donkeys; and twice as much for buffaloes and camels. [45]In the case of working bullocks and milk cows used to suckle calves, rations should be allocated according to the time of the work and according to the yield, respectively; [45]for all, as much grass and water as they want.

[47]That is the explanation of the cattle herd.

> [48]He should create herds of 100—with five studs in the case of donkeys and horses, with ten studs in the case of goats and sheep, and with four studs in the case of cows, buffaloes, and camels.

THAT CONCLUDES THE TWENTY-NINTH CHAPTER: "SUPERINTENDENT OF CATTLE" OF THE SECOND BOOK: "ON THE ACTIVITIES OF SUPERINTENDENTS."

Chapter 30

Topic 47: Superintendent of Horses

[1]The Superintendent of Horses should get the total number of horses recorded in writing—those received as gifts, those acquired by purchase, those gained by war, those born to the herd, those procured in return for assistance, those pledged in a treaty, and those temporarily borrowed—according to their pedigree, age, color, marks, class, and provenance. [2]He should report those that are defective, crippled, or sick.

[3]The horse keeper should take care of them, collecting the monthly allotment from the treasury and the storehouse.*

[4]He* should have a stable constructed, a stable whose length corresponds to the number of horses, whose width is twice a horse's length, which has four doors and a central area for rolling on the ground, as well as an entrance hall, and which is equipped with planks for seating near the main door and teeming with monkeys, peacocks, spotted deer, mongooses, Cakora-partridges, parrots, and myna birds.* [5]He should have a stall facing east or north constructed for each horse, a stall that is square in shape with each side the length of a horse and with a floor made of smooth planks, that is equipped with a hamper for feed and an outlet for urine and excrement. [6]Alternatively, he may adjust the direction in accordance with the requirements of the stable. [7]The stalls for mares, stallions, and foals should be at separate ends.

[8]A mare that has just given birth should be given a Prastha of ghee to drink for three nights, [9]and afterwards for ten nights a Prastha of barley meal and a stimulating drink of fat and medicine, [10]and thereafter porridge (2.15.33 n.), green fodder, and food appropriate for the season.

[11]After the first ten days, a foal's food should consist of one Kuḍuba of barley meal together with one-quarter as much of ghee and one Prastha of milk until it is six months old. [12]Thereafter, its food is one Prastha of barley, increased by half a Prastha per month, until it is three years old, and one Droṇa until it is four years old. [13]After that time, when it is four or five years old, it has reached its full size and is capable of working.

[14]The finest type of horse is one whose face is 32 Aṅgulas, whose length is five times its face, whose shank is 20 Aṅgulas, whose height is four times its shank*—[15]the middling and the lowest being successively three Aṅgulas less—[16]and whose girth is 100 Aṅgulas—[17]the middling and the lowest being successively one-fifth less.

[18]The ration* for the finest type of horse is two Droṇas of Śāli-rice, Vrīhi-rice, barley, or panic grain, half dry or half cooked, or a porridge (2.15.33 n.) of Mudga-beans or Māṣa-beans; a Prastha of fat; five Palas of salt; 50 Palas of meat (2.29.43 n.); an Āḍhaka of juice or double that amount of curd to moisten the lumps; a Prastha of liquor (2.29.43 n.) with five Palas of sugar or twice that amount of milk as a stimulating drink (2.25.10 n.). [19]In order to make them eat, horses that are tired after a long journey or after pulling a heavy load should be given a Prastha of fat as an enema, a Kuḍuba of fat for the nose, half a load (2.29.43 n.) of green fodder, double that amount of grass, or a bundle of grass six Aratnis in circumference. [20]One-quarter successively less than that should be given to the middling and the lowest. [21]A chariot horse and a stallion of the middling type get the same ration as the finest type of horse, [22]and those of the lowest type get the same as the middling type of horse. [23]One-quarter less than that is the ration for mares and mules; [24]and half of the latter for foals. [25]That is the scheme of rations.

[26]Those who cook the rations, those who hold the reins, and the doctors are obliged to taste the food.

[27]Horses unable to work due to war, sickness, or old age should receive sufficient food to maintain themselves. [28]Those that are unfit for battle should be employed as stallions to service mares for the benefit of people in the cities and the countryside.

[29]Of those fit for battle, the best are those bred in Kamboja, Sindhu, Āraṭṭa, and Vanāyu;* the middling are those bred in Bāhlīka, Pāpeya,

Sauvīra, and Titala; the rest are the lowest. [30]According to whether their dispositions are ardent, gentle, or sluggish, he should assign them to activities relating to the military or to transportation.

[31]The military activity of a horse is comprehensive.*

[32]Gallop, canter, leap, trot, and response to signals are the movements of a riding horse. [33]Among these, the gallop consists of *upaveṇuka, vardhamānaka, yamaka, ālīḍhapluta, pr̥thuga,* and *tūpacālī.** [34]The same, when the head and ears remain unaffected, is canter; or else, it has 16 gaits. [35]The gaits of canter are *prakīrṇaka, prakīrṇottara, niṣaṇṇa, pārśvānuvr̥tta, ūrmimārga, śarabhakrīḍita, śarabhapluta, tritāla, bāhyānuvr̥tta, pañcapāṇi, siṃhāyata, svādhūta, kliṣṭa, ślingita, br̥ṃhita,* and *puṣpābhikīrṇa.* [36]The types of leaping are monkey-leap, frog-leap, one-leap,* one-foot-leap, cuckoo-gait, chest-motion, and crane-gait. [37]The types of trotting are heron-gait, heron's-gait-on-water, peacock-gait, half-peacock-gait, mongoose-gait, half-mongoose-gait, boar-gait, and half-boar-gait. [38]Response to signals is acting in accordance with cues.

[39]The journey* of a chariot horse is six, nine, or 12 Yojanas, while that of a riding horse is five, seven and a half, or ten Yojanas. [40]The gaits are stride, gentle-breath-gait, and load-carrying-gait, [41]while the speeds are stride, gallop, leap, semi-fast, and fast.

[42]The training masters should give directions concerning their fastenings and equipment and the charioteers concerning the military trappings of chariot horses. [43]Horse veterinarians should provide remedies for the decrease or increase in body weight and food appropriate for each season.

[44]Those who hold the reins, tie the horses, give green fodder, cook the rations, guard the stalls, and groom the hair, and experts in the cure of poisons should take care of the horses according to their respective tasks. [45]And if any of them neglects his tasks, moreover, he should deduct a day's wages. [46]If someone rides a horse kept locked up for the rite of lustration* or on the orders of the veterinarian, he is to be fined 12 Paṇas. [47]In case a sickness becomes worse because treatment or medicine was delayed, the fine is twice the amount spent for the cure. [48]If because of their fault something unfortunate happens,* the fine is the price of the animal.

[49]This also explains what pertains to a herd of cows, as also to donkeys, camels, and buffaloes, and to goats and sheep.

> [50]He should have the horses bathed twice a day and given perfume and garlands. On new-moon days, oblations to spirits

should be offered, and on full-moon days, the proclamation of blessings (see 2.32.21).

[51]Devoted to pacificatory rites, he should have the lustration rite performed on the ninth day of Āśvayuja (September-October), at the beginning or end of an expedition, or during a sickness.

THAT CONCLUDES THE THIRTIETH CHAPTER: "SUPERINTENDENT OF HORSES" OF THE SECOND BOOK: "ON THE ACTIVITIES OF SUPERINTENDENTS."

Chapter 31

Topic 48: Superintendent of Elephants

[1]The Superintendent of Elephants should provide for the following: the protection of the elephant forests; stables, stalls, and places for lying down for male and female elephants and cubs that are under training or capable of work; the amount of work, rations, and green fodder assigned for them; allotting of work to them; their fastenings and equipment; their military trappings; and the retinue of attendants such as veterinarians and elephant trainers.*

[2]He should have a stable constructed, a stable whose height, width, and length are twice the length of an elephant; that has additional stalls for female elephants, an entrance hall, and a "princess" configuration;* and that faces the east or the north. [3]He should have each stall constructed square in shape with each side the length of an elephant, a stall that is equipped with a smooth tying post and a floor made of smooth planks, and that has an outlet for urine and excrement. [4]He should have a place for lying down that is the same in size as a stall but half as high prepared, within the fort for military and transport elephants, and outside the fort for elephants under training and for vicious elephants.

[5]Within the eightfold division of a day (1.19.7), the first and the seventh are the times for bathing, and immediately thereafter for feeding. [6]The time for exercise is the forenoon, and the time for the stimulating drink (2.25.10 n.) is the afternoon. [7]Two parts of the night are for sleeping, while a third part is for lying down and getting up.*

[8]The time for capturing elephants is the summer. [9]A 20-year-old should be captured, [10]while cubs, ones with small tusks, ones without tusks, the sick, and female elephants that are pregnant or suckling should not be captured.*

[11]The best is a 40-year-old elephant measuring seven Aratnis in height and nine in length,* with a girth of ten; the middling* is a 30-year-old one; and the lowest* is a 25-year-old one. [12]The rations for the latter two are successively one-quarter less.

[13]Per Aratni, the ration* is one Droṇa of rice kernels, half an Āḍhaka of oil, three Prasthas of ghee, ten Palas of salt, 50 Palas of meat (2.29.43 n.), one Āḍhaka of juice or twice that amount of curd to moisten the lumps, one Āḍhaka of liquor (2.29.43 n.) or double that amount of milk along with ten Palas of sugar as a stimulating drink, one Prastha of oil for anointing the limbs, one-eighth of that for the head and for the lamp, two and a quarter loads (2.29.43 n.) of green fodder, two and a half loads of dry grass, and an unlimited amount of leaves. [14]Outside the time of rut, an eight-Aratni elephant gets the same amount of food as a seven-Aratni one. [15]The remaining types of elephant, namely, the six-Aratni and the five-Aratni, are treated according to their measurement in Hastas.*

[16]In order to play with, one may capture a cub, feeding it milk and green fodder.

[17]The appearances* are as follows: emergence of redness, being covered, sides that have become smooth, even girth, flesh evenly distributed, with even back muscles,* and having a trough formed.

> [18]To a gentle and a sluggish one, as also to an animal with mixed characteristics, he should give exercise (by employing them) in various tasks in accordance with either their appearance or the season.

THAT CONCLUDES THE THIRTY-FIRST CHAPTER: "SUPERINTENDENT OF ELEPHANTS" OF THE SECOND BOOK: "ON THE ACTIVITIES OF SUPERINTENDENTS."

Chapter 32

Topic 48a: Activities of Elephants

[1]There are four who are mainly devoted to work:* trainee, war elephant, riding elephant, and vicious elephant.

[2]Of these, trainees are of five kinds:* one becoming accustomed to someone getting on its shoulders, one becoming accustomed to being tied to the post, one becoming accustomed to water,* one becoming

accustomed to pits,* and one becoming accustomed to the herd. [3]Its preparatory regimen consists of the activities of a cub.*

[4]The war elephant has seven types of activities (2.32.2 n.): standing in attendance, walking around, marching together, killing and trampling, battling elephants, attacking cities, and engaging in warfare.* [5]Its preparatory regimen consists of putting on the girth and the neck chain, and activities of the elephant corps.

[6]Riding elephants are of eight kinds (2.32.2 n.): one that is led, one that can be ridden only with the help of another elephant, one that trots, one that uses various gaits,* one that can be ridden only with the help of a stick, one that can be ridden only with the help of a goad, one that can be ridden without any help, and one that is used in hunting. [7]Its preparatory regimen consists of autumnal work, inferior work,* and responding to signals.

[8–9]The vicious elephant has just one type of activity. Its preparatory regimen consists of keeping it under restraint and guarding it individually. It is one that is apprehensive, obstinate,* erratic, and in rut; one whose rut is diagnosed; and one the cause of whose inebriation is diagnosed.* [10]A vicious elephant that is lost to all activities may be simple, firmly resolved, erratic, and vitiated by all the defects.*

[11]Their fastenings and equipment fall under the authority of the elephant trainer. [12]The fastenings consist of tying post, neck chain, girth, stirrup ropes, foot chain, upper chain, and the like. [13]The equipment consists of goad, bamboo, mechanical device,* and the like. [14]The ornaments consist of Vaijayantī-garland, Kṣurapra-necklace, covering, blanket, and the like. [15]The military ornaments consist of armor, lance, quiver, mechanical device, and the like.

[16]The retinue of attendants consists of veterinarian, trainer, mahout, groom, guard, decorator, cook, feeder, foot restrainer, stall guard, sleep attendant, and the like. [17]The veterinarian, the stall guard, and the cook should each receive one Prastha of boiled rice, one Prasṛti of fat, and two Palas of sugar and salt; and, except the veterinarians, also ten Palas of meat.* [18]Veterinarians should treat elephants suffering as a result of a journey, sickness, work, rut, or old age.

[19]These are the occasions for imposing a penalty: keeping the stall unclean, not giving green fodder, making an elephant sleep on bare ground, striking it on an improper area, letting someone else ride on it, making it travel at an improper time or on unsuitable ground, taking it to water at a place that is not a ford, and letting it go into a thicket of trees. [20]He should deduct this from their rations and wages.

[21]Three lustrations (2.30.46 n.) should be performed at the junctures of the four-month seasons,* and offerings to spirits on new-moon days and to Senānī* on full-moon days (2.30.50). [22]Leaving aside a length equal to twice the circumference at the root of the tusk, he should cut the tusks every two and a half years in the case of those born near rivers and every five years in the case of those inhabiting mountain regions.

THAT CONCLUDES THE THIRTY-SECOND CHAPTER: "ACTIVITIES OF ELEPHANTS" WITHIN "SUPERINTENDENT OF ELEPHANTS" OF THE SECOND BOOK: "ON THE ACTIVITIES OF SUPERINTENDENTS."

Chapter 33

Topic 49: Superintendent of Chariots

[1]The discussion of the Superintendent of Horses explains also what pertains to the Superintendent of Chariots. [2]He should have factories for chariots constructed.

[3]Ten-man* high with a 12-man interior is a standard chariot. [4]When the interior is reduced successively by one-man up to a six-man interior, we obtain seven kinds of chariot.

[5]He should have these kinds of chariots built: chariots for gods, festive chariots, ones for military use, ones for travel, ones for assaulting an enemy city, and ones for training purposes.

[6]He should have a thorough knowledge of the arrangements of bows, javelins, armor, and equipment, and the assignment of charioteers, chariot attendants, and chariot horses to various activities, as well as giving rations and wages to both servants and non-servants* until the completion of the tasks, providing exercise and protection to them, and regaling them with gifts and honor.

Topic 50: Superintendent of the Infantry

[7]The above explains also what pertains to the Superintendent of the Infantry. [8]He should have a thorough knowledge of the following: the strengths and weaknesses of hereditary, hired, corporate, ally's, enemy's, and tribal troops;* military operations carried out in water and on land, openly and in secret, in trenches and in the open, and during day and night (7.10.34–37); and the deployment and non-deployment* in various tasks.

Topic 51: Activities of the Chief of the Armed Forces

[9]The Chief of the Armed Forces—trained in the science of every kind of warfare and weaponry and a renowned expert in riding elephants, horses, and chariots—should have a thorough knowledge of the very same things, as well as of the management of the activities carried out by the four divisions of the army.* [10]He should keep an eye out for the terrain suitable for his side,* the proper time for war, configuring the right counter array, breaking through unbroken ranks (10.4.14–15), closing up broken ranks, breaking through compact ranks, destroying broken ranks, destroying a fort, and the proper time to start a military expedition.

> [11]Devoted to the training of the troops, he should arrange signals for the different arrays using musical instruments, standards, and flags when the army is stationary, on the march, and on the attack.

THAT CONCLUDES THE THIRTY-THIRD CHAPTER: "SUPERINTENDENT OF CHARIOTS," "SUPERINTENDENT OF THE INFANTRY," AND "ACTIVITIES OF THE CHIEF OF THE ARMED FORCES" OF THE SECOND BOOK: "ON THE ACTIVITIES OF SUPERINTENDENTS."

Chapter 34

Topic 52: Superintendent of Passes

[1]The Superintendent of Passes should give a pass for payment of one Māṣaka.

[2]Only someone who possesses a sealed pass should be authorized to enter or to exit the countryside. [3]A person living in the countryside without a sealed pass should pay 12 Paṇas. [4]In the case of a forged seal, the punishment is the lowest seizure fine (2.1.29 n.); for one not belonging to the countryside, the highest fine.

Topic 53: Superintendent of Pasture Land

[5]The Superintendent of Pasture Land should check the sealed pass.

[6]He should, moreover, establish pasture land between villages.* [7]He should rid the marshy lands and the wild tracts of the dangers posed by thieves and vicious animals.

[8]In areas lacking water, he should construct wells, reservoirs, and springs, as well as flower gardens and fruit orchards.

[9]Fowlers and hunters should patrol the wild tracts. [10]At the approach of robbers or enemies, they should sound an alarm with conchs or drums, without letting themselves be caught either by climbing on to hills or trees or by using a swift conveyance.*

[11]He should, moreover, communicate to the king the movement of enemies and forest tribes by sending sealed letters through homing pigeons or by means of a series of fires sending smoke signals.

> [12]He should get the following carried out: maintenance of those in the produce and elephant forests, road tolls, defense against thieves, escorting caravans, protecting cattle, and trade.

THAT CONCLUDES THE THIRTY-FOURTH CHAPTER: "SUPERINTENDENT OF PASSES" AND "SUPERINTENDENT OF PASTURE LAND" OF THE SECOND BOOK: "ON THE ACTIVITIES OF SUPERINTENDENTS."

Chapter 35

Topic 54: Activities of the Collector

[1]The Collector, after dividing the countryside into four, should make a record of the total number of villages classified into best, middling, and lowest, stating which is exempt from tax, which supplies soldiers, and which provides grain, farm animals, money, forest produce, labor, or counter-levy (2.29.1, 5), and how much.

[2]Under his supervision, a Revenue Officer should look after a five-village unit or a ten-village unit. [3]He should have a written record made of the total number of villages according to their boundary limits,* and the total number of fields by enumerating the plowed and unplowed fields, dry and wetlands, parks, vegetable plots, flower gardens and orchards (2.24.28 n.), forests, buildings, sanctuaries, temples, reservoirs, cemeteries, rest houses (7.15.22 n.), water-dispensing sheds, holy places, pasture lands, and roads. In accordance with that, he should, with reference to the boundaries and the fields,* have a written record made of the dimensions of the borders, wild tracts, and roads, and of grants, sales, favors, and tax-exemptions, as well as of the houses, enumerating which ones pay taxes and which are tax-exempt, [4]and stating—in them, there are so many who belong to the four social classes; so many who are farmers, cowherds, traders, artisans, workers, and slaves; there are so many who are two-footed and four-footed;

and this is the money, labor, duty, and fines accruing from them. [5]With regard to men and women of the families, furthermore, he should find out how many are children and old people, what their occupations and customs are, and the amount of their earnings and expenditures.

[6]In the same manner, furthermore, the County Supervisor should look after one-quarter of the countryside.*

[7]In the offices of the Revenue Officers and County Supervisors, Magistrates should carry out their duties and the collection of tributes.*

Topic 55: Secret Agents Working Undercover as Householders, Traders, and Ascetics

[8]Agents appointed by the Collector and working undercover as householders, moreover, should find out the total number of fields, houses, and families located in the villages to which they have been assigned—fields in terms of size and output, houses in terms of benefits and exemptions,* and families in terms of class and occupation. [9]They should also find out the number of individuals in them and their incomes and expenditures (2.36.3). [10]They should also find out the reason for leaving or for stopping over in the case of those who have gone away or arrived and of pernicious men and women, as well as the activities of informants.

[11]Agents working undercover as traders, likewise, should find out the quantity and the value of king's goods originating in his own country and produced in pit mines, reservoirs, forests, factories, and fields. [12]In the case of goods of high and low value originating in other lands and transported by water and land routes—and with respect to activities*—they should find out the amount of duty, road toll, escort charges, payments to security stations, ferry tolls, payments to employees, taxes, rations, and royal gifts (2.16.18 n.).

[13]Likewise, agents appointed by the Collector and working undercover as ascetics should find out the honesty or dishonesty of farmers, cowherds, and traders, as well as of superintendents. [14]Their apprentices, moreover, operating undercover as veteran thieves in sanctuaries, crossroads, deserted spots, wells, rivers, ponds, fords, temple precincts, hermitages, wild tracts, hills, woods, and thickets, should discover the purpose for the entry, residence, and exit of thieves and of eminent warriors of enemies.

> [15]Exerting himself in this manner, the Collector should look after
> the countryside. Those clandestine establishments also should

look after it, as also other clandestine establishments having specific origins of their own.*

THAT CONCLUDES THE THIRTY-FIFTH CHAPTER: "ACTIVITIES OF THE COLLECTOR" AND "SECRET AGENTS WORKING UNDERCOVER AS HOUSEHOLDERS, TRADERS, AND ASCETICS" OF THE SECOND BOOK: "ON THE ACTIVITIES OF SUPERINTENDENTS."

Chapter 36

Topic 56: Regimen of the City Manager

[1]Just like the Collector, the City Manager should look after the city, [2]while a Revenue Officer should look after a unit of ten households, 20 households, or 40 households (2.35.1–2). [3]The latter should find out the number of individual men and women within each unit in terms of their castes, lineages, names, and occupations, as well as their incomes and expenditures.

[4]In like manner, a County Supervisor should look after one-quarter section* of a fort.

[5]Those in charge of religious rest houses should give lodgings to members of religious orders and travelers after informing the authorities, and to recluses and Vedic scholars on simply their own assessment.*

[6]Craftsmen and artisans should provide lodgings to their colleagues in their own workplaces, and traders should give lodgings to each other in their own workplaces. [7]They should inform on anyone who sells commodities at unauthorized places and times or without proof of ownership.

[8]Vendors of liquor, cooked meat, and boiled rice, and prostitutes should provide lodgings to people well known to them. [9]They should inform on anyone who incurs extravagant expenditures or engages in reckless activities.

[10]A physician who informs the Revenue Officer or the County Supervisor about a man who has made him treat a wound secretly or has done something pernicious is to be released—and so would a head of household; otherwise he becomes guilty of the same crime. [11]He should also inform on anyone who departs or arrives; otherwise he becomes guilty of a night offense;* [12]on secure nights,* he should pay three Paṇas.

[13]Secret agents deployed on roads and in roadless tracts should arrest anyone with a wound, carrying harmful tools, hiding behind a package, agitated, overcome by intense sleep, or tired from travel, or any stranger within or outside the city, in temples, holy places, woods, and cemeteries.

[14]Likewise, inside the city they should carry out searches in empty houses, workshops, taverns, places for selling boiled rice and cooked meat, gambling halls, and residences of religious orders.

[15]In the summer, moreover, there should be safeguards against fire. [16]During the two middle quarters* of the day, the fine for lighting a fire is one-eighth (of a Paṇa). [17]Alternatively, people should do their cooking outdoors. [18]For not keeping ready five jars,* as well as a pot, trough, ladder, ax, winnow, hook, "hair-grabber,"* and water skin, the fine is a quarter (Paṇa). [19]He* should remove all coverings of grass or thatch. [20]He should have people whose occupation involves fire live together in one area.

[21]Heads of household should reside near the main entrances to their houses, without roaming together at night.

[22]Collections of water jars in their thousands should be positioned along streets, and also at crossroads, gates, and royal precincts.

[23]If the head of a household does not run to a house on fire, he is fined 12 Paṇas; a tenant, six Paṇas. [24]When houses catch fire through negligence, the fine is 54 Paṇas. [25]An arsonist should be executed by burning.

[26]For throwing dirt in a street, the fine is one-eighth (of a Paṇa).; for obstructing the flow of dirty water, a quarter (Paṇa). —[27]if it is done on a royal highway, the fine is doubled. [28]For voiding excrement in a holy site, a place for water, a temple, or a royal precinct, the fine is one Paṇa successively increased* by one Paṇa; for voiding urine, the fines are halved. [29]If this is caused by medicine, sickness, or fear, they should not be fined.

[30]For discarding a dead cat, dog, mongoose, or snake within the city, the fine is three Paṇas; a dead donkey, camel, mule, horse, or farm animal, six Paṇas; and a dead human being, 50 Paṇas. [31]For changing the route and for taking a corpse out through a gate other than the gate for taking out corpses, the punishment is the lowest seizure fine (2.1.29 n.); [32]and the gatekeepers are fined 200 Paṇas. [33]For depositing or cremating a corpse in a place other than the cemetery, the fine is 12 Paṇas.

[34]The instrument for signaling a watch* shall be sounded six Nālikās* after the beginning and before the end of the night. [35]When the instrument has sounded, the punishment for moving about during curfew near the king's residence during the first and the last watch is one and a quarter Paṇas; during the middle watch, it is double that; and for moving outside,* it is four times that.

[36]He should question anyone arrested in a suspicious place, with a suspicious mark, or because of a previous offense. [37]For approaching the royal

precincts and for climbing the city defenses, the punishment is the middle seizure fine (2.1.29 n.). [38]People moving about on account of childbirth, to get a physician, because of a death, with a lamp, in a carriage, when the City Manager has sounded the instrument,* to see a show, or because of a fire, as also those carrying a sealed pass, are not subject to arrest.

[39]During nights of free movement, people wearing secretive or incongruous attire,* renouncers, and people carrying clubs or weapons should be punished in accordance with their offense.

[40]For restricting the movement of someone who should not be restricted and for not restricting someone who should be restricted, the guards are subject to a fine double that for movement during curfew. [41]For molestation, they should be assessed the lowest seizure fine (2.1.29 n.) in the case of a slave woman; the middle fine in the case of a non-slave women; the highest fine in the case of a woman kept confined;* and execution in the case of a woman from a respectable family.

[42]For not reporting an offense committed deliberately or accidentally at night, the City Manager should be assessed a fine proportionate to the offense; so also in case of negligence.* [43]He should keep under constant watch places for water, roads, drainage ditches, clandestine passages,* ramparts, walls, and fortifications, and keep safe what has been lost or forgotten, or what has run away.*

[44]Children, old people, the sick, and the helpless, moreover, are released from prison on the day of the birth constellation* and on full-moon days. [45]Pious men or individuals belonging to a group governed by conventions* may pay a ransom for an offense.

> [46]Every day or every fifth day, he should discharge the prisoners
> through bonded manual labor* or monetary compensation.
> [47]Release of prisoners is decreed when new territory is acquired,
> at the anointing of the Crown Prince, and at the birth of a son.

THAT CONCLUDES THE THIRTY-SIXTH CHAPTER: "REGIMEN OF THE CITY MANAGER" OF THE SECOND BOOK: "ON THE ACTIVITIES OF SUPERINTENDENTS."

THAT CONCLUDES THE SECOND BOOK: "ON THE ACTIVITIES OF SUPERINTENDENTS" OF KAUṬILYA'S *ARTHAŚĀSTRA*.

Book Three

On Justices

Chapter 1

Topic 57: Enunciation of Transactions

[1]Justices* of ministerial rank* in groups of three* should conduct trials—in frontier posts, collection centers, district municipalities, and provincial capitals*—of lawsuits arising from transactions.*

[2]They should invalidate transactions carried out in absentia* and those executed inside a house, at night, in the wilderness, by fraud, or in secret. [3]Both the person executing it and the person who gets it executed receive the lowest seizure fine (2.1.29 n.); [4]each of the witnesses individually receives half that fine. [5]Those taking part in good faith, however, forfeit the object.*

[6]Transactions carried out in absentia shall be valid when a debt is secured with an absent pledge or when they are viewed as not blameworthy. [7]Transactions executed inside a house shall be valid when they are connected with inheritance, consignments, deposits,* and marriage or contracted by secluded women (4.13.32 n.) and sick persons of sound mind. [8]Transactions executed at night shall be valid when they are connected with forcible seizure, trespass,* brawl, marriage, and royal command, and when they are contracted by individuals carrying out business in the early part of the night.* [9]Transactions executed in the wilderness shall be valid when they are done by people moving about in the wilderness amidst caravans, herds, hermitages, hunters, and bards. [10]Transactions executed by fraud, moreover, shall be valid when they are among individuals with secret occupations (4.4); [11]and transactions executed in secret shall be valid when they are done within a secret association.*

[12]Transactions other than these shall not be valid,* as also those executed by dependents, by a son living with his father, by a father living with his son, by a brother excluded from the family, by a younger son who is a coparcener, by a woman living with her husband or son,* by a slave or a person given as a pledge,* by one who is below or beyond the legal age,* and by a notorious criminal,* renouncer, cripple, or someone who has fallen on hard times—except when they have been appointed to execute the transaction.

[13]Even in such cases,* transactions executed by a person who is enraged, deeply afflicted, intoxicated, insane, or under someone else's control* shall not be valid. [14]Those who execute such transactions, those who get them executed, and those who act as witnesses should be individually assessed the prescribed fine (3.1.3).

[15]In each respective group,* however, all transactions shall be valid when they are executed at the proper place and time, by someone with proof of ownership (3.16.17–18), observing all the formalities, with valid documentation (3.1.19), and noting down the appearance, distinctive marks, quantity, and quality. [16]And among these, the last document should be trusted, except in the case of a directive or a pledge.*

That concludes the "Enunciation of Transactions."

Topic 58: Writing Down the Grounds for Litigation*

[17]He* should first write down the year, the season, the month, the fortnight, the day, the Karaṇa,* the court, and the debt, as also the region, village, caste, lineage, name, and occupation of the plaintiff and the defendant, after they have provided competent sureties. Then he should record the interrogations of the plaintiff and the defendant according to the sequence of topics; [18]and he should review* what he has recorded.

[19]The man casts aside the plaint as recorded and moves on to another plaint; does not make a point made subsequently accord with what was stated previously; after challenging an unchallengeable statement of the opponent, remains obstinate; promises to produce a document (*deśa*), but when told, "Produce it," does not produce it, or produces a defective document (*hīnadeśa*) or something that does not constitute documentary evidence (*adeśa*);* puts forward a document (*deśa*) different from the document (*deśa*) specified; denies a significant statement in the document (*deśa*) he has put forward, saying, "It is not so"; does not accept what has been ascertained through witnesses; secretly carries on a discussion with

witnesses with regard to a document (*deśa*) that is prohibited from being discussed*—these are the reasons for loss of suit.

[20]The fine for loss of suit is one-fifth of the amount.* [21]The fine for voluntary admission is one-tenth of the amount.*

[22]Wages for the men* are one-eighth.* [23]Provisions for travel are assessed according to the prevailing prices. [24]The losing party has to pay both these.

[25]An accused shall not bring a countersuit, except in the case of a brawl, a forcible seizure, a caravan, and an association.* [26]An accused, furthermore, cannot be subjected to another lawsuit.

[27]If, after receiving a response,* the plaintiff does not offer a reply on that very day, he loses the case; [28]for it is the plaintiff who made the decision with regard to the lawsuit, not the defendant. [29]If the latter does not offer a reply, he may be allowed three or seven days. [30]Thereafter, he should fine the man a minimum of three Paṇas and a maximum of 12 Paṇas. [31]If he does not offer a reply after three fortnights, he should impose the fine for loss of suit, and pay the plaintiff's claim from whatever property the defendant may possess, with the exception of the tools of his trade. [32]He should do the very same to a defendant who absconds.* [33]The plaintiff loses the case the moment he absconds; [34]if he is dead or has fallen on hard times, upon the testimony of witnesses.*

[35]When the man is a pauper, the plaintiff may pay the fine and get work done by him.* [36]Or he* may, if he so wishes, provide a pledge. [37]Or else, guarded by the demon-killing rite, he should be forced to make payment through labor, with the exception of a Brāhmaṇa.*

> [38]Because he secures the proper conduct of the people consisting of the four social classes and four orders of life, at a time when all Laws are perishing, the king is the promoter of Law.
>
> [39]Law, convention, custom, and royal edict: these are the four feet of the subject of a legal dispute; each succeeding one countermands each preceding one.*
>
> [40]Among these, Law rests on truth, convention on witnesses, and custom on the consensus of people, while royal edict is a king's command.*
>
> [41]The Law proper to the king leads him to heaven when he protects his subjects according to Law; the reverse awaits him when he fails to protect or inflicts improper punishment.

[42]For punishment alone protects this world and the next when the king dispenses it evenly to both his son and his enemy according to the offense.

[43]When he renders verdicts* according to Law, convention, canon,* and, fourthly, edict, he will conquer the earth up to its four ends.

[44]When, with regard to a lawsuit, the law treatise contradicts a canon or the conventional treatise,* he should decide the case according to Law.*

[45]When the treatise* is contradicted by any edict with regard to Law, on that matter the edict is authoritative; for there the text is nullified.

[46]An evident offense, voluntary admission, being candid in questioning with respect to one's side and to the opponent's side, reasoning, and oath are ways of proving a case.

[47]When there is a contradiction between earlier and later statements, when the witnesses are proved to be reprehensible, and when someone escapes from the custody of the guards, one should declare the loss of the suit.

THAT CONCLUDES THE FIRST CHAPTER: "ENUNCIATION OF TRANSACTIONS" AND "WRITING DOWN THE GROUNDS FOR LITIGATION" OF THE THIRD BOOK: "ON JUSTICES."

Chapter 2

Topic 59: Matters Relating to Marriage

Topic 59a: Law of Marriage

[1]Transactions presuppose marriage* (1.15.2; 2.8.1; 8.1.23–53).

[2]Brāhma marriage is the gift of a girl after adorning her; [3]Prājāpatya is jointly fulfilling the Law; [4]Ārṣa results from the receipt of a pair of cattle; [5]Daiva results from the gift of her to the officiating priest within the sacrificial enclosure; [6]Gāndharva results from a secret union;* [7]Āsura results from the receipt of the bride price; [8]Rākṣasa results from forcible seizure; [9]and Paiśāca results from the seizure of a sleeping or intoxicated girl.*

[10]The first four are in keeping with the Law when they are sanctioned by the father; the others when they are sanctioned by both the mother and the father, [11]for these two take their daughter's bride price, or one of them in the absence of the other. [12]The second bride price* should be taken by the woman. [13]In all of them, it is not forbidden to shower her out of affection.*

That concludes the Law of marriage.

Topic 59b: Rules regarding Woman's Property

[14]Woman's property* consists of livelihood or ornaments. [15]Livelihood is an endowment with a maximum of 2,000 Paṇas. There is no limit on ornaments.

[16]The wife incurs no fault if she uses it to support a son or a daughter-in-law and when the husband has gone away without providing for her support; nor does the husband if he uses it for countermeasures against bandits, sickness, famine, and dangers or for obligations relating to Law; nor the couple if they use it jointly after they have produced a son and a daughter. [17]When it has been used for three years in the most righteous forms of marriages,* moreover, he should not subject it to an inquiry.* [18]When it has been used within a Gāndharva or Āsura marriage, the husband should be forced to return both* with interest. When it has been used in a Rākṣasa or Paiśāca marriage, he should pay the penalty for theft.*

[19]When the husband has died, if the wife desires to dedicate herself to the Law, she should receive immediately the endowment and ornaments, as well as the remainder of the bride price.* [20]If, on the other hand, after receiving them she gets remarried, she should be forced to return both with interest. [21]If she desires a family, however, at the time of her remarriage, she should receive what was given to her by her father-in-law and husband.* [22]We shall explain the time for remarriage in "Long Absence from Home" (3.4.39–41). [23]If, on the other hand, she remarries against the wishes of her father-in-law, she loses what was given to her by her father-in-law and her husband.

[24]When a woman has been taken from the custody of her relatives, the relatives should return all she had received.* [25]When she has remarried according to the proper rules, the person who marries her must protect her woman's property.

[26]When a woman remarries, she shall lose the inheritance from her husband;* [27]but a woman who dedicates herself to the Law* can make use of it. [28]If a woman who has sons remarries, she loses her woman's

property; [29]and her sons shall take that woman's property of hers. [30]Alternatively, a woman who gets married to maintain her sons should augment it for the sake of her sons.

[31]When she has sons from several husbands, she should allocate to each son the woman's property according to what was given by his own father. [32]A woman who has remarried should allocate to her sons even the woman's property that she can dispose of as she pleases.

[33]A sonless woman who faithfully guards her husband's bed may use her woman's property until her death, remaining close to her elders; [34]for woman's property is intended for a time of adversity. [35]After her death, it shall go to her heirs.

[36]If a woman dies while her husband is still alive, her woman's property should be partitioned by her sons and daughters; if she has no son, by her daughters; and if there are no daughters, by her husband. [37]Her relatives should take her bride price, what she has received subsequent to her marriage, or whatever else has been given by her relatives.

That concludes the rules regarding woman's property.

Topic 59c: Compensation for Supersession

[38]A man should wait for eight years if his wife does not produce offspring, does not have a son, or is barren; for ten years, if her offspring are stillborn; and for 12 years, if she gives birth only to girls. [39]Thereafter, desiring a son, he may marry a second wife. [40]If he violates this, he should give* the bride price, the woman's property, and half the compensation for supersession,* as well as a fine not to exceed 24 Paṇas.

[41]After giving her the bride price and woman's property—and, in the case of a woman who has no bride price or woman's property, a compensation for supersession equal to that—as well as appropriate maintenance, he may marry even many wives; [42]for the purpose of women is sons.*

[43]When their menstrual periods coincide, moreover, he should have sexual relations according to the marriage, or with the wife he married earlier, or with the wife who has living sons.* [44]For concealing menstruation and for not having sex at the time of menstruation,* the fine is 96 Paṇas.

[45]He should not have sex with a wife who has borne a son, who desires to pursue the Law, who is barren, whose offspring are stillborn, or who has reached menopause, if she is unwilling. [46]A husband, moreover, is not obliged to have sex with a wife who has leprosy or who is insane, if

he is unwilling. [47]A wife, on the other hand, should have sex even with a husband of that sort for the sake of a son.*

> [48]A husband who has become degraded, who has gone to a foreign country, who has committed an offense against the king, who is a danger to her life, or who has fallen from his caste may be abandoned; so also a husband who is impotent.

THAT CONCLUDES THE SECOND CHAPTER: "LAW OF MARRIAGE," "RULES REGARDING WOMAN'S PROPERTY," AND "COMPENSATION FOR SUPERSESSION" WITHIN "MATTERS RELATING TO MARRIAGE" OF THE THIRD BOOK: "ON JUSTICES."

Chapter 3

Topic 59d: Obedience

[1]A woman 12 years old has reached the age for legal transactions,* as also a man 16 years old. [2]Thereafter, in the case of disobedience, for a woman the fine is 12 Paṇas; for a man, double that amount.

That concludes obedience.*

Topic 59e: Alimony

[3]When a time for the payment of alimony has not been fixed, he should give an amount sufficient for food and clothing or in excess of that, according to the retinue of people (1.16.5 n.) or even more.* [4]If the time has been fixed, after calculating the same, he should provide a security;* [5]so also if she has not been given the bride price, woman's property, and compensation for supersession.

[6]If she has moved into at her father-in-law's family, or if she lives separately after receiving her share of the estate, the husband cannot be sued.

That concludes alimony.

Topic 59f: Assault

[7]Instilling proper conduct should be carried out without using the following language: "You doomed wench! You ruined wench! You cripple! You fatherless wench! You motherless wench!" [8]Or she may be beaten on the back three times with one of these: a bamboo strip, a piece of rope, and the hand. [9]For violating this, the fine is half that for verbal or physical assault

(3.18–19). [10]The same applies to a wife vis-à-vis her husband, a wife who is a well-known offender and who is jealous.* [11](When it is done) on excursions outside the house or by the doors, the penalty is as laid down.*

That concludes assault.

Topic 59g: Hatred

[12]When a wife who hates her husband does not adorn herself* for seven menstrual periods, she should surrender right then her endowment and ornaments (3.2.14–15) and consent to her husband sleeping with another woman.

[13]Alternatively, if the husband hates his wife, he should consent to her staying alone in the household of any one of these: a female religious mendicant, a guardian,* and a relative.[14]When he has cheated with regard to sexual intercourse and there is clear evidence of this or it has been discovered through a female spy of the same social class,* and he lies about it, he should pay 12 Paṇas.

[15]A wife who hates her husband should not be granted a divorce from him if he is unwilling, or a husband from his wife. [16]Mutual hatred is grounds for divorce. [17]Alternatively, if the man seeks a divorce because of an offense by the woman, she should give him what she has taken. [18]If, on the other hand, the woman seeks a divorce because of an offense by the man, she should not give him what she has taken.* [19]There is no divorce in marriages contracted in keeping with the Law (3.2.10).

That concludes hatred.

Topic 59h: Wrongdoing

[20]A wife who, although forbidden, arrogantly entertains herself with liquor should pay a fine of three Paṇas. [21]For going during the day to a women's show or excursion, the fine is six Paṇas, and for going to a men's show or excursion, 12 Paṇas; [22]double that if it is done at night.

[23]For going away when the husband is sleeping or drunk, and for not opening the door to him, the fine is 12 Paṇas; [24]double that for going out at night.

[25]When a woman and a man, intending to have sexual intercourse, make indecent movements of their limbs or secretly engage in lewd conversation, the fine for the woman is 24 Paṇas; double that for the man. [26]For caressing the hair, the knot of the lower garment, teeth, or nails, the lowest seizure fine (2.1.29 n.);* double that for the man.

[27]For carrying on a conversation in a suspicious place, moreover, lashes are substituted for the Paṇas.* [28]For women, a Caṇḍāla should give five

lashes between the shoulders in the middle of the village; [29]or she may redeem herself by paying one Paṇa for each stroke.

That concludes wrongdoing.

Topic 59i: Prohibition of Gifts and Transactions

[30]When a woman and a man, although forbidden, give gifts to each other, the fine is 12 Paṇas if they consist of small articles; 24 Paṇas, if they consist of large articles; and 54 Paṇas, if they consist of money or gold*—double that for the man. [31]These same, when they are between two who are forbidden to have sex with each other,* carry half those fines, as also in the case of transactions with forbidden men.*

That concludes prohibition.

> [32]By enmity to the king and by wrongdoing, as also by going away
> on her own, a woman loses ownership of her woman's property,
> what she has brought, and her bride price.

THAT CONCLUDES THE THIRD CHAPTER: "OBEDIENCE," "ALIMONY," "ASSAULT," "HATRED," "WRONGDOING," AND "PROHIBITION OF GIFTS AND TRANSACTIONS" WITHIN "MATTERS RELATING TO MARRIAGE" OF THE THIRD BOOK: "ON JUSTICES."

Chapter 4

Topic 59j: Going Away

[1]For a wife who goes away from her husband's home, the fine is six Paṇas, unless she has been ill-treated; [2]twelve Paṇas, if she had been forbidden to do so.

[3]For a wife going over to a neighbor's* house, the fine is six Paṇas. [4]For a neighbor, a mendicant, or a trader who gives her accommodation, alms-food, or merchandise, respectively, the fine is 12 Paṇas; [5]if they had been forbidden to do so, the lowest seizure fine (2.1.29 n.).

[6]For a wife who goes over to some other man's house, the fine is 24 Paṇas. [7]For giving accommodation to some other man's wife, the fine is 100 Paṇas, except in times of adversity. [8]If he prohibits her or is unaware, he is not at fault.

[9]"She is not at fault for going to one of the following places because of an offense on the part of her husband, as long as there are no men in

it: relative of the husband, custodian (3.4.26), village headman, guardian (3.3.13 n.), female religious mendicant, and home of a relative," so state the teachers. [10]"The home of a relative even with men in it, [11]for how could there be deceit in a virtuous woman? [12]Surely, this is easy to understand!" So says Kauṭilya.

[13]There is no prohibition at all against going to the home of a relative on the occasion of a death, illness, tragedy, or childbirth. [14]For a man preventing her from going on such an occasion, the fine is 12 Paṇas. [15]If she absconds even on such an occasion, she loses her woman's property; or her relatives hiding her lose the remainder of the bride price (3.2.19 n.).

That concludes going away.

Topic 59k: Accompaniment on the Road

[16]For running away from her husband's home and going to another village, the fine is 12 Paṇas and the loss of her endowment (3.2.15) and ornaments. [17]For traveling with a man with whom sexual relations are permitted (3.3.31 n.), the fine is 24 Paṇas and the exclusion from all that pertains to Law,* except for providing maintenance and sexual relations during her season; [18]for the man, the lowest seizure fine (2.1.29 n.) if he is of equal or superior rank, and the middle fine if he is of inferior rank. [19]If he is a relative, he should not be fined; [20]if he was forbidden, his fines are half the above amounts.

[21]If she goes to a secret place halfway along the road or is accompanied on the road by a suspicious or a forbidden man with the intention of having sexual relations, he (3.5.26 n.) should recognize it as adultery.

[22]Accompaniment on the road is not a fault for wives of dancers, minstrels, fishermen, hunters, cowherds, and tavern keepers, and of other men who give free rein to their wives. [23]Alternatively, if prohibited, for the man taking her and for the woman going with him, the fines are half the above amounts.

That concludes accompaniment on the road.

Topic 59l: Brief Absence from Home

[24]Wives of Śūdras, Vaiśyas, Kṣatriyas, and Brāhmaṇas who are briefly absent from home should wait for a period of one year—increased successively by one year—if they have no children; if they have children, one extra year in each case.* [25]Those who have been provided for should wait double those periods. [26]Their custodians should support those who are

not provided for,* and their relatives for four or eight years beyond that. [27]Thereafter, they* should take back what they had given and release* them.

[28]A wife of a Brāhmaṇa who is studying should wait for ten years if she has no children and for 12 years if she has children, while the wife of a royal official should wait until death. [29]She shall not incur censure by bearing a child from a man of her own class.

[30]Alternatively, if she is released (3.4.27 n.) by her custodians at a time when the family fortunes have ebbed, she may remarry as she wishes—or for the sake of livelihood, when she has fallen in dire straits.

[31]After a marriage contracted in keeping with the Law (3.2.10), when the man who married her* has gone away without informing her, a maiden shall wait for seven menstrual periods if she has not heard from him; for one year if she has heard from him. [32]If he went away after informing her, she should wait for five menstrual periods if she has not heard from him; for ten if she has heard from him. [33]If only a part of the bride price has been paid (3.2.19 n.), she should wait for three menstrual periods if she has not heard from him; for seven if she has heard from him. [34]If the bride price has been paid, she should wait for five menstrual periods if she has not heard from him; ten if she has heard from him. [35]After that time, discharged by the Justices, she may remarry as she wishes. [36]"For, frustrating menses is the destruction of Law," says Kauṭilya.

That concludes brief absence from home.

Topic 59m: Long Absence from Home

[37]The wife of a man who is absent from home for a long time, who has become a renouncer, or who is dead, should wait for seven menstrual periods; for one year, if she has children. [38]After that time she should go to a uterine brother of her husband;* [39]if there are several, to the one who is closest, the one who is righteous (*dhārmika*), the one capable of maintaining her, the youngest, or the one without a wife; [40]and in their absence, even to one who is not a uterine brother: a man of the same ancestry or a member of the same family who is close by. [41]This is the strict order among them.

> [42]Passing over these heirs,* if she remarries or takes a lover, the lover, the woman, the giver, and the man who marries her receive the penalty for adultery.

THAT CONCLUDES THE FOURTH CHAPTER: "GOING AWAY," "ACCOMPANIMENT ON THE ROAD," "BRIEF ABSENCE FROM HOME," AND "LONG ABSENCE FROM HOME" WITHIN "MATTERS RELATING TO MARRIAGE" OF THE THIRD BOOK: "ON JUSTICES."

Chapter 5

Topic 60: Partitioning of Inheritance

Topic 60a: Order of Inheritance

[1]Sons who have a father—whose father and mother are still there*—are without power. [2]After the father has passed on, there is a partitioning of the father's property among them.

[3]What has been earned by oneself is not subject to partition, except those things that have been generated using the father's property.

[4]Sons or grandsons, up to the fourth generation, receive shares of things that have come down without partition from the father's property. [5]Until then the funerary rice ball remains unbroken. [6]All, in the case of whom the funerary rice ball is broken, should partition into equal shares.*

[7]Those who have not received anything from the father's property or those who have received shares of the father's property through partition,* if they are living together, may partition it again. [8]The one because of whom the property was generated* should receive a double share.

[9]The property of a man without sons should be taken by his uterine brothers or those living together with him, as also by his unmarried daughters; [10]and the estate of a man with sons, by his sons or by his daughters born in the most righteous marriages (3.2.10), [11]in their absence, by his father if he is alive, [12]and in the absence of the father, by his brothers and the sons of his brothers.

[13]Even if they are many, fatherless brothers and sons of brothers receive a single share of their father.* [14]The partition of inheritance among uterine brothers from more than one father takes place according to their respective fathers. [15]Among father, brother, and son, when one listed earlier is present, they do not depend on one listed afterward, and when the eldest is alive, on the youngest even if he has received wealth.*

[16]At a partition carried out when the father is still alive, the father should neither favor any one [17]nor exclude any one from partition without a reason.

[18]When the father has left no wealth, the older brothers should look after the younger ones, except those who behave dishonestly.

[19]Partition takes place among those who have reached the age for legal transactions (3.3.1). [20]The shares of those who have not reached the age for legal transactions, after clearing any dues,* should be deposited with their mother's relatives or village elders until they reach the age for legal transactions, as also the shares of someone who is away on a journey. [21]They should give to those who are unmarried marriage expenses equal to the expenses provided to those who are already married; and to unmarried girls, a sum to be presented at their wedding.

[22]There is an equal division of debts and estate.

[23]"Those who are utterly destitute may divide even water pots," so state the teachers. [24]"That is wordplay," says Kauṭilya. [25]"Partition takes place of existent wealth, not of the nonexistent."*

[26]He* should have the partition carried out in the presence of witnesses, saying with specific statements: "This is the extent of the common property. Of that, this is the extent of each share."

[27]They should repartition the following: what has been wrongly partitioned, what has been stolen from each other, what has been concealed, and what has come to light that was previously unknown.

[28]The king should take a property that has no heir, excluding what is required for the maintenance of the wife and for funeral expenses, [29]with the exception of property belonging to Vedic scholars. [29]He should present that to experts in the triple Veda.

[30]A man fallen from caste, someone born to a man fallen from caste, and an impotent man do not receive shares, as also someone who is an idiot, insane, blind, or a leper. [31]In case they have a wife,* their* offspring shall take a share, if the offspring are not like them. [32]Others receive food and clothing, except those who have fallen from caste.

> [33]If they lose the capacity to procreate after they have married, moreover, their relatives should produce sons for them (3.4.38 n), and he (3.5.26 n) should apportion shares to them.

THAT CONCLUDES THE FIFTH CHAPTER: "ORDER OF INHERITANCE" WITHIN "PARTITIONING OF INHERITANCE" OF THE THIRD BOOK: "ON JUSTICES."

Chapter 6

Topic 60b: Division into Shares

[1]Among sons born from the same wife, the share of the eldest consists of goats among Brāhmaṇas, horses among Kṣatriyas, cows among Vaiśyas, and sheep among Śūdras. [2]The one-eyed and the lame among these are the share of the middle son, and those of mixed colors, the share of the youngest. [3]In the absence of quadrupeds, the eldest should take one share out of each ten items, except for jewels, [4]for he is bound with the fetter of ancestral offerings. [5]That is the partitioning according to Uśanas.

[6]From the father's personal belongings, carriage and ornaments are the share of the eldest; bed and seat, as well as brass eating utensils he has used, are the share of the middle son; black grain, iron, household furniture, and bullock cart are the share of the youngest. [7]The rest of the articles, or a single article,* are divided equally.

[8]Sisters do not partake of the inheritance;* they receive from their mother's personal belongings the brass eating utensils she has used and her ornaments.

[9]An eldest son who lacks manly qualities should receive one-third of the share reserved for the eldest; one-quarter, if he behaves unjustly or has given up obligations relating to the Law. [10]If he follows a licentious lifestyle, he loses the entire amount.

[11]That also explains what pertains to the middle and the youngest sons. [12]Of these two, the one who has manly qualities should receive one-half of the share reserved for the eldest.

[13]Among sons born to different wives, however, seniority derives from being born earlier—except when one wife was married with the proper rites while another was married without them, and when one wife was married as a virgin while another was married after she had lost her virginity—as also between two sons of the same wife and between twins.

[14]Among Sūtas, Māgadhas, Vrātyas, and Rathakāras (3.7.24–35), partition is made according to proficiency. [15]The others should live under him. [16]If no one has acquired proficiency, the partition is equal.

[17]Among sons from wives belonging to the four social classes, the son of a Brāhmaṇa wife should take four shares; the son of a Kṣatriya wife, three shares; the son of a Vaiśya wife, two shares; and the son of a Śūdra wife, one share. [18]That also explains the partition among sons of a Kṣatriya or a Vaiśya by wives belonging to three or two social classes.*

[19]The son of a Brāhmaṇa born to a wife of the class immediately next receives an equal share; [20]the son of a Kṣatriya or Vaiśya, half a share; an equal share if he possesses manly qualities.*

[21]When between two wives, one of the same class as the husband and the other not, there is only one son, he takes the entire estate; and he should support the relatives. [22]Among Brāhmaṇas, however, a Pāraśava son (3.7.21) shall receive one-third of a share, while someone of the same ancestry or a close member of the same family receives two-thirds for the purpose of offering ancestral rites; [23]in their absence, the father's teacher or pupil.

> [24]Or else, an appointed man—either a relative of the mother or a man belonging to the same lineage—should beget through his wife a son "begotten on the wife" (3.7.6) and allot that property to him.

THAT CONCLUDES THE SIXTH CHAPTER: "DIVISION INTO SHARES" WITHIN "PARTITIONING OF INHERITANCE" OF THE THIRD BOOK: "ON JUSTICES."

Chapter 7

Topic 60c: Classification of Sons

[1]"A seed deposited in someone else's property belongs to the owner of the field," so state the teachers. [2]"Mother is a sack. The offspring belongs to the owner of the seed," so state others. [3]"Both are to be found,"* says Kauṭilya.

[4]When a man* fathers a son by himself through a wife he has married with the proper rites, he is the *natural son*. [5]The *son of a female-son* (1.17.49 n.) is equal to him. [6]When he is fathered through his wife by a man of the same lineage or of a different lineage who has been duly appointed, he is the *son begotten on the wife*. [7]When the biological father does not have another son, this one son has two fathers and two lineages, and he offers the ancestral rites to and inherits the property from both. [8]Having the same qualities as the latter, but born secretly in the house of her kin, is the *son born in secret*. [9]One forsaken by his kin is the *son adopted after being abandoned*; he belongs to the man who performs his rites of passage. [10]The child of a maiden is the *son born to an unmarried woman*. [11]A son of a woman who gets married while she is pregnant is the *son received with marriage*. [12]A son born to a woman who has married again is the *son of a*

remarried woman. [13]If fathered by oneself, he is the heir to the estate of his father and of his relatives; [14]if fathered by another, he is the heir to the estate of only the one who performed his rites of passage, not of the relatives. [15]Having the same qualities as the latter is the *son given in adoption,* who is given up by his mother and father with the pouring of water. [16]One who has offered to be a son either on his own or through his relatives is the *son who has been offered.* [17]One appointed to the position of son is the *constituted son.* [18]One who has been bought is the *purchased son.*

[19]When a natural son is born, however, those* belonging to the same class as the father receive a one-third share each, while those not belonging to the same class receive food and clothing.

[20]Sons of a Brāhmaṇa or a Kṣatriya born to a wife belonging to the very next class* belong to the same class as their father, while those born to a wife belonging to the next but one class* do not belong to the same class as their father. [21]A son of a Brāhmaṇa through a Vaiśya wife is an Ambaṣṭha, and through a Śūdra wife, a Niṣāda or a Pāraśava. [22]Through a Śūdra wife, the son of a Kṣatriya is an Ugra, [23]while the son of a Vaiśya is simply a Śūdra. [24]Among these,* moreover, sons born to wives belonging to the same class by men who have not undergone initiation are Vrātyas. [25]These are the ones born in the natural order.*

[26]From a Śūdra male are born the Āyogava, Kṣatta, and Caṇḍāla; [27]from a Vaiśya male, the Māgadha and Vaidehika; [28]from a Kṣatriya male, the Sūta.* [29]The Sūta of the Purāṇas, however, is someone different, as also the Māgadha, getting their distinction from the Brāhmaṇa and the Kṣatriya.* [30]These are the ones born in the inverse order (3.7.25 n.) on account of the king transgressing the Law specific to him.

[31]From an Ugra male through a Naiṣāda female is born a Kukkuṭa; in the inverse case, a Pulkasa. [32]From an Ambaṣṭha male through a Vaidehika female is born a Vaiṇa; in the inverse case, a Kuśīlava. [33]From an Ugra male through a Kṣatta female is born a Śvapāka.* [34]These listed here, as well as others, are intermediate classes.

[35]In terms of his occupation, a Rathakāra is a Vaiśya.

[36]Their marriages are with their own kind; their rules of precedence and hereditary occupations—he should establish as the Law specific to them.* [37]Alternatively, they have the same qualities* as Śūdras, with the exception of Caṇḍālas.

[38]Only by acting in this manner will the king attain heaven; otherwise, hell. [39]Among all the intermediate classes, there is equal partitioning of property.*

[40]Whatever Law is customary in a particular region, caste, association, or village, according to that alone should he (3.5.26 n.) administer the Law of inheritance.

THAT CONCLUDES THE SEVENTH CHAPTER: "CLASSIFICATION OF SONS" WITHIN "PARTITIONING OF INHERITANCE" OF THE THIRD BOOK: "ON JUSTICES."

Chapter 8

Topic 61: On Immovable Property

[1]Disputes concerning immovable property depend on the neighbors' assessment (2.36.5 n.). [2]House, field, grove, dike, reservoir, or pond constitutes immovable property.

Topic 61a: On Immovable Property Consisting of Houses

[3]Alongside the house there is a boundary line with a border marker of Karṇa posts or iron.* [4]He should get the house built in keeping with the boundary line;* [5]or, in its absence, he should have the foundation wall constructed* two Aratnis or three Padas away from the wall of the neighbor's house.

[6]The latrine, drain, or well should not be located in places suitable for a house, except a water ditch during childbirth until the tenth day.* [7]For violating this, the punishment is the lowest seizure fine (2.1.29 n.). [8]That also explains the cutting of firewood and trenches for water used for sipping during festive celebrations.

[9]He should have a water duct constructed with a deep flow or with cascades three Padas or one and a half Aratnis removed (from the neighbor's property). [10]For violating this, the fine is 54 Paṇas.

[11]He should have the place for carts and animals, the fireplace, the place for the water tank, the grinding mill, or the pounding machine constructed one Pada or one Aratni removed (from the neighbor's property). [12]For violating this, the fine is 24 Paṇas.

[13]Between any two residential properties (1.20.1 n.) or two protruding halls,* there should be a passageway* of one Kiṣku or three Padas. [14]Between the eaves of their roofs, there should be a gap of four Aṅgulas, or they may overlap.

[15]He should get a side door a full Kiṣku wide built in such a way that it would not collide and permit the door pane to open wide in the passageway.* [16]He should get a small window built high up to let in light. [17]When the house is occupied, he should have it covered.*

[18]Alternatively, the house owners may come together and jointly get them constructed as they like and prevent what they do not like (3.9.2 n.).

[19]Over the verandah, he should have the section requiring shelter covered with a thatch screen or equipped with a wall touching (the roof) built, because of the danger of damage from rain.* [20]For violating this, the punishment is the lowest seizure fine, as well as for obstructing a door or a window against the normal procedure*—except in the case of a royal highway or a road*—[21]as also for causing an obstruction outside the house by a section of a ditch, a stairway, a water duct, a ladder, or a latrine, and for causing a hindrance to the use (by others).

[22]For anyone damaging the wall of someone else's house with water, the fine is 12 Paṇas; double that for damaging it with urine or feces.

[23]Free flow should be allowed along a water duct during rain; otherwise the fine is 12 Paṇas; [24]as also for someone living in a house when forbidden to do so and for someone throwing out a tenant, except in the case of assault,* theft, forcible seizure, sexual misconduct, or wrongful use.* [25]If he leaves on his own, he should pay the remainder of the annual rent.*

[26]For someone not offering assistance in a common household, for someone obstructing a common property—for causing a hindrance to its use—* the fine is 12 Paṇas; [27]double that for someone destroying it.

> [28]Common use is prescribed of storerooms, courtyards, and
> latrines, of fire stalls and pounding sheds, and of all open spaces.

THAT CONCLUDES THE EIGHTH CHAPTER: "ON IMMOVABLE PROPERTY CONSISTING OF HOUSES" WITHIN "ON IMMOVABLE PROPERTY" OF THE THIRD BOOK: "ON JUSTICES."

Chapter 9

Topic 61b: Sale of Immovable Property

[1]Relatives, neighbors, and creditors, in that order, should have the first right to purchase landed property; [2]after that outsiders.

[3]They should auction a residence in front of the house and in the presence of 40 neighboring families;* a field, a park, an embankment, a reservoir, or a pond, at its borders* and in the presence of elders from neighboring villages, saying: "In conformity with its boundary lines, who will buy this at this price?"* [4]When it has been announced three times without being countered, the man who wished to buy gets to purchase it.

[5]If the price increases* because of competition, on the other hand, the increase in price together with the duty goes to the treasury. [6]The successful bidder at the sale should pay the duty. [7]For bidding by one who is not an owner,* the fine is 24 Paṇas. [8]After seven days have passed and he does not turn up, the person offering the property for sale may sell it. [9]In the case of a transgression* by the person offering the property for sale, the fine is 200 Paṇas in the case of immovable property; in other cases, the fine is 24 Paṇas.

That concludes the sale of immovable property.

Topic 61c: Disputes concerning Boundaries

[10]A group of five or ten villages that neighbor both the villages should settle a boundary dispute between the two based on immovable or man-made boundary markers.

[11]Elders of agriculturists or cattle herders, or outsiders who were former users of the place—many or even one, so long as they are knowledgeable about the boundaries—after disclosing the boundary markers and wearing incongruous attire,* should point out the boundary. [12]When the boundary markers pointed out are not seen, the fine is 1,000 Paṇas. [13]He* should impose the same fine on those who, after the boundary has been pointed out, remove the boundary or destroy the boundary markers.

[14]When the line demarcating the boundary is missing (3.8.4 n.), the king should apportion the boundary* in a way that is beneficial.

That concludes the disputes concerning boundaries.

Topic 61d: Disputes concerning Fields

[15]Elders of neighboring villages should settle disputes concerning fields. [16]When these are divided, they* should settle in favor of the party supported by a majority, by those who are honest, or by those who have been endorsed;* or else they should adopt the middle course.* [17]The king shall take an immovable property concerning which both sides have lost their case, as also anything whose owner is missing. [18]Or else, he may apportion it in a way that is beneficial.

[19]In the case of immovable property, the punishment for forcible seizure is the fine for theft (2.7.39 n.). [20]If it is seized for a good reason, he should pay an amount after deducting for effort and for profit.*

That concludes the disputes concerning fields.

Topic 61e: Fixing Borders

[21]For removing a border (3.9.2 n.), the punishment is the lowest seizure fine (2.1.29 n.); [22]for breaking a border, 24 Paṇas.

[23]The above discussion also explains disputes concerning ascetic groves, grazing lands, highways, cemeteries, shrines, sacrificial grounds, and holy places.

That concludes the fixing of borders.

Topic 61f: On Impairment and Encroachment

[24]All disputes depend on the neighbors' assessment (2.36.5 n.).

[25]Among grazing land, dry farmland, wet farmland, vegetable plots, threshing floors, sheds, and stalls for draught animals, each previous one will have to bear with encroachment.* [26]Areas comprehended by dry farmland exclude* wild tracts for Vedic study and Soma sacrifices, shrines, sacrificial grounds,* and holy places.

[27]When the plowed land or seeds of another's field are damaged by the use of a pond, canal, or wet farmland, they should pay the cost proportionate to the loss. [28]When wet farmland, groves, and dikes cause damage to each other, the fine is double the damage. [29]A reservoir on a lower level built more recently should not inundate with water the wet farmland served by a reservoir on a higher level. [30]A reservoir built at a higher level should not obstruct the flow of water into a lower reservoir, unless it has been left unused for three years. [31]For violating this, the punishment is the lowest seizure fine (2.1.29 n.), as well as the emptying of the reservoir.

[32]When a dike is left unused for five years, ownership to it ceases, unless during times of adversity.

[33]When reservoirs and dikes are newly constructed,* they are exempt from taxes for five years; when those that are dilapidated and abandoned (2.29.1 n.) are renovated, for four years; when overgrown ones are cleared, for three years; and when dry farmland is newly brought under cultivation, for two years. [34]That person* has the power to mortgage or sell it.

[35]They may give water from their canals, dams on rivers, and reservoirs to wet farmland, groves, and vegetable plots in return for a share of

various crops produced from them;* or to others according to the benefits they may accrue.

[36]Those who use these on lease, on fixed rent, as a pledge, for a share of the crop, or with the permission for use should keep them in repair. [37]For not keeping them in repair, the fine is double the loss.

> [38]For someone releasing water from dikes out of turn, the fine is six Paṇas, as also for someone obstructing the water to others through negligence when it is their turn.

THAT CONCLUDES THE NINTH CHAPTER: "SALE OF IMMOVABLE PROPERTY," "DISPUTES CONCERNING BOUNDARIES," "DISPUTES CONCERNING FIELDS," "FIXING BORDERS," AND "ON IMPAIRMENT AND ENCROACHMENT" WITHIN "ON IMMOVABLE PROPERTY" OF THE THIRD BOOK: "ON JUSTICES."

Chapter 10

Topic 61g: Damage to Grazing Land, Fields, and Roads

[1]For someone who obstructs a customary canal for irrigation water* or makes one that is not customary, the punishment is the lowest seizure fine (2.1.29 n.), as also for anyone who constructs a dike, well, holy place, sanctuary, or temple on another man's land. [2]For anyone who puts up or gets someone to put up a longstanding dike constructed as an act of piety (*dharma*) for mortgage or sale, the punishment is the middle seizure fine; and for those who act as witnesses, the highest fine, unless it is dilapidated and abandoned (2.29.1 n.).

[3]In the absence of the owner, villagers (2.28.2 n.) or pious individuals should make repairs to them.

[4]The size of roads has been explained under "Layout of a Fort" (2.4.3–5). [5]For someone obstructing a road for small animals and humans, the fine is 12 Paṇas; a road for large animals, 24 Paṇas; a road for elephants or in fields, 54 Paṇas; a road on a dike or in a forest, 106 Paṇas; a road in a cemetery or a village, 200 Paṇas; a road in a district municipality, 500 Paṇas; and a road in a provincial capital, province, or pasture land, 1,000 Paṇas. [6]For reducing their size,* furthermore, these fines are reduced to one-quarter. [7]For plowing over them, the fines are the ones given above.

[8]For an owner taking away a field or for a tenant leaving during the time of sowing, the fine is 12 Paṇas, except in the case of a defect, a disaster, or unacceptability (3.15.1–4).

[9]People subject to taxes must mortgage or sell only to others subject to taxes, and those entitled to Brāhmaṇa land grants (2.1.7), to others entitled to Brāhmaṇa land grants; [10]otherwise, the punishment is the lowest seizure fine (2.1.29 n.)—[11]or for a man subject to taxes settling in a village exempt from taxes. [12]A person settling in a village subject to taxes has the freedom to procure anything except a house. [13]Even that he may give to him.*

[14]When a man does not till a field that cannot be alienated, someone else may use it for five years and then return it after receiving compensation for his efforts.

[15]Persons exempt from tax living elsewhere may live on the revenue.*

[16]When a village headman goes on a journey for village business, the tenants should accompany him by turns. [17]Those who refuse to accompany him should pay one and a half Paṇas per Yojana.

[18]For a village headman who expels from the village someone who is not a thief or an adulterer, the fine is 24 Paṇas, and for that village, the highest fine (2.1.29 n.). [19]The entry by someone who has been expelled is explained under trespass (4.13.3–4).

[20]He should have a fence with posts erected all around at a distance of 100 Dhanuṣes from the village.

[21]They should live by cutting the grass on the pasture land meant for cattle grazing.* [22]They should charge one-quarter of a Paṇa per animal for camels and buffaloes that graze there and leave; for cows, horses, and donkeys, one-eighth of a Paṇa; for small farm animals (2.21.24 n.), one-sixteenth; [23]for those that lie down after grazing, the fines are double the same amounts; and for those that remain overnight, four times. [24]Bulls belonging to a god or a village,* or a cow within ten days of calving, as well as old bulls and stud bulls,* are exempt from fines.

[25]If crops are eaten, he (3.5.26 n.) should calculate the loss to the crop in accordance with the expected harvest and make the man pay twice that amount. [26]For an owner, moreover, who gets his herd to graze without informing (the owner of the field), the fine is 12 Paṇas; for letting them roam freely, 24 Paṇas. [27]For the herdsmen, the fines are half those amounts. [28]The very same fines should be levied for grazing in a vegetable plot. [29]The fine is doubled for breaking a fence, as also for eating grain from a shed or the round enclosure of a threshing floor.

[30]One should take care to avoid causing injury. [31]When animals from forest sanctuaries (2.26.1) or those in preserves (2.26.3) are grazing, the owner should be informed and the animals should be driven away in

such a way as not to cause them injury. [32]Farm animals should be turned away with a whip or a goad. [33]For those who injure them in other ways, the fine is that for physical assault (3.19.26–27). [34]Animals who attack or whose offense is evident should be subdued through every possible means.

That concludes damage to fields and roads.

Topic 62: Non-Observance of Conventions

[35]The penalty paid by a farmer who, after entering into an agreement with a village,* does not keep to it, should be taken by the village itself. [36]For not performing the work, he should pay twice the wages for that work; for not paying the money,* twice the amount of the share of each individual; and for not providing food and drink during festivities, double the share.

[37]When someone does not give his share to stage a show, he along with his people shall not see it. [38]For listening or viewing it secretly, moreover, he should be forced to pay double his share, as also in the case of an activity for the common good.

[39]They* should carry out the orders of the one who prescribes something for the common good. [40]For not carrying them out, the fine is 12 Paṇas. [41]If they conspire and beat him up, on the other hand, each shall pay twice the fine for that offense; [42]it shall be more severe for those who cause injury to him.

[43]Seniority among them should be determined beginning with the Brāhmaṇa. [44]And in their festivities, Brāhmaṇas shall not do work if they are unwilling; nevertheless, they should receive their share.

[45]That explains also the non-observance of conventions within regions, castes, families, and associations.

> [46]When people build dikes that benefit the region and concourses* along roads, and undertake projects to beautify and to protect villages, the king should do what is pleasing and beneficial to them.

THAT CONCLUDES THE TENTH CHAPTER: "DAMAGE TO GRAZING LAND, FIELDS, AND ROADS" WITHIN "ON IMMOVABLE PROPERTY" AND "NON-OBSERVANCE OF CONVENTIONS" OF THE THIRD BOOK: "ON JUSTICES."

Chapter 11

Topic 63: Non-Payment of Debts

RATES OF INTEREST

[1]One and a quarter Paṇas per month on 100 Paṇas is the righteous* rate of interest; five Paṇas, the commercial rate; ten Paṇas for travelers through wild tracts; and 20 Paṇas for seafarers. [2]For anyone charging or making someone charge more than that, the punishment is the lowest seizure fine (2.1.29 n.), and half that fine for each of the witnesses individually. [3]When, however, the king is not providing security, he (3.5.26 n.) should take into account the customs among lenders and borrowers.

[4]Interest on grain is up to one-half if paid at the time when crops are harvested; after that, it is monetized and will continue to bear interest on that capital.* [5]Interest on investment capital is half of the profit; that interest is laid aside in a depository and paid annually. [6]Someone who has gone away for a long time or who remains obstinate* should pay twice the principal.

[7]When someone has not set an interest rate and then tries to enforce payment or to increase the rate, or when someone produces witnesses to claim a principal with interest added to it, he is fined four times that amount;* [8]if the sum claimed through witnesses is a trifling amount,* four times that fictive amount. [9]Of that fine, the claimant should pay three-quarters,* and the enabler the rest.

[10]A debt shall cease to bear interest in the case of a person detained by a long sacrificial session, an illness, or in a teacher's house, and in the case of a child or a pauper.

RECOVERY OF DEBTS

[11]For someone not accepting a debt that is being paid off, the fine is 12 Paṇas. [12]If he gives a valid excuse, the debt, which ceases to bear interest, should be held by a third party.

[13]A debt that is ignored for ten years cannot be recovered, except in the case of children, the old, the sick, and people who have fallen on hard times, gone abroad, or emigrated, or when there is an upheaval in the kingdom.

[14]A money lender's loan to a man who has died should be paid by his sons, or by the heirs who inherited his estate or the sureties who assumed co-responsibility*—[15]and not any other liability of a surety.* [16–17]A surety's liability, however, relating to a pauper or a child, when its place and time have not been specified, should be paid by sons, grandsons, or heirs who

take the estate.* [18]A surety's liability relating to life, marriage, and land, when its place and time have not been specified, on the other hand, should be borne by sons or grandsons.*

[19]When several debts come due at the same time, two should not sue a single individual* concurrently, except when he is about to go away. [20]Even in this case, he should make the payment in the order in which the debts were contracted, or else he should pay first a debt owed to the king or to a learned Brāhmaṇa.

[21]A debt contracted between a husband and wife and a father and son, and between brothers who are coparceners cannot be legally recovered.

[22]Farmers and king's officials shall not be detained during times when they must work; [23]a wife, likewise, for a debt incurred by her husband to which she has not formally agreed, except in the case of herdsmen and sharecroppers.* [24]A husband, on the other hand, may be detained for a loan taken by his wife, if he had gone away without providing for her.

TOPIC OF WITNESSES

[25]It is the best if an admission is made.* [26]When there is no admission, however, witnesses provide the evidentiary proof, witnesses who are trustworthy, honest, or endorsed (3.9.16 n.), and a minimum of three; [27]or, if approved by the parties, even two; but never one with regard to a debt.*

[28]The following are forbidden: a brother of the wife, an associate, a dependent, a lender, a borrower, an enemy, a cripple, and a man subjected to judicial punishment; as also those previously mentioned as ineligible to execute transactions (3.1.12); [29]the king, a learned Brāhmaṇa, a village servant (2.1.11 n.), a leper, and a man with sores;* an outcaste, a Caṇḍāla, and one following a despicable profession; anyone who is blind, deaf, dumb, or self-appointed;* and a woman or an official of the king—except within their own groups. [30]In cases concerning assault (3.18–19), theft, and sexual offenses, however (all these are allowed), except an enemy, a wife's brother, and an associate. [31]In the case of secret transactions, a single woman or man who has heard or seen it can be a witness, except the king and an ascetic.

[32]Masters may testify for their servants, priests and teachers for their pupils, and a father and mother for their sons—and vice versa—without being forced to do so. [33]When they sue each other, moreover, the superiors who lose the case shall pay one-tenth of the amount under litigation (2.7.21 n.), and the inferiors one-fifth.

That concludes the qualification of witnesses.

EXAMINATION OF WITNESSES

[34]He should impanel the witnesses in the presence of Brāhmaṇas, a pot of water, and fire. [35]In that context, to a Brāhmaṇa he should say: "Speak the truth!" [36]To a Kṣatriya or a Vaiśya: "May you not receive the fruit of your sacrifices and good works! May you go, a potsherd in hand, to your enemy's house to beg for almsfood!"—[37]and to a Śūdra: "Any fruit of your* meritorious deeds between your birth and death, all that will go to the king, and the sins of the king to you!—if an untruth is spoken.* Punishment will also follow. Afterwards, furthermore, facts as seen and heard will become known. Single-mindedly present the truth." [38]Those who fail to present it are fined 12 Paṇas* after seven days; after three fortnights they should pay the claim.

[39]When the witnesses are divided, they* should settle in favor of the party that has the support of the majority, or of those who are honest, or of those who have been endorsed (3.9.16 n.); alternatively, they should adopt the middle course (3.9.16). [40]Or else, the king should take that property.

[41]If the witnesses attest to an amount less than the claim, the plaintiff should pay the excess amount as a penalty.* [42]If they testify to an amount in excess of the claim, the king should take the excess.

[43]With respect to anything that has been poorly witnessed* or badly written down through the folly of the plaintiff, or where the person providing the affidavit has died, the ascertainment, after a thorough examination, should be based solely on witnesses (2.36.5 n.).

[44]"When through the folly of the witnesses, they give conflicting answers to questions with regard to place, time, and subject of the lawsuit, they should be imposed the lowest, the middle, and the highest fine (2.1.29 n.), respectively," so state the Auśanasas. [45]"When false witnesses sustain a bogus lawsuit or overturn a truthful lawsuit, they should pay ten times that* as a fine," so state the Mānavas. [46]"Or, for those who, through their folly, break their trust,* execution with torture," so state the Bārhaspatyas. [47]"No," says Kauṭilya; [48]"for witnesses perforce must testify truthfully. [49]Twenty-four Paṇas is the fine for those who fail to testify truthfully, half of that amount for those who do not speak."*

> [50]He (3.5.26 n.) should produce witnesses located not too distant
> in place and time; he should produce those who are far away or
> do not budge by means of a royal summons.

THAT CONCLUDES THE ELEVENTH CHAPTER: "NON-PAYMENT OF DEBTS" OF THE THIRD BOOK: "ON JUSTICES."

Chapter 12

Topic 64: On Deposits

[1]The discussion of debts also explains deposits.*

[2]In the event that a fort or province is plundered by an enemy king or a tribal chief; or a village, caravan, or herd station is plundered by bandits; or a carriage is lost; or when one is besieged by flames or rushing water at a time of calamity in the middle of the village caused by fire or flood during which nothing was saved or just a portion of the property was salvaged;* or the boat has sunk or has been robbed—and he himself has been affected—he shall not be liable for the deposit.

[3]Someone who makes use of a deposit should pay compensation for that use according to place and time, and in addition a fine of 12 Paṇas. [4]If it is lost or damaged as a result of its use, he shall be liable, and in addition pay a fine of 24 Paṇas; or if it flees under other conditions.*

[5]He shall not be liable for a deposit that has died or has been stricken by some calamity. [6]In case he mortgages or sells the deposit or denies receiving it, the fine is four times one-fifth the amount,* [7]and in the case of substituting the deposit or being responsible for its fleeing, the fine is equal to its full value.

PLEDGES

[8]The above discussion also explains the loss, use, sale, mortgage, and theft of a pledge.*

[9]A pledge that provides a benefit cannot be forfeited, and the principal it guarantees does not bear interest unless it is permitted. [10]A pledge that does not provide a benefit can be forfeited, and the principal it guarantees bears interest.

[11]For someone who does not return a pledge to the man who has come to redeem it, the fine is 12 Paṇas. [12]Or, if the lender is absent, he may deposit the amount due with the village elders and take back the pledge. [13]Alternatively, after fixing its value at that time and halting all further interest, it may be kept right there or in the care of the facility for safeguarding against loss or destruction.* [14]Or, if the borrower is absent and he fears the destruction of the pledge, he may sell it at the highest price with the consent of the Justices or the acquiescence of the guardian of pledges.

[15]An immovable pledge, however—whether it can be enjoyed only with exertion or it yields fruits that can be enjoyed—may provide a return over

and above the amount of the interest on the loan without causing a reduction in the principal. [16]Anyone who enjoys it without permission should give the return above the amount of the interest, as also a security.*

[17]The rest has been explained under deposits.

DIRECTIVE AND ASSIGNMENT

[18]The above discussion also explains directives and assignments.*

[19]If a man carrying an assignment and traveling with a caravan fails to reach the designated place or is assaulted and abandoned (2.29.1 n.) by robbers, he shall not be liable for the assignment. [20]Or, if he dies on the way, even his heir shall not be liable.

[21]The rest has been explained under deposits.

BORROWING AND RENTING

[22]People who borrow or rent anything should return it in the very same condition that they received it. [23]They shall not be liable for anything that was given with restriction as to place and time if it is lost or destroyed through decay or a disaster.

[24]The rest has been explained under deposits.

SALE THROUGH AN AGENT

[25]Now, in the case of a sale through an agent, the sales agents, selling the merchandise at the right place and time, should give the original price* and profit exactly as realized. [26]Or, in the event they miss the right place and time, and the price goes down, they should give the price and profit calculated according to its worth at the time the goods were consigned. [27]Or, if they do not make a profit by selling according to the agreement, they should give only the original price. [28]Or, if due to a fall in prices there is a reduction, then they should give an amount less than the original in keeping with the reduction. [29]Or, in the case of trustworthy businessmen who have not received any reprimand from the king, when the merchandise is lost or destroyed through decay or disaster, they do not have to give even the original price. [30]In the case of merchandise intended for distant places and times,* however, they should give the price and the profits after deducting losses and expenses; in the case of a collection of merchandise, each according to his share.

[31]The rest has been explained under deposits. [32]This also explains sale through an agent.

CONSIGNMENTS

[33]The discussion on deposits, moreover, explains consignments.*

[34]When someone hands over a consignment given by one person to another person, he forfeits it.* [35]In the case of the theft of a consignment, a previous offense and those making the consignment constitute adequate proof; [36]for artisans are dishonest. [37]Among them, the Law of consignments requiring written receipt* does not exist.

[38]When someone denies a consignment made without a written receipt, the consignor should place witnesses within a false wall and get them to learn about it by imploring the man in secret or by infusing confidence in him during a drinking bout in a park.

[39]An old* or sick trader should secretly consign in the man's hand an article that has been marked and go away. [40]At his direction, his son or brother should go to the man and request it. [41]If he gives it, he is honest; otherwise, he should both give back the consignment and pay the fine for theft (2.7.39 n.). [42]Alternatively, a trustworthy man about to go abroad should consign in his hand an article that has been marked and then depart. [43]Then, returning after some time, he should request it. [44]If he gives it, he is honest; otherwise, he should both give back the consignment and pay the fine for theft.

[45]Or else, he should draw him in by means of a marked article.*

[46]Alternatively, a man looking naturally a dimwit, afraid of the royal guard during the night curfew, should consign in his hand a valuable article at night and go away. [47]While he is in prison, he should request it. [48]If he gives it, he is honest; otherwise, he should both give back the consignment and pay the fine for theft.

[49]By showing the identity card (4.5.7 n.), he should request both from the people in the house. [50]If either is not given—the same as that stated above.*

[51]He (3.5.26 n.) should question the man about how he obtained the articles in his possession, about circumstantial evidence* connecting the article to the transaction, and about the capacity of the plaintiff to own that object.

[52]The above discussion also explains secret associations.*

> [53]One should, therefore, conclude transactions with people of one's own group or with outsiders openly in the presence of witnesses, properly disclosing the place, time, quantity, and quality.

THAT CONCLUDES THE TWELFTH CHAPTER: "ON DEPOSITS" OF THE THIRD BOOK: "ON JUSTICES."

Chapter 13

Topic 65:* Rules Governing Slaves and Laborers

Topic 65a: Rules concerning Slaves

[1]Except in the case of a subsistence slave,* when someone belonging to his own people* makes a sale or pledge of an Ārya individual who has not reached the age for legal transactions (3.3.1 n.), he is fined 12 Paṇas if that individual is a Śūdra, double that if he is a Vaiśya, three times if he is a Kṣatriya, and four time if he is a Brāhmaṇa. [2]If he belongs to a different group of people,* the punishment is the lowest, the middle, and the highest fines (2.1.29 n.), and execution, respectively; the same for the buyers and the witnesses.

[3]It is not an offense for barbarians to sell or to give as pledges their offspring. [4]An Ārya,* however, can never be reduced to slavery.

[5]Alternatively, having pledged an Ārya in a time of distress for Āryas when the family has become bonded,* when they have obtained the price of redemption, they should redeem first a child or one who has been of assistance.

[6]Someone who has offered himself as a pledge succumbs* the first time he flees; one who was given as a pledge by someone else, the second time. Both succumb the first time if they are heading to the realm of an enemy king or have stolen money.* [7]Someone who deprives a slave of his Ārya status should pay half the fine.*

[8]When a pledge has fled, died, or has fallen on hard times, the one who made the pledge becomes liable for the capital.

[9]When a man given as a pledge is made to handle a corpse, urine, feces, or leavings, or when women given as pledges are made to bathe a naked man, are subjected to corporal punishment, or are violated, it causes the loss of the capital; the same acts also cause the freeing of nurses, female attendants, sharecroppers, and maidservants.

[10]It is legitimate for a servant who has had a child* to go away.

[11]For having sex with an unwilling female nurse given as a pledge,* the punishment is the lowest seizure fine (2.1.29 n.) if she is under his control; the middle, if she is under the control of someone else.* [12]For violating a virgin given as a pledge by himself or through someone else, he loses the capital and has to pay her bride price and twice that much as a fine.

[13]The offspring of someone who has sold himself should be recognized as an Ārya. [14]He should receive what he has earned on his own without impairing his work for his master, as well as his paternal inheritance. [15]He can

get back his Ārya status,* moreover, by paying the original price. [16]This also explains a subsistence slave (3.13.1 n.) and someone given as a pledge; [17]and the amount to redeem him is proportionate to the amount of the loan.

[18]Someone who is assessed a fine may pay off the fine through manual labor (2.12.21 n.).

[19]An Ārya individual who is captured in battle must be freed either by appropriate work during a specified period or by paying half the price.*

[20]If someone employs in vile work or in a foreign land against his will a slave less than eight years old, without relatives, and belonging to any of these categories: born in the house, received as inheritance, obtained as a gift, and purchased;* or if someone sells or pledges a pregnant female slave without providing support for her confinement, the punishment is the lowest seizure fine, as also for the buyers and the witnesses.

[21]For anyone who does not make a slave an Ārya (3.13.15 n.) upon the payment of suitable price for redemption, the fine is 12 Paṇas and imprisonment until he does.

[22]The paternal relatives are heirs to the property of a slave; in their absence, the owner.

[23]The child fathered by an owner on his slave woman should be recognized as a non-slave* along with the mother. [24]If the mother works within the house looking after the affairs of the family, even her brother and sister* shall be non-slaves.

[25]For someone who, after redeeming a male or a female slave, either sells or pledges that person once again, the fine is 12 Paṇas, except when those persons themselves agree to it.

That concludes the rules concerning slaves.

Topic 65b: Rules concerning Laborers

SUBJECT OF EMPLOYERS

[26]Those nearby should keep an eye on a laborer's application to his work. [27]He should receive the wage agreed upon; one without a wage agreement, a wage proportionate to the work and the time. [28]An agricultural worker, a cowherd, and a trader without a wage agreement should receive one-tenth of the crops, butter, and merchandise, respectively, in which each has had a hand; [29]one with a wage agreement, however, the wage agreed upon.

[30]Groups who work with the expectation of remuneration, however, such as artisans, craftsmen, performers, physicians, bards, and attendants, should receive wages similar to others in their profession or as experts may determine.

[31]The ascertainment should be based solely on witnesses (2.36.5 n.). [32]If witnesses are unavailable, he (3.5.26 n.) should make inquiries at the place where the work was carried out. [33]For non-payment of wages, the fine is one-tenth* of the amount due (2.7.21 n.) or six Paṇas. [34]In case of denial, the fine is 12 Paṇas or one-fifth* of the amount due.

[35]If someone in distress, besieged by the current of a river, flames, robbers, or ferocious animals, cries for help promising to give all his possessions, his sons, his wife, and himself, and he is rescued, he should give a wage determined by experts. [36]That explains also the retraction of a promise made in distress under any circumstances.

> [37]A prostitute should receive her fee for sex when there is clear circumstantial evidence (3.12.51 n.) that a union has taken place. If she asks for too much, however, she loses, as also if she shows meanness of spirit or immodesty.

THAT CONCLUDES THE THIRTEENTH CHAPTER: "RULES CONCERNING SLAVES," AND "RULES CONCERNING LABORERS" OF "RULES GOVERNING SLAVES AND LABORERS" OF THE THIRD BOOK: "ON JUSTICES."

Chapter 14

SUBJECT OF EMPLOYEES

[1]For an employee who takes the wages but does not do the work, the fine is 12 Paṇas and detention until the work is done. [2]If he lacks the strength, if the work is repulsive, or if he is sick or struck by a calamity, he should have the right either to rescind the contract or to get the work done by someone else. [3]Alternatively, the employer should have the right to get the work done at the employee's expense.

[4]If there is a restrictive clause: "You must not get the work done by someone else, and I shall not work for anyone else," the fine for an employer who does not get him to do the work or for an employee who does not do the work is 12 Paṇas. [5]After completing the work of his employer, he does not have to continue to work for him if he is unwilling and has received wages from elsewhere.

[6]"When he* does not give work to one who has come to him,* that work should indeed be regarded as done," so state the teachers. [7]"No," says Kauṭilya. [8]"Wages are given for work done, not for work left undone. [9]If he

gets someone to do even a little amount of work and then stops him from working, his work should indeed be regarded as done."*

[10]When work has been carried out contrary to the right place and time or in a different manner, he may not, if he is unwilling, accept the work as done. [11]If someone does a greater amount of work than agreed upon, he should not make that exertion fruitless.

[12]That also explains issues relating to employees from an association. [13]A pledge of theirs* must remain for seven days. [14]After that, it must supply another and ensure the completion of the work. [15]An association, moreover, must neither remove nor bring in anyone without first informing the employer. [16]For violating this, the fine is 24 Paṇas; [17]for the person removed by the association the fine is half that.

That concludes the subject of employees.

Topic 66: Partnerships

[18]Employees from an association or associates in a partnership should receive the wages either as agreed upon or in equal shares.

[19]Alternatively, agriculturists and traders may give a share proportionate to the work he has done to someone who falls ill between the time of inception and conclusion of work relating to crops and merchandise. [20]If he supplies a substitute worker, they should give him a full share. [21]If the merchandise picked out becomes lucrative, however, they should immediately give the person who has taken ill his individual share; [22]for on the road, both success and failure are jointly shared.

[23]Once the work has commenced, on the other hand, for a healthy person who quits the fine is 12 Paṇas; [24]and no one is at liberty to quit.*

[25]A swindler, however, should be ensnared* by first granting a promise of safety and then offering an individual share for work; he should be given safety and his individual share. [26]If he steals again, he should be banished; so also if he goes elsewhere.* [27]In the event of a very serious offense, however, he should be treated like a traitor.*

[28]Priests officiating at a sacrifice should apportion the wages either as agreed upon or in equal shares, except for the items given for the special activities of each.* [29]In sacrifices such as the Agniṣṭoma, moreover, a priest falling ill after the sacrificial consecration should receive one-fifth of a share; after the selling of the Soma, one-quarter of a share; after the heating of the Pravargya vessel on the middle Upasad day, one-third of a share; after the middle Upasad day, one-half of a share; after the morning

pressing on the day of the Soma pressing, three-quarters of a share;* [30]and after the midday pressing, he should receive the full share,* [31]for then the sacrificial fees have been conveyed. [31]For, except at the pressing for Bṛhaspati,* the sacrificial fees are given at each pressing.

[33]That also explains what pertains to sacrificial fees of sacrifices lasting many days. [34]The remaining employees should do the work of those who are sick for up to ten days and nights, or others in whom they have confidence.

[35]If, on the other hand, the patron of the sacrifice becomes ill before the rite is completed, the officiating priests should complete the rite and take the sacrificial fee. [36]For anyone abandoning either the sacrificer or the priest while the rite remains incomplete, however, the punishment is the lowest seizure fine (2.1.29 n.).

> [37–38]An owner of 100 cows who has not established the three sacred fires,* an owner of 1,000 cows who has not offered a sacrifice, one who drinks liquor, a husband of a Śūdra woman, a murderer of a Brāhmaṇa, a man who has sex with his elder's wife, one addicted to receiving gifts from evil persons, a thief, and someone who officiates at the sacrifices of degraded persons—in such cases it is not a fault to abandon each other, because of the certainty of defiling the rite.

THAT CONCLUDES THE FOURTEENTH CHAPTER: "SUBJECT OF EMPLOYEES" OF "RULES GOVERNING SLAVES AND LABORERS" AND "PARTNERSHIPS" OF THE THIRD BOOK: "ON JUSTICES."

Chapter 15

Topic 67: Cancellation of Sale or Purchase

SALE

[1]For someone selling a merchandise and not delivering it, the fine is 12 Paṇas, except in the case of a defect, a disaster, or unacceptability.* [2]A defect is a defect of the merchandise. [3]A disaster is a hardship caused by the king, thieves, fire, or water. [4]Unacceptability is when it lacks numerous attributes or is contracted by someone in distress.*

[5]For traders, the period for cancellation is one day; for agriculturists, three days; for cattle herders, five days; [6]for people of mixed or the highest social classes, when they have sold their means of livelihood, seven days.*

[7]In the case of perishable merchandise, cancellation must be done with the restrictive clause: "It shall not be sold elsewhere." [8]For its violation, the fine is 24 Paṇas or one-tenth of the value of the merchandise.

PURCHASE

[9]For someone buying a merchandise and refusing to accept it, the fine is 12 Paṇas, except in the case of a defect, a disaster, or unacceptability (3.13.1, 4 n.). [10]Cancellation (by the buyer), moreover, is identical to cancellation by the seller.

[11]In the case of marriages among the three upper classes, however, revocation is valid until the joining of hands;* among Śūdras, until consummation. [12]Even after the couple have joined their hands, if a sexual defect is detected, revocation is valid, [13]but clearly not after the couple have had a child.

[14]For a man giving a girl in marriage without revealing a defect of the girl, the fine is 96 Paṇas and the return of the bride price and the woman's property (3.2.14–37); [15]for a suitor getting married without revealing a defect of the groom,* double the amount and the loss of the bride price and the woman's property.

[16]In the case of bipeds and quadrupeds, however, for declaring sluggish, sick, and ill-disposed* ones to be lively, healthy, and well-disposed,* the fine is 12 Paṇas. [17]Revocation is permitted for up to three fortnights in the case of quadrupeds and for up to one year in the case of humans, [18]for within that period of time it is possible to determine whether they are well-disposed or ill-disposed.*

> [19]In the case of a gift or a sale, the court officials should make a
> cancellation in such a way that neither the donor nor the receiver
> is harmed.*

THAT CONCLUDES THE FIFTEENTH CHAPTER: "CANCELLATION OF SALE OR PURCHASE" OF THE THIRD BOOK: "ON JUSTICES."

Chapter 16

Topic 68: Non-Delivery of Gifts

[1]The non-payment of debts has also explained the non-delivery of gifts.

[2]In the event of cancellation, a gift must remain in one location without being subject to transaction.* [3]To a person who, after gifting all his

possessions or his sons or wife, cancels it, he (3.5.26 n.) should give permission; [4]as also a gift for the purpose of Law to sinful persons or for harmful activities, a gift for the purpose of Success to people who do not help or who cause harm, and a gift for the purpose of Pleasure to unworthy people.*

[5]Experts, moreover, should arrange a cancellation in such a way that neither the donor nor the receiver is harmed (3.15.19).

[6]For someone receiving a gift given out of fear—fear of punishment, fear of an upbraiding, or fear of harm—the fine for theft (2.7.39 n.); [7]as also for someone giving* a gift out of anger to hurt another person and a gift out of arrogance surpassing gifts of kings—[8]in this case, the fine is the highest.*

[9]A liability arising out of suretyship (3.11.16–17 n.), the balance of a fine or bride price, a gambling debt, a debt related to liquor, and a gift out of love—these need not be paid, if unwilling, by a son or an heir who inherits the estate.

That concludes the non-delivery of gifts.

Topic 69: Sale by a Non-Owner

[10]With reference to sale by a non-owner, however—an owner, when he discovers a lost or stolen article, should get a Justice to impound it. [11]Or else, if there is an urgency* with regard to place and time, he may impound it himself and deliver it to him. [12]The Justice, moreover, should interrogate the owner:* "From where did you obtain this?" [13]If he points out a customary method of acquisition but not the seller, he is freed by surrendering the article. [14]If the seller is discovered, he should pay the price* and the fine for theft (2.7.39 n.). [15]If he were to find someone who would exonerate him, he shall be exonerated—until persons providing exonerations are exhausted. [16]When exhausted, that person should pay the price and the fine for theft.*

[17]The one who lost the article, furthermore, should receive the lost article that was recovered by showing proof of ownership. [18]If there is no proof of ownership, the fine is one-fifth the amount,* [19]and that article shall become legally the property of the king. [20]For an owner retrieving a lost or stolen article without informing (a Justice), the punishment is the lowest seizure fine (2.1.29 n.).

[21]A lost or stolen article that has been recovered should remain in the customs house (3.12.13 n.). [22]What remains unclaimed after three

fortnights, the king may take, or the owner by showing proof of ownership. [23]He should pay a charge of five Paṇas for each biped, four Paṇas for a single-hoofed animal, two Paṇas for a cow or buffalo, and a quarter Paṇa for small farm animals; [24]for gems, articles of high or low value, and forest produce, he should pay 5 percent of the value.

[25]Things robbed by an enemy king or a tribal chief, however, the king should recover and restore to their respective owners. [26]Anything stolen by thieves that cannot be found—or that he is powerless to recover—the king should restore from his own property. [27]What has been seized as a result of individual plunder,* he should recover and restore or pay compensation.

[28]Alternatively, what a man has brought from an enemy territory by his own valor he may enjoy as directed by the king, with the exception of Ārya individuals and the property of gods (1.19.29 n.), Brāhmaṇas, and recluses.

That concludes sale by a non-owner.

Topic 70: Relation between Owner and his Property

[29]With reference to the relation between owner and his property, however—for assets to which the documentary evidence* has been lost, their continuous enjoyment establishes the respective ownership.

[30]When someone pays no heed while his property is being enjoyed by others for ten years, he forfeits it, except in the case of children, old people, the sick, those who have fallen on hard times, those who have gone abroad, and those who have migrated, and when there is a tumult in the country. [31]He should not subject to an inquiry* an immovable property (3.8.2) that has been left unoccupied and to which no one has paid any heed for 20 years.

[32]Relatives, Vedic scholars, or members of religious orders residing—outside the presence of kings*—in immovable properties belonging to others do not obtain ownership over them through enjoyment; nor over a deposit, a pledge, a treasure trove, a consignment (3.1.7 n.), a woman, a boundary, and the property of the king or a Vedic scholar.*

[33]Hermits or members of religious orders should live in a large compound without disturbing each other. [34]They should put up with a little disturbance. [35]Or, one who arrives first should provide lodgings in turn.* [36]He (3.5.26 n.) should expel anyone who does not provide them.

[37]Teacher, pupil, brother in the Law, and fellow student, in that order, inherit the property of a forest hermit, an ascetic, and a Vedic student.

[38]In legal disputes among them, moreover, they should perform fasts, bathing, fire worship, and worship of Mahākacca* for the benefit of the king during as many nights as the number of Paṇas in the corresponding fine. [39]Holy men belonging to religious orders do not have money or gold. [40]They should propitiate with fasts and observances according to the practices of each, except in cases of assault, theft, forcible seizure, and sexual misconduct. [41]In these cases, the prescribed punishments should be carried out.

> [42]The king should restrain through punishment those who behave improperly in the various ascetic orders, for when righteousness (*dharma*) is struck by unrighteousness (*adharma*), it strikes the ruler who remains indifferent.

THAT CONCLUDES THE SIXTEENTH CHAPTER: "NON-DELIVERY OF GIFTS," "SALE BY A NON-OWNER," AND "RELATION BETWEEN OWNER AND HIS PROPERTY" OF THE THIRD BOOK: "ON JUSTICES."

Chapter 17

Topic 71: Forcible Seizure

[1]Forcible seizure is a violent act in the presence of the victim.* [2]When it is committed in his absence, it is theft, as also in the case of denial.*

[3]"When jewels, articles of high or low value, and forest produce are seized forcibly, the fine is equal to the value of the property," so state the Mānavas. [4]"Twice the value of the property," say the Auśanasas. [5]"According to the crime," says Kauṭilya.

[6]"For small items such as flowers, fruits, vegetables, roots, bulbs, cooked food, and vessels made with leather, reed, or clay, the fine is a minimum of 12 Paṇas and a maximum of 24 Paṇas. [7]For big items such as goods made of iron, wood, or rope, small farm animals, and cloth, the fine is a minimum of 24 Paṇas and a maximum of 48 Paṇas. [8]For big items such as vessels made of copper, steel, bronze, glass, and ivory, the fine is a minimum of 48 Paṇas and a maximum of 96 Paṇas, which is the lowest seizure fine (2.1.29 n.). [9]For big items such as large farm animals, humans, land, houses, money, gold, and fine clothes, the fine is a minimum of 200 Paṇas and a maximum of 500 Paṇas, which is the middle seizure fine. [10]For a man who confines, gets someone to confine,

or releases from confinement a woman or a man through the use of force, the fine is a minimum of 500 Paṇas and a maximum of 1,000 Paṇas, which is the highest seizure fine." So state the teachers.

[11]"A man who gets someone to commit forcible seizure, saying, 'I will take responsibility,' should pay double. [12]One who does so, saying, 'I will give as much money as will be needed,' should pay a quadruple fine. [13]One who makes someone do so, saying, 'I will give so much money,' and specifying an amount, should pay the specified amount of money, as well as the fine." So state the Bārhaspatyas.

[14]"If he offers anger, intoxication, or folly as an excuse, he should be assessed the prescribed fine," so states Kauṭilya.

> [15]Whenever fines are assessed, one should know that there is an impost* of eight Paṇas per 100, and when fines exceed 100, also a surcharge (2.6.10 n.) of five Paṇas per 100.
>
> [16]Impost and surcharge are illegitimate, existing because of the profusion of crimes among the subjects or the natural iniquity of kings; only the basic fine, according to tradition, is legitimate.*

THAT CONCLUDES THE SEVENTEENTH CHAPTER: "FORCIBLE SEIZURE" OF THE THIRD BOOK: "ON JUSTICES."

Chapter 18

Topic 72: Verbal Assault

[1]Insult, abuse, and threat constitute verbal assault.*

[2]Among insults relating to body, character, learning, occupation, and country, for an insult relating to the body with words such as "one-eyed" and "lame," the fine is three Paṇas if it is true, and six Paṇas if the insult is untrue.

[3]For disdain couched as praise of people who are one-eyed, lame, and the like, saying, "What beautiful eyes you have!" the fine is 12 Paṇas.

[4]For abuse by referring to people as lepers, insane, impotent, and the like, depending on whether it is true, false, or disdain couched as praise, the fines are 12 Paṇas increased progressively by 12 (2.36.28 n.), if it is among equals. [5]If it is directed at superiors, the fines are doubled; if it is directed at inferiors, the fines are cut in half; and if it is directed at the wives of others, the fines are doubled. The fines are cut in half if it is done

through negligence, intoxication, folly, and the like. [6]Leprosy and insanity are authenticated by physicians and men living nearby, while impotency is authenticated by women and by froth in the urine and the sinking of feces in water.*

[7]For an insult relating to character among Brāhmaṇas, Kṣatriyas, Vaiśyas, Śūdras, and the lowest-born, if it is directed by one listed later at one listed earlier, the fines are three Paṇas increased progressively by three (2.36.28 n.); if it is directed by one listed earlier at one listed later, the fines are decreased progressively by two Paṇas;* the same applies to abuse with such words as "Vile Brāhmaṇa!"

[8]That also explains insults relating to the learning of bards, insults relating to the occupation of artisans and performers, and insults relating to the country of people coming from Prājjūna, Gandhāra, and the like.

[9]A man who issues a threat to do something to another, saying, "I will do this to you!" but who does not carry it out, should pay half the fine prescribed for actually carrying it out. [10]If he is incapable of carrying it out or if he offers the excuse of anger, intoxication, or folly, he should pay a fine of 12 Paṇas. [11]If he harbors feelings of hostility and is capable of doing harm, he should provide a surety for as long as he lives.

> [12]For reviling his own country or village, a man deserves the lowest fine (2.1.29 n.); for reviling the caste and association, the middle fine; and for reviling gods and sanctuaries, the highest fine.

THAT CONCLUDES THE EIGHTEENTH CHAPTER: "VERBAL ASSAULT" OF THE THIRD BOOK: "ON JUSTICES."

Chapter 19

Topic 73: Physical Assault

[1]Touching, menacing, and striking constitute physical assault.

[2]For someone touching someone's body below the navel with the hand, mud, ashes, or dust, the fine is three Paṇas; for doing so with the same that are impure or with the foot or spit, it is six Paṇas; and for doing so with vomit, urine, feces, and the like, it is 12 Paṇas. [2]For doing so above the navel, the fines are doubled, and for doing so on the head, the fines are quadrupled—these apply among equals. [4]When directed at superiors,

the fines are doubled; when directed at inferiors, the fines are cut in half; and when directed at the wives of others, the fines are doubled. The fines are cut in half if these are done through negligence, intoxication, folly, and the like (3.18.5).

[5]For pulling the feet, garment, hands, or hair, the fine is six Paṇas increased progressively by six (2.36.28 n.). [6]For pressing, squashing, twisting, dragging, and pinning down, the punishment is the lowest seizure fine (2.1.29 n.). [7]For running away after throwing someone down, the fine is half that amount.

[8]When* a Śūdra uses a particular limb to injure a Brāhmaṇa, he (3.5.26 n.) should have that limb of his cut off—[9]for menacing, compensation;* and for touching, half the fine. [10]That explains also issues relating to Caṇḍālas and impure persons.*

[11]For menacing with the hand, the fine is a minimum of three Paṇas and a maximum of 12 Paṇas; with the feet, double that; with an object that can cause pain, the lowest seizure fine (2.1.29 n.); with an object that can endanger life, the middle fine.

[12]For someone causing pain without drawing blood using any of the following objects: stick, clod, stone, metal rod, or rope, the fine is 24 Paṇas; it is doubled if blood is drawn, except in the case of infected blood.* [13]For someone beating a man almost to the point of death without drawing blood, or for dislocating a hand or a foot, the punishment is the lowest seizure fine; as also for breaking a hand, foot, or tooth; for cutting an ear or the nose; and for opening up a wound, except in the case of infected wounds. [14]For breaking the thigh or neck, for damaging an eye, or for causing an impediment to speech, movement, or eating, the punishment is the middle seizure fine, and in addition the expenses for recovery. [15]In the case of death, he should be brought before the agency for the Eradication of Thorns (4.1.1).

[16]For a group of people beating a single man, each is assessed double the fine.

[17]"A brawl or trespass that took place a while back should not be the subject of litigation," so state the teachers. [18]"A criminal should never be allowed to go free," says Kauṭilya. [19]"With respect to a brawl, the one who comes (to the court) first wins, for it is the one who is unable to bear that runs (to the court)," so state the teachers. [20]"No," says Kauṭilya. [21]"Whether one comes earlier or later, it is the witnesses who provide the proof; and when there are no witnesses, the injury or circumstantial evidence (3.12.51 n.) regarding the quarrel."

[22]When someone does not respond to a lawsuit relating to an injury, he is convicted* that very day.

[23]For someone who steals an item during a brawl, the fine is ten Paṇas; for damaging a small item, its restitution and an equal amount as a fine; for damaging a big item, its restitution and double the amount as a fine; and for damaging clothes, jewelry, money, or articles of gold, their restitution and the lowest seizure fine (2.1.29 n.).

[24]For a man who makes the wall of someone else's house shake by battering it, the fine is three Paṇas; for cutting or breaking it, six Paṇas, as well as its repair. [25]For a man who throws an object that can cause pain into someone else's house, the fine is 12 Paṇas; for throwing an object that can endanger life, the lowest seizure fine.

[26]For causing pain to small farm animals with sticks and the like, the fine is one or two Paṇas; for drawing blood, the fine is doubled. [27]For doing the same to large farm animals, the fines are doubled, plus the expenses for recovery.

[28]For cutting sprigs from trees in city parks that produce flowers and fruits and give shade, the fine is six Paṇas; for cutting small branches, 12 Paṇas; for cutting stout branches, 24 Paṇas; for cutting the trunk, the lowest seizure fine; for uprooting, the middle. [29]In the case of bushes and creepers that produce flowers and fruits and provide shade, the fines are cut in half, as also in the case of trees growing in a holy place, ascetic grove, or cemetery.

> [30]In the case of trees marking boundaries, sanctuary trees, distinguished trees, and those in royal forests, double the same fines should be imposed.

THAT CONCLUDES THE NINETEENTH CHAPTER: "PHYSICAL ASSAULT" OF THE THIRD BOOK: "ON JUSTICES."

Chapter 20

Topic 74: Gambling and Betting

[1]The Superintendent of Gambling should have gambling carried out in one location—[2]for anyone gambling elsewhere the fine is 12 Paṇas—so as to find out those who have secret occupations.*

[3]"In a lawsuit relating to gambling, the winner receives the lowest seizure fine (2.1.29 n.), and the loser the middle fine;* [4]for the latter, being

foolish by nature, craves to win and cannot bear to lose," so state the teachers. [5]"No," says Kauṭilya. [6]"If a loser is assessed a double fine, then no one will come to the king. [7]For, by and large, gamblers cheat when they play."

[8]The Superintendents should provide for them genuine shells and dice. [9]For substituting other shells or dice, the fine is 12 Paṇas; for cheating at play, the lowest seizure fine and the forfeiture of the winnings; if there is fraud,* in addition the fine for theft (2.7.39 n.).

[10]The Superintendent should take 5 percent of the winnings, as well as the rental charges for shells, dice, leather straps, and ivory cubes;* and charges for water, ground, and play. [11]He should carry out the pledging and sale of articles. [12]For not interdicting offenses with respect to dice, ground, and hands, the fine is doubled.

[13]That also explains betting,* with the exception of betting on learning and craftsmanship.

Topic 75: Miscellaneous

[14]With regard to the miscellaneous, on the other hand—for not returning at the appointed place and time anything borrowed, rented, pledged, or deposited; for missing the place and time for assembling or staying at a particular time of night or day; for someone charging a Brāhmaṇa the toll at a military checkpoint or a ferry (2.28.18); and for an invitation that bypasses one's neighbors to the front and back,* the fine is 12 Paṇas.

[15]For someone who does not deliver an article as directed,* who violates his brother's wife with his hand, who has sex with a prostitute in the exclusive keeping of another, who buys* a piece of merchandise reserved for another person, who breaks into a sealed house, or who causes trouble to any of the 40 neighboring families (3.9.2 n.), the fine is 48 Paṇas.

[16]For someone who has received the family valuables and denies it, for someone who violently rapes a widow living on her own, for a Caṇḍāla who touches an Ārya woman, for someone who does not rush to the aid of a neighbor in distress or who rushes without a reason, for someone who feeds rabble recluses such as Śākyas and Ājīvakas* at divine and ancestral rites, the fine is 100 Paṇas.

[17]For someone who carries out an interrogation by administering an oath without being authorized to do so, who performs an official's duties without being appointed as an official, who castrates small farm animals used for stud, or who causes an abortion of a female slave through medication, the punishment is the lowest seizure fine.

[18]A father and son, a husband and wife, a brother and sister, a maternal uncle and nephew, a pupil and teacher—for any one of these abandoning the other who has not fallen from caste, and for someone who abandons another man who has come in the same caravan in the middle of a village, the punishment is the lowest seizure fine (2.1.29 n.); for doing so in a wild tract, the middle; for causing him harm as a result of that, the highest; for others going in the same caravan, half those fines.

[19]For someone who confines or gets another to confine a man who should not be confined, who releases a man who has been confined, or who confines or gets another to confine a child who is still a minor (3.3.1), the fine is 1,000 Paṇas.

[20]Distinctive fines should be imposed in keeping with the distinctive character of the person and the offense.

[21]A head of a religious order, a recluse, a sick person, someone wearied by hunger, thirst, or travel, a foreigner, someone oppressed by a fine, and a pauper should be shown compassion. [22]In the case of gods (1.19.29 n.), Brāhmaṇas, recluses, women, children, the aged, the sick, and the helpless,* who may not come (to the court) themselves, the Justices should initiate lawsuits on their behalf, and they should not dismiss their cases under the pretext of place, time, or enjoyment.

[23]Men are to be honored on the basis of preeminence in learning, intelligence, bravery, birth, and deeds.

> [24]In this way, Justices should try lawsuits without engaging in deceit, being impartial to all persons, inspiring trust, and being loved by the people.

THAT CONCLUDES THE TWENTIETH CHAPTER: "GAMBLING AND BETTING" AND "MISCELLANEOUS" OF THE THIRD BOOK: "ON JUSTICES."

THAT CONCLUDES THE THIRD BOOK: "ON JUSTICES" OF KAUṬILYA'S *ARTHAŚĀSTRA*.

Book Four

Eradication of Thorns

Chapter 1

Topic 76: Surveillance of Artisans

[1]Magistrates of ministerial rank in groups of three (3.1.1 n.) should carry out the Eradication of Thorns.

ARTISANS

[2]Those able to indemnify a valuable article—supervisors of artisans, collectors of deposits, and artisans working with their own capital—acting under the authority of their guild may accept deposits.* [3]In the event of death,* the guild shall assume liability for the deposit.

[4]They should perform any task, moreover, only after stipulating the time it would take, the place, and the kind of work involved; the kind of work may be an excuse for leaving the time and place unstipulated. [5]If the stipulated time is exceeded, the result is the loss of one-quarter of the pay and a fine of twice that amount. [6]They shall be liable for anything that is lost or damaged, except in case of decay or disaster (3.12.23, 29). [7]If the work is done in a different way, the result is the loss of pay and a fine of twice that amount.*

WEAVERS

[8]Weavers should increase the weight of yarn by one-tenth. [9]If there is a reduction in the increase, the fine is twice the amount of the reduction.*

[10]Pay* for weaving is equal to the value of the yarn; in the case of flax and Kauśeya silk, one and a half times the value; and in the case of "leaf-wool" silk (2.11.107 n.), blankets, and Dukūla (2.11.102 n.), double the value.

[11]In case there is a reduction of size,* the pay is reduced by the amount of the reduction; in addition, double that amount as a fine.* In case there is a reduction in weight, the fine is four times the amount of the reduction. In case the yarn is switched, the fine is double its value. [12]This also explains issues relating to the weaving of double cloth (2.11.105).

[13]In the case of wool, five Palas is the reduction in one Tulā while carding, as also in the case of hair.

WASHERMEN

[14]Washermen* should wash clothes on planks of wood or smooth stones. [15]Those who wash them elsewhere should pay compensation for any damage to the clothes and a fine of six Paṇas.

[16]Those who wear garments other than ones marked with a club sign* should pay a fine of three Paṇas. [17]For selling, renting, or pledging the clothes of others, moreover, the fine is 12 Paṇas; and for exchanging clothes, the fine is double the value and the return of the clothes.

[18]They should return one that is cleansed white like a bud in one day; one that is scrubbed on a stone slab in two days; one that has the color of washed yarn in three days; and one that is burnished white in four days.*

[19]One that is dyed light red takes five days; one that is dyed blue, six days; and a high-quality garment that is dyed the color of saffron flower, lac, or madder, a process requiring arduous work and careful treatment, seven days.* [20]After that time, they incur the loss of pay.* [21]In case of disputes regarding dyeing, trustworthy experts should make a determination regarding pay.

[22]For garments of the highest value, the pay is one Paṇa; for those of mid-value, half a Paṇa; for those of lowest value, a quarter Paṇa; for coarse ones, one or two Māṣakas; and for those that are dyed, double.* [23]At the first wash, the loss of value amounts to one-fourth, and at the second, to one-fifth.* [24]That also explains amounts beyond those.

[25]The discussion of washermen also explains issues pertaining to tailors.

GOLDSMITHS

[26]For goldsmiths purchasing silver or gold in its original form* from a dishonest person without reporting it, the fine is 12 Paṇas; in an altered form, 24 Paṇas; from a thief, 48 Paṇas; [27]for purchases made at a price below the value, secretly, or in an altered form, the fine for theft (2.7.39 n.), as also for deceit with respect to a manufactured article.

[28]For a man stealing one Māṣaka from a Suvarṇa of gold, the fine is 200 Paṇas; for a man stealing one Māṣaka from a Dharaṇa of silver, the fine is 12 Paṇas. [29]That also explains amounts beyond those. [30]For a man who carries out the enhancement of the color or the strategy of removal,* the fine is 500 Paṇas. [31]When there is deceit with regard to these two, he should regard it as extraction of color.*

[32]For one Dharaṇa of silver, the pay is one Māṣaka; for one Suvarṇa of gold, one-eighth.* [33]Corresponding to the excellence of skill, the pay may be doubled. [34]That also explains amounts beyond those. [35]In the case of copper, steel, bell metal, Vaikṛntaka (2.12.16 n.), and brass (2.12.23 n.), the pay is five per 100.*

[36]One-tenth is the loss from a lump of copper. [37]For a loss of one Pala,* the fine is double the amount lost. [38]That also explains amounts beyond those. [39]One-twentieth is the loss from a lump of lead or tin; [40]and the pay for it is one Kākaṇī per Pala. [41]One-fifth is the loss from a lump of iron; [42]and the pay for it is two Kākaṇīs per Pala. [43]That also explains amounts beyond those.

COINS

[44]For an Examiner of Coins (2.12.25) who proscribes as inauthentic an established Paṇa currency that ought not to be proscribed or refuses to proscribe as inauthentic one that ought to be proscribed, the fine is 12 Paṇas. [45]A Paṇa becomes legitimate currency upon the payment of the surcharge (2.12.26). [46]For someone earning* one Māṣaka on a Paṇa, the fine is 12 Paṇas. [47]That also explains amounts beyond those.

[48]For a man who orders the manufacture of a counterfeit coin, or receives or passes into circulation such a coin, the fine is 1,000 Paṇas; for one who deposits such a coin in the treasury, execution.

TREASURE TROVES

[49]Bearers and dust washers (2.13.33) should receive one-third of a valuable article (they find), and the king shall take two-thirds, as well as any gem. [50]For stealing a gem, the punishment is the highest fine (2.1.29 n.).

[51]When someone provides information about pit mines, gems, or treasure troves, the informant should receive one-sixth; one-twelfth if he is a state employee. [52]In the case of a treasure trove, anything over 100,000 Paṇas goes to the king; [53]of what is below that amount, he should give one-sixth.* [54]An inhabitant of the countryside, if he is upright, should receive the entire amount of a treasure trove belonging to his ancestors by

producing proof of ownership. [55]If he has no proof of ownership, the fine is 500 Paṇas; if he appropriates it secretly, the fine is 1,000 Paṇas.

PHYSICIANS

[56]For a physician who employs a life-threatening treatment without reporting it, the punishment is the lowest seizure fine in the case of death; in the case of death due to malpractice, the middle fine. [57]When an injury to a vital part or a physical impairment* is caused, he should regard it as a case of physical assault (3.19).

ACTORS

[58]Performers should live together in the same place during the rainy season. [59]They should avoid conferring excessive affection or excessive insults on one person.* [60]For violating this, the fine is 12 Paṇas. [61]They may freely perform satirical acts poking fun at various regions, castes, lineages, schools,* and love affairs.

[62]The discussion of actors explains also issues pertaining to wandering troubadours and mendicants. [63]For the latter, when they declare a certain amount of Paṇas with their iron spike, the punishment is an equal number of strokes with a whip.*

[64]In the case of further kinds of activities, he should fix the pay for craftsmen in accordance with the products they manufacture.

> [65]In this manner, he should prevent traders, artisans, and performers, as well as mendicants and other charlatans (1.20.18 n.)—who are all thieves although not called thieves—from oppressing the country.

THAT CONCLUDES THE FIRST CHAPTER: "SURVEILLANCE OF ARTISANS" OF THE FOURTH BOOK: "ERADICATION OF THORNS."

Chapter 2

Topic 77: Surveillance of Traders

[1]The Superintendent of the Marketplace should organize within the marketplace the pawning or sale of secondhand implements that have been authenticated with proof of ownership.

[2]He should inspect equipment for weighing and measuring, moreover, because of cheating in standard weights and measures (2.19). [3]In the case of a Parimāṇī or a Droṇa, to be half a Pala less or more is not an offense.* [4]If it is one Pala less or more, the fine is 12 Paṇas. [5]That also explains the increase in the fine for every additional Pala. [6]In the case of a Tulā, to be one Karṣa less or more is not an offense.* [7]If it is two Karṣas less or more, the fine is six Paṇas. [8]That also explains the increase in the fine for every additional Karṣa. [9]In the case of an Āḍhaka, to be half a Karṣa less or more is not an offense.* [10]If it is one Karṣa less or more, the fine is three Paṇas. [11]That also explains the increase in the fine for every additional Karṣa. [12]In the case of specific weights and measures other than these, he should make an inference.*

[13]For someone who, after buying with weights or measures larger than the standard, sells the same using ones that are smaller than the standard,* these same fines are doubled. [14]In the case of commodities sold by number, for someone pilfering anything that is one-eighth of the price of the commodities,* the fine is 96 Paṇas. [15[20]]For a weigher or a measurer who by sleight of hand causes a diminution* that amounts to one-eighth of an article valued at one Paṇa, the fine is 200 Paṇas. [16[21]]That also explains successive 200-Paṇa increases in the fines.

[17[22]]For adulterating grain, fat, sugar, salt, perfume, or medicine with substances of similar kind, the fine is 12 Paṇas. [18[15]]For someone presenting for sale or pawn as genuine an article that is not genuine—whether it is made of wood, metal, or gems; or made of rope, leather, or clay; or made of yarn, bark fiber, or hair—the fine is eight times its price. [19[16]]For someone presenting for sale or pawn an article that is not of high value as one of high value, an article not belonging to a particular class as one belonging to that class, an article containing a fake luster, a sham article, or an article whose container is switched,* the fine is 54 Paṇas if its price is trifling; double that if the price is one Paṇa; and 200 Paṇas if the price is two Paṇas. [20[17]]That also explains the proportional increase of the fine corresponding to the increase in price.

[21[18]]For artisans and craftsmen who collude in generating profit derived from lowering the quality of their work or impeding sales and purchases,* the fine is 1,000 Paṇas. [22[19]]For traders too who collude in withholding commodities or in selling them at an inordinate price, the fine is 1,000 Paṇas.

[23[20, 23]]After adding up* the total earnings of the day, the Trader should allot to them an allowance on which they should be able to live, an allowance distinct from weights and measures, or from price and kind.*

[24]Whatever has fallen between buyer and seller that is distinct from the amount taken in, [25]with that they may create, when permitted, stockpiles of grain and commodities.* [26]The Superintendent of Commodities should confiscate from them stockpiles created in any other way. [27]With that, he should engage in the sale of grain and commodities as a favor to the subjects (2.16.5).

[28]He should fix for them (4.2.23 n.), moreover, a profit above the authorized purchase price of 5 percent in the case of local commodities, and of 10 percent in the case of foreign commodities. [29]For those who increase the price beyond that or, in buying or selling, realize a profit beyond that, the fine is 200 Paṇas for every five Paṇas of additional profit per 100 Paṇas. [30]That also explains the proportional increase in the fine corresponding to the increase in the price.

[31]When a joint purchase by them remains unsold, furthermore, he should not permit another joint purchase; [32]and when commodities become damaged, he should act favorably toward them.

[33]If there is an oversupply of commodities, the Superintendent of Commodities should have all the commodities sold* in one location. [34]As long as these remain unsold, others should refrain from selling. [35]They should sell those commodities for a daily wage* as a favor to the subjects.

[36]In the case of commodities remote in terms of place or time, however,

> he* should, being an expert in pricing, fix their prices, after calculating the outlay, the production of the commodity, duty, interest, rent, and other expenses.

THAT CONCLUDES THE SECOND CHAPTER: "SURVEILLANCE OF TRADERS" OF THE FOURTH BOOK: "ERADICATION OF THORNS."

Chapter 3

Topic 78: Remedial Measures against Disasters

[1]There are eight great dangers arising from fate: fire, water, disease, famine, rats, vicious animals, snakes, and demons. [2]He* should protect the countryside from these.

FIRE

[3]In the summer, villagers (2.28.2 n.) should do their cooking either outdoors or overseen by a group of ten households.* [4]Prevention of fires has been explained in the "Regimen of the City Manager" (2.36) and, with reference to the royal compound, in the "Regimen of the Residence" (1.20). [5]Further, he should have rites of fire worship carried out on days of the moon's change* with Bali offerings, fire offerings, and the proclamation of blessings.

WATER

[6]During the rainy season, villagers (2.28.2 n.) along river banks should live away from the flood plain. [7]They should also keep at hand planks, bamboos, and boats. [8]They should rescue anyone being carried away, using gourds, skin bags, floats, wooden blocks, and twisted rope. [9]For those who do not run to his aid, the fine is 12 Paṇas, except for those without floats.

[10]Further, on the days of the moon's change (4.3.5 n.), he should have rituals of river worship carried out. [11]Those proficient in magical practices or those knowledgeable in the Vedas should perform spells against rain.

[12]During a drought, he should have rites of worship of Indra, Gaṅgā, mountains, and Mahākaccha (3.16.38 n.) carried out.

DISEASE

[13]They should counteract* the danger of disease through occult remedial measures, physicians through medicines, and thaumaturgic ascetics through pacificatory rites and penances.

[14]That also explains an epidemic. [15]He should have these carried out: bathing at sacred fords, worship of Mahākaccha (3.16.38 n.), milking cows in the cemetery, burning a headless trunk,* and a gods' night.*

[16]In the case of disease or epidemic affecting farm animals, he should have lustration rites of the stalls and equipment and the worship of their respective gods carried out.

FAMINE

[17]During a time of famine, the king should first gather a stockpile of seeds and foodstuffs and then grant favors: work on forts or irrigation projects in exchange for foodstuffs, or distribution of foodstuffs, or handing over the region.* [18]Alternatively, he may seek refuge with allies or bring about a reduction or a transfer of population.* [19]Or else, he may migrate along with the people of the countryside to another region (1.17.42 n.) where

crops have flourished, or repair to an area by the sea, a lake, or a reservoir. [20]Or, he should take to growing cereals, vegetables, roots, and fruits along reservoirs, or to slaughtering deer, game animals, birds, vicious animals, and fish.

RATS

[21]When there is a danger from rats, cats and mongooses should be released. [22]If these are captured or killed, the fine is 12 Paṇas, as also for not keeping dogs confined, except in the case of foresters. [23]He should strew grains smeared with the milk of the Snuhi-plant or mixed with secret compounds. [24]Or, he should institute a rat tax;* [25]or thaumaturgic ascetics should perform a pacificatory rite. [26]On the days of the moon's change (4.3.5 n.), moreover, he should have rites of rat worship carried out.

[27]That also explains remedial actions in the case of locusts, birds, and insects.

VICIOUS ANIMALS

[28]When there is a danger from vicious animals, he should scatter corpses of farm animals mixed with a coma-inducing liquid or entrails filled with Madana and Kodrava-grain.* [29]Fowlers or hunters should set to work with concealed cages and pits. [30]Men with protective armor and carrying weapons should kill the vicious animals.

[31]For anyone not rushing to render assistance, the fine is 12 Paṇas. [32]The same amount is the reward for anyone who kills a vicious animal. [33]On the days of the moon's change (4.3.5 n.), moreover, he should have rites of mountain worship carried out.

[34]That also explains the remedial measures against herds of deer or game animals, flocks of birds, or crocodiles.

SNAKES

[35]When there is a danger from snakes, experts in the cure of poisons should set to work with incantations and medicines. [36]Or else, people should get together and kill the snakes. [37]Or, experts in the Atharvaveda should perform magic spells. [38]On the days of the moon's change (4.3.5 n.), moreover, he should get the rites of cobra worship performed.

[39]That also explains the remedial measures against dangers from aquatic creatures.

DEMONS

[40]When there is a danger from demons, experts in the Atharvaveda or those proficient in magical practices should perform demon-killing rites (3.1.37 n.). [41]On the days of the moon's change (4.3.5 n.), moreover, he should get the rites of sanctuary worship performed with offerings of platforms, umbrellas, food, pennants, and goats.

[42]During any danger, they should make offerings day and night, saying, "We offer you the porridge." [43]In all cases, moreover, like a father, he should render support to those who have been afflicted.

> [44]Therefore, those proficient in magical practices and thaumaturgic ascetics should reside in his territory, being honored by the king as those who remedy adversities arising from fate.

THAT CONCLUDES THE THIRD CHAPTER: "REMEDIAL MEASURES AGAINST DISASTERS" OF THE FOURTH BOOK: "ERADICATION OF THORNS."

Chapter 4

Topic 79: Surveillance of People with Secret Income

[1]Surveillance of the countryside has been dealt with in "Regimen for the Collector" (2.35). [2]With respect to it, we will describe the Eradication of Thorns.

[3]The Collector should post in the countryside agents acting undercover as thaumaturgic ascetics, renouncers, traveling holy men,* wandering troubadours, charlatans (1.20.18 n.), entertainers,* diviners, soothsayers, astrologers, physicians, madmen, mutes, deaf persons, idiots, blind persons, traders, artisans, craftsmen, performers, brothel keepers, tavern keepers, and vendors of flat bread, cooked meat, and boiled rice. [4]They should find out the honesty and dishonesty of village officials (2.28.2 n.) and superintendents. [5]And when he suspects anyone of them of having a secret source of income, he should employ a secret agent to spy on him.

[6]After winning his confidence, a secret agent should tell a Justice or Magistrate:* "A lawsuit has been filed against this relative of mine. Remedy this misfortune of his, and do accept this money."* [7]If he does

so, he should be sent into exile* as a bribe taker. [8]That also explains issues pertaining to Magistrates.

[9]A secret agent should tell a village official or a corrupt superintendent:* "That scoundrel is very wealthy. He has fallen into this misfortune.* Using that, do blackmail him." [10]If he does so, he should be sent into exile as an extortionist.

[11]Or, posturing as the target of a lawsuit, he should instigate those well known as bearing false witness with a lot of money. [12]If they do so, they should be sent into exile as false witnesses. [13]That also explains issues pertaining to those who suborn false testimony.

[14]Or, if he considers someone to be a wizard inducing love through incantations and root witchcraft,* or through cremation-ground rituals, a secret agent should tell him: "I love that man's wife—*or* daughter-in-law *or* daughter. Make it such that she loves me in return. And accept this money." [15]If he does so, he should be sent into exile as a love-inducing wizard. [16]That also explains issues pertaining to those who are given to black magic and sorcery.

[17]Or, if he considers someone to be a manufacturer, buyer, or seller of poison, or a dealer in medicine or food to be a poisoner, a secret agent should tell him: "That man is my enemy. Bring about his death. And accept this money." [18]If he does so, he should be sent into exile as a poisoner. [19]That also explains issues pertaining to one who deals in coma-inducing mixtures (4.3.28 n.).

[20]Or, if he considers someone to be a manufacturer of counterfeit currency—one who is a frequent buyer of various metals and acids, and of coal, bellows, tongs, vices, anvils, dies, chisels, and crucibles; one who is betrayed by his hands and clothes being soiled with soot, ash, and smoke; one in whose possession are found the tools of a blacksmith—a secret agent should gain his trust by becoming his pupil and establishing dealings with him, and then expose him. [21]Once he is exposed, he should be sent into exile as a manufacturer of counterfeit currency (4.1.48). [22]That also explains issues pertaining to an extractor of color (4.1.31 n.) and dealer in counterfeit gold.

> [23]The 13* with secret income and engaged in causing injury, however, should be sent into exile; or they may give a sum as reparation according to the gravity of the offense.

THAT CONCLUDES THE FOURTH CHAPTER: "SURVEILLANCE OF PEOPLE WITH SECRET INCOME" OF THE FOURTH BOOK: "ERADICATION OF THORNS."

Chapter 5

Topic 80: Disclosing Criminals Using Agents Working Undercover as Thaumaturgic Ascetics

[1]After the employment of secret agents*—agents working undercover as thaumaturgic ascetics should entice criminals with magic skills for crime: bandits with a spell that induces sleep, makes one invisible (see 14.3.4–50), or opens doors; and adulterers with a love-inducing spell.

[2]When they have been roused, they should take a large group of them at night and aim to go to one village. Going, however, to a different village where people posing as husbands and wives have been stationed, they should tell them: "Right here you will behold the might of our magic skills! It is difficult to go to that other village." [3]Then, having opened the doors with the door-opening spell, they should tell them: "Enter!" [4]With the spell that makes one invisible, they should make the criminals pass between guards while they remain awake. [5]With the sleep-inducing spell, they should put the guards to sleep and get the criminals to move them around along with their beds. [6]With the love-inducing spell, they should get women disguised as wives* of others to have sexual pleasures with the criminals. [7]Once they have become convinced of the might of their magical skills, they should instruct them to perform the preparatory rites and the like to provide a mark of identity.*

[8]Or, they should get them to carry out their activities in houses containing marked articles. [9]Or, once they have won their confidence,* they should get them arrested in a single location. [10]They should get them arrested while buying, selling, or pawning marked articles, or when they are intoxicated with doped liquor.

[11]Once they have been arrested, he* should question them about their previous offenses and their associates.

[12]Alternatively,* agents working undercover as veteran thieves, after they have won the confidence of thieves, should, in the same manner, get them to carry out activities and have them arrested. [13]Once they have been arrested, the Collector should show them to the people of the cities and the countryside, saying: "The king has learnt the magical lore for catching thieves. Under his direction, these thieves have been caught. I will catch others too. You should restrain your relatives who engage in criminal conduct."

[14]When he finds out through information provided by spies that someone has stolen a yoke pin, a goad, or the like, he should expose him to them, saying: "This is the king's might!"

[15]Veteran thieves, cowherds, fowlers, and hunters, moreover, having won the confidence of forest thieves and forest tribes, should incite them to raid caravans, cattle camps, and villages abounding in fake money, forest produce, and wares. [16]During the raid, they should get them killed by concealed soldiers or by means of provisions for the journey mixed with coma-inducing juice (4.3.28 n.). [17]They should have them arrested as they fall sound asleep, worn out by a long journey carrying heavy loads of stolen goods, or as they lie intoxicated with doped liquor at festive celebrations.

> [18]Having arrested them, moreover, the Collector should show them publicly as before, ordering the broadcast of the king's omniscience among the inhabitants of the realm.

THAT CONCLUDES THE FIFTH CHAPTER: "DISCLOSING CRIMINALS USING AGENTS WORKING UNDERCOVER AS THAUMATURGIC ASCETICS" OF THE FOURTH BOOK: "ERADICATION OF THORNS."

Chapter 6

Topic 81: Arrest on Account of Suspicion, Articles, or Activities

[1]After the employment of thaumaturgic ascetics (4.5.1 n.)—arrest on account of suspicion, articles, or activities.

ARREST ON ACCOUNT OF SUSPICION

[2]Someone whose inheritance and family fortune* have been depleted; someone receiving a paltry wage; someone who gives false information regarding his native land, caste, lineage, name, or occupation; someone with a covert occupation or undertaking; someone addicted to meat, liquor, food, delicacies,* perfume, garlands, clothes, or ornaments; someone undertaking extravagant expenditures; someone addicted to prostitutes, gambling, or taverns; someone traveling abroad constantly; someone with merchandise regarding which one does not know where it is located or where it is being transported to;* someone who visits lonely places, the wilderness, and parks at inappropriate times; someone who holds frequent meetings or discussions at a place that is concealed or has victims he could

prey on; someone who gets recently inflicted wounds treated secretly; someone who always remains indoors; someone going here and there;* someone who haunts wild tracts;* someone who is constantly inquiring about other people's possessions, and about other people's wives, assets, or houses;* someone in possession of implements associated with a reprehensible activity or science; someone moving clandestinely along the shadows of walls at night's end;* someone selling articles in an altered form (4.1.26 n.) at an improper place or time; someone whose heart is filled with animosity; someone with a low occupation or caste; someone concealing his appearance; someone who, although not an ascetic, carries the emblems of an ascetic, or who, although an ascetic, follows a contrary behavior pattern (2.28.20); someone who has previously committed a crime; someone betrayed by his own activities; someone who, at the sight of the City Manager or high official,* absconds, flees, remains seated without voiding excrement,* or becomes agitated, or whose voice or facial complexion becomes parched or transformed; someone frightened by a throng of men carrying weapons—he (4.5.11 n.) should suspect such a man to be a murderer, a thief, or a man who has secret income through the appropriation of a treasure trove or deposit or through a commission by an enemy.

That concludes arrest on suspicion.

ARREST ON ACCOUNT OF ARTICLES

[3]With regard to arrest, however, on account of articles—when something is lost or stolen* and cannot be found, he (4.5.11 n.) should report it to traders who deal in that type of goods. [4]If, after coming across the reported article, they conceal it, they incur the same guilt as that of accomplices. [5]If they were ignorant, they may be released by surrendering the article. [6]And they should never pawn or sell old articles without informing the Superintendent of the Marketplace (4.2.1).

[7]If he comes across the reported article, he should ask the man arrested with the article about his legal title* to it, saying, "Where did you get this?" [8]If he were to say, "I obtained it through inheritance. I received it—bought it, got it made, received it secretly as a pledge—from that individual. This is the place and the time of its acquisition. These are its price, size, distinguishing marks, and value," he should be released when his legal title to it has been substantiated. [9]If the person who lost the article were to establish the same, he should recognize that the article belongs to the person who possessed it first and longer, or who has a valid document of title;*

[10]for even among quadrupeds and bipeds, there is similarity in appearance and distinguishing marks—how much more among forest produce, ornaments, and wares produced with material from the same source and by the same manufacturer?

[11]If he were to say,* "This is something borrowed—something rented *or* received as a pledge; *or* a deposit; *or* a security; *or* something received for sale on commission (3.12.25–31)—belonging to so-and-so," he should be released when he is corroborated by the person who is to provide his exoneration. [12]Or, if the person who is to provide his exoneration were to say, "It wasn't so," the man arrested with the article may corroborate (2.7.30 n.) the reason for giving on the part of the other man, the reason for accepting on his part, or the circumstantial evidence (3.12.52 n.), by means of the giver, the man who facilitated the giving, the recorder, the receiver, and witnesses who saw or heard.

[13]In the case of anything found after it has been abandoned, lost, or run away (2.36.43 n.), a man is exculpated by providing circumstantial evidence (3.12.51 n.) regarding the place, time, and acquisition. [14]And if he is not exculpated, he should return it and pay an equal amount as a fine; [15]otherwise he should receive the fine for theft (2.7.39 n.). That concludes arrest on account of articles.

ARREST ON ACCOUNT OF ACTIVITIES

[16]With regard to arrest, however, on account of activities, when, in the case of a house that has been burgled, there has been an entry or exit other than through the door—that is, a breach of the door through a joint or the hinge,* a breach of a latticed window or eaves of the upper floor, a breach of the wall while ascending and descending, or a hole dug as a means of depositing and taking articles secretly—he should know that it was done by an insider if it could have been found out* only through information that has been supplied and if the chiseling, the debris, the crushing, and the implements are found inside. [17]If the opposite is true, he should know that it was done by an outsider; if both are true, by both of them.*

[18]If it has been done by an insider, he should investigate the following: a man close by* who has fallen on hard times; one who associates with cruel people or has burglar's tools in his possession; a woman from a poor family or enamored of another man; a domestic servant of similar conduct; someone who is sleeping a lot, overcome by sleep, or agitated, whose voice or facial complexion is parched or transformed, who is nervous or prattling excessively, whose legs have become stiff by climbing

high, whose body and clothes are cut, frayed, rent, or torn, whose hands and feet are scarred or stiffened, whose hair and nails are full of dust, or whose hair and nails are cut and twisted; someone who has bathed and anointed himself thoroughly, massaged his legs with oil, or just washed his hands and feet; someone whose exact footprints are found on dusty or wet surfaces; or someone whose garland, liquor, perfume, pieces of clothing, unguents, or sweat match those found at the point of entry or exit. [19]He should recognize that person as the thief or the adulterer.

> [20]The Magistrate, along with the Revenue Officer and the County Supervisor, should conduct the search for thieves outside, while the City Manager should do so within the fort, using the clues given above.

THAT CONCLUDES THE SIXTH CHAPTER: "ARREST ON ACCOUNT OF SUSPICION, ARTICLES, OR ACTIVITIES" OF THE FOURTH BOOK: "ERADICATION OF THORNS."

Chapter 7

Topic 82: Investigation into a Person Who Has Died Suddenly

[1]He* should examine a person who has died suddenly after he has been coated with oil.

[2]When urine and feces have spurted out, the abdominal skin is bloated with wind, the hands and feet are swollen, the eyes are open wide, and the throat has marks on it, he should know that the man was killed by suffocation through strangulation. [3]When a man with those same marks has his arms and thighs drawn together, he should know that the man was killed by hanging.

[4]When the hands, feet, and stomach are swollen, the eyes are drawn in, and the navel is bulging out, he should know that the man was taken down* (from a stake).

[5]When the anus and eyes are closed, the teeth have bitten into the tongue, and the stomach is distended, he should know that the man has drowned.

[6]When blood is smeared around and the limbs are broken or disjointed, he should know that the man was killed with sticks or stones.

[7]When the limbs are broken up and blown apart, he should know that the man was thrown from on high.

[8]When the hands, feet, teeth, and nails have turned dark; the flesh, bodily hair, and skin droop; and the mouth is coated with foam, he should know that the man was killed with poison. [9]When a man with those same marks has bloody fang marks, he should know that the man was killed by a snake or insect.*

[10]When the clothes and limbs are contorted and excessive vomiting and purging have taken place, he should know that the man was killed by a coma-inducing mixture (4.3.28 n.).

[11]He should find out whether a man was killed in one of the above ways, or whether, after killing him, his neck was lacerated by hanging* because of the fear of punishment.

[12]He should examine the leftover food of a man killed by poison using birds (1.21.6). [13]When material extracted from the heart is thrown in fire, if it makes a crackling sound or becomes rainbow-colored, he should know that it contains poison; or when he sees that the heart remains unburned after he has been cremated. [14]He should initiate a probe into any domestic servant of his who was subjected to severe verbal or physical abuse, or a wife of his who has been aggrieved or is enamored of another man, or a relative of his who covets his inheritance, livelihood, or wife.

[15]He should investigate the same things in the case of a man who has been killed and then hanged. [16]Or, in the case of a man who has hanged himself, he should initiate a probe into whether any inordinate hurt was involved.

[17]Or else, in all cases, the occasion for rage may be a wrong done to wife or inheritance, professional rivalry, hostility toward an opponent, or a partnership in the marketplace, or else any one of the grounds for litigation (3.1.17 n.). [18]Murder results from rage.

[19]Through people who were nearby, he should investigate the murder of a man who has been killed by someone on his own or using men who have been commissioned, or by thieves for the sake of his property, or by enemies of some other man because the two look alike. [20]He should interrogate any man by whom the murdered man was summoned, with whom he stayed or departed, and by whom he was brought to the place of the murder. [21]And he should ask individually those who were moving about in the vicinity of the place where he was murdered: "Who brought this man here? *or* Who killed him? Did you see anyone who was carrying a weapon,

trying to hide himself, or agitated?" [22]He should continue with the interrogation according to their responses.

> [23–24]Having noted what is on the body of that helpless man—things he has used, his personal effects, clothes, costume, or ornaments—he should interrogate dealers in those things: what their association with him was, where they live, the reason for their sojourn, their occupation, and their transactions. Thereafter, he should initiate the probe.
>
> [25–26]If anyone, overpowered by love or hatred—or a woman, led astray by an evil man—were to kill himself with a rope, weapon, or poison, he should have a Caṇḍāla drag them by a rope along the royal highway. No cremation rites are to be performed for them, and likewise no rites by relatives.
>
> [27]If, however, a relative of theirs performs the rites for a newly departed for them, hereafter he will endure the same condition as they, or he is banished by his people.
>
> [28]When someone associates with an outcaste by officiating at sacrifices, by teaching, and by contracting marriages, in one year, he himself becomes an outcaste; so also even someone else who associates with such people.*

THAT CONCLUDES THE SEVENTH CHAPTER: "INVESTIGATION INTO A PERSON WHO HAS DIED SUDDENLY" OF THE FOURTH BOOK: "ERADICATION OF THORNS."

Chapter 8

Topic 83: Investigation through Interrogation and Torture

[1]In the presence of the victim of the theft, as well as external and internal* witnesses, he should interrogate the accused about his country, caste, lineage, name, occupation, wealth, associates, and residence. [2]He should corroborate (2.7.30 n.) these by checking them against other depositions.* [3]Then he should interrogate him about what he did the previous day and where he spent the night until his arrest. [4]If he is corroborated by the person providing his exoneration, he is to be considered innocent; otherwise, he is to undergo torture.

[5]A suspect may not be arrested after the lapse of three days, because questioning becomes infeasible*—except when the tools are found on him.

[6]For a man who calls someone a thief when he is not a thief, the fine is the same as that for a thief; so also for anyone who hides a thief.

[7]When a person accused of being a thief has been inculpated because of enmity or hatred, he is to be considered innocent. [8]For someone who keeps an innocent man in custody, the punishment is the lowest seizure fine (2.1.29 n.).

[9]Against someone on whom suspicion has fallen, he should produce tools, advisers, accomplices, stolen goods, and agents (2.5.18 n.); [10]and he should corroborate (2.7.30 n.) his action by checking it against the entry, the receipt of the goods, and the partition of shares.

[11]When these kinds of evidence are lacking, he should consider him as just a blabbermouth and not the thief. [12]For we see that even a person who is not a thief, when by chance he runs into thieves making their way and is arrested because his clothing, weapons, and goods are similar to those of the thieves or because he was lingering where the stolen goods of the thieves were found,* may, just like Māṇḍavya-of-the-Stake,* confess "I am a thief" even though he is not a thief, because he fears the pain from torture. [13]Therefore, he should punish only a man against whom there is convincing evidence.

[14]He should not subject to torture a person who has committed a small offense, a child, an old person, a sick person, an intoxicated person, an insane person, a person wearied by hunger, thirst, or travel, a person who has eaten too much or whose food is still undigested, or a weak person. [15]He should have such people spied on by persons of the same character, prostitutes, attendants at water booths, or those who give them advice, accommodation, or food. [16]He should outwit them in this way, or in the manner explained in the section on the theft of a consignment (3.12.38–51).

[17]When there is likelihood of someone's guilt, he should subject him to torture, but never a woman who is pregnant or within a month after giving birth—[18]for a woman, however, half the normal torture or just oral questioning; [19]for a Brāhmaṇa, the employment of secret agents, as also for learned men and ascetics.* [20]When this rule is violated, both the torturer and the one who authorized the torture should be assessed the highest fine (2.1.29 n.), as also for a death resulting from torture.

[21]There are four kinds of conventional torture: six strokes with a stick, seven lashes with a whip, two suspensions, and the water tube.* [22]Beyond that, for those who have committed grave crimes there are nine strokes with a cane, 12 lashes with a whip, two thigh bindings, 20 strokes with a

Naktamāla-twig, 32 slaps, two scorpion bindings, two hangings, needle in the hand, burning one digit of a finger of a man after he has drunk gruel, heating in the sun for one day for a man after he has drunk oil, and sleeping during a winter night on a bed with points of Balbaja-grass.* [23]These are the 18* types of torture.

[24]The instruments used in it, its extent, the manner of inflicting it, its prognosis, and its restriction:* These he should learn from the *Kharapaṭṭa*.* [25]He should subject a person to torture on alternate days, and only to a single torture on any one day.

[26]Someone who has previously committed a crime, someone who confesses and then retracts, someone in whose possession a portion of the loot is found, someone who has been arrested by reason of the act or the stolen goods (4.6), someone who embezzles from the king's treasury, or someone subject to death by torture on the king's orders—he should subject these to torture administered collectively, individually, or repeatedly.

[27]A Brāhmaṇa should not be subjected to corporal punishment for any type of crime. [28]A mark relating to his offense should be branded on his forehead so as to bar him from social dealings—a dog for theft, a headless trunk for the murder of a human being, a vagina for sex with an elder's wife, and a liquor flag (2.25.11 n.) for drinking liquor.

> [29]When a Brāhmaṇa has committed a crime, the king should proclaim it publicly, scar him with the mark, and either exile him from his territory or make him reside in mines.

THAT CONCLUDES THE EIGHTH CHAPTER: "INVESTIGATION THROUGH INTERROGATION AND TORTURE" OF THE FOURTH BOOK: "ERADICATION OF THORNS."

Chapter 9

Topic 84: Surveillance of All Agencies

[1]The Collectors and Magistrates* should first exercise control over the superintendents and their assistants.

MALFEASANCE BY OFFICIALS

[2]For someone* who steals an article of high value or a gem from pit mines or factories producing articles of high value, the punishment is clean

execution;* [3]for someone who steals an article of low value or a tool from factories producing articles of low value, the lowest seizure fine (2.1.29 n.). [4]For someone who, from sites for merchandise,* steals king's merchandise valued more than one Māṣa up to a quarter Paṇa, the punishment is 12 Paṇas; valued up to two-quarters of a Paṇa, 24 Paṇas; valued up to three-quarters of a Paṇa, 36 Paṇas; valued up to one Paṇa, 48 Paṇas; valued up to two Paṇas, the lowest seizure fine (2.1.29 n.); valued up to four Paṇas, the middle; valued up to eight Paṇas, the highest; and valued up to ten Paṇas, execution.

[5]These same punishments apply in cases of theft of forest produce, wares, or tools with half the above values from storehouses, depots for merchandise, storage facilities for forest produce, or armories. [6]Double those same punishments apply in cases of theft of articles with quarter of the above values from the treasury, a warehouse,* or a precious metals workshop (2.13.1). [7]In the case of breaking and entry, the punishment for thieves is vivid execution (4.9.2 n.), [8]as explained with reference to royal properties (2.5.16–20).

[9]With regard to property outside of those, however, for someone who secretly steals from a field, threshing floor, house, or shop during the day forest produce, wares, or tools valued more than one Māṣa up to a quarter Paṇa, the punishment is three Paṇas or broadcasting his crime after smearing him with a daub of cow dung; valued up to two quarters of a Paṇa, six Paṇas or broadcasting his crime after smearing him with cow dung and ashes; valued up to three quarters of a Paṇa, nine Paṇas or broadcasting his crime after smearing him with cow dung and ashes or putting a girdle of potsherds around him; valued up to one Paṇa, 12 Paṇas or shaving his head and sending him into exile; valued up to two Paṇas, 24 Paṇas or sending him into exile with a brickbat* after shaving his head; valued up to four Paṇas, 36 Paṇas;* valued up to five Paṇas, 48 Paṇas; valued up to ten Paṇas, the lowest seizure fine (2.1.29 n.); valued up to 20 Paṇas, 200 Paṇas; valued up to 30 Paṇas, 500 Paṇas; valued up to 40 Paṇas, 1,000 Paṇas; and valued up to 50 Paṇas, execution. [10]These same punishments apply in the case of articles with one-half the above values when someone steals them forcibly by day or night during periods of curfew.* [11]Double those same punishments apply in the case of articles with one-quarter of the above values when someone steals them forcibly by day or night using a weapon.

[12]For making forged documents or seals of heads of household, superintendents, chief officers, and the king, the punishments are the lowest

fine, the middle fine, the highest fine (2.1.29 n.), and execution, respectively, or else in accordance with the crime.

MALFEASANCE BY JUSTICES AND COURT OFFICIALS

[13]If a Justice threatens, reprimands, drives out, or suppresses* a man who has filed a lawsuit, he* should impose on him the lowest seizure fine (2.1.29 n.); if there is a verbal assault (3.18), the fine is doubled. [14]If he questions someone* who should not be questioned; does not question someone who should be questioned; or after questioning brushes it aside; or if he tutors, reminds, or prompts him, he should impose on him the middle seizure fine. [15]If he does not request a document (*deśa*; 3.1.19 n.) that needs to be produced, requests a document that need not be produced, lets the case proceed without documentary evidence, dismisses it under some pretext, drives away by delays someone who becomes tired, rejects a statement properly presented, assists witnesses with their memory, or takes up a case that has already been adjudicated and a verdict rendered, he should impose on him the highest seizure fine. [16]In the case of a repeat offense, the fine is doubled and he is removed from office.

[17]If the court clerk does not write down what was said, writes down what was not said, writes correctly what was badly said, writes incorrectly what was correctly said, or alters a clear meaning, he should impose on him the lowest seizure fine, or else a punishment corresponding to the crime.

[18]If a Justice or a Magistrate imposes a monetary punishment on a person who does not deserve punishment, he should impose on him a fine equivalent to double the amount he imposed; or eight times the amount by which it is less or more than (the prescribed fine). [19]If he imposes corporal punishment, he should himself suffer corporal punishment; or double the standard reparation (4.10). [20]Alternatively, when he dismisses a truthful lawsuit or sustains a bogus lawsuit, he should pay eight times that* as a fine.

CORRUPTION IN PRISONS

[21]For preventing someone from sleeping, sitting down, eating, answering calls of nature, or moving about, or for keeping him tied up in a court lockup, a jail, or a prison,* the fine on the perpetrator and on the person ordering it is three Paṇas increased progressively by three (2.36.28 n.).

[22]For anyone releasing an accused from a jail or letting him escape, the punishment is the middle seizure fine, as also the payment of the amount

under litigation; if it is from a prison, the confiscation of all his property and execution.

[23]For a prison superintendent who, without informing, allows freedom of movement to a prisoner, the fine is 24 Paṇas; who orders his torture, double that amount; who transfers him to a different station* or deprives him of food and water, the fine is 96 Paṇas; who inflicts excruciating pain or maiming, the middle seizure fine (2.29.1 n.); who kills him, 1,000 Paṇas; [24]who violates a married female prisoner who is a slave or a pledge, the lowest seizure fine; a wife of a thief or rioter, the middle fine; an Ārya female prisoner, the highest fine. [25]For a prisoner doing that, execution on the spot. [26]The same, he should know, applies in the case of an Ārya woman arrested during night curfew (2.36.34–35); when it is a slave, the lowest seizure fine.

[27]For someone assisting an escape from a jail, the punishment is the middle seizure fine if done without breaching, and execution if it is breached; and if the escape is from a prison, both the confiscation of all his property and execution.

> [28]In this manner, he should discipline officials in charge of money (2.9.32) by means of fines; and, so disciplined, they in turn should discipline the people of the city and the countryside by means of punishments.

THAT CONCLUDES THE NINTH CHAPTER: "SURVEILLANCE OF ALL AGENCIES" OF THE FOURTH BOOK: "ERADICATION OF THORNS."

Chapter 10

Topic 85: Reparation in Lieu of Cutting Individual Limbs

[1]In the case of someone striking at a river crossing, a cutpurse, and someone with raised hand,* the punishment for a first offense is cutting off the thumb and forefinger (2.23.15 n.) or a fine of 54 Paṇas; for the second offense, cutting off five fingers (2.14.14 n.) or a fine of 100 Paṇas; for the third offense, chopping the right hand or a fine of 400 Paṇas; and for the fourth offense, execution in any way desired.*

[2]For stealing or killing a fowl, mongoose, cat, dog, or pig that is valued under 25 Paṇas, the punishment is a fine of 54 Paṇas or cutting the tip of the nose; half that fine when it is done by Caṇḍālas or forest dwellers. [3]For

carrying off* deer, game animals, birds, vicious animals, or fish that have been caught in snares, nets, or pitfalls, the punishment is their restitution and an equal amount as a fine. [4]For carrying off deer or forest produce from reserves for deer or forest produce, the fine is 100 Paṇas; [5]the fine is doubled for stealing deer or birds meant for exhibition or entertainment or for killing them.

[6]For stealing small implements* from artisans, craftsmen, performers, or ascetics, the fine is 100 Paṇas; for stealing large implements, 200 Paṇas, as also for stealing agricultural implements.

[7]For someone entering a fort without being granted permission, or for someone making a getaway carrying a deposit through a hole in the rampart, the punishment is chopping the tendon* or a fine of 200 Paṇas; [8]for someone stealing a carriage, a boat, or a small farm animal, chopping one foot or a fine of 300 Paṇas; [9]for someone cheating* with false shells, dice, leather straps, or ivory cubes (3.20.10 n.), or by sleight of hand, chopping one hand or a fine of 400 Paṇas; [10]for providing assistance to a thief or an adulterer and to a woman who is kept under guard, chopping the ears and nose or a fine of 500 Paṇas—to the man, double that;* [11]for someone stealing a large farm animal or a single male or female slave, or for someone selling an article from a corpse, chopping both feet or a fine of 600 Paṇas.

[12]For striking persons of the highest class and elders with one's hands or feet, and for climbing onto the king's vehicle, mount, and the like, the punishment is chopping one hand and one foot or a fine of 700 Paṇas; [12]for a Śūdra calling himself a Brāhmaṇa, and for someone embezzling property belonging to a deity (1.19.29 n.), directing actions inimical to the king, or causing blindness of both eyes, the punishment is blinding through the use of toxic collyrium (14.1.15) or a fine of 800 Paṇas; [14]for someone freeing a thief or an adulterer, writing a royal edict with omissions or additions, abducting a young woman or a female slave along with money, engaging in fraudulent transactions, or selling unfit meat, the punishment is cutting the left hand and both feet or a fine of 900 Paṇas; [15]for selling human flesh, execution.

[16]For someone stealing an animal, an icon, a man, a field, a house, money, gold, gems, or crops belonging to a deity (1.19.29 n.), the punishment is the highest fine (2.1.29 n.) or clean execution (4.9.2 n.).

> [17–18]In inflicting punishment, the Magistrate, standing between the king and the subjects,* should first examine carefully the

person, the crime, the motive, whether the crime is slight or serious, the future proclivity,* the current condition, the place, and the time, and then impose the highest, middle, or lowest fine (2.1.29 n.).

THAT CONCLUDES THE TENTH CHAPTER: "REPARATION IN LIEU OF CUTTING INDIVIDUAL LIMBS" OF THE FOURTH BOOK: "ERADICATION OF THORNS."

Chapter 11

Topic 86: Rules on the Clean and the Vivid Forms of Capital Punishment

[1]For someone killing a man during a brawl, the punishment is vivid execution (4.9.2 n.); [2]if the man dies within seven days, clean execution (4.9.2 n.); within a fortnight, the highest fine (2.1.29 n.); within a month, 500 Paṇas—and, in addition, the cost of treatment.

[3]For someone striking with a weapon, the punishment is the highest fine; [4]for doing so because of intoxication, chopping the hand; for doing so because of delusion, 200 Paṇas—[5]when death ensues, execution.

[6]For someone who causes a miscarriage by striking a blow, the punishment is the highest fine; by administering medicine, the middle fine; and by causing excessive pain, the lowest seizure fine (2.1.29 n.).

[7]They should impale on stakes the following: those who kill,* attack, hold down, threaten, assault, or stab a man or a woman violently; highway or house robbers; and those who kill or steal an elephant, horse, or chariot belonging to the king. [8]And anyone who cremates them or takes them away should receive the very same punishment, or the highest seizure fine.

[9]For providing food, shelter, tools, fire, or advice, and for rendering assistance to murderers or thieves, the punishment is the highest fine; a reprimand if it was done out of ignorance.[10]Of murderers and thieves, he should set free sons and wives if they are not co-conspirators; if they are co-conspirators, he should apprehend them.

[11]He should kill by setting the head and hands on fire anyone who covets the kingdom, attacks the royal residence, incites tribal chiefs or enemies, or causes rebellions in the fort, the provinces, or the army; [12]if it is a Brāhmaṇa, he should consign him to darkness.*

[13]He should kill by setting the skinless head on fire anyone who kills his mother, father, son, brother, or teacher, or a recluse. [14]For reviling any

of these, his tongue is to be cut off; for injuring a limb, he is to be deprived of that same limb.

[15]For the involuntary* killing of a man and for the theft of a herd of farm animals, the punishment is clean execution (4.9.2 n.); [16]and he should know that a herd consists of at least ten.

[17]For someone breaking a dike that holds water, the punishment is drowning in that very place; if it is without water, the highest seizure fine (2.1.29 n.); and if it is dilapidated and abandoned (2.29.1 n.), the middle fine.

[18]He should drown a man who has given poison and a woman who has killed a man,* unless she is pregnant; in case she is pregnant, he should delay it for at least one month after the delivery. [19]He should have cattle tear asunder a woman who kills her husband, elder, or child; who is an arsonist or poisoner; or who breaks into a house.

[20]He should have someone who sets fire to a pasture, a field, a threshing ground, a house, a produce forest, or an elephant forest burnt with fire.

[21]He should tear out the tongue of anyone who reviles the king or reveals his secret counsel, who spreads pernicious news reports, or licks a Brāhmaṇa's cooking utensils.

[22]He should have anyone who steals weapons or armor killed with arrows if he is not a soldier; [23]if he is a soldier, the punishment is the highest fine.

[24]If a man damages the penis or testicles of someone, he should have that same organ of his cut off; [25]for damaging the tongue or nose, the cutting off of the thumb and forefinger (2.23.15 n.).

> [26]These are the punishments involving torture laid down in the treatises of great men. For crimes, however, that do not inflict pain, tradition lays down clean execution (4.9.2 n.) as the righteous punishment.

That concludes the Eleventh Chapter: "Rules on the Clean and the Vivid Forms of Capital Punishment" of the Fourth Book: "Eradication of Thorns."

Chapter 12

Topic 87: Deflowering of Virgins

[1]For someone deflowering a virgin who has not attained puberty and belongs to the same social class, the punishment is chopping off the hand

or a fine of 400 Paṇas; [2]if she dies, execution. [3]For someone deflowering a virgin who has attained puberty, the punishment is chopping the forefinger and the middle finger or a fine of 200 Paṇas; [4]in addition, he should pay compensation to her father for the loss.*

[5]If she did not consent, furthermore, he does not get the right to have her.* [6]If she did consent, he is fined 54 Paṇas, but the woman, half that amount. [7]If she has been secured through the payment of a bride price by another man, the punishment is chopping his hand or a fine of 400 Paṇas, along with the repayment of the bride price.

[8]If a man does not get possession of a girl after she has had seven menstrual cycles following the betrothal, he may obtain the right to have her by deflowering her. And he does not have to pay compensation to the father for the loss (4.12.4 n.); [9]he forfeits his ownership of her by frustrating her menses.

[10]A woman does not incur guilt by going to a man of equal status when she has been menstruating for three years; thereafter even to a man of unequal status, but without wearing her ornaments. [11]If she takes her father's property, she shall become guilty of theft.

[12]For a man who solicits a girl for one man and procures her for another, the fine is 200 Paṇas. [13]And that man does not get the right to have her if she is unwilling.

[14]For a man who shows one girl and gives another, the fine is 100 Paṇas if she is of equal status;* twice that amount if she is of a lower status.

[15]For a woman who is not a virgin at the time of consummation of the marriage, the fine is 54 Paṇas, and in addition she should return the bride price and the wedding expenses. [16]A woman found guilty by experts in these matters should give double the amount to the surety.* [17]In the event she substitutes other blood, the punishment is 200 Paṇas, as also for a man who accuses her falsely. [18]And he shall forfeit the bride price and the wedding expenses [19]and not get the right to have her if she is unwilling.

[20]A virgin deflowered by a woman of similar status should pay a fine of 12 Paṇas, if she consented; the woman who deflowered her should pay double that amount. [21]If she did not consent, the woman should pay a fine of 100 Paṇas for satisfying her passion,* as well as the bride price. [22]A virgin who deflowers herself becomes a slave of the king. [23]When a girl is deflowered outside the village and when there is a false accusation, the fine is doubled.

[24]For someone who forcibly abducts a virgin, the fine is 200 Paṇas; if she is abducted along with her gold, the highest seizure fine (2.1.29 n.). [25]When many individuals abduct a virgin, the prescribed fines are assessed on each individually.

[26]For someone deflowering a daughter of a courtesan, the fine is 54 Paṇas and a bride price of 16 times the fee for sex paid to her mother. [27]For someone deflowering the non-slave daughter of a slave man or woman, the fine is 24 Paṇas, and in addition giving her the bride price and ornaments. [28]For someone deflowering a female slave who is ready to be redeemed, the fine is 12 Paṇas, and in addition giving her clothes and ornaments.

[29]For giving assistance and accommodation, the fine is equal to that of the perpetrator.

[30]When a woman whose husband has gone abroad behaves improperly, a relative or servant of the husband should keep her under guard. [31]While under guard, she should await her husband. [32]If the husband were to forgive her, both* should be set free. [33]If she is not forgiven, the woman's ears and nose should be cut off, and her paramour shall be put to death. [34]For someone carrying the paramour away, saying he is a thief,* the fine is 500 Paṇas; for someone getting him released by giving money, eight times the amount given.

[35]Adultery is indicated by the caressing of each other's hair; or else by circumstantial evidence (3.12.51 n.) of carnal enjoyment, through experts in these matters, or through the woman's confession.

[36]After rescuing a wife of another man who had been abducted by an enemy force or tribal chief, carried away by a flood, or abandoned in the wilderness during a time of famine or left there for dead, a man may enjoy her according to the agreement they had made; [37]if she is of a higher caste, is unwilling, or has children, he should hand her over upon receiving compensation.

> [38–40]After rescuing a woman belonging to others from robbers, from the current of a river, from a famine, from an upheaval in the region, or from a wild tract, or when she had been lost, abandoned, or left for dead, a man may enjoy her according to the agreement they had made; but not a woman who has been banished by the prowess of the king or by her kinsmen, who is of a higher class or unwilling, or who already has children. Such a woman, however, he should hand over after receiving an equitable ransom.

That concludes the Twelfth Chapter: "Deflowering of Virgins" of the Fourth Book: "Eradication of Thorns."

Chapter 13

Topic 88: Punishments for Transgressions

[1]For someone who causes the consumption of forbidden drink or food by a Brāhmaṇa, the punishment is the highest fine (2.1.29 n.); by a Kṣatriya, the middle; by a Vaiśya, the lowest; and by a Śūdra, 54 Paṇas. [2]Those who consume these on their own should be sent into exile.*

[3]For storming into someone else's house during the day, the punishment is the lowest seizure fine; during the night, the middle. [4]Whether it is during the day or the night, for someone entering with a weapon in his hand, the punishment is the highest fine. [5]A mendicant or trader, the intoxicated or the insane, close neighbors under threat of force or in an emergency, and people who are customarily granted entry should not be punished, unless they have been forbidden. [6]For someone climbing over the perimeter wall of his own house after the end of night (4.6.2 n.), the punishment is the lowest seizure fine; if it is the house of another, the middle fine,* as also for anyone breaking the fence around a village park.

[7]Traders in a caravan may lodge within village perimeters after declaring the value of their goods. [8]From among these, anything stolen or killed—unless it has gone out at night—should be compensated by the village headman.* [9]What is stolen or killed between villages, on the other hand, should be compensated by the Superintendent of Pasture Lands; [10]in areas beyond the pasture lands, by the officer in charge of catching thieves. [11]For areas not provided with such security, they should permit a search in accordance with the boundary limits; [12]if it is outside boundary limits, a group of five or ten villages.*

[13]When an injury has been caused by someone making a flimsy house, a cart without a support for its pole head, a weapon without a case, or a hole, well, or pitfall without a cover, he (4.7.1 n.) should regard it as physical assault (3.19).

[14]When a man shouts "Get out!" while cutting a tree, tugging an untrained animal by the reins, handling or riding an untrained animal, or twirling around a piece of wood, a clod, a stone, a stick, an arrow, or his arms, or when about to collide with a cart or an elephant, he should not be punished.

[15]A man (wanting to be) killed by an enraged elephant should present it with one Droṇa of food, a Kumbha of liquor, a garland and unguents, and a cloth to clean its tusks. [16]The washing of the feet is done because being killed by an elephant is equal to participating in the bath at the conclusion of a horse sacrifice. [17]In the event a bystander is killed, the highest fine is imposed on the mahout.*

[18]For an owner who does not rescue a man being mauled by a horned or tusked animal of his, the punishment is the lowest seizure fine (2.1.29 n.); double that amount if the man called to him for help. [19]For someone permitting horned or tusked animals to kill one another, the punishment is restitution* and an equal amount as a fine.

[20]For someone riding on an animal dedicated to a god, a bull, a stud bull, or a heifer, the punishment is 500 Paṇas; for killing it, the highest fine. [21]For seizing small animals useful for fur, milk, riding, or breeding, the punishment is restitution and an equal amount as a fine; so also for killing them, except for a divine or ancestral rite.

[22]The driver should not be punished for injuries caused by a cart when the nose-string strap has been severed or its yoke has broken, when it skids forward sideways, when it slides back,* or when men or animals are crowding around. [23]Otherwise, he shall be liable (2.28.26 n.) for the prescribed fine for injuring men or creatures; [24]in addition, if a nonhuman creature is killed, for compensation for that creature.

[25]If the driver is a minor, the owner, if he is riding in the vehicle, should be punished and, if the owner is not present, the man riding in the vehicle; or else, the driver, if he has attained majority (3.3.1). [26]The king should confiscate a vehicle that is operated by a minor or that is without a man.*

[27]Whatever affliction a man causes another person through witchcraft or sorcery, the same should be inflicted on him. [28]Love-inducing rites may be freely used on a disaffected wife, on a young woman by a man who wants to marry her, or on a husband by his wife. [29]In other cases, when there is an injury, the punishment is the middle seizure fine (2.1.29 n.).

[30]For someone who has sex with the sister of his mother or father, the wife of his maternal uncle, the wife of his teacher, or his daughter-in-law, daughter, or sister, the punishment is the cutting off of his penis and testicles and then execution. [31]If the woman consented, she should receive the same punishment, as also a woman who has sex with a slave, a servant, or a man kept as a pledge.

[32]For a Kṣatriya having sex with an unguarded* Brāhmaṇa woman, the punishment is the highest fine (2.1.29 n.); for a Vaiśya, the confiscation

of all his property; while a Śūdra should be burnt with a straw fire. [33]In all cases of sex with a wife of the king, the punishment is to be boiled in a vat.

[34]If someone has sex with a Śvapāka (3.7.33 n.) woman, he should go to another country branded with a headless trunk; or, if he is a Śūdra, he shall be reduced to the level of a Śvapāka. [35]For a Śvapāka having sex with an Ārya woman, the punishment is execution; and for the woman, cutting off of her ears and nose.

[36]For having sex with a female wandering ascetic, the fine is 24 Paṇas. [37]If the woman was willing, she should receive the same punishment.

[38]For having sex with a prostitute by force, the fine is 12 Paṇas; [39]for many men raping a single (prostitute), the fine is 24 Paṇas each.

[40]For someone having sex with a woman in a place other than the vagina, the punishment is the lowest seizure fine (2.1.29 n.), as also for someone ejaculating in a man.

> [41]For the wretch who performs a sexual act in vaginas of animals, the fine is 12 Paṇas; double that, tradition says, for performing a sexual act on divine statues.
>
> [42]For a king fining someone who does not deserve to be fined, the fine is 30 times that amount. He should place it in water for Varuṇa, and then give it to Brāhmaṇas.
>
> [43]By that, the king's sin caused by wrongful infliction of fines is cleansed, for Varuṇa is the one who disciplines kings when they act wrongly with respect to men.

THAT CONCLUDES THE THIRTEENTH CHAPTER: "PUNISHMENT FOR TRANSGRESSIONS" OF THE FOURTH BOOK: "ERADICATION OF THORNS."

THAT CONCLUDES THE FOURTH BOOK: "ERADICATION OF THORNS" OF KAUṬILYA'S *ARTHAŚĀSTRA*.

Book Five

On Secret Conduct

Chapter 1

Topic 89: On the Infliction of Punishment

[1]We have described the eradication of thorns from the fort and the provinces. [2]We will now explain their eradication from the king and his regime.

[3]Against those chief officers who live off the king by bringing him under their grip or who are equally partial to the enemy,* success is achieved by employing clandestine operatives or by recruiting seducible factions, as described above; or else through instigation to sedition or espionage in the manner we will describe in the section on capturing an enemy settlement.*

[4]Against those chief officers, however, who, being either favorites or banded together, impair the regime—traitors who cannot be subdued openly—he* should employ secret punishment (1.11.21 n.), finding delight in his duty.*

USE OF KINSMEN IN SECRET PUNISHMENT

[5]A secret agent should incite a brother of a traitorous high official, a brother who has not been treated with respect, and present him to the king. [6]The king should urge him to attack the traitor by granting the use of the traitor's property.* [7]Once he has attacked him with a weapon or poison, he should have him executed on the spot, proclaiming, "This man is a fratricide!" [8]This explains also the Pāraśava and the son of a female attendant.*

[9]Alternatively, the brother, incited by a secret agent, should request a traitorous high official for his inheritance.* [10]At night, as he is lying down in front of the door of the traitor's house*—or staying elsewhere*—an assassin should kill him and announce: "This fellow has been killed as he was longing for his inheritance!" [11]Then, taking the side of the dead man, he should arrest the other. [12]Or else, secret agents positioned near the traitor should threaten the brother with death as he is requesting his inheritance. [13]"At night, as he . . ." (5.1.10)—the rest is the same as above.

[14]Alternatively, when, between two traitorous high officials, a son violates the wife of the father, the father the wife of the son, or a brother the wife of a brother—a brawl between them initiated by a crafty student spy is explained by the foregoing.

[15]Alternatively, a secret agent should instigate the conceited son of a traitorous high official, saying, "You are the king's son. You have been placed here out of fear of the enemy." [16]Once he is convinced, the king should pay him honor in secret, saying, "You have reached the age for becoming the Crown Prince, but I am not anointing you out of fear of the high official." [17]The secret agent should prod him to kill the high official. [18]When he has carried out the attack, he should have him executed on the spot, proclaiming, "This man is a parricide!"

[19]Alternatively, a female mendicant agent should win the confidence of the traitorous high official's wife by providing her with love-inducing medications and then trick her by substituting poison.

[20]That concludes the strategy using kinsmen.

PUNISHMENT THROUGH DEVIOUS PRACTICES

[21]He should dispatch a traitorous high official with a weak army that includes assassins to destroy a forest tribe or an enemy town, or to install a Frontier Commander or a commander of a province in a region separated by a wild tract, or to pacify a sector under the City Manager that is in revolt, or to take charge of a caravan escort* along the frontier together with an area subject to recapture.* [22]As the battle is engaged during night—or during the day—the assassins or agents in the guise of bandits should kill him, announcing: "He was killed during the offensive."

[23]Alternatively, while he is engaged in an expedition or a recreational activity, he should summon traitorous high officials to visit him. [24]When they enter accompanied by assassins with concealed weapons, they should submit themselves to be searched in the middle courtyard* in order to

gain entry into the interior. [25]Then, the assassins, when they are arrested by the gate guards, should say, "We are employed by the traitors." [26]After publicizing that, they should kill the traitors. [27]And others should be executed in place of the assassins.

[28]Alternatively, while he is out on an excursion, he should grant honors to traitors, providing them quarters near him. [29]A woman of bad character disguised as the queen should be arrested at night within their quarters—the rest is the same as before.

[30]Alternatively, by complimenting "Your chef—*or*, your baker*—is marvelous!," he should ask a traitorous high official for food and delicacies or, at a time when he has been out on the road, for drinks. [31]Having mixed them both with poison, he should press both* to taste them first. [32]After publicizing it, he should execute both* as poisoners.

[33]Alternatively, he should get an agent working undercover as a thaumaturgic ascetic to bring one who is given to black magic under his control by telling the man: "You will obtain your wishes by eating one of the following possessing auspicious marks: monitor lizard, tortoise, crab, and an ox with broken horns." [34]Once he is convinced, he should kill him during the rite with poison or metal clubs, announcing: "He was killed due to a mishap in the rite."

[35]Alternatively, an agent working undercover as a physician, after establishing that a traitor has an evil or incurable disease, should trick him by putting poison into the preparations of food and medicine.

[36]Alternatively, agents employed to work undercover as chefs or cooks (1.12.9 n.) should trick the traitor with poison.

[37]That concludes suppression by secret practices.

SUPPRESSION OF TWO TRAITORS

[38]With regard to the suppression of two traitors, however— [39]he should dispatch a person who is himself a traitor along with a weak army that includes assassins to the place where there is a traitor who needs to be suppressed, saying: "Go and in that fort—*or*, province—raise a military force—*or*, money—; *or*, seize money from the favorite; *or*, abduct the favorite's daughter by force; *or*, carry out any one of these tasks: building a fort, undertaking an irrigation project, making a trade route, settling a vacant land, starting a pit mine, and establishing a produce or elephant forest; *or*, function as a commander of a province or a Frontier Commander. Imprison anyone who may oppose you or refuses to render assistance to you." [40]In like manner, he should notify other officers: "You

must oppose the misbehavior of this man." [41]While he is arguing during these incidents of altercation or interference with his tasks, assassins should hurl their weapons and kill him stealthily. [42]The others should be punished for this crime.

[43]In the case of traitorous cities, villages, or families, assassins should hurl their weapons during an altercation relating to village boundaries and borders (3.9.2 n.) between fields, threshing floors, and houses, or due to injuries caused to property, implements, crops, and draught animals, or during spectacles, performances, and festivals, and declare: "This is what happens to those who altercate with this man!" [44]The others should be punished for this crime.

[45]Alternatively, in the case of traitorous persons among whom there have been deep-rooted altercations, assassins should set fire to their fields, threshing floors, or houses, or hurl weapons at their kinsmen, relatives, or draught animals, and declare likewise: "We have been dispatched by that person." [46]The others should be punished for this crime.

[47]Alternatively, secret agents should get traitors in the fort or the provinces to invite each other as guests. [48]On that occasion, poisoners should give them poison. [49]The others should be punished for this crime.

[50]Alternatively, a female mendicant agent should instigate a traitorous provincial chief: "The wife—*or*, daughter-in-law, *or*, daughter—of that traitorous provincial chief is in love with you." [51]Once he is convinced, she should take an ornament belonging to him and show it to the master, saying, "That chief, arrogant due to his youth, covets your wife—*or*, your daughter-in-law, *or*, your daughter." [52]An altercation between the two at night . . .—the rest is the same as above.

[53]In the case, however, of traitors surrendering with their troops (7.2.9)—the Crown Prince or the Chief of the Armed Forces should commit some offense and flee, after which he should mount an offensive. [54]Then the king should dispatch those same traitors surrendering with their troops accompanied by a weak army including assassins—all the secret measures are the same as above. [55]As the sons are brooding,* moreover, the one who remains steadfastly true should receive the paternal estate.

[56]In this way, the kingdom, free from dangers posed by officials, passes in regular succession to his sons and grandsons.

> [57]He should employ the secret punishment on his own circle and that of his enemy without hesitation, displaying mercy both in the present and with regard to the future.

THAT CONCLUDES THE FIRST CHAPTER: "ON THE INFLICTION OF PUNISHMENT" OF THE FIFTH BOOK: "ON SECRET CONDUCT."

Chapter 2

Topic 90: Stocking the Treasury

[1]When his treasury is depleted and things have started to go badly for him (1.15.35 n.), he should fill up the treasury.

DEMANDS ON FARMERS

[2]He should solicit one-third or one-fourth part* from a district, whether it is large or small in extent, that is not dependent on rain* and produces abundant crops; and from a middling and inferior region, according to its productivity. [3]He should not solicit from one that is helpful in building a fort, undertaking an irrigation project, making a trade route, settling a vacant land, starting a pit mine, or establishing a produce or elephant forest, or from a small one near the frontier.

[4]He should give grain, farm animals, money, and the like to someone who is establishing a new settlement. [5]He should purchase for money one-quarter of the crops, after deducting the amount for seed corn and food.

[6]He should exempt forest produce and the property of Vedic scholars. [7]Even these he may purchase as a favor.*

[8]Alternatively, if that does not work (5.2.31), officers of the Collector should have the farmers thrown out in the summer.* [9]At the time for sowing seeds, they should execute a document regarding seeds,* laying down a penalty of double the amount lost through negligence. [10]Once the crop is produced, they should prevent the pilfering of green or ripe crop, with the exception of handfuls of vegetables or grain stalks plucked by hand for use in divine and ancestral worship, for gifting, and for cows; [11]and they should leave remnants at the bottom of heaps, moreover, for mendicants and village servants (2.1.11 n.).

[12]For someone filching from his own crop, the compensation is eight times the amount. [13]For someone filching from the crops of others, the royal-land penalty (2.22.14 n.) is 15 times the amount if the man belongs to the same group; for an outsider, however, execution.

[14]They should take one-fourth of grains; one-sixth of forest produce, of merchandise consisting of silk-cotton, lac, linen, bark, cotton, wool, silk,

medicines, perfumes, flowers, fruits, and vegetables, and of wood, bamboo, meat, and dried meat; and one-half of ivory and skins. [15]For someone selling these without permission, the punishment is the lowest seizure fine (2.1.29 n.).

[16]That concludes the demand on farmers.

DEMANDS ON TRADERS

[17]Dealers in gold, silver, diamonds, gems, pearls, corals, horses, and elephants are subject to a tax of one-fiftieth.* [18]Dealers in thread, clothes, copper, steel, bronze, perfumes, medicines, and liquor are subject to a tax of one-fortieth. [19]Dealers in grains, juices, and metals, as well as traders who use carts, are subject to a tax of one-thirtieth. [20]Traders in glass and major artisans are subject to a tax of one-twentieth. [21]Minor artisans and keepers of prostitutes are subject to a tax of one-tenth. [22]Dealers in wood, bamboo, stoneware, earthenware, prepared food, and greens are subject to a tax of one-fifth. [23]Performers and prostitutes should give half their earnings.

[24]They should extract a monetary tax from those who are not upright in their work,* and they should not condone any transgression of theirs; [25]for they may sell things, presenting these as not belonging to them.

[26]That concludes the demand on traders.

DEMANDS ON KEEPERS OF LIVING BEINGS

[27]A man should give a half in the case of fowls and pigs; one-sixth in the case of small farm animals; and one-tenth in the case of cattle, buffaloes, mules, donkeys, and camels.

[28]Using royal maids who are young women of exquisite beauty, keepers of prostitutes should replenish the treasury.*

[29]That concludes the demand on keepers of living beings.

[30]This should be employed only once, not twice.*

EMERGENCY MEASURES

[31]Alternatively, if that does not work (5.2.8), the Collector should solicit contributions from the people of the city and the countryside under the pretense of a project that has to be carried out. [32]At the outset, moreover, covert agents should contribute lavish amounts for that purpose. [33]Using that as an example, the king should solicit contributions from the people of the city and the countryside. [34]And crafty student spies should berate those among them who give little.

[35]Alternatively, he should solicit money from rich people according to their means or according to the assistance they have received; or whatever they may proffer of their own free will. [36]And he should award them positions, parasols, turbans, and ornaments in exchange for money.

[37]Executive officers* should bring over the property of religious orders or the property of temples, except what is meant for use by Vedic scholars, stating that it was deposited with a person who has died or whose house has been burnt down.* [38]The Temple Superintendent should gather individually the treasures belonging to the temples of the city and the provinces in one place, and bring them over in the same manner.

[39]Alternatively, having erected a divine shrine or a holy place of a theurgist at night, claiming it to have arisen spontaneously, he should make a living through pilgrimages and fairs. [40]Or, he should publicize the advent of a divinity via a tree in a sanctuary grove bearing flowers and fruit out of season. [41]Or, after disclosing the danger of a demon in a tree demanding a human being as a tax, agents working undercover as thaumaturgic ascetics should counteract it for the people of the city and the countryside in exchange for money. [42]Or, for a monetary gift, he should show a snake with several heads in a well equipped with an underground tunnel.* [43]He should show to credulous people the sight of a snake put into a trance with food in a snake statue containing a cavity within it or in a hole of a sanctuary or an anthill.* [44]In the case of those who are not credulous, after administering poison to them when they are sipping water or washing, he should declare it to be a curse of the deity—or after getting a man condemned to death stung.* [45]Or, he should replenish the treasury by counteracting occult appearances.*

[46]Alternatively, an agent working undercover as a trader, provided with plenty of merchandise and apprentices, should conduct business. [47]When he has become prosperous with deposits and loans taken against the value of his merchandise, he should have him robbed at night. [48]This also explains the Examiner of Coins and the Goldsmith.*

[49]Alternatively, an agent working undercover as a trader renowned for his business should borrow or rent a lot of silver and gold articles on the occasion of a festivity. [50]Or, at a fair, he should collect large amounts of money and gold on loan using the display of all his merchandise as collateral, as well as the price for each piece of merchandise.* [51]He should have both these robbed at night.

[52]After getting traitorous men infatuated through female secret agents in the guise of holy women,* they should apprehend them in the houses of those same women and confiscate all their property.

[53]Alternatively, when a dispute has arisen among traitorous men of distinguished families, poisoners deployed there should administer poison. [54]The others should have all their property confiscated (2.9.24 n.) for this crime.

[55]Alternatively, a man condemned to death (2.5.4 n.) should request from a traitor on some credible pretext the return of a commodity, a monetary deposit, the principal of a loan,* or an inheritance. [56]Or, he should importune the traitor by calling him "slave," or his wife, daughter-in-law, or daughter by calling them "slave woman" or "servant woman."* [57]At night, as he is lying down in front of the door of the traitor's house*—or staying elsewhere (5.1.10 n.)—an assassin should kill him and announce: "This fellow has been killed as he was pursuing a just desire!"* [58]Others* should have all their property confiscated (2.9.24 n.) for this crime.

[59]Alternatively, an agent working undercover as a thaumaturgic ascetic, after he has enticed a traitorous man with magical lores, should say to him, "I know a rite that will secure inexhaustible wealth—*or* open royal doors, *or* capture a woman's heart, *or* strike an enemy with a disease, *or* secure long life, *or* produce a son."* [60]Once he is convinced, he should get him to make an offering with plenty of liquor, meat, and perfume during the night at the site of a sanctuary. [61]And at that location, money consisting of a single coin* should have been buried beforehand, where the limb of a corpse or a dead child had been planted.* He should show the man the money from there, and tell him: "That is too little;" [62]adding, "To get a lot of money, another offering must be made. So, tomorrow using this money, you yourself should buy a lot of material for the offering." [63]He should be arrested in the act of purchasing the material for the offering using that money.

[64]Alternatively, a secret agent in the guise of a mother, saying, "You have killed my son!" should remain in great anguish.* [65]As his night sacrifice, forest sacrifice,* or forest sport is in progress, assassins should kill a condemned man who has been well prepared* and bring him there stealthily.

[66]Alternatively, an agent working undercover as a servant of the traitorous man should expose him by inserting a counterfeit coin into the money he received as wages. [67]Or, an agent working undercover as a workman

should plant the implements of a thief or a maker of counterfeit coins while he is carrying out work inside the house; or an agent working undercover as a physician should plant poison disguised as medicine.

[68]Alternatively, a secret agent who is close to a traitorous man should send word* through a crafty student spy about implements for royal anointing and the royal dispatch of the enemy that have been planted there, and also communicate the reason.*

[69]He should pursue this conduct with respect to traitors and unrighteous people, not with respect to others.

> [70]As one plucks one ripe fruit after another from a garden, so should he from his kingdom. Out of fear for his own destruction, he should avoid unripe ones, which give rise to revolts.

THAT CONCLUDES THE SECOND CHAPTER: "STOCKING THE TREASURY" OF THE FIFTH BOOK: "ON SECRET CONDUCT."

Chapter 3

Topic 91: On Remuneration for Officials

[1]According to the capacity of the fort and countryside, he should fix the wages of officials at one-quarter of the revenue raised, or at a level that the payment to an official would be sufficient for the completion of the work.* [2]Let him pay attention to the corpus (of revenue),* and not harm Law or Success.

[3]Officiating priest, teacher, Counselor-Chaplain (1.10.1 n.), Chief of the Armed Forces, Crown Prince, queen mother, and chief wife of the king—these receive 48,000 Paṇas. [4]With this level of remuneration, they would not become susceptible to instigation (cf. 1.13.17) or liable to revolt.

[5]Chief Gate Guard, Head of the Palace Guard, Administrator, Collector, and Treasurer—these receive 24,000 Paṇas. [6]With this level of remuneration, they become upright in their work (5.2.24 n.).

[7]Princes, mothers of princes, Commander, City Overseer, Director of Factories, Council of Counselors (1.12.6 n.), Commander of a province, and Frontier Commander—these receive 12,000 Paṇas. [8]For they become helpful in strengthening the retinue of the lord with this level of remuneration.

[9]Chiefs of corporate troops, chiefs of elephant, horse, and chariot corps, and Magistrates—these receive 8,000 Paṇas. [10]For they are able to keep their groups in line with this level of remuneration.

[11]Superintendents of infantry, horse, chariot, and elephant corps, and wardens of produce and elephant forests—these receive 4,000 Paṇas.

[12]Charioteers, elephant trainers, physicians, horse trainers, and carpenters, as well as keepers of living beings (5.2.27–29)—these receive 2,000 Paṇas.

[13]Diviners, soothsayers, astrologers, chroniclers,* bards, and panegyrists; assistants to the chaplain; and all the superintendents—these receive 1,000 Paṇas.

[14]Trained foot soldiers, as well as those in the ranks of accountant, scribe, and the like—these receive 500 Paṇas.

[15]Performers, on the other hand, receive 250 Paṇas, while those who make their musical instruments receive twice that amount in wages.

[16]Artisans and craftsmen receive 120 Paṇas.

[17]Servants, helpers, attendants, guards of quadrupeds and bipeds,* and purveyors of laborers receive 60 Paṇas, as also climbers, manikins, and hill diggers* overseen by Āryas, and all attendants.

[18]Teachers and men of learning should receive honoraria as deserved: a minimum of 500 and a maximum of 1,000 Paṇas.

[19]A mid-level envoy receives ten Paṇas for each Yojana. Beyond ten Yojanas, he receives double the wage up to 100 Yojanas.

[20]In sacrifices such as the royal consecration, the "king"* should receive double the wage given to those of equal learning.

[21]The king's charioteer receives 1,000 Paṇas.

[22]Crafty student spies, apostate recluse spies, and agents working undercover as householders, traders, and ascetics receive 1,000 Paṇas.

[23]Village servants (2.1.11 n.), secret agents, assassins, poisoners, and female mendicant agents receive 500 Paṇas.

[24]Carriers of secret information (1.12.24) receive 250 Paṇas, or have their wages increased proportionate to their efforts.

[25]Superintendents in charge of units* of 100 and 1,000 should distribute their rations and wages, give them orders, and order their disbandment.* [26]There is to be no disbandment when they are attending to guarding royal property, the fort, or the provinces. [27]They should be under a permanent command and under separate commands (2.4.29–30).

[28]When they die in the performance of their duties, their sons and wives should receive rations and wages; [29]children, old folks, and sick persons

of theirs should receive assistance; [30]and during ceremonies relating to death, sickness, or birth among them, he should offer monetary gifts and honors.*

[31]One with a meager treasury should give forest produce, farm animals, and fields, as well as a small amount of money. [32]Or else, if he has set out to settle vacant land, he should give only money and not a village, so as to provide stability to conventions pertaining to the total revenue from the villages.* [33]With that,* he should increase the rations and wages of his servants and temporary workers corresponding to their knowledge and work. [34]Taking one Āḍhaka for a person receiving a wage of 60 Paṇas as the basis, he should allocate rations in accordance with their monetary wages.*

[35]Infantry, cavalry, and chariot and elephant corps should carry out exercises in their skills outside (the city) at sunrise, except on the liminal days.* [36]The king should constantly attend to them and inspect their skills frequently.

[37]He should have weapons and armor deposited in the armory after they have been marked with the king's seal. [38]People should travel unarmed, except when they have a permit bearing the seal. [39]When something is destroyed or lost, he* should pay double the amount; [40]and he should keep an account of what has perished.

[41]Frontier Commanders should confiscate the weapons and armor of traders in caravans, or permit them to proceed after placing them under seal.

[42]Or,* when he is set to march on an expedition, he should rouse up his army. [43]Then, at the time of the expedition, agents working undercover as traders should give all kinds of merchandise to the soldiers to be returned twofold. [44]In this manner is made the secret sale of merchandise belonging to the king, as also the recovery of the salaries.*

[45]When he keeps close watch over income and expenditure in this manner, nothing untoward will happen to his treasury or the army.

[46]That concludes the discussion of the different rates of rations and wages.

> [47]Secret agents, prostitutes, artisans, performers, and old soldiers should diligently find out whether the soldiers are loyal or disloyal.

THAT CONCLUDES THE THIRD CHAPTER: "ON REMUNERATION FOR OFFICIALS" OF THE FIFTH BOOK: "ON SECRET CONDUCT."

Chapter 4

Topic 92: On the Conduct Appropriate for Dependents

[1]An expert in worldly matters should seek service with a king through people who are dear to and intimate with him, a king who possesses the exemplary qualities both of the self (6.1.6) and of material constituents (6.1.8–11; 6.2.28). [2]Or, were he to consider someone thus: "As I am seeking to obtain service, so he is seeking to obtain training and is endowed with the qualities of a man who is approachable (6.1.3)," he should seek service with him even if he lacks material constituents, but never with one who lacks the exemplary qualities of self. [3]For a man without the exemplary qualities of self (1.5.16 n.) comes to nothing even after achieving great sovereignty, because such a man hates political science and associates with nefarious people.

[4]When he has obtained an audience with one who possesses the exemplary qualities of the self, he should subject himself to questioning regarding the science,* [5]for he obtains stability in his position by not contradicting it. [6]When questioned about activities that require intellectual acumen, he should speak like an expert, presenting what is achievable relating to Law and Success at the present time and in the future, without being afraid of the council.

[7]Once he is chosen, he should negotiate, saying, "You should not do these: question undistinguished people about Law and Success, inflict punishment on people associated with powerful individuals, or inflict punishment in connection with me and on the spur of the moment.* You should not harm my party, my livelihood, and my secrets. I should be allowed through the use of signs to prevent you from imposing punishment out of lust or anger."

[8]Once he is appointed, he should enter the designated place with permission. And he should sit on one side if placed close by, and on a farther seat if placed at a distance.* [9]He should not do the following: combative speech;* statements that are impolite, indistinct,* incredible, or untrue; laughing loudly outside the context of a joke; and passing wind or expectorating noisily. [10]He should refrain from doing the following: speaking secretly with another man; speaking stridently during arguments between people; wearing clothes fit for a king or ones worn by the haughty and charlatans (1.20.18 n.); openly soliciting gems or prominence; contracting one eye or lip, knitting the eyebrows, or interrupting when another

person is speaking; opposing those associated with powerful individuals; and close contact, cooperation, and congress with women, people looking after women, envoys of neighboring lords, people belonging to an enemy faction, persons who have been dismissed, and nefarious persons.

[11]He should speak what conforms with Law and Success—what is profitable to the king without delay, what is profitable to himself in the company of people who are dear to and intimate with him, and what is profitable to others at the proper place and time.

[12]When questioned, he should state what is both pleasing and beneficial,* not what is pleasing but not beneficial; or he may state what is beneficial but not pleasing, in private and after receiving permission, while he is paying attention.

[13–14]Or else, during a reply, he may remain silent and not talk about enemies and the like. Even those out of favor and who have been ejected because of that sentiment may well be skilled, and even nefarious persons who act according to their knowledge of his mind are seen to become his favorites. He should laugh on humorous occasions, but refrain from offensive laughter.*

[15]He should let offensive words from another pass by, not utter offensive words at another, and bear patiently when they are directed at him, remaining full of forbearance like the earth.

[16]For a wise man must always protect himself first; for the conduct of those who serve the king is said to be like (that of those who work with) fire.

[17]Fire, when it reaches someone, will burn one part or the whole body; but a king kills or fosters a man along with his wife and sons.*

That concludes the Fourth Chapter: "On the Conduct Appropriate for Dependents" of the Fifth Book: "On Secret Conduct."

Chapter 5

Topic 93: On Sanctioned Conduct

[1]When he* is appointed to carry out activities, he should show the income after deducting the expenses. [2]He should, moreover, specify the

task—whether it is internal or external, secret or public, urgent or permitting delay—saying, "This is a task of this type."

[3]He should not be an enabler through his praises when the king becomes addicted to hunting, gambling, drinking, and women. [4]Remaining close to him, moreover, he should strive to eradicate his vices and protect him from instigations, trickery, and deceit of his enemies.

[5]He should scrutinize his* gestures and bearing, [6]for a wise man, in order to conceal his counsel, displays gestures and bearing (1.15.8–9) that invert these pairs—love and hatred, excitement and dejection, resolve and fear.

[7]He* is delighted at seeing him; receives what he says favorably; offers him a seat; gives him private audience; on an occasion for suspicion does not overly suspect; takes delight in his conversation; pays attention to matters that need to be communicated; bears with him when he gives him salutary advice; gives him assignments with a smile; touches him with his hand; does not mock him in a matter that deserves praise; talks about his virtues outside his earshot; thinks of him at mealtimes; goes on pleasure trips with him; comes to his help when he is in trouble; honors those who are devoted to him; tells him secrets; enhances his honors; does what is beneficial; and averts what is harmful—this is the way he knows that he is pleased.

[8]These same factors are inversed when he is displeased, and we will present additional factors: [8]anger at seeing him; not paying attention to or contradicting his statements; not giving him a seat; not looking at him; alteration of color or voice; contraction of an eye, eyebrow, or lip; breaking out in a sweat, sighing, or smiling at inappropriate times; taking counsel with someone else; leaving abruptly; fostering someone else; scratching the ground or the body; goading another person;* disdaining his learning, social class, and region; criticizing those with similar faults as he;* criticizing every fault of his; praising those who are antagonistic to him; not paying heed to things he does right; broadcasting things he does wrong; paying attention to the back;* being completely ostracized; speaking falsely;* and change in behavior toward him on the part of the king's confidants.

[10]He should, moreover, pay attention to a change in behavior of even nonhuman beings. [11]Kātyāyana went away, thinking, "This one is sprinkling from high above;"* Kaṇiṅka Bhāradvāja, thinking, "A Krauñca-crane is to the left;" Dīrgha Cārāyaṇa, thinking, "Grass!";* Ghoṭamukha, thinking, "The garment is cold;"* Kiñjalka, thinking, "An elephant has sprayed

outward;"* Piśuna, thinking, "Chariot and horse have cried out;"* and the son of Piśuna, when he heard the barking of a dog.

[12]Furthermore, when money and honor are refused, he should abandon him; [13]or, taking note of the lord's character and his own transgression, he should redress it. [14]Alternatively, he should go to a close ally of his.*

> [15]While remaining there,* he should work through allies to remove the offense he has committed toward his master. Thereafter, he should come back whether his master is alive or dead.

THAT CONCLUDES THE FIFTH CHAPTER: "ON SANCTIONED CONDUCT" OF THE FIFTH BOOK: "ON SECRET CONDUCT."

Chapter 6

Topic 94: Transition of Regime

[1]With regard to a calamity* that has befallen the king, the minister* should take the following remedial measures.

[2]Well before he fears that the king is in danger of dying, by winning over people dear to and intimate with the king, he should arrange for him to be seen publicly at intervals of one or two months, under the pretext: "The king is carrying out a rite for removing the tribulations of the country—*or* for removing an enemy, *or* for promoting long life, *or* for securing a son" (5.2.59 n.). [3]He should show someone disguised as the king to his subjects at a time when it is difficult to distinguish features, as also to the envoys of allies and enemies. [4]Further, he should arrange for appropriate conversations with them to be carried out through a minister; [5]and through the Chief Gate Guard and the Head of the Palace Guard, he should have the prescribed regimen of the king carried out (1.19). [6]Toward those who do him harm, moreover, he should show either wrath or kindness, whichever may please the subjects; and toward those who do him favors, only kindness.

[7]He* should arrange for the treasury and the army to be collected in one place under the charge of trustworthy men, either in the fort or by the frontier; as also members of the royal household, princes, and chief officers under various pretexts.

[8]When a chief officer with a following or posted in a fort or a tribal region becomes antagonistic, moreover, he should work to win him over.

[9]Alternatively, he should dispatch him on an expedition fraught with many dangers or to the household of an ally.

[10]Further, when he becomes aware that a neighboring lord poses a danger, he should have him arrested under the pretext of a festival, marriage, capturing elephants, sale of horses, or land grant, or else through an ally of that man. [11]Then, he should make him enter into an inviolable* pact. [12]Alternatively, he should foster enmity between him and tribal chiefs or enemies. [13]Or else, he should win over a pretender from the royal family or a prince in disfavor by the offer of a portion of that man's territory.

[14]Alternatively, after winning over members of the royal household, princes, and chief officers, he should publicly display a prince who has already been anointed.

[15]Alternatively, he should carry on the administration of the kingdom after eradicating the thorns of the kingdom in the manner given in "On the Infliction of Punishment" (5.1).

[16]If, on the other hand, any chief officer or one of the neighboring lords were to contemplate a revolt, he should summon him, saying, "Come, I will make you king," and then kill him. [17]Or else, he should subdue him using the remedial measures against calamities.*

[18]Alternatively, he should first transfer the burden of the kingdom progressively on the Crown Prince and then announce the calamity that has befallen the king.

[19]When a calamity has befallen the king within an enemy territory, he should negotiate a pact with the foe using an ally in the guise of an enemy and then retreat. [20]Alternatively, he should install one of these—a neighboring lord and so forth*—in his fort and then retreat. [21]Or else, he should anoint a prince and then counterattack. [22]Or, when attacked by the enemy, he should resort to the prescribed remedial measures against calamities (5.6.17 n.).

Topic 95: Continuity of Sovereignty

[23]"In this manner, the minister should arrange for the continuity of sovereignty," says Kauṭilya.

[24]"That's not so," says Bhāradvāja. [25]"When the king is dying, the minister should either get the members of the royal household, the princes, and the chief officers to attack each other or chief officers*—[26]when someone attacks, he should have him killed by a revolt of the constituents—[27]or, after subduing the members of the royal household, the princes, and the

chief officers by the use of secret punishment (1.11.21 n.), he should seize the kingdom himself. [28]For, on account of the kingdom, a father turns hostile against his sons, and sons against their father; how much more then the constituent who is a minister (6.1.1 n.), the sole anchor of the kingdom. [29]Let him not disdain it when it comes to him on its own. [30]There is the popular saying: 'For a woman approaching on her own curses when she is spurned.'

> [31]Time comes but once to a man who is waiting for his time; that
> time is hard to come by for him when he wants to accomplish
> a task."

[32]"That incites the constituents to revolt, is unrighteous, and is uncertain," says Kauṭilya.

[33]He should install a son of the king endowed with the exemplary qualities of self (6.1.6) over the kingdom. [34]In the absence of someone so endowed, he should put forward a prince not prone to vice, a princess, or a pregnant queen,* assemble the High Officials, and say to them, "This one is your charge. Have regard for his father and for his* character and high birth. This one is only the emblem; you alone are the masters. Or, how shall we proceed?" [35]As he is speaking this way, covert agents should tell him: "Who else but this king, with you to guide him, has the capacity to protect the four social classes?" [36]Saying, "So be it!," the minister should appoint the prince, the princess, or the pregnant queen and present that person to the kinsmen and relatives, as well as to the envoys of allies and enemies.

[37]He should have the rations and wages of ministers and soldiers increased and declare: "When this one is grown up, he will make further increases." [38]He should speak in like manner to the chief officers of the fort and the provinces, as also to the partisans of allies and enemies as appropriate. [39]He should also work strenuously at training the prince.

[40]Alternatively, he should get a man of the same caste to father a child through the princess and anoint him. [41]Because of the fear that the mother's mind may become agitated,* he should keep near her a family member of hers without much drive and a pupil with auspicious marks;* [42]and he should guard her during her season (1.3.9 n.).

[43]He should not get any luxurious amenities, moreover, to be prepared for his own use. [44]For the use of the king, however, he should have vehicles,

mounts, ornaments, garments, women, houses, and such personal effects prepared.

> [45]When he has become a young man, further, he should ask his permission to retire to test his disposition. If he is not satisfied, he should abandon him; if he is satisfied, he should continue to protect him.
>
> [46]If he has fallen out of favor, he should retire to the wilderness or perform a long sacrificial session, after instructing secret and powerful groups to protect the prince.
>
> [47]Alternatively, when the king is in the grip of chief officers, he, being learned in the science of Success (*arthaśāstra*), should enlighten him using Itihāsas and Purāṇas (1.5.14 n.), supported by those who love the king.
>
> [48]Alternatively, putting on the appearance of a thaumaturgic ascetic, he should secure the king by resorting to secret measures and, after securing him, he should employ the "Infliction of Punishment" (5.1) on traitors.

THAT CONCLUDES THE SIXTH CHAPTER: "TRANSITION OF REGIME" AND "CONTINUITY OF SOVEREIGNTY" OF THE FIFTH BOOK: "ON SECRET CONDUCT."

THAT CONCLUDES THE FIFTH BOOK: "ON SECRET CONDUCT" OF KAUṬILYA'S *ARTHAŚĀSTRA*.

Book Six

Basis of the Circle

Chapter 1

Topic 96: The Exemplary Qualities of the Constituent Elements

[1]Lord, minister, countryside, fort, treasury, army, and ally are the constituent elements.

[2]Of these, the following constitute the exemplary qualities of the lord: [3]Coming from a noble family; endowed with good fortune, intelligence, and spirit; visiting elders; righteous; truthful; not breaking his word; grateful; generous; with immense energy; not given to procrastination; with pliant neighboring rulers; with a resolute mind; with a council that is not petty; eager to be trained*—these are the qualities of a man who is approachable. [4]Desire to learn, attentive listening, grasping, retention, comprehension, reasoning, rejection, devotion to truth—these are the qualities of intelligence (1.5.5 n.). [5]Bravery, indignation, quickness, skill—these are the qualities of energy. [6]Articulate; bold; endowed with memory, intellect, and strength; exalted; easy to manage; trained in the crafts; free of vices; providing leadership to the army; providing the prescribed retribution for benefits provided and wrongs done; modest; taking the appropriate action in times of adversity and normalcy; judicious and farsighted; placing emphasis on tasks undertaken at the proper place and time and with the right human effort; able to discriminate between entering into a peace pact and initiating hostilities, releasing and detaining, and keeping to the agreement and seeking the enemy's vulnerable points; guarding himself well; not laughing in an undignified manner; looking without squinting or frowning; free of lust, hatred, greed, rigidity, inconstancy,

brutality, and slander; affable; speaking with a smile and with dignity; and acting according to the instructions of elders—these are the exemplary qualities of the self.

[7]The exemplary qualities of a minister have been given above (1.9.1).

[8]Having strongholds* in the center and on the frontiers; capable of supporting itself and others during a time of adversity; easy to protect; providing an easy living; showing antipathy toward enemies; with pliant neighboring rulers; free of mud, stones, brackish soil, rugged land, criminals,* gangs, vicious animals, wild animals, and forest tribes; charming; abounding in agricultural land, pit mines, produce forests, and elephant forests; good for cattle and for humans; with secure pasture land; abounding in farm animals; with land not dependent on rain (5.2.2 n.); containing water and land routes; containing valuable, diverse, and ample commodities; capable of bearing fines and taxes; containing agricultural workers with a good work ethic and landlords who are prudent;* populated mainly by the lower social classes (2.1.2); and with people who are loyal and honest—these are the exemplary qualities of the countryside.

[9]The exemplary qualities of the fort have been given above (2.3).

[10]Acquired lawfully either by his ancestors or by himself; consisting mainly of gold and silver; with a variety of large gems and coins; one that can withstand even a prolonged adversity when there is no income—these are the exemplary qualities of the treasury.

[11]Bequeathed by the father and grandfather; consistent; submissive; one in which the sons and wives of hired soldiers are content; not prone to insubordination during long marches; without obstacles anywhere; able to bear hardships; one that has experienced many battles; expert in the science of all kinds of warfare and weaponry; not prone to duplicity, being partners in both prosperity and decline (7.1.25–29); and consisting mainly of Kṣatriyas—these are the exemplary qualities of the army.

[12]Bequeathed by the father and grandfather; consistent; submissive; not prone to duplicity; eminent; and able to mobilize quickly—these are the exemplary qualities of an ally (7.9).

[13]Without royal pedigree; greedy; with an insignificant council and disaffected subjects; not behaving righteously; without focus; fallen on hard times; without energy; relying on fate; acting aimlessly; without a refuge;* not following up;* effeminate; and always doing what is harmful—these are the exemplary qualities of an enemy.* [14]For a foe of this type can be easily vanquished.

[15]Excluding the enemy, these are the seven constituents displaying the qualities of each. These constituents have been described as subsidiary elements of the exemplary qualities of the king.

[16]When a king is endowed with the exemplary qualities of the self (1.5.16 n.), he endows the constituents with the exemplary qualities that they lack, while a king lacking the exemplary qualities of the self destroys the constituents, even when they are prosperous and loyal (see 8.1.16).

[17]Then this king, lacking the exemplary qualities of the self and surrounded by flawed constituents, even if he rules all four corners of the earth, is killed by his constituents or comes under the power of his enemies.

[18]When, however, he possesses the exemplary qualities of the self, is linked to the exemplary qualities of the constituents, and knows good policies, he is sure to conquer the entire earth and is never laid low, even if he rules over a small territory.

THAT CONCLUDES THE FIRST CHAPTER: "THE EXEMPLARY QUALITIES OF THE CONSTITUENT ELEMENTS" OF THE SIXTH BOOK: "BASIS OF THE CIRCLE."

Chapter 2

Topic 97: On Rest and Exertion

[1]Rest and exertion form the basis of enterprise and security.* [2]Exertion consists of the enterprise that one furnishes to activities that are being undertaken. [3]Rest consists of the security that one furnishes to the enjoyment of the fruits of one's activities.

[4]The basis of rest and exertion is the sixfold strategy (7.1.2). [5]Its outcomes are decline, stability, and prosperity (7.1.25–29).

[6]Good and bad policy pertain to the human realm, while good and bad fortune pertain to the divine realm. [7]Divine and human activity, indeed, makes the world run. [8]The divine consists of what is caused by an invisible agent. [9]Of this, attaining a desirable result is good fortune, while attaining an undesirable result is bad fortune. [10]The human consists of what is caused by a visible agent. [11]Of this, the success of enterprise and security is good policy, while their failure is bad policy. [12]This is within the range of thought, whereas the divine is beyond the range of thought.

[13]The seeker after conquest is a king who is endowed with the exemplary qualities both of the self (6.1.6; 1.9.1 n.) and of material constituents (6.2.28), and who is the abode of good policy. [14]Forming a circle all around him and with immediately contiguous territories is the constituent comprising his enemies. [15]In like manner, with territories once removed from his, is the constituent comprising his allies.

[16]A neighboring ruler possessing the exemplary qualities of an enemy (6.1.13 n.) is the "foe"; when he is facing a calamity, he is the "vulnerable";* when he is without support or with weak support, he is the "vanquishable";* and in the opposite case, he is the "oppressable"* or the "enfeebleable."* [17]These are the different types of enemies.

[18]Beyond him in a series of contiguous territories toward the front are located the ally, the enemy's ally, the ally's ally, and the ally of the enemy's ally; and toward the back, the rear enemy, the rear ally, the rear enemy's backer, and the rear ally's backer.

[19]One with an immediately contiguous territory is a natural enemy; one of equal birth is an innate enemy; and one who is hostile or acts with hostility is a contingent enemy.

[20]One with a territory once removed is the natural ally; one related to the mother or father is an innate ally; and one who has sought refuge for money or life* is a contingent ally.

[21]One with a territory immediately contiguous to both the enemy and the seeker after conquest, and who is able to assist them both when they are united and when they are not and to overpower them when they are not united is the intermediate.*

[22]One who is apart from the enemy, the seeker after conquest, and the intermediate, and more powerful than the constituents,* and who is able to assist the enemy, the seeker after conquest, and the intermediate both when they are united and when they are not and to overpower them when they are not united is the neutral.

[23]These are the constituents (6.2.22 n.).

[24]Alternatively, its* constituents are three: the seeker after conquest, the ally, and the ally's ally. [25]These, with each individually connected to his five constituents—minister, countryside, fort, treasury, and army—form the 18-fold circle.* [26]This also explains the separate circles associated with the enemy, the intermediate, and the neutral. [27]That is the sum of the four circles.

[28]There are 12 royal constituents and 60 material constituents—in sum, 72.* [29]Each of these has its own set of exemplary qualities.

[30]Power and success—[31]power is strength, [32]and success is happiness.

[33]Power is threefold: power of counsel comprising the strength of intellect, power of might* comprising the strength of treasury and army, and power of effort comprising the strength of valor.

[34]Success, likewise, is threefold: success of counsel to be achieved through the power of counsel, success of might* to be achieved through the power of might,* and success of effort to be achieved through the power of effort.

[35]When he has been strengthened by these, he becomes stronger; when he is weakened with respect to these, he becomes inferior; and when he has equal power, he becomes coequal.* [36]Therefore, he should strive to bring power and success to himself or, if he is similar,* to his material constituents (6.2.28) in accordance with their contiguity or integrity.

[37]Or else, he should strive to take these away from traitors and enemies. [38]Alternatively, if he were to foresee—

> My enemy, if he were to have power, will oppress his subjects through verbal and physical abuse and by confiscating property; or, if he were to have success, he will become careless because of hunting, gambling, drinking, and women. When his subjects are disaffected, and he is weakened or careless, it will be possible for me to overpower him.
>
> Or, when he is attacked during a time of hostilities, he will stay in one place or outside his fort gathering his army there. With his troops brought together and separated from his allies and fort, it will be possible for me to overpower him.
>
> Or, he will render me assistance either when I am being attacked by a powerful king, thinking, "This powerful king seeks to vanquish an enemy somewhere else, and after vanquishing him he will vanquish me"; or when the projects I have undertaken have failed; or while seeking to overpower the intermediate king—

for reasons such as these, he may seek to provide power and success even to an enemy.

> [39]Making the kings who are once removed the felly, those who are immediately contiguous the spokes, and himself the hub, the leader* should stretch himself out in the circle of constituents.

[40]For, when the enemy is positioned between the leader and his ally, he will turn out to be "vanquishable" or "oppressable" (6.2.16 n.) even if he is powerful.

THAT CONCLUDES THE SECOND CHAPTER: "ON REST AND EXERTION" OF THE SIXTH BOOK: "BASIS OF THE CIRCLE."

THAT CONCLUDES THE SIXTH BOOK: "BASIS OF THE CIRCLE" OF KAUṬILYA'S *ARTHAŚĀSTRA*.

Book Seven

On the Sixfold Strategy

Chapter 1

Topic 98: Enumeration of the Sixfold Strategy

[1]The basis of the sixfold strategy* is the circle of constituents.

[2]"The sixfold strategy consists of peace pact, initiating hostilities,* remaining stationary, marching into battle, seeking refuge, and double stratagem," so state the teachers.

[3]"Strategy is twofold," says Vātavyādhi, [4]"for by means of a peace pact and initiating hostilities, the sixfold strategy is accomplished."

[5]"This is indeed a sixfold strategy, because there are different circumstances," says Kauṭilya.

[6]Of these, peace pact is a negotiated agreement; [7]initiating hostilities is harmful action; [8]remaining stationary is awaiting patiently; [9]marching into battle is strength (6.2.35); [10]seeking shelter is surrendering to another; [11]and double stratagem is pursuing a peace pact and initiating hostilities at the same time.* [12]These are the six strategies.

[13]When he is getting weaker in comparison to the enemy, he should arrange a peace pact, [14]and when he is getting stronger, he should initiate hostilities. [15]When he realizes, "Neither is my enemy able to hurt me, nor am I able to hurt my enemy," he should remain stationary. [16]When he possesses an abundance of the strategic advantages, he should march into battle. [17]When he lacks power, he should seek refuge. [18]With respect to a task achievable only with an accomplice, he should resort to the double stratagem. [19]So are established the strategic measures.

Topic 99: Decisions during Decline, Stability, and Prosperity

[20]Among these, when by resorting to a particular strategic measure, he foresees, "By resorting to this I will be able to advance my activities relating to forts, irrigation works, trade routes, settling vacant lands, pit mines, and produce and elephant forests, and to hurt these same activities of my enemy," then he should adopt it. [21]This constitutes prosperity. [22]When he realizes, "My prosperity will be quicker or greater, or will lead to further prosperity, and the opposite will be true of my enemy," he should tolerate the prosperity of his enemy. [23]Or else, when their prosperity takes equal time and brings the same results, he should enter into a peace pact.

[24]Alternatively, when by resorting to a particular strategic measure, he foresees that his own activities will become ruined and not those of the other, he should not resort to it. [25]This constitutes decline. [26]When he realizes, "I will decline more slowly or to a smaller extent, or in such a way as to lead to greater prosperity, and the opposite will be true of my enemy," he should tolerate a decline. [27]Or else, when their decline takes equal time and brings the same results, he should enter into a peace pact.

[28]Alternatively, when by resorting to a particular strategic measure, he foresees that his activities will neither prosper nor decline, it constitutes stability. [29]When he realizes, "I will remain stable for a shorter period or in such a way as to lead to greater prosperity, and the opposite will be true of my enemy," he should tolerate stability.

[30]"Alternatively, when stability lasts for an equal time and brings the same results, he should enter into a peace pact," so state the teachers. [31]"That is not an alternative,"* says Kauṭilya.

[32]Alternatively, he should promote prosperity through a peace pact if he were to foresee the following:

> By resorting to a peace pact, I will hurt the activities of my enemy by means of my own activities bearing copious fruit.
>
> Or, I will enjoy my own activities bearing copious fruit or those of my enemy.
>
> Or, by creating confidence through a peace pact, I will hurt the activities of my enemy by employing secret activities (book 5) and occult practices (book 14).
>
> Or, facilitated by benefits and exemptions, I will easily lure away the people who can carry out the activities of my enemy by

creating greater profit for them through engagement in my own activities.

Or, by entering into a peace pact with an exceedingly powerful king, the enemy will suffer the ruin of his activities.

Or, when he enters into a peace pact with me as hostilities are initiated against him by someone, I will ensure that his state of hostility with that man is prolonged.

Or, he will harass the countryside of the one who has entered into a peace pact with me but is antagonistic toward me.

Or, people of his countryside, oppressed by his enemy, will come to me; thereby I will achieve prosperity in my activities.

Or, given that my enemy finds himself in a difficult situation with his activities in ruins, he cannot threaten my activities.

Or, initiating my activities far away and entering into peace pacts with both,* I will achieve prosperity in my activities.

Or, by entering into a peace pact with my foe, I will split off from him the circle that is loyal to that foe and, once it has split off from him, I will secure it for myself.

Or, when my foe is attempting to overpower the circle, I shall create hostility toward him by supporting him with the supply of troops; and once he faces hostilities, I shall get him killed by the same circle.

[33]Alternatively, he should promote prosperity by initiating hostilities if he were to foresee the following:

My countryside consists predominantly of martial people or fighting groups or is protected by a single entry point consisting of a hill fort, a forest fort, or a river fort (2.3). Thus it will be able to repel an enemy attack.

Or, taking refuge in an impregnable fort at the edge of my territory, I will be able to hurt the activities of my enemy.

Or, my enemy, with his efforts undermined by the havoc resulting from calamities, has reached the point when his activities face devastation.

Or, when hostilities have been initiated against him by someone else, I will be able to force people out from his countryside (2.1.1 n.).

[34]Alternatively, he should promote prosperity by remaining stationary if he thinks the following:

> My enemy is not capable of hurting my activities; nor am I capable of hurting his activities.
>
> Or, he is suffering from a calamity.
>
> Or, he is engaged in a conflict similar to that between a dog and a boar.*
>
> Or, intent on carrying out my activities, I will become prosperous.

[35]Alternatively, he should promote prosperity by marching into battle if he thinks, "The ruining of my foe's activities can be accomplished by marching into battle; and I have made arrangements to protect my own activities."

[36]Alternatively, if he thinks, "I am not capable of hurting the activities of my enemy or of preventing the hurting of my activities," having sought refuge with someone powerful, he should endeavor to advance from decline to stability and from stability to prosperity, by carrying out his own activities.

[37]Alternatively, if he thinks, "By entering into a peace pact, on the one hand, I will promote my activities, and by initiating hostilities, on the other hand, I will hurt the activities of my enemy," he should promote prosperity by means of the double stratagem.

> [38]Establishing himself within the circle of constituents in this way, by means of these six strategic measures, he should seek to progress from decline to stability and from stability to prosperity in his activities.

THAT CONCLUDES THE FIRST CHAPTER: "ENUMERATION OF THE SIXFOLD STRATEGY" AND "DECISIONS DURING DECLINE, STABILITY, AND PROSPERITY" OF THE SEVENTH BOOK: "ON THE SIXFOLD STRATEGY."

Chapter 2

Topic 100: Conduct when Seeking Refuge

[1]When* equal prosperity results from a peace pact and from initiating hostilities, he should resort to a peace pact; [2]for initiating hostilities brings

about losses, expenses,* absence from home, and setbacks. [3]That also explains remaining stationary when faced with remaining stationary or marching into battle.

[4]When faced with double stratagem and seeking refuge, he should resort to double stratagem; [5]for someone who employs double stratagem focuses on his own activities and serves only his own interests, whereas someone who takes refuge serves the interests of the other and not his own.*

[6]He should seek refuge with someone whose strength is greater than that of his neighbor.* [7]If someone whose strength is greater than the latter is not available, he should take refuge with the latter himself and, remaining out of sight, strive to render assistance to him with one of the following: treasury, army, and land; [8]for consorting with someone of greater strength is an enormous peril for kings, except when he is in a state of war with an enemy.

[9]If he is unable to do that, he should conduct himself in the same way as someone surrendering with his troops (7.15.21–30). [10]When he sees, moreover, that the man is suffering from a lethal disease, or he is facing an internal revolt, or his foe is becoming prosperous, or a calamity has befallen his ally, and that as a result he himself can become prosperous, then he should go away under the convincing pretext of an illness or a religious duty. [11]Or, if he is residing in his own territory, he should not visit him. [12]Or else, if he is residing near him, he should strike him at his vulnerable points.

[13]Alternatively, if he finds himself in the middle of two stronger individuals, he should seek refuge with the one who is capable of providing him protection, or with the one with reference to whom he is the interposed (7.13.25), or with both. [14]He should abide resorting to the "potsherd" pact (7.3.30–31), spreading the false rumor to the one that the other intends to seize his home territory. [15]Or, he should cause alienation between the two by spreading false rumors about each other; once they are alienated, he should employ the secret punishment (1.11.21 n.) on them.

[16]Alternatively, if he finds himself on the flank of two strong kings, he should take countermeasures against an immediate danger. [17]Or, finding a haven in the fort, he should remain there adopting the double stratagem. [18]Or, he should occupy himself with the reasons for resorting to a peace pact or to initiating hostilities.* [19]He should bolster the treasonable individuals, enemies, and forest chieftains associated with both. [20]Going over

to one of these two, he should, with the help of these same people, strike the other one when a calamity has befallen him.

[21]Alternatively, if he is attacked by both, finding a haven in the circle, he should remain there; or take refuge with the intermediate king or the neutral king. [22]Together with him, he should, by bolstering the one, vanquish the other or both of them.

[23]Alternatively, if he is vanquished by both, he should seek refuge with someone of righteous conduct among the intermediate king, the neutral king, or kings who are their partisans. [24]Or, among those whose behavior is equally upright, he should seek refuge with the one whose constituents would make him happy, or by staying with whom he would be able to lift himself up, or to whom his ancestors were in the habit of going, or with whom he has a close relationship, or where he has numerous and very powerful friends.

> [25]Which of these two—the one to whom he is dear or the one
> who is dear to him? He should go to the one to whom he is dear.
> This is the best course in seeking refuge.

That concludes the Second Chapter: "Conduct when Seeking Refuge" of the Seventh Book: "On the Sixfold Strategy."

Chapter 3

Topic 101: Adherence to Strategic Measures on the Part of Equal, Weaker, and Stronger Kings

[1]The seeker after conquest should employ the sixfold strategy with due regard to his power. [2]He should enter into a peace pact with someone who is equal or stronger, whereas he should initiate hostilities against one who is weaker. [3]For, in initiating hostilities against someone stronger, he is as if engaging in a fight with an elephant while on foot; [4]while initiating hostilities against an equal brings losses to both, like an unbaked pot being struck by another unbaked pot. [5]When he initiates hostilities against someone weaker, he attains certain success, like a stone striking a clay pot.

[6]If someone stronger does not want to enter into a peace pact, he should resort to the conduct of someone surrendering with his troops (7.15.21–30) or to the methods recommended for a weaker king (Book 12).

[7]If an equal does not want to enter into a peace pact, he should inflict the same amount of damage on him as the latter has inflicted on him. [8]For, heat is the cause of joining; [9]an unheated piece of metal does not become joined to another piece of metal.*

[10]If someone weaker remains subservient in all matters, he should enter into a peace pact with him. [11]For, like a forest fire, the blazing rage born of grief and rancor makes a person charge boldly; [12]and he would be looked upon with favor by the circle.

[13]If, after making a peace pact, he were to foresee, "My enemy's subjects, being greedy, destitute, or rebellious, or because they fear being seized again, will not come over to me," then he should initiate hostilities even if he is weaker.

[14]If, after initiating hostilities, he were to foresee, "My enemy's subjects, being greedy, destitute, or rebellious, or being alarmed by the hostilities, will not come over to me," then he should enter into a peace pact even if he is stronger; or he should assuage the alarm caused by the hostilities.

[15]Even in the case of concurrent calamities, if he were to foresee, "My calamity is more serious. My enemy's calamity is minor. He will easily redress his calamity and attack me," he should enter into a peace pact even if he is stronger.

[16]If he were to foresee that neither a peace pact nor the initiation of hostilities will bring about the weakening of his enemy or the strengthening of himself, he should remain stationary even if he is stronger.

[17]If he were to foresee that the calamity that has struck his enemy cannot be redressed, he should march into battle even if he is weak.

[18]When he is faced with an imminent calamity that cannot be redressed, he should seek refuge even if he is stronger

[19]If he were to foresee the success of his undertaking by entering into a peace pact on one front and by initiating hostilities on another, then he should resort to double stratagem (7.1.11 n.) even if he is stronger.

[20]The sixfold strategy is employed by an equal in the same manner.

Topic 102: Peace Pacts by Weaker Kings

[21]With regard to that, however, there are these special provisions:

> [22]When a weaker king is overwhelmed by a stronger king with a superb army, he should quickly submit with a peace pact by offering his treasury, his army, himself, or his land.

[23]He himself is required to render service with a stipulated number of troops or with the full strength of the army; this is considered a "peace pact with himself as the bait."

[24]The Chief of the Armed Forces or the prince is required to render service; this is a "peace pact using another person" and not himself; it is, therefore, one that provides protection to himself.

[25]Either just himself or just his army is required to retire elsewhere; this is a "peace pact with an unseen person,"* and it provides protection to the army chief and to himself.

[26]In the first two kinds of pacts, he should establish a marriage alliance for the chief,* while in the last he should get rid of the enemy in secret. These are the peace pacts entered into by someone surrendering with his troops.

[27–28]When the remaining constituents are rescued by surrendering the treasury, that peace pact is "purchase." The same with the amount to be delivered successively in installments at one's leisure should be known as the "support" peace pact. A tribute limited as to place and time is support.

[29]One that is bearable because it involves payment of a sustainable amount in the future, and also because of a marriage alliance, is the "golden peace pact"; it brings about harmony because of mutual confidence.

[30]The opposite is the "potsherd," so called because of exorbitant payments. In the first two kinds, he should hand over forest produce, or elephants and horses that have been administered poison.*

[31]In the third (7.3.29), he should hand over the amount. In the fourth (7.3.30), he should linger, explaining the decline of his activities. These are the peace pacts of someone surrendering with his treasury.

[32]Protecting the remaining constituents by surrendering a portion of his land is the "preplanned peace pact," desirable when one intends to attack by using clandestine operatives and thieves.

[33]Surrendering lands—with the exception of his home territory—from which all the valuable resources have been removed, is the "peace pact using what has been vanquished," desirable when one expects a calamity to befall the enemy.

[34]Saving lands by offering their produce is "renting." When there is a total surrender of the produce from the lands, the peace pact is "ravaging."

[35]In the case of the first two (7.3.32–33), he should wait vigilantly, while in the case of the last two (7.3.34), he should adopt the conduct of a weaker king (Book 12), while taking the produce for himself. These are the peace pacts of someone surrendering with his territory.

[36]These are the three kinds of peace pacts by someone who is weaker commended at the proper place and time as demanded by one's undertakings and to be carried out in keeping with the conduct of a weaker king.

That concludes the Third Chapter: "Adherence to Strategic Measures on the Part of Equal, Weaker, and Stronger Kings" and "Peace Pacts by Weaker Kings" of the Seventh Book: "On the Sixfold Strategy."

Chapter 4

Topic 103: Remaining Stationary after Initiating Hostilities

[1]Remaining stationary and marching into battle in the context of concluding a peace pact or initiating hostilities have not yet been explained.*

[2]Remaining still, remaining stationary, and waiting patiently; these are synonyms for remaining stationary. [3]Their peculiarities, however, are the following: When strategic advantages are partially present, it is remaining still; when the intention is to achieve one's own prosperity, it is remaining stationary; and when strategic measures are not employed, it is waiting patiently.

[4]Remaining stationary either after initiating hostilities or after entering into a peace pact is meant for an enemy and the seeker after conquest who desire to outwit each other, but who are incapable of hurting each other.

[5]Alternatively, if he were to foresee, "I have the power to weaken an equal or a stronger individual using either my own troops or the troops of my allies or tribal chiefs," then, after doing the needful* in the outer and the interior regions, he should initiate hostilities and then remain stationary.

[6]Alternatively, if he were to foresee, "My constituents are energetic, unified, and prosperous, and will carry out their activities unhindered or hurt the activities of my enemy," then he should initiate hostilities and then remain stationary.

[7]Alternatively, if he were to foresee the following, then, in order to hinder the prosperity of his enemy and to demonstrate his prowess, he should initiate hostilities and then remain stationary:

> My enemy's subjects are rebellious, impoverished, greedy, or harassed by his troops, thieves, or tribal forces, and they will come over to me on their own or through instigation.
>
> My commercial undertakings are thriving, while those of my enemy are languishing. His subjects, oppressed by famine, will come over to me.
>
> My commercial undertakings are languishing, while those of my enemy are thriving. Yet my subjects will not go over to him, and, after initiating hostilities, I shall plunder his grains, farm animals, and money.
>
> Or, when hostilities have been initiated against him, I will obstruct my enemy's merchandise that undermines my own merchandise, or valuable goods will come to me from his trade route and not to him.
>
> Or, when hostilities have been initiated against him, he will not suppress his traitors, enemies, and tribal chiefs, or else he will be plunged into a state of hostility with those very people.
>
> After marching against my ally possessing the disposition of an ally (7.9.43), within a short time and with minimal losses and expenses (7.2.2 n.), he will acquire abundant wealth or fertile land that is easy to seize.
>
> When, after gathering together his entire army, he wishes to march into battle with total disregard of me, how would he not march?

[8]"Having turned around, he may actually devour him," say the teachers. [9]"No," says Kauṭilya. [10]"He will only cause his weakening, if the latter is not facing a calamity. When his own prosperity is enhanced by that of his enemy, on the other hand, he will vanquish him. [11]Thus, remaining unvanquished, the vulnerable opponent of his enemy will offer him assistance. [12]Therefore, against someone who has gathered together his entire army, he should declare war and then remain stationary."*

Topic 104: Remaining Stationary after Entering into a Peace Pact

[13]When the reverse of the reasons for initiating hostilities and then remaining stationary is the case, then, after entering into a peace pact, he should remain stationary.

Topic 105: Marching into Battle after Initiating Hostilities

[14]When he has become strengthened by the reasons for declaring war and then remaining stationary, after initiating hostilities, he should march into battle, taking care not to gather together his entire army.

[15]Alternatively, if he were to foresee the following, then, after initiating hostilities, he should march into battle:

> My foe is facing a calamity.
>
> Or, the calamity affecting a constituent of his cannot be remedied by the remaining constituents.
>
> Or, his subjects are oppressed by his army or are disaffected; they are weakened, bereft of energy, or are divided the one from the other. They are thus able to be enticed.
>
> My enemy's draught animals, men, stocks, and defensive arrangements have become weakened as a result of fire, water, disease, epidemic, or famine.

[16]Alternatively, if he were to foresee the following, after initiating hostilities, he should march into battle:

> My ally in the front and my rear ally* have subjects who are brave, prosperous, and loyal, whereas the opposite is true of the subjects of my enemy, my rear enemy, and his backer. After initiating hostilities against the rear enemy's backer through my ally in the front, or against my rear enemy through my rear ally, I will be able to march into battle.

[17]Alternatively, if he were to foresee that the result can be secured alone and within a brief period of time, then, after initiating hostilities against the rear enemy and his backer, he should march into battle.

Topic 106: Marching into Battle after Entering into a Peace Pact

[18]Under opposite circumstances, after entering into a peace pact, he should march into battle.

Topic 107: Marching Forth into Battle after Forming a Partnership

[19]Alternatively, if he were to foresee, "I am unable to march into battle alone, but it is imperative that I march into battle," then he should march into battle after forming a partnership with consociates who may be equal, or weaker, or stronger, agreeing to fixed shares if conducted in one place, or to shares that are not fixed if conducted in more than one place.* [20]If a formal coalition with them is not feasible, he should request troops from any one of them for a set share. [21]Or else, he should hire them with the pledge to march in partnership with them—with a fixed share if the winnings are certain, or with a share of the winnings if they are uncertain.

> [22]A share equal to the amount of troops is the lowest, and one equal to the effort is the highest; or the plundered amount in accordance with what is seized; or an amount proportionate to the investment.

THAT CONCLUDES THE FOURTH CHAPTER: "REMAINING STATIONARY AFTER INITIATING HOSTILITIES," "REMAINING STATIONARY AFTER ENTERING INTO A PEACE PACT," "MARCHING INTO BATTLE AFTER INITIATING HOSTILITIES," "MARCHING INTO BATTLE AFTER ENTERING INTO A PEACE PACT," AND "MARCHING FORTH INTO BATTLE AFTER FORMING A PARTNERSHIP" OF THE SEVENTH BOOK: "ON THE SIXFOLD STRATEGY."

Chapter 5

Topic 108: Reflections on Attacking a Vulnerable Ruler and an Enemy

[1]When neighboring rulers are facing equal calamities, should it be the vulnerable ruler or the enemy? It is the enemy against whom he should march into battle; after he has been suppressed, against the vulnerable king. [2]For, when the enemy has been suppressed, the vulnerable ruler

may give him assistance, but not the enemy when the vulnerable ruler has been suppressed.

[3]Should it be the vulnerable ruler facing a serious calamity or the enemy facing a minor calamity? "It is the one facing a serious calamity against whom he should march into battle, because it is easier," say the teachers. [4]"No," says Kauṭilya. [5]"He should march into battle against the enemy facing a minor calamity; [6]for when someone is attacked, even a minor calamity becomes dangerous. [7]True, a serious calamity also will become even more serious. [8]But when he is not attacked, the enemy facing a minor calamity, after easily redressing that calamity, will come to the rescue of the vulnerable ruler or will launch an attack from the rear."

[9]When several rulers become vulnerable at the same time, should it be the one facing a serious calamity but behaving righteously, or the one facing a minor calamity but behaving unrighteously, or the one whose subjects are disaffected? It is the one whose subjects are disaffected against whom he should march into battle. [10]When attacked, subjects render assistance to a ruler facing a serious calamity but behaving righteously; they show indifference to a ruler facing a minor calamity but behaving unrighteously; when they are disaffected, they vanquish even a powerful ruler. [11]Therefore, it is against the one whose subjects are disaffected that he should march into battle.

[12]Should it be the ruler with destitute and greedy subjects or the ruler with rebellious subjects? "It is the one with destitute and greedy subjects against whom he should march into battle, for destitute and greedy subjects submit easily to instigation or harassment; not the rebellious, who can be subdued only by suppressing their leaders," say the teachers. [13]"No," says Kauṭilya; [14]"for destitute and greedy subjects, when they love their lord, are devoted to what is beneficial to their lord or frustrate any instigation—as it is said: 'In loyalty is every strategy.'* [15]Therefore, it is against the ruler with rebellious subjects that he should march into battle."

[16]Should it be the strong ruler behaving unrighteously, or the weak ruler behaving righteously? He should march into battle against the strong ruler behaving unrighteously. [17]When attacked, the subjects will not render assistance to a strong ruler behaving unrighteously; they will make him flee, or they will go over to his enemy. [18]On the other hand, when attacked, the subjects will embrace a weak ruler behaving righteously or follow him when he flees.

Topic 109: Causes of the Impoverishment, Greed, and Disaffection among the Subjects

> [19]For,* by casting away good people and embracing evil people, by initiating unprecedented and unrighteous acts of violence;
>
> [20]by discontinuing customary and righteous practices, by addiction to what is unrighteous, and by severing himself from what is righteous;
>
> [21]by doing what ought not be done, by scrapping what ought to be done, by not giving what ought to be given, and by securing what ought not to be given;
>
> [22]by not punishing those who ought to be punished, by punishing those who ought not to be punished, by apprehending those who ought not to be apprehended, and by not apprehending those who ought to be apprehended;
>
> [23]by doing what is unprofitable, by wrecking what is profitable, by not providing protection against robbers, and by himself engaging in thievery;
>
> [24]by denigrating courageous activities, by disparaging the quality of accomplishments, by harming leading men, and by dishonoring honorable men;
>
> [25]by contradicting elders, by favoritism and falsehood, by not rewarding what has been done, and by not carrying out what has been established;
>
> [26]through the negligence and laziness of the king or the destruction of enterprise and security, there arise the impoverishment, greed, and disloyalty of the subjects.
>
> [27]When impoverished, subjects become greedy; when they are greedy, they become disloyal; and when they are disloyal, they either go over to the enemy or kill their lord themselves.

[28]Therefore, he should not create the reasons for the impoverishment, greed, and disloyalty of his subjects; or, when they have been created, he should immediately redress them.*

[29]Is it the subjects who are impoverished, or who are greedy, or who are disaffected?* [30]The impoverished, because they fear being harassed or vanquished, prefer immediately a peace pact, war, or flight. [31]The greedy,

not satisfied because of greed, respond favorably to enemy instigations. [32]The disloyal start a revolt in response to an enemy attack.*

[33]Of these, impoverishment relating to money and grain destroys everything and is difficult to redress, while impoverishment relating to draught animals and men can be overcome with money and grain. [34]Greed, having a limited scope and restricted to the chiefs, can be redirected against properties of the enemy or can be removed. [35]Disloyalty can be overcome by suppressing the leaders; [36]for leaderless subjects are easily exploited and not receptive to instigations by others, but they are incapable of withstanding adversities. [37]When the subjects are divided into many groups through the favors granted to their leaders, they become protected and capable of withstanding adversities.

Topic 110: Discussion of Consociates

[38]Among the consociates also, after examining the reasons for a peace pact and for initiating hostilities and after forming a partnership with those who are strong and honest, he should march into battle. [39]For, one who is strong has the ability to attack from the rear and to render assistance in the military expedition, while one who is honest carries out the stipulations both in success and in failure.

[40]Among these, should one march into battle after forming a partnership with one ruler who is stronger or with two equals? It is better to do so with two equals; [41]for with a stronger ruler, he operates under his control, while when he is in partnership with two equals, he operates with plenty of opportunities to outwit them. [42]For it is easy to cause dissension between the two; and, if one becomes traitorous, for the two to restrain him; and to seize the one who is in the grip of dissension.

[43]With one who is equal or with two who are weaker? It is better to do so with two who are weaker; [44]for they accomplish two tasks and remain under his control.

[45]When the task has been accomplished, however,—

> he should go away secretly under some pretext from a stronger ruler who has accomplished his goal if he is dishonest; if he is of honest behavior, he should wait until he is dismissed.
>
> [46]Or, after moving away his family, he should make every effort to flee from a secure location (7.15.22 n.), for even an equal who

has achieved his goal poses a danger to someone who places his trust in him.

[47]Even an equal who has achieved his goal has a tendency to become stronger, and when he has become strengthened, he becomes untrustworthy; prosperity tends to alter the mind.

[48]Even if he receives a small share or no share at all from a distinguished ruler, he should leave with a happy face. Then, striking him when he is within reach, he should seize double the amount.

[49]When the leader himself has achieved his goal, however, he should dismiss the consociates. Even if he is shortchanged, he should not win it by force. Thus he will become well liked by the circle.

THAT CONCLUDES THE FIFTH CHAPTER: "REFLECTIONS ON ATTACKING A VULNERABLE RULER AND AN ENEMY," "CAUSES OF THE IMPOVERISHMENT, GREED, AND DISAFFECTION AMONG THE SUBJECTS," AND "DISCUSSION OF CONSOCIATES" OF THE SEVENTH BOOK: "ON THE SIXFOLD STRATEGY."

Chapter 6

Topic 111: Concerning the Marching into Battle after Concluding a Pact

[1]The seeker after conquest should outwit the second constituent* in the following manner. [2]He should urge a neighboring ruler* to march into battle after concluding a pact, saying, "You should march in this direction, and I will march in that direction. The spoils shall be equal." [3]If the spoils are equal, there shall be a peace pact; if they are unequal, an attack.*

Topic 112: Peace Pacts with and without Stipulations, and Those Made with Deserters

[4]A peace pact may be with stipulations and without stipulations.

PACTS WITH STIPULATIONS

[5]"You should march into that region, and I will march into this region"; this is one with a stipulation relating to region. [6]"You should conduct

operations for this length of time, and I will conduct operations for this length of time"; this is one with a stipulation relating to time. [7]"You should carry out this kind of task, and I will carry out this task"; this is one with a stipulation relating to objective.

[8]Alternatively, if he were to think, "My enemy will march into a region containing hill, forest, and river forts; separated by a forest; cut off from grains, men, supplies, and reinforcements; bereft of green fodder, firewood, and water; a region that is unfamiliar, distant, with a hostile population, or without land suitable for military operations. I will march into a region with the opposite characteristics"; in this sort of a situation, he should enter into a peace pact with a stipulation relating to region.

[9]Alternatively, if he were to think, "My enemy will operate during a time when there is excessive rain, heat, or cold; when diseases are prevalent; when food and amenities are scarce; when there are obstacles for military operations; a time that is too short or too long for accomplishing the task. I will operate during a time with the opposite characteristics"; in this sort of a situation, he should enter into a peace pact with a stipulation relating to time.

[10]Alternatively, if he were to think, "My enemy will carry out a task from which the opponent can recover;* or which makes the subjects revolt; takes a long time; entails enormous losses and expenses (7.2.2 n.); is trivial; entails persistent difficulties; or is unwholesome, unrighteous, opposed by the intermediate or neutral kings, or detrimental to the ally. I will carry out a task with the opposite characteristics"; in this sort of a situation, he should enter into a peace pact with a stipulation relating to the objective.

[11]Thus, by fixing the region and time, the time and objective, the region and objective, and the region, time, and objective, we get seven types* of peace pacts with stipulations.

[12]In the context of that kind of pact, having initiated and properly established his own activities beforehand, he should attack the activities of his enemy.

PACTS WITHOUT STIPULATIONS

[13]When he wishes to outwit a foe who is corrupt, hasty, disrespectful, and lazy or who is ignorant, he should tell him, "We have entered into a peace pact" without fixing the region, time, or task. After finding out his vulnerable points through the confidence generated by the peace pact, he should attack him—that is a peace pact without stipulations.

[14]On this, there is the following:

> [15]A wise man, after getting one neighbor to initiate hostilities against another neighbor, should then seize the land of another, cutting off the faction completely.*

[16]With regard to a peace pact, there are the desire to make one not yet made, adhering to one already made, violating one already made, and repairing one that is damaged. [17]With regard to warfare, there are open war, covert war, and silent war. [18]These are the kinds of peace pact and warfare.

[19]The desire to make a peace pact not yet made consists of (1) the pursuit of a completely new pact through strategies such as conciliation along with their consequences, and (2) locating the equal, weaker, and stronger rulers according to their strength. [20]Adhering to a peace pact already made consists of complying with a pact already made on the part of both parties by means of what is pleasing and beneficial, and of carrying out and safeguarding the contracts as agreed upon, thinking how he may not be divided from the other. [21]Violating a peace pact already made consists of transgressing it, after establishing that the enemy deserves to have a pact with him violated by outwitting him through traitorous persons.*

PACTS WITH DESERTERS

[22]Repairing a peace pact that is damaged consists of renewing the alliance with a vassal or an ally who had deserted due to some fault. [23]In this case, those who have left and returned are of four types: one who left and returned for a proper reason, and the opposite of this; one who left for a proper reason but returned without a proper reason, and the opposite of this.

[24]One who left due to a fault of his lord and returned due to his lord's virtue, or one who left due to the enemy's virtue and returned due to the enemy's fault, is a person who has left and returned for a proper reason; he is a fit person with whom to conclude a pact.

[25]One who left and returned due to his own fault overlooking the virtues of both* is a person who has left and returned without a proper reason; he has a fickle mind and is not a fit person with whom to conclude a pact.

[26]One who left due to a fault of his lord and returned from the enemy because of his own fault is a person who left for a proper reason but

returned without a proper reason. Regarding such a person, he should deliberate: "Does he intend to harm me either at the urging of my enemy or through his own fault? Has he returned because he fears retaliation, knowing that my enemy vanquishes his foe?* Or, has he returned out of compassion, after abandoning my enemy who intends to vanquish me?" [27]After he has found out, he should honor a man with noble intentions and make a man with contrary intentions live far away.

[28]One who left due to his own fault and returned because of the enemy's fault is a person who left without a proper reason and returned for a proper reason. Regarding such a person, he should deliberate: "Will he shore up my vulnerable points? Is he accustomed to living here? Do his people not like to live at the enemy's place? Has he made pacts with my allies? Has he initiated hostilities against my foes? Is he apprehensive of the greedy and cruel enemy, or of the enemy who has concluded a pact with his own foe?" [29]After he has found out, he should deal with him according to his intentions.

[30]"Wiping out what has been done, loss of power, commodifying learning,* dashed hopes, longing to visit countries, lack of trust, or conflict with a powerful person are the bases for abandoning someone," so say the teachers. [31]"Fear, lack of livelihood, and resentment," says Kauṭilya.

[32]One should abandon a man who has caused harm here* and enter into a peace pact with a man who has caused harm to the enemy; about a man who has caused harm to both, one should deliberate—the rest is the same as above (7.6.26, 28).

[33]If, however, it is necessary to make a pact with someone with whom one should not make a pact, then he should take countermeasures against his areas of might.

> [34]In arranging the repair of a pact already made, he should allocate a dwelling in a distant location to a person belonging to the enemy's faction who brings benefits, keeping him under guard until his death.
>
> [35]Either he should get him to attack his master or, if he is of proven loyalty, he should make him lead troops against enemies or forest tribes; or he should dispatch him to a corner of the frontier.
>
> [36]Or, if he is not of proven loyalty, he should turn him into a commodity, or even if he is a man of proven loyalty, covering him

with the former and censuring him for the crime of the former, for the sake of a pact that must be concluded with his enemy.*

[37]Or else, he should do away with him silently for the sake of the future; and seeing that someone who left and returned will seek to kill him in the future, he should slay him.

[38]Someone returning from an enemy has the drawback caused by his living with the foe; because it is similar to living with a snake, he suffers the drawback created by constant apprehension.

[39]He becomes a source of constant apprehension, posing a danger even afterwards, like a pigeon that has eaten a Plakṣa fruit to a Śālmali tree.*

[40–41]Attacking at an announced place and time is open war. Causing fright, surprise attack, striking during carelessness or calamity, and withdrawing and charging at the same place are the kinds of covert war. Employing secret measures (Book 5) and instigations through clandestine operatives are the marks of silent war.

THAT CONCLUDES THE SIXTH CHAPTER: "CONCERNING THE MARCHING INTO BATTLE AFTER CONCLUDING A PACT" AND "PEACE PACTS WITH AND WITHOUT STIPULATIONS, AND THOSE MADE WITH DESERTERS" OF THE SEVENTH BOOK: "ON THE SIXFOLD STRATEGY."

Chapter 7

Topic 113: Peace Pact and Attack Linked to Double Stratagem

[1]The seeker after conquest should bolster the second constituent (7.6.1 n.) in this manner. [2]He should march into battle against one neighbor after forming a partnership with another neighbor, if he were to think:

> He will not attack me from the rear.
> He will thwart my rear enemy.
> He will not go to the help of the vulnerable king.
> My troops will be doubled.
> He will enhance my supplies and reinforcements and thwart those of my enemy.

He will crush the thorns on my path strewn with numerous obstacles.

He will move with his army against the hideaways in forts and forests.

He will put the vulnerable king in a situation of unbearable jeopardy or force him to conclude a peace pact.

Or, receiving his share of the spoils, he will inspire confidence in my other enemies.

[3]Alternatively, resorting to the double stratagem, he should seek to obtain from one of the neighbors troops in return for treasure or treasure in return for troops. [4]Among these, when he obtains them from a stronger one for a larger share, from an equal for an equal share, or from a weaker one for a smaller share, it constitutes an equal peace pact. [5]In the opposite case, it is an unequal peace pact. [6]Among these two, gaining a special advantage results in an "outwitting" pact.*

[7]A weaker ruler may bargain with a stronger one with the offer of a gain equal to the troops provided when the latter is beset by a calamity, is addicted to harmful activities, or is facing dangers.* [8]The one with whom the bargain is made* should attack the other if he is able to harm him; otherwise, he should conclude a pact.

[9]Alternatively, a weaker ruler in the same situation* may bargain with a stronger one with the offer of a gain larger than an equal share in terms of the troops provided either to recoup his own dwindled strength and prowess or, if he is pursuing an achievable objective, to protect his home territory and his rear. [10]The one with whom the bargain is made should offer support if the other has noble intentions; otherwise, he should attack.

[11]A weaker ruler who is firmly ensconced in a fort or with an ally and who wishes to march across a short route against an enemy or to secure a gain that does not require combat or whose attainment is certain may bargain with a stronger one who is facing calamities, or has vulnerable points within his constituents, or who is facing dangers, with the offer of a gain smaller than an equal share in terms of the troops provided. [12]The one with whom the bargain is made should attack the other if he is able to harm him; otherwise, he should conclude a pact.

[13]Alternatively, a stronger ruler free from vulnerabilities or calamities may accept a smaller gain if he intends to burden a weaker king whose activities have taken off to a bad start with further losses and expenses (7.2.2 n.), or if he intends to get rid of his own traitorous troops, or if he

intends to win over the (other's) traitorous troops, or if he intends to use the weaker ruler to harass someone who ought to be oppressed or vanquished, or if he places great importance on peace pacts and has noble intentions. [14]Having formed a partnership with one possessing noble intentions, he should seek to achieve his object; otherwise, he should attack.

[15]In this way, an equal should outwit an equal or offer his support to him.

[16]An equal may bargain with the offer of a gain equal to the troops provided when those troops are a match against those of the enemy or of his allies or tribal chiefs, or when those troops are able to act as guides over terrain unsuitable to the enemy or to provide protection to his home territory or his rear. [17]The one with whom the bargain is made should offer support if the other has noble intentions; otherwise, he should attack.

[18]An equal may bargain with the offer of a gain smaller than an equal share in terms of the troops provided if the other is facing calamities, or has vulnerable points within his constituents, or is opposed by many, or if he himself is able to obtain troops from someone else. [19]The one with whom the bargain is made should attack the other if he is able to harm him; otherwise, he should conclude a peace pact.

[20]Alternatively, an equal in the same situation (7.7.9 n.) may bargain with the offer of a gain larger than an equal share in terms of the troops provided if his activities are dependent on the neighbor, or if his army needs to be built up. [21]The one with whom the bargain is made should offer support if the other has noble intentions; otherwise, he should attack.

[22]Someone may demand more from a stronger, weaker, or equal ruler if he intends to attack the latter while he is facing calamities or has vulnerable points within his constituents, or if he intends to hurt his undertakings that have taken off to a fine start and are assured of success, or if he intends to launch an assault on his home territory or military expedition, or if he is going to receive more from the vulnerable ruler.* [23]The one from whom more is demanded should give more in order to protect his own army when he intends, by using the enemy's troops, to crush another's unassailable fort or the rear enemy's backer or the tribal troops; when he intends to burden the enemy troops with losses and expenses (7.2.2 n.) on a distant or prolonged expedition; when he intends to vanquish the enemy himself after he has become strong by means of the enemy troops; or when he intends to appropriate the enemy troops for himself.

[24]Alternatively, a stronger ruler may bargain with a weaker one with the offer of a gain larger than an equal share in terms of the troops provided

when he intends to bring the latter into his grip under the pretext of attacking a vulnerable king; when he intends to vanquish that very ruler after he has vanquished his enemy; or when, after making a gift,* he intends to recover it. [25]The one with whom the bargain is made should attack the other if he is able to harm him; otherwise, he should conclude a peace pact. [26]Or, he should remain after entering into a pact with the vulnerable king, or hand over to him traitorous troops, troops of the enemy, or troops of tribal chiefs.*

[27]Alternatively, a stronger ruler who is facing calamities and has vulnerable points within his constituents may bargain with a weaker one with the offer of a gain equal to the troops provided. [28]The one with whom the bargain is made should attack the other if he is able to harm him; otherwise, he should conclude a peace pact.

[29]A stronger ruler may bargain with a weaker king in the same situation (7.7.9 n.) with the offer of a gain smaller than an equal share in terms of the troops provided. [30]The one with whom the bargain is made should attack the other if he is able to harm him; otherwise, he should conclude a peace pact.

> [31]At the outset, both the one with whom the bargain is made and the one who is proposing the bargain should ascertain the reason. Then, after pondering it from both sides, one should adopt the course that provides prosperity.

THAT CONCLUDES THE SEVENTH CHAPTER: "PEACE PACT AND ATTACK LINKED TO DOUBLE STRATAGEM" OF THE SEVENTH BOOK: "ON THE SIXFOLD STRATEGY."

Chapter 8

Topic 114: Proper Behavior on the Part of a Vulnerable Ruler

[1]A vulnerable ruler who is about to be attacked, if he wants to remove or to thwart the reason for the pact,* should bargain with any one of the consociates by offering double the gain. [2]Proposing the bargain, he should describe to the other the losses, expenses (7.2.2 n.), absence from home, setbacks, benefits to the enemy, and dangers to his own person (7.2.2). [3]When he agrees, he should urge him on with money. [4]Or he should provoke in him animosity toward the others and alienate him from them.*

EXCURSUS

[5]When one intends to burden someone whose activities have taken off to a bad start with further losses and expenses, or to obstruct the success of an expedition that has taken off to a fine start, or to launch an assault on the home territory or military expedition, or, having made a pact with the vulnerable ruler, to make further demands, or when things are going badly for himself (1.15.35 n.), or when he has lost his confidence in the other, he should accept a small gain in the present and a greater gain in the future.

[6]When he foresees a benefit to the ally and a harm to the enemy that redound to his own advantage, or when he wants to get someone who has helped him before to carry on doing so, he may forgo a large gain in the present and seek a small gain in the future.

[7]When he wants to rescue someone who is threatened by a traitor or an enemy or by a stronger ruler seeking to seize his home territory, or to get the other to provide him the same kind of assistance, or when he takes relationships into consideration, he may not accept a gain either in the present or in the future.

[8]When he wants to violate a peace pact he has entered into, or to weaken the enemy's subjects, or to break up his pacts with an ally or enemy, or when he is worried about an attack from the enemy, he should demand a gain that is not yet realized or that is more than what is realized. [9]With regard to him, the other should reflect on the sequence* both in the present and in the future. [10]This also explains the earlier cases.*

Topic 115: The Kinds of Allies Deserving Assistance

[11]When, however, the enemy and the seeker after conquest are providing assistance each to his own ally, there is a distinction: one whose undertakings are feasible, one whose undertakings are sound, one whose undertakings are promising, one who is resolute in his activities, and one who has loyal subjects. [12]One whose undertakings are feasible takes up activities that can be accomplished; one whose undertakings are sound, activities that are faultless; and one whose undertakings are promising, activities that lead to a happy outcome. [13]One who is resolute in his activities never rests before he has completed his activity. [14]One whose subjects are loyal, because he has good companions, accomplishes his goal with even a little help. [15]These kinds of people, once they have attained their goals, provide assistance easily and in abundance. [16]Those who have characteristics opposite of these do not deserve to be assisted.

[17]In the event both give assistance to the same individual, the one who gives assistance to the individual who is an ally or a stronger ally* outwits the other; [18]for through the ally he attains his own prosperity, while the other is left with losses, expenses, absence from home, and providing benefits to the enemy. [19]The foe,* moreover, once he has attained his goal, becomes antagonistic.

[20]In the event both give assistance to the intermediate ruler, however, the one who gives assistance to the intermediate who is an ally or a stronger ally (7.8.17 n.) outwits the other; [21]for through the ally he attains his own prosperity, while the other is left with losses, expenses, absence from home, and providing benefits to the enemy. [22]If the intermediate ruler, after he has received assistance, becomes antagonistic to him, the enemy outwits him; [23]for he secures the intermediate's enemy,* who has expended effort but deserted the intermediate, and who has now made common cause with him.

[24]This also explains the rendering of assistance to the neutral ruler.

[25]When a part of someone's army is given to the intermediate or the neutral ruler, the one who gives troops who are brave, skilled in weapons, able to endure distress, and loyal, becomes outwitted by the other; [26]while the one who acts in the opposite manner outwits the other.

[27]Where the troops, when deployed,* will accomplish that goal, as well as others, however, he should give* any one of these kinds of troops—hereditary, hired, corporate, ally's, and tribal chief's—when the place and duration are known, or troops of the enemy or tribal chief, when the place is far away and the duration is long.

[28]He should not give him assistance under the pretext that the troops are occupied elsewhere, however, if he thinks:

> Once his goal is achieved, he will seize my troops.
>
> Or, he will make them encamp with the troops of the enemy or the tribal chief, in unsuitable terrain, or during an improper season.
>
> Or, he will make them ineffective.

[29]If it is necessary to provide assistance in this manner, however, he should give him troops able to endure for just that duration. [30]Until completion, moreover, he should encamp them, make them fight, and guard them against calamities that may strike an army. [31]Further, once that person's goal has been attained, he should take them away from him under some pretext. [32]Alternatively, he should give him troops that are traitorous

or belonging to the enemy or tribal chief; [33]or he should outwit him by concluding a pact with the vulnerable ruler.

> [34]For, when the gain is equal, one should conclude a peace pact; when the gain is unequal, an attack is recommended for the equal, weaker, and stronger ruler. Thus are described the peace pacts and attacks.

THAT CONCLUDES THE EIGHTH CHAPTER: "PROPER BEHAVIOR ON THE PART OF A VULNERABLE RULER" AND "THE KINDS OF ALLIES DESERVING ASSISTANCE" OF THE SEVENTH BOOK: "ON THE SIXFOLD STRATEGY."

Chapter 9

Topic 116: Peace Pacts for Allies, Money, Land, and Projects

[1]Among the gain of an ally, money, and land, the gain of each subsequent one is better than each preceding when undertaking a military expedition after making a pact; [2]for an ally and money result from gaining land, and an ally from gaining money—[3]or else, that gain which, when secured, secures one of the remaining two.*

Topic 116a: Peace Pacts for Allies and Money

[4]"Let both you and I each acquire an ally"; a pact such as this is an equal pact. [5]"You acquire an ally"*; a pact such as this is an unequal pact. [6]Between these two, gaining a special advantage results in an "outwitting" pact (7.7.6 n.).

[7]In an equal pact, however, the man who acquires an ally possessing the exemplary qualities (6.1.12) or an ally during a time of hardship for that ally is the one who outwits; [8]for adversity causes the strengthening of friendship.

[9]Even during a time of hardship for the ally, is it the ally who is consistent although non-submissive, or the ally who is submissive although inconsistent (7.5.29 n.)? "The one who is consistent although non-submissive is better, for, although he may not provide assistance, yet he does no harm," say the teachers. [10]"No," says Kauṭilya. [11]"The one who is submissive although inconsistent is better. [12]Someone is an ally only to the extent that he provides assistance, given that providing assistance is the defining characteristic of an ally."

[13]Of two who are submissive also, is it the one who is of great benefit but is inconsistent, or the one who is of small benefit but is consistent? "The one who is of great benefit but inconsistent is better. Someone who is of great benefit but inconsistent helps defray large areas of expenditure by providing great assistance in a short period of time," so state the teachers. [14]"No," says Kauṭilya. [15]"The one who is of little benefit but consistent is better. [16]One who is of great benefit but inconsistent will run away because he fears having to provide assistance, or, after providing assistance, he will try to recover it. [17]One who is of little benefit but consistent, by providing small assistance constantly, will over a long period of time provide great assistance."

[18]Is it a great ally who is slow to mobilize, or a small ally who is quick to mobilize? "A great ally who is slow to mobilize provides prowess, and, when he does mobilize, he accomplishes his task," say the teachers. [19]"No," says Kauṭilya. [20]"A small ally who is quick to mobilize is better. [21]A small ally who is quick to mobilize does not let the time for the task pass by and, because of his weakness, can be made use of at will; but not the other, who controls a vast territory."

[22]Is it one whose troops are dispersed, or one whose troops are non-submissive?* "Dispersed troops can be mustered because they are submissive," say the teachers. [23]"No," says Kauṭilya. [24]"One with non-submissive troops is better; [25]for the non-submissive troops can be brought under control through means such as conciliation, but the other, being engaged in diverse tasks,* cannot be mustered."

[26]Is it an ally helpful with men, or an ally helpful with money? "An ally helpful with men is better. An ally helpful with men provides prowess and, when mobilized, he accomplishes his goal," say the teachers. [27]"No," says Kauṭilya. [28] "An ally helpful with money is better, [29]for money is used continuously, while troops are used occasionally. [30]With money, moreover, one obtains troops, as well as other things one desires."

[31]Is it an ally helpful with money, or an ally helpful with land? "An ally helpful with money, because of its portable nature, will assist in defraying all expenses," say the teachers. [32]"No," says Kauṭilya; [33]"for it has already been stated (7.9.2) that an ally and money result from gaining land. [34]Therefore, an ally helpful with land is better."

[35]When they are equal in being helpful with men, then the special advantage consists of bravery, ability to withstand distress, loyalty, or gaining all the troops from the ally's household. [36]When they are equal in being helpful with money, then the special advantage consists of obtaining

what is requested, copiousness, the need for minimal effort, and being uninterrupted.

[37]On this, there is the following (7.6.14–15 n.):

> [38]He who—being consistent, submissive, able to mobilize quickly, bequeathed by the father and grandfather, mighty, and not prone to duplicity—possesses the exemplary qualities, is said to be an ally possessing the six qualities:*
>
> [39]He who protects and is protected out of love and without regard to money, and the connection to whom has grown from ancient times, is said to be a consistent ally.
>
> [40]A submissive ally is said to be threefold: one of total utility, one of diverse utility, and one of great utility. Being useful on one side, on both sides, and on all sides is another threefold division (7.16.10–15).
>
> [41]He who, whether receiving or giving assistance, lives by inflicting injury on enemies, is a consistent but non-submissive ally; as also he who has a hideaway in a fort or forest.
>
> [42]He who, when another has initiated hostilities against him or when facing a slight calamity, enters into a pact to obtain assistance is a submissive but fickle ally.
>
> [43]He who is connected by common advantages and disadvantages,* provides assistance, and does not change is an ally possessing the disposition of an ally and not prone to duplicity in times of adversity.
>
> [44]An ally is constant when he has the disposition of an ally; he is fickle when he is equally partial to the foe; he is neutral when he is not partial to either; and he has the disposition of both when he is partial to the two.*
>
> [45]He who, being an enemy of the seeker after conquest, has become an interposed king,* or who is either not obliged (7.18.37) or unable to provide assistance, is an ally offering no assistance.
>
> [46]He who, while he is dear to, protected and honored by, or simply related to the enemy, provides assistance is an ally equally partial to the foe.

[47]He who controls a vast territory and is content, strong, and lazy is a neutral ally; as also one who is held in disregard because of a calamity.

[48]He who, because of his weakness, is dependent on the prosperity of the enemy and the leader (6.2.39 n.), and who is not hated by either, should be known as having the disposition of both (7.9.44 n.).

[49]When a man overlooks an ally who abandons him with or without a reason and returns with or without a reason, he embraces death.

[50]Is it a quick but small gain, or a large but slow gain? "The quick but small gain that corresponds to the task, place, and time is better," say the teachers. [51]"No," says Kauṭilya. [52]"A large but slow gain is better when it is not evanescent and has a seminal nature; in the opposite case, the former is better."

[53]Having seen in this manner the blossoming of strategy* with regard to a gain or a portion of a gain that is enduring and intent on attaining his own goal, he should march into battle after entering into a pact with consociates.

THAT CONCLUDES THE NINTH CHAPTER: "PEACE PACTS FOR ALLIES AND MONEY" WITHIN THE "PEACE PACTS FOR ALLIES, MONEY, LAND, AND PROJECTS" OF THE SEVENTH BOOK: "ON THE SIXFOLD STRATEGY."

Chapter 10

Topic 116b: Peace Pacts for Land

[1]"Let both you and I each acquire land"; this is a pact for land.

[2]Of these two, the man who obtains quality land* when the need for it has arisen is the one who outwits.

[3]When the acquisition of quality land is equal, then the man who obtains the land by attacking a powerful ruler is the one who outwits; [4]for he achieves the gain of land, the weakening of the enemy, and prowess. [5]True, the gaining land from a weak ruler is easy; [6]yet gaining of land is itself quite weak, while the neighboring king, who was an ally, turns into an enemy.*

[7]When their strength is equal, the man who obtains the land by overthrowing an entrenched enemy* is the one who outwits; [8]for the acquisition of a fort protects his own territory and repels enemies and tribal chiefs.

[9]When land is gained from a mobile enemy,* the special advantage comes from having a pliant neighbor; [10]for enterprise and security (6.2.1 n.) are quickly augmented when a land has a weak neighbor. [11]A land with a strong neighbor is the opposite of this and becomes detrimental to the treasury and the army.

[12]Is it a quality land with permanent enemies or a land of lesser quality with impermanent enemies (7.5.29 n.)? "A quality land with permanent enemies is better, for a quality land makes the treasury and army prosper, and these two repulse the enemy," say the teachers. [13]"No," says Kauṭilya. [14]"In gaining land with permanent enemies, the gain of foes becomes larger. [15]A permanent foe, furthermore, remains a foe whether one assists him or harms him, whereas an impermanent foe is pacified by assisting him or by not harming him."

[16]A land whose frontiers have many forts* and are never devoid of bandit gangs or barbarians and forest tribes* is one with permanent enemies; in the opposite case, however, it is one with impermanent enemies.

[17]Is it a nearby land that is small or a distant land that is large? The nearby land that is small is better, [18]for it is easy to obtain, to govern, and to rescue. [19]A distant land has the opposite characteristics.

[20]Between two distant lands also, is it the land that is controlled by the army or by itself? The land controlled by itself is better; [21]for it is controlled by the treasury and army generated by itself. [22]The land controlled by the army has the opposite characteristics, being the place where the army is stationed.

[23]Is it the gain of land from a foolish ruler or from an intelligent one? Gaining land from a foolish ruler is better; [24]for it is easy to acquire and to govern, and it cannot be taken back. [25]Land gained from an intelligent ruler has the opposite characteristics, the people there being loyal to him.

[26]Between an "oppressable" and a "vanquishable" (6.2.16 n.), gaining land from a "vanquishable" is better; [27]for the "vanquishable" has no support or has weak support, and, seeking, when attacked, to flee taking with him the treasury and the army, he is abandoned by the subjects. Not so the "oppressable," firmly entrenched in a fort or with an ally.

[28]Between two entrenched in forts also, one in a land fort and one in a river fort (2.3.1–2), gaining land from one in a land fort is better; [29]for a

land fort is easy to besiege, easy to storm, and easy to launch a surprise attack against, and the foe cannot sneak out of it. [30]A river fort, on the contrary, demands twice as much strain, and the water provides drink and livelihood to the enemy.

[31]Between one in a river fort and one in a hill fort, gaining land from one in a river fort is better; [32]for a river fort can be captured by means of elephants, bridges of tree trunks, dikes, and boats (10.2.14); its depth is not constant; and its water can be drained (13.4.9). [33]A hill fort, on the contrary, is easy to defend, difficult to besiege, and hard to scale; even if one part is breached, it is not entirely destroyed; and rocks and trees can be thrown on those perpetrating great damage.

[34]Between those who fight in water and those who fight on land, gaining land from those who fight in water is better; [35]for those who fight in water are limited as to place and time, whereas those who fight on land can fight in any place and at any time.

[36]Between those who fight in trenches and those who fight out in the open, gaining land from trench fighters is better; [37]for those who fight in trenches fight employing both trenches and weapons, whereas those who fight out in the open employ only weapons.

> [38]Gaining land from these kinds of rulers, one who knows the Treatise on Success (*arthaśāstra*) wins a special advantage over both confederates and enemies.

That concludes the Tenth Chapter: "Peace Pacts for Land" within the "Peace Pacts for Allies, Money, Land, and Projects" of the Seventh Book: "On the Sixfold Strategy."

Chapter 11

Topic 116c: Peace Pacts for Unsettled Land

[1]"Let us both you and I settle vacant land"; that is a pact for unoccupied land (2.24.17 n.).

[2]Between these two, the man who settles a land possessing the recommended qualities when the need for it has arisen is the one who outwits.

[3]Even in that case, is it un-irrigated or irrigated land (7.5.29 n.)? A small tract of irrigated land is better than a large tract of un-irrigated land, because its crops are constant and fixed.

[4]Between two un-irrigated tracts also, the one that yields earlier and later crops in abundance, whose crops ripen with little rain, and that permits unobstructed operation is better.

[5]Between two irrigated tracts also, the one in which grain can be sowed is better than the one in which grain cannot be sowed. [6]Between two such tracts where the one is large and the other is small, a large tract not favorable to grain crops is better than a small tract favorable to grain crops; [7]for in a large area, there are wetland and dry-land plants. [8]Further, there is a lot of scope for carrying out projects such as building forts, [9]for the qualities of land are produced by human activity.

[10]Between the benefits from pit mines and those from grain, the benefits from pit mines enhance the treasury, while the benefits from grain enhance the treasury and the storehouse (2.5; 2.15); [11]for initiating activities such as the building of forts depends on grain. [12]Alternatively, the benefits from pit mines are better, given the large scope for their sale.

[13]"Between the benefits from a produce forest and from an elephant forest, the benefits from a produce forest are the basis for all activities and are able to create an extensive store; the benefits from an elephant forest have the opposite characteristics," so state the teachers. [14]"No," says Kauṭilya. [15]"It is possible to plant any number of produce forests in any number of tracts, not so an elephant forest; [16]for the extermination of an enemy's army depends principally on elephants."

[17]Between the benefits from a water route and a land route, the benefits from a water route are not constant, while the benefits from a land route are constant.

[18]Is it a land containing a divided population or a land containing a population organized into bands? The land containing a divided population is better. [19]A land containing a divided population is easy to exploit and not receptive to instigations by others, but it is unable to bear adversity. [20]A land containing a population organized into bands has the opposite characteristics and is extremely dangerous during a revolt.

[21]With regard to settling people of the four social classes in that land, one containing predominantly people from the lower social classes is better, because such a land is able to yield all kinds of benefits. One with agriculturists is better, because agriculture is profuse and constant. One with cowherds is better, because they promote both agriculture and other kinds of activities. One with rich traders is better, because of the assistance provided by stores of merchandise and loans.

[22]Among the qualities of land, providing a haven is the best.

[23]Is it the land providing a haven in the form of a fort, or the land providing a haven in the form of men? The one providing a haven in the form of men is better, [24]for a kingdom consists of men. [25]Like a barren cow, what would a land bereft of men yield?

[26]When, however, someone seeks to acquire a land that entails enormous losses and expenses to settle,* he should first bargain with a purchaser who is weak, or without a royal pedigree, or without drive, or without a following, or given to improper behavior, or given to vice, or trusting in fate, or doing whatever he pleases.

[27]For when a weak person of royal pedigree settles in a land entailing enormous losses and expenses to settle, he, along with his constituents with close family ties* to him, perish on account of those losses and expenses. [28]A strong person without royal pedigree is forsaken by his constituents without close family ties to him, being afraid of losses and expenses. [29]A person without drive, however, not deploying the army even though he possesses an army, is crushed along with his army on account of losses and expenses. [30]Even though he possesses a treasury, a person without a following does not get anything out of it because he is deprived of the benefits from the losses and expenses.* [31]A person given to improper behavior will drive people out from even a settled land. [32]How can such a man settle an unsettle land? [33]This also explains a person who is given to vice. [34]A person trusting in fate and devoid of human effort perishes, as he does not undertake tasks, or the tasks he undertakes flounder. [35]A person who does whatever he pleases never realizes anything, [36]and he is the worst among these. [37]"For as he undertakes whatever he pleases, he may sometimes realize a vulnerable point of the seeker after conquest," say the teachers. [38] "Just as he realizes a vulnerable point, so he may realize also his destruction," says Kauṭilya.

[39]When these are not available, he should deal with the land according to what we will say in the context of securing the rear enemy (7.16.16).

[40]That is a solicited pact.*

[41]When a strong person requests to buy an excellent tract of land or one that can be recovered, he should give it to him after concluding a pact. [42]That is a non-secretive pact.

[43]Or, when an equal requests, he should give it to him after examining the reason: "I can recover the land or it will be under my control. The enemy, when he is bound to it, will come under my control. Or, by selling the land I will gain allies and money that will strengthen my undertakings." [44]This also explains the weaker purchaser.

[45]Gaining in this manner an ally, money, and land with and without people, one who knows the treatise* outwits the consociates.

THAT CONCLUDES THE ELEVENTH CHAPTER: "PEACE PACTS FOR UNSETTLED LAND" WITHIN THE "PEACE PACTS FOR ALLIES, MONEY, LAND, AND PROJECTS" OF THE SEVENTH BOOK: "ON THE SIXFOLD STRATEGY."

Chapter 12

Topic 116d: Peace Pacts for Projects

[1]"Let us both you and I get a fort built"; that is a pact for projects.

[2]Between these two, the man who gets a fort built that is naturally formed, unassailable, and constructed at a small expense is the one who outwits. [3]Even in that case, among a land fort, a river fort, and a hill fort (2.3.1–2), the ones listed later are better than the ones listed earlier.

[4]Between two reservoirs (2.1.20 n.) also, a naturally watered reservoir is better than a reservoir with water channeled from elsewhere. [5]Even between two naturally watered reservoirs, one with a large area for sowing is better.

[6]Between two produce forests also, the man who harvests a produce forest that is large, with forest land containing valuable products, located at the frontier of the territory, and watered by a river is the one who outwits; [7]for one watered by a river provides an easy living and becomes a haven during a time of adversity.

[8]Between two elephant forests also, the man who establishes an elephant forest that has many brave animals and a weak neighbor, causes distress to the adjoining enemy,* and is located at the frontier of the territory is the one who outwits. [9]Even in that case, "Between one with many sluggish elephants and one with a few brave elephants, the one with a few brave elephants is better; for a battle depends on brave ones. A few brave ones will rout many timid ones. When they are routed, they turn into slayers of their own troops," so say the teachers. [10]"No," says Kauṭilya. [11]"Many sluggish elephants are better. Because of their employment in the army, they perform numerous tasks and during battle they become a haven for their own troops and unconquerable and dreadful for the enemy troops. [12]For, through training, it is possible to instill bravery into many dull elephants, whereas it is not possible to turn a few brave elephants into many."

[13]Between two pit mines also, the man who has a pit mine dug yielding a lot of valuable materials, with accessible roads, and needing little expenditure to operate is the one who outwits. [14]Even in that case, is it a pit mine (1.10.15 n.) yielding a small quantity of very valuable material, or a mine yielding a large quantity of less valuable material (7.5.29 n.)? "A mine yielding a small quantity of very valuable material is better, for diamonds, gems, pearls, corals (1.10.15 n.), and gold and silver ores eclipse by reason of their extremely high price a mine yielding a large quantity of less valuable material," say the teachers. [15]"No," says Kauṭilya. [16]"A buyer for items of great value is found rarely and infrequently, while there are numerous buyers found all the time for items of small value."

[17]This also explains the trade route. [18]Even in that case, "Between a water route and a land route, a water route is better; it requires little expenditure and effort, and it yields plenty of merchandise," say the teachers. [19]"No," says Kauṭilya. [20]"A water route has restricted movement, does not operate at all times, contains great dangers, and is not open to remedial measures. A land route has the opposite characteristics."

[21]In the case of a water route, however, between a route along the shore and a route in the open sea, a route along the shore is better, because there are many ports; or a river route is better, because it operates at all times and because its hazards can be overcome.

[22]In the case of a land route also, "Better than the southern route is the Himalayan route, with merchandise of greater value consisting of elephants, horses, perfumes, ivory, antelope skins, silver, and gold," say the teachers. [23]"No," says Kauṭilya. [24]"The same merchandise, with the exception of blankets, antelope skin, and horses, and also merchandise consisting of conch shells, diamonds, gems, pearls, and gold is more abundant in the southern route."

[25]Even in the southern route, a trade route containing many pit mines, merchandise of high value, and well-established passages, and demanding little expenditure and effort is better; or, one with merchandise of low value but with an extensive scope for their sale.*

[26]This also explains the eastern and western trade routes.

[27]Even in that case, between a route for wheeled carts and a route for travel by foot, a route for wheeled carts is better because it permits large-scale undertakings; or, as befitting the place and time, a route for travel by donkeys and camels. [28]These two also explain a route for men carrying goods on their shoulders.

[29]The flourishing of the enemy's projects results in the decline of the leader's projects; in the opposite case, his projects prosper. When the course of their projects is the same, the seeker after conquest should realize that it is his stable condition (7.1.20–38).

[30]Decline consists of a small income and a large expenditure; the opposite constitutes prosperity. When income and expenditure are equal, he should know it as the stable condition of his projects.

[31]Therefore, when from among a fort and the like, he undertakes a project that requires little expenditure and yields large profits, he gains a special advantage. Thus have been described the pacts for projects.

THAT CONCLUDES THE TWELFTH CHAPTER: "PEACE PACTS FOR PROJECTS" WITHIN THE "PEACE PACTS FOR ALLIES, MONEY, LAND, AND PROJECTS" OF THE SEVENTH BOOK: "ON THE SIXFOLD STRATEGY."

Chapter 13

Topic 117: Reflections on the Attacker from the Rear

[1]When the enemy and the seeker after conquest band together and attack from the rear two enemies engaged in battle with their opponents, the one who attacks the rear of the powerful man is the one who outwits; [2]for a powerful man, after vanquishing his enemy, might vanquish the attacker from the rear; not so a powerless man who has not secured any gain.

[3]In case they are of equal power, the one who attacks the rear of the man with vast operations is the one who outwits; [4]for a man with vast operations, after vanquishing his enemy, might vanquish the attacker from the rear; not so a man with few operations, with his army stranded.

[5]In case their operations are equal, the one who attacks the rear of the man who has marched into battle gathering together his entire army is the one who outwits; [6]for, with his home territory empty,* it is easy for him to overpower the man; not so a man who has marched into battle with only a portion of his army and has made provisions for guarding his rear.

[7]In case they deploy troops equally, the one who attacks the rear of the man who has marched into battle against a mobile enemy (7.10.9 n.) is the one who outwits; [8]for a man who has marched into battle against a mobile

enemy, after easily attaining success, will vanquish the attacker from the rear; not so a man who marches into battle against an entrenched enemy (7.10.7 n.). [9]For the latter, repulsed by the fort and turning against the attacker from the rear, is thwarted by the entrenched enemy.

[10]This also explains those who were mentioned earlier.*

[11]In case the foes are equal, the one who attacks the rear of the man who is attacking a righteous ruler is the one who outwits; [12]for a man who attacks a righteous ruler becomes the object of hatred to his own people and to his enemies; a man who attacks an unrighteous ruler is much loved.

[13]This also explains the attack in the rear of those who attack a squanderer of his patrimony, a spendthrift, and a miser (2.9.20–23).

[14]These are the very reasons for attacking in the rear two individuals who are attacking their allies.

[15]When between two, the one attacks his ally and the other his enemy, the one who attacks in the rear the man who is attacking his ally is the one who outwits; [16]for the man who is attacking his ally, after easily attaining success, might vanquish the one attacking from the rear. [17]For it is easy to make a pact with an ally, not so with an enemy.

[18]When between two, the one exterminates his ally and the other his enemy, the one who attacks in the rear the man who exterminates his enemy is the one who outwits; [19]for the king who exterminates his enemy, with a strengthened ally, might vanquish the one attacking from the rear, not the other who destroys his own faction.

[20]In case the two go away without obtaining any gain, the attacker from the rear whose enemy is deprived of a large gain or incurs heavy losses and expenses is the one who outwits. [21]In case they go away after obtaining a gain, the attacker from the rear whose enemy is worsted in terms of gain or strength is the one who outwits, or the one whose enemy is attacking someone who is able to harm him during hostilities.*

[22]Between two attackers from the rear also, the one who raises a larger number of troops for a feasible operation, whose foe is entrenched (7.10.7 n.), or who is located on the flank is the one who outwits; [23]for someone located on the flank can run to the rescue of someone under attack and poses a danger to the home territory, whereas one located in the rear only poses a danger to the home territory.

> [24]Attackers from the rear who thwart the activities of an enemy,
> one should recognize, are of three kinds: the group of neighbors
> in the rear and the two neighbors located on the two flanks.

> [25]A weak king located in the middle of the enemy and the leader (7.9.48 n.) is called "interposed." When he has a haven in a fort or a forest, he is a deterrent to a stronger king.

[26]The enemy and the seeker after conquest, however, while attempting to overpower the intermediate ruler, attack the intermediate ruler from the rear. Of these two, in the event the intermediate ruler returns after securing his gain, the one who alienates him from his ally and obtains him, who was his enemy, as his ally is the one who outwits.* [27]Now it is proper to conclude a pact with a foe who renders assistance, but not with an ally who has cast aside the disposition of an ally.

[28]This also explains the attempt to overpower the neutral ruler.

[29]"In the event of an attack in the rear and frontal march into battle, however, prosperity comes from the battle of wits (12.2.1–7); [30]for in a battle involving military operations, prosperity is denied to both because of losses and expenses. [31]For even if one is victorious, he stands in fact defeated with the depletion of his army and treasury," so state the teachers. [32]"No," says Kauṭilya. [33]"Even by incurring very great losses and expenses, he must bring about the defeat of his foe."

[34]In case the losses and expenses are equal, the one who gets his traitorous troops killed by deploying them in the front and, with his thorns eliminated, fights at the rear with his submissive troops is the one who outwits. [35]Even between two who get their traitorous troops killed by deploying them in the front, the one who secures the killing of a larger number of them, of the more powerful of them, and of the most traitorous of them is the one who outwits.

[36]This also explains the killing of enemy and tribal troops.

> [37]When the seeker after conquest finds himself in the role of an attacker from the rear, an attacker from the front, or one being attacked, he should then observe the following course of action for a leader.
>
> [38]The leader becomes an attacker from the rear to a foe who is attacking his own ally from the front. He should do so after he has first got the rescuer of the rear attacker to engage in battle the enemy's ally in the rear.*
>
> [39]While he attacks in the front, he should thwart his rear enemy using his rescuer at the rear, and likewise thwart the ally of his rear enemy using the ally of his rescuer at the rear.

[40]He should get his ally in the front, moreover, to engage in battle the ally of his enemy, and get his own ally's ally to thwart the ally of his enemy's ally.

[41]When he is attacked from the front, he should get his ally to attack the rear of the one attacking from the front, and get the ally of his own ally to keep away the rescuer at the rear from the rear enemy.

[42]In this way, the seeker after conquest should set up in the front and the rear a circle with the exemplary qualities of the ally constituent (6.1.1) so as to promote his own interests.

[43]He should, moreover, always station envoys and clandestine operatives throughout the entire circle, becoming an ally of his rivals and operating secretly as he kills over and over again.

[44]The operations of someone who is not secretive, even if they produce spectacular results, will inevitably flounder, like a damaged boat in the ocean.

That concludes the Thirteenth Chapter: "Reflections on the Attacker from the Rear" of the Seventh Book: "On the Sixfold Strategy."

Chapter 14

Topic 118: Augmenting Weakened Power

[1]The seeker after conquest, when he is attacked in this manner* by consociates, should tell the one who is their chief: "I want to make a peace pact with you. Here is the money, and I will be your ally. Your prosperity will double. It does not befit you to promote the prosperity of your enemies pretending to be allies by suffering losses yourself; for once they become prosperous, they will subjugate you yourself."

[2]Alternatively, he should foment disunity: "Just as they have joined together and attacked me, although I have done no wrong to them, so when they are doing well or facing a calamity, they will combine their strengths and attack you also; for strength transforms the mind. Destroy that strength of theirs."

[3]When they have become disunited, he should provide support to the chief and get him to attack the weaker ones; or get support provided to the

weaker ones and get them to attack the chief; or proceed in a manner that he would consider more advantageous. [4]Alternatively, provoking in one of them animosity toward the others, he should alienate him from them.

[5]Alternatively, secretly promising the chief a larger profit, he should get him to negotiate a peace pact. [6]Then, double agents, disclosing his larger profit, should subvert the minds of the consociates by saying, "You have been outwitted!" [7]When their minds have been subverted, he should subvert the pact. [8]Then, double agents should again create disunity among them, saying, "This is exactly what we told you!" [9]When they are disunited, he should proceed by providing support to one of them.

[10]If there is no chief, he should secure from among the consociates one of the following: One who galvanizes them, one who perseveres in his undertakings, one with loyal subjects, one who joined the confederation out of greed or fear, one who is afraid of the seeker after conquest, one who is anchored to his kingdom, an ally, or a mobile enemy (7.10.9 n.)—selecting those listed earlier in the absence of those listed later—the one who galvanized them by offering himself, the one who perseveres in his undertakings with conciliatory prostrations, the one with loyal subjects by giving and receiving girls in marriage, the greedy one by offering a double share, the one afraid of them by providing support with treasure and troops, the one naturally afraid by building up his confidence and giving a surety, the one anchored to his kingdom by entering into close coalition with him, the ally by doing things cherished by and beneficial to both or by handing over benefits he has received, and the mobile enemy who is confined by halting injurious actions and offering assistance. [11]Alternatively, he should secure any one of them using any means by which he may become disunited, or through conciliation, gifts, dissension, and military force as we will explain in the section on dangers (9.5–7).

[12]Alternatively, when he is buffeted by calamities and is thus in a hurry, he should enter into a peace pact confined with respect to place, time, and task by offering treasure and troops. [13]Once he has concluded the pact, he should redress his own weakness.

[14]When he finds himself weak with respect to his following, he should create a following consisting of kinsmen and allies, or build an unassailable fort; [15]for when he finds support in a fort or with allies, he becomes worthy of honor by his own people and by enemies.

[16]When he finds himself weak with respect to the power of counsel, he should gather together a group of wise men or affiliate himself to people of deep learning; [17]for thus he attains immediate well-being.

[18]When he finds himself weak with respect to might, he should work hard to bring about enterprise and security to his subjects. [19]The countryside is the source of all undertakings, and from it is derived might. [20]The fort is the refuge for it and for himself in a time of danger. [21]Irrigation works are the source of crops, [22]for irrigated crops produce constant fruits, as good as when they are watered by rain. [23]The trade route is the source of outwitting the enemy; [24]for the infiltration of troops and clandestine operatives and the purchase of weapons, armor, vehicles, and draught animals are carried out using trade routes, as well as import and export. [25]Pit mines are the source of military armaments; produce forests, of fort construction and of carriages and chariots; elephant forests, of elephants; and herd stations of cattle, horses, donkeys, and camels. [26]When these are unavailable, he should obtain them from the households of kinsmen and allies.

[27]When he finds himself weak with respect to energy, he should gather together eminent warriors from corporate militia, robber bands, forest tribes, barbarian groups, and clandestine operatives able to cause harm to enemies, according to their availability.

[28]He should deploy against the enemies what is given in the "redress for a joint-enemy danger" (9.6.11f) or "on the weaker king (book 12.)."

> [29]Endowed in this manner with a following, counsel, material resources, and an army, he should march out to overcome the obstruction thrown against him by the enemy.

THAT CONCLUDES THE FOURTEENTH CHAPTER: "AUGMENTING WEAKENED POWER" OF THE SEVENTH BOOK: "ON THE SIXFOLD STRATEGY."

Chapter 15

Topic 119: Reasons for Barricading Oneself after Initiating Hostilities against a Strong King

[1]When a weak king is attacked by a strong king, he should seek refuge with a king of greater strength than the latter, a king whom the other would not outwit by the power of his counsel. [2]Among those with equal power of counsel, superiority derives from the presence of exemplary qualities in his dependents* or from association with elders.

[3]When someone of greater strength is not available, he should remain after forming a partnership with kings or confederacies that are equal in

strength to the strong king and that the latter cannot outwit by the power of his counsel and might. [4]Among those with equal power of counsel and might, superiority derives from the vastness of the undertakings.

[5]When those of equal strength are not available, he should remain after forming a partnership with kings of inferior strength who are honest, energetic, and hostile to the strong king and whom the latter cannot outwit by the power of his counsel, might, and enterprise. [6]Among those with equal power of enterprise, superiority derives from finding a terrain suitable for one's own technique of warfare. [7]Among those with equally suitable terrain, superiority derives from finding a season suitable for one's own technique of warfare. [8]Among those with equally suitable terrain and season, superiority derives from draught animals, weapons, and armor.

[9]When a partner to provide assistance is not available, he should seek refuge in a fort where the enemy would not be able to cut off his supply of food, green fodder, firewood, and water even with a large army and would himself incur losses and expenses. [10]Among forts of equal merit, superiority derives from stocks and hideaways. [11]"For, he should seek to obtain a fort defended by men and equipped with stocks and hideaways," says Kauṭilya.

[12]He should take refuge in it for the following reasons:

I will win over the rear enemy, his backer, the intermediate king, or the neutral king.

I will get his kingdom seized or destroyed by a neighbor, a tribal chief, a pretender from his family, or a prince in disfavor.

Or, by supporting a seducible party, I will stir up a revolt in his fort, province, and military camp.

When he is nearby, I will kill him at will employing a weapon, fire, or poison, or through occult practices (book 14).

Or, I will entangle him in losses and expenses through secret measures employed by myself.*

Or, I will prevail in gradually instigating his set of allies or his army when they are deeply troubled by losses, expenses, and absence from home.

Or, by destroying his supplies, reinforcements, and foraging raids, I will subjugate his military camp.

Or, after creating a vulnerable point by infiltrating troops, I will storm him by gathering together my entire army.

Or, I will conclude whatever pact I desire with him when his spirit of enterprise has been crushed.

Or, while he is engaged in a conflict with me, revolts will arise all around him.

Or, I will get his home territory, bereft of reinforcements, pillaged by troops of an ally or tribal troops.

Or, remaining right here,* I will protect the enterprise and security of a vast territory.

Or, as I remain right here,* my forces dispersed by myself or by my ally will gather in one place and become unassailable.

Or, my forces, skilled in combat in water, in trenches, and at night and freed from the perils of the road, will carry out the assignment when he is close by.

Or, when he arrives here over a terrain or during a season unfavorable to him, he will fall apart on this own due to losses and expenses. This region is accessible only at the cost of enormous losses and expenses, because it contains a lot of fort and forest hideaways. In it, enemies face incessant sickness, and it provides no terrain suitable for military operations. He will enter it beset by adversity, and once he has entered it, he will not escape.

13"In the absence of any reason* or when the enemy's strength has swelled, he should abandon the fort and flee. 14Or, he should fall on the enemy like a moth into a fire, 15for a man who is ready to lay down his life is bound to achieve one thing or the other," so state the teachers. 16 "No," says Kauṭilya. 17"After ascertaining that he and his enemy are disposed toward a peace pact, he should conclude a pact. 18In the opposite case, he should seek either a pact or an escape by means of an assault. 19Or, he should send an envoy to the one disposed toward a peace pact. 20Or, after receiving with deference an envoy sent by the other with money and honors, he should tell him: 'Here are the gifts for the king. Here are the gifts for his queen and the princes in the name of my queen and princes. This kingdom and I myself are at your disposal.' "

Topic 120: Behavior Proper for a King Surrendering with his Troops

21When he has found a refuge, he should behave toward his master according to what is stated in the section on sanctioned conduct (5.5). 22He should carry out activities relating to the fort and the like, as well as giving and receiving in marriage, anointing a prince, purchasing horses, capturing elephants, visiting secure locations,* undertaking an expedition, or going on an excursion, only with his permission. [23]He should carry out everything—pacts with the constituents still remaining in his territory or the punishment of deserters—only with his permission.

[24]If the people of his city and countryside become hostile to him, although he has conducted himself justly, he should either request another territory [25]or deal with them like traitors using silent punishment (1.11.21 n.). [26]He should not accept even a suitable territory given after it has been taken from an ally.

[27]When he cannot get an audience with the master, he should see the Counselor, Chaplain,* the Chief of Armed Forces, or the Crown Prince; and he should help him according to his ability. [28]During divine worship and pronouncements of good luck, he should have blessings proclaimed on his behalf. [29]He should speak everywhere about his surrender as something admirable.

> [30]Someone surrendering with his troops should behave in this manner toward his master by uniting himself with him, by serving those in power, and by opposing those under suspicion and other similar people.

THAT CONCLUDES THE FIFTEENTH CHAPTER: "REASONS FOR BARRICADING ONESELF AFTER INITIATING HOSTILITIES AGAINST A STRONG KING" AND "BEHAVIOR PROPER FOR A KING SURRENDERING WITH HIS TROOPS" OF THE SEVENTH BOOK: "ON THE SIXFOLD STRATEGY."

Chapter 16

Topic 121: Behavior Proper for a King Enforcing a Surrender with Troops*

[1]When a strong king wishes to conquer someone who has transgressed the terms of a pact to which he has agreed, he should march into battle where the terrain, season, and livelihood are suitable for his own troops, and where the enemy has no fort to serve as a hideaway, no help in the rear, and no rear backup.* [2]When conditions are the reverse, he should march into battle after taking countermeasures.

[3]He should subjugate weak kings through conciliation and gifts, and strong kings by creating dissension and by using military force. [4]He should secure the constituents who are immediately next to him or once removed from him (6.2.14–15) by the use of the strategies, either restrictively or cumulatively (9.7.73–76).

[5]Protecting people living in villages and wild tracts; protecting herd stations and trade routes; handing over those who have been jettisoned, who have deserted, and who have committed hostile acts—that is how he should practice conciliation. [6]Giving land and property; giving girls in marriage; and giving safety—that is how he should practice gift-giving. [7]Demanding treasure, troops, land, and inheritance by supporting a neighbor, a tribal chief, a pretender from the royal family, or a prince in disfavor—that is how he should practice dissension. [8]Attacking the enemy by open, covert (10.3), and silent warfare (12.4–5), and through the employment of the means for capturing a fort (book 13)—that is how he should practice warfare.

[9]In this manner, he should install those full of enterprise to assist with the army; those possessing their own might to assist with the treasury; and those endowed with intellect to assist with the territory.

[10]Among them,* when someone provides many kinds of assistance with products from ports, villages, and pit mines; with gems, articles of high and low value, and forest produce; with products from produce forests, elephant forests, and herd stations; or with carts and draught animals, he is of varied utility. [11]When someone provides great assistance with troops or treasure, he is of great utility. [12]When someone provides assistance with troops, treasure, and land, he is of total utility.

[13]When someone counters the enemy from one side, he is useful on one side. [14]When someone counters the enemy and his backer from both sides, he is useful on both sides. [15]When someone counters from all sides the enemy, the backer, the neighbor on the flank (7.12.8 n.), and the tribal chief, he is useful on all sides.

[16]If he finds, furthermore, that any rear enemy—whether he is a tribal chief, a principal officer of the foe, or the foe—can be secured by land grants, he should win his support with land of poor quality:

someone settled in a fort, with noncontiguous land;
a tribal chief, with land not yielding a livelihood;
a pretender from the enemy's side, with recoverable land;

a prince in disfavor on the enemy's side, with land that has been cut off;*

someone possessing corporate troops, with land containing permanent enemies (7.10.16);

someone whose troops are gathered together,* with land that has strong neighbors.

an opponent in war, with land having both characteristics;*

an enterprising person, with land unsuitable for military exercises;

someone belonging to the enemy's faction, with barren land;

someone lured away,* with unproductive land;

a deserter who has returned, with land involving enormous losses and expenses to be settled;

a deserter who has come over from the enemy, with land providing no shelter.

With land that cannot be occupied by the enemy, he should himself win the support of the master.

[17]Of these, he should permit the continuance of anyone who provides great assistance and is of unchanging loyalty. [18]He should secretly get rid of anyone who is antagonistic. [19]Anyone who renders assistance, he should gratify with assistance according to his ability; [20]and, corresponding to his effort, he should offer him money and honor, and help in calamities. [21]To those who have come over of their own accord, he should grant an audience when they desire it and make provisions for them. [22]Further, he should not employ toward them insults, hurtful speech, contemptuous words, or abusive language; [23]and, after granting them safety, he should support them like a father.

[24]When someone does him harm, on the other hand, he should publicize his offense and publicly execute him. [25]Or else, because it may cause alarm to others, he may act according to "infliction of secret punishments" (5.1). [26]Further, after he has killed him, he should not covet his land, property, sons, or wife. [27]He should also place members of his family in appropriate positions. [28]If he is killed in action, he should install his son over the kingdom.

[29]In this way, those who have surrendered with their troops will remain loyal to his sons and grandsons.

[30]When, however, a man kills or imprisons those who have surrendered and covets their land, property, sons, and wives, his circle, becoming alarmed, will rise up to destroy him. [31]Those ministers who, living in their own lands, are subject to him,* moreover, will also become alarmed and seek refuge with the circle. [32]Or else, they will plot against his kingdom or life.

> [33]Kings living in their own lands, therefore, and maintained by conciliation become favorably disposed toward the king and remain loyal to his sons and grandsons.

THAT CONCLUDES THE SIXTEENTH CHAPTER: "BEHAVIOR PROPER FOR A KING ENFORCING A SURRENDER WITH TROOPS" OF THE SEVENTH BOOK: "ON THE SIXFOLD STRATEGY."

Chapter 17

Topic 122: Making a Peace Pact

[1]Peace, pact, and hostage;* these have the same meaning, [2]given that peace, pact, and hostage* all create confidence in kings.

[3]"Truth or oath constitutes an unstable pact. A surety or a hostage* constitutes a stable pact," so state the teachers. [4]"No," says Kauṭilya. [5]"Truth or oath constitutes a stable pact here and in the hereafter, while a surety or a hostage, depending on strength, is of use only here."

[6]"We have entered into a pact"; so did the kings of old, true to their agreements, make pacts with truth.

[7]In case it is transgressed, they touched with an oath the following: fire, water, a furrow, a clod from a rampart, the shoulder of an elephant, the back of a horse, the seat of a chariot, a weapon, a gem, seeds, perfume, poison, gold, and money, saying: "May these kill or abandon the man who breaks his oath."

[8]In case the oath is transgressed, there is a surety consisting of the binding into suretyship of great men, recluses, or chiefs. [9]In this event, the man who takes sureties capable of suppressing the enemy is the one who outwits. [10]One who does the opposite is outwitted.

[11]The taking of a kinsman or a chief constitutes a hostage. [12]In this event, the one who gives a traitorous minister or a traitorous offspring is the one who outwits. [13]One who does the opposite is outwitted; [14]for the

enemy strikes without remorse at the vulnerable points of someone who is full of confidence because of receiving a hostage.

[15]In giving an offspring as a hostage, however, as between a daughter and a son, the man who gives a daughter is the one who outwits; [16]for a daughter is not an heir, is intended only for others, and cannot be tortured. [17]A son has the opposite characteristics.

[18]Even between two sons, the man who gives a son who is legitimate, intelligent, brave, skilled in the use of arms, or a single son is the one who is outwitted. [19]One who does the opposite outwits. [20]For giving an illegitimate son is better than giving a legitimate son, because the latter would result in the succession of heirs being erased; an unintelligent son is better than an intelligent one, because the latter would erase the power of counsel; a timid son is better than a brave one, because the latter would erase the power of enterprise; a son unskilled in the use of arms is better than one who is skilled in the use of arms, because the latter would erase the abundance of targets to strike;* and one who is not the only son is better than an only son, because hopes do not ride on him.

[21]Between a legitimate son and an intelligent son, the attribute of sovereignty attends a son who is legitimate but not intelligent, while the capacity for counsel attends a son who is intelligent but illegitimate. [22]Even with regard to capacity for counsel, a legitimate son through his association with elders outwits an intelligent son.

[23]Between an intelligent son and a brave son, the application to feats of intelligence attends a son who is intelligent but timid, while the capacity for valor attends a son who is brave but not intelligent. [24]Even with regard to the capacity for valor, an intelligent son outwits a brave son, like a hunter an elephant.

[25]Between a brave son and a son skilled in the use of arms, resolve in valor attends a son who is brave but not skilled in the use of arms, while the capacity to hit the mark attends a son who is skilled in the use of arms but timid. [26]Even with regard to the capacity to hit the mark, a brave son outwits a son skilled in the use of arms due to his steadfastness, quick wit, and vigilance.

[27]Between a king with many sons and a king with a single son, the king with many sons, after giving one and bolstered by the rest, can break the pact, but not the other.

[28]When a pact involves the giving of the son who is all he has, the special advantage derives from the son's offspring. [29]When both have the same number of offspring from their sons, the special advantage derives

from the ability to procreate.* [30]Even when both have the ability to procreate, the special advantage derives from an imminent birth.

[31]When his single son has that ability,* however, a king who has lost his capacity to procreate a son should give himself up, and not that single son.

Topic 123: Liberating a Hostage

[32]Once he has grown in strength, he should bring about the release of the hostage. [33]Secret agents operating undercover as artisans and craftsmen and carrying out activities near the prince should spirit him away through an underground tunnel that they have dug at night.

[34]Alternatively, actors, dancers, singers, musicians, bards, performers, rope dancers, and dramatic storytellers (2.27.25 n.), who had been infiltrated beforehand, should wait upon the enemy. [35]They should wait upon the prince one after another, [36]and he should dictate that they may enter, stay, and exit without time restrictions. [37]Then he should go away at night disguised as one of them. [38]This also explains courtesans and women disguised as wives. [39]Or else, he should get out carrying the packages of their musical instruments.

[40]Alternatively, he should be taken out by chefs, cooks, bath attendants, masseurs, preparers of beds, barbers, valets, and water servers (1.12.9), along with packages of articles, garments, and utensils, and beds and seats after they have been used.

[41]Alternatively, he should get out during a time when it is difficult to distinguish features either disguised as a servant and carrying something or through an underground tunnel carrying a nightly offering.*

[42]Alternatively, he should resort to the Varuṇa ruse* in a body of water.

[43]Alternatively, agents operating undercover as traders should administer poison to the guards by selling to them cooked food and fruits.

[44]On the occasion of a divine offering, ancestral offering, or festivity, he should flee after giving poison or food and drink mixed with a coma-inducing drug (14.1.16–17) to the guards, or by enticing the guards.

[45]Alternatively, agents operating undercover as men about town, performers, physicians, or vendors of flat bread should set fire at night to houses of the rich or of the guards. [46]Or, agents operating undercover as traders should set fire to the market place. [47]Or, after depositing another body, he* should set fire to his own house out of fear that he would be

tracked down. [48]Then he should flee through a hole in the wall, a trench, or an underground tunnel.

[49]Alternatively, he should leave at night disguised as a man carrying a load of goods in pots hung from a shoulder pole.

[50]Alternatively, he should infiltrate a convoy of shaven-headed or matted-haired ascetics and leave at night disguised as one of them or by one of these means: disfiguring himself, contracting an illness, or in the guise of a forest dweller.

[51]Alternatively, he should be carried out by clandestine operatives disguised as a corpse; [52]or he should follow a corpse dressed as a woman.

[53]Agents operating undercover as forest dwellers, moreover, should point them in a direction other than the one he has taken; [54]and he should go in a direction different from that.* [55]Or else, he should get away with cart convoys of traveling holy men (4.4.3 n.).

[56]Or, when the pursuit is closing in, he should get into a secure location (7.15.22 n.). [57]If a secure location is not available, he should spread on both sides of the road money or poisoned foodstuff, [57]and he should flee in a different direction.

[59]Or, if he is caught, he should outwit the pursuers through strategies such as conciliation, or with food for the journey that has been poisoned.

[60]Or, in the case of the Varuṇa ruse (7.17.42 n.) or arson, after depositing another body, he* should accuse the foe, saying, "You have killed my son!"

> [61]Or, carrying concealed weapons, he should launch an assault on the guards at night and get away on swift horses accompanied by clandestine operatives.

THAT CONCLUDES THE SEVENTEENTH CHAPTER: "MAKING A PEACE PACT" AND "LIBERATING A HOSTAGE" OF THE SEVENTH BOOK: "ON THE SIXFOLD STRATEGY."

Chapter 18

Topic 124: Conduct toward the Intermediate King

[1]With respect to the intermediate king—he himself and the third and the fifth constituents are the friendly constituents. [2]The second, the fourth, and the sixth are the hostile constituents.*

[3]If the intermediate king assists both those,* the seeker after conquest should have friendly relations with that intermediate. [4]If he does not assist them, he should have friendly relations with the friendly constituents.

[5]If the intermediate king seeks to overpower an ally of the seeker after conquest, an ally possessing the disposition of an ally, he should rescue his ally by rousing his own allies and those of that ally and by causing disunity between the intermediate king and his allies. [6]Or he should entice the circle, saying, "This intermediate king has become overly powerful. He has risen up for the destruction of us all. Joining together in partnership, let us repel his military expedition." [7]If the circle welcomes that, he should enhance himself by suppressing the intermediate. [8]If it does not welcome that, he should support his ally with treasure and troops and win over through conciliation and gifts the chief or the nearest among the kings who hate the intermediate—a large number of whom may be assisting each other, or by securing one of whom many can be secured, or who would not rise up because they are afraid of each other. [9]Becoming thus twofold, he should win over a second; and becoming threefold, he should win over a third. [10]Having become strong in this manner, he should suppress the intermediate king. [11]Or, if the place and time were to pass by, he should make a pact with the intermediate and provide assistance to his ally; or, with regard to traitorous officials,* he should make a pact for a project (7.12).

[12]Or, if the intermediate king seeks to overpower his ally who needs to be weakened, he should bolster him by saying, "I will rescue you," until he is weakened. [13]Once he is weakened, he should rescue him.

[14]Or, if the intermediate king seeks to overpower his ally who needs to be vanquished, he should rescue him when he is weakened, fearing that the intermediate may increase his power. [15]Or, if he is vanquished, he should get him into his grip by granting him land, fearing that he may flee elsewhere.

[16]If the allies of a king who needs to be weakened and of a king who needs to be vanquished offer assistance to the intermediate, he should conclude a pact using another person.* [17]Or, if the allies of those two are capable of suppressing the seeker after conquest, he should conclude a pact.

[18]Or, if the intermediate king seeks to overpower his* enemy, he* should conclude a pact. [19]In this way, he* accomplishes his* own goal, and the intermediate becomes pleased.

[20]If the intermediate king seeks to overpower his own ally possessing the disposition of an ally, he* should conclude a pact using another person (7.3.24). [21]Or, if the man were to have some regard,* he* should prevent him, saying, "It is not right for you to vanquish an ally." [22]Or, he* should remain indifferent, thinking, "Let the circle become incensed with him for killing someone of his own faction."

[23]Or, if the intermediate king seeks to overpower his own enemy, he* should assist him behind the scene with treasure and troops. [24]Or, if the intermediate king seeks to overpower the neutral king, he* should render assistance to him, thinking, "Let him be separated from the neutral." [25]Between the intermediate and the neutral, he* should resort to the one who is favored by the circle.

Topic 125: Conduct toward the Neutral King

[26]The conduct toward the intermediate king also explains the conduct toward the neutral king.

[27]If the neutral king seeks to overpower the intermediate, he* should adopt the course by which he would outwit his foe, render assistance to his ally, or get the neutral king to assist him with troops.

Topic 126: Conduct toward the Circle

[28]Enhancing his own power in this way, he should weaken the constituent who is an enemy and support the constituent who is an ally.

[29]Even though an inimical disposition is omnipresent,* the following are neighbors who have the disposition of an enemy:

> the foe in the front without the exemplary qualities of the self (1.5.16 n.) and constantly doing harm; the rear enemy allied with the foe in the front; a vulnerable king facing a calamity; one who attacks the leader facing a calamity.

The following are neighbors who have the disposition of an ally:

> someone going into battle for a common objective; someone going into battle for a separate objective; someone marching into battle after forming a partnership; someone going into battle after entering into a pact; someone going into battle for his own objective;

someone rising up together; someone who, undertaking a double stratagem, purchases or sells treasure and troops.

And the following are neighbors who have the disposition of a dependent:

a neighbor placed in between or on the side as a check on a strong king; the rear enemy of a strong king; one who surrenders with his troops either on his own or in the face of stronger prowess.

[30]These also explain those who are separated by one intervening territory (6.2.15).

[31]Among these, when an ally assumes the same objective as he in a conflict with a foe, he should assist him with the power that would enable him to resist the enemy.

[32]When an ally, after conquering the foe and enhancing his power, becomes non-submissive, he should put him into conflict with two constituents, his immediate neighbor and the one separated by one intervening territory.

[33]Alternatively, he should have his territory seized by a pretender from that family or by a prince in disfavor. Or, he should act in a manner that would bring him into submission in consideration of the assistance he has provided.

[34]If an ally, when excessively weakened, cannot offer assistance or may go over to the enemy, he, versed in political science, should keep him neither weak nor strong.

[35]When a wavering ally enters into a pact to further his own objective, he should eliminate the reason why he may leave, so he may not waver.

[36]Or, when an ally is in league with the enemy, he should separate that cheat from the enemy; and when he is separated, he should vanquish him first and immediately thereafter that foe.

[37]When an ally remains neutral, he should put him into conflict with his neighbors. Then, after he is distressed by hostilities, he should get him to seek assistance.

[38]When a weak ally turns to both the enemy and the seeker after conquest, he should assist him with troops so that he may not turn away from him.

[39]Alternatively, he should take that ally from there and settle him in another territory, after first settling another ally there* because of the assistance with troops he has given.

[40]When an ally does harm to him or refuses to help him in a time of adversity even when he is able, he should definitely vanquish him when his trust in him makes him fall into his hand.

[41]Or, when an enemy has risen to power unrestrained because of a calamity that has struck the ally, he should be overpowered through that very ally by surmounting that calamity of his.

[42]When an ally, who has risen to power because of a calamity that has befallen the enemy, becomes disaffected, he can be overpowered through that very foe by surmounting the enemy's calamity.

[42]Prosperity, decline, stability, weakening, and vanquishing—knowing the science of politics, he should employ all these strategies.

[44]When he realizes in this way that the sixfold strategy works in tandem, he plays as he pleases with kings bound by the chains of his intelligence.

THAT CONCLUDES THE EIGHTEENTH CHAPTER: "CONDUCT TOWARD THE INTERMEDIATE KING," "CONDUCT TOWARD THE NEUTRAL KING," AND "CONDUCT TOWARD THE CIRCLE" OF THE SEVENTH BOOK: "ON THE SIXFOLD STRATEGY."

THAT CONCLUDES THE SEVENTH BOOK "ON THE SIXFOLD STRATEGY" OF KAUṬILYA'S *ARTHAŚĀSTRA*.

Book Eight

On the Subject of Calamaties

Chapter 1

Topic 127: Set of Calamities Affecting the Constituent Elements

[1]When calamities arise simultaneously,* should one march into battle or take protective measures according to the ease with which it can be carried out? Hence, the reflection on calamities.

[2]A calamity affecting a constituent element is either divine or human and comes about either through bad fortune or bad policy (6.2.6–12).

[3]The inverse of qualities, absence, great defect, addiction, or affliction is a calamity.* [4]It separates (*vy-as*) him from prosperity; that is how we get the term calamity (*vyasana*).

[5]"Lord, minister, countryside, fort, treasury, army, and ally—a calamity affecting each previous one is more serious," say the teachers.

[6]"No," says Bhāradvāja. [7]"Between calamities affecting the lord and a minister, a calamity affecting a minister is more serious. [8]Counsel, achieving the fruits of counsel, carrying out activities, managing income and expenditure, imposing punishments, keeping enemies and tribal chiefs in check, protecting the kingdom, redressing calamities, guarding the princes, and the anointing of the princes—all these are dependent on ministers. [9]In the absence of ministers, these cease to be, and the king's activities come to an end, like those (of a bird) with its wings clipped. [10]When calamities affect them, moreover, instigations of the enemy are close at hand; [11]and when they turn hostile, there is a danger to the king's life, because they operate near the king's person."

[12]"No," says Kauṭilya. [13]"It is the king who appoints the various kinds of functionaries, such as Counselor-Chaplain (1.9 n.), directs the activities of the superintendents, and redresses calamities affecting the human and material constituents (6.2.28 n.), as well as makes them flourish. [14]Or, when the ministers are afflicted by calamities, he appoints others who are not afflicted by calamities. [15]He remains always intent on honoring those worthy of honor and on suppressing traitorous people. [16]When the lord is endowed with the exemplary qualities (6.1.6), moreover, by means of his own exemplary qualities, he endows his constituents with their exemplary qualities.* [17]His constituents will come to have the same character as he, because they are dependent on him both in exertion and in carelessness; [18]for the lord stands at their head."

[19]"Between calamities affecting a minister and the countryside, a calamity affecting the countryside is more serious," says Viśālākṣa. [20]"Treasury, army, forest produce, labor, draught animals, and stocks are derived from the countryside. [21]In the absence of the countryside, these cease to be and, immediately thereafter, also the king and minister."

[22]"No," says Kauṭilya. [23]"In the minister are rooted all the undertakings—the success of operations in the countryside, securing its enterprise and security against one's own people and those of the enemy, providing countermeasures against calamities, settling vacant land and developing them, and procuring the benefits of fines and taxes."

[24]"Between calamities affecting the countryside and the fort, a calamity affecting the fort is more serious," says Pārāśara. [25]"For the fort is where the treasury and army originate, and it is a secure place for the people of the countryside in times of danger. [26]The people of the fort, furthermore, are stronger than the people of the countryside and are steadfast associates of the king in times of danger. [27]The people of the countryside, on the other hand, are equally partial to the enemy."

[28]"No," says Kauṭilya. [29]"In the countryside are rooted the undertakings relating to fort, treasury, army, irrigation projects, and commerce. [30]In the people of the countryside are found bravery, steadfastness, expertise, and large numbers; [31]and hill forts and forts formed by an island in the middle of water cannot be populated if there is no countryside. [32]When the countryside is populated mostly by agriculturalists, however, a calamity affecting the fort is more serious, whereas when the countryside is populated mostly by fighters, a calamity affecting the countryside is more serious."

[33]"Between calamities affecting the fort and the treasury, a calamity affecting the treasury is more serious," says Piśuna. [34]"For, in the treasury

are rooted the construction of the fort; the protection of the fort; keeping the countryside, allies, and enemies in check; instigating those who have gone to another region to sedition; and commercial transactions of army troops.* [35]The fort is vulnerable to instigations to sedition by enemies through disbursements from the treasury. [36]Further, in a calamity it is possible to flee taking along one's treasury, but not the fort."

[37]"No," says Kauṭilya. [38]"Treasury, army, silent war (7.6.41), keeping one's own partisans in check, commercial transactions of army troops (8.1.34 n.), receiving rear reinforcements,* and the suppression of enemy forces and tribal chiefs—all this relies on the fort. [39]When there is no fort, moreover, the treasury will fall into enemy hands; [40]for we see that kings who have forts are not vanquished."

[41]"Between calamities affecting the fort and the army, a calamity affecting the army is more serious," says Kauṇapadanta. [42]"For, the army serves as the foundation for keeping allies and enemies in check, instigating the enemy troops to sedition, and getting reinforcements (8.1.38 n.) into one's own army. [43]In the absence of an army, moreover, the treasury will certainly perish; [44]while in the absence of a treasury, it is possible to raise an army using forest produce or land, or through individual plunder (3.16.27n.) of enemy land; and it is possible for one who has an army to amass a treasury. [45]Because it operates close to the lord, furthermore, the army has the same characteristics as a minister."

[46]"No," says Kauṭilya. [47]"For the the treasury serves as the foundation of the army. [48]When there is no treasury, the army goes over to the enemy or kills the lord. [49]The treasury facilitates offensive operations; it sustains religious activities and sensual pleasures. [50]According to the requirements of place, time, and task, however, either the treasury or the army is of greater moment; [51]for the army is instrumental in acquiring and protecting the treasury, whereas the treasury is instrumental in acquiring and protecting both the treasury and the army. [52]A calamity affecting the treasure is more serious, because all material objects originate from the treasury."

[53]"Between calamities affecting the army and an ally, a calamity affecting an ally is more serious," says Vātavyādhi. [54]"An ally carries out his activities without payment and at a distance; thwarts the rear enemy, his backer, the enemy, and the tribal chief; and, united in times of calamity, offers assistance with treasury, army, and land."

[55]"No," says Kauṭilya. [56]"When he (7.18.18–27 n.) has an army, his ally maintains the disposition of an ally, or an enemy takes on the disposition of an ally. [57]When, however, a task can be accomplished equally by both

the army and an ally, the special advantage comes from their respective capacity and from obtaining the terrain and the season suited for their own type of warfare. [58]When one has to move quickly against an enemy or a tribal chief, however, and when there is an internal revolt, an ally is of no avail. [59]When calamities are concurrent and when the enemy has become prosperous, an ally will seek his own interests."

[60]Thus, the way one assesses the calamities affecting the constituent elements has been explained.

> [61]What leads to the accomplishment of a task, however, is the large number, the loyalty, or the power of individual members of the constituent elements, according to the special nature of the calamity.
>
> [62]When, however, the calamity affecting two constituents is equal, the difference is based on the loss in terms of their qualities, if it does not preclude the other constituents from possessing their qualities.
>
> [63]But when the calamity of one results in the ruin of the other constituents, then that calamity is more serious, whether it affects the principal or some other constituent.

THAT CONCLUDES THE FIRST CHAPTER: "SET OF CALAMITIES AFFECTING THE CONSTITUENT ELEMENTS" OF THE EIGHTH BOOK: "ON THE SUBJECT OF CALAMITIES."

Chapter 2

Topic 128: Reflection on Calamities Affecting the King and his Reign

[1]King and reign—that is the epitome of the constituent elements.

[2]For a king, is it an internal revolt or an external revolt (7.5.29 n.)? [3]An internal revolt (9.3.12), because of the snake-like danger it poses, is more harmful than an external revolt; likewise, a revolt among the interior ministers (9.3.20 n.) is more harmful than an internal revolt. [4]Therefore, he should keep the power of the treasury and the army under his own control.

[5]"Between a dual reign and an illegitimate reign—a dual reign is destroyed either through mutual hatred and loyalty on the part of their

factions or through jealousy toward each other. Others, however, enjoy an illegitimate reign just the way it is, given that it depends on winning the hearts of the constituents," so state the teachers.

[6]"No," says Kauṭilya. [7]"A dual reign by a father and a son, or by two brothers—with enterprise and security held in common and exercising mutual restraint—does endure.* [8]In the case of an illegitimate reign, on the other hand, having wrenched it from an enemy who is still alive, and thinking, 'This is not mine,' he will impoverish it, depopulate it (2.1.1n), or sell it; or else, if it is disaffected with him, he will abandon it and go away."

[9]Is it a "blind" king or a king deviating from the provisions of the science?* "A king blind because he lacks the eye of science (1.14.7) does anything he pleases, is stubbornly tenacious, or is manipulated by others, and thus hurts the kingdom through unjust rule. In the case of a king deviating from the provisions of the science, on the other hand, it is possible to bring him around in those matters where his mind deviates from the science," so state the teachers.

[10]"No," says Kauṭilya. [11]"A blind king can be made to proceed in one way or the other through the exemplary qualities of his associates (1.9.1 n.). [12]A king deviating from the provisions of the science, on the other hand, with his mind firmly set on what is contrary to the provisions of the science, will hurt his reign and himself through unjust rule."

[13]Is it a sick king or a new king? "A sick king faces either the overthrow of his reign brought about by the ministers or a threat to his own life brought about by his reign. A new king, on the other hand, carries on with the discharge of his own duties, bestowing favors, granting exemptions, giving gifts, and conferring honors, which gratify and benefit the subjects," so state the teachers.

[14]"No," says Kauṭilya. [15]"A sick king continues to carry out the royal functions as he did before. [16]A new king, on the other hand, thinking, 'This is my kingdom won by force,' behaves as he pleases, uncontrolled; [17]or, under the control of his associates in the uprising, he will condone the plunder of the kingdom. [18]Given that he is not firmly rooted among the subjects, he can be easily vanquished."

[19]With respect to a sick king, there is a difference between one suffering from an evil disease* and one not suffering from an evil disease. [20]With respect to a new king also, there is a difference between one who is of noble birth and one who is not of noble birth.

[21]Is it a weak king of noble birth or a strong king not of noble birth? "The subjects, taking into account his weakness, respond to the instigations of a weak king of noble birth with great difficulty, while they respond easily to those of a strong king who is not of noble birth, taking into account his strength," so state the teachers.

[22]"No," says Kauṭilya. [23]"The subjects submit on their own to a weak king of noble birth, as it is said: 'The attribute of sovereignty attends a man of noble birth' (7.17.21); [24]and they frustrate the instigations of a strong king who is not of noble birth, as it is said: 'In loyalty is every strategy'" (7.5.14).

[25]The loss of the crop, because it entails the loss of the entire labor, is more harmful than the loss of what has been sowed; and, likewise, lack of rain, because it entails the loss of livelihood, is more harmful than too much rain.

> [26]The relative seriousness of calamities affecting the constituents, taking them two at a time, has been explained according to the traditional order, as the reason for marching into battle and for remaining stationary.

THAT CONCLUDES THE SECOND CHAPTER: "REFLECTION ON CALAMITIES AFFECTING THE KING AND HIS REIGN" OF THE EIGHTH BOOK: "ON THE SUBJECT OF CALAMITIES."

Chapter 3

Topic 129: Set of Human Vices

[1]Not being trained in the sciences (1.5–6) is the cause of human vices;* [2]for an untrained man does not see the harmful effects of vices. [3]We will spell these out.

[4]There is a set of three that stem from wrath, and a set of four that stem from pleasure.*

[5]Of the two, wrath is more serious, [6]for wrath is operative everywhere. [7]One hears, moreover, that for the most part kings under the sway of wrath have been killed through the wrathful revolts* of the subjects, while those under the sway of pleasure have been killed by enemies and diseases as a result of their decline.

[8]"No," says Bhāradvāja. [9]"Wrath is conduct proper for a good man; it exacts retribution for enmity, snuffs out insults, and instills dread in people.

[10]Resorting to wrath, furthermore, always has as its goal the stamping out of evil. [11]Pleasure relates to the attainment of success, conciliation, propensity for generosity, and an endearing nature. [12]Resorting to pleasure, furthermore, always has as its goal the enjoyment of the fruits of one's labor."

[13]"No," says Kauṭilya. [14]"Wrath consists of being the object of hatred, making enemies, and association with grief. [15]Pleasure consists of disgrace, the depletion of resources and association with undesirable people: robbers, gamblers, hunters, singers, and musicians. [16]Of the two,* being the object of hatred is more serious than disgrace, [17]given that a disgraced man is under the grip of his own people and of his enemies, whereas a man who is the object of hatred is totally vanquished. [18]Making enemies is more serious than the depletion of resources, [19]given that the depletion of resources endangers one's treasury, whereas making enemies endangers one's life. [20]Association with grief is more serious than association with undesirable people, [21]given that the association with undesirable people can be rectified in a moment, whereas the association with grief causes prolonged distress. [22]Therefore, wrath is more serious."

[23]Verbal abuse, injury to property, and physical assault (8.3.4 n.)—

[24]"Between verbal abuse and injury to property, verbal abuse is more serious," says Viśālākṣa. [25]"For, a spirited man, when abusive speech is directed at him, retaliates with spirit. [26]The dart of offensive speech plants itself in the heart, inflames the spirit, and burns the senses."

[27]"No," says Kauṭilya. [28]"Obsequious offer of property pulls out the dart of speech, whereas injury to property cuts off one's livelihood."

[29]Not giving property, seizing it, destroying it, or throwing it away constitutes injury to property.

[30]"Between injury to property and physical assault, injury to property is more serious," says Pārāśara. [31]"Property (*artha*) is the foundation of Law (*dharma*) and Pleasure (*kāma*), [32]and the world functions only when it is joined to property* (*artha*). [33]Injury to it is more serious."

[34]"No," says Kauṭilya. [35]"No one wishes the destruction of his body even for a lot of property. [36]As a result of physical assault, moreover, one will face the same danger at the hand of others."

[37]—these constitute the set of three stemming from wrath (see 8.3.23; 8.3.4 n.).

[38]The set of four stemming from pleasure, however, consists of hunting, gambling, women, and drinking.

[39]With regard to that, "Between hunting and gambling, hunting is more serious," says Piśuna. [40]"There is a risk to life in it resulting from

dangers posed by thieves, enemies, vicious animals, forest fires, and falling down; from losing the way; and from hunger and thirst. [41]In gambling, on the other hand, an expert in dice is sure to win, just like Jayatsena and Duryodhana."*

[42]"No," says Kauṭilya. [44]"The fact that, of the two, the one or the other sustains defeat is illustrated by Nala and Yudhiṣṭhira.* [45]The very same object that one has won becomes a bait and a continuous source of enmity. [45]Aversion to legitimate wealth, securing illegitimate wealth,* loss of wealth before it has been enjoyed, and getting sick because of hunger, the retention of urine or feces, and the like—these are the harmful effects of gambling. [46]In the case of hunting, on the other hand, we have exercise; the elimination of phlegm, bile, fat, and perspiration; practice in hitting moving and still bodies; and discerning the minds of animals when they are angry, afraid, and at ease; as well as travel that is not constant."

[47]"Between the vices of gambling and women, the vice of gambling is more serious," says Kauṇapadanta. [48]"For a gambler plays at dice all the time, at night by lamplight, and even when his mother has died. [49]And if someone questions him when he is in difficulties, he gets angry. [50]In the case of the vice of women, on the other hand, there are indeed occasions, such as bath, toilet, and meals, when questions regarding Law and Success can be posed to him. [51]It is possible, moreover, to enlist a woman to do what is beneficial to the king, or by means of silent punishment (1.11.21 n.) or through a disease to turn her away or to get rid of her."

[52]"No," says Kauṭilya. [53]"In gambling there is the possibility of rehabilitation, while the vice of women does not permit rehabilitation [54]and results in keeping out of sight, aversion to work, harm to Success and transgression of Law owing to procrastination, ineptitude in administrative work, and addiction to drinking."

[55]"Between the vices of women and drinking, the vice of women is more serious," says Vātavyādhi. [56]"For the many kinds of folly associated with women have been explained in 'Regimen of the Residence' (1.20.14–17). [57]In the case of drinking, on the other hand, we have the enjoyment of sensual objects such as sound, giving gifts out of affection, paying respect to waiters, and relieving the fatigue of work."

[58]"No," says Kauṭilya. [59]"With regard to the vice of women, there are the begetting of offspring and the protection of himself in the case of wives inside the home, the opposite in the case of those outside, and the devastation of everything in the case of women with whom sex is forbidden. [60]Both these* are present in the vice of drinking. [61]The aftermath of

drinking* is loss of consciousness; insane behavior on the part of someone who is not insane; appearing like a dead man on the part of someone who is not dead; showing the private parts; loss of learning, intelligence, life, wealth, and friends; separation from good people; association with harmful people; and addiction to the mastery of the lute and singing that causes the despoiling of wealth."

[62]Between gambling and liquor, gambling is more serious. [63]The victory or defeat at betting of some people causes clashes among the subjects by creating two factions with respect to animals and non-animate things. [64]In particular, moreover, dissension caused by gambling affects confederacies and royal houses having the character of confederacies (1.17.53), and they are destroyed on account of that. Thus, favoring evil people, it is the worst of all vices, because it causes ineptitude in administrative work.

> [65]Pleasure favors evil people and wrath represses good people. Both are considered to be an unending calamity,* because they generate numerous harmful effects.
>
> [66]A man, therefore, who possesses the exemplary qualities of the self (1.5.16 n.), serves the elders, and controls his senses, should abandon both wrath and pleasure, which initiate calamities and plunder the patrimony.

THAT CONCLUDES THE THIRD CHAPTER: "SET OF HUMAN VICES" OF THE EIGHTH BOOK: "ON THE SUBJECT OF CALAMITIES."

Chapter 4

Topic 130: Set of Afflictions

[1]Divine afflictions are fire, flood, disease, famine, and epidemic (6.2.6–12).

[2] "Between fire and flood, the affliction from fire is without remedy and burns up everything, whereas affliction from flood is something from which one can flee and whose danger can be overcome," say the teachers.

[3]"No," says Kauṭilya. [4]"A fire burns a village or a half of a village. The velocity of a flood, however, carries away a hundred villages."

[5]"Between disease and famine, disease hurts undertakings by impeding the activities of workers who die or are sick or afflicted,* whereas famine does not hurt undertakings and yields taxes in money and farm animals," say the teachers.

[6]"No," says Kauṭilya. [7]"A disease afflicts a single region and remedies can be found for it, whereas a famine afflicts all the regions and deprives living beings of their livelihood."

[8]This also explains an epidemic.

[9]"Between the loss of common people and the loss of chiefs, the loss of common people deprives undertakings of enterprise and security, whereas the loss of chiefs has the nature of impeding the execution of the undertakings," say the teachers.

[10]"No," says Kauṭilya. [11]"It is possible to rectify the loss of common people, because they are numerous, but not the loss of chiefs, [12]for among a thousand, there may be one chief or none at all, because he must possess a high degree of spirit and intelligence, and because common people depend on him."*

[13]"Between one's own army and the army of an enemy, one's own army oppresses through excessive punishment and taxes, and it is impossible to restrain it, whereas one can counterattack the army of an enemy or it can be evaded through flight or a peace pact," say the teachers.

[14]"No," says Kauṭilya. [15]"Oppression by one's own army can be prevented by appeasing or vanquishing the leaders of the ranking officials, or it oppresses only one region, whereas the army of an enemy oppresses all the regions, and it oppresses by pillage, carnage, arson, laying waste, and abduction."*

[16]"Between disputes among the subjects and among the royals, disputes among the subjects create divisions among the subjects and open the door to enemy attacks, whereas disputes among the royals provide the subjects with double the rations, wages, and exemptions," say the teachers.

[17]"No," says Kauṭilya. [18]"Disputes among the subjects can be prevented by appeasing the leaders of the subjects or by removing the reasons for the disputes. [19]The subjects, as they dispute among themselves, however, provide benefits through their mutual rivalry. [20]Disputes among the royals, on the other hand, lead to the oppression and extermination of the subjects and can be resolved only with a doubling of effort."

[21]"Between merrymaking by the country people and by the king, merrymaking by the country people destroys the fruits of activities throughout the three times,* whereas merrymaking by the king provides benefits to artisans, craftsmen, performers, bards, prostitutes, and traders," say the teachers.

[22]"No," says Kauṭilya. [23]"Merrymaking by the country people, meant to alleviate the fatigue from work, consumes little, and after such

consumption once again leads them to engage in their undertakings, whereas merrymaking by the king oppresses through individual plunder (3.16.27n.), levies, gifts, and seizure of undertakings by the king himself and by his favorites."

[24]"Between the beloved wife and the prince, the prince oppresses through individual plunder (3.16.27n.), levies, gifts, and seizure of undertakings by the prince himself and by his favorites, whereas the beloved wife oppresses through enjoying amusements," say the teachers.

[25]"No," says Kauṭilya. [26]"It is possible to restrain the prince through the Counselor or the Chaplain (7.15.27 n.), but not the beloved wife because of her foolishness and association with evil people."

[27]"Between a corporate regiment and a chief, a corporate regiment, unchecked because of its large numbers, oppresses through theft and forcible seizure, whereas a chief oppresses by supporting or wrecking undertakings," say the teachers.

[28]"No," says Kauṭilya. [29]"A corporate regiment is easily restrained because all its members have similar traits and vices, or it can be restrained by appeasing the leader of the corporate regiment or one segment of that regiment. [30]A chief, puffed up with arrogance, oppresses by destroying other people's lives and property."

[31]"Between the Treasurer and the Collector, the Treasurer oppresses by disparaging work that has been done and by imposing penalties, whereas the Collector, guided by the bureau of experts (2.5.8; 2.11.1), enjoys the rewards assigned to him," say the teachers.

[32]"No," says Kauṭilya. [33]"The Treasurer accepts items that have been verified by others as suitable for deposit in the treasury, whereas the Collector first secures wealth for himself and only then secures wealth for the king or lets it perish; and in taking the property of others acts according to his own assessment (2.36.5 n.)."

[34]"Between the Frontier Commander and traders, the Frontier Commander oppresses the trade route by allowing thieves to operate and by charging excessive levies, whereas traders enrich it through the benefits of commodities exported and the commodities imported in return," say the teachers.

[35]"No," says Kauṭilya. [36]"The Frontier Commander promotes it through the benefit of bringing together commodities, whereas traders, conspiring with each other and raising or lowering the prices of commodities, live off of it by making a profit of a hundred Paṇas on a single Paṇa, or a hundred Kumbhas on a single Kumbha (2.19.32)."

[37]Is it a land obstructed by a man of noble birth, or a land obstructed by a herd station for farm animals (7.5.29 n.)? "A land obstructed by a man of noble birth may yield ample produce; yet, being a supplier of soldiers, it is not suitable for recovery, because one fears the peril of a calamity. A land obstructed by a herd station for farm animals, on the other hand, is suitable for recovery when it is suitable for agriculture; [38]for pasture lands must yield to cultivated fields," say the teachers.

[39]"No," says Kauṭilya. [40]"A land obstructed by a man of noble birth, though it may provide exceedingly great benefits, is suitable for recovery, because one fears the peril of a calamity. A land obstructed by a herd station for farm animals, on the other hand, being a supplier of articles for the treasury and draught animals, is not suitable for recovery, except when it obstructs the sowing of crops."*

[41]"Between highwaymen and forest tribes, highwaymen lurk under the cover of night,* cause physical harm, are ever present, rob hundreds of thousands, and incite chiefs to revolt, whereas, remaining far away and operating in frontier forests, forest tribes go about openly and in plain sight, and they plunder a single region," say the teachers.

[42]"No," says Kauṭilya. [42]"Highwaymen rob those who are heedless, are few in number and sluggish, and are easy to recognize and apprehend, whereas, living in their own region and being numerous and brave, forest tribes fight in the open, plunder and destroy regions, and behave like kings."

[44]Between a deer forest and an elephant forest, deer are abundant, provide benefits with an abundance of meat and skin, cause little trouble with regard to fodder, and are easily controlled. [45]The opposite is true of elephants; and when, being captured, they turn out to be vicious, they tend to destroy a region.

[46]Between benefits conferred on one's own provincial capital (2.3.3) and on that of the enemy, benefits conferred on one's own provincial capital—benefits in the form of grain, farm animals, money, and forest produce—maintain the lives of people in the countryside during a time of adversity, [47]whereas the opposite is true in the case of benefits conferred on the provincial capital of the enemy.

These are the afflictions.

Topic 131: Set of Hindrances

[48]The internal is the hindrance from the chiefs, while the external is the hindrance from enemies and tribal chiefs.

That is the set of hindrances.

Topic 132: Set of Factors Blocking Revenue to the Treasury

[49]Afflicted by these two* and by afflictions as enumerated (8.4.1), obstructed among the chiefs,* undermined by exemptions, scattered, fraudulently collected, and stolen by neighboring rulers or tribal chiefs—that is the set of obstructions to the flow of revenue to the treasury.

> [50]He should strive to prevent the rise of afflictions, to surmount those that have risen, and to eliminate hindrances and blocking of revenue, in order to promote the prosperity of the country.

THAT CONCLUDES THE FOURTH CHAPTER: "SET OF AFFLICTIONS," "SET OF HINDRANCES," AND "SET OF FACTORS BLOCKING REVENUE TO THE TREASURY" OF THE EIGHTH BOOK: "ON THE SUBJECT OF CALAMITIES."

Chapter 5

Topic 133: Set of Calamities Affecting the Army

[1]These are the calamities affecting the army: not honored,* dishonored, unpaid, sick, arrived recently, journeyed from afar, fatigued, depleted, repulsed, trounced in the initial assault, caught in an unsuitable season, caught in an unsuitable terrain, given up hope, buffeted by desertions, having wives within it, containing darts within it, having a rebellious base, having internal divisions, fled, widely dispersed, settled nearby, completely absorbed, obstructed, encircled, with grain, men, and supplies cut off, dispersed in one's own territory, dispersed in an ally's territory, containing traitorous individuals, with a vicious rear enemy, with an empty home territory (7.13.6 n.), not united with the lord, with its chief knocked out, and "blind" (8.2.9–10).

[2]Among these—between one that is not honored and one that is dishonored, the one not honored will fight when presented with money and honor, but not the one that is dishonored, given that it is burning inside with anger.

[3]Between one that is unpaid and one that is sick, the one that is unpaid will fight when salaries are paid immediately, but not the one that is sick, given that it is unfit for work.

[4]Between one that has arrived recently and one that has journeyed from afar, the one that has arrived recently will fight after it has acquired the knowledge of the country from others and has been merged with one that is not new, but not the one that has journeyed from afar, given that it is worn out by a long march.

[5]Between one that is fatigued and one that is depleted, the one that is fatigued will fight after it has been refreshed by bathing, eating, and sleeping, but not the one that is depleted, given that its men and draft animals have been expended in a battle elsewhere.

[6]Between one that has been repulsed and one that has been trounced in the initial assault, the one that has been repulsed, battered in the initial combat, will fight after it has been pulled together by eminent warriors, but not the one that has been trounced in the initial assault, given that its eminent warriors have been killed in the initial combat.

[7]Between one caught in an unsuitable season and one caught in an unsuitable terrain, the one caught in an unsuitable season will fight when equipped with draught animals, weapons, and armor appropriate for that season, but not the one caught in an unsuitable terrain, given that its foraging raids and military maneuvers are thwarted.

[8]Between one that has given up hope and one buffeted by desertions, the one that has given up hope will fight when it has obtained its wishes, but not the one buffeted by desertions, given that its chiefs have run away.

[9]Between one having wives within it and one containing darts within it, the one having wives within it will fight after sending away the wives, but not the one containing darts within it, given that it contains enemies within it.

[10]Between one having a rebellious base and one having internal divisions, the one having a rebellious base will fight when the rebellion has been allayed by means of conciliation and the like (1.13.25 n.), but not the one having internal divisions, given that each is divided from the other.

[11]Between one that has fled and one that is widely dispersed, the one that has fled, that is, retreated to a single realm, will fight through counsel and military maneuvers, finding shelter in a secure location (7.15.22 n.) or with an ally, but not the one that is widely dispersed, given that it has retreated to numerous realms because it faced numerous perils.

[12]Between one that has settled nearby and one that is completely absorbed, the one that has settled nearby, marching and remaining stationary independently, will fight after outwitting the enemy, but not the

one that is completely absorbed, given that it remains stationary and marches in unison with the enemy.*

[13]Between one that is obstructed and one that is encircled, the one that is obstructed will break out in another direction and counterattack the obstructer, but not the one that is encircled, given that it is blocked off from all sides.

[14]Between one with its grain cut off and one with its men and supplies cut off, the one with its grain cut off will fight, bringing in grain from elsewhere or eating mobile and immobile creatures, but not the one with its men and supplies cut off, given that it lacks a rescue.

[15]Between one dispersed in one's own territory and one dispersed in an ally's territory, the one dispersed in one's own territory, given that an army dispersed in one's own land can be mobilized in an emergency, but not the one dispersed in an ally's territory, because of the long distance and time involved.

[16]Between one containing traitorous individuals and one with a vicious rear enemy, the one containing traitorous individuals will fight when led by trustworthy officers and not kept unified, but not the one with a vicious rear enemy, given that it is terrified of an attack from the rear.

[17]Between one with an empty home territory (7.13.6 n.) and one not united with the lord, the one with an empty home territory will fight by gathering together the entire army after providing protection to the people of the city and the countryside, but not the one not united with the lord, given that it is bereft of the king and the Chief of the Armed Forces.

[18]Between one with its chief knocked out and one that is "blind" (8.2.9–10), the one with its chief knocked out will fight when led by someone else, but not the one that is blind, given that it is without a guide.

> [19]Purging defects, injecting fresh troops, outwitting by resorting to a secure location, and making a peace pact with a stronger party—these are the means of surmounting calamities that affect the army.
>
> [20]In a calamity, he should guard his own army against enemies, remaining always assiduous, and strike at vulnerable points of the army of his foes, remaining always assiduous.
>
> [21]From whichever source he might suffer a calamity to his constituent elements, he should, at the very outset, tirelessly take countermeasures against that source.

Topic 134: Set of Calamities Affecting the Allies

[22]An ally whom he himself has attacked either in partnership with others or at someone else's behest; an ally whom he has abandoned because of weakness, greed, or affection;*

[23]an ally whom he has sold to an antagonist by turning back during a battle, or by pursuing a double stratagem, or by plotting to march elsewhere against another enemy;

[24]an ally whom, by inspiring confidence in him, he has outwitted either in a separate or a joint military expedition; an ally whom he has not rescued in a calamity because of fear, contempt, or lethargy;

[25]an ally who, being barred from his own lands, flees from his vicinity in fear; an ally who has been treated with contempt by expropriating, by refusing to give, or even in giving;

[26]an ally from whom he has extorted money either by himself or through someone else; an ally who, assigned to a very onerous task, is brought to his knees and has fled to the enemy;

[27]an ally whom he has ignored because of his impotence and whom he has now antagonized by making requests;

such an ally is won over with great difficulty, and even when he is won over, he becomes quickly disaffected.

[28]An ally who, although he has worked hard or is worthy of honor, is, through folly, either not given honor or is given an honor that does not befit him; or an ally who has been prevented from gaining strength;

[29]or an ally who is frightened because of a harm done to an ally; or an ally who is suspicious because of a pact concluded with his enemy; or an ally who has been alienated by traitorous men;

such an ally is easily won over, and remains firm once he has been won over.

[30]Therefore, he should not let these defects arise, defects that cause harm to allies; or, once they have arisen, he should remove them by means of good qualities that are capable of eliminating the defects.

That concludes the Fifth Chapter: "Set of Calamities Affecting the Army" and "Set of Calamities Affecting the Allies" of the Eighth Book: "On the Subject of Calamities."

That concludes the Eighth Book: "On the Subject of Calamities" of Kauṭilya's *Arthaśāstra*.

Book Nine

Activity of a King Preparing to March into Battle

Chapter 1

Topic 135: Ascertaining the Relative Strengths and Weaknesses with Respect to Power, Place, and Time

[1]The seeker after conquest should first ascertain the relative strength and weakness of himself and his enemy with respect to power, place, time, proper times for military expeditions, proper times for mustering troops, revolt in the rear, losses, expenses, gains, and dangers.* Then, if he is of superior strength, he should march into battle; otherwise, he should remain stationary.

POWER

[2]"Between energy* and might, energy is superior; [3]for a king who is brave, strong, healthy, and skilled in weapons, even with the assistance of just his army, is able to defeat by himself a king possessing might. [4]Even a small army of his has the capacity to accomplish its goal by reason of its spirit. [5]A king possessing might but without energy, on the other hand, overpowered by aggressive force, perishes," so state the teachers.

[6]"No," says Kauṭilya. [7]"A king possessing might outwits a king possessing energy through his might by beckoning another king stronger than the other, and by hiring or purchasing eminent warriors. [8]His army, moreover, possessing abundant might, horses, elephants, chariots, and equipment, proceeds everywhere unhindered. [9]Those who possess might—even women, children, the lame, and the blind—have conquered the earth by winning over and purchasing those who possess energy."

[10]"Between might and counsel, might is superior; [11]for, when a man endowed with the power of counsel lacks might, his intellect becomes barren. [12]His lack of might, moreover, undoubtedly hurts his activities based on counsel, just as the lack of rain hurts the germinating grain," so state the teachers.

[13]"No," says Kauṭilya. [14]"The power of counsel is superior; [15]for a king, with the eyes of wisdom and science (8.2.9 n.), is able with even the slightest effort to embrace counsel and to outwit even enemies possessing energy and might through strategies such as conciliation (1.13.25 n.) and by means of secret measures (Book 5) and occult practices (Book 14)."

[16]Thus, among the powers of energy, might, and counsel, it is the man who has more of each later one who outwits.

PLACE

[17]Place means the earth (9.1.2 n.). [18]Within it, between the Himalayas and the sea longitudinally and 1,000 Yojanas* in extent latitudinally constitutes the territory of a universal sovereign.* [19]Within it, the special divisions are wild land, village land, hilly land, wet land, dry land, flat land, and rugged land. [20]In these, he should engage in activities that would enhance his strength. [21]Where the land is suitable for military operations of one's own army and unsuitable for those of the enemy's army, that is the best place; one that is the opposite of this is the worst; and one that is the same to both is middling.

TIME

[22]Time comprises cold, heat, and rain. [23]Its special divisions are night, day, fortnight, month, season, half-year, year, and Yuga (2.20.65–66 n.). [24]In these, he should engage in activities that would enhance his strength. [25]When the season is suitable for military operations of one's own army and unsuitable for those of the enemy's army, that is the best time; one that is the opposite of this is the worst; and one that is the same to both is middling.

[26]"Among power, place, and time, however, power is superior," say the teachers. [27]"For one who has power is able to employ countermeasures with respect to a place that contains water and dry land, and with respect to a time that is cold, hot, or rainy." [28]"Place is superior," say some. [29]"For a dog, when it is on dry land, drags around a crocodile, and a crocodile, when it is in water, drags around a dog." [30]"Time is superior," say some. [31]"During the day, a crow kills an owl, while during the night an owl kills a crow."* [32]"No," says Kauṭilya. [33]"For power, place, and time reinforce one another."

Topic 136: Proper Times for Military Expeditions

[34]When he has become strengthened by these, he should deploy one-third or one-fourth of his army in the home territory, at the rear, and in the tribal areas along the frontier for their protection and, taking a sufficient treasury and army to accomplish the mission, he should undertake a military expedition in Mārgaśīrṣa (November–December) against an enemy whose old food stocks have been depleted and new food stocks have not been gathered and whose fort has not been repaired, in order to destroy his rainy-season crop and his winter sowing. [35]He should undertake a military expedition in Caitra (March–April) to destroy his winter crop and his spring sowing. [36]Against an enemy whose grass, wood, and water have been depleted and whose fort has not been repaired, he should undertake a military expedition in Jyeṣṭhā (May–June) to destroy his spring crop and his rainy-season sowing.

[37]Against a region that is very hot and has little green fodder, firewood, and water, he should march in the winter. [38]Against a region that has bad snowy weather, a lot of unfordable waterways, or dense growths of grass and trees, he should march in the summer. [39]Against a region that is suited for the military operations of his own army and unsuitable for those of his enemy, he should march in the rainy season. [40]He should undertake a military expedition of long duration between the full-moon days of Mārgaśīrṣa (November–December) and Taiṣa (December–January); one of medium duration between the full-moon days of Caitra (March–April) and Vaiśākha (April–May); and one of short duration between the full-moon days of Jyeṣṭha (May–June) and Āṣāḍha (June–July); the fourth kind of military expedition is when one wants to burn things down during a calamity.* [41]Marching during a calamity has been explained in "Marching into Battle after Initiating Hostilities (7.4.14–17)."

[42]Further, teachers for the most part counsel: "One should march during a calamity affecting the enemy." [43]"One should march when one has grown in power, given the uncertainty surrounding calamities," says Kauṭilya; [44]"or else, one should march when after marching one is able to weaken or to vanquish the enemy."

[45]During a time when excessive heat has abated, he should march with regiments consisting mostly of elephants; [46]for elephants sweat internally and thus become leprous, [47]and when they cannot immerse in water and drink water, they have internal secretions and thus become blind.

[48]Therefore, one should march with regiments consisting mostly of elephants only in a region with abundant water and during the rainy season. [49]When conditions are opposite, he should march into a region with little rain or muddy areas with regiments consisting mostly of donkeys, camels, and horses. [50]In the rainy season, he should march into a region that is mostly desert with all four divisions of the army (2.33.9 n.).

[51]Or else, he should arrange his military expedition depending on whether the land is flat or rugged, or wet or dry, and whether the expedition is short or long.

> [52]Alternatively, all military expeditions may be of short duration when the mission is easy, or of long duration when the mission is difficult; and one may set up camp during the rains in the territory of the enemy.

THAT CONCLUDES THE FIRST CHAPTER: "ASCERTAINING THE RELATIVE STRENGTHS AND WEAKNESSES WITH RESPECT TO POWER, PLACE, AND TIME" AND "PROPER TIMES FOR MILITARY EXPEDITIONS" OF THE NINTH BOOK: "ACTIVITY OF A KING PREPARING TO MARCH INTO BATTLE."

Chapter 2

Topic 137: Proper Times for Deploying Troops

[1]These are the proper times for deploying hereditary troops, hired troops, corporate troops, troops supplied by the ally, troops supplied by the enemy, and tribal troops.

[2]The proper times for deploying hereditary troops are when there are hereditary troops in excess of what is required to defend the home territory; when hereditary troops containing an over-insertion unit (10.5.28 n.) could undermine the home territory; when it is necessary to fight using military operations against an opponent equipped with an army containing a large number of loyal hereditary troops or with an army containing strong men; when the distance or duration is long, because hereditary troops are able to bear losses and expenses; when a large number of loyal troops has been assembled and there is no confidence in other troops, such as hired troops, because of the fear that they may be subject to instigation by the adversary; and when all other kinds of troops have lost their strength.

[3]The proper times for deploying hired troops are when one thinks, "My hired troops are plentiful, and my hereditary troops are few"; or "The hereditary troops of my enemy are few or disloyal, and his hired troops contain mostly weak men or no strong men"; or "The war is to be waged through diplomatic strategy with limited military operations"; or "The distance and duration are short, entailing few losses and expenses"; or "My troops have few insertion units (10.5.28 n.), instigations within it have been suppressed, and I have confidence in it"; or "A small incursion by the enemy has to be repulsed."

[4]The proper times for deploying corporate troops are when one thinks, "My corporate troops are plentiful and capable of being deployed both in the home territory and in the expedition"; or "The time away from home is short"; or "The opponent has mostly corporate troops and intends to wage war through diplomatic strategy and military operations"; or "There is a commercial transaction of army troops (8.1.34 n.)."

[5]The proper times for deploying troops supplied by the ally are when one thinks, "The troops supplied by my ally are plentiful and capable of being deployed both in the home territory and in the expedition"; or "The time away from home is short, and the war using military operations will be more productive than the war of wits"; or "After first waging war against the tribal troops, the capital city, or the reinforcements* (8.1.38 n.), using the troops supplied by my ally, I will then wage war with my own troops"; or "I have a common mission with my ally"; or "The success of my mission depends on my ally"; or "My ally is nearby and deserves assistance"; or "I will destroy his over-insertion unit (10.5.28 n.)."

[6]The proper times for deploying troops supplied by the enemy are when one thinks, "Troops supplied by my foe are plentiful. I will wage war against the capital city or the tribal troops using the troops supplied by my foe.* In that situation, I will benefit by either outcome, like a Caṇḍāla at a fight between a dog and a boar (7.1.34 n.)"; or "I will make them the means of crushing the thorns among allied reinforcements or tribal troops." Now, he should always station troops supplied by the enemy that have swelled in numbers close at hand because of the danger of revolt, except when there is a concern that a revolt may arise in the interior (9.3.20)—or when the time for waging his own war is later than that of his foe.*

[7]That explains the proper times for deploying tribal troops. [8]These are the proper times for deploying tribal troops: when they are needed to guide the way; when they are suitable for the enemy terrain; when they are best at countering the enemy's mode of fighting; or when the enemy has

mostly tribal troops, thinking, "Let a wood apple be squashed by a wood apple;"* or when a small incursion has to be squashed.

[9]When an army is not a cohesive unit, is drawn from different places, and, whether sanctioned or not, rises up in order to plunder, it is an enterprising army (3.16.27n.). It receives no rations or wages and engages in plunder, forced labor, and rapine, and it can be divided by enemies. It cannot be divided when it is large and unified, and mostly consists of men from the same region, caste, and profession.

These are the proper times for deploying troops.

[10]Among these, he should provide forest produce or booty as wages for troops supplied by the enemy and for tribal troops. [11]Alternatively, when the time has come for the enemy to raise an army, he should confine the troops supplied by the foe,* dispatch them elsewhere, make them ineffective, make them live dispersed, or discharge them after that time has passed. [12]He should thwart the enemy, moreover, from deploying the army and secure it for himself.

Topic 138: Relative Values of Equipping for War

[13]Further, it is better to equip for war each previous one among these.* [14]Hereditary troops, because they have the same sentiment as he and always enjoy his respect, are better than hired troops. [15]Hired troops, being always nearby, quickly mobilized, and submissive, are better than corporate troops. [16]Corporate troops, coming from the countryside, coalescing for the common goal, and having the same rivalries, animosities, successes, and gains, are better than troops supplied by an ally. [17]Troops supplied by an ally, having no limitations as to place and time and because they coalesce for a common goal, are better than troops supplied by an enemy. [18]Troops supplied by an enemy, commanded by Āryas, are better than tribal troops. [19]Both the latter two have plunder as their aim, [20]and in the absence of plunder, as also during a calamity, they pose the same danger as a snake.

[21]"Among Brāhmaṇa, Kṣatriya, Vaiśya, and Śūdra troops, it is better to equip for battle each preceding one based on the predominance of spirit," say the teachers.

[22]"No," says Kauṭilya. [23]"An enemy may win over a Brāhmaṇa force by humble prostrations. [24]A Kṣatriya force that is trained in the science of weaponry, however, is better, or a Vaiśya or Śūdra force with a large number of strong men."

Topic 139: Deployment of Counterforces

[25]Therefore, he should deploy forces with the thought, "My enemy has these kinds of forces, and these are the counterforces against him."

[26]A force with elephants, mechanical devices, and carts at its center, and equipped with lances, javelins, spears, bamboos, and darts (2.18.7) is the counterforce for an elephant force. [27]The same, but with a large quantity of stones, clubs, armor, hooks, and "hair-grabbers," (2.36.18 n.), is the counterforce for a chariot force. [28]The counterforce for a cavalry force is the very same, or else elephants with armor or horses with armor. [29]Chariots with defensive coverings and infantrymen with protective armor are the counterforce for an army with the four divisions (2.33.9 n.).

> [30]In this manner, he should deploy forces that would repel the enemy's troops consistent with the strength of his own troops and the diversity of the troop divisions.

THAT CONCLUDES THE SECOND CHAPTER "PROPER TIMES FOR DEPLOYING TROOPS," "RELATIVE VALUES OF EQUIPPING FOR WAR," AND "DEPLOYMENT OF COUNTERFORCES" OF THE NINTH BOOK: "ACTIVITY OF A KING PREPARING TO MARCH INTO BATTLE."

Chapter 3

Topic 140: Reflection on the Revolt in the Rear

[1]Is it a small revolt in the rear or a large gain in the front (7.5.29 n.)? A small revolt in the rear is more serious; [2]for when the king has marched into battle, traitors, enemies, and tribal chiefs—or else a revolt of the constituents*—will amplify on all sides a small revolt in the rear. [3]Furthermore, when this happens, even after acquiring a large gain in the front, it will be consumed by his servants, allies, losses, and expenses. [4]Recognizing, therefore, that, when there is a revolt in the rear, the advantage from a gain in the front is one-thousandth part or perhaps one-hundredth, he should not march forth; [5]for there is a saying among the people: "Misfortunes have a mouth not bigger than a needle."*

[6]In the event of a revolt in the rear, he should employ conciliation, gifts, dissension, and military force (1.13.25 n.). [7]In the event of a gain in the front, he should appoint the Chief of the Armed Forces or the prince

to command the troops. [8]Alternatively, if the king is strong and is able to suppress a revolt in the rear, he should march into battle to secure a gain in the front.

Topic 141: Countermeasures against Revolts by Constituent Elements in Outlying Regions and in the Interior

[9]If he suspects that there may be a revolt in the interior, he should march into battle, taking with him those under suspicion or, if he suspects that there may be a revolt in the outlying regions, taking with him their* sons and wives. [10]After suppressing a revolt in the interior and installing a Regent* with various kinds of troops led by different commanders, he should march into battle; or else, he should not march into battle. [11]It has been stated earlier that a revolt in the interior is more dangerous than a revolt in the outlying regions.*

[12]A revolt in the interior is one initiated by one of the following: Counselor, Chaplain (7.15.27 n.), Chief of the Armed Forces, or Crown Prince. [13]He should subdue that person either by eliminating his own faults or in conformity with that person's power and crime. [14]Even in the case of a serious crime, the Chaplain is subdued by imprisonment or exile; the Crown Prince, by imprisonment or by execution if he has another virtuous son.

[15]He should subdue energetically a son or brother, or any other member of his family, who intends to usurp the kingdom; if he lacks energy, by ceding what he has seized or by entering into a pact with him, because of the fear that he may enter into a pact with the enemy. [16]Or else, he should reassure him by providing land grants to others similar to him. [17]Alternatively, he should deploy against him a military force stronger than his, a force that is permitted individual plunder (3.16.27n.), or else neighboring rulers or tribal chiefs. When he is engaged in hostilities with them, he should outwit him. [18]He should resort to the method for securing a prince in disfavor (1.18.13–16) or to the secret method of capturing an enemy settlement (13.1). [19]This also explains the counselor and the Chief of the Armed Forces.

[20]A revolt by any one of the interior ministers* apart from the Counselor and the rest (9.2.12) constitutes a revolt by interior ministers. [21]In this case also he should employ strategies (1.13.25 n.) as appropriate.

[22]A revolt by any one of the following—Provincial Chief, Frontier Commander, tribal chief, and a king who has surrendered with his troops

(7.15.21–30)—is a revolt in the outlying regions. [23]He should have that person suppressed using one another. [24]Or, if the man is firmly ensconced within a fort, he should have him suppressed using one of these: a neighbor, a tribal chief, a pretender from his family, and a prince in disfavor.

[25]Alternatively, he should get an ally to win him over, so that he does not go over to the enemy; [26]or else, a secret agent should divide him from the enemy by telling him:

> This man thinks that you are a covert agent, and he will make you attack the lord himself. When his aim has been achieved, he will make you lead troops against enemy kings and tribal chiefs or in a difficult enterprise; or he will make you reside at the frontier without your wife and sons. [27]When your attack has been repulsed, he will make a deal with your lord for you; or else, he will make a pact using you and propitiate that very lord. [28]Alternatively, go to the close ally of his (see 5.5.14).

[29]If he agrees, he should honor him by fulfilling his fondest wishes. [30]If he does not agree, he should divide him from the one with whom he has sought refuge, telling the latter: "That man has been deployed as a covert agent against you." [31]And a secret agent should have him killed by means of royal decrees carried by men condemned to death* or through clandestine operatives. [32]Alternatively, he should win over eminent warriors who had left with that man by fulfilling their wishes; [33]and a secret agent should expose them as deployed by him.* [34]Thus is success achieved!

[35]Furthermore, he should arrange for these sorts of revolts to rise up against the enemy and suppress the ones against himself.

[36]One should instigate to sedition someone who has the capacity to foment a revolt or to suppress one.

[37]When the man is true to his agreements and has the capacity to render assistance in carrying out a task and in securing its reward and to rescue him in case of failure, he should respond favorably to his instigation; and he should ponder whether that man has an honest intent or is a fraud.

[38]For thinking that,

> If he kills his master and installs me as the king, I will secure a double gain: death of the enemy and the acquisition of land. Or else, the

> enemy will kill him; and because of that, the faction consisting of the slain man's relatives and those alarmed at being punished for a similar crime will provide me with a faction that is large and unseducible. Or, he will become suspicious also of others like that man; and I will get his other chiefs killed one by one by means of royal decrees carried by men condemned to death* (9.3.31 n.);

a fraud from the outlying regions will instigate an official in the interior.[39]Alternatively, thinking that

> I will loot his treasury. Or, I will kill his troops. Or, I will get him to kill the wicked master. If the official from the outlying region complies, I will make him attack the enemies or tribal chiefs. Let his troops get stuck. Let his enmity become cemented. Then he will fall under my control. Thereafter, I will propitiate the master himself or seize the kingdom myself. Alternatively, I will first imprison him, and then I will take possession of both the territory of the official from the outlying region and the territory of the master. Or else, when he has rebelled, I will invite the official of the outlying region who has placed his confidence in me and then have him killed. Or, I will seize his empty home territory* (7.13.6 n.);

a fraud from the interior will instigate an official of the outlying regions.

[40]A man with honest intent, however, undertakes an instigation for the benefit of those who live with him. [41]One should make a pact with a man with honest intent, whereas one should agree with a fraud, saying "Yes," and then outwit him.

[42]Having comprehended this,—

> a wise man should protect outsiders from outsiders, his own people from his own people, his own people from outsiders, outsiders from his own people, and his own self both from his own people and from outsiders.

THAT CONCLUDES THE THIRD CHAPTER: "REFLECTION ON THE REVOLT IN THE REAR" AND "COUNTERMEASURES AGAINST REVOLTS BY CONSTITUENT ELEMENTS IN OUTLYING REGIONS AND IN THE INTERIOR" OF THE NINTH BOOK: "ACTIVITY OF A KING PREPARING TO MARCH INTO BATTLE."

Chapter 4

Topic 142: Discussion of Losses, Expenses, and Gains

[1]A decrease of draught animals and men constitutes loss, [2]while a decrease in money and grain constitutes expenditure.

[3]When the gain is many times greater than these two, he should march into battle.

[4]The attributes of a successful gain* are as follows: it is fit to be seized, it is fit to be recovered, it causes gratification, it causes revolt, it is done in a short time, it entails a small loss, it requires little expenditure, it is large, it gives rising profits, it is safe, it is righteous, and it is a forerunner.*

[5]When it is easy to obtain and to protect, and it cannot be recovered by the enemies, then it is fit to be seized. [6]When the opposite is true, it is fit to be recovered. [7]A man who seizes it or who dwells in it will perish.

[8]Or, if he were to foresee,

After seizing what can be recovered,

> I will dismantle its treasury, army, stocks, and defensive arrangements;
>
> I will make its pit mines, produce forests, elephant forests, irrigation works, and trade routes robbed of everything valuable;
>
> I will impoverish its subjects, abduct them (2.1.1 n.), or win them over with agreeable measures, whereas later (the enemy) will inflame them with disagreeable measures;
>
> I will sell it to an opponent of his, or present it to his ally or a prince in disfavor;
>
> I will stay right here and take counter measures against harassment of my country or that of my ally by robbers and adversaries;
>
> I will make his ally or patron understand his iniquity, and then, disaffected with the enemy, he will turn to a pretender from his family;
>
> Or I will honor him and give the land to him, so that I will have for a long time an ally who is allied with me and will act in concert with me;

he should seize even a gain that can be recovered.

[9]Thus, what is fit to be seized and what is fit to be recovered have been explained.

[10]When a righteous king secures a gain from an unrighteous king, it gratifies both his own people and those of his enemy. [11]A gain that is the opposite of it causes revolt.

[12]When he fails to secure a gain that was recommended by counselors, it provokes a revolt, because they think, "We have caused him to incur losses and expenses." [13]When he secures a gain ignoring the advice of traitorous counselors, it provokes a revolt, because they think, "Having secured his object, he will destroy us." [14]A gain that is the opposite of it is what causes gratification.

[15]Thus, what causes a revolt and what causes gratification have been explained.

[16]Because it can be secured by an expedition alone, it is done in a short time. [17]Because it can be secured by diplomatic strategy, it entails a small loss. [18]Because the only expenditure is food, it requires little expenditure. [19]Because of its current immensity, it is large. [20]Because of continuous advantages, it gives rising profits. [21]Because it is not beset with perils, it is safe. [22]Because it is obtained in an honorable manner, it is righteous. [23]Because it accrues to the consociates without restrictions, it is a forerunner.

[24]When the gain is equal, he should consider the place and time, the power and strategy, and whether it is going to be agreeable or disagreeable, fast or slow, near or far, immediate or gradual, valuable or continuous, and abundant or with a lot of advantages, and then secure the gain possessing a lot of advantages.

[25]These are the obstacles for securing gains: lust, anger, anxiety, pity, bashfulness, an ignoble disposition, pride, compassion, concern for the other world, righteousness, lack of liberality, dejection, envy, contempt for what one has, wickedness, lack of trust, fear, failure to take countermeasures, inability to bear cold, heat, and rain, and attachment to auspicious days and constellations.

> [26]Riches pass over the fool who overly consults constellations, for riches are the constellation of riches; what will stars do?
> [27]Men without means do not obtain riches even if they try 100 times. Riches are captured with riches, like elephants with elephants.

THAT CONCLUDES THE FOURTH CHAPTER: "DISCUSSION OF LOSSES, EXPENSES, AND GAINS" OF THE NINTH BOOK: "ACTIVITY OF A KING PREPARING TO MARCH INTO BATTLE."

Chapter 5

Topic 143: Dangers from the Outlying Regions and from the Interior

[1]The employment of a peace pact and the like in a manner contrary to what is prescribed* is bad policy. [2]From that arise dangers.

[3]An instigation originating in the outer regions and responded to from the interior; an instigation originating in the interior and responded to from the outer regions; an instigation originating in the outer regions and responded to from the outer regions; and an instigation originating in the interior and responded to from the interior—these are the dangers.

[4]In a situation where those in the outer regions instigate those in the interior or those in the interior instigate those in the outer regions, it is more advantageous, when there is guile at both ends, to suppress the one who responds to the instigation; [5]for those who respond to an instigation are the ones who are most deceitful, and not the instigators. [5]When they have been subdued, the instigators will not be able to instigate any others; [6]for people in the outer regions find it difficult to instigate those in the interior, and the latter, the former. [8]For the enemies, moreover, this constitutes the frustration of an enormous effort, and for oneself a continuous advantage.

[9]When those in the interior are responding to instigations, he should employ conciliation and gifts. [10]Conciliation consists of conferring a position or bestowing honors. [11]Gifts consist of favors and exemption or employment in tasks.

[12]When those in the outer regions are responding to instigations, he should employ dissension and military force. [13]Or else, secret agents posing as allies of people in the outer regions should communicate to them this secret information: "This king intends to outwit you using people posing as traitors. Be on your guard." [14]Alternatively, individuals posing as traitors and assigned to the traitors should alienate the traitors from those in the outer regions, or those in the outer regions from the traitors.

[15]Or else, assassins, gaining the trust of the traitors, should kill them with weapons or poison; [16]or, having invited those in the outer regions, they should have them killed.

[17]In a situation where those in the outer regions instigate others in the outer regions, or those in the interior instigate others in the interior, it is more advantageous, when there is guile at only one end, to suppress the one initiating the instigation; [18]for once treachery has been purged, there will be no traitors, [19]whereas once the traitors have been purged, treachery will again incite others to treason.*

[20]Therefore, when those in the outer regions instigate, he should employ dissension and military force. [21]Or else, secret agents posing as allies should tell them: "This king himself intends to seize you. This king has initiated hostilities against you. Be on your guard!" [22]Alternatively, assassins, gaining the trust of the envoys or troops of the man who responds favorably to the instigations, should attack them at their weak points with weapons, poison, and the like. [23]Thereupon, secret agents should accuse the man who responded to the instigations of that crime.

[24]When those in the interior instigate others in the interior, he should employ a strategy that is appropriate. [25]Against someone who is discontented but shows signs of contentment—or against someone who is the inverse of this—he should employ conciliation. [26]Gifts consist of bestowing honors under the pretext of recognizing someone's honesty or skill, or in consideration of a calamitous or propitious occasion. [27]Or else, an agent posing as an ally should tell them: "The king will subject you to a secret test to discover your inner thoughts. You should disclose them to him." [28]Or, he should alienate them from each other: "This man and that other man are secretly communicating this to the king about you"—that is dissension. [29]And force is used as in the infliction of punishment (5.1).

[30]Among these four dangers, it is the internal danger that he should suppress first. [31]It has been already stated above that an internal revolt, because of the snake-like danger it poses, is more harmful than an external revolt (8.2.3).

> [32]One should understand that among the dangers (9.5.3), each prior one is less serious than each subsequent one, or that the one posed by more powerful men is more serious and the opposite is less serious.

THAT CONCLUDES THE FIFTH CHAPTER: "DANGERS FROM THE OUTLYING REGIONS AND FROM THE INTERIOR" OF THE NINTH BOOK: "ACTIVITY OF A KING PREPARING TO MARCH INTO BATTLE."

Chapter 6

Topic 144: Dangers Associated with Traitors and Foes

[1]Danger* from traitors and danger from enemies: These are the two kinds of simple danger.

[2]In the case of a simple danger coming from traitors, he should use strategies against people in the city or in the countryside with the exception of military force (2.10.47); [3]for it is not possible to use military force against a large number of people. [4]Or, even when it is used, it does not achieve the desired result, on the one hand, and gives rise to some other undesirable result, on the other. [5]Against their leaders, however, he should act as in the infliction of punishment (5.1).

[6]In the case of a simple danger coming from enemies, he should seek to subdue the enemy, whether he is the principal or a subordinate official, through strategies such as conciliation at the location where the enemy resides. [7]Subduing the principal depends on the lord, while subduing the dependents depends on the counselors, and subduing the principal and the dependents depends on both.

[8]When traitors and non-traitors join together, it is called a joint danger. [9]In the case of a joint danger, the subduing is accomplished through the non-traitorous party; [10]for when the prop is gone, there will be no one who is propped up.

[11]When allies and enemies collaborate, it is called a joint-enemy danger. [12]In the case of a joint-enemy danger, the subduing is accomplished through the ally; [13]for it is easy to make a pact with an ally, not with an enemy (7.13.17).

[14]If the ally does not want to enter into a pact, he should constantly instigate him. [15]Then, getting secret agents to alienate him from the enemy, he should win over the ally. [16]Or else, he should win over the one located at the outer edge of the confederacy of allies.* [17]Once the one located at the outer edge is won over, those located at the center become alienated. [18]Alternatively, he should win over the one located at the center. [19]Once the one located at the center is won over, those located at the outer edge will not stand united.

[20]He should employ those strategies, furthermore, that would alienate them from their base of support.

[21]He should appease a righteous king by praising his ancestry, family, learning, and conduct, by pointing out the relationship of their ancestors, or by offering assistance to him or refraining from harming him during all three times (8.4.21 n.).

[22]He should subdue through conciliation a king of upright intentions who is bereft of enterprise, who is exhausted by hostilities, whose strategies have been thwarted, who is tormented by loses and expenses and by absence from home, who is seeking another ally because of his honesty, who is apprehensive of some other ally, or who prizes friendship.

[23]He should subdue a king who is greedy or impoverished through gifts preceded by the appointment of a recluse or a chief (7.17.8) as surety. [24]Gifts fall into five categories: surrendering one's claim to what the other owes, allowing the other to keep what he has seized, giving back what one has taken, giving one's own property never given before, and giving permission for individual plunder (3.16.27n.) of an enemy's property. [25]That is the giving of gifts.

[26]When a king is apprehensive because of mutual hatred or enmity or fearing the seizure of his land, he should cause him to be alienated using one of them.* [27]Or else, he should alienate a timid king by pointing out the risk of reprisal: "After making a peace pact, this man will move against you. He has dispatched his ally. You are not part of the peace negotiation."

[28]Or, when merchandise is delivered to someone as royal gifts either from his own territory or from that of someone else, secret agents should spread the rumor: "He has received this from the king against whom a military expedition has been planned." [29]When this rumor has been spread wide, he should send a royal decree through a man condemned to death (2.5.4 n.): "I have sent you this merchandise *or** this royal gift. Either attack the consociates or flee. After that you will receive the rest of the amount we have agreed upon." [30]Thereafter, secret agents should spread the word among the enemies: "This was given by your enemy."

[31]Alternatively, a piece of merchandise widely known to belong to the foe should be transferred without his knowledge to the seeker after conquest. [32]Agents working undercover as traders associated with the latter should offer it for sale among the chiefs of the foe. [33]Then secret agents

should spread the word among the enemies: "This piece of merchandise was given to your enemy."

[34]Alternatively, he should regale men guilty of serious crimes with money and honors and deploy them against the enemy with weapons, poison, and fire. [35]Then he should get one of his ministers to defect* [36]and, after placing his wife and sons under protective custody, have it proclaimed that they were killed at night. [37]Then the minister should reveal those criminals to the enemy one by one—[38]he should not get them arrested if they carry out their instructions, [39]or get them arrested if they are unable to carry them out. [40]When he has secured a position of trust, he should inform the enemy that he should guard himself against his chief. [41]Then a double agent should get the enemy's royal decree for the killing of the chief impounded.

[42]Or else, he should send a decree to one who possesses the power of energy (7.15.5), saying, "Seize that man's kingdom. Our pact will continue as before." [43]Then secret agents should have it impounded in the midst of the enemies.

[44]They* should destroy the military camp, military supplies, or reinforcements of one (of the confederates). [45]While they professes friendship with the others, they should secretly instigate him: "You have been targeted by them for assassination."

[46]Or, when an eminent warrior, elephant, or steed of someone dies or is killed or abducted by clandestine operatives, secret agents should spread the word that it has been killed by one of them.* [47]Then he should send a royal decree to the accused, saying, "Do more similar things. Then you will receive the rest of the amount we have agree upon." [48]Double agents should get it impounded.

[49]When they are alienated from each other, he should win over one of them.

[50]The above also explains* the Chief of the Armed Forces, the prince, and military commanders.

[51]Furthermore, he should employ methods of creating dissension recommended for confederacies (11.1). [52]These are the activities fostering dissension.

[53]Clandestine operatives should subdue a foe who is fierce or energetic, or who has been struck by a calamity or is entrenched (7.10.7 n.), using weapons, fire, poison, and the like. Or else, one of them should carry it out depending on the ease with which it can be accomplished, [54]for a single assassin may subdue someone with weapons, poison, or

fire. [55]Such a man will do the work of an entire army gathered together, or even more.

[56]Those are the four kinds of strategy.* [57]Among them, each preceding one is simpler. [58]Conciliation is singular. [59]Giving gifts is twofold, being preceded by* conciliation. [60]Sowing dissension is threefold, being preceded by* conciliation and giving gifts. [61]Military force is fourfold, being preceded by* conciliation, giving gifts, and sowing dissension.

[62]These have been prescribed with reference to those who initiate attacks.

[63]With regard to those who are located in their own territories, however, the strategies are the very same. [64]The following, however, are the special steps: [65]He should frequently dispatch well-known leading envoys carrying royal gifts with them to one of the confederates located in their own territories. [66]They should urge him either to enter into a peace pact or to kill the others. [67]If he does not agree, they should broadcast the news: "He has entered into a pact with us!" [68]Double agents should expose him to the others, saying, "This king of yours is a traitor."

[69]Alternatively, if fear, enmity, or hatred is directed by one of them toward another, they should alienate the latter from the former by saying, "This man has entered into a peace pact with your foe. Before he outwits you, quickly conclude a peace pact and strive to subdue him."

[70]Or else, after forging an alliance by giving and taking wives, he should divide those who are outside the alliance.

[71]He should, furthermore, get neighboring rulers, tribal chiefs, pretenders from their families, or princes in disfavor to devastate their realms, or their caravans, herds, and forests, or troops coming to render assistance. [72]Castes and confederacies that are supported by each other* should strike at their vulnerable points, and clandestine operatives should strike them with fire, poison, and weapons.

> [73]When there is a joint-enemy danger (9.6.11), resorting to trickery, he should kill the enemies by employing secret measures, like a fowler using a cloak and a lure, by creating confidence and offering a bait.

THAT CONCLUDES THE SIXTH CHAPTER: "DANGERS ASSOCIATED WITH TRAITORS AND FOES" OF THE NINTH BOOK: "ACTIVITY OF A KING PREPARING TO MARCH INTO BATTLE."

Chapter 7

Topic 145: Dangers Associated with Advantage, Disadvantage, and Uncertainty

[1]Indiscretions such as a love affair (1.15.11) incite the constituents* of his own realm to revolt, while bad policy incites outside constituents.* [2]These two together constitute demonic conduct. [3]Revolt consists of the disaffection of one's own people.

[4]With reference to things that cause an enemy to prosper, there could be an advantage coupled with danger, a disadvantage, and an uncertainty.

[5]An advantage that, if not secured for oneself, will cause an enemy to prosper, that when secured may be recovered by the foes, or that entails losses and expenses while it is being secured is an advantage coupled with danger. [6]For example, a gain available due to a calamity affecting a neighboring ruler and thus a bait for the neighboring rulers; or a gain coveted by a foe and obtainable by him because of its very nature; a gain in the front that generates hostilities through a revolt in the rear or by the rear enemy; a gain that is opposed by the circle because it entails the vanquishing of an ally or the contravention of a pact—these are examples of an advantage coupled with danger.

[7]When there is a danger arising from his own people or from an enemy, it is a disadvantage.

[8]Between these two,* when one questions: "Is this an advantage or not?" "Is this a disadvantage or not?" "Is this advantage actually a disadvantage?" "Is this disadvantage actually an advantage?"—it is uncertainty. [9]There is uncertainty as to whether it is an advantage or not to rouse up an ally of the foe. [10]There is uncertainty as to whether it is a disadvantage or not to entice troops of the foe with money and honors. [11]There is uncertainty as to whether the advantage in seizing land from people with powerful neighbors is actually a disadvantage. [12]There is uncertainty as to whether the disadvantage in marching after joining forces with a more powerful king is actually an advantage. [13]Among these, he should opt for the uncertainty relating to an advantage.*

[14]An advantage followed up by an advantage; an advantage without a follow-up; an advantage followed up a disadvantage; a disadvantage followed up by an advantage; a disadvantage without a follow-up; and a disadvantage followed up by a disadvantage—these are the six kinds of follow-ups. [15]Capturing the rear enemy after extirpating the foe is an

advantage followed up by an advantage. [16]Assisting a neutral king with troops in exchange for a reward is an advantage without a follow-up. [17]Vanquishing an intermediate king of the enemy is an advantage followed up by a disadvantage. [18]Assisting the neighbor of a foe with treasure and troops is a disadvantage followed up by an advantage. [19]Remaining inactive after rousing up a weak king is a disadvantage without a follow-up. [29]Remaining inactive after provoking a stronger king is a disadvantage followed up by a disadvantage. [21]Among these, it is better to pursue each preceding one.

[22]So are laid down the tasks.*

[23]When advantages present themselves simultaneously from all sides, that constitutes a danger from advantages from all sides. [24]The same, when it is opposed by the rear enemy, constitutes a danger from uncertainty concerning advantages from all sides. [25]In these two cases, success is achieved through the assistance of the ally and the rear ally.

[26]When perils from foes present themselves from all sides, that constitutes a danger from disadvantages from all sides. [27]The same, when it is opposed by an ally, constitutes a danger from uncertainty concerning disadvantages from all sides. [28]In these two cases, success is achieved through the assistance of a mobile enemy (7.10.9 n.) and the rear ally, or by employing the methods for counteracting a joint-enemy danger (9.6.11f).

[29]There is a gain from this side and a gain from the other side: This constitutes a danger from advantages from both sides. [30]In this case and in the case with advantages from all sides, he should march into battle to secure the advantage that possesses the qualities of a gain (9.4.4). [31]In case the qualities of a gain are the same, he should march into battle to secure the one that is eminent, or that is close by, or that does not permit a delay, or in which he is deficient.

[32]There is a disadvantage from this side and a disadvantage from the other side: This constitutes a danger from a disadvantage from both sides. [33]In this case and in the case of a danger from a disadvantage from all sides, he should seek to achieve success by means of allies. [34]If allies are unavailable, he should surmount a danger from a disadvantage from one side by means of a constituent element of lesser importance,* and a danger from a disadvantage from two sides by means of a constituent element of greater importance; while he should deal with a danger from a disadvantage from all sides by means his home territory.* [35]If he is unable to do that, he should abandon everything and flee; [36]for we see examples of people who, remaining alive, made a comeback, such as Suyātra and Udayana.*

[37]There is a gain from this side and an attack on the kingdom from the other side: This constitutes a danger from an advantage and a disadvantage from both sides. [38]In this case, he should march into battle to secure the advantage that would overcome the disadvantage; [39]for, otherwise, he would simply thwart the attack on the kingdom.* [40]This also explains the danger from advantages and disadvantages from all sides.

[41]There is a disadvantage from this side and uncertainty concerning an advantage from the other side: This constitutes a danger from a disadvantage and uncertainty concerning an advantage from both sides. [42]In this case, he should first overcome the disadvantage and, when that is overcome, deal with the uncertainty concerning the advantage. [43]This also explains the danger from a disadvantage and uncertainty concerning an advantage from all sides.

[44]There is an advantage from this side and uncertainty concerning a disadvantage from the other side: This constitutes a danger from an advantage and uncertainty concerning a disadvantage from both sides.* [45]This also explains the danger associated with an advantage and uncertainty concerning a disadvantage from all sides. [46]In this latter case, he should try to rescue each earlier one among the constituent elements (6.1.1) from the uncertainty concerning a disadvantage before each later one; [47]for it is better that the ally remain uncertain concerning a disadvantage and not the army, or the army and not the treasury. [48]When it is not possible to rescue an entire constituent, he should try to rescue segments of the constituents. [49]Of these, among the human constituents, he should rescue the ones that are more numerous or loyal, except the fierce and the greedy; and among the material constituents (6.1.8–11), the ones that are valuable or of greater benefit. [50]He should rescue the less important ones using the strategies of a peace pact, remaining stationary, and the double stratagem, and the more important ones using their opposites.* [51]Among decline, stability, and prosperity (6.2.5), he should seek to achieve each succeeding one over each preceding. [52]Alternatively, he may do the reverse if he foresees a special future advantage in decline and so forth.

[53]So are laid down the places (9.7.22 n.).

[54]This also explains the encountering of an advantage, a disadvantage, and uncertainty at the beginning, middle, and end of a military expedition.

[55]Because advantage, disadvantage, and uncertainty have an immediate effect, moreover, it is better to encounter an advantage at the beginning of a military expedition with respect to overcoming the rear enemy and his

backer, compensating for losses, expenses, and absence from home, and protecting the home territory. [56]Likewise, a person remaining in his own territory is able to endure a disadvantage or uncertainty.

[57]This also explains the encountering of an advantage, a disadvantage, and uncertainty in the middle of a military expedition.

[58]It is better, however, to encounter an advantage at the end of a military expedition, after he has weakened someone who needed to be weakened or vanquished someone who needed to be vanquished, but not a disadvantage or an uncertainty, because of the fear of perils posed by the enemy.

[59]Among consociates, on the other hand, it is better for one who is not the leader to encounter a disadvantage or an uncertainty in the middle or at the end of a military expedition, because it will affect all without restrictions.

[60]Advantage (*artha*), righteousness (*dharma*), and pleasure (*kāma*): These constitute the Triple Set relating to advantage.* [61]Of that, it is better to encounter each preceding one than each following.

[62]Disadvantage (*anartha*), unrighteousness (*adharma*), and sorrow (*śoka*): These constitute the Triple Set relating to disadvantage. [63]Of that, it is better to counteract each preceding one than each following.

[64]Is it an advantage or a disadvantage (7.5.29 n.)? Is it righteous or unrighteous? Is it pleasure or sorrow? These constitute the Triple Set relating to uncertainty. [65]Of that, it is better to encounter the first alternative after subduing the second.

[66]So are laid down the times (9.7.22 n.).

These are the dangers.

Topic 146: Overcoming These Dangers through Various Means

[67]Next, overcoming them.

[68]The appropriate way to overcome them in the case of sons, brothers, and relatives is through conciliation and giving gifts; in the case of leaders among the people of the city and the countryside, and among the troops, through giving gifts and sowing dissension; in the case of neighboring rulers and tribal leaders, through sowing dissension and military force. [69]These are the normal ways of overcoming; the opposite are the abnormal.*

[70]In the case of allies and enemies, they are overcome through a combination of these; [71]for strategies bolster each other.

[72]In the case of the ministers of a foe who are under suspicion, the use of conciliation obviates the use of the others; in the case of treasonable ministers, the use of gifts; in the case of confederates, the use of dissension; and in the case of powerful individuals, the use of military force.

[73]Depending on the gravity or the triviality of the dangers, there is restriction, option, or combination. [74]"Only by this strategy and none other"—that is restriction. [75]"By this or by that"—that is option. [76]"By this and by that"—that is combination.*

[77]Among these, there are four operations when used singly, as also when used in threes; six when used in twos; and one when used in fours.* [78]Thus, there are 15 strategies; [79]and the same number when they are used in the abnormal way.

[80]Among these, overcoming through one strategy constitutes a single overcoming; overcoming using two strategies constitutes a double overcoming; overcoming using three strategies constitutes a triple overcoming; and overcoming using four strategies constitutes a quadruple overcoming. [81]Given that advantage (*artha*) is rooted in righteousness (*dharma*) and results in pleasure (*kāma*), the achievement* of advantage resulting in continuous righteousness, advantage, and pleasure constitutes achievement in all objectives* (9.7.60 n.).

These constitute overcoming (9.7.67).

[82]These dangers are caused by fate: fire, water, disease, epidemic, panic, famine, and demonic creation.* [83]These are overcome by homage paid to gods and Brāhmaṇas.

> [84]Excessive rain, lack of rain, or a demonic creation; these are overcome through Atharvan rites and interventions by thaumaturgic ascetics.

THAT CONCLUDES THE SEVENTH CHAPTER: "DANGERS ASSOCIATED WITH ADVANTAGE, DISADVANTAGE, AND UNCERTAINTY" AND "OVERCOMING THESE DANGERS THROUGH VARIOUS MEANS" OF THE NINTH BOOK: "ACTIVITY OF A KING PREPARING TO MARCH INTO BATTLE."

THAT CONCLUDES THE NINTH BOOK: "ACTIVITY OF A KING PREPARING TO MARCH INTO BATTLE" OF KAUṬILYA'S *ARTHAŚĀSTRA*.

Book Ten

On War

Chapter 1

Topic 147: Setting up the Military Camp

[1]On a site recommended as a building site (1.20.1 n.), the commander, carpenters, and astrologers should have a military camp constructed during a time of danger and when it is time to halt, a military camp that is circular, rectangular, or square, or in accordance with the terrain, that has four gates, six paths, and nine zones, and is outfitted with a moat, a rampart, a parapet, gates, and turrets.*

[2]The royal compound should be located in the one-ninth sector to the north of the middlemost (2.4.7). It should be 100 Dhanuṣes long and half as much wide. The royal residence should be located in its western half. [3]At its perimeter, moreover, he should station the palace guard. [4]At the front, he should set up the assembly hall; to the right, the treasury and the offices for issuing royal commands and for assigning tasks; to the left, the yard for elephants, horses, and carriages for the use of the king.

[5]Beyond that are to be located four enclosures, each separated from the next by 100 Dhanuṣes, constructed with posts in a cart formation, columns in a creeper formation, or a parapet.*

[6]Within the first, the Counselor and Chaplain are housed in the front; the storehouse and kitchen on the right (2.4.8); and the depot for forest produce and the armory on the left (2.4.10). [7]Within the second are the quarters for hereditary and hired troops, for horses and chariots, and for the Chief of the Armed Forces. [8]Within the third are housed the elephants, corporate troops, and the camp administrator (10.1.17). [9]Within the fourth

are housed the laborers and the commander, as well as troops supplied by the ally and the enemy and tribal troops, all under the command of his own officers.

[10]Traders and prostitutes should be located along the main highway. [11]Fowlers and those who hunt with dogs should be located outside the camp carrying drums and fire,* as also undercover sentries. [12]Along the path through which an enemy may attack, he should have pits, hidden traps, and barbed strips positioned (2.3.15). [13]He should have the guards of the 18 groups* rotated [14]and daytime watches also maintained in order to spot spies.

[15]He should stamp out disputes, drinking, fairs, and gambling, and keep the seal guarded.

[16]The Regent (9.3.10 n.) should arrest any soldier who returns from the army without a written permit.

> [17]The camp administrator should travel ahead on the road and get the carpenters and laborers to construct properly the defenses and water sources.

THAT CONCLUDES THE FIRST CHAPTER:"SETTING UP THE MILITARY CAMP" OF THE TENTH BOOK: "ON WAR."

Chapter 2

Topic 148: Marching into Battle from the Military Camp

[1]He should undertake a military expedition after estimating the encampments in villages and wild tracts along the way contingent on the supply of green fodder, firewood, and water, as well as the time for sojourns, stopovers, and travel. [2]He should arrange for the transport of double the quantity of rations and equipment needed to take care of those eventualities. [3]Alternatively, if he is unable to do so, he should either delegate it to the soldiers or stockpile them at intervals along the way.

[4]The commander in the front, the lord and his family in the center, horses on the flanks to repel attacks (10.4.13), elephants or expansive foraging raids* at the borders of the wheel formation (10.1.5 n.), and the Chief of the Armed Forces in the rear—so should they march and encamp.

[5]Obtaining subsistence from forests on all sides constitutes a foraging raid. [6]Influx from one's own country constitutes supplies. [7]Troops

supplied by an ally constitute reinforcements. [8]The location of the family is the hideaway.*

[9]If an attack is expected from the front, he should march in the crocodile formation (10.6.27); if from the rear, in the cart formation (10.6.26); if from the two flanks, in the harpoon formation (10.6.35 n.); if from all sides, in the "propitious-on-all-sides" formation (10.6.31); and in a terrain where only marching single file is possible, in the needle formation (10.6.20).

[10]When there are two alternate routes, he should march on terrain best suited for him; [11]for in a battle those who operate on terrain best suited for them get the better of those operating in terrain least suitable for them.

[12]Traveling one Yojana is the lowest speed;* one and a half Yojanas, the middle speed; and two Yojanas, the highest speed; or else the speed should be determined according to what is achievable.

[13]When he has to take countermeasures against a rear enemy, his backer, the intermediate king, or the neutral king who is providing shelter or destroying quality land (7.10.2 n.); when he has to clear a dangerous route; when he has to wait for the treasury, the army, the troops supplied by an ally or an enemy, tribal troops, laborers, or the proper season; or when he thinks, "A degradation of the fortification, stockpiles, and defensive measures undertaken by him, despondency on the part of the troops he has purchased, and despondency on the part of troops supplied by his ally will come about"; or "Those who have been dispatched to instigate sedition are not acting very swiftly"; or "My foe will accede to my demands"—under these conditions he should march slowly, and under opposite conditions, quickly.

[14]He should arrange the crossing of bodies of water using elephants, bridges of tree trunks, dikes, boats, and pontoons of wood and bamboo, as well as gourds, leather baskets, skin bags, rafts, tree trunks, and ropes (7.10.32). [15]If the ford is in enemy hands, he should cross at another point during the night with the help of elephants and horses and get to a secure location (7.15.22 n.).

[16]In a waterless region, he should have wagons and draught animals transport according to their capacity the amount of water needed for the journey.

Topic 149: Guarding at a Time of Calamity to the Army and of a Surprise Attack

[17]He should provide protection for his own troops and launch an attack against enemy troops in the following situations: When they are in a long

stretch of wasteland, in a waterless region, without green fodder, firewood, and water, or on an arduous road; when they are shattered by an attack, exhausted by hunger, thirst, and travel, or engaged in climbing up or down hills, canyons, or rivers filled deep with mud or water; when they are crowding in large numbers along a path requiring travel in a single file, a rugged and hilly terrain, or a narrow route; when they are bereft of equipment within the camp or on the road; when they are occupied with a meal, exhausted by a long march, sleeping, or troubled by diseases, epidemics, or famine; when they contain sick infantrymen, horses, and elephants; when they are in an unsuitable terrain; or during calamities affecting an army (8.5.1–18).

[18]An assessment of the enemy's army is made by counting the soldiers marching through a route requiring travel in a single file, as also the fodder, foodstuffs, beds, bedding, fire receptacles, banners, and weapons. [19]He should conceal these same items belonging to him.

> [20]He should fight as well as set up camp on terrain suitable for him, after he has set up at his rear a hill fort or a forest fort equipped with a place of retreat and rear reserve troops (8.1.38 n.).

THAT CONCLUDES THE SECOND CHAPTER: "MARCHING INTO BATTLE FROM THE MILITARY CAMP" AND "GUARDING AT A TIME OF CALAMITY TO THE ARMY AND OF A SURPRISE ATTACK" OF THE TENTH BOOK: "ON WAR."

Chapter 3

Topic 150: Kinds of Covert Military Operations

[1]When he has the stronger military force, when secret instigations to sedition have been carried out, when precautionary measures have been taken with regard to the season, and when operations are carried out on terrain suitable for himself, he should undertake open military operations; [2]in the opposite case, covert military operations.

[3]He should attack the enemy during times of calamity affecting an army (8.5.1–18) or at an opportune time for a surprise attack (10.2.17); or when he is operating on terrain suitable for himself, while the enemy is operating in a terrain unsuitable for him; or even when the enemy is in a suitable terrain, but he himself has the strong support of his constituents.

[4]Alternatively, after creating a fake breach through traitorous troops, troops supplied by the enemy, or tribal troops, he should attack him when he has reached an inhospitable terrain. [5]He should breach a compact military formation with the use of elephants. [6]When someone who had first given him chase after he has faked a breach is now himself breached, he, remaining unbreached, should turn around and attack him.

[7]He should attack him from the front first and, when he is tottering or turns back, he should attack him from the rear with elephant brigades and cavalry. [8]He should attack him from the rear first and, when he is tottering or turns back, he should attack him from the front with his most powerful troops. [9]This also explains attacks on the two flanks. [10]Or else, he should attack at the point where there are traitorous or weak troops.

[11]When the terrain in the front is rugged, he should attack from the rear; [12]when the terrain in the rear is rugged, he should attack from the front; [13]and when the terrain on one flank is rugged, he should attack from the other flank.

[14]Or else, he should first engage him in battle using traitorous troops, troops supplied by the enemy, or tribal troops, and then, when the enemy is wearied while he himself is unwearied, he should attack him. [15]Alternatively, after creating a fake breach of himself at the hands of traitorous troops, when he is off guard thinking that he has won, being on guard himself, he should repair to a secure location (7.15.22 n.) and attack him.

[16]When the enemy lets down his vigilance while he is engaged in plundering a caravan, a herd station, a military camp, or a market place, remaining vigilant himself, he should attack him. [17]Or else, with his powerful troops concealed within weak troops, he should penetrate the ranks of enemy warriors and kill them. [18]Or, having lured the enemy warriors for raiding cattle or hunting game and remaining hidden in an ambush, he should attack them.

[19]After keeping them awake at night by launching a surprise attack, he should attack them during the day while they are overpowered by sleep or are fast asleep. [20]Or, he should launch an attack on sleeping troops using elephants with their feet encased in leather covers.

[21]He should attack during the afternoon those who are tired after carrying the fighting equipment during the day. [22]Or, when the enemy is breached, with his elephant and horse contingents rendered ineffective by frightened herds of cattle, buffaloes, and camels carrying bags of dried skin and round pebbles, and turns back,* he should, remaining unbreached, attack him. [23]Or, he should attack everyone who is facing the sun or the wind (10.3.48 n.).

[24]The following are places for an ambush (7.15.22 n.): a desert region, a forest, a narrow path, a muddy place, a hill, a marsh, a rugged terrain, a boat, cattle,* a cart formation (10.6.26), a fog, and nighttime.

[25]Further, the times given above (10.2.17) for launching an assault are also occasions for covert military operations.

Topic 151: Rousing One's Own Troops

[26]War at a pre-announced time and place, however, is the most righteous.

[27]Having gathered the army together, he should proclaim, "I receive the same remuneration as you. It is imperative that I enjoy this kingdom along with you. It is my request to you that you should attack the enemy."

[28]In the Vedas too,* at the baths that conclude sacrifices where the sacrificial fees have been fully distributed, it is announced, "Your state will be that of heroic warriors." [29]In this regard, further, there are these two verses:

> [30]Heroic warriors who lay down their lives in righteous wars will in a moment reach even beyond the worlds attained by Brāhmaṇas desirous of heaven through a multitude of sacrifices, through ascetic toil, and through numerous gifts to worthy recipients.
>
> [31]A new cup filled with water, well consecrated, and covered with Darbha grass—may that not be his lot and may he go to hell who will not fight for the sake of the sustenance provided by his master.*

[32]He should get the Counselor and the Chaplain to rouse the soldiers, pointing out the eminence of their military formations. [33]His astrologers and similar groups, moreover, should embolden his own faction and terrify his enemy's faction by proclaiming his omniscience and his intimacy with gods (13.1.1–3).

[34]When it is announced that "The battle is tomorrow," he should observe a fast and sleep alongside his weapons and mount; [35]make fire offerings reciting Atharvan formulas; [36]have blessings connected with victory and with winning heaven pronounced; [37]and surrender himself to Brāhmaṇas.

[38]He should make the central core of his military formation consist of soldiers who are brave, skilled, of high birth, and loyal, and who have not

been slighted with respect to money and honors. [39]A plain formation without flags and consisting of soldiers related to each other as fathers, sons, and brothers is the location for the king. [40]The conveyance for the king is either an elephant or a chariot with a cavalry escort. [41]He should mount the one most used by the troops or on which he was trained. [42]A man disguised as the king should be placed at the front of the military formation.

[43]Bards and panegyrists should proclaim heaven for the brave and exclusion from heaven for the timid, and extol the castes, associations, families, deeds, and conduct of the soldiers. [44]Assistants of the Chaplain should speak about the employment of black magic and sorcery, and mechanics, carpenters, and astrologers about the success of their own activities and the failure of those of the enemies.

[45]The Chief of the Armed Forces should address the army in battle array after it has been gratified with money and honors: "100,000 Paṇas for killing the king; 50,000 Paṇas for killing the Chief of the Armed Forces or the Crown Prince; 10,000 Paṇas for killing a leader of eminent warriors; 5,000 Paṇas for killing an elephant or chariot fighter; 1,000 Paṇas for killing a cavalryman; 100 Paṇas for killing a leader of infantry; and 20 per head; and, in addition, double the pay and individual plunder (3.16.27 n.)." [46]The leaders of groups of ten should determine that with regard to them.*

[47]Physicians carrying surgical instruments, medical devices, medicines, oils, and bandages, and women in charge of food and drink with the duty of emboldening the men should be stationed at the rear.

Topic 152: Deployment of One's Troops against Enemy Troops

[48]He should organize his battle formations in a terrain best suited for him and in such a way that they do not face the south, and do have the sun at the back and the wind blowing from a favorable direction.* [49]And in the event that his battle formations are in a terrain more suitable for his enemy, he should make his horses move about there.

[50]Where the terrain is unsuitable both for standing firm and for swift movement of a battle formation, he will be defeated either way, whether he stands firm or moves swiftly. [51]In the opposite case, he will win either way, whether he stands firm or moves swiftly.

[52]He should find out whether the terrain to the front, on the flanks, and in the rear is flat, rugged, or mixed. [53]If it is flat, he should employ

the staff and the circle formations (10.6.4, 6); if it is rugged, the snake and the non-compact formations (10.6.5, 7, 24); and if it is mixed, the uneven formations (10.5.17).

[54]After crushing someone of superior strength, he should petition for a peace pact. [55]If he is so petitioned by someone of equal strength, he should enter into a peace pact. [56]He should keep on striking someone of inferior strength, but never a person who has reached terrain suitable for himself or who is ready to lay down his life.

> [57]The vehemence of someone who reenters a battle without regard for his life becomes irrepressible. Therefore, he should not harass a man who has been crushed.*

THAT CONCLUDES THE THIRD CHAPTER: "KINDS OF COVERT MILITARY OPERATIONS," "ROUSING ONE'S OWN TROOPS," AND "DEPLOYMENT OF ONE'S TROOPS AGAINST ENEMY TROOPS" OF THE TENTH BOOK: "ON WAR."

Chapter 4

Topic 153: Terrains Suitable for Fighting

[1]For both fighting and setting up camp in the case of infantry, horses, chariots, and elephants, it is advantageous to find a terrain suitable for each. [2]For men fighting in deserts and forests and on water and dry land; for men fighting in trenches and open spaces and during day and night; and for elephants operating in rivers, mountains, marsh land, and lakes; as well as for horses—the desirable terrains and times for fighting are to be determined according to the needs of each.

[3]A terrain suitable for chariots is one that is flat, hard, clear, and without holes; in which wheels, hooves, or axles will not get stuck; that does not contain hazards caused by trees, shrubs, creepers, tree trunks, swampland, craters, anthills, sand, or mud; and that is free of clefts. Such a terrain is also suitable for elephants and horses, as well as for men, in fighting and in setting up camp, in both an even and an uneven battle formation.*

[4]A terrain suitable for horses is one in which there are small stones and trees, shallow and traversable craters, and whose only drawback is minor clefts. [5]A terrain suitable for infantry is one that has large tree trunks, rocks, trees, creepers, anthills, and shrubs. [6]A terrain suitable for elephants is one that contains traversable hills, water, or rugged land, trees

that can be ripped up, creepers that can be lopped off, and mud hazards, and that is free of clefts.

[7]The most excellent for foot soldiers is a terrain that is without thorns and not overly rugged, and that provides room for retreat. [8]The most excellent for horses is a terrain that provides double the room for retreat, is free of mud, water, and marshes, and contains no gravel. [9]The most excellent for elephants is a terrain that has places containing dust, mud, water, reeds, and rushes, is devoid of "dog's teeth" (2.3.15), and is free of obstructions created by large tree branches. [10]The most excellent for chariots is a terrain that contains water reservoirs and havens, has no holes, is devoid of swampland, and permits turning around.

[11]For all, the suitable terrain has been described. [12]Through that, explanations have been given regarding encampment and fighting by all elements of the military.

Topic 154: Respective Tasks for Infantry, Cavalry, Chariot Corps, and Elephant Corps

[13]These are the tasks of the cavalry: scouting the terrain, places for camping, and forests; securing a route with unrugged land, water, fords, favorable winds, and sunshine (10.3.48 n.); destroying or guarding* supplies and reinforcements; clearing and stabilizing* the army; undertaking expansive foraging raids (10.2.5); repelling attacks; undertaking first strikes; penetrating; piercing through; reassuring; gathering; dispatching;* altering the course of a pursuit; carrying away the treasury and the Crown Prince; charging the hind and the tips (10.5.12 n.); pursuing the weak; escorting; and rounding up.

[14]These are the tasks of the elephant corps: marching at the vanguard; making new roads, camping places, and fords; repelling attacks; crossing and descending into water; holding the ground, marching forward, and descending; entering rugged and crowded places; setting and putting out fires; scoring a victory with a single army unit; reuniting a broken formation; breaking an unbroken formation; providing protection in a calamity; charging forward; causing fear; terrorizing; demonstrating grandeur; gathering; dispatching (10.4.13 n.); shattering parapets, doors, and turrets; and taking the treasury safely in and out.

[15]These are the tasks of the chariot corps: guarding one's own army; obstructing the army of four divisions (2.33.9 n.) during battle; gathering; dispatching (10.4.13 n.); reuniting a broken formation; breaking an

unbroken formation; terrorizing; demonstrating grandeur; and making terrifying noises.

[16]These are the tasks of the infantry: carrying weapons in all places and times,* and engaging in military exercises.

[17]These are the tasks of the labor corps: activities relating to clearing military camps, roads, reservoirs, wells, and fords; transporting mechanical devices, weapons, armor, equipment, and food; and carrying away from the battlefield weapons, armor, and the wounded.

> [18]A king who has few steeds should yoke oxen and horses to chariots, while a king with few elephants should place at the center carts drawn by donkeys and camels.

THAT CONCLUDES THE FOURTH CHAPTER: "TERRAINS SUITABLE FOR FIGHTING" AND "RESPECTIVE TASKS FOR INFANTRY, CAVALRY, CHARIOT CORPS, AND ELEPHANT CORPS" OF THE TENTH BOOK: "ON WAR."

Chapter 5

Topic 155: Arrangement of Battle Formations in the Wings, Flanks, and Breast according to the Total Troop Strength

[1]He should initiate a battle after setting up a fortified stronghold at a distance of 500 Dhanuṣes, or as dictated by the terrain.

[2]Having dispatched (10.4.13 n.) the army out of sight* with its various units apportioned to chief officers, the Chief of the Armed Forces and the commander should organize the battle formations.

[3]He should space foot soldiers one Śama apart, horses three Śamas apart, and chariots or elephants five Śamas apart. [4]He should position the battle formations separated by two or three times those distances. [5]In this way, one can fight comfortably without being crammed.

[6]A Dhanuṣ is five Aratnis* long. [7]He should place an archer at that distance, a horse at a distance of three Dhanuṣes, and a chariot or an elephant at a distance of five Dhanuṣes.

[8]At five Dhanuṣes is the link point of wings, flanks, and breast of a battle formation.

[9]There should be three men fighting in front of a horse; [10]fifteen in front of a chariot or an elephant, as also five horses. [11]The same number of foot guards should be employed for a horse, a chariot, and an elephant.

[12]He should deploy a chariot formation consisting of three rows of three chariots each at the breast,* and the same on the flank* and wing* on both sides. [13]Thus, in a chariot formation there are 45 chariots, 225 horses, 675 men fighting in the front, and an equal number of foot guards.

[14]This is the even formation. [15]It may be increased beginning with two chariot rows up to 21 rows. [16]In this way, odd numbers become the ten basic constituents of an even formation.

[17]When there is an uneven number in the wings, flanks, and breast with respect to each other,* it is an uneven formation. [18]It also may be increased beginning with two chariot rows up to 21 rows. [19]In this way, odd numbers become the ten basic constituents of an uneven formation.

[20]Then, he should create an insertion unit* with the troops left over after constituting the military formations. [21]He should insert two-thirds of the chariots in the limbs and keep the rest at the breast. [22]In this manner, one should make an insertion unit of chariots consisting of one-third less.*

[23]This also explains the insertion units of elephants and horses. [24]He should make an insertion in such a manner that it will not cramp the fighting of horses, chariots, and elephants.

[25]A surplus of troops constitutes an insertion unit. [26]A surplus of infantry constitutes a counter-insertion unit. [27]A surplus of one outer section is a side-insertion unit. [28]A surplus of traitorous troops is an over-insertion unit.*

[29]Insertions should be made, according to his troop strength, up to four or eight times the insertion and the counter-insertion made by the enemy.

[30]The chariot formation also explains the elephant formation.

[31]Alternatively, a mixed formation consists of elephants, chariots, and horses—elephants at the borders of the army, horses in the two flanks, and chariots in the breast. [32]When elephants are in the breast, chariots in the two flanks, and horses in the two wings, it is a formation where the breakthrough is done with the center. [33]When the formation is the reverse of this, the breakthrough is done with the edges.

[34]A pure formation, however, consists only of elephants—with war elephants forming the breast, riding elephants the hind, and vicious elephants the two tips; [35]a horse formation—with armored horses forming the breast and unarmored horses, the flanks and the wings; [36]an infantry formation—with men in protective armor at the front and archers in the rear. [37]These are the pure formation.

[38]Infantrymen in the two wings, horses in the two flanks, elephants in the back, and chariots in the front—or the reverse depending on the formations employed by the enemy—[39]that is the troop arrangement containing two limbs. [40]This also explains the troop arrangement with three limbs.

Topic 156: Arrangement of Strong and Weak Troops

[41]With respect to men, the best troops are endowed with the exemplary qualities of the army (6.1.11). [42]With respect to elephants and horses, the special distinction comes from pedigree, breed, spirit, youth, stamina, height, speed, vigor, skill, steadfastness, stateliness, obedience, auspicious marks, and good conduct.

[43]He should position one-third of the best infantrymen, horses, chariots, and elephants as the breast; two-thirds as the flank and wing on either side; the next best directly behind; the third best directly in front; and the weakest directly in front. [44]In this way, he would put everyone to good use.

[45]By deploying the weakest troops at the edges, he will be able to resist an onslaught.

[46]Having deployed the best troops at the front, he should deploy the next best at the tips, the third best in the hind, and the weakest in the middle. [47]In this way, it will become capable of resistance.

[48]After positioning the formation, however, he should attack using one or two from among the wings, flanks, and breast and use the rest as back-up reserve.

[49]When an enemy's army is weak and bereft of elephants and horses, contains traitorous ministers, or has been subject to secret instigations, he should attack it with a large number of his best troops. [50]Alternatively, when an enemy's army consists of the very best troops, he should attack it with twice the number of his best troops. [51]When a division of his has few of the best troops, he should reinforce it with a large number of them. [52]He should deploy his formations near the location where the enemy has suffered a depletion, or from where he foresees a danger.

Topic 157: Methods of Fighting for Infantry, Cavalry, Chariot Corps, and Elephant Corps

[53]For horses, the techniques of fighting* are as follows: charging straight on; charging in a circular pattern; charging past; charging back; remaining

attentive after dealing a crushing blow; pincer movement; zigzag movement;* encirclement; scattering; turning back to attack after a feigned flight; protecting one's broken ranks along columns, in the front, on the two wings, and in the rear; and pursuing the broken ranks (of the enemy).

[54]For elephants, the techniques of fighting are as follows: all the above ones with the exception of scattering; and in addition the annihilation of the four divisions (2.33.9 n.), whether they are combined or separate; crushing the wings, flanks, and breast; sudden assault; and attack on sleeping troops.

[55]For chariots, the techniques of fighting are as follows: all the above ones (10.5.53) with the exception of remaining attentive after dealing a crushing blow; and in addition charging forward, retreating, and fighting from a stationary position on a terrain suitable to them.

[56]For infantrymen, the techniques of fighting are as follows: launching assaults in all places and at all times, and silent punishment (1.11.21 n.).

> [57]In this manner, he should create the formations in odd or even numbers, such that the strength of the four divisions (2.33.9 n.) becomes suitably employed.
>
> [58]Withdrawing to a distance of 200 Dhanuṣes, the king should remain with the reserve regiment (8.1.38 n.), which enables the restoration of broken ranks. Hence, he should not fight a war without a reserve regiment.

That concludes the Fifth Chapter: "Arrangement of Battle Formations in the Wings, Flanks, and Breast according to the Total Troop Strength," "Arrangement of Strong and Weak Troops," and "Methods of Fighting for Infantry, Cavalry, Chariot Corps, and Elephant Corps" of the Tenth Book: "On War."

Chapter 6

Topic 158: Arraying the Battle Formations of Staff, Snake, Circle, and Non-Compact

[1]Two wings, breast, and reserves (8.1.38 n.)—that is the arrangement of battle formations according to Uśanas; [2]two wings, two flanks, breast, and reserves—according to Bṛhaspati. [3]According to both, the primary battle

formations are staff, snake, circle, and non-compact containing wings, flanks, and breast.

[4]Of these, the staff is the one in which operations are conducted transversely; [5]the snake is the one in which all the divisions operate sequentially; [6]the circle is the one in which advancing divisions conduct operations on all sides; [7]and the non-compact is the one in which stationary divisions conduct separate military operations.

[8]When operations are conducted evenly with wings, flanks, and breast, it is the staff formation. [9]The same formation, when it breaks through with the flanks, is the "cleaver"; [10]when it pulls back with the wings and flanks, it is the "buttresser"; [11]when it breaks through with the two wings, it is the "irresistible"; [12]and when it keeps the two wings stationary and breaks through with the breast, it is the "falcon." [13]When these are carried out in the opposite way, they are "bow," "bow belly," "fixed," and "firmly fixed," respectively. [14]The one whose wings are like bows is the "victor." [15]The same formation, when it breaks through with the breast, is the "conqueror"; [16]when its wings are like stout ears, it is "pillar-eared"; [17]when it has double wing pillars, it is the "wide conqueror"; [18]when its wings are increased threefold, it is the "army-faced"; [19]in the opposite case, it is the "fish-mouthed." [20]The staff, when it is in a straight line, is the "needle." [21]Two staffs constitute the "pincer"; [22]and four, the "invincible." [23]These are the staff formations.

[24]When operations are conducted unevenly with wings, flanks, and breast, it is the snake formation. [25]It consists of either the "snake motion" or the "zigzag motion" (10.5.53 n.). [26]The same formation, when its breast has a pair of divisions and its wings have staff formations, is the "cart"; [27]in the opposite case, it is the "crocodile." [28]The cart, when interspersed with elephants, horses, and chariots, is "flying about." [29]These are the snake formations.

[30]When the wings, flanks, and breast are unified, it is the circle formation. [31]The same formation, when it faces all directions, is the "propitious-on-all-sides";* [32]and when it has eight arrays, it is the "invincible." [33]These are the circle formations.

[34]When the wings, flanks, and breast are not compact, it is the non-compact formation. [35]The same formation is called "harpoon" or "monitor lizard" when five arrays are used to resemble their forms;* [36]when four arrays are used, it is called "hearth" or "crow's feet"; [37]when three arrays are used, it is called "half-moon" or "crab-horned." [38]These are the non-compact formations.

[39]When the breast consists of chariots, the flanks of elephants, and the hind of horses, it is the "invulnerable." [40]When infantrymen, horses, chariots, and elephants are in formation the one behind the other, it is the "immovable." [41]When elephants, horses, chariots, and infantrymen are in formation the one behind the other, it is the "impregnable."

Topic 159: Deployment of Counter Formations against Them

[42]Among these, he should attack a "cleaver" with a "buttresser"; a "buttresser" with an "irresistible"; a "falcon" with a "bow"; a "fixed" with a "firmly fixed"; a "victor" with a "conquerer"; a "pillar-eared" with a "wide conqueror"; and a "flying about" with a "propitious-on-all-sides." [43]He should use the "invincible" formation to counter all the formations.

[44]In the case of infantrymen, horses, chariots, and elephants, he should use each latter one to attack each former; and a deficient unit with a superabundant unit.

[45]The single leader of ten units is a lieutenant; the single leader of ten lieutenants is a general; and the single leader of ten generals is a commander.* [46]It is the latter who should establish the signals using drumbeats, flags, and banners for the units to split up, to join together, to remain stationary, to march, to retreat, and to attack.

[47]When the military formations are equally matched, success comes from having the suitable terrain, season, and strength.

> [48–50]He should cause panic in his enemy by employing the following strategies: mechanical devices, esoteric practices (14.1–4), assassins killing people engaged in other matters, magical exercises, demonstrations of intimacy with gods (13.1.1–3), carts, causing fright with elephants,* rousing treasonable men, herds of cattle (10.3.22), setting fire to the military camps, attacks on the tips and the hind (10.4.13), creating dissension through agents posing as envoys, and announcing, "Your fort has been burnt down—or captured; a member of your family—or your enemy or tribal chief—has staged a revolt."
>
> [51]An arrow unleashed by an archer may kill a single man or not kill anyone; but a strategy unleashed by a wise man kills even those still in the womb.

THAT CONCLUDES THE SIXTH CHAPTER: "ARRAYING THE BATTLE FORMATIONS OF STAFF, SNAKE, CIRCLE, AND NON-COMPACT" AND "DEPLOYMENT OF COUNTER FORMATIONS AGAINST THEM" OF THE TENTH BOOK: "ON WAR."

THAT CONCLUDES THE TENTH BOOK: "ON WAR" OF KAUṬILYA'S *ARTHAŚĀSTRA*.

Book Eleven

Conduct Toward Confederacies

Chapter 1

Topic 160: Ways of Fomenting Dissension

[1]Gaining a confederacy is the best among gains, whether it is army or ally;* [2]for confederacies, because they are closely knit, are impervious to enemy assaults. [3]He should exploit the ones that are favorably disposed through conciliation and gifts, and those not favorably disposed by sowing dissension and using military force.

[4]The Kāmbojas, the Surāṣṭras, the Kṣatriyas, the Śreṇis, and the like live by commerce and the use of weapons. [5]The Licchivikas, the Vr̥jikas, the Mallakas, the Madrakas, the Kukuras, the Kurus, the Pāñcālas, and the like live by using the title "king." *

[6]In the case of all these, secret agents operating nearby should find out the grounds for mutual abuse, hatred, enmity, and quarrels among members of confederacies, and sow dissension in anyone whose confidence they have gradually won, saying, "That person defames you." [7]When ill will has thus been built up among adherents of both sides, agents posing as teachers should provoke quarrels among their young boys with respect to their knowledge, skill, gambling, and sports.*

[8]Or else, assassins should provoke quarrels among the partisans of chiefs of the confederacy by praising their antagonists (5.5.9) in brothels and taverns, or by supporting seducible factions.

[9]They* should instigate princelings enjoying inferior* luxuries with the prospect of superior* luxuries. [10]They should, moreover, prevent the superiors from eating or contracting marriages with inferiors. [11]Or else,

they should urge the inferiors to eat or to contract marriages with superiors; [12]or urge the most inferior to aspire to equal status by reason of family or bravery, or through a reversal of rank.

[13]Alternatively, they should get them to nullify a settled convention* by establishing the contrary. [14]Or, when there are matters under legal dispute, assassins should provoke quarrels by attacking property, animals, and humans at night.

[15]On all occasions of quarrel, moreover, the king, after giving support to the inferior side with treasure and troops, should urge it to destroy the opposing side. [16]Or, he should remove (2.1.1 n.) those who have split apart [17]and resettle them in groups of five or ten families on land suitable for agriculture; [18]for, should they live in the same place, they might become capable of bearing arms. [19]Furthermore, he should fix a penalty in the event of their forming a coalition.

[20]He should appoint as the Crown Prince a man from a good family and of noble birth, but who has been detained or expelled by those bearing the title "king" (11.1.5 n.). [21]His band of astrologers and the like, moreover, should spread the news among the confederates that he possesses the marks of royalty. [22]He should also secretly instigate deeply righteous chiefs of the confederacy, saying, "Carry out your specific duties with regard to the son or brother of that king." [23]When they agree, he should dispatch money and troops to support the seditious parties. [24]At the time of fighting, agents working undercover as tavern keepers should offer hundreds of pots containing liquor mixed with coma-inducing juices (4.3.28 n.) under the pretext of the death of a son or wife, saying, "This is a funerary libation" (12.4.4–6).

[25]Secret agents, moreover, should disclose a deposit—sealed boxes containing money and containers with money—connected with the execution of a compact, a deposit buried at the gate of a sanctuary or temple or near a fortified area. [26]And when the confederates are within sight, they should inform them: "These belong to the king." [27]Then he* should launch a surprise attack.

[28]Alternatively, after procuring draught animals or money at a periodic interest* from the confederates, he should present to a chief of the confederacy the specified material. [29]When they request it, he should say, "I gave it to that chief."

[30]The above also explains the ways of sowing dissension in a military camp or among tribal chiefs.

Topic 161: Secret Punishments

[31]Alternatively, a secret agent should convince the conceited son of a chief of a confederacy, saying, "You are the son of that king. You have been placed here out of fear of the enemy" (5.1.15–18). [32]Once he is convinced, the king should support him with treasure and troops and get him to attack the confederates. [33]When the king has achieved his objective, he should have him also killed.

[34]Keepers of prostitutes, or else rope dancers, actors, dancers, or dramatic storytellers deployed there should get the chiefs of a confederacy to become infatuated with young and extremely beautiful women (12.2.11). [35]When these have fallen in love, they should provoke quarrels among them by creating confidence in one of them and then going to another, or by forcible abduction.* [36]During the quarrel, assassins should do their task and say, "This fellow has been killed as he was longing for just this much" (5.2.57 n.) [37]Or else, when someone bears with his disappointment, the woman should hasten to him and say, "I am in love with you, but that chief harasses me. So long as he is alive, I will not remain here." Thus she should urge him to kill that man. [38]Or, if she has been forcibly abducted, she should get an assassin to kill the abductor at night near a grove or in a pleasure house; or she should kill him herself with poison. [39]Then she should announce: "My lover was killed by that man."*

[40]Alternatively, an agent operating undercover as a thaumaturgic ascetic should win the confidence of the man fallen in love by providing him with love-inducing medications, then trick him by substituting poison, and run away. [41]When he has fled, secret agents should declare that it was the work of a rival.

[42]Female covert agents posing as rich widows or women with a clandestine livelihood—or wives of Kauśikas who are actresses or singers*—while engaged in a dispute over an inheritance or a deposit, should make the chiefs of a confederacy infatuated with them. [43]When they have consented and entered clandestine houses at night to have sex, assassins should kill them or bind and abduct them.

[44]Or else, a secret agent should describe to a chief of a confederacy who has a fondness for women: "A family of a poor man has been banished to that village. His wife is fit for a king. Seize her!" [45]Once she has been seized, after a fortnight, an agent in the guise of a thaumaturgic ascetic should cry out in the midst of treasonable chiefs of the confederacy, "That chief is violating my wife—*or* daughter-in-law, *or* sister, *or* daughter"

(9.6.29 n.). [46]If the confederacy were to arrest him, the king should support him and get him to attack those who are hostile to him. [47]If he is not arrested, assassins should kill that agent in the guise of a thaumaturgic ascetic at night. [48]Then other agents appearing in the same guise should cry out, "He is a murder of a Brāhmaṇa! And he is the paramour of a Brāhmaṇa woman!"

[49]Or else, an agent working undercover as an astrologer should describe to one man a girl who has been chosen by another: "That man's daughter is bound to become the wife of a king and the mother of a king. Get her by giving all you have got or by using force." [50]If he fails to get her, he should stir up the opponent's side. [51]If he gets her, a quarrel is assured.

[52]Or else, a female mendicant should tell a chief who loves his wife: "That chief, arrogant due to his youth, sent me to your wife. Because I fear him, I have come here carrying his letter and ornaments. Your wife is innocent. You should deal with him secretly. In the meantime, I will carry on"* (5.1.50–51).

[53]On these and similar occasions of quarrel, whether a quarrel has arisen on its own or has been provoked by assassins, the king, after giving support to the weaker side with treasure and troops, should get him to attack those who are hostile or have him spirited away.

[54]A sovereign king* should behave in this manner toward confederacies. [55]Confederacies too should guard themselves in this manner against these kinds of deceptive practices perpetrated by a sovereign king.

> [56]The chief of a confederacy, behaving justly toward confederates and doing what is beneficial and pleasing to them, should remain self-controlled and devoted to his people, and act in accordance with the wishes of all.

THAT CONCLUDES THE FIRST CHAPTER: "WAYS OF FOMENTING DISSENSION" AND "SECRET PUNISHMENTS" OF THE ELEVENTH BOOK: "CONDUCT TOWARD CONFEDERACIES."

THAT CONCLUDES THE ELEVENTH BOOK: "CONDUCT TOWARD CONFEDERACIES" OF KAUṬILYA'S *ARTHAŚĀSTRA*.

Book Twelve

On the Weaker King

Chapter 1

Topic 162: Work of an Envoy*

[1]"When a weaker king is attacked by a stronger king, he should remain submissive in all circumstances, assuming the characteristics of a reed; [2]for he who bows before a stronger king bows before Indra," so says Bhāradvāja.

[3]"Gathering together all his troops, he should fight; [4]for prowess triumphs over a calamity. [5]This is also the specific duty of a Kṣatriya: victory or defeat in war," so says Viśālākṣa.

[6]"No," says Kauṭilya. [7]"A man who is submissive in all circumstances remains with no interest in life, like a herd ram,* [8]while a man with few troops who engages in a fight flounders like a man without a boat plunging into the ocean. [9]On the contrary, he should keep on striving after taking refuge either with a king who is superior to the other or in an impregnable fort."

[10]There are three kinds of attackers: one who conquers righteously, one who conquers out of greed, and one who conquers demoniacally. [11]Of these, one who conquers righteously is satisfied with submission. [12]He should submit to such a man; he should do so also when there is danger from enemies. [13]One who conquers out of greed is satisfied with plundering his land and property. [14]He should submit to such a man by giving money. [15]One who conquers demoniacally is satisfied with plundering his land, property, sons, wives, and life. [16]He should appease such a man with land and property and then, making himself unsusceptible to capture, take countermeasures.

[17]If one of these were to rise up, he should make a countermove against him by offering a peace pact, by waging a battle of wits, or by waging a covert war—[18]against that man's enemy faction through conciliation and giving gifts, and against that man's own faction by sowing dissension and through military force.

[19]Clandestine operatives should subdue his fort, province, or military camp using weapons, poison, and fire. [20]He should arrange for his rear to be attacked on all sides. [21]Or, he should get tribal chiefs to sack the kingdom, or get a pretender from his family or a prince in disfavor to seize it. [22]And when such hostile acts have ended, he should dispatch an envoy to him; [23]or, without resorting to hostile acts, conclude a peace pact with him.

[24]Should he, in spite of that, march against him, he should seek a peace pact* by increasing the offer of treasure or troops by one-quarter each time or by successively increasing the numbers of days and nights.*

[25]Should he seek a peace pact* entailing the army, he should give the man elephants and horses that are sluggish, or energetic ones that have been administered poison (7.3.30 n.).

[26]Should he seek a peace pact* entailing men, he should give him traitorous troops, troops supplied by the enemy, or tribal troops under the command of covert agents. [27]He should handle this in such a manner that both* are destroyed. [28]Or else, he should give him vicious troops who, when they are disparaged, will cause him harm. Alternatively, he should give hereditary troops who are loyal and who, when he is facing a calamity, will cause him injury.

[29]Should he seek a peace pact* entailing treasure, he should give him a valuable article for which he cannot find a buyer, or some forest produce that is unsuitable for war.

[30]Should he seek a peace pact entailing land,* he should give him a piece of land that can be recovered, that is constantly beset by enemies, that provides no haven (7.11.23), and that requires a great deal of losses and expenses to settle (7.11.26).

[31]Alternatively, he should seek a peace pact* with a stronger king offering all that he owns, with the exception of his capital city.

> [32]Whatever the other may seize by force he should offer to him as
> part of his strategy. He should protect his body and not his wealth;
> for what pity can there be for wealth, which is ephemeral.

THAT CONCLUDES THE FIRST CHAPTER: "WORK OF AN ENVOY" OF THE TWELFTH BOOK: "ON THE WEAKER KING."

Chapter 2

Topic 163: War of Wits

[1]If he* does not accede to a peace pact, he should tell him, "These are the kings who, falling under the power of the set of six enemies (1.6), have perished. It does not become of you to follow in the footsteps of them, who lacked the exemplary qualities of the self (1.5.16 n.)."

[2]"Pay attention to what is righteous and profitable,* [3]for those who urge you to do things that are reckless, unrighteous, and detrimental to profit are enemies in the guise of allies—"

> [4]"'to fight with brave men who are ready to lay down their lives is reckless; to cause the annihilation of people on both sides is unrighteous; to forsake a profit that is at hand or an ally who is not duplicitous is detrimental to profit—*.'"*

[5]"That king, moreover, has allies, and using these resources, he will rouse up further allies. They will attack you from all sides. [6]He has not been abandoned, moreover, by the intermediate or neutral kings or by the circle. You, on the other hand, have been abandoned, given that they simply watch you as you mobilize, thinking, 'Let him incur further losses and expenses! Let him be alienated from his ally! Then, when he has abandoned his home territory, we will vanquish him easily.' [7]It does not become of you, sir, to listen to enemies in the guise of allies; to intimidate your allies and to confer benefits on your enemies; and to wade into a misadventure that puts your life at risk."

In this way, he should constrain him.

Topic 164: Assassination of Army Chiefs

[8]In spite of that, should he nevertheless march against him, he should incite a revolt among his constituent elements as described in "Conduct toward Confederacies" (11.1) and "Drawing out by Trickery" (13.2), [9]and deploy assassins and poisoners. [10]He should deploy the assassins and

poisoners at those points that are singled out in "Personal Protection of the King" (1.21) as the ones to be guarded.

[11]Keepers of prostitutes should get the army chiefs to become infatuated with young and extremely beautiful women (11.1.34). [12]When several or two chiefs fall in love with one woman, assassins should provoke quarrels among them. [13]They should urge the party that was at the losing end in the quarrel to flee elsewhere or to render assistance to their master in the military expedition.

[14]Alternatively, agents working undercover as thaumaturgic ascetics, in order to trick those who are under the sway of lust by using love-inducing medications, should have poison administered to the chiefs.*

[15]Or else, an agent working undercover as a trader should shower wealth on a personal maid of the favorite queen as a token of love and then forsake her. [16]Then, an agent working undercover as a thaumaturgic ascetic recommended by an agent working undercover as a servant of that very trader should give the maid some love-inducing medication, telling her, "Put this on the body of that trader." [17]When this has been accomplished, he should instruct the favorite queen also in the same secret measure, saying, "Put this on the body of the king." [18]Then, he should trick her by substituting poison.

[19]Or else, an agent working undercover as an astrologer should tell a high official, whose confidence he has gradually won, that he possesses royal marks. [20]A female mendicant should tell his wife, "You will become the wife of a king—or the mother of a king."

[21]Or, a female agent working undercover as a wife should tell the high official, "The king, it has been reported, will lock me up. This letter and ornaments have been brought to your place by a female wandering ascetic."*

[22]Or, an agent working undercover as a chef or cook (1.12.9 n.) should inform him about the king's instruction regarding the administration of poison to him and the money given to entice him to do this. [23]An agent working undercover as a trader should corroborate that information and tell him about the success of the undertaking.*

[24]In this manner, using one or two or three strategies, he should urge each of his high officials individually either to launch an attack or to flee.

[25]In his forts, moreover, secret agents who have drawn close to the Regent should announce among the inhabitants of the cities and the countryside as a token of friendship, "The Regent has given these instructions

to the soldiers and heads of departments: 'The king is in deep trouble. It is unclear whether he will return alive or not. You should expropriate wealth by force and kill the enemies.'" [26]When the rumor has spread, assassins should have inhabitants of the city abducted at night and kill the chiefs, saying, "This is what happens to those who do not obey the Regent." [27]They should, moreover, discard blood-stained weapons, articles, and fetters in the offices of the Regent. [28]Then, secret agents should announce: "The Regent is murdering and plundering."

[29]In this manner, they should alienate the inhabitants of the countryside from the Collector. [30]Assassins, however, should kill officers of the Collector at night in the middle of villages and declare, "This is what happens to those who unrighteously oppress the countryside."

[31]When troubles have started, they should have the Regent or the Collector killed through a revolt by the subjects, [32]and a pretender from his family or a prince in disfavor installed.

> [33]They should set fire to the royal palace and the city gates and to the stores of equipment and grain, or kill them,* and then, uttering cries of pain, accuse him.*

That concludes the Second Chapter: "War of Wits" and "Assassination of Army Chiefs" of the Twelfth Book: "On the Weaker King."

Chapter 3

ASSASSINATION OF ARMY CHIEFS: CONTINUED

[1]Secret agents who have drawn close to the king or to the king's favorites should announce on a confidential basis as friends to people who are regarded as allies of the chiefs of infantry, cavalry, chariot corps, and elephant corps: "The king is angry." [2]When the rumor has spread, assassins, after taking precautions for traveling at night,* should go to their houses and tell them, "Come with us on the orders of the lord." [3]As soon as they come out, they should kill them, telling those nearby, "This is the lord's message." [4]To those who have not been executed, moreover, secret agents should say, "This is exactly what we told you. If you wish to live, you should flee."

[5]When the king does not give what some persons have requested, secret agents should tell them, "The king has told the Regent: 'This man and that other man requested from me something that should not be

requested. When I refused them, they have allied themselves with the foe. Make every effort to eliminate them.'" [6]Then, he should proceed as before.

[7]When the king does give what some persons have requested, secret agents should tell them, "The king has told the Regent: 'This man and that other man requested from me something that should not be requested. I have given them that thing so as to create confidence. They have allied themselves with the enemy. Make every effort to eliminate them.'" [8]Then, he should proceed as before.

[9]When some persons do not request something that should be requested, secret agents should say, "The king has told the Regent: 'This man and that other man do not request from me something that should be requested. What other reason could there be other than that they are anxious because of their own guilt. Make every effort to eliminate them.'" [10]Then, he should proceed as before.

[11]This explains also all the seducible factions.

[12]A secret agent who has drawn close to the king should apprise him: "This and that other high official of yours are in conversation with agents of the enemy." [13]When the king is convinced, he should show him traitorous men carrying royal messages, saying, "This is it!"

[14]Or else, after enticing army chiefs or ranking officials* with the offer of land or money, he should get them to attack their own people or take them away (2.1.1 n.).

[15]He should get a secret agent to instigate a son of his who is residing nearby or in a fort, telling him, "You are the son who possesses in the highest degree the exemplary qualities of the self (6.1.6). Yet, you have been overshadowed. So why do you remain apathetic? Attack and seize it before the Crown Prince destroys you."

[16]After enticing a pretender from his family or a prince in disfavor with money, he should tell him, "Demolish his interior troops and troops on the frontier and in the frontier fort."

[17]After giving support to tribal chiefs with money and honors, he should get them to destroy his kingdom.

Topic 165: Stirring up the Circle

[18]Alternatively, he should tell the man's rear enemy, "This king will surely vanquish me first and then will vanquish you. Attack his rear. If he turns around to face you, I will attack his rear."

[19]Or, he should tell his allies, "I am your dike. When I am breached, this king will engulf all of you. Let us form a partnership and thwart his expedition."

[20]He should send messages both to those who are allied with him and to those who are not, saying, "This king will surely exterminate me first and then take action against you. Take heed! It is better for you to help me."

> [21]In order to save himself, he should send a message to the intermediate king or to the neutral king, depending on who is near, offering him all his possessions.

That concludes the Third Chapter: "Assassination of Army Chiefs: Continued" and "Stirring up the Circle" of the Twelfth Book: "On the Weaker King."

Chapter 4

Topic 166: Secret Deployments of Weapons, Fire, and Poison

Topic 167: Destroying Supplies, Reinforcements, and Foraging Raids*

[1]Agents operating undercover as traders in his forts, agents operating undercover as householders in his villages, and agents operating undercover as cattle herders and ascetics in his frontier posts (3.1.1) should send a message accompanied by royal gifts to a neighboring ruler, a tribal chief, a pretender from his family, or a prince in disfavor, saying, "This region can be captured." [2]When their clandestine operatives arrive at the fort, moreover, they should welcome them with money and honors and show them the vulnerable points in the constituent elements (6.1.1) [3]and attack those points along with those men.

[4]Alternatively, in his military camp, an agent operating undercover as a tavern keeper, after establishing that a man condemned to death is his son, should kill him by administering poison during the time of a surprise attack; and then he should offer hundreds of pots containing liquor mixed with coma-inducing juices (4.3.28 n.) under the pretense of the death of a son or wife,* saying, "This is a funerary libation." [5]Or, on the first day, he should give unadulterated liquor—or liquor containing one-quarter

poison*—and on the next day, he should offer liquor mixed with poison. [6]Or, he should first give unadulterated liquor to the army chiefs and then, once they are intoxicated, offer them liquor mixed with poison. [7]Or, an agent operating undercover as an army chief should claim that a man condemned to death is his son—the rest is the same as above.

[8]Alternatively, agents operating undercover as vendors of cooked meat or boiled rice, or as tavern keepers or vendors of flat bread, after publicizing that they have vendibles of exceptional quality, should, while competing with each other, invite the enemies, saying, "I give on credit!" (11.1.28 n.) or "This is very cheap!" and then blend their vendibles with poison.

[9]Or, taking liquor, milk, curd, ghee, or oil from those who deal in them, women and children should pour them into their own receptacles containing poison. [10]Then, protesting "Give it at this price," or "Give a better quality product again," they should pour it back into the same vessels. [11]Agents working undercover as traders or those who bring commodities for sale (should sell) these same products.*

[12]Those residing nearby should put poison into the rations and green fodder of elephants and horses. [13]Or, agents operating undercover as laborers should sell green fodder or water mixed with poison.

[14]Alternatively, cattle traders who have established close connections over a long period of time should release herds of cattle or of goats and sheep—as well as the ferocious ones among horses, donkeys, camels, buffaloes, and the like—at times of surprise attack in locations that would cause confusion to the enemies. [15]Or, agents operating undercover as such traders should release animals whose eyes have been smeared with the blood of musk rats (14.1.29). [16]Or, agents operating undercover as hunters should release ferocious wild animals from their pens; or snake catchers should release virulently poisonous snakes; or elephant keepers should release elephants; [17]or people whose occupation involves fire should make a fire spread.

[18]Alternatively, clandestine operatives should attack chiefs of infantry, cavalry, and chariot and elephant corps as they turn back from battle, or they should set fire to the houses of the chiefs.

[19]Secret agents posing as traitorous troops, troops supplied by the enemy, or tribal troops deployed (with the enemy) should carry out an attack in the enemy's rear or provide reinforcements (8.1.38 n.) for a surprise attack on him.

[20]Or, operatives concealed in the forest should lure a frontier regiment out and attack them or, on a path that permits travel only in single file, destroy its supplies, reinforcements, and foraging raids.

[21]Or else, arranging a signal beforehand, they should sound a lot of drums during a nighttime battle and proclaim, "We have entered! The kingdom has been captured!"

[22]Alternatively, having gained entry into the king's quarters, they should kill the king during the commotion. [23]Or, as he is fleeing, leaders of barbarian or tribal troops from all sides, taking cover in places of ambush or a fence of tree trunks, should kill him. [24]Or, agents operating undercover as hunters should slay him during commotions created by a surprise attack with the means used in a fight by clandestine operatives.* [25]Or, they should slay him either on a path that permits travel only in single file or on a mountain, behind a fence of tree trunks, in a marshy land, or in water, using troops for whom that terrain is suitable. [26]Or, they should engulf him with the strong current created by breaking dams in rivers, lakes, and reservoirs. [27]If he is staying within a desert fort, forest fort, or water fort, they should destroy him with occult fire or smoke.* [28]Assassins should dispose of him with fire if he is in tight quarters; with smoke if he is in a desert fort; with poison if he is in his residence; with ferocious crocodiles or people moving in water if he has plunged into water; or when he comes out of his residence that has been set on fire.

> [29]He should outwit his enemy when he is holding fast to the locations mentioned by drawing him out through secret strategies,
> by secret means, or by any one of the secret means.*

THAT CONCLUDES THE FOURTH CHAPTER: "SECRET DEPLOYMENTS OF WEAPONS, FIRE, AND POISON" AND "DESTROYING SUPPLIES, REINFORCEMENTS, AND FORAGING RAIDS" OF THE TWELFTH BOOK: "ON THE WEAKER KING."

Chapter 5

Topic 168: Outwitting through Trickery*

Topic 169: Outwitting through Military Force*

Topic 170: Victory of a Lone King*

[1]During a pilgrimage for worshipping a divinity, there are numerous places that (the enemy) will visit to pay homage according to his devotion. [2]At those places, he should employ trickery on him. [3]Upon him, as

he enters a temple, he should make a false wall or a stone fall by releasing a mechanical device; [4]or set off a shower of stones or weapons from an upper chamber; or let a door panel plunge; or release a door bar attached to a wall and secured at one end. [5]Or, he should make the statue, banner, or weapons of the god fall upon him. [6]Or, in places where he stands, sits, or walks, he should arrange for poison to be used against him by means of the cow dung that is smeared, the scented water that is sprinkled, or the flowers and powders that are offered. [7]Or, he should waft over to him lethal smoke concealed by perfume. [8]Or, by releasing a pin, he should make him plunge into a well with spikes or a pitfall that is located beneath his bed or seat and whose top surface is held together by a mechanical device.

[9]Alternatively, when the enemy has drawn near, he should bring over people from the countryside who are able to withstand a siege [10]and drive out of the fort people unable to withstand a siege, or dispatch them to an area of the enemy's territory* that can be recovered. [11]He should, moreover, relocate the people of the countryside in a single location—in a mountain, forest, or river fort, or in regions separated by forests—under the control of a son or brother of his.

[12]The reasons for barricading oneself have been explained in the section "Behavior Proper for a King Surrendering with his Troops."*

[13]He should have grass and trees burnt all around up to one Yojana, [14]and water sources poisoned and discharged. [15]He should, moreover, locate pits, hidden traps, and barbed wires on the outside (2.3.15; 10.1.12).

[16]Having constructed an underground tunnel with multiple openings into the enemy camp, he should have the heads of the stores abducted or the enemy himself. [17]Or, if the enemy has built an underground tunnel, he should have the moat dug up—or else the well enclosure by the side of the parapet—until water reaches the tunnel. [18]He should have pots with water or brass vessels* placed on locations that are suspect so as to discover any digging. [19]Once the path of the underground tunnel is discovered, he should have a counter tunnel dug there. [20]Breaking it in the middle, he should force smoke or water into it.

[21]Alternatively, after making provisions for the defense of the fort and appointing a kinsman over the home territory, he should go to a quarter opposite to that from which he is coming—

> or to a quarter where he will be united with his allies, kinsmen, or
> tribal chiefs, or with powerful enemies or traitors of his enemy;

or to a quarter by going to which he could separate the enemy from his allies, attack him from the rear, have his kingdom seized, or cut off his supplies, reinforcements, and foraging raids;
or to a quarter from where he will be able to strike him with a sneak attack in the manner of a gambler's crooked throw;
or to a quarter from where he could rescue his kingdom or bolster his home territory.

[22]Or else, he should go to a place from which he could secure a desirable peace pact.

[23]Alternatively, those who have marched out with him should send a message to the enemy: "This foe of yours has fallen into our hands. Under the pretext of purchase or plunder, send money and also a strong military contingent to which we may hand him over bound or killed." [24]Once the enemy has agreed to this, he should seize the money and the strong military contingent.

[25]Or else, the Frontier Commander should bring over a portion of his army inside by surrendering the fort and then, when trust has been establish, exterminate it.

[26]Or else, he should invite the enemy's army to exterminate the country people gathered in one location. [27]Then, he should bring it over into a confined area and, when trust has been established, exterminate it.

[28]Alternatively, an agent appearing as an ally should send a message to the enemy outside: "In this fort, the grain supply—*or* oil, *or* sugar, *or* salt (9.6.29 n.)—is exhausted. It will be brought in at this location and time. Capture it." [29]Then, he should have poisoned grain, oil, sugar, or salt brought in by traitorous men, enemies, or tribal chiefs, or else by other men condemned to death. [30]This also explains the capture of all kinds of goods and supplies.

[31]Alternatively, after concluding a peace pact, he should hand over to him one portion of the money, but delay the payment of the remaining portion. [32]In the meantime, he should arrange for the enemy's defensive arrangements to be undermined; [33]or attack him with fire, poison, or weapons; [34]or shower favors on his favorites who come to accept the money.

[35]Or else, if he is completely drained, he should surrender the fort to him and flee; [36]he should flee through an underground tunnel or through a side opening cut through the rampart.

[37]He should launch a surprise attack at night and, if successful, remain there; or, if unsuccessful, escape through some trick (see 7.17.50–52). [38]He

may flee disguised as a member of a religious order and accompanied by a small retinue; [39]or he may be carried away camouflaged as a corpse by clandestine operatives; [40]or, wearing the clothes of a woman, he may follow a corpse; [41]or (he may flee) after leaving behind poisoned food and drink at an offering to a god, at an ancestral offering, or a festivity (7.17.44).

[42]After conducting secret instigations, he should rush out with agents posing as traitorous troops and, accompanied by clandestine forces, slay him.*

[43]Alternatively, if his fort has been thus captured, he should equip a sanctuary with plenty of food and remain there after entering the hollow within a statue of a god, or a false wall, or an underground chamber equipped with a statue of a god.* [44]When things have been forgotten, he should gain entrance into the king's bedroom at night through an underground tunnel and kill the enemy as he sleeps. [45]Or, letting loose something that can be let loose through a mechanical device, he should make it drop down on him. [46]Or, he should arrange for a house coated with a poisonous incendiary mixture or a house of lac in which the enemy is sleeping to be set on fire. [47]Or, when the enemy lets his guard down in a place for relaxation such as pleasure parks or recreational fields, assassins, gaining entry through an underground chamber, a tunnel, or a false wall, should assassinate him; or clandestine operatives deployed there should assassinate him with poison. [48]Or, as he is sleeping in a confined place, female clandestine operatives should release upon him snakes or poisonous incendiary devices or smoke (12.4.27 n.).

[49]Alternatively, when the occasion presents itself, moving about in secret, he should employ any measure whatsoever that is opportune against the enemy when he is residing in the palace. [50]Then, he should escape in secret and give the signal to his own men.

> [51]Summoning by signals of drumbeats, doorkeepers, eunuchs, and others secretly put to work for the enemy, he should get them to kill the rest of the enemies.

THAT CONCLUDES THE FIFTH CHAPTER: "OUTWITTING THROUGH TRICKERY," "OUTWITTING THROUGH MILITARY FORCE," AND "VICTORY OF A LONE KING" OF THE TWELFTH BOOK: "ON THE WEAKER KING."

THAT CONCLUDES THE TWELFTH BOOK: "ON THE WEAKER KING" OF KAUṬILYA'S *ARTHAŚĀSTRA*.

Book Thirteen

Means of Capturing a Fort

Chapter 1

Topic 171: Enticing to Sedition

[1]The seeker after conquest, when he desires to capture an enemy settlement (1.18.10 n.), should embolden his own faction and terrify his enemy's faction by proclaiming his omniscience and his intimacy with gods (10.3.33).

[2]The proclamation of his omniscience, however, is as follows: finding out secret news from their houses and communicating it to the chiefs; discovering people who do what is inimical to the king through spies working for the agency for the eradication of thorns and exposing them; revealing what is about to be requested or presented by detecting signals according to the science of association (1.12.1 n.) that are not seen by anyone; knowing news from a distant region the very day it happened, gathered by means of homing pigeons carrying sealed messages.

[3]The proclamation of his intimacy with gods,* however, is as follows:

conversing with and worshipping agents posing as gods of a fire sanctuary, agents who have entered the hollows of divine statues in the fire sanctuary through an underground tunnel;
or conversing with and worshipping agents disguised as Nāga and Varuṇa* emerging from water;
displaying at night a circle of fire within water by placing there sheaths of sea sand;*
standing on a raft held submerged by a sling with stones;

applying to the nose oil boiled a hundred times with the entrails of a spotted deer or the fat of crabs, crocodiles, dolphins, and otters, the nose whose surrounding head is covered with a urine bladder or a chorion.

[4]By this means, the bands of the night move about. [5]These are the ways of moving about in water. [6]Through them are produced the speech of and conversation with Varuṇa and Nāga maidens, and on occasions for anger, the emission of fire and smoke from the mouth.

[7]These powers of his should be broadcast throughout his territory by diviners, soothsayers, astrologers, chroniclers, fortune tellers, and clandestine operatives, as well as by those who have assisted and those who have witnessed these things. [8]In the territory of the enemy, they should proclaim how gods have appeared to him and how divine treasures and troops have come to him. [9]And while dealing with questions to gods, omens, flight of crows, interpretation of limbs (1.11.17 n.), dreams, and cries of animals and birds, they should predict victory for him and the opposite for the enemy; [10]and they should point out to the accompaniment of drums a meteor in the constellation of the enemy.*

[11]Agents operating undercover as envoys, as they advise the chief officers of the enemy out of friendship, should inform them that their lord held them in high regard and that his side is being strengthened while the enemy's side is being undermined. [12]They should announce that the ministers and the soldiers will retain the same enterprise and security as before. [13]He should show consideration for them when they face calamities and during festive occasions and honor their children.

[14]In this manner, he should stir up his enemy's side, as explained before (1.14.6f). [15]And we will explain it further: [16]skilled individuals by the proverb of the communal donkey; leaders of the army by the proverb of stick and beating the branch; those who are alarmed by the proverb of the "herd ram"; those who have been insulted by the proverb of the thunderbolt shower; those whose hopes have been dashed by the proverbs of the barren reed, the crow's rice ball, and the magically created cloud; those receiving honor as rewards by the proverb of jewelry given to an ugly woman by the man who hates her; those who have been subjected to secret tests by the proverbs of the tiger skin and the deathtrap; and those who are steadfast in rendering assistance by the proverbs of chewing Pīlu, camel-shaped water jug, and churning a female donkey's milk.*

[17]He should bestow wealth and honors on those who agree; [18]and when there are scarcities of goods and food, he should assist them by providing them goods and food. [19]They should carry off the wives, children, and jewelry of those who fail to agree.*

[20]When there is a famine or harassment caused by thieves or forest tribes, secret agents should stir up the inhabitants of the cities and the countryside and tell them, "Let us ask the king* for help. If he refuses to help, let us go elsewhere."

> [21]When they agree, saying "Yes!," assistance should be given to them with the provision of goods and grain. That is the great marvel of instigation.

THAT CONCLUDES THE FIRST CHAPTER: "ENTICING TO SEDITION" OF THE THIRTEENTH BOOK: "MEANS OF CAPTURING A FORT."

Chapter 2

Topic 172: Drawing Out by Trickery

[1]A shaven-headed or a matted-haired ascetic, saying that he lives in a mountain cave and is 400 years old, should station himself in the vicinity of the city, accompanied by a lot of matted-haired pupils. [2]His pupils, moreover, approaching the ministers and the king with roots and fruits, should urge them to visit their lord. [3]And when the king visits him, he should narrate the identification marks and the countries of former kings and say, "Every time I complete 100 years, I enter the fire and become a child once again. So, here in your presence I will enter the fire for the fourth time. It is imperative that I pay honor to you. Choose three boons." [4]When he agrees, he should tell him, "For seven nights you should reside here along with your sons and wives, after you have organized a festival with shows." [5]While he is residing there, he* should launch a surprise attack on him.

[6]An agent posing as a diviner of underground objects, being either a shaven-headed or a matted-haired ascetic accompanied by a lot of matted-haired pupils, should first coat a bamboo strip—or else a gold tube—with goat's blood, smear it with gold dust, and then insert it into an anthill so that ants would follow it. [7]Then, a secret agent should inform the king, "The thaumaturgic ascetic over there knows a blossoming treasure

trove." [8]When the man is questioned by the king, he should reply, "Yes," and point out the evidence—alternatively, he may do this after hiding there more money. [9]And he should tell the king, "This treasure trove is guarded by a snake, and it can be secured only by worship." [10]When he agrees, he should tell him, "For seven nights . . ."—the rest is the same as above.

[11]Or, while an agent posing as a diviner of underground objects, enveloped by a fire of glowing (oil)* at night, stays in a solitary spot, secret agents, after getting the king gradually to have faith in him, should tell the king, "The thaumaturgic ascetic over there is able to secure prosperity." [12]Undertaking to procure whatever the king asks him for, he should tell him, "For seven nights . . ."—the rest is the same as above.

[13]Or, an agent posing as a thaumaturgic ascetic should entice the king with magical lores. [14]"Undertaking to procure . . ."—the rest is the same as above.

[13]Or, an agent posing as a thaumaturgic ascetic, finding shelter near a highly honored divinity of the region, and winning the confidence of the chiefs of the subjects by organizing frequent festivities, should gradually outwit the king.

[16]Or, an agent posing as a matted-haired ascetic made completely white should reside under water, exiting through a tunnel or an underground chamber built under the bank. Secret agents, after getting the king gradually to have faith in him, should inform him that he is Varuṇa or the king of Nāgas (13.1.3 n.). [17]"Undertaking to procure . . ."—the rest is the same as above.

[18]Or, an agent posing as a thaumaturgic ascetic residing at the frontier of the countryside should urge the king to come and view the enemy. [19]When the king agrees, after making an image and summoning the foe,* he should kill the king in a secluded spot.

[20]Agents working undercover as traders coming to trade horses should invite the king so as to purchase them or to receive them as gifts. While he is engrossed in inspecting the horses or is swarmed by horses, they should kill him or charge at him with horses.

[21]Alternatively, assassins, climbing a sanctuary tree in the vicinity of the city and blowing into pots through tubes or reeds, should say indistinctly, "We will eat the flesh of the king or the chiefs. Let offerings be made to us." [22]Agents working undercover as soothsayers or astrologers should report this to them.

[23]Or, agents assuming the form of Nāgas (13.1.3 n.), their bodies anointed with glowing oil (13.2.11 n.) and pounding iron clubs and pestles at night in a holy lake or in the middle of a reservoir, should say the same thing.

[24]Or, agents wearing bearskin jackets, blowing fire and smoke, and bearing the aspect of demons should go around the city three times counterclockwise and say the same thing in between the cries of dogs and jackals.

[25]Or, after making a statue of a god in a sanctuary blaze at night using glowing oil (13.2.11 n.) or fire covered by a layer of mica, they should say the same thing. [26]Others should report this.

[27]Or, from highly honored statues of gods, they should cause an excessive flow of blood. [28]Then, others should say that the flow of god's blood predicts defeat in war.

[29]Or else, on nights of the junctures (2.31.21 n.), they should point out a sanctuary with men eaten up while erect* in a prominent area of the cemetery. [30]Thereafter, someone assuming the appearance of a demon should demand a human offering. [31]And others should kill whomever comes there to see it, whether he claims to be brave or is just some man, by beating him with iron pestles in such a way that people will reckon that he was killed by demons. [32]People who have witnessed this, as well as secret agents, should report that wonder to the king. [33]Then, agents working undercover as soothsayers or astrologers should recommend a pacificatory rite and penance, saying, "Otherwise a great affliction will strike the king and the country." [34]When he agrees, they should tell him, "On these occasions,* the king himself should perform a fire offering with mantras each night for seven nights." [35]Thereafter, it is the same as before.

[36]Alternatively, he should demonstrate how, when these tricks are employed against himself, he counteracts them, so that it could be a lesson for his enemies.* [37]Then, he should employ those tricks.

[38]Or, he should replenish the treasury by counteracting occult appearances (5.2.45 n.).

[39]Alternatively, wardens of elephant forests should entice a king who is fond of elephants with an elephant possessing auspicious marks. [40]When he agrees, after leading him into a dense forest or a place that permits only travel in a single file, they should either kill him or tie him up and take him away.

[41]This also explains a king who loves hunting.

[42]Secret agents should entice a king who loves wealth and women with rich widows or extremely beautiful young women brought to him with regard to an inheritance or a deposit.* [43]When he agrees, remaining hidden in an ambush at night, they should kill him at the place of the tryst with weapons or poison.

[44]Alternatively, assassins, gaining entry through an underground chamber, a tunnel, or a false wall, should kill the enemy during his frequent visits to thaumaturgic ascetics, wandering mendicants, sanctuaries, Stūpas,* or statues of gods.

> [45]In those places where the king himself goes to see a show; or where he diverts himself in an expedition or excursion or plays in water;
>
> [46]when words of reproof are spoken and all other similar occasions; or during sacrifices and festivities; or on occasions of childbirth, death, or sickness, or of joy, sorrow, or fear;
>
> [47]or when he, being trustful, lets down his guard during a festive occasion of his own people; or where he moves about without a guard; or on a rainy day; or in crowded places;
>
> [48–49]or when he has strayed from the route; or during a fire; or when he has entered a deserted spot—having gained entrance with packages containing clothes, ornaments, and garlands, with beds and seats, with containers of liquor and food, or with musical instruments; assassins, along with agents who had been infiltrated beforehand, should strike the enemy.
>
> [50]They should get away, moreover, in the same way that they entered on the occasions of an ambush of the enemy.
>
> So has been explained the drawing out of the enemy by trickery.

THAT CONCLUDES THE SECOND CHAPTER: "DRAWING OUT BY TRICKERY" OF THE THIRTEENTH BOOK: "MEANS OF CAPTURING A FORT."

Chapter 3

Topic 173: Deployment of Spies

[1]He should get a trustworthy chief of corporate troops to defect. [2]The latter, after taking refuge with the enemy, should bring over from his own country aides and associates on the pretext that they belong to his faction. [3]Or, after bringing in a number of spies and obtaining the approval of the enemy, he should destroy a traitorous settlement (1.18.10 n.), or a contingent of troops without horses or elephants and led by a traitorous minister, or a (traitorous) rear ally and send a message to the enemy. [4]He

should turn to a section of the countryside, to a corporate regiment, or to a tribal unit in order to obtain assistance. [5]After he has won the enemy's confidence, he should send a message to his lord. [6]Thereupon, the lord, under the pretext of capturing elephants or vanquishing forest tribes, should attack the enemy secretly.

[7]This also explains ministers and tribal chiefs.

[8]After developing a friendship with the foe, he should dismiss some ministers. [9]They should send a message to his foe: "Placate the master for us." [10]When he sends an envoy, he should reproach him, saying, "Your master is sowing dissension between me and my ministers. Never come back here." [11]Then, he should get one of the ministers to defect. [12]After taking refuge with the enemy, he should bring to the enemy's notice the disaffected and the traitorous among his clandestine spies who are weak,* as well as thieves and tribal chiefs who are harmful to both sides. [13]When he has secured a position of trust, he should bring to his notice the harm caused by prominent men, such as a Frontier Commander, a tribal chief, or a military chief, saying, "It is certain that this man and that other man has entered into a pact with your foe." [14]Then, after some time, he should have them killed by means of royal decrees carried by men condemned to death (9.3.31 n.).

[15]Alternatively, he should have him killed after rousing up his foe* by a commercial transaction of army troops (8.1.34 n.).

[16]Or else, after getting the king who is the enemy of his enemy to cause him harm by supporting the seducible people of his side, he should attack that king.* [17]Thereupon, he should send a message to his enemy: "That adversary of yours is causing me harm. Come, we will join forces and kill him. You will get a share of the land or money." [18]When he agrees, he should pay honor to him, and when he comes, he should get him killed by his foe through either a surprise attack or an open battle. [19]Or, under the pretext of granting land, anointing a prince, or providing protection in order to create confidence, he should have him seized. [20]Or, if he is unassailable, he should get him killed through secret punishment (1.11.21 n.). [21]If he provides the troops but does not come himself, he should get him* killed by his adversary. [22]Or, if he wishes to march with his troops and not with the seeker after conquest, even then he should get him killed by a pincer movement from both sides. [23]Or, if he is distrustful and wants each to march separately, or wants to seize one part of the kingdom of the man against whom they are marching, even then he should get him killed either through his adversary or by gathering together all his troops. [24]Or,

while he is occupied with his adversary, he should get his home territory seized by sending troops from another direction.

[25]Alternatively, he should bargain with the ally* with the offer of the land of the foe,* or with the foe with the offer of the ally's land. [26]Then, getting that ally to cause him harm in his greed to acquire the land of his foe, he should attack that ally—after that all the tricks are the same as stated above (13.3.16–18). [27]Or, when the foe has agreed in his greed to acquire the ally's land, he should support him with troops. [28]Then, as he marches against the ally, he should outwit him.

[29]Alternatively, after taking due precautions, he should reveal a calamity that has befallen him. Then, he should get an ally to rouse the enemy and to attack him. [30]Thereupon, he should either kill the enemy with a pincer movement or, taking him alive, he should force him to bargain away his kingdom.

[31]If the foe, taking shelter with his ally, seeks to remain in an inaccessible location, he should get the neighboring rulers and the like (5.6.20 n.) to seize his home territory. [32]Or, if he attempts to protect it with his army, he should get that army of his destroyed.

[33]If the two do not become disunited (13.3.25 n.), then he should openly bargain with them with the offer of each other's land. [34]Then, either agents posing as allies or agents in the pay of both should send envoys to the one and the other, saying, "This king, in alliance with his foe, wants to seize your land." [35]When one of the two becomes apprehensive or angry, he should act in the same way as before.

[36]Alternatively, he should send into exile chiefs of the fort, provinces, or army, after publicizing the reasons why they should be viewed as belonging to the seducible faction. [37]They should outwit the foe on the occasion of a battle, surprise attack, siege, or calamity. [38]Or else, they should create a division between him and the people of his own group, [39]and provide corroboration (2.7.30 n.) through royal decrees carried by men condemned to death (9.3.31 n.).

[40]Alternatively, agents operating undercover as hunters, remaining near the gate to sell meat and given shelter by the gate guards, should gain the enemy's trust by informing him two or three times about the approach of robbers. Then, they should get the master's army located in two places to destroy a settlement (1.18.10 n.) and to launch a surprise attack and tell the enemy, "A band of robbers is nearby and the call for help is loud. A large contingent of troops must come." [41]After handing it over to the portion of the army deployed to destroy the settlement, they should take the

other portion of the army at night to the gates of the fort and say, "The band of robbers has been killed. This army has returned after a successful expedition. Open the gate." [42]Or, agents deployed there beforehand should throw open the gates. [43]Along with them, they should attack.

[44]Alternatively, he should position soldiers posing as artisans, craftsmen, members of religious orders, performers, and traders within the enemy's fort. [45]Agents operating undercover as householders should bring to them weapons and armor in wagons carrying wood, grass, grain, and merchandise, or in flags and statues of gods. [46]Then, agents disguised as them* should announce the killing of those who were inattentive, the provision of reinforcements (8.1.38 n.) for a surprise attack, the launch of a rear attack, or, with the sound of conchs and drums, "They have entered!" [47]They should throw open the rampart gates and turrets and divide or destroy the army.

[48]The infiltration of troops is carried out using people going around with caravans or bands, or using escorts, bridal parties, dealers in horses or merchandise, transporters of equipment, buyers and sellers of grain, people wearing the emblems of renouncers, and envoys. A peace pact should be negotiated to build trust.

[49]These are the spies directed at the king.

[50]Spies directed at forest tribes are the very same, and in addition those mentioned in the section on the "Eradication of Thorns" (4.4–5). [51]Spies should get robbers to destroy a herd station or a caravan in the vicinity of the forest tribe. [52]As previously agreed, they should place there food and drink mixed with coma-inducing juices (4.3.28 n.) and flee. [53]Then, the cattle herders or the traders should get a surprise attack launched on the robbers carrying the loads of stolen goods as they succumb to the coma-inducing juices (4.3.28 n.).*

[54]Alternatively, an agent posing as a shaven-headed or matted-haired ascetic devoted to god Saṃkarṣaṇa* should outwit them with a drink mixed with coma-inducing juices at a festival. [55]Thereupon, he should launch a surprise attack.

[56]Alternatively, an agent operating undercover as a tavern keeper should outwit the tribals with drink mixed with coma-inducing juices on the occasion of selling or presenting liquor during a rite for gods or ancestors, a festival, or a fair. [57]Thereupon, he should launch a surprise attack.

> [58]Or, after dispersing the forest tribe that has entered to plunder
> a settlement, he should kill them. Thus have the spies directed at
> robbers been described.

THAT CONCLUDES THE THIRD CHAPTER: "DEPLOYMENT OF SPIES" OF THE THIRTEENTH BOOK: "MEANS OF CAPTURING A FORT."

Chapter 4

Topic 174: Task of Laying Siege

[1]The work of laying siege* is preceded by weakening.

[2]He should keep the countryside, to the extent that it is settled, out of danger. [3]He should get anyone who is setting out to remain by providing favors and exemptions. [4]He should settle those fleeing elsewhere on land away from the fighting or make them live in one location.* [5]"For, there is no countryside without people and no kingdom without a countryside," says Kauṭilya.

[6]He should destroy the sowings or crops of someone ensconced in an inaccessible place, as also his supplies and foraging raids.

> [7]By demolishing foraging raids and supplies, by also destroying sowings and crops, by depopulating, and by secret killings, one brings about the weakening of the constituents (6.2.24–26).

[8]He should lay siege when he thinks, "My army is fully supplied with grain, forest produce, mechanical devices, weapons, armor, laborers, and ropes in large quantities and of the finest quality. A good season is ahead, but it is a bad season for my enemy. His stores and defenses are weakening because of disease and famine. The troops he has bought, as well as the troops supplied by his ally, are despondent."

[9]He should first make arrangements for the protection of the military camp, supplies, foraging raids, and the road; encircle the fort around the moat and ramparts; poison the water; and drain the moats or fill them up. Then he should have the rampart and palisade taken by means of an underground tunnel or a cave room,* and the gate with an armored elephant.* [10]He should have the wetlands covered with a mantle of dirt.* [11]He should destroy a massive fortification with mechanical devices. [12]Drawing them out from the egress door (2.3.14 n.), they should attack them with horses. [13]During pauses between attacks, moreover, he should seek to achieve success by employing the strategies restrictively, optionally, or in combination (9.7.73–79).

[14]After getting hawks, crows, nightjars, vultures, parrots, mynas, owls, and pigeons living within the fort captured, he should attach an incendiary mixture (13.4.19–21) to their tails and release them into the enemy's fort. [15]From his military camp that has been moved back a distance or is being protected by raised flags and bows, he should set fire to the enemy's fort with "human fire" (14.2.38). [16]Clandestine operatives, moreover, working as guards within the fort should attach an incendiary mixture to the tails of mongooses, monkeys, cats, and dogs and release them among reeds, stocks, defenses, and houses. [17]They should place fire in the abdomens of dried fish or in dried meat and get birds to carry it away by offering it to crows.

[18]Balls of Sarala-pine, Devadāru-pine, stinkgrass, bdellium, pine resin, Sal resin, and lac, as well as the dung of donkeys, camels, goats, and sheep—these retain fire well.

[19]Powder of Priyāla, soot of Avalguja, beeswax, and the dung of horses, donkeys, camels, and cattle—these form an incendiary mixture that is to be hurled. [20–21]Either the powder of all metals with a fiery color or the powder of Kumbhī,* lead, and tin, along with the flowers of Pāribhadraka and Palāśa, the soot of Keśa, oil, beeswax, and pine resin form an incendiary mixture that is attached or is a Viśvāsaghātin, that is, an arrow coated with it and wrapped with hemp or the bark of Trapusa. Such is an incendiary mixture.*

[22]He should, however, never hurl fire when there is an opportunity for an assault; [23]for fire is treacherous and is a divine affliction (8.4.1), causing the destruction of innumerable creatures, grains, farm animals, money, forest produce, and goods. [24]Even if acquired, a kingdom with all its stocks lost leads only to further losses.

That concludes the work of laying siege.

Topic 175: Taking by Storm

[25]When he thinks, "I have all the equipment and laborers needed for the task. My enemy is ill, his constituents have turned against him because of secret tests (1.10), or the construction of his fort and the procurement of stocks have not been carried out. Whether he is without reinforcements or has reinforcements, he will soon conclude a peace pact with his allies"—that is the time for taking by storm.*

[26]When a fire has erupted spontaneously or has been deliberately set; during a festivity; when people are engrossed in seeing a show or military formation; during a drunken brawl; when his troops are exhausted by

constant battles; when his men have been injured and killed in numerous battles; when people have fallen asleep, being wearied by keeping watch; on a rainy day; when the river is flooded; or when there is a thick fog—on these occasions he should take by storm.

[27]Alternatively, abandoning the military camp and hiding in the forest, he should kill the foe when he comes out.

[28]Alternatively, an agent posing as a chief ally or backer of his should develop a friendship with the one under siege and dispatch to him a man condemned to death as an envoy with the message: "This is your vulnerable point. These are the traitorous men;" *or* "This is the vulnerable point of the man laying siege. This is the seducible faction for you." [29]The seeker after conquest, seizing him as he comes out with a return envoy and publicizing his guilt, should kill him and withdraw. [30]Then, the agent posing as his ally or backer should tell the one under siege, "Come out here to rescue me. Or, joining forces with me, kill the man laying siege." [31]When he agrees, he should get him killed by a pincer movement from both sides; or, taking him alive, he should force him to bargain away his kingdom (13.3.22, 30). [32]Or else, he should lay waste to his capital city; [33]or, forcing his best troops to come out, he should launch an attack.

[34]The above also explains the case of a king who surrenders with his army and a tribal chief. [35]Alternatively, one of the two, either the king who surrenders with his army or the tribal chief, should send a message to the one under siege: "This man who is laying siege is ill;" *or* "He is being attacked by the rear enemy;" *or* "Another vulnerable point has emerged;" *or* "He intends to withdraw to another region." [36]When he agrees, the man laying siege should burn down his military camp and withdraw. [37]Then, he should proceed as before (13.4.31).

[38]Or else, making a stockpile of merchandise, he should outwit him with poisoned merchandise.

[39]Alternatively, an agent posing as a backer should send an envoy to the one under siege with the message: "I have attacked the man outside. Come out here to attack him." [40]When he agrees, he should proceed as before.

[41]Covert agents, carrying official passes with seals under the pretext of visiting a friend or a relative, should enter the fort and get it seized.

[42]Alternatively, an agent posing as a backer should send the following message to the one under siege: "At this place and time, I will attack the military camp. You should also enter the battle." [43]When he agrees, he should make it seem like there is a commotion caused by an attack as

already described, and when he comes out of the fort at night he should kill him.

[44]Or else, he should invite an ally or a tribal chief* and urge him on, saying, "While he is under siege, launch an assault and take over his land." [45]When he launches his assault, he should have him killed by his subjects or by lending support to traitorous chiefs, or by himself with poison. He achieves his aim by announcing, "This man is an assassin of his ally."*

[46]Or, an agent posing as an ally should inform the enemy about the other's intention to launch an assault. [47]When he has secured a position of trust, he should have his eminent warriors killed (13.3.14).

[48]Or, after concluding a peace pact with him, he should get him to settle the countryside with people. [49]When his countryside has been settled, he should attack it without revealing his identity.

[50]Or, after getting harm done to him and luring a portion of his army against treasonable people or tribal chiefs, he should capture the fort through a surprise attack.*

[51]Further, traitorous men, enemies, tribal chiefs, people who hate him, and deserters who have returned—all of whom have been provided with money, honors, signals, and emblems—should launch a surprise attack against the enemy's fort.

[52]Having launched a surprise attack against the enemy's fort or military camp, they should grant safety to those who have fallen down, turned back, surrendered, loosened their hair, or put down their weapons, or who are contorted through fright, as well as to noncombatants.

[53]Having captured the enemy's fort, he should enter it after he has cleared it of people belonging to his foe's faction and taken precautions inside and out against secret punishment (1.11.21 n.).

[54]In this way, after gaining the enemy's territory, the seeker after conquest should seek to seize the intermediate king and, when he has been subdued, the neutral king. [55]This is the first path to conquering the earth.

[56]If there is no intermediate or neutral king, he should subdue the enemy constituents through strategic preeminence and then the constituents beyond that.* [57]This is the second path.

[58]If there is no circle, he should subdue the ally by means of the enemy, and the enemy by means of the ally, using a pincer movement from both sides (13.3.22). [58]This is the third path.

[60]He should first subdue a weak or a solitary neighbor. Becoming by means of him twice as powerful, he should subdue a second; and

becoming thrice as powerful, a third. [61]This is the fourth path to conquering the earth.

[62]After conquering the earth, he should enjoy it, divided into social classes and orders of life, in accordance with the duties specific to him.

> [63]Instigation to sedition, agents, drawing out, laying siege, and taking by storm—these are the five means of capturing a fort.

THAT CONCLUDES THE FOURTH CHAPTER: "TASK OF LAYING SIEGE" AND "TAKING BY STORM" OF THE THIRTEENTH BOOK: "MEANS OF CAPTURING A FORT."

Chapter 5

Topic 176: Pacifying the Territory Gained

[1]The venture of the seeker after conquests is of two kinds: the one directed at forests and the like, and the other directed at a single settlement (1.18.10 n.) and the like. [2]And its capture is of three kinds: new, formerly possessed, and ancestral.

[3]After acquiring a new territory, he should eclipse the enemy's faults with his own virtues, and the enemy's virtues with twice as many virtues of his. [4]He should, moreover, promote what is cherished by and beneficial to the subjects by carrying out his own duties and by granting favors, exemptions, gifts, and honors. [5]And he should have favors granted to the seducible party according to agreements; more, if they have made extraordinary efforts. [6]For a man who does not keep to an agreement is not to be trusted either by his own people or by his enemies, as also a man whose conduct is contrary to that of the subjects. [7]Therefore, he should adopt the habits, dress, language, and conduct similar to theirs, [8]and demonstrate his devotion to them during festivals in honor of the gods of the region, festivities, and recreational activities.

[9]Secret agents, moreover, should constantly point out to the chiefs of districts, settlements, castes, and associations the misdeeds of the enemy, as also the lord's extraordinary fortune and devotion to them, and the lord's palpable respect for them. [10]And he should exploit them by preserving their customary privileges, exemptions, and protection.

[11]He should arrange for the veneration of all gods and hermitages and for the donation of land, wealth, and exemptions to men preeminent

in knowledge, eloquence, and righteousness, as also for the release of all prisoners and for assistance to the wretched, the helpless, and the sick. [12]There is to be a suspension of slaughter for a fortnight at the beginning of each four-month season; for four nights at each full moon; and for one night at the constellations of the king and the region.* [13]He should prohibit the killing of breeding females and the young, as well as castration.

[14]Whatever custom he may consider to be detrimental to the treasury and army or to be very unrighteous, he should set it aside and establish a righteous convention.

[15]He should have the residences of congenital robbers and barbarian groups changed, dispersing them in several locations; as also those of the chiefs of the fort, the provinces, and the army. [16]He should also make the counselors and chaplains who have been favored by the enemy reside dispersed in several locations in the frontier regions of the enemy's territory. [17]He should eliminate through secret punishment (1.11.21 n.) those who are capable of causing harm or who are brooding (5.1.55 n.) the destruction of the master. [18]He should settle his own countrymen or people who had been expelled by the enemy in places from which these have been removed.

[19]If there is a pretender from his family who is able to take back easily recoverable land, or a noble man residing in a forest region at the frontier who has the capacity to cause him problems, he should grant him land of inferior quality or one-quarter of the land that is of superior quality. He should do so after fixing a tribute in treasure and troops, such that in paying it, he will cause the inhabitants of the fort and the countryside to revolt. [20]When they are in revolt, he should get them to kill him. [21]He should send away anyone who is denounced by the subjects or settle him in a perilous region.

[22]In the case of land possessed before, he should cover up that fault of the constituents owing to which he withdrew and amplify the good quality because of which he returned.

[23]In the case of ancestral land, he should cover up the faults of his father and publicize his good qualities.

> [24]He should promote righteous customs, both those that are not
> yet established and those that have been established by others.
> And he should not promote unrighteous ones and put an end to
> those established by others.

THAT CONCLUDES THE FIFTH CHAPTER: "PACIFYING THE TERRITORY GAINED" OF THE THIRTEENTH BOOK: "MEANS OF CAPTURING A FORT."

THAT CONCLUDES THE THIRTEENTH BOOK: "MEANS OF CAPTURING A FORT" OF KAUṬILYA'S *ARTHAŚĀSTRA*.

Book Fourteen

On Esoteric Practices

Chapter 1

Topic 177: Secret Means of Killing Enemy Troops

[1]For the sake of protecting the four social classes, he should employ esoteric practices against very unrighteous people.

[2]Well-liked* women and men from barbarian groups, masquerading as hunchbacks, dwarfs, Kirātas (1.12.9 n.), or persons who are dumb, deaf, insane, or blind, and with credible disguises in terms of region, attire, craft, language, and birth (1.12.9), should slip in the set of poisons beginning with Kālakūṭa (2.17.12) into articles used on the body of the enemy.

[3]Clandestine operatives should insert weapons into sports equipment for the king's use and into articles of the storehouse used by him; while night patrols making a living as secret agents, as well as people whose occupation involves fire, should insert fire.*

[4]Powder made from the speckled frog, Kauṇḍinyaka-insect, Kṛkaṇa-insect, Pañcakuṣṭha-insect, and centipede; powder made from the Uccidiṅga-crab, Kambalī-insect, Śatakanda-insect, Idhma, and Kṛkalāsa-lizard; powder made from the house lizard, Andhāhika-snake, Krakaṇṭaka, Pūtikīṭa-stinkbug, and Gomārikā—all this mixed with the sap of Bhallātaka-tree and Avalguja-plant causes instant death; or even the smoke of these.

> [5]Or, after boiling any one of these insects along with a black snake and panic grain, he should desiccate that mixture. It is considered to cause instant death.*

[6]The root of Dhāmārgava and Yātudhāna mixed with powder made from Bhallātaka flowers causes death within a fortnight. [7]The root of Vyāghātaka mixed with powder made from Bhallātaka flowers, along with the insect mixture (14.1.4), causes death within a month. [8]The dose for men is just one grain;* double that for donkeys and horses; and four times that for elephants and camels.

[9]Smoke created by Śatakardama, Uccidiṅga-crab, Karavīra-plant, bitter gourd, and fish, along with the stalks of Madana-plant and Kodrava-grain (4.3.28 n.) or with the stalks of Hastikarṇa-plant and Palāśa-tree, when carried downwind by the breeze kills everything in its path.

[10]Powder made from Pūtikīṭa-stinkbug, fish, bitter gourd, Śatakardama-plant, Idhma, and Indragopa-insect, or powder made from Pūtikīṭa-stinkbug, Kṣudrā, Arālā, Hema, and Vidarī, mixed with power made from the horns and hooves of a goat—smoke from that causes blindness.

[11]Leaves of Pūtikarañja, yellow orpiment, antimony, Guñja-berries, and stalks of the red cotton tree made into a paste with the sap of Āsphoṭa, Kāca, and cow dung—smoke from that causes blindness.

[12]Slough of a snake, dung of cows and horses, and the head of an Andhāhika—smoke from that causes blindness.

[13]Urine and dung of pigeons, frogs, and carnivores, as well as of elephants, men, and boars; green vitriol, asafetida, and the husk, grain fragments, and whole grains of barley; seeds of cotton, Kutaja, and Kośātakī; roots of Gomūtrikā and Bhāṇḍi; pieces of neem, drumstick, Phaṇirjaka, Akṣīva, and Pīluka; skin of snakes and of female carp; powder made from the nails and tusks of elephants—smoke from that generated with stalks of the Madana-plant and Kodrava-grain or with the stalks of Hastikarṇa and Palāśa kills each and every one wherever it spreads.

[14]Roots of Kālī, Kuṣṭha, Naḍa, and Śatāvarī, or powder made from snakes, Pracalāka, Kṛkaṇa, and Pañcakuṣṭha—smoke from that generated according to the procedure given above (14.1.13) or with wet and dry stalks, when directed at men rushing into battle or crowding during a surprise attack by men who have taken precautions to protect their eyes with "cleansing water" (14.4.2), destroys the eyesight of all living creatures.

[15]Dung of myna bird, pigeon, Baka-heron, Balākā-flamingo, made into a paste with the milk of the plants Arka, Akṣi, Pīluka, and Snuhi, produces a collyrium that causes blindness and poisons water.

[16]A mixture of the roots of barley and Śāli-rice, fruits of Madana, leaves of nutmeg, and urine of men, when combined with the roots of Plakṣa and

Vidārī, or with a decoction of Mūka, Udumbara, Madana, and Kodrava, or with a decoction of Hastikarṇa and Palāśa, forms a coma-inducing mixture (4.3.28 n.).

[17]A mixture of ginger, Gautama-vṛkṣa, Kaṇṭakāra, and Mayūrapadī; a mixture of Guñjā, Lāṅgalī, Viṣamūlikā, and Iṅgudī; a mixture of Karavīra, Akṣi, Pīluka, Arka, and Mṛgamāraṇī, when combined with a decoction of Madana and Kodrava, or with a decoction of Hastikarṇa and Palāśa, forms a coma-inducing mixture.

[18]Or, all of these together* poison green fodder, firewood, and water.

[19]The smoke of Kṛtakaṇḍala, lizard, house lizard, and Andhāhika destroys eyesight and causes madness.

[20]A mixture of lizard and house lizard causes leprosy. [21]The same mixture when combined with the entrails of a speckled frog and honey brings about urinary disease, and when combined with human blood, consumption.

[22]Dūṣīviṣa together with the powder of Madana and Kodrava is a formula for the paralysis of the tongue.

[23]A mixture of Mātṛvāhaka, Añjalikāra, Pracalāka, frog, Akṣi, and Pīluka causes cholera.

[24]A mixture of Pañcakuṣṭhaka, Kauṇḍinyaka, Rājavṛkṣa flowers, and honey causes fever.

[25]A mixture of Bhāsa-vulture, mongoose, Jihvā-plant, and Granthikā-plant, made into a paste with donkey milk causes a person to be dumb and deaf within a month or a fortnight.

[26]The dose for men is just one grain . . .—the rest is the same as before (14.1.8).

[27]In the case of plants, employing a decoction made with fragments; in the case of animals, powder; or in all cases, employing a decoction—in this way it becomes more potent. [28]These are the effects of mixtures (1.9.1 n.).

[29]When an arrow, boiled* with the seeds of Śālmalī and Vidārī, containing Mūla and Vatsanābha, and smeared with an ointment of blood of muskrats, pierces a man, the man so pierced bites ten other men; and those who are so bitten, bite ten other men.

[30]A decoction of Elaka, Akṣi, bdellium, and Hālāhala, together with the flowers of Bhallātaka, Yātudhāna, Avānu, Dhāmārgava, and Bāṇa, combined with the blood of a goat and man, is a mixture that induces biting. [31]Half a Dharaṇa of this mixture put in water with barley meal and oilcake poisons a body of water 100 Dhanuṣes in extent; [32]for a shoal of fish bitten or touched by this becomes poisonous, as also anyone who drinks or touches that water.

[33]When a monitor lizard is placed together with red and white mustard seeds in a camel-shaped vessel buried in the ground for three fortnights and then taken out by a man condemned to death, it causes death wherever it looks; or else, a black snake.

[34]When a piece of charcoal or a fire kindled by lightning is caught and maintained in pieces of wood burnt by lightning, that fire, into which a ritual offering to Rudra has been made under the constellation Kṛttikā (Pleiades) or Bharaṇī (Arietis), when directed against anyone burns, and there is nothing that can counteract it.

> [35]Fetching fire from a blacksmith, he should offer honey—and, separately, liquor in a fire from a tavern keeper; ghee in a fire from a brothel;*
>
> [36]garland flowers in a fire from a woman devoted to a single husband; mustard seeds in a fire from a prostitute; curd in a fire from a woman who has just given birth; rice grains in a fire from a man who maintains the three sacrificial fires (3.14.37 n.);
>
> [37]meat in a fire from a Caṇḍāla; human flesh in a fire from a funeral pyre; and in all these fires together the fat of a goat, human flesh, and fig wood.*
>
> [38]He should offer pieces of wood from the Rājavṛkṣa with the ritual formula to Fire. This is a fire that nothing can counteract; it bewilders the eyes of enemies.
>
> [39]Hail to you, Aditi! Hail to you, Anumati. Hail to you Sarasvatī. Hail to you, God Savitar. [40]To Fire, Svāhā! To Soma, Svāhā! Earth, Svāhā! Atmosphere, Svāhā!

THAT CONCLUDES THE FIRST CHAPTER: "SECRET MEANS OF KILLING ENEMY TROOPS" OF THE FOURTEENTH BOOK: "ON ESOTERIC PRACTICES."

Chapter 2

Topic 178: Deception

Topic 178a: Creating Prodigious Effects

[1]Mixing the powder made from Śirīṣa, Udumbara, and Śamī with ghee is a mixture for keeping hunger away for a fortnight; [2]for one month, when it

is boiled with Kaśeruka, bulbous root of lotus, sugarcane root, lotus fiber, milk, ghee, and cream.

[3]By drinking the power made from Māṣa-bean, barley, Kulattha, and Darbha root together with milk and ghee, or Vallī-plant, milk, and ghee, boiled together in equal quantities; or a paste of the roots of Sāla and Pṛśniparṇī together with milk; or by consuming milk boiled with it, together with honey and ghee, a man is able to fast for one month.

[4]Sesame oil that has been kept in a bitter gourd for one and a half months and then boiled with white mustard seeds left in the urine of a white goat for seven nights causes disfigurement in quadrupeds and bipeds. [5]White mustard oil boiled with barley grains from the dung of a white donkey seven nights after it has been fed with buttermilk and barley causes disfigurement.

[6]White mustard oil boiled with the urine and dung of either of these two,* and with the admixture consisting of the powder made from Arka, silk-cotton, and Pataṅga, causes leukoderma. [7]A mixture of the dung of a white fowl and a white boa constrictor causes leukoderma. [8]White mustard seeds left in the urine of a white goat for seven nights, buttermilk, milk of Arka, salt, and grain—this mixture kept for a fortnight causes leukoderma.

[9]A paste of white mustard seeds kept for a fortnight in a bitter gourd while the gourd is still attached to the vine causes body hair to turn white.

> [10]The insect known as Alojunā* and the white house lizard—
> when a paste made from these is applied to head hair, they turn
> as white as a conch.

[11]Rubbing the body of a man with cow dung or a paste of Tinduka and Ariṣṭa and smearing it with the sap of Bhallātaka is a formula for giving him leprosy within a month. [12]Guñja-seeds kept in the mouth of a black snake or of a house lizard for seven nights is a formula for causing leprosy. [13]Applying the bile and the fluid in the egg of a parrot to the entire body is a formula for causing leprosy.

[14]A decoction made with the pulp of Priyāla is a remedy for leprosy.

[15]A man who consumes a preparation containing the roots of Kukkuṭa, Kośātakī, and Śatāvarī becomes fair in complexion within a month. [16]A man who bathes in a decoction of banyan and is smeared with a paste of

Sahacara becomes black in complexion. [17]Orpiment and red arsenic mixed with the oil of Śakuna and Kaṅgu cause a dark complexion.

[18]Powder of fireflies mixed with mustard oil glows at night. [19]Powder of fireflies and Gaṇḍūpada-worms, or powder made from the flowers of Samudrajantu, Bhṛṅgakapāla, Khadira, and Karṇikāra, mixed with the oil of Śakuna and Kaṅgu, produce a glowing powder (13.2.11 n.).

[20]Soot from the bark of Pāribhadraka mixed with the fat of a frog makes the limbs glow with fire. [21]A body smeared with a paste made from the bark of Pāribhadraka and sesame glows with fire. [22]A lump made with the soot from the bark of Pīlu glows in the hand. [23]A man smeared with the fat of a frog glows with fire. [24]A body glows when smeared with that or sprinkled with the oil of Kuśāmra fruit (see 2.15.39 n.) mixed with the powder of a female sea frog, sea foam, and the resin of Sarja. [25]Equal parts of sesame oil and the fat of frogs, crabs, and the like boiled together cause the limbs to glow with fire when applied all over. [26]A body glows with fire when coated with bamboo root and Śaivala water plant and smeared with the fat of a frog.

[27]A man whose feet have been smeared with sesame oil boiled with the pulp of the roots of Pāribhadraka, Pratibalā, Vañjula, Vajra, and banana tree and with the fat of a frog can walk on burning coal.

> [28–29]Upodakā, Pratibalā, Vañjula, and Pāribhadraka—he should boil sesame oil with a paste made from the roots of these along with the fat of a frog. With that he should anoint his well-cleaned feet. He would walk on a heap of burning coal as on a bed of flowers.

[30]Torches made with reed and tied to the tails of ruddy geese, Krauñca-cranes, peacocks, and other large birds that swim on water present a meteor display at night.

[31]Ash from a lightning strike is a means of extinguishing fire.

[32]Māṣa-beans soaked in a woman's menstrual discharge and the root of Vajrakulī mixed with the fat of a frog are means of preventing a blazing fireplace from cooking. [33]The remedy for it is to clean the fireplace.

[34]A ball made of Pīlu wood with fire placed within it, with a plug of Suvarcalā root or of thread and wrapped all around with cotton, is a means of blowing fiery smoke through the mouth.

[35]Fire, when sprinkled with the oil of Kuśa-grass and mango fruit, burns even in rain and wind; [36]when it contains sea foam and is combined with oil, it burns while floating on water. [37]Fire produced by drilling the

bones of aquatic birds with a speckled bamboo stick is not extinguished by water, but burns with water.

[38]Fire produced by drilling with a speckled bamboo stick the left rib bones of a man killed by a weapon or impaled on a stake, or fire produced by drilling the bones of a man or a woman with a human rib—when this fire is taken around some place three times counterclockwise, no other fire will burn there.

> [39]Muskrat, wagtail, and Khārakīṭa—when these are ground into a powder and mixed with horse urine, it is a means of breaking chains;

[40]or even a loadstone made twice as strong by smearing it with the fat of crabs, frogs, and Khārakīṭa.

[41]A bovine fetus ground together with the sides of Kaṅka-heron and Bhāsa-vulture, and with lotus and water, is a balm for the feet of quadrupeds and bipeds.

[42]By coating camel-skin shoes with the fat of an owl and a vulture and wrapping them with banyan leaves, a man is able to walk for fifty Yojanas without getting tired; [43]with the bone marrow or semen of a hawk, Kaṅka-heron, crow, vulture, ruddy goose, Krauñca crane, and Vīcīralla, for 100 Yojanas—or with the bone marrow or semen of a lion, tiger, leopard, crow, and owl; [44]with the fat produced from pressing the aborted fetuses of all the social classes—or dead children within a cemetery—in a camel-shaped vessel (13.1.16 n.), for 100 Yojanas.

> [45]He should strike terror into his enemy by creating pernicious prodigies, with the abusive words: "May you be kingdomless!"*
> This is said to be equal to a revolt.

That concludes the Second Chapter: "Creating Prodigious Effects" within "Deception" of the Fourteenth Book: "On Esoteric Practices."

Chapter 3

Topic178b: Use of Medicines and Mantras

[1]He should get two sets of powders prepared, the one from the right eyes and the other from the left eyes of one, two, or several of the following: cat,

camel, wolf, boar, porcupine, flying fox, Naptṛ-nightjar, crow, and owl, or of other animals that roam at night. [2]Then, by anointing thoroughly the right eye with the left-eye powder and the left eye with the right-eye powder, he is able to see at night and in the dark.

> [3]One Amlaka fruit, the eye of a boar, a firefly, and the black Śārivā—a man whose eyes are anointed with this is able to see things at night.

[4]After fasting for three nights, on a Puṣya day, he should plant barley seeds in soil placed in the skull of a man killed by a weapon or impaled on a stake and sprinkle them with sheep's milk. [5]Then, by wearing a garland made with the barley sprouts, he is able to move about with his shadow and shape invisible. [6]After fasting for three nights, on a Puṣya day, he should get two sets of powders prepared, the one from the right eyes and the other from the left eyes of a dog, cat, owl, and flying fox. [7]Then, by anointing each eye with the powder from the corresponding eye, he is able to move about with his shadow and shape invisible. [8]After fasting for three nights, on a Puṣya day, he should get an applicator and a collyrium receptacle made with the thighbone of a murderer. [9]Then, by anointing the eyes with the eye powder of any one of them,* he is able to move about with his shadow and shape invisible. [10]After fasting for three nights, on a Puṣya day, he should get an applicator and a collyrium receptacle made of iron. [11]Then, he should fill the skull of any animal that roams at night with collyrium, insert it into the vagina of a dead woman, and set fire to it. [12]Taking out that collyrium on a Puṣya day, he should place it in that collyrium receptacle. [13]When his eyes are anointed with that, he is able to move about with his shadow and shape invisible.

[14]When he sees a Brāhmaṇa who had maintained the three sacred fires (3.13.37 n.) burnt or being burnt in some place, after fasting there for three nights, on a Puṣya day, he should make a pouch out of the clothes of a man who has died naturally and fill it with ash from the pyre. By tying it, he is able to move about with his shadow and shape invisible. [15]A snakeskin bag filled with powder made from the bones and marrow of a bull killed on the occasion of the funeral rites of a Brāhmaṇa is a means of making farm animals invisible. [16]A bag made from a skin of a venomous snake filled with the ash of a man killed by a snakebite is a means of making wild animals invisible. [17]A snakeskin bag filled with powder made from the

tail, dung, and knee bone of an owl and a flying fox is a means of making birds invisible.

[18]These are the eight means of making someone invisible.

> [19]I pay homage to Bali, the son of Virocana, to Śambara of 100 tricks, and to Bhaṇḍīpāka, Naraka, Nikumbha, and Kumbha.
>
> [20]I pay homage to Devala and Nārada. I pay homage to Sāvarṇigālava. At the direction of these, a great sleep has been brought on you.
>
> [21]As sleeps the pythons, as sleeps the Camūkhalas* too, so may the men sleep, as also those who are prying in the village.
>
> [22]With 1,000 receptacles and 100 chariot rims, I will enter this house; may the receptacles remain silent.
>
> [23–24]Having paid homage to Manu and shut the dog cages—those gods in the divine realms, the Brāhmaṇas among the human, the perfected beings who have mastered their studies, and the ascetics on Kailāsa—having paid homage to all these perfected beings, a great sleep has been brought on you.
>
> [25]And as I go beyond, may those who have gathered together run away.
>
> [26]O Alitā! O Valitā! To Manu, Svāhā!

[27]The following is its* application. [28]After fasting for three nights, on the 14th day of the dark fortnight when the moon is in conjunction with the Puṣya constellation, he should purchase from the hand of a Śvapāka woman (3.7.33 n.) the scrapings of a Bilakhā.* [29]He should place them along with Māṣa-beans in a basket and have it buried in an undisturbed cremation spot. [30]Taking it out on the 14th lunar day of the next dark fortnight and getting a virgin to pound them, he should have pills made out of them. [31]Then, he should recite the ritual formula over one pill. Wherever he throws that pill while reciting this ritual formula, it makes everyone there fall asleep.

[33]Using this same procedure, he should have a porcupine quill with three black and three white stripes buried in an undisturbed cremation spot. [33]He should take it out on the 14th lunar day of the next dark fortnight. Wherever he throws it along with the ash from the cremation ground while reciting this ritual formula, it makes everyone there fall asleep.

[34]I pay homage to Brahmāṇī with golden flowers and to Brahmā with the flag of Kuśa-grass. I pay homage to all the divinities, and I pay homage to all the ascetics.

[35]May Brāhmaṇas come under my power, as also Kṣatriya kings! May Vaiśyas and Śūdras come under my power! May they always come under my power!

[36]Svāhā! O Amilā! O Kimilā! O Vayucārā! O Prayogā! O Phakkā! O Vayuhvā! O Vihālā! O Dantakaṭakā! Svāhā!

[37]May the dogs sleep soundly, as also those who are prying in the village. And this porcupine quill with three white stripes has been created by Brahmā.

[38]For all men who have attained wealth are fast asleep! This sleep has been brought on you up to the boundary of the village and until rising of the sun.

[39]Svāhā!

[40]The following is its (14.3.27 n.) application. [41]The porcupine quills should have three white stripes. After fasting for seven nights, on the 14th day of the dark fortnight, collecting 108 pieces of Khadira-wood kindling sticks, he should offer them in the fire along with honey and ghee while reciting this ritual formula. [42]Thereafter, wherever one of those quills is buried—at the entrance to a village or at the door of a house—with this ritual formula, it makes everyone there fall asleep.

[43]I pay homage to Bali, the son of Virocana, to Śambara of 100 tricks, to Nikumbha, Naraka, Kumbha, and Tantukaccha, the great Asura;

[44]to Armālava, Pramīla, Maṇḍolūka, and Ghaṭobala;* to the attendant of Kṛṣṇa and Kaṃsa and to Paulomī full of fame.

[45]Having consecrated it with the ritual formula, I take the dead myna bird for the sake of success. May it be victorious! And it is victorious! Homage to quilled creatures. Svāhā!

[46]May the dogs sleep soundly, as also those who are prying in the village. May the men who have attained wealth sleep soundly—the very wealth that we seek—from the setting of the sun until its rise, until the money has become my reward.

[47]Svāhā!

[48]The following is its (14.3.27 n.) application. [49]After fasting for four mealtimes,* on the 14th day of a dark fortnight, he should offer a Bali-oblation on an undisturbed cremation spot, take a dead myna bird using this ritual formula, and tie it in a bag made of a hog's snout. [50]Then, he should pierce it in the middle with a porcupine quill. Wherever it is buried using this ritual formula, it makes everyone there fall asleep.

> [51]I seek refuge with Fire, the divinities, and the ten directions.
> May all flee! May they always come under my power!
> [52]Svāhā!

[53]The following is its (14.3.27 n.) application. [54]After fasting for three nights, on a Puṣya day, he should make a collection of 21 pebbles and offer them in the fire with honey and ghee. [55]Then, he should worship them with perfumes and garlands and bury them. [56]On the next Puṣya day, he should take them out. He should recite the ritual formula over one of those pebbles and strike the door panel with it. [57]Within four pebble strikes, the door will open.

[58]After fasting for four mealtimes (14.3.49 n.), on the 14th day of a dark fortnight, he should get a bull made out of the bones of a broken-bodied man (4.7.6) and recite this ritual formula over it. [59]There will be an oxcart yoked with a pair of oxen brought. [60]Thereafter, he will traverse through the sky. [61]Becoming akin* to the sun, he will penetrate everything beyond the gate bar.

[62]"You are the torrent of the harsh power of the gourd pitcher of the Caṇḍāla woman, possessing a woman's vagina, Svāhā!" [63]This is the means of opening locks and causing sleep.

[64]After fasting for three nights, on a Puṣya day, he should plant Tuvarī seeds in soil placed in the skull of a man killed by a weapon or impaled on a stake and sprinkle them with water. [65]When they have sprouted, he should gather them specifically on a Puṣya day and braid them into a rope. [66]Thereafter, when it is cut in front of bows and mechanical devices equipped with strings, it causes those strings to snap.

[67]He should fill a bag made from the skin of a water snake with toilet soil used by a man or a woman. It is the means of blocking the nostrils and gagging the mouth.

[68]After filling a bag made from the skin of a boar with toilet soil, he should tie it with a monkey's tendons. It causes epistasis.

[69]On the 14th day of a dark fortnight, he should anoint a statue of his enemy carved from Rājavṛkṣa wood with bile taken from a tawny-colored cow killed by a weapon. It causes blindness.

[70]After fasting for four mealtimes (14.3.49 n.), on the 14th day of a dark fortnight, he should make a Bali-offering (1.21.5 n.) and get pegs made from the bones of a man who has been impaled on a stake. [71]When one of these is buried in someone's urine or feces, it causes epistasis. When it is buried in a place where he places his foot or sits, it causes his death by consumption. When it is buried in his shop, field, or house, it destroys his livelihood. [72]This very procedure explains pegs made out of a tree burnt by lightning.

> [73–74]When someone buries Punarnava growing downward, neem, Kāmamadhu,* monkey's hair, and a human bone, tied together with the clothes of a dead person, in the house of a man, or plants it at a spot where he sees him placing his foot, that man, along with his sons, wives, and wealth, will not last beyond three fortnights.
>
> [75–76]When someone buries Punarnava growing downward, neem, Kāmamadhu, Svayaṃguptā, and a human bone in a place where a man places his foot, or at the door to his house, army camp, village, or city, that man, along with his sons, wives, and wealth, will not last beyond three fortnights.
>
> [77]He should collect the hair of the following: goat, monkey, cat, mongoose, Brāhmaṇa, Śvapāka (3.7.33 n.), crow, and owl. When a man's feces are pounded with these, it causes his immediate destruction.
>
> [78]When someone buries the flowers from a corpse, ferment (2.25.26, 33), hair of a mongoose, and the skin of a scorpion, bee, and snake in a place where a man places his foot, he becomes impotent immediately until that is removed.

[79]After fasting for three nights, on a Puṣya day, he should plant Guñja seeds in soil placed in the skull of a man killed by a weapon or impaled on a stake and sprinkle them with water. [80]When they have sprouted, he should have the Guñja creepers collected on a new-moon or a full-moon day when the moon is in conjunction with the Puṣya constellation and get rings made out of them. [81]When vessels containing food and drink are placed on them, they do not become exhausted.

[82]When a show is going on at night, he should have the udders of a dead cow cut out and burnt in the flames of a lamp. [83]When they are burnt, he should get them pounded with the urine of a bull and coat the inside of a new pot with it. [84]When he carries that pot counterclockwise around the village and puts it down on a spot, to it comes all their fresh butter.

[85]On the 14th day of a dark fortnight when the moon is in conjunction with the Puṣya constellation, he should insert into the vagina of a female dog in heat an iron signet ring. [86]He should gather it when it has fallen down on its own. [87]When summoned with it, fruits from trees come to him.

> [88]With secret measures accompanied by ritual formulae and medicines and those produced by magical means, he should annihilate his enemies and protect his own people.

THAT CONCLUDES THE THIRD CHAPTER: "USE OF MEDICINES AND MANTRAS" WITHIN "DECEPTION" OF THE FOURTEENTH BOOK: "ON ESOTERIC PRACTICES."

Chapter 4

Topic 179: Countermeasures against Harm to One's Own Troops

[1]These are the countermeasures against poisons such as Dūṣīviṣa employed against one's side by the enemy.

[2]"Cleansing water"* mixed with a decoction of Śleṣmātaka, Kapittha, Danti, Dantaśaṭha, Goji, Śirīṣa, Pāṭalī, Balā, Syonāga, Punarnavā, Śvetā, and Vāraṇa* and blended with sandalwood and the blood of a female hyena is a cleanser for the private parts of women who are to have sex with the king; it is also an antidote for poison directed at the army.

[3]The powder of Mahīrājī mixed with the bile of the spotted deer, mongoose, peacock, and monitor lizard, and a mixture of Sinduvārita, Varaṇa, Vāruṇī, Taṇḍulīyaka, tips of Śataparva, and Piṇḍītaka remove the evil effects of a coma-inducing drug. [4]A drink made with the decoctions of the roots of one or all of the following: Sṛgālavinnā, Madana, Sinduvārita, Varaṇa, Vāraṇa, and Vallī, and mixed with milk removes the evil effects of a coma-inducing drug.

[5]The oil of Kaiḍarya, Pūti, and sesame, put in the nostrils, is a cure for madness.

[6]A mixture of Priyaṅgu and Naktamāla is a cure for leprosy.

[7]A mixture of Kuṣṭha and Lodhra removes gray hair and consumption.

[8]The powder of Kaṭa fruit,* Dravantī, and Vilaṅga, put in the nostrils, is a cure for headaches.

[9]A mixture of Priyaṅgu, Mañjiṣṭhī, Tagara, lac juice, liquorice, turmeric, and honey revives those who have lost consciousness by hanging, drowning, poisoning, beating, and falling. [10]The dose for humans is just one Akṣa,* double that for cattle and horses, and four times that for elephants and camels. [11]A ball made of these with gold inside is a cure for every kind of poison.

[12]A ball made of Jīvantī, Śvetā, Muṣkaka, Puṣpa, and Vandākā, and of an Aśvattha tree growing on a drumstick tree* removes every kind of poison.

> [13]The sound of drums smeared with these destroys poison. By looking at a flag or banner smeared with them, a man becomes free of poison.
>
> [14]Having taken countermeasures using these with regard to his troops and himself, he should employ poisonous smoke and the poisoning of water against his enemies.

THAT CONCLUDES THE FOURTH CHAPTER: "COUNTERMEASURES AGAINST HARM TO ONE'S OWN TROOPS" OF THE FOURTEENTH BOOK: "ON ESOTERIC PRACTICES."

THAT CONCLUDES THE FOURTEENTH BOOK: "ON ESOTERIC PRACTICES" OF KAUṬILYA'S *ARTHAŚĀSTRA*.

Book Fifteen

Organization of a Scientific Treatise

Chapter 1

Topic 180: Organizational Elements of a Scientific Treatise*

[1]Success (*artha*) is the livelihood of human beings; Success means land containing human beings. [2]The science (*śāstra*) that provides the means of gaining and protecting that earth is Treatise on Success (*arthaśāstra*).

[3]It contains 32 organizational elements: subject matter, arrangement, employment, meaning of a term, goal of a reason, allusion, explanation, advice, reference, extension, intimation, analogy, implication, doubt, correspondence, inverse, the rest of a sentence, agreement, elucidation, derivation of words, illustration, exception, one's own technical term, prior view, subsequent view, absolute rule, reference to a future statement, reference to a past statement, restriction, option, combination, and what is to be inferred.

[4]Subject matter is the object with respect to which a statement is made, [5]such as: "This singular Treatise on Success has been composed for the most part by drawing together the Treatises on Success composed by former teachers for gaining and administering the earth" (1.1.1).

[6]Arrangement is the sequence of topics in the treatise, [7]such as: "Enumeration of Knowledge Systems; Association with Elders; Mastery over the Senses; Establishment of Ministers" (1.1.3), and the like.

[8]Employment is the arrangement of sentences, [9]such as: "People belonging to the four social classes and orders of life" (1.4.16).

[10]Meaning of a term has the term as its limit. [11]"Squanderer of patrimony" is a term. [12]"A man who consumes in improper ways the property

of his father and grandfather is a squanderer of patrimony" (2.9.21) is its meaning.

[13]Goal of a reason is a reason that accomplishes a goal, [14]such as: "for Success is the foundation of Law and Pleasure." (1.7.7).

[15]Allusion is a terse sentence, [16]such as: "Mastery over the senses results from training in the knowledge systems" (1.6.1).

[17]Explanation is a comprehensive sentence, [18]such as: "Mastery over the senses consists of the senses—ear, skin, eye, tongue, and nose—not wandering inappropriately among sounds, touches, visible forms, tastes, and smells" (1.6.2).

[19]"Thus should a man behave." That is advice, [20]such as: "He should pursue Pleasure without transgressing Law or Success; he should not deprive himself of enjoyments." (1.7.3).

[21]"Thus says so and so." That is a reference, [22]such as: "'He should constitute a council of counselors consisting of 12 ministers,' state the Mānavas. 'Sixteen,' say the Bārhaspatyas. 'Twenty,' say the Auśanasas. 'According to ability,' says Kauṭilya" (1.15.47–50).

[23]Extension is exposition by means of what has already been said, [24]such as: "The non-payment of debts has also explained the non-delivery of gifts" (3.16.1).

[25]Intimation is exposition by means of what will be said, [26]such as: "or through conciliation, gifts, dissension, and military force as we will explain in the section on dangers" (7.14.11).

[27]Analogy is the exposition of what is unknown through what is known, [28]such as: "Like a father, he should assist those whose exemptions have come to an end" (2.1.18).

[29]Implication is when something, although unstated, is discerned by the very connotation, [30]such as: "An expert in worldly matters should seek service with a king through people who are dear to and intimate with him, a king who possesses the exemplary qualities both of the self and of material constituents" (5.4.1).[31]Here, by its very connotation, one discerns: "He should not seek service through people who are not dear to and not intimate with him."

[32]Doubt is an issue for which there are reasons on both sides, [33]such as: "Should it be the ruler with destitute and greedy subjects or the ruler with rebellious subjects?" (7.5.12).

[34]Correspondence is when the matter is the same as that given within a different topic, [35]such as: "In a place assigned to him for agriculture . . .—the rest is the same as above" (1.11.10).

[36]Inverse is the exposition of something through its opposite, [37]such as: "(He should interpret) the inverse of these (as signs that) he is displeased" (1.16.12).

[38]The rest of a sentence is what completes a sentence, [39]such as: "the king's activities come to an end, like those (of a bird) with its wings clipped" (8.1.9). [40]Here, "of a bird" constitutes the rest of the sentence.

[41]Agreement is when the statement of another is not contradicted, [42]such as: "Two wings, breast, and reserves—that is the arrangement of battle formations according to Uśanas" (10.6.1).

[43]Elucidation is a thorough description, [44]such as: "[64]In particular, moreover, dissension caused by gambling affects confederacies and royal houses having the character of confederacies, and they are destroyed on account of that. Thus, favoring evil people, it is the worst of all vices, because it causes ineptitude in administrative work" (8.3.64).

[45]Derivation of words is tracing the origin of a word by means of its component parts, [46]such as: "It separates (*vy-as*) him from prosperity; that is how we get the term calamity (*vyasana*)" (8.1.4).

[47]Illustration is the exemplification using an example, [48]such as: "For, in initiating hostilities against someone stronger, he is as if engaging in a fight with an elephant while on foot" (7.3.3).

[49]Exception is retraction of a general rule, [50]such as: "He should always station troops supplied by the enemy . . . close at hand . . ., except when there is a concern that a revolt may arise in the interior" (9.2.6).

[51]One's own technical term is a word not acknowledged by others, [52]such as: "(The seeker after conquest) is the first constituent. One with a territory immediately contiguous to his is the second. One with a territory once removed is the third" (cf. 6.2.13–15).

[53]Prior view is a statement that must be rejected, [54]such as: "Between calamities affecting the lord and a minister, a calamity affecting a minister is more serious" (8.1.7).

[55]The subsequent view is a statement presenting the verdict on it, [56]such as: "because they are dependent on him . . . for the lord stands at their head" (8.1.17–18).

[57]Absolute rule is what is pertinent to all occasions, [58]such as: "Therefore, he should make himself energetic" (1.19.5).

[59]Reference to a future statement is saying, "This is determined later," [60]such as: "We shall discuss balances and weights in the section on the Superintendent of Standardization" (2.13.28).

[61]Reference to a past statement is saying, "This was determined earlier," [62]such as: "The exemplary qualities of a minister have been given above" (6.1.7).

[63]Restriction is saying,: "This way, and in no other way," [64]such as: "Therefore, one should teach him what accords with Law and Success, never something that is contrary to Law and Success." (1.17.33).

[65]Option is saying, "This way or that," [66]such as: "or by his daughters born in the most righteous marriages" (3.5.10).

[67]Combination is saying, "This way and that," [68]such as: "If fathered by oneself, he is the heir to the estate of his father and of his relatives" (3.7.13).

[69]What is to be inferred is doing what is not prescribed, [70]such as: "Experts, moreover, should arrange a cancellation in such a way that neither the donor nor the receiver is harmed" (3.16.5).

> [71]In this manner, this treatise, arranged with these organizational elements of a scientific treatise, has been proclaimed for the gain and protection of this world and the next.
>
> [72]This treatise brings into being and protects Law (*dharma*), Success (*artha*), and Pleasure (*kāma*), and suppresses those who are unrighteous (*adharmān*) and those who hate Success.
>
> [73]The man who out of indignation quickly rescued the treatise (*śāstra*) and the weapon (*śastra*), as also the land that had fallen into the hands of the Nandas, it is he who composed this treatise.

THAT CONCLUDES THE FIRST CHAPTER: "ORGANIZATIONAL ELEMENTS OF A SCIENTIFIC TREATISE" OF THE FIFTEENTH BOOK: "ORGANIZATION OF A SCIENTIFIC TREATISE."

THAT CONCLUDES THE FIFTEENTH BOOK: "ORGANIZATION OF A SCIENTIFIC TREATISE" OF KAUṬILYA'S *ARTHAŚĀSTRA*.

> [Noticing the many errors committed by commentators on treatises, Viṣṇugupta himself composed both the aphoristic text and the commentary.]*

THAT CONCLUDES KAUṬILYA'S *ARTHAŚĀSTRA*

APPENDIX I

Fauna and Flora

COMMON FAUNA AND flora that can be readily translated are not listed here; they are found in the Index. Identifying Sanskrit names for flora and fauna is beset with difficulties. As Wujastyk (2003, xxxv) has observed: "Anyone who has worked with the Sanskrit medical texts has, at one time or another, been driven to desperation by the problem of plant nomenclature and identification." I am no exception. Below I give the best identifications I can come up with; sometimes they are multiple, because different scholars provide different identifications. All the places where these terms occur are listed after each entry. One problem with Kangle's translation is that he has made no effort to identify the flora and fauna mentioned in the *AŚ*. My hope is that this index, imperfect though it is, will help those readers interested in the use of plants and animals in ancient Indian statecraft.

For further information on flora, see Nadkarni 1976; P. V. Sharma 1979. For animals, see Prater 1997. For birds, see Dave 2005. For reptiles and amphibians, see Daniel 2002. See also the many online resources: http://www.plantago.nl/; Table of Ayurvedic Plants and Minerals with Sanskrit (and Synonyms), Common, and Botanical Names: http://ayurveda-florida.com/Ayurvedic_Materia_Medica_Articles/Table2.htm; Ayurvedic Medicinal Plants: http://ayurvedicmedicinalplants.com/.

Akṣi. I have been unable to identify this plant. If it is a short term for Matsyākṣi, then it is Sessile Joyweed; Hindi: Gudrisag; *Alternanthera sessilis*. Or it could be *Enhydra fluctuans*. There are also other plants with *akṣi* at the end of their names: Gavākṣi (*Citrullus colocynthis*); Kuberākṣi (*Caesalpinia bonduc*). 14.1.15, 17, 23, 30.

Akṣīva. In general, it is the common drumstick tree (*Moringa pterygosperma*). Given that it is listed at 14.1.13 along with *śigru*, which is the most common name for the drumstick tree, it probably refers to a different plant.

Amlaka. Indian gooseberry, emblic myrobalan, *Emblica officinalis*, 14.3.3.

Anavadya. Probably the stamen of saffron crocus. See 2.11.29 n.

Andhāhika. Literally, "blind snake," the term probably refers to a particular reptile with this name. Daniel (2002, 76–78) identifies three kinds of worm snakes called blind snakes: *Ramphotyphlops braminus, Typhlops diardii,* and *Rhinotyphlops acutus*. This term is also identified with a fish called Kucikā (*Unibranchapertura cuchiya*). 14.1.4, 12, 19.

Añjalikāra. Appearing between two animals at 14.1.23, it probably refers to a kind of lizard or animal that brings its paws together. It could also be a variant of Añjalikārikā, *Mimosa natans*.

Apāmārga. Commonly called prickly chaff flower or devil's horsewhip, *Achyranthes aspera*. 2.25.33.

Arālā. The tree *Shorea robusta*, more commonly known in Sanskrit as *sāla*. 14.1.10.

Arjuna. Arjuna myrobalan; Hindi: Arjuna, Kahu, *Terminalia arjuna*, 2.17.4.

Arka. Madder tree. See Wojtilla 2011, 6. *Calotropis procera* or *gigantea*. 2.17.7; 2.18.9; 14.1.15, 17; 14.2.6, 8.

Āsphota. Wild jasmine, *Jasminum angustifolium*. Also identified as *Jasminum sambac, Evolvulus alsinoides, Clitoria ternatea, Ichnocarpus frutescens, Salvadora persica*. 2.25.33; 14.1.11.

Aśvattha. Peepal or sacred fig tree, *Ficus religiosa*. 1.20.5; 14.4.12.

Atasī. Linseed, flax plant, *Linum usitatissimum* (Wojtilla 2011, 5). 2.17.7.

Avalguja. Possibly Babchi, psoralea seed. Hindi: Bavchi, Bakshi, *Psoralea corylifolia*. 13.4.19; 14.1.4.

Avānu. I have been unable to identify this plant. The reading at 14.1.30 is also uncertain.

Badara. The jujube tree, *Ziziphus jujuba*. 2.14.33.

Baka. Dave 2005, 383–387, 408–409. This term is applied to a wide variety of water fowl, including the heron, ibis, stork, and common flamingo. 14.1.15.

Bakula. Bullet-wood tree, *Mimusops elengi*. 2.11.108, 111.

Balā. Indian country mallow, flannel weed, *Sida cordifolia*. 14.4.2.

Balākā. Dave 2005, 409–421. Flamingo; the term is sometimes applied to other water fowl, such as the egret. 14.1.15.

Balbaja. A type of coarse grass; crowfoot grass, crab grass, *Eleusine indica*. 2.17.8; 4.8.22.

Bāṇa. Generally means arrow and possibly refers to the reed *Saccharum sara*. 14.1.30.

Bhallātaka. Marking nut, oriental cashew, *Semecarpus anacardium*, or black varnish tree of Malabar. Hindi: Halgery, *Holigarna arnottiana*. 14.1.4, 6, 7, 30; 14.2.11.

Bhallātakī. Possibly another spelling of Bhallātaka. 2.2.10.

Bhāllūka. A variety of reed (2.17.5). I have not been able to identify this further. The form Bhalluka is identified by Macri (1988, 105) as *Calosanthes indica* (also named *Oroxylum indicum*), but this is a large tree and cannot be classified as a reed.

Bhāṇḍi. Siris tree, Indian walnut, Indian madder. Many plants and trees bear this name: *Albizia lebbeck, Albizia julibrissin, Operculina turpethum, Clerondendrum viscosum, Rubia munjesta, Hydrocotyle asiatica*. 14.1.13.

Bhāsa. A species of vulture, identified by Dave (2005, 188) as the bearded vulture. 14.1.25; 14.2.41.

Bhṛṅgakapāla. Perhaps the trailing eclipta plant. Hindi: Bangrah, Moprant, *Eclipta alba* or *prostrata*. 14.2.19.

Bhṛṅgarāja. The large racket-tailed drongo (Dave 2005, 64). 1.20.7; 2.26.5.

Cakora. Partridge, *Perdix rufa*. 1.20.8; 2.26.5; 2.30.4.

Cakravāka. The ruddy sheldrake called the Brahmani duck. The fidelity of a mated pair to each other and their grief when separated are celebrated in Indian poetry and folklore (Dave 2005, 450f.). 2.26.5.

Cāpa. A kind of reed or bamboo. 2.17.5; 2.18.8.

Cimiya. A kind of reed or bamboo. 2.17.5.

Cirbhiṭa. Snake cucumber, *Cucumis melo* or *utilissimus*. 2.15.17.

Citraka. White or Ceylon leadwort, doctorbush, *Plumbago zeylanica*. 2.25.29, 33.

Coraka. According to Macri (1988), *Trigonella corniculata*; a kind of fenugreek. According to the *Table of Ayurvedic Plants*: Angelica, *Angelica glauca*, called Cora in Punjabi (Kirtikar and Basu 2001, 1687). Kangle identifies it as anise seed. 2.15.20.

Damanaka. Sagebrush, *Artemisia siversiana*. Dona in Bengali; Davana in Marathi; Dauna in Hindi (Kirtikar and Basu 2001, 1933). 2.15.20.

Daṇḍāsana. It is unclear whether this is simply the name of an arrow or refers to a reed from which the arrow was made. See 2.18.10.

Dantaśaṭha. Perhaps sour orange, *Citrus aurantium*, or Chinese gooseberry, *Averrhoa carambola* (Macri 1988). 14.4.2.

Danti. Wild castor, wild croton. Hindi: Hastidanti, *Baliospermum montanum*. According to Macri (1988), *Croton polyandrus*. 14.4.2.

Darbha. A type of grass used for ritual purposes, most commonly the same as Kuśa; specifically the grass *Saccharum cylindricum*. Sometimes, Darbha can mean simply a tuft or bundle, as in *VaDh* 21.2, *lohitadarbha* (Lohita grass). 10.3.31; 14.2.3.

Dāruharidrā. Indian barberry, tree turmeric, *Berberis aristata*.

Dātyūha. This term is given to a variety of birds, including the hawk cuckoo and several water birds, such as the black ibis, the white-breasted waterhen, and the purple moorhen (Dave 2005, 294). 2.25.27, 33.

Devadāru. The Himalayan cedar, *Cedrus deodara*. 13.4.18.

Dhāmārgava. Wash sponge, sponge gourd, *Luffa cylindrica* or *Luffa acutangula*. Hindi: Dhundhul. 14.1.6, 30.

Dhanvana. Dhaman, *Grewia tiliaefolia*. According to Macri (1988), *Grewia elastica*. 2.17.4.

Dhava. Identified by Shamasastry as *Mimosa hexandra*, and by Macri (1988) as *Grislea tomentosa* and *Anogeissus latifolia* (axle-wood, button tree). 2.17.4.

Dravantī. Physic nut, purging nut, *Jatropha curcas*. 14.4.8.

Dūṣīviṣa. In its usage, it is unclear whether it is a plant from which a poison is derived, or the name of a poison. 14.1.22; 14.4.1.

Elaka. Also spelled *eḍaka*, a variety of cardamom, *Elletaria cardamomum*. 14.1.30.

Elāvāluka. Identified by Shamasastry as *Solanum melongena* (eggplant), and by Meyer and Macri (1988) as *Feronia elephantum* (wood apple). 2.25.27.

Eṇa. The black buck (also called Kṛṣṇasāra in *MDh* 2.23), an antelope with black fur on its back and sides and white fur on its belly, *Antilope cervicapra* (Prater 1997, 270). 2.15.55.

Gajapippalī. A large perennial climber, *Scindapsus officinalis*. Hindi: Gajapippal, Barippali. 2.25,29.

Gaṇḍūpada. A kind of worm, earthworm. 14.2.19.

Gautama-vṛkṣa. I have been unable to identify this species. 14.1.17

Gavedhukā. Job's tear, coixseed, tear grass, *Coix lacryma-jobi*. 2.17.7.

Goji. The identity is unclear. According to Macri (1988), *Trophis aspera*. 14.4.2.

Gomārikā. The identity is unclear. Meyer thinks it could be a reptile, insect, or plant that is poisonous to cows. 14.1.4.

Gomūtrikā. The identity is unclear; dictionaries call it a reddish grass, with the synonyms *raktatṛṇā*, *tāmbaḍu*, and the like. 14.1.13.

Granthikā. Macri (1988, 76) gives the form *granthika* and identifies it as *Piper longum*, the long pepper. 14.1.25.

Guñja. Indian licorice, Jequirity, rosary pea, *Abrus precatorius*. 2.19.2; 14.1.11; 14.2.12; 14.3.79, 80.

Hālāhala. At 2.17.12, this appears within a list of poisons and is perhaps a name of a particular poison. But the poison may get its name from the plant from which it is derived, as at 14.1.30, where it is listed among other ingredients of a mixture. I have not been able to identify it; Macri (1988, 145) simply calls it a poisonous vegetable.

Hastikarṇa. Castor-oil plant, *Ricinus communis*. 14.1.9, 13, 16, 17

Hema. Perhaps the same as Hemamālatī, *Myxopyrum serratulum*. 14.1.10.

Hrībera. Hindi: Vālak. *Plectranthus vettiveroides, Coleus vettiveroides*. 2.24.22.

Idhma. I have been unable to identify this plant, animal, or insect. It is also unclear whether the readings at 14.1.4, 10 are correct.

Indīvara. Heartleaf, false pickerelweed, oval-leafed pondweed. A flowering plant in the water hyacinth family, *Monochoria vaginalis*. 2.25.33.

Indragopa. The precise zoological species is unclear. Lienhart (1978) shows that earlier translations of firefly and cochineal are inaccurate. The term refers to the tiny bright-red velvet mites (*Thrombidiiae*) that appear in large numbers early in the rainy season. 14.1.10.

Iṅgudī. Indian almond, *Terminalia catappa* (Wojtilla 2011, 7), or *Sarcostigma kleinii*, Tamil Oṭal. 2.15.40; 14.1.17.

Jātī. Spanish jasmine, royal jasmine, *Jasminum grandiflorum*. Hindi: Chameli. 2.11.66.

Jihvā. The identity of this plant is uncertain, as is the reading at 14.1.25.

Jīvaṃjīvaka. The peacock pheasant (Dave 2005, 273). 1.20.8; 2.26.5.

Jīvantī. Hindi: Arkapuṣpi, Cakṣuṣya, etc. *Leptadenia retriculata*. 1.20.5; 14.4.12.

Kāca. I have been unable to identify this. Shamasastry and Meyer take it as a kind of salt. 14.1.11.

Kaiḍarya. Possibly the curry leaf tree, *Murraya koenigii*. 14.4.5.

Kākāṇḍa. The tree *Diospyros tomentosa* (Macri 1988, 33, 62) and also identified as *mahānimba*. 2.12.16.

Kalāya. Mallow, jute, *Corchorus capsularis*; or yellow pea, yellow vetch, *Lathyrus aphaca*. 2.11.31; 2.12.6; 2.15.29, 37; 2.24.14.

Kāleyaka. Macri (1988), with the spelling *kālīya(ka)*, identifies this as *Curcuma zanthorrhiza*, a kind of turmeric. 2.11.69.

Kālī. Indian stinging nettle, *Tragia involucrata*, according to Shamasastry. 14.1.14.

Kaliṅgayava. Snowflakes, milky way, *Wrightia antidysenterica* or *Holarrhena pubescens*. 2.25.33.

Kambalī. Probably a small insect, but I have been unable to identify it. 14.1.4.

Kaṅgu. Foxtail millet, *Setaria italica*, or *Panicum frumentaceum*, or *Papaver dubium* (Wojtilla 2011, 9). 14.2.17.

Kaṅka. The name is used for several varieties of eagle, heron, stork, and kite. Its feathers were used in making arrows (Dave 2005, 242). Fitzgerald (1998, 258) has argued that the term refers to a carrion-eating stork. 14.2.41, 43.

Kaṇṭaka. A kind of reed or bamboo. 2.17.5.

Kaṇṭakāra. Also Kaṇṭakāri and Kaṇṭakārikā. Macri (1988): *Solanum jacquini*. Shamasastry: *Solanum xanthocarpum*. 14.1.17.

Kapittha. Wood apple, *Limonia acidissima; Feronia elephantum*. 14.4.2.

Karamarda. Jasmine flowered carrisa, *Carissa carandas*. 2.15.18.

Karañja. Indian beech, *Pongamia glabra* or *pinnata*. Hindi: Karanj. 2.25.33.

Karavīra. Indian oleander, *Nerium oleander*. 14.1.9, 17.

Karṇa. Golden shower tree, also called Aragvadha, Caturangula, Kritamala, Suvarnaka, *Cassia fistula*. 3.8.3.

Karṇikāra. Commonly known as Kanak Champa, Muchakunda, or Karnikar tree, *Pterospermum acerifolium*. 14.2.19.

Kaśeruka. A kind of bulrush gowing in wetlands, *Scirpus kysoor*. 14.2.2.

Kaṭa. Clearing-nut tree; Hindi Nirmali, the fruits of which are used for medicinal purposes and to purify water, *Strychnos potatorum*. 14.4.8.

Kaṭaśarkarā. A kind of sugarcane, *Saccharum officinarum*. 2.25.28, 33.

Kauṇḍinyaka. Perhaps a venomous insect. 14.1.4, 24.

Keśa. The identity of this plant is unclear; if it is the same as *keśara*, it would be *Mimusops elengi*, the Spanish cherry. 13.4.20, 21.

Khadira. Black catechu, cutch tree, *Acacia catechu*. 14.2.19; 14.3.41.

Khārakīṭa. The identity is unclear. With *kīṭa* at the end, it must refer to some kind of insect, perhaps one that makes a loud noise. 14.2.39, 40.

Kodrava. Kodo millet, *Paspalum scrobiculatum*. 2.15.25, 34; 2.24.12; 4.3.28; 14.1.9, 13, 16, 17, 22.

Kola. Identified by Shamasastry as "small jujube," and by Meyer as "Brustbeere" or jujube fruit. Macri (1988) gives Cavya (*Piper chaba*), Citra(ka), (*Plumbago zeylanica*), and Badara (*Ziziphus jujuba*) as synonyms. 2.15.18.

Kośātakī. Ribbed gourd, *Luffa pentandra, Luffa acutangula*. 14.1.13; 14.2.15.

Kovidāra. Kodo millet, *Paspalum scrobiculatum*. 2.12.6.

Krakaṇṭaka. The identity and the correct reading are unclear. Meyer thinks that there may be an initial syllable missing, perhaps *vakrakaṇṭaka, śukrakaṇṭaka,* or *takrakaṇṭaka*. Shamasastry identifies it as a kind of partridge. 14.1.4.

Kramuka. Arecanut, betel nut, *Areca faufel*. 2.25.29.

Krauñca. A species of large water bird, probably the common crane (Dave 2005, 312). 1.20.8; 2.15.58; 2.26.5; 5.5.11; 14.2.30, 43.

Kṛkalāsa. Lizard, chameleon. 14.1.4.

Kṛkaṇa. The identity is uncertain; probably a kind of insect. 14.1.4, 14.

Kṛtakaṇḍala. The identity is uncertain; probably some kind of lizard or small animal. 14.1.19.

Kṣīravṛkṣa. Perhaps any of the four milky trees: banyan, Udumbara (*Ficus glomerata*), peepal (*Ficus religiosa*), and Madhūka (*Madhuca longifolia*). 2.25.33.

Kṣudrā. Macri (1988) identifies this as *Mimosa pudica*. Several plants appear to bear this name: *Solanum Jacquini*, commonly called Badi Katehri, *Oxsalis pusilla, Coix barbata*. 14.1.10.

Kukkuṭa. Four-leaf clover, *Marsilia quadrifolia*. 14.2.15.

Kulattha. Horse gram, *Dolichos biflorus* or *uniflorus* (Macri 1988). 2.24.14; 14.2.3.

Kuraṇḍaka (also Kuraṇḍika). Blistering ammannia, *Ammannia baccifera*. Hindi: Dadamari, Kuranta. 2.13.26.

Kuraṅga. The four-horned antelope, Chowsingha, *Tetracerus quadricornis*. 2.15.55.

Kuśa. The most common of the sacred grasses (see Darbha) used for rituals and sacred purposes, *Poa cynosuroides*. 14.3.34.

Kuśāmra. Manuscripts at 2.17.4 record the spelling Kaśāmra. I have been unable to identify this tree. See 2.15.39 n.

Kuṣṭha. Canereed, wild ginger, *Saussurea lappa*, *Costus speciosus*. 2.11.68; 2.17.12; 14.1.14; 14.4.7.

Kutaja. The ivory tree, *Holarrhena antidysenterica*, *Wrightia antidisenterica*. Hindi: kurchi, kuda. 14.1.13.

Lāṅgalī. According to Shamasastry, *Jusseina repens* (creeping primrose willow). 14.1.17.

Likuca (or Lakuca). Monkey jack, *Artocarpus lacucha*. 2.11.110.

Lodhra. Lodh tree, *Symplocos racemosa*. 2.25.29; 14.4.7.

Madana. Emetic nut, *Randia dumetorum*. 4.3.28; 14.1.9, 13, 16, 17, 22; 14.4.4.

Madanaśārikā. The hill myna, *Gracula religiosa* (Dave 2005, 81). 2.26.5.

Madhūka. Indian butter tree, Mahwa, Mahua, *Madhuca longifolia*. Macri (1988) identifies it as *Bassia latifolia*. 2.15.40; 2.17.4.

Madhurasā. Macri (1988) provides several identifications: *Sansevieria Roxburghiana* (Indian bowstring hemp), *Gmelina arborea* (Candahar tree, white teak), *Vitis vinifera* (wine grape), *Glycyrrhiza glabra* (liquorice). 2.25.27.

Mahīrājī. The identity is unclear; equally unclear is whether we are dealing with one or two plants. Rājī is identified by Meyer as *Veronia anthelmintica* (purple fleabane). 14.4.3.

Mālatī. Refers to a variety of Jasmine. Given that it is listed at 2.17.7 among plants that yield fiber, it is unclear what species this refers to. Macri (1988) gives *Jasminum grandiflorum*, *Bignonia suaveolens*, *Aganosma caryophyllata*.

Mañjiṣṭhī. Indian madder, cultivated for the red pigment from its roots, *Rubia cordifolia*. 14.4.9

Māṣa. Mung bean, *Phaseolus radiatus*. 2.12.5, 9; 2.15.27, 30, 51; 2.19.2, 29; 2.24.13; 2.25.26; 2.29.43; 2.30.18; 14.2.3, 32; 14.3.29.

Masūra. A kind of lentil, *Ervum lens*, *Ervum hirsutum*. 2.11.4; 2.15.31; 2.24.14.

Mātṛvāhaka. This is probably a variant of Mātṛvāhinī, a bat. 14.1.23.

Mattakokila. Probably the same as Kokila (Dave 2005, 128), the Asian koel or cuckoo. 1.20.8; 2.26.5.

Mayūrapadī. Macri spells *mayūra(ka)*. *Celosia cristata*, cockscomb. 14.1.17.

Meṣaśṛṅgī (Meṣaśṛṅga). According to Macri (1988), *Odina wodier*, *Gymnema sylvestre*, Indian Ipecacuanha. 2.15.17; 2.17.12; 2.25.22, 33.

Moraṭā. *Sansevieria roxburghiana*. Moraṭa: root of *Saccharum officinarum*; flower of *Alangium hexapetalum*. 2.25.26, 33.

Mṛgamāraṇī. Literally, a plant that kills deer. I have failed to identify this plant. 14.1.17.

Mudga. Green gram, *Vigna radiata*. Macri 1988: *Phaseolus mungo*. 2.12.5; 2.13.21, 54; 2.15.27, 30; 2.24.13; 2.30.18.

Mūka. I have been unable to identify this plant. 14.1.16.

Mūla. According to Macri (1988), a vegetable in the group *pañcamūla*. 14.1.29.

Mūlāṭī. This term occurs at 2.11.32, 39, with reference to a particular color or the sparkle of gems and diamonds. The reading and the meaning are unclear. I have not been able to identify the plant.

Muñja. A species of rush belonging to the sugarcane family used for basket weaving, *Saccharum munja*. 2.17.8.

Mūrvā. A species of hemp used in the manufacture of bow strings, *Sanseviera roxburghiana*. 2.17.7; 2.18.9.

Muṣkaka. Weaver's beam tree, *Schrebera swientenioides*. Hindi: Moka. 1.20.5; 14.4.12.

Naḍa. I have been unable to identify this; it is perhaps another spelling for Naḷa. 14.1.14.

Nāgalatā. Betel leaf plant, Paan, *Piper betle*. 2.17.6.

Nāga-vṛkṣa. Indian rose chestnut, Ceylon ironwood, *Mesua ferrea*. 2.11.108, 109.

Naktamāla. Indian beech, *Pongamia glabra* or *pinnata*. Same as Karañja. Hindi: Karanj. 4.8.22; 14.4.6.

Naptṛ. Nightjar (Dave 2005, 170). 14.3.1.

Nārāca. At 2.18.10, this plant is identified among those supplying material for the manufacture of arrows. Therefore, it must refer to some kind of reed or bamboo. The commentary *Cāṇakyaṭīkā* and Gaṇapati Śāstrī, however, take it to mean either iron or any kind of metal. 2.18.10.

Navamālikā. Arabian jasmine, Tuscan jasmine, Double jasmine, *Jasminum sambac*. 2.11.59.

Palāśa. A variety of fig tree called Dhak with a beautiful trunk and abundant leaves, *Butea frondosa*. 2.12.9; 2.25.33; 13.4.20, 21; 14.1.9, 13, 16, 17.

Pañcakuṣṭha. I have been unable to identify this. Perhaps the reference is to five kinds of ginger (Kuṣṭha). 14.1.4, 14, 24.

Pāribhadraka. Indian coral tree, Moochy wood tree, tiger's claw, *Erythrina indica*; has fiery red flowers. 13.4.20, 21; 14.2.20, 21, 27–29.

Pārijāta. Same as the previous. 2.11.29.

Parūṣaka. Phalsa or Falsa, *Grewia asiatica*, the fruit of which is sweet, sour, and acidic. 2.15.18.

Pāṭalī. Trumpet flower, yellow snake tree, *Bignonia suaveolens*, *Stereospermum suaveolens*. 2.12.6; 14.4.2.

Pataṅga. At 14.2.6, it is unclear whether this term refers to a flying insect or a plant species. If it is the latter, as I think it is, then the reference is to Sappan, *Caesalpina sappan*.

Pāṭhā. *Clypea hernandifolia*, *Stephania hernandifolia*. 2.25.27, 33.

Pattūra. Species of red sandalwood, *Achyranthes trianda*. 2.25.33.

Phaṇirjaka. Also called *phaṇijjha(ka)*, this is a kind of marjoram (*Oreganum*) or basil. 14.1.13.

Pīlu. The tree *Careya arborea* (patana oak) growing in grassy expanses, or the toothbrush tree, *Salvadora persica*. 2.12.8, 9; 13.1.16; 14.2.22, 34.

Pīluka. Probably the same as Pīlu. 14.1.13, 15, 17, 23.

Piṇḍāluka. Perhaps the same as Piṇḍālu, sweet potato, *Ipomoea batatas*. 2.24.22.

Piṇḍītaka. According to Macri (1988), *Vangueria spinosa; Tabernaemontana coronaria* (crape jasmine); *Randia dumetorum* (emetic nut). 14.4.3.

Plakṣa. Wavy-leaf fig tree, *Ficus lacor*. According to Macri (1988), *Ficus infectoria*. 7.6.39.14.1.16.

Pracalāka. Either a chameleon or a poisonous snake. 14.1.14, 23.

Pratibalā. I have been unable to identify this plant. 14.2.27–29.

Priyaka. Laurel. According to Shamasastry, yellow Sal tree, *Terminalia tomentosa*. 2.17.4.

Priyāla. Cuddapa almond, Chironji tree, *Buchanania lanzan*. According to Macri (1988), *Buchanania latifolia*. Hindi: Chār. 13.4.19; 14.2.14.

Priyaṅgu. Foxtail millet, *Setaria italica*. According to Macri (1988), *Panicum italicum*. 2.25.27; 14.4.6, 9.

Pṛśniparṇī. Cyprus, *Cyperus sp. Cyperaceae*. According to Macri (1988), *Hemionitis cordifolia, Uraria lagopodioides*. 14.2.3.

Punarnava. Spreading hogweed, tar vine, red spiderling, *Boerhavia diffusa*. 14.3.73–76.

Puṣpa. I have been unable to identify this. If at 14.4.12, we take Muṣkaka-puṣpa as a compound, then it would simply mean the flower of Muṣkaka. 1.20.5; 14.4.12.

Pūti. If this is the same as *pūtika*, then (according to Macri 1988) it would be *Guilandina bonduc* or *Pongamia glabra* (Indian beech, Pongam oil tree). 14.4.5.

Pūtikarañja. Bonduc fruit, fever nut, physic nut, *Guilandina Bonducella*. 14.1.11.

Pūtikīṭa. A kind of stinkbug. 14.1.4, 10.

Rājavṛkṣa. According to Macri (1988), *Cassia fistula* (Indian laburnum, purging cassia, golden shower), *Buchanania latifolia* (almondette tree, chironji, Buchanan's mango), *Euphorbia tirucalli* (milk-bush, milk hedge, Indian tree spurge). 2.12.8; 14.1.24, 38; 14.3.69.

Raṅku. A species of deer or antelope producing high-quality wool. Some identify this as the goat from which we get pashmina wool. Others take it to be the Himalayan ibex. 2.23.8.

Sahacara. Wild cowry fruit, Saptarangi, *Casearia esculanta*. According to Macri (1988), *Barleria prionitis* or *Barleria cristata*. 14.2.16.

Śaimbya. Probably a generic name to refer to legumes (*śimba*). 2.24.13.2.24.13.

Śaivala. According to Macri (1988), *Blyxa octandra* (a kind of duck-weed or water plant) or *Cerasus puddum*. 14.2.26.

Śakuna. I have been unable to identify this plant species. It is given with Kaṅgu, which is a kind of millet. So it is possibly also a kind of grain from which oil could be produced. Macri (1988) gives *śakunāhṛta* as a variety of rice. 14.2.17, 19.

Sāla. Sal tree, *Shorea robusta*. 14.2.3.

Śalākā. At 2.18.10, it is listed among the material for manufacturing arrows. If it does not refer to a particular kind of tree, then it probably refers to splinters or strips of wood.

Śāli. A variety of rice, different from Vrīhi. The commentators call this red winter rice. 2.15.25, 34; 2.24.12, 20; 2.30.18; 14.1.16.

Śālmalī. Red silk-cotton tree. *Bombax ceiba*. 2.1.3; 14.1.29.

Śamī. The name covers two plants: *Mimosa suma* (Hindi: *chikkur*), a thorny shrub, and *Prosopis spicigera*. 2.1.3; 14.2.1.

Samudrajantu. Identified by Meyer as *Trigonella corniculata*, commonly known as Kasuri methi or Marwari methi. 14.2.19.

Śaṇa. Indian hemp, *Cannibis sativa*, or sun hemp, *Crotolaria juncea*. 2.17.7, 9.

Saptaparṇa. Indian snakeroot, *Rauvolfia serpentina*. Macri (1988) identifies it as *Alstonia scholaris* (devil's tree, dita bark tree). 2.25.33.

Śara. A kind of reed used for arrows. *Saccharum sara*. 2.18.10.

Sarala. Long-leaved pine, *Pinus roxburghii*. 13.4.18.

Śārivā. Sebesten plum, *Cordia wallichii*. 14.3.3.

Sarja. White babool, Distiller's acacia, *Acacia leucophloea*. Hindi: Revaṃjā. Macri (1988) identifies it as *Vatica robusta* (Sal tree). 14.2.24.

Śatakanda. Identified by Shamasastry as *Phyalis flexuosa*, commonly called Aśvagandha. 14.1.4.

Śatakardama. I have been unable to identify this plant or animal. 14.1.9, 10.

Śataparva. According to Macri (1988), a variety of millet, *Panicum*. 14.4.3.

Śatapuṣpā. Munja grass, *Saccharum munja*. According to Macri (1988), *Anethum sowa* (Indian dill, Sowa); *Andropogon aciculatus*. 2.25.33

Śatāvarī. Flax hemp, *Crotalaria verrucosa Papilionaceae*. 14.1.14; 14.2.15.

Sauvīraka. Indian trumpet tree, *Oroxylum indicum*. Hindi: Bhūtvṛkṣa. 2.15.18.

Seraka. Occurring at 2.17.13 with regard to a group of animals providing valuable body parts, neither Meyer nor Shamasastry is able to identify it. 2.17.13.

Śīkavallī. A kind of vine. I have been unable to identify this. 2.17.6.

Sinduvāra. Three-leaved chaste tree, *Vitex trifolia*. Hindi: Nichinda. 2.12.15.

Sinduvārita. Meyer identifies this as *Vitex negundo* (five-leaved chaste tree); perhaps this is a different spelling for Sinduvāra. 14.4.3, 4.

Śirīṣa. The siris tree, Lebbeck, flea tree, *Albizia lebbeck*. Also identified as Pomela, *Citrus decumana*. 2.11.30, 39; 14.2.1; 14.4.2.

Śleṣmātaka. Also called Śleṣmānta and Śelu; ash-colored fleabane, *Vernonia cinerea*. Macri (1988) identifies it as *Cordia latifolia* (Sebesten fruit). Hindi: Lasoda. 14.4.2.

Snuhi. Milkhedge, *Euphorbia antiquorum; Euphorbia neriifolia*. 2.24.25; 4.3.23; 14.1.15.

Sṛgālavinnā. With the reading *sṛgvṛntā*, Meyer identifies this as *Hemionitis cordifolia* (heart fern, tongue fern, mule fern); also called *Hemionitis arifolia*. 14.4.4.

Suvarcalā. Also called Brahmasuvarcalā, the word refers either to a variety of sunflower (*Heriantus*) or to *Clerodendron siphonanthus*. 14.2.34.

Śvetā. Macri (1988) says that this is the name of numerous vegetables. But Śveta, Macri says, is a variety of Jīvaka (*Terminalia tomentosa*). Shamasastry identifies this as *Aconitum ferox*, Indian aconite, wolfsbane. 1.20.5; 14.4.2.

Śyāmalatā. Several identifications have been offered, but given the category under which it is listed at 2.17.6, it must be some kind of vine. Shamasastry: *Ichnocarpus* (black creeper); Meyer: *Echites frutescens*, which is a synonym of *Ichnocarpus fructescens*. 2.17.6.

Syonāga. According to Shamasastry and Meyer, *Bignonia indica*, also named *Oroxylum indicum*, Indian trumpet flower. 14.4.2.

Tagara. Indian valerian, *Valeriana jatamansi*. Macri (1988) identifies this as *Tabernaemontana coronaria*, East Indian rosebay. 14.4.9.

Tailaparṇika. Probably a generic term for wood for incense. 2.11.61.

Tālamūla. Black musale, golden eye grass, *Curculigo orchioides* or *Desmodium oojeinense*. 2.18.17.

Tālī palm. A kind of palm identified by Shamasastry and Meyer as *Corypha taliera*, similar to a fan palm. It is close to extinction in the wild, with some specimens on the campus of Dhaka University. 2.17.9.

Taṇḍulīyaka. Prickley amaranth, *Amarantus spinosus*. 14.4.3.

Tejovatī. Java long pepper *Piper chaba*. 2.25.27

Tilaka. Identified by Shamasastry as *Barleria cristata* (Philippine violet, bluebell barleria), and by Meyer as *Clerodendrum plumoides* (a flowering plant, including glory bower, bagflower, bleeding heart). These identifications are doubtful because it is listed at 2.17.4 under the category of hardwoods.

Tinduka. Gaub tree, Indian ebony, embroypteris, *Diospyros tomentosa*. 14.2.11.

Tiniśa. Chariot tree, Punjab kino, Sandan, *Ougeinia dalbergioides*. 2.17.4.

Trapusa. Cucumber, *Cucumis sativus*. 13.4.20, 21.

Tripuṭa. Grass pea, chickling vetch, Indian pea, *Lathyrus sativus*. 2.11.4.

Tuvarī. Gaṇapati Śāstri identifies this as Āḍhakī, the pulse *Cajanus indicus Spreng* called pigeon pea. Meyer, without comment, identifies it as *Asparagus racemosus* (Indian asparagus). 14.3.64.

Uccidiṅga. Also spelled Ucciṭiṅga, identified as a crab or a poisonous water animal. 14.1.4, 9.

Udāraka. Possibly a variety of millet (Wojtilla 2011, 8). 2.15.27, 34; 2.24.12.

Udumbara. A type of fig tree the wood of which is used for ritual purposes, *Ficus glomerata* or *Ficus racemosa*. 14.1.16; 14.2.1.

Upodakā. Indian spinach, *Basella rubra*. 14.2.28–29.

Urvāruka. Identified by Shamasastry as cucumber, and by M-W as *Cucumis utilissimus*. 2.15.17.

Uśīra. Khus or cuscus grass, *Vetiveria zizanioides*. 2.11.59, 67; 2.24.22.

Uṭaja. A species of bamboo. 2.17.5.

Utkrośaka. Refers to several varieties of sea eagles that have a loud cry (Dave 2005, 214). 2.26.5.

Vajra. According to Shamasastry, *Andropogon muricatus* (vetiver, cuscus) or *Euphorbia* (spurge). Macri (1988) has Vajravṛkṣa and identifies it as *Euphorbia antiquorum* (triangular spurge) or *Cactus opuntia* (a kind of prickly-pear cactus). 2.12.9; 2.13.9; 14.2.27.

Vajrakulī. Its identity is unclear. Meyer thinks it is a Solanum (nightshades, horsenettles, and related species). 14.2 32.

Vallī. The common meaning is simply a creeper, but here it must refer to a specific creeper. 14.2.3; 14.4.4.

Vaṃśa. The thorny bamboo, *Bambusa arundinacea*. 2.17.5.

Vandākā. Identified by Shamasastry as *Epidendrum tesseloides*, and by Meyer as *Vanda roxburghii* (Banda-Rasna). 1.20.5; 14.4.12.

Vañjula. *Calamus rotang, Dalbergia ougeinensis, Jonesia Asoca, Hibiscus mutabilis*. 14.2.27; 14.4.28, 29.

Varaka. A kind of inferior grain, wild gram, Jangali mung, *Phaseolus trilobus*. 2.15.25, 34; 2.24.12.

Vāraṇa. Identified by Dave (2005, 327) as the great bustard. 14.4.2, 4.

Vāruṇī. Meyer thinks it may be the Durvā grass. With the spelling Varuṇa(ka), Macri (1988) takes it to be *Crataeva roxburghii* and Shamasastry as *Teriandium indicum*. 14.4.3.

Vāśī. A kind of vine, identified by Shamasastry as *Justicia gendarussa* (Krishna vasa, Nila-nirgundi). 2.17.6.

Vatsanābha. Indian aconite, *Aconitum ferox* or *nepellus*. 2.17.12; 14.1.29.

Veṇu. Thorny bamboo, *Bambusa arundinacea*. 2.17.5.

Vetra. Common rattan, *Calamus rotang*. 2.17.6.

Vīcīralla. I have been unable to identify this animal, and all the translators leave it unidentified. 14.2.43.

Vidarī. Indian kudzu, *Pueraria tuberosa, Batatas paniculata, Desmodium gangeticum*. Hindi: Vidarikand or Sural; Malayalam: Mutukku. 14.1.10.

Vilaṅga. Meyer gives several possible identifications. According to Stein (1921), *Embelia ribes*. Gaṇapati Śāstrī identifies it with Amoghā, the trumpet flower (*Bignonia suaveolens*). 2.25.29, 33; 14.4.8.

Viṣamūlikā. Literally, a plant with poisonous roots. I have not been able to identify this. 14.1.17.

Vrīhi. A variety of long-grained rice different from *śāli* and one that ripens, according to commentators, in 60 days. 2.15.25, 34; 2.24.12; 2.30.18.

Vyāghātaka. Identified by Shamasastry as *Cassia fistula* (Indian laburnum, purging cassia, golden shower). 14.1.7.

Yātudhāna. I have been unable to identify this plant. 14.1.6, 30.

APPENDIX 2

Weights and Measures

N.B.: Weights and measures have varied over time in India. The values given below are approximations derived mostly from sources later than the *AŚ* (see tables A2.1 and A2.2). These conversions, however, will give the reader some idea of the quantities involved.

Measures of Weight and Volume [AŚ 2.19]

Unfortunately, we cannot get an accurate chart of the weights, because weights with the same names had differing values depending on the uses to which they were put. For example, weights for articles coming into the treasury were different from those used for ordinary trade. Further, weights for gold, silver, and other substances had different values. Here is one example: "a Droṇa used as a measure for revenue holds 200 Palas of Māṣa-beans; while a Droṇa for trade holds 187.5 Palas; a Droṇa for payments, 175 Palas; and a Droṇa for palace payments, 162 Palas" (2.19.29). However, in general we have come up with the following chart (see table A2.3) of measures of volume, sometimes also used for weight.

We can get a rough glimpse of the system of weights at *AŚ* 2.19.19–21 in table A2.4.

Āḍhaka: a measurement of volume and weight, one-quarter of a Droṇa, approximately 2.4 kg.

Akṣa: a measurement of weight used once at 14.4.10. Gaṇapati Śāstri says that it is 16 Māṣakas, which equal 4 gm.

Table A2.1 Measures of Space and Distance (*AŚ* 2.20.2–27)

8 Paramāṇu	=	1 Rathacakravipruṣ
8 Rathacakravipruṣ	=	1 Likṣā
8 Likṣā	=	1 Yūka
8 Yūka	=	1 Yavamadhya
8 Yavamadhya	=	1 Aṅgula
4 Aṅgula	=	1 Dhanurgraha
8 Aṅgula	=	1 Dhanurmuṣṭi
12 Aṅgula	=	1 Vitasti
12 Aṅgula	=	1 Chāyāpauruṣa
14 Aṅgula	=	1 Śama
14 Aṅgula	=	1 Śala
14 Aṅgula	=	1 Pariraya
14 Aṅgula	=	1 Pada
2 Vitasti	=	1 Aratni (= Prajāpati-hasta)
2 Vitasti + 1 Dhanurmuṣṭi	=	1 Kiṣuka or 1 Kaṃsa
42 Aṅgula	=	1 saw Kiṣuka of carpenters
54 Aṅgula	=	1 Hasta for produce forests
84 Aṅgula	=	1 Vyāma for ropes
84 Aṅgula	=	1 Pauruṣa for digging
4 Aratni	=	1 Daṇḍa
4 Aratni	=	1 Dhanuṣ
4 Aratni	=	1 Nālikā
4 Aratni	=	1 Pauruṣa for householder
108 Aṅgula	=	1 Dhanuṣ for roads and walls
108 Aṅgula	=	1 Pauruṣa for fire altar
6 Kiṃsa	=	1 Daṇḍa measure for gifts
10 Daṇḍa	=	1 Rajju
2 Rajju	=	1 Parideśa
3 Rajju	=	1 Nivartana
3 Rajju + 2 Daṇḍa	=	1 Bāhu
2,000 Dhanuṣ	=	1 Goruta
4 Goruta	=	1 Yojana

Aṅgula: a measurement of length, approximately 2 cm.
Aratni: a measurement of length, approximately 48 cm.
Ayana: one-half of the year when the sun moves north or south.
Bāhu: a measurement of length, approximately 61 m.

Table A2.2 Measures of Time (*AŚ* 2.20.28–64)

2 Tuṭa	=	1 Lava
2 Lava	=	1 Nimeṣa
5 Nimeṣa	=	1 Kāṣṭā
30 Kāṣṭā	=	1 Kalā
40 Kalā	=	1 Nālikā [see alternative]
2 Nālikā	=	1 Muhūrta
15 Muhūrta	=	1 day or 1 night [in Caitra and Āśvayuja]
15 days + nights	=	1 fortnight
2 fortnights	=	1 month
2 months	=	1 season
2 Ayana	=	1 year
4 years	=	1 Yuga

Table A2.3 Measures of Volume

4 Kuḍuba	=	1 Prastha
4 Prastha	=	1 Āḍhaka
4 Āḍhaka	=	1 Droṇa
16 Droṇa	=	1 Khari
20 Droṇa	=	1 Kumbha
10 Kumbha	=	1 Vaha
21 Kuḍuba	=	1 Ghaṭikā of ghee
84 Kuḍuba	=	1 Vāraka of ghee
16 Kuḍuba	=	1 Ghaṭikā of oil
64 Kuḍuba	=	1 Vāraka of oil

Bhāra: a measurement of weight, approximately 755.2 kg.
Chāyāpauruṣa: a measurement of length, approximately 24 cm.
Daṇḍa: a measurement of length, approximately 1.92 m.
Dhanurgraha: a measurement of length, approximately 8 cm.
Dhanurmuṣṭi: a measurement of length, approximately 16 cm.
Dhanus: a measurement of length, approximately 1.92 m.
Dharaṇa: a measurement of weight, approximately 377.6 gm.
Dharaṇika: a measurement of weight, approximately 3.78 gm.

Table A2.4 Measures of Weight

10 Dharaṇika	=	1 Pala
4 Karṣa	=	1 Pala
100 Pala	=	1 Tulā
20 Tulā	=	1 Bhāra

Droṇa: a measurement of capacity, especially of grains, probably about 5 liters. When it is a measurement of weight, it is approximately 9.6 kg.

Ghaṭikā: a measurement of volume or weight, approximately 3.15 kg or 2.4 kg.

Goruta: a measurement of length, approximately 3,840 meters. At 2.2.2, however, the measurement appears to be that of an area; perhaps a square Goruta is meant.

Hasta: a measurement of length, approximately 47 cm, or 108 cm when measuring produce forests.

Kākaṇī: a copper coin with a probable value of a quarter Māṣaka or 1/64th of a Paṇa. It is also given as a particular weight, especially in the manufacture of gold and silver. Taking a Māṣa as 0.59 gm, a Kākaṇī would be about 0.15 gm.

Kalā: a measurement of time, approximately 1 minute and 36 seconds.

Kaṃsa: a measurement of length, approximately 64 cm.

Karṣa: a measurement of weight, approximately 151 gm.

Kāṣṭā: a measurement of time, approximately 3.2 seconds.

Khārī: a measurement of volume or weight, 16 Droṇas, possibly 153.6 kg.

Kiṣku: a measurement of length, probably the same as a Hasta, approximately 48 cm.

Kiṣuka: a measurement of length, approximately 64 cm.

Krośa: a measurement of distance, approximately 3.6 km.

Kuḍuba: a measurement of volume or weight,one-quarter of a Prastha, possibly 0.15 kg.

Kumbha: a measurement of capacity, 20 Droṇas, possibly 192 kg.

Kumbhī: probably the same as a Kumbha.

Lava: a measurement of time, given as half a Nimeṣa, which is approximately 0.107 second.

Likṣā: "egg of a louse," a very minute measurement of weight equal to 8 Trasareṇus.

Māṣa: "a bean," a measurement of weight, approximately 0.59 gm.

Muhūrta: a measurement of time, approximately 48 minutes.

Nālikā: a measurement of time, approximately 24 minutes; a measurement of length, approximately 1.92 m.

Nimeṣa: a measurement of time, approximately 0.2133 seconds.

Nivartana: a measurement of length, approximately 57.6 m.

Pada: a measurement of length, approximately 28 cm.

Pala: a measurement of weight, approximately 37.76 gm.

Paṇa: the basic currency in ancient India. In the *AŚ*, it is a silver coin.

Paramāṇu: the smallest unit of measurement of length (2.20.2); theoretically it would be 5 mm.

Parideśa: a measurement of length, approximately 38.4 m.

Parimāṇī: a particular kind of balance for weighing heavy objects (2.19.17), and also a particular weight (4.2.3).

Pariraya: a measurement of length, approximately 28 cm.

Pauruṣa: a measurement of length. Three values are given: for householder, 192 cm; for digging, 168 cm; for fire altar, 216 cm.

Prastha: a measurement of volume or weight, one-quarter of an Āḍhaka, possibly 0.6 kg.

Rajju: a measurement of length, approximately 19.2 m.

Rathacakravipruṣ: a measurement of length, approximately 6.25 mm.

Śala: a measurement of length, approximately 28 cm.

Śama: a measurement of length, approximately 28 cm.

Suvarṇa: a measurement of weight, approximately 9.44 gm.

Tulā: a measurement of weight, approximately 37.76 kg.

Tuṭa: a minute measurement of time, theoretically about 0.053 second.

Vaha: a measurement of volume or weight, 10 Kumbha, possibly 1,920 kg.

Vāraka: a measurement of volume or weight, approximately 12.6 kg or 9.6 kg.

Vitasti: a measurement of length, approximately 24 cm.

Vyāma: a measurement of length, approximately 168 cm.

Yavamadhya: a measurement of length, approximately 25 mm.

Yojana: a measurement of length, approximately 14.5 km.

Yuga: four years.

Yūkā: a measurement of length, approximately 12.5 mm.

APPENDIX 3

Geographical Names

Alakanda. Probably Alexandria in Egypt. See 2.11.42 n.

Aṅgara. The reference and the reading are unclear, some manuscripts giving Aṅga and Vaṅga. The commentator Yoggama says that it is a forest between the region of Vidiśā/Narmadā and the Pāriyātra mountains (western Vindhya)—that is, probably somewhere in southern Madhya Pradesh or Chhattisgarh. 2.2.15.

Antaravatī. A place where wood for incense is obtained, probably located in Assam. 2.11.67.

Aparānta. Konkan and the coastal regions of Maharashtra. 2.2.15; 2.11.115 n.; 2.24.5.

Āraṭṭa. Possibly a region of Punjab (Meyer). 2.30.29.

Āroha. A region that produces a variety of valuable animal skins. The Malayalam commentary locates it in the Himalayas. 2.11.81.

Aśmaka. A region of northern Maharashtra along the Godavari River with its capital in Pratiṣṭhāna, modern Paithan. 2.24.5.

Aśokagrāma. A region that produces wood for incense, but the location is uncertain. 2.11.61.

Avantī. A region in Madhya Pradesh roughly corresponding to the Malwa region, and also around Ujjain. 2.24.5.

Bāhlava. Probably another way of pronouncing Bāhlīka, the region of Bactria. 2.11.88.

Bāhlīka. The region of Bactria in the far northeastern corner of Persia. 2.30.29.

Bhoja. A region in southwestern Gujarat, around modern Surat. 1.6.5.

Cakravāla. The identity of this region, in which a particular kind of silver was mined, is uncertain. The commentators think it is the name of a mountain. 2.13.10.

Cedi. A region roughly in Bundelkhand of Madhya Pradesh, south of the Yamuna River and along the Betwa River. 2.2.15.

Cīna. China or western regions of China. 2.11.114.

Cūrṇī. This is identified by the commentators as a river in Kerala. 2.11.2.

Daśārṇa. A region in Madhya Pradesh just to the southeast of Chedi. 2.2.15.

Devasabhā. The identity of this region is unclear, but the commentators place it in Kerala, which is plausible, given that red sandalwood comes from this region. 2.11.47.

Doṅga. A place for sandalwood, located by the commentators in Assam. 2.11.58 n.

Dvādaśagrāma. At 2.11.77, this is a region producing two valuable kinds of animal skins. The commentators place it in the Himalayas or in the northern trade route (*uttarāpatha*).

Gandhāra. A region in the northwestern corner of Pakistan and eastern Afghanistan. 3.18.8

Gauḍa. The identity of this region, in which a particular kind of silver was mined, is uncertain. The commentators and Meyer think it is located in today's Assam. 2.13.10.

Gośīrṣa. A place where sandalwood was obtained, probably the name of a mountain. 2.11.44

Grāmeru. A place for sandalwood, located by the commentators in Assam. 2.11.48, 63.

Hari. A region from which a particular kind of sandalwood came. The identity is unclear. 2.11.45.

Hāṭaka. A place where a variety of gold originated. The identity is unclear. 2.13.3.

Himavat. The Himalayas. 2.11.2

Hrāda. Either the name of a lake or perhaps a generic term for freshwater pearls harvested from lakes (see Srotasī). 2.11.2.

Indravāna. A region with diamond mines identified with Kaliṅga, that is, Orissa. 2.11.37.

Jambū River. An area producing gold. The identity is unclear. 2.13.3.

Jāpa. A place for sandalwood, located by the commentators in Assam. 2.11.47.

Joṅga. A place for sandalwood, located by the commentators in Assam. 2.11.48, 57 n., 61.

Kailāsa. The mythical mountain in the Himalayas, the abode of Śiva and holy ascetics. 14.3.24.

Kāla Mountain. This mountain or mountainous region cannot be identified, but most of the areas from which sandalwood comes are in Kerala or Assam. 2.11.51.

Kaliṅga. A region in modern Orissa. 2.2.15, 115; 2.13.21.

Kamboja. A region north of Gandhāra in what is today northwestern Pakistan and eastern Afghanistan. 2.30.29.

Kambu. The identity of this region, in which a particular kind of silver was mined, is uncertain. The commentators think it is the name of a mountain. 2.13.10.

Kardamā. Probably the name of a river from which pearls were harvested. 2.11.2.

Karūṣa. A region close to and just south of Cedi in Madhya Pradesh. 2.2.15.

Kāśī. The same as Vārāṇasī or Benares. 2.11.106, 115.

Kāstīrarāṣṭra. A region with diamond mines that the commentators locate around Vārāṇasī or Benares. 2.11.37.

Kośāgāra. This mountain or region cannot be identified, but most of the areas from which sandalwood comes are in Kerala or Assam. 2.11.52

Koṭi. Probably a region of Kerala. 2.11.28.

Kṣatriya. This region containing military guilds or groups is difficult to identify. Jayaswal (1924, I, 61) identifies this with the Greek Xathroi, placing them somewhere in Sindh. 11.1.4.

Kukura. The appellation of a confederacy, probably part of the Andhaka-Vṛṣṇi league located in western Gujarat around Dwaraka. 11.1.5.

Kulā. Probably the name of a river in Sri Lanka. It could possibly be the Kalu Ganga in southwestern Sri Lanka. 2.11.2.

Kuru. A famous ancient clan, the land of the Kurus broadly corresponds to the region north of present-day Delhi. 11.1.5.

Lauhityā. A place where wood for incense is obtained, probably located in Assam. See note to 2.11.66.

Licchivika. Probably the same as Licchavi, a confederacy with Vaiśāli as the capital, located in northern Bihar. 11.1.5.

Madhurā. The reference could be to either Mathura in northern India or the Madurai in Tamil Nadu. 2.11.115.

Madraka. This confederacy is probably located in the Punjab. 11.1.5.

Magadha. The region of modern Bihar. 2.11.107; 2.19.10.

Mahendra. Perhaps the name of a mountain but, given that it is the source of pearls, the reference must be to a river of that name. 2.11.2.

Mahiṣa. The location of this region is uncertain. 2.11.115.

Mālā. Probably a region of Kerala. 2.11.28, 49.

Mallaka. Probably the same as Malla, a region of northwestern Bihar and eastern Uttar Pradesh. 11.1.5

Maṇimanta. A region with diamond mines. The commentators identify this as Mount Maṇimanta in the northern country (*uttarāpatha*). 2.11.37.

Mekala. A mountainous region in Madhya Pradesh. 2.19.10

Nāga Mountain. The identity of this hill region is unclear, but it is probably in Kerala, the primary source of sandalwood. 2.11.54.

Nepal. A region broadly coinciding with modern Nepal. 2.11.100.

Odra. Kangle tentatively identifies this region as Orissa. 2.11.92.

Pāñcāla. This is the central region of Vedic culture located in the northern region of the Yamuna-Ganges Doab. 11.1.5.

Pañcanada. Probably a forest region between today's Sindh and Uttar Pradesh. 2.2.16.

Pāṇḍyakavāṭa. Identified as Mount Malayakoṭi in the Pāṇḍya country of southern Tamil Nadu by the commentators, it probably rather refers to Negapatam or Ramnad, ports of embarkation to Sri Lanka. 2.11.2.

Pāpeya. The name could also be Pāpī. Probably a region in the northwest frontier where horses were obtained. 2.30.29.

Pārasamudra. Sri Lanka. 2.11.28, 59.

Pāśikā. Possibly the name of a river in the Pāṇḍya country in southern Tamil Nadu. 2.11.2.

Prājjūna. The identity of this region is unclear, as also whether it is a reference to the Huns. It is probably located in the northwestern border region because it is coupled with Gandhāra. 3.18.8

Puṇḍra. A region of northeastern India around modern Bihar and west Bengal. 2.11.102, 106, 107.

Pūrṇakadvīpa. A region where wood for incense was obtained; its identity is unclear. 2.11.65.

Sabhārāṣṭra. An area with diamond mines, identified as the region of Vidarbha in eastern Maharashtra. 2.11.37.

Śālaka. A region with sandalwood, probably located in Kerala. 2.11.55.

Śatakumbha. An area producing gold. The identity is unclear. 2.13.3.

Sātana. A region with red sandalwood, probably located in Kerala. 2.11.43.

Sauvīra. This region lies along the Indus to the north of Sindh. 1.6.7; 1.20.16; 2.30.29.

Sindhu. The region of Sindh in southeastern Pakistan. 2.13.47, 49; 2.30.29.

Śītodakā. A region with sandalwood, probably located in Kerala. 2.11.53.

Śreṇi. This region containing military guilds or groups is difficult to identify. Jayaswal (1924, I, 64) identifies this with the Greek Agesinae (i.e., *agra-śreṇi*) and places them in Sindh. 11.1.4.

Śrīkaṭana. A region with diamond mines located probably in the Jabalpur District in Madhya Pradesh. 2.11.37.

Śṛṅgaśukti. An area producing gold, identified by the commentators with Suvarṇabhūmi (probably Burma). 2.13.3.

Srotasī. Either the name of a river producing pearls or simply a term to describe freshwater pearls from rivers (see Hrāda). 2.11.2.

Surāṣṭra. A region in southwestern Gujarat. 2.2.16; 11.1.4.

Suvarṇakuḍya. Probably a region located in Assam. 2.11.64, 104, 107, 113.

Svarṇabhūmi. Probably Burma, 2.11.69; see note to 2.11.61–70.

Tajjamārāṣṭra. A region with diamond mines located by the commentators in Orissa or Kosala in Uttar Pradesh. The reading and the identity are uncertain. 2.11.37 n.

Tāmraparṇī. Although this term often refers to Sri Lanka, it appears that the reference at 2.11.2 is to a river in south India.

Tāpī. Probably the Tāpī River in northern Maharashtra and Gujarat. 2.13.21.

Titala. Some identify this as a region of Orissa, but given that good horses are bred there, it is possibly a region in the northwest. 2.30.29.

Tṛṇasā. A region with sandalwood, possibly located in Kerala. 2.11.45.

Turūpa. A place for sandalwood, located by the commentators in Assam. 2.11.48.

Tuttha. The identity of this region, in which a particular kind of silver was mined, is uncertain. The commentators think it is the name of a mountain. 2.13.10.

Uttaraparvata. Literally, "northern mountain," it is probably the Himalayan region. 2.11.70, 73.

Vanāyu. This has been identified either as Arabia or, more plausibly, as Persia. 2.30.29.

Vaṅga. The area close to the mouth of the Ganges, today's Bengal/ Bangladesh. 2.11.102, 115.

Vatsa. An area around Kausambi in Uttar Pradesh near the confluence of the rivers Yamuna and Ganges. 2.11.115.

Veṇu. An area producing gold, either a river or a mountain. 2.13.3.

Videha. A region in what is today northern Bihar, north of Patna. 1.6.5.

Vivarṇa. Probably a place where coral was obtained, either in the Mediterranean or in the Persian Gulf. 2.11.42.

Vṛjika. Probably the same as Vṛjjis, a confederacy located in northern Bihar and extending to southern Nepal. 1.11.5.

Vṛṣṇi. The Andhaka-Vṛṣṇi league was probably located in western Gujarat around Dwaraka. 1.6.10.

Notes

BOOK 1

1.1.18. *Contents of the treatise* (*śāstrasamuddeśa*): Kangle takes this as a nominal sentence: "The enumeration of the (contents of the) Science amounts to." I think this initial statement refers to the first chapter (1.1), which bears the title Enumeration of Topics and Books (*prakaraṇādhikaraṇasamuddeśa*). Thus, the entire text consists of this initial chapter, plus 15 books, etc.

1.2.1. *Critical inquiry... systems*: For a detailed analysis of "critical inquiry" (*anvīkṣikī*) in the *AŚ* and other ancient texts, see Hacker 1958; Halbfass 1988, 273–286; Bronkhorst 2007, 171–172. The term refers to rational investigations based on proper logical reasoning (see 1.2.11). "Economics" (*vārttā*) here refers specifically to the texts that deal with agriculture, commerce, and other such economic activities. These same four areas of knowledge are mentioned in *MBh* 12.59.33. I translate *daṇḍanīti* as government, because it encompasses both the discipline of political science (there are departments of government in modern universities) and the art of governance, both of which are implied in the Sanskrit. See Scharfe 1993, 47, for parallels in the *MBh*; Scharfe suspects that what we have here is a fragment of an original verse.

1.2.2. *The Triple... assert*: For this view, see *MBh* 3.49.31, where it is presented as the norm without comment and without ascription to any school. At *MBh* 3.49.29, however, mention is made of Bṛhaspati and Uśanas. Triple here (*trayī* in the feminine) refers to *vidyā* (knowledge), that is, the Veda (1.3.1).

1.2.7. *pursuit of all the knowledge systems* (sarvavidyārambhāḥ): Kangle translates this as "undertakings connected with all the sciences." The term *ārambha* does mean practical undertakings; however, the expression *vidyārambha* is so closely connected with the beginning and pursuit of knowledge, especially in the rite of passage of that name, it is more probable that it has a similar meaning here also.

1.2.9. *comes to know... systems*: A common practice among ancient Indian scholars is to draw the inner and essential meaning of a term using either etymologies or phonetic similarities. These give both the origin of the term and its deepest meaning, in the present case the meaning of *vidyā* (knowledge system).

1.2.10. *Sāṃkhya... Lokāyata*: Sāṃkhya is one of the oldest philosophical systems. It is especially important because it provided many of the cosmological categories that become commonplace in later Indian thought. Yoga in this context probably refers to the system of logic, later known as Nyāya, rather than to the well-known system of mental training (Halbfass 1988, 278). Lokāyata (also called Cārvāka) was an old system of materialistic or natural philosophy that rejected the existence of a spiritual realm and the belief in rebirth (Bronkhorst 2007, 150–159).

these constitute critical inquiry: Hacker (1958) and, following him, Scharfe (1993) think that this statement does not constitute a definition of critical inquiry (*anvīkṣikī*). Rather, this statement simply states that critical inquiry is to be found in these three traditions. Even though the statement may not amount to a formal *definition* of critical inquiry, I am doubtful about Hacker's interpretation. The parallel passages that deal with the other two knowledge systems, the Triple Veda and economics, have identical wording. It is clear that the Triple Veda is not simply *found* in Sāma, Ṛg, and Yajur, but that the latter constitutes the Triple (1.3.1). Likewise, economics consists of agriculture, animal husbandry, and trade (1.4.1).

1.2.12. *Critical... laws*: This verse is found in Vātsyāyana's *Nyāyabhāṣya* (1.1.1) and was probably borrowed by the śāstric redactor (see Introduction, p. 14f) from a text on logic. See Halbfass 1988, 275.

1.3.2. *Atharva Veda*: This Vedic text is traditionally counted as the fourth Veda. However, in the earlier enumeration expressed in the terse *trayī* (Triple), only three are recognized as authoritative.

Itihāsa Veda: The category *itihāsa* (narratives that are viewed within the tradition as historical) generally applies to the two major Sanskrit epics, the *Mahābhārata* and the *Rāmāyaṇa*. Whether that is the meaning here is unclear, even though the *Mahābhārata* itself claims to be the fifth Veda. However, later the *AŚ* (1.5.14) gives a longer list of texts comprehended by this term, where *Itihāsa* appears to have the broader meaning of traditionally authoritative texts.

1.3.3. *limbs*: There are the six supplementary knowledge systems that helped in exploring and understanding the Vedic texts. The notion of limbs (*aṅga*) evokes the image of an animal with the six extremities (head, four feet, and tail) protruding out of the main torso, which in this conception would constitute the Veda proper.

1.3.8. *economic activities* (vārttā): This term was used at 1.2.1–4 with the meaning of a knowledge system, where it refers to the expert tradition focusing on economic activities within society. Clearly the meaning here is different and must refer to various kinds of economic activities themselves, especially agriculture and trade, rather than to a knowledge system focused on those activities. Elsewhere also, we see the fine line separating a knowledge system (*śāstra*) from the real-world activities analyzed by that system.

1.3.9. *during her season*: This technical expression refers to the time in a woman's monthly cycle when she is assumed to be fertile. This period consists of the days immediately following her menstrual period.

venerating (pūjā): This term refers both to the ritual aspects of veneration and especially to the offering of food that invariably accompanies such rites of homage.

servants (bhṛtya): This term in the *AŚ* generally refers to a servant, rather than to a dependent kinsman or a slave, when the context is a normal household. See Vigasin and Samozvantsev 1985, 130.

eating what is left over: The practice of eating leftovers is associated with mendicant ascetics. However, in the reevaluation of a householder's religious life, he is often compared favorably with such ascetics, because he also eats what is left over after he has fed all his dependents, as well as gods, ancestors, and guests. See Wezler 1977.

1.3.12. *abstaining from ritual activities*: The term *anārambha* is used with a technical meaning in ascetic literature. It refers to the abstention from activities, especially ritual activities, that is the hallmark of Brāhmaṇical ascetics. See *GDh* 3.25. Pandey (1979) is quite off the mark in taking the term to mean selfless action.

1.3.15. *intermixture* (saṃkara): This term probably refers specifically to the intermixture of classes (*varṇasaṃkara*) that results when people do not observe the norms specifically enjoined on them, especially those relating to marriage.

1.4.2. *By means... army*: Throughout this treatise, it is emphasized that money and material are needed in order to fill the treasury and equip the army. Without these material resources provided by economic activities, a king loses his power. For the concept of circles of kingdoms, see 6.2.13–23.

1.4.3. *Government seeks... recipients*: For parallel passages expressing the same doctrine, see *MDh* 7.99–101; *MBh* 12.59.57. See Scharfe 1993, 47.

1.4.5. *Seeking... punishment*: See the parallel at *MDh* 7.102. As Scharfe (1993, 46–48) has pointed out, several sections of these prose passages scan and are probably derived from preexisting verses.

1.4.6. *Teachers*: The *AŚ* contains numerous Kauṭilya dialogues, where opinions of different authorities are given as opposing views (*pūrvapakṣa*), at the end of which the authoritative view of Kauṭilya is presented. "Teachers" here is a generic term to refer to views of past authorities, although in other places names of individuals and schools are given. See Introduction, p. 21.

1.4.11. *Law, Success, and Pleasure* (dharma-artha-kāma): Although the first two concepts have been already introduced, this is the first time all three concepts are used together. These constitute the *trivarga* (Triple Set) or the three areas of human activity and aspiration. The *AŚ* uses the concept of the Triple Set frequently throughout the treatise.

1.4.13. *law of the fish*: This is a well-known proverb in ancient Indian literature with reference to an anarchical society not governed by the stern rule of a king. In such a society, the strong devour the weak, as the big fish eat the smaller fish. This maxim is invoked in connection with the creation of the institution of king; see 1.13.5.

1.4.15. *protected...prevails*: "[B]y him" here probably refers to the king who dispenses punishment. The referent of "he" is somewhat unclear; I have taken it to be the weak in society who are protected by the shield provided by punishment.

1.5.1. *three knowledge systems*: At 1.2.1, four such systems were listed. Given that punishment is the core of government (*daṇḍanīti*), the three must refer to the remaining knowledge systems: critical inquiry, the Triple, and economics.

1.5.2. *training* (vinaya): This term is usually translated as discipline, especially in its usage in Buddhist texts with reference to the Buddhist monastic rules. Within the present context, however, it appears that the term refers to a program of training, both physical and intellectual/moral (see 2.33.11; 5.6.39), and especially training in military skills (1.5.12). The term can also have a broader meaning of good conduct, which is the result of such moral training. Given that the term is used both as a noun and as a verb (2.5.4), "training" can capture both usages. In other places, the term is used in the sense of disciplining, namely, punishment (see 2.1.25).

1.5.5. *desire to learn...truth*: These qualities of the intellect are noted again at 6.1.4. "Reasoning" (*ūha*) is the ability to deduce proper conclusions, while "rejection" is negative argumentation aimed at refuting false views. A verse given in several sources presents these as qualities of the mind: *śuśrūṣā śravaṇaṃ caiva grahaṇaṃ dhāraṇā tathā | ūho 'poho 'rthavijñānaṃ tattvajñānaṃ ca dhīguṇāḥ || Kāmandakīya Nītisāra*, 4.22. These are probably the ones referred to as the "eight elements of intelligence" (*buddhyā aṣṭāṅgayā*) in a passage added after *Rām* 6.101.22; see the translation by Goldman et al., p. 1415. The same verse is given in three manuscripts after *MBh* 3.2.16 or 17.

1.5.7. *tonsure* (caula): This is a rite of passage when the child's hair is shaved, generally in the third year. After this rite and before the Vedic initiation (*upanayana*), the formal teaching of the alphabet is done in a rite called "beginning of knowledge" (*vidyārambha*), generally performed in the fifth year. According to the Brāhmaṇical texts, Vedic initiation is generally performed in the eighth year for a Brāhmaṇa, in the 11th year for a Kṣatriya, and in the 12th year for a Vaiśya.

1.5.10. *hair cutting*: This rite of passage called *godāna* (literally, giving of a cow) consists of shaving the hair and beard when the young man is 16 years of age. See 2.21.18, where *caula* as childhood tonsure is distinguished from *godāna*.

1.5.14. *Lore... Success*: It is probable that this sentence was a commentarial or marginal gloss explaining the term *itihāsa* of the previous sentence, a gloss that found its way into the text proper. Even though the texts referred to here are given in the singular, I think they refer to genres of literature, and thus I have translated the terms in the plural (see Rocher 1986, 26). Purāṇas, at least in later times, are texts dealing with a variety of topics, including creation and dissolution of the universe, genealogies of gods and dynasties, as well as other didactic and sectarian teachings. They are grouped into 18 major and 18 minor Purāṇas. The meaning of Reports (*itivṛtta*) is unclear, although a commentary identifies the epics *Mahābhārata* and *Rāmāyaṇa*. Probably this category includes reports of incidents and events that were thought to have happened in the past, what could be called history. It is also unclear what Narratives (*ākhyāyikā*) and Illustrations (*udāharaṇa*) refer to, although some think that they may refer to fables and stories, such as the *Pañcatantra*, also called *Tantrākhyāyikā*.

1.5.16. *exemplary qualities of the self* (ātmavattā): This term and the related *ātmavat*, which occur frequently in the *AŚ*, are translated by Kangle as self-possession or self-control. I think, however, this expression refers more specifically to the exemplary qualities (see 1.9.1 n.) of the self described at 6.1.6. This fuller meaning of *ātmavān* is clearly expressed in 6.1.16.

1.6.5. *Dāṇḍakya*: The story of Daṇḍa, who raped Arajā, the daughter of the seer Uśanas, and was destroyed by the curse of the seer, is narrated in the *Rāmāyaṇa* (7.71–72). Examples of ancient kings who got into trouble for a variety of reasons, especially for sexual transgressions, are common in ancient Indian literature. Aśvaghoṣa (second century C.E,) in his *Buddhacarita* (1.40–46; 4.16–20, 71–81; 9.67–71; 11.31) and especially in *Saundarananda* (7.25–46) presents numerous examples of such arguments. On this and the following examples, see Hultzsch 1919, 230–231.

Karāla: A Karāla Janaka is mentioned in Aśvaghoṣa's *Buddhacarita* (4.80), where he is said to have abducted a Brāhmaṇa girl and come to ruin thereby. The *Majjhima Nikāya* (11.82) and *Jātaka* (541) of the Pāli Buddhist Canon identify this king as the son of Nimi, the king of Mithilā. Karāla is said to have brought his dynasty to an end.

1.6.6. *Janamejaya*: There are several Janamejayas recorded in the *Mahābhārata*, the most famous being the one who performed the immense fire sacrifice, into which snakes fell, in revenge for the killing of his father, Parikṣit, by a poisonous snake. Regarding the assailing of Brāhmaṇas, there is a Janamejaya mentioned in *MBh* 12.146.3 who killed a Brāhmaṇa and was therefore abandoned by his subjects. The commentary on this passage of the *AŚ* mentions a Janamejaya who beat Brāhmaṇas whom he suspected of having violated his wife. Aśvaghoṣa (*Saundarananda* 7.44), however, gives the story of a Janamejaya who has sex with Kālī after the death of her husband, Śantanu. For this outrage, he was killed in battle by Bhīṣma.

Tālajaṅgha: Aśvaghoṣa in his *Saundarananda* (7.39) says that this king became infatuated with Menakā, a celestial nymph, and for this indiscretion was kicked by her husband, Viśvāvasu. The extirpation of Tālajaṅghas and Haihayas (1.6.9) by Sagara is recorded in *MBh* 3.104.7.

1.6.7. *Aila*: Also called Purūravas, he is presented in the *MBh* (1.70.16–20) as the son of Ilā, who was both his father and mother. Purūravas arrogantly seized gems of Brāhmaṇas. He was cursed by the seers and perished.

Ajabindu: Nothing is known about this king from other sources.

1.6.8. *Rāvaṇa*: the famous demon king of Laṅkā who abducted Rāma's wife, Sītā, and set the scene for the epic battle of the *Rāmāyaṇa*.

Duryodhana: the oldest of the 100 Kaurava brothers in the great battle with their five Pāṇḍava cousins in the *Mahābhārata*. The refusal of Duryodhana to share the kingdom with his cousins led to the war and his own destruction.

1.6.9. *Dambhodbhava*: The story of this ancient king is narrated in *MBh* 5.94. He was obsessed with defeating everyone in battle. When he had conquered the whole earth and could not find anyone with whom to fight, he was told of Nara and Nārāyaṇa, who were practicing austerities. He was defeated by them using nothing but sacred grass.

Arjuna: The story of Arjuna of the Haiyayas is narrated in *MBh* 12.49.30–45. Arjuna conquered the whole world and with the help of the fire god burnt down the entire earth. He and his sons were killed in battle by Jamadagni and his sons.

1.6.10. *Vātāpi*: The story of the demon Vātāpi and his older brother Ilvala is narrated in *MBh* 3.94–97 and *Rām* 3.10.55–66. Ilvala, disguised as a Brāhmaṇa, would invite other Brāhmaṇas for an ancestral offering (*śrāddha*), at which he would cook Vātāpi, who had taken the form of a goat. After the Brāhmaṇas had eaten the meal, Ilvala would call out to his brother, and he would come out bursting open the bellies of the Brāhmaṇas. This was put to an end by Agastya who ate the Vātāpi-goat and actually digested him.

Vṛṣṇi confederacy: The story is recorded in the *Ghaṭa Jātaka* (no. 454) and more briefly in the *Saṃkicca Jātaka* (no. 530). The Vṛṣṇis (called Andhaka-Vṛṣṇis in the Jātakas and Vṛṣṇi-Andhakas in the *Buddhacarita* 11.31) teased Dvaipāyana (also called Vyāsa, the reputed creator of the *Mahābhārata*) by asking him what a boy dressed like a pregnant girl will deliver. The angry sage said that "she" would deliver a knot of Khadira wood. When it was delivered, the Vṛṣṇis ground the wood into powder and threw it into the river. The powder gathered downstream and an Eraka plant grew from it. In a fight with each other, the Vṛṣṇis struck each other with that plant's branches, which turned into clubs. The clan was thus destroyed. The account in the *MBh* 16.9 is somewhat different, and the *AŚ* reference is taken from the earlier version preserved in the Jātakas. For a detailed discussion of this story, see Sullivan 1999, 102–107. See also Banerjee 1925.

1.6.12. *Jāmadagnya*: In all likelihood, he is the same as Paraśu-Rāma, the son of Jamadagni (see 1.6.9 n.). His conquering the senses and ruling the earth for a long time are not recorded elsewhere.

Ambarīṣa: The virtues of this king are narrated in *MBh* 12.29.93–98.

1.7.1. *gain mastery...beneficial*: It appears that the first four of this series of eight refer to the king himself, while the last four deal with the benefits his subjects receive through the activities of the king. The only exception is the penultimate, but even there, the people are involved in loving the king because he makes them successful in their undertakings.

1.7.3–5 *He should pursue...other two*: It appears that this passage constitutes an opponent's view (*pūrvapakṣa*), to which a response is made by Kauṭilya in the very next sentence, unless the Kaulīya opinion is an interpolation; see Introduction, p. 21f.

1.7.8. *wastes...private*: Commentators refer to his addiction to pleasures within his harem. The term *pramādyantam* can mean both to be neglectful of duties and to indulge in sex.

sundial and the water clock: The reference is to measures of time. The implication is that these individuals would tell the king when it is time for him to perform particular functions or reproach him for being negligent when he has failed to perform his duties at the proper time. For the sundial, see 1.19.6–8 and 2.20.39; and for the water clock, see 2.20.34–36. For the existence of the water clock in ancient India, see Hinüber 1978.

1.7.9. *move*: The reference is clearly to a cart or a chariot that requires more than one wheel to move. The kingdom can be moved forward only through the work of many royal associates and servants.

1.8. *Establishment of Ministers*: As many scholars have observed (see Scharfe 1993, 32 and 67f), chapters 8 and 9 are confused. The topic of ministers does not really begin until chapter 9, and the presumed topic of chapter 9 does not start until 9.9. I agree with Scharfe (1993, 24) that the insertion of topic titles at the beginning of the respective chapters is not original; on the relation of topics to chapters, see Introduction, p. 9f. The topic of ministers actually begins at 9.1 and the topic of Counselor-Chaplain at 9.9. The problem of the long debate in chapter 8 (Kauṭilya dialogue) can be easily eliminated if we accept (see Introduction, p. 21f) that these are later interpolations. The extant text has simply put the fourth topic title in front of it, and mistakenly put a chapter boundary at the end of it. The very brevity of the fifth topic may have made the śāstric redactor manipulate the text here to come up with two substantial chapters.

1.8.1. *ministers*: For the meaning of the term *amātya* in the *AŚ* and the possible distinctions between the various technical terms for state officials, see the Note to the Translation, Table 0.1.

1.8.7. *mutual*: The meaning is that the drawback Viśālākṣa points out with respect to the ministers affects the king as well; as he knows their vulnerabilities, so do they know his.

1.8.17. *common smell*: The expression *sagandha* derives from animals, especially cows as indicated in the next passage, who identify their own herd by the smell. This animal behavior is extended in a metaphorical way to humans, who generally prefer to remain with their own close relatives and associates.

1.9. *Counselor-Chaplain*: I take the compound *mantri-purohita* here and elsewhere in the *AŚ* as a Karmadhāraya compound referring to a single office of the chaplain who acts as a king's counselor (Falk 1986b, 69). I have presented the reasons for this interpretation at 1.12.6 n. Indeed, within this topic, there is no discussion of counselors at all. Most earlier translators take the two words of the compounds as referring to two classes of officers, the counselors and the chaplain. See the note to 1.8.

1.9.1. *exemplary qualities of a minister* (amātyasampad): The term *sampad* (and its participial equivalent *sampanna*) have a rather technical and specific meaning here, indicating all the requisite qualities that would make up an ideal entity (minister, self, enemy, army, etc.; see 6.1). For this interpretation of the term, see Wezler 2000b, along with the critique of Wezler's interpretation by Bodewitz 2003, who has shown that the term carries multiple meanings. The "ideal" is always from the perspective of the king to whom the text is addressed, the so-called seeker after conquest (*vijigīṣu*). Thus, the ideal qualities of an enemy would be those that would make it easy for the king to subdue him. In many places, we have a list with a final *iti* indicating what constitutes *sampad*: 1.9.1; 2.10.6; 6.1.6, 8, 10–13; 8.3.61. Often the term refers to the successful outcome or the consequences: success of crops, *sasyasampad* (2.8.2); the aftermath of drinking, *pānasampad* (8.3.61); effects of certain poisonous mixtures, *yogasampad* (14.1.28). At 2.10.6, *lekhasampad* refers to the qualities of an exemplary document. I have not attempted to adopt a uniform translation of *sampad*, given its diverse connotations.

1.9.8. *appointment*: I take the term *karman* here not as activity (activities) but to mean the appointment of officials. The verbal form of this term (*kurvīta*) is used with precisely this meaning in the very next sentence.

1.9.9. *Atharvan*: These are ritual means for warding off impending catastrophes given in the *Atharva Veda* or in literature and practices connected to that Vedic tradition.

1.9.10. *follow*: The meaning of this pregnant term appears to be that the king should honor his chaplain, obey him, and abide by his advice.

1.9.11. *Royal power... conquered*: Note here the metaphoric use of sacrificial terminology: "set ablaze" (*edhita*) refers to the kindling of the sacrificial fire. I think here that *edhita* (lit., "prospered") is linked to *indh* ("to set ablaze" or "to kindle"); perhaps the original reading was *indhita*. Counsel (*mantra*) is homologized with the mantras of a ritual, and the weapon (*śastra*) is connected to the authoritative text *(śāstra)* that provides the procedures of the ritual and of political science. The term *śāstra,* however, has a broad meaning and here may refer simply to political science as a system of knowledge rather than to a particular text.

1.10.1. *Counselor-Chaplain*: For an explanation, see 1.9 n. The assistance of the Counselor-Chaplain appears to extend both to the appointments (see 1.11.1 n.) and the subsequent tests.

1.10.2. *The Chaplain... dismiss him*: This is not a true dismissal of the Chaplain, but an elaborate hoax to make other officials believe that the Chaplain has fallen out with the king. He is dismissed for not obeying the king in doing something unrighteous, so that he may instigate the ministers to revolt against the unrighteous king and thus test their loyalty.

1.10.3. *He*: The referent of the pronoun is unclear. It is clear, however, that the test of ministers is to be carried out by the dismissed Chaplain both for the reasons I have given in the previous note, and because in the next test, it is the dismissed general who tests the loyalty of the ministers.

in his place: The Sanskrit is cryptic: *asya* ("his"). I think the *Jayamaṅgalā* commentary may be correct in taking this word to stand for *asya sthāne,* "in his place."

sole support: The term *ekapragraha* is used also at 5.6.28 with reference to the minister (perhaps the chief minister) as the constituent of the state (*prakṛti,* 6.1.1) coming right next to the king himself.

man who has risen to power: The meaning of *aupapādika* is not altogether clear. The commentator Bhikṣu Prabhāmati thinks that it refers to a man not of royal descent who has risen to eminence, giving the example of Candragupta, who overthrew the Nandas and established the Maurya dynasty.

1.10.4, 6, 8. *righteousness* (dharma), *money* (artha), *lust* (kāma): At one level, a relation is made to the Triple Set (1.7.4; 1.10.16). However, given the last test relating to fear, I think these tests relate not simply to the objective goals delineated in the Triple Set, but also to inner qualities and propensities of individuals.

1.10.13. *Justices*: The office of the Justices is described in detail in book 3.

Eradication of Thorns: This office is described in detail in book 4.

Collector: For this officer, see 2.6.

storage facilities of the Treasurer: See 2.5.

outer and inner compounds (bāhyābhyantaravihāra): I follow the explanation of the *Jayamaṅgalā* commentary. The reference is to the quarters occupied by the queens (inner quad) and those by other women of the royal household and harem (outer quad). The test regarding lust to which these officers are put indicates that they were employed in functions relating to royal women.

1.10.15. *pit mines*: Two terms are used in the *AŚ* for a mine: *khani*, a term derived from digging and which I have, for want of a better term, translated as pit mine; and *ākara*, literally a scattering, indicating a place abounding in something, a term that I have translated as mine. Of the two, *khani* is clearly the older term; it is unclear when *ākara* was coined. In the second part of the *AŚ* (books 6–14), only *khani* is used, while in the first part (books 1–5), both terms are used. See the superintendent of *ākara* at 2.12.1f, and the superintendent of *khani* at 2.12.27. With the dominance of *ākara* as the common term for mine, the semantic range of *khani* became restricted to underwater mining for coral, pearls, and even diamonds. For a discussion of the two terms, see Introduction, p. 12, and Olivelle 2012a.

1.10.16–20. These verses appear to engage in a debate with what is given in the prose section. The first verse appears to ascribe the four tests ascribed in the preceding section to "teachers," often the strawman opponent of Kauṭilya. The remaining verses describing Kauṭilya's view take quite a different position from that enunciated in the prose section, either minimizing the need for such tests or, in the final two verses, rejecting such tests altogether. This is another example that demonstrates the different provenance of the prose and verse segments of this text (see Introduction, p. 15).

1.11.1. *he*: once again, as in 1.10.3, the referent of the pronoun is unclear. Given that the appointment of ministers in 1.10.1 is carried out by the king with the assistance of the Counselor-Chaplain, it is likely that the king is the subject of this sentence as well. On the issue of spies in the *AŚ*, see Scharfe 1989, 159–165; 1993, 204–239.

crafty students: The meaning of the Sanskrit *kāpaṭika* (and the variant *kārpaṭika*) is unclear. The term literally means crafty and deceitful. It appears to have acquired other specialized meanings, such as flatterer and parasite, and lexicons also give the meaning of student. See Scharfe 1993, 204–208.

apostate recluses: It is a common assumption in ancient Indian law that a person who has renounced the world and become a wandering mendicant cannot return to society. An apostate renouncer becomes a slave of the king. These vulnerable individuals are here targeted for recruitment into spy establishments. For a detailed study, see Olivelle 1987.

undercover: The term *vyañjana* has often been translated as "disguised" or "seeming." Scharfe (1993, 209) has pointed out the inadequacy of these translations. The term *vyañjana* indicates the sign or mark of a person; these secret agents assume the marks of a householder, merchant, or ascetic, so that they pass themselves off as such individuals. Indeed, they may be "actual" householders or ascetics and may continue these lifestyles; they need not only appear to be so. However, they have a double life as secret agents, and these professions are a cover for their spying activities. Nevertheless, *vyañjana* is also used frequently to indicate a disguise or camouflage, or simply pretense: as an ascetic or corpse (7.17.50–51; 12.5.39), as a treasonable man (9.5.14; 12.4.19), or as the king himself (10.3.42) or a divinity (13.1.3).

crafty students...female mendicant agents: The four types of agents from crafty student to fake ascetic are stationary and connected with spy establishments. They report to various officials (Scharfe 1993, 216). The last four, who are distinguished from the preceding in the Sanskrit by being put into a different compound, are roving spies reporting directly to the king.

1.11.5. *economic activity* (vārttā): At 1.4.1, three occupations are listed under economic activities: agriculture, animal husbandry, and trade. Given that the spy has assistants, it is likely that he is engaging in some business or artisan activity.

1.11.17. *the interpretation of limbs*: The expression *aṅgavidyā* may refer to a variety of prognostications using signs present on the body of a person. Varāhamihira's *Bṛhatsaṃhitā* devotes an entire chapter (51) to this topic. It appears that the astrologer puts a question to his client, and interprets the future by observing which part of the body the client touches, what sorts of persons or animals he sees, and the like.

1.11.18. *bring that about* (saṃpādayeyuḥ): The meaning of the Sanskrit is not altogether clear. Jolly (1920) and Meyer translate "bestätigen," and Kangle "should cause that (prophecy) of his to be fulfilled." The former approach is adopted by Scharfe (1993, 226): "should provide him with that [information]." He argues that "it is politically unthinkable that the 'ascetic' could force the king's hand, or even that of other agents, with spontaneous predictions." This point is well taken. I think, however, that Kangle also has a point, in that sentence 20 makes the Counselor do pretty much the same thing. I think the term *saṃpādayeyuḥ* is sufficiently ambivalent to include both meanings: The ascetic does not make predictions on his own but is instructed by the secret agents. The latter not only inform the ascetic but see to it that these predictions actually happen. Further, it is clear that the two proclamations at the end of 17 are separated from the preceding announcements regarding incidents in the family (so also Meyer); these were communicated to him by his pupils, who must have done some advance work! It is only the two proclamations regarding future matters, especially the activities of the king, with which the secret agents are involved.

1.11.19. *Counselor*: This is probably the same as the major state functionary identified as Counselor-Chaplain (*mantripurohita*), 1.9 n.

1.11.21. *silent punishment* (tūṣṇīṃdaṇḍa): More commonly called *upāṃśudaṇḍa*, this is a euphemism for secret assassination. Often such assassinations are carried out in a way that makes the death appear an accident or the result of a quarrel. See 11.1.31–55 and also 5.1.5–57. Regarding the need to carry out these kinds of secret punishments against powerful individuals within a kingdom, see Scharfe 1979.

1.11.22. *clandestine establishments* (saṃsthā): These are secret agents who set up bogus institutions, either religious or commercial, and conduct their spy activities from them. These are distinguished from roving spies (*saṃcāra*) dealt with in 1.12.

1.12.1. *Secret agents who…maintained*: For a detailed study of this passage and for the meaning of *sattrin* (secret agent), see Scharfe 1993, 216–230; for the connection of *sattrin* to the Vedic sacrifice and the bands of aggressive young men to which they belonged, see Falk 1986a, especially 58. Falk has shown that an *āpya* is precisely such a band of young men. The *Jayamaṅgalā* also reads *āpya* and takes it to mean kinsmen (*svajana*, see Harihara Sastri 2011, 87). All previous scholars have misunderstood the expression *cāpyasaṃbandhinaḥ*, taking it as *ca apy asaṃbandhinaḥ*, when it should be read as *ca āpya-saṃbandhinaḥ*. Given their function within the *AŚ*, however, I have maintained the translation "secret agent" rather than adopting Scharfe's "comrade." These agents belonged to respectable families, and this explains their functions within the spy establishment, including employment to test the loyalty of princes and high officials.

interpretation of signs: The meaning is unclear. Kangle takes this to mean the interpretation of bodily marks. It is, however, unclear how this is different from the next. The signs here may have a broader meaning than simply bodily marks, such as natural phenomena, crying of birds, sightings of various animals, and the like. This is the interpretation offered by Meyer.

the interpretation of limbs: See 1.11.17 n.

creating illusions: This probably refers to various kinds of magical tricks.

Law of hermitages: Kangle and Scharfe (1993, 216) take *āśrama* here to mean the orders of life. This category is somewhat anomalous here. I take it to mean the duties relating to religious hermitages. Perhaps the reference is to spies who assume the guise of matted-haired ascetics mentioned often in the *AŚ*.

interpretation of the interstices of a circle (antaracakra): This method of prognostication is explained by Varāhamihira in the 87th chapter of his

Bṛhatsaṃhitā. The circle has 32 sections (interstices). When the omen, the cry of a bird or animal (explained in chapter 86), comes from the direction of a particular part of this circle, a particular interpretation is given. Thus, if it comes from the eastern division, it indicates the arrival of an officer of the king, the gaining of honor, or the acquisition of wealth.

science of association: The meaning is unclear, and the commentators take it to mean the magical arts associated with love and sex. Meyer prefers "gesellschaftliche Kunst." The term *saṃsarga* can also refer to certain planetary conjunctions. See also 13.1.2.

1.12.4. *she should visit... officials*: These words coming at the end of this sentence appear to be a gloss that found its way into the text. The three previous passages defined the first three mobile agents listed at 1.11.1. One would have expected the "female mendicant" (*bhikṣukī*) to be defined here. It is possible that this very term may have been the last word of this sentence, parallel to the previous three definitions. The difference is that a *bhikṣukī* could be a Brāhmaṇa woman (in this case a widow and apparently without a shaven head) or a regular non-Brāhmaṇical mendicant woman with a shaven head (1.12.5). Indeed, I think that the term *parivrājikā* with reference to the Brāhmaṇa woman may simply mean a poor woman who goes around to houses begging (*bhikṣukī*, see the same term at 1.12.13). The statement that this female agent should visit the houses of high officials is misplaced here, because we have that explicit statement with regard to all these agents at 1.12.6. In any case, the job of these women, as described in 1.12.10, is not to gain employment in these houses (so Scharfe 1993, 219), but to carry messages from the poisoners employed in the households of these high officials.

1.12.5. *mobile agents* (saṃcāra): These agents are distinguished from spy establishments (*saṃsthā*); see 1.11.22 n. As indicated in 1.12.7–12, the roving spies report to those running the spy establishments, and they in turn transmit the information to the central authorities.

1.12.6. *them*: The referent of this pronoun is not altogether clear. In all likelihood, it refers to both the roving spies and the spy establishments dealt with under topics 7a and 7b.

devotion: The term *bhaktitaḥ* may mean loyalty to the king. However, Scharfe (1993, 219) has noted the related expression *yadbhaktiḥ* at 1.14.6, where an agent is assigned to a person who has some religious or emotional attachment to that agent. So, here also, the agents may be assigned to officials who have some ties to them.

Counselor-Chaplain... Tribal Chief: As indicated in verse 1.12.20, this list includes 18 high officials or, more likely, high offices; some of these offices, such as magistrate and council of counselors, may contain more than one official. Kangle's list, taking *mantripurohita* as two individuals (counselor and chaplain), actually contains 19 offices instead of the standard 18 (see 1.12.20). This is one more proof that *mantripurohita,* at least in the early portions of the AŚ, was a single office. Some take *mantripariṣadadhyakṣa* to be "the administrator (president) of the council of counselors"; but this is unlikely both because such an office is not recorded elsewhere in the text and because, at 5.3.7 and 13, we have the *mantripariṣad* and *adhyakṣa* listed separately. Scharfe (1993, 177) objects to viewing superintendent (*adhyakṣa*) as a separate category also because it is evident from the salary list that he is paid a low salary. The salary list, however, is probably a later addition to the text and cannot be used as a criterion to judge other parts of the text. Further, in the *Pañcatantra* text regarding *mahāmātras* that Scharfe (1993, 189) himself cites, several such *adhyakṣas* are listed, including those overseeing elephants and the treasury.

1.12.9. *Poisoners*: It is likely that all the individuals mentioned in the passage are secret agents within the category of poisoner, in the same way as in the previous passage, assassins spied on the outdoor activities.

chefs, cooks: The exact meanings of the terms *sūda* (chef) and *ārālika* (cook) are unclear. They are both types of cooks. The first term is quite common. The second is found four times in the *AŚ*, here and at 5.1.36; 7.17.40; 12.2.22, always in the compound *sūdārālika*. It is found just twice in the *MBh* (4.2.7; 15.1.17), in the first juxtaposed with *govikartā* (cow butcher) and *sūpakartā* (sauce maker); and in the second juxtaposed with *sūpakartā* (sauce maker) and *rāgakhāṇḍavika* (maker of sweet meats). If the connection of *arāla* (3.20.10; 4.10.9) with a leather strap is confirmed, then the juxtaposition of *ārālika* with a butcher may hint at a cook specializing in meat. The *sūda* is connected to making *vyañjana* (sauces or curries) in *MBh* 4.7.5.

disguised as: It is, of course, difficult to see how someone could disguise himself as a dwarf or a hunchback. The likely meaning is that such people were recruited by the state as secret agents, because there were jobs for them within the rich households. It appears that such deformed people were employed to walk in front of the king to divert the evil eye from the king (Scharfe, personal communication).

Kirātas: The reference is probably to some kind of tribal people, who must have been fierce warriors. At 1.21.1, they are part of the king's personal bodyguard.

1.12.11. *signs and written messages*: Kangle and Scharfe (1993, 220), following the commentators, take the compound *saṃjñālipi* to mean "sign alphabets," that is, some kind of coded writing. However, in 1.12.13, we have letters and signs as two separate means of communication. The signs were probably prearranged with their handlers.

1.12.17. *Eradication of Thorns*: This is the topic of book 4. These secret agents stationed in the countryside are mentioned in 4.4.3.

1.12.19. *agents of the same type*: If a double agent is disguised as a merchant, for example, the king should deploy another agent pretending to be a merchant to test the integrity of his double agent.

1.12.20. *eighteen high officials*: For the use of the term *tīrtha* as a synonym of *mahāmātra* (1.12.6 n.), see Scharfe 1993, 189. On these 18 officers and the significance of the term *tīrtha*, see Wilhelm 1967–1968.

1.12.24. *mobile agents…as clandestine operatives*: This line of the verse is quite obscure. I have taken *saṃsthāgūḍhāḥ* as a compound, paralleling *cārasaṃcāriṇaḥ* and meaning spies within spy establishments (2.7). I have also adopted the reading *agūḍhasaṃjñitaiḥ* (instrumental) of the *Jayamaṅgalā* commentary; it parallels *tādṛśaiḥ* of the first line. What this compound actually means, whether as a nominative or an instrumental plural, is unclear. In some sense, it must mean secret agents who are unrecognizable as such, in contrast to those in the first line who are similar to the spies whom they try to detect. The meaning, however, remains uncertain.

1.12.25. *officials who are…seducible factions*: The meaning of this phrase is quite unclear. The interpretation of the commentator Yogghama, followed by Kangle, seems to be the most plausible. These officials ostensibly act as if they have been offended by being sent to the frontier posts; we must assume that certain postings, much like those of diplomats today, can be viewed as punishment. Thus they may appear to be in collusion with seducible factions. When the double agents try to recruit these officials, they would be exposed.

1.13.5. *Manu*: In several accounts of the origin of the human race, Manu is presented both as the first man and as the first king. This theory of kingship sees the selection of the first king by the people as a contract between the people and the king.

1.13.6. *They allocated…money*: As part of the original agreement, people pay taxes to the king in exchange for his providing security, especially security from theft and robbery. This contractual agreement at the beginning of history is presented as the reason for the legitimacy of taxation. It is unclear whether cash payments of an unspecified amount are in addition to the shares of grain and merchandise, or the amount in cash is also one-tenth of the money earned by a person, in the same way as merchandise. Ghoshal (1929) thinks that "money" (*hiraṇya*) in some inscriptions refers to a monetary tax on certain goods (Scharfe 1993, 161).

1.13.10. *The position…manifest*: Indra is the king of gods, and Yama is the king of the realm of the dead, as well as the judge of good and bad deeds performed on earth by those who die. The king occupies these positions on earth as their visible representative. Often kings are viewed as being created with portions of the guardian deities of the world, as spelled out, for example, in the *MDh* 7.3–7: "To protect this whole world the Lord created the king by extracting eternal particles from Indra, Wind, Yama, Sun, Fire, Varuṇa, Moon, and the Lord of wealth. Because the king was fashioned out of particles from these chiefs of the gods, he overpowers all beings by reason of his energy. Like the sun, indeed, he burns eyes and minds; no one on earth can bear to gaze upon him. He is Fire, he is Wind, he is the Sun, he is the Moon, he is the King of the Law [Yama], he is Kubera, he is Varuṇa, and he is the Great Indra—by reason of his power."

1.13.13–14. *he, they*: The switch in the pronoun from singular to plural probably means that the restraining of the common people is done by the second agent who had given the philosophy of kingship. The discovery of rumors is done by all the agents involved in this kind of altercation.

1.13.15. *its* (asya): Kangle translates as "his," thus taking these people to receive wages and benefits from the king. But that is unlikely, because they are said to provide these supplies to the king in times of need. The likely referent of the pronoun is the countryside (*janapada*), on whose produce these people subsist (see also sentence 19). They are the target of the state's spying activities.

1.13.25. *conciliation... military force*: These are the four strategies (*upāya*) for overcoming enemies (see also 2.10.47; 7.14.11). Manu (*MDh* 7.198–200), among other authorities, recommends the first three applied individually or collectively, with military force as a last recourse. Often these four are mentioned in abbreviated form, conciliation etc. (*sāmādi*); *MDh* 7.107, 109, 159; *AŚ* 7.6.19; 7.9.25; 7.17.59; 8.5.10; 9.1.15; 9.6.6.

1.14.2–5. *set*: For these groups of people who are open to instigation, see 1.13.22.

1.14.2. *put in prison*: The reading here is uncertain. Kangle and Meyer suggest that the word *kārā* (prison) should be *kāra* or *kara* (tax), and the sentence should be something like "some who are oppressed by taxes."

1.14.3. *hurt another*: I follow Kangle in taking the passive past participle *upahata* (and *viprakṛta* that follows) with an active meaning. It is he who has committed these offenses; that is why he is afraid. If he had been the subject of these acts, he would rather be angry.

surrendered with his troops: For this expression, see topic 120 (at 7.15). Kangle, however, thinks that the expression *daṇḍenopanataḥ* here refers to someone who has been subdued by force.

1.14.7. *intoxication*: The term *mada* in the context of the elephant refers to its rut, which makes it difficult to manage, while the mahout is simply drunk.

king... science: The term *śāstra* may refer either to this particular treatise of Kauṭilya or to the science of government. The Malayalam commentary adds the words *andhena mantriṇādhiṣṭhitaḥ* (and guided by a blind counselor), which would parallel the blind elephant and its blind mahout.

1.14.9. *lacking spirit... eloquence*: See the parallel at 1.11.19.

1.14.10. *made use of*: The same Sanskrit term *upabhogya* is used with reference to both the well and the king. In the case of the well, it means that only Caṇḍālas can draw water from it, while in the case of the king, only vile people will serve him and receive remuneration and honors from him.

1.14.11. *employ them*: The context makes it clear that these individuals from the enemy territory who have been recruited to work against the enemy carry out their tasks in that territory. They become a sort of a fifth column.

1.15.1. *factions... enemies*: The compounds *svapakṣa* and *parapakṣa* are understood literally by Kangle and Meyer ("his own party and the party of the enemy"). However, the reference is to the subjects covered in topics 9 and 10, where the activities of the king and spies are directed at not simply his party and the enemy's party but at seducible and non-seducible factions within the territories of both. Therefore, I have taken the two compounds to be abbreviations for the factions located within one's own and the enemy's territories.

1.15.10. *All that*: The referent of the pronoun *tasya* ("of that") is unclear. It probably refers back to the discussion that took place during the time of counsel.

1.15.19. *affairs of a king... inferred*: For this expression and comments on the three categories, see 1.9.4–7.

1.15.20. *bringing certainty... is certain*: The readings of the extant manuscripts here (*upalabdhasya niścitabalādhānam*) appear to be defective. I have followed the reading adopted by Jolly (1923) and approved by Meyer: *upalabdhasya niścayo niścitasya balādhānam*. This reading, which is clearly superior, is found in the citation of this passage in Somadeva's *Nītivākyāmṛta*.

1.15.22. *child*: The Sanskrit term *bāla* may also mean a fool or simpleton.

1.15.33. *instability* (anavasthā): The meaning appears to be that, if the king selects a different group of counselors every time he wants to do something, it would create a lack of continuity and cohesion in the advice he gets from his counselors.

1.15.35. *when things are going badly* (arthakṛcchreṣu): The meaning of this expression is not altogether clear. Kange translates it as "in difficult matters," similar to Meyer's "bei schwieringen Dingen." The same expression occurs also at 5.2.1 and 7.8.5 in the compound *pratyutpannārthakṛcchraḥ*. At 5.2.1, Kangle translates "when difficulties concerning money have arisen" (in a similar way also at 7.8.5). In all these, *arthakṛcchra* refers to difficult circumstances, when things are not going well (including money). This expression is found frequently in the *MBh* (1.77.18; 1.196.15;

2.5.24; 2.69.19; 3.2.18; 3.64.3; 3.198.41; 5.70.77; 12.94.11; 12.219.15), and in these places, the meaning is broader than simply money.

1.15.39. *if it…catastrophe*: As Kangle observes, this appears to have been a marginal gloss on the previous sentence that found its way into the text proper.

1.15.41. *take counsel…or two*: The text in Kangle's edition reads *ekena saha dvābhyām eko vā*, and he translates: "with one or two, or alone by himself." This provision seems rather odd, given that the dispute focuses on the number of counselors who should be present. I suggest that the text be emended to change *eko* to *eva;* in any case, it is problematic for *eko* to come before *vā*, when one would have expected the latter to follow *dvābhyām*. So my emendation would change the current text to read *ekena saha dvābhyām eva vā*. I thank Professor Albrecht Wezler for this conjecture.

1.15.42. *five components*: That is, counsel has to deal with the five parts of any undertaking listed in this passage.

1.15.45. *not waste time*: Initial consultations will lead to a decision to pursue a particular project. Once that decision is made, he should not waste time and immediately begin consultations with his counselors, probably as to the best strategies to follow in accomplishing the objectives.

1.15.50. *According to ability*: The expression *yathāsāmarthyam* is used also at 1.15.41, with the probable meaning of "as far as he is able." Here also, it probably means that, according to Kauṭilya, the king should appoint as many counselors as he is able; there is no fixed number. It is unclear whether the Kauṭilya quotation ends with this or extends to the end of passage 52.

1.15.55–57. *Indra's council…thousand-eyed*: It is quite likely that this reference to Indra was a marginal gloss that found its way into the text. It disturbs the continuity between the passages 53–54 and 58–59 that deal with the process of royal consultation. "Thousand-eyed" (sahasrākṣa) is an epithet of Indra, here interpreted as referring to his thousand counselors.

1.15.58. *urgent*: The term *ātyayika*, which also occurs in Aśoka's sixth Rock Edict, is contrasted with *upekṣatavya* at 5.5.1, where the latter term probably means a task that permits a delay. The translation "urgent" fits that context, as well as the three other places where it occurs: 1.15.58; 1.19.29, 30. Scharfe (1989, 136; 1993, 176) suggests that the term refers to a "matter of life and death." I think the term *urgent* covers both these situations: requiring immediate action *and* a matter of pressing importance.

counselors and the council of counselors: This is a rather awkward statement. We must assume that these constitute two distinct groups of individuals, even though they bear the same title. Scharfe (1993, 176–177) thinks that only the first group consisted of true counselors, of whom there were probably three or four, whereas the council of counselors consisted of a variety of senior officials spread throughout the country.

1.15.59. *or* (vā): The important northern manuscript D reads *ca* ("and"), and Scharfe (1993, 176) thinks that this is a superior reading. One must be sure that the advice has the support of the majority *and* should assure success. The owl king of the *Pañcatantra* (book 3) followed the advice of the majority but not the wise counsel of one counselor that would have led to success. Taking *vā* as presenting the preferred option, however, may make this emendation unnecessary.

1.15.60. *He must not...limbs*: This verse with slight variants is found in *MDh* 7.105 and *MBh* 12.84.46. It probably belonged to a group of proverbial (*subhāṣita*) verses on the king.

1.15.61. *As none...counsel*: There is a play on the words here; only a person learned in the Vedas (*śrotriya*) can eat a funeral offering (*śrāddha*), and only a learned person (*śruta*) can listen (*śrotum*) to counsel.

1.16.5. *retinue of assistants* (puruṣaparivāpa): This expression occurs also at 2.24.28 and 3.3.3. The term *puruṣa* in these contexts has a wide spectrum of meaning, from assistant or servant to people under one's care or dependents. Here the reference is to the officials and servants who would normally accompany the envoy. In the other two instances, the term probably refers to dependents.

1.16.12. *his good qualities*: The Sanskrit does not have a pronoun, and it is unclear whose good qualities are being mentioned. It could refer to the envoy himself or to the master who has sent him.

1.16.16. *This is the statement*: That is, the formal statement the envoy has just delivered from his master.

1.16.24. *vulnerable...kingdom*: The seven constituents of a kingdom are listed at *AŚ* 6.1.1: king, minister, countryside, fort, treasury, army, and ally. Regarding the vulnerable points, one can especially think of ministers who may be disaffected, the fort that may have weaknesses, the treasury that may be depleted, the army that may be weak, or an ally who may be disaffected or double-crossing.

1.16.25. *with them*: The reference is to the spies he has deployed. In this case, he should obtain the information they have gathered (*cāra*) through these methods. It is actually these spies who appear to blather or draw pictures, so they would not be seen in the company of the envoy. I think Kangle is incorrect here to think that the envoy himself obtains secret information through these means, the assumption then being that he is unable to make use of spies. The term *cāra* does not refer simply to secret information but to information gathered by spies, who are also called *cāra*.

1.16.29. *rear enemy, rear ally*: For this and other allies and enemies around a king, see 6.2.18 and the Note to the Translation, Table 0.3.

ally in front: The term *mitra* simply means ally. But in contexts where the term is contrasted with *ākranda* (the ally at the back to whom one can cry for help), the term means an ally located in front. See *AŚ* 7.4.16; *MDh* 7.177, 208.

1.17.1–3. *The king... surveillance of sons*: Here we have the author playing on the two meanings of the Sanskrit term *rakṣ-*: surveillance or keeping watch, and protection or guarding. The princes are kept under surveillance, and this in turn enables the king to protect himself and his kingdom.

1.17.16. *as one milks... the calf*: The reference is to the cow that yields milk only if the calf is present and she can smell it. The analogy may refer more specifically to a practice where, if the calf is dead or has been slaughtered, the herdsman would keep the stuffed head of the calf (probably prepared by a taxidermist) so that the mother can smell it and thus yield milk. The Malayalam commentary states: "In the way of men milking a cow after killing the calf." I thank Professor Hartmut Scharfe for pointing this out. Evidently, in a similar manner, the neighboring king could use the presence of the prince to get whatever he wants from the father.

1.17.19. *Aditi-Kauśikas*: The reference and the analogy are totally opaque. The *Jayamaṅgalā* commentary takes the compound as a Dvandva, with *Aditi* as people who beg by showing statues of gods and *Kauśika* as people who do so exhibiting snakes (i.e., snake charmers). Some kind of people who used various devices to extract money from householders appears to be meant (see also 11.1.42 and my note to it). In the play *Mudrārākṣasa* (Act 1) by Śūdraka, who is deeply versed in the Arthaśāstric tradition and makes Cāṇakya (*alias* Kauṭilya) the hero of the play, a spy comes to a house disguised as a religious itinerant carrying a *yamapaṭa*, a cloth with a depiction of god Yama.

1.17.26. *rite of passage* (saṃskāra): This probably refers to the rites immediately following birth and/or during the early years of life (1.5.7–10; 2.21.18). It may also include the most significant childhood rite of passage, the Vedic initiation (*upanayana*).

1.17.31. *fresh object*: The reference is to a fresh pot, either unbaked or unglazed, that would absorb any color or odor when something is smeared on it.

1.17.33. *Therefore... and Success*: For the importance of concentrating on the positive and avoiding negative instructions in the training of students, see Scharfe 2002, 237–239, 267.

1.17.34. *The secret agents*: It is unclear where the Kauṭilya quotation ends in the absence of a concluding *iti*. It is possible that the passage 1.17.34–40 may also be part of the quotation.

1.17.39. *to attack*: For this meaning of the verb *prārthayati*, see 3.10.34; 6.2.38.
smash you like a clod: The exact meaning of the difficult compound *ekaloṣṭavadha* is unclear. The most probable meaning is that the people would destroy the king as easily as a man plowing a field would break up a clod of earth. See Scharfe 1989, 67.

1.17.42. *another region* (anyaviṣaya): For the meaning of the term *viṣaya,* see Scharfe 1993, 118–119. In the *AŚ*, the term generally refers to the entire territory of a kingdom, especially when *svaviṣaya* ("own territory") and *paraviṣaya* ("territory of another or of an enemy") are contrasted (1.14.1; 2.16.17–18; 13.1.7–8). In inscriptions, however, *viṣaya* may mean a part of a kingdom; see Kane 1962–1975, III: 138. The compound *anyaviṣaya* occurs only twice in the *AŚ*, here and at 4.3.19. The issue is whether this is a Tatpuruṣa compound ("territory of another" as in the case of *paraviṣaya*) or a Karmadhāraya ("other territory"); in the latter case, the distinction may be not between kingdoms, but between the place where the king is residing and another region of his kingdom. The fact that in these two places the author has used *anya,* whereas when reference is made to another king's territory, the term *para* (which is also the term for an enemy) is used, indicates that the reference probably is to a distinct area of the king's own territory.

a son, a bargaining chip, or an embryo: The meanings of the three Sanskrit terms, *garbha, paṇya,* and *ḍimba,* are quite unclear. Commentators and translators alike appear to be guessing. It is also unclear whether the readings are accurate; Meyer's suggested reading of *garbha, ṣaṇḍa, ḍimba,* and *vāna* (fetus, impotent prince, silly prince, and exhausted prince) does not improve the text. The possible meaning is that the leaders or people in the region where the prince is exiled will not use him as a bargaining chip against his father. I take *paṇya,* therefore, not as commodity but as something to be bargained with. The meaning of the passage, however, remains quite uncertain.

1.17.49. *female-son*: The Sanskrit term *putrikā*, which is a feminine construction from *putra* ("son"), has generally been translated as "appointed daughter," an institution that is also found in other Indo-European cultures, where a daughter is ritually appointed to bear a son for her own father. Such a son is ritually constituted as his maternal grandfather's son; he is not the son of his biological father. This translation, however, is misleading, because, as Jolly (1885, 147–9) has pointed out, such a daughter is not merely the one who produces a son for her father but is actually a "son" in her own right. Many legal texts list her immediately after the natural son and before other kinds of sons (see *MDh* 8.158–60). See also *MDh* 9.130 about her right to inherit the paternal estate. Although somewhat awkward, I have opted for "female-son" to highlight the fact that she is legally a son who happens to be female. See *The Law Code of Gortyn* (ed. Ronald F. Willetts. Berlin: de Gruyter, 1967, 23–27 and 45–47), a fifth-century b.c,e. text from Crete, which devotes a substantial section to the "heiress," that is, a daughter who inherits the paternal property in the absence of sons.

1.17.50. *field* (kṣetra): Namely, his wife; a woman is often compared to a field in which a man sows the seed. For an extensive discussion of this topic, see *MDh* 9.32–55.

mother's kinsman: It appears that kings favored their maternal relatives over paternal ones. During the last centuries B.C.E., we also find textual and epigraphic evidence of kings and others identifying themselves as sons of their mothers in preference to their fathers. One can understand this in light of the fact that Indian kings had multiple wives, whose sons often vied with each other for the right of succession. See below at 1.18.11, where a prince in his father's disfavor is advised to form an alliance with his mother's relatives. A king's paternal relatives are also related to his brothers, whereas his maternal relatives are connected only to him.

1.18.8. *coloring gems*: The coloring of crystals to look like expensive gems was a technique known in the ancient world at least by the first century C.E., according to Wojtilla (2009, 40), who cites Pliny the Elder. Such artificial gems may be the ones referred to as *kācamani* at 2.11.36.

and mines: Kangle translates "mines and factories for gold-smelting...." This would involve an impossible dissolution of the compound *suvarṇa pāka...ākarakarmāntān*, joining the first elements with *karmānta* (factory) in a Tatpuruṣa compound, and taking the intervening *ākara* (mine) in a Dvandva relation to the rest of the compound. I think the compound *ākarakarmānta* in all its occurrences (1.13.21; 2.1.19) are Tatpuruṣa compounds and deal with factories or workshops associated with mining operations. The term *karmānta* is used in this way frequently with produce forests (2.2.5; 2.17.2), with various metals (2.12.23; 2.13.1; 2.15.60), with diamonds, gems, and the like (2.12.27), with textiles (2.23.8), for armor (2.23.10), for chariots (2.33.2), and for mines and valuable articles (4.9.2). I have taken the compound generally to be a Tatpuruṣa, except in the title of topic 30 (2.12) and its mention at 1.1.4. This is the interpretation also of Bhikṣu Prabhāmati in his commentary on these passages.

1.18.10. *secret method...settlement*: For a similar provision, see 9.3.18. Secret methods of conquering an enemy's fortified town are given in 13.1 and 3. The term used here, *pāragrāmika*, occurs also at 5.1.3 and 9.3.18, where it clearly refers to a section of this treatise. But no section with that title exists in the text as we currently have it, although book 13 clearly deals with this subject, albeit in the title the term *durga* ("fort") is used. Yet the very first sentence of that book uses the term *grāma*, which is probably an old term to refer to a fortified settlement. See also 5.1.3 n.

1.19.7. *A shadow...Aṅgulas*: For the dimensions of these measurements, see 2.20.39–42 and appendix 2.

1.19.10. *try cases*: The Sanskrit *kāryāṇi paśyet* could simply mean "look into the affairs" (Kangle's translation). However, in the *MDh*, this expression is used repeatedly within the context of adjudicating lawsuits. Thus, at *MDh* 8.2 and 24, we have: "he should try the cases of the plaintiffs" (*paśyet kāryāṇi kāryiṇām*), and at 8.10, "he should try the cases" (*so 'sya kāryāṇi saṃpaśyet*). See also *MDh* 7.140–141; 8.174, 178, 390. I think here and later at 1.19.30–32 of the *AŚ* this technical meaning is also intended. It appears that this section has been deeply influenced by the Brāhmaṇical Dharmaśāstric tradition; note the use of the technical term *svādhyāya* (Vedic recitation) at 1.19.11, 20, the only occurrences of that term in the *AŚ* apart from 1.3.10 dealing with the duties of a Vedic student, once again a deeply Brāhmaṇical topic. See also the mention of *saṃdhyā*, the worship of the sun during especially the evening twilight, at 1.19.17, once again the only occurrence of this term in the *AŚ*, and the equation of various royal duties with the components of a Vedic sacrifice (1.19.33). For a discussion of the compositional history of the *AŚ*, see Introduction, p. 6f.

1.19.12. *monetary... superintendents*: The reference appears to be to checking the income generated by the treasury and to assigning tasks to the superintendents, who are dealt with in book 2. The expression *adhyakṣān kurvīta* could also include the appointment of new superintendents.

1.19.21. *Treatise*: The term *śāstra* here may refer to the treatise, as well as to the knowledge system, comprehended by Arthaśāstra or political science. The Sanskrit term comprehends both meanings, but even when a system of knowledge is meant, the textualization of it is always present in the background. See Pollock 1985, 1989a, 1989b, 1990; Olivelle 2005, 62–66.

1.19.26. *plead their cases*: See the note to 1.19.10 on the meaning of *kārya* as a legal case, even though here the term may have a broader meaning. In the very next sentence (1.19.27), however, the term is used in a more general sense; I think the author is playing on the two meanings of the term in this passage. See a similar play with *artha* at 1.19.34, where its meaning is clearly Success as a component of the Triple Set (1.7.4–6). See 2.7.10 for the expression *kāryārthin*, where the meaning clearly is not limited to legal cases.

1.19.29. *relating to gods*: In general, disputes concerning a god or property of a god refer to temples of individual gods. It is the god enshrined in a temple who is the owner of both the temple and any property or slaves attached to that temple. On the juridical position of a god in Indian jurisprudence, see Sontheimer 2004.

1.20.1. *recommended as a building site* (vāstukapraśaste): The precise meaning of *vāstuka* is unclear. I take it as a variant of *vāstu* (building site; so also Jolly 1920 and Meyer), while Kangle, following several commentators, and Scharfe (1993, 142) take it to mean a person who is an expert in prognosticating auspicious sites for houses. However, in all the places where the term occurs (1.20.1; 2.3.3, 22; 2.6.2; 2.13.43; 2.14.35, 39, 46; 3.8.13; 10.1.1, 2, and in the title of topic 61), the term invariably refers to a compound where a building may be erected or a building site. Either way, however, the meaning is not very different.

courtyards (kakṣyā): I take this Sanskrit term to refer to courts or courtyards that gave access to dwellings. We find a series of such courtyards mentioned at 1.21.1. On these courtyards around which rooms are built, see Schlingloff 1969, 24f.

1.20.2. *He should get…calamity*: This long sentence is somewhat unclear and has a convoluted syntax. Kangle places *madhye* ("in the center") also in the first phrase and translates: "He should cause to be constructed a living chamber in the centre in accordance with the procedure laid down for the treasury." I do not think this addition is necessary. In this translation, I have followed the persuasive explanation of Schlingloff (1968). The meaning appears to be that one should follow the basic plan for the treasury (see 2.5.2–3 and the notes there). The author then gives three alternatives. The final clause "as well as a floor…time of calamity" is a separate provision for an emergency exit and defense not directly connected to the construction of the living quarters.

1.20.3. *Or he may…students*: The purpose of this provision is obscure. Commentators take "fellow students" to mean enemy kings who may have access to this same treatise. This seems doubtful; see the similar view on appointing fellow students at 1.8.1–6. The term *sahādhyāyin* generally refers to those who have been classmates. The meaning probably is that such students may know all these hidden tricks and use them for their own advantage during a time of crisis.

1.20.4. *When a fire…mixed with earth*: Setting fire to a fort was a favorite method during a siege; see *AŚ* 13.4.14–21. For occult means of preventing fires, see also *AŚ* 14.2.38.

1.20.5. *Snakes…Aśvattha tree*: For the poison-destroying properties of these trees and their magical uses, see 14.4.12. The exact method of application is unclear. I take *pratāna* as the aerial roots of the Aśvattha tree, while Kangle takes it to mean a string of shoots hung around a house, which may, indeed, be the way these plant materials were used. With regard to which parts of Jīvantī, etc. are meant, Meyer takes them to be the flowers, while Kangle thinks they are also shoots. It is unclear whether Puṣpa refers to a flower or is a particular kind of tree. The *Jayamaṅgalā* commentary takes it to mean the flowers of the trees mentioned before it. Meyer restricts it to the immediately preceding Muṣkaka. Both Gaṇapati Śāstrī and Kangle take Puṣpavandākā as the name of a tree, although Gaṇapati at 14.4.12 separates the two and calls Puṣpa a kind of plant. Clearly, there is a lot of guessing going on here.

drumstick tree (akṣībe): The meaning of this term is unclear. Kangle, following the *Jayamaṅgalā* commentary, takes it to mean wetland, although he does not provide any other source for this meaning. Meyer takes it as sea salt. I think the reading *akṣība* or *akṣīva* here has the meaning of the drumstick tree (Moringa). The Aśvattha tree, in the fig family, grows on many surfaces, and here apparently it has grown on the stem of a drumstick tree. For this meaning, see EDS I: 227, which gives a citation from the medical treatise *Suśrutasaṃhitā* (Kalpasthāna, 8.120) for the compound *akṣīvapippala* meaning "Pippal [= Aśvattha] tree grown on *Moringa pterigosperma* [i.e., the drumstick tree]."

1.20.10. *yard with trees and water*: This may refer to a park or a garden with trees and ponds.

1.20.11. *outside*: The Sanskrit is terse with simply *bahiḥ* ("outside"). It is unclear outside of what these residences are to be located. The uses of *madhye* ("in the center") for the king's chamber, *pr̥ṣṭhataḥ* ("at the back") for the women's quarters, *bahiḥ* ("outside") for the residence of younger royals, and *purastāt* ("in the front") for the various public rooms seem to suggest that these directional terms refer to the royal residence (*antaḥpura*) that is mentioned in the very first sentence (1.20.1). If this is the case, the term "outside" probably means not outside the compound of the royal residence, but the "outer area" of that residence.

1.20.15–16 *For Bhadrasena…her braids*: For examples of ancient kings who got into trouble for a variety of reasons, see the notes to 1.6.5–12. Some of the episodes listed in this passage are given in greater detail in Bāṇa's *Harṣacarita* (tr. Cowell and Thomas, 192–194) and more briefly in Varāhamihira's *Br̥hatsaṃhitā* (78.1–2). Bhadrasena was a king of Kaliṅga (broadly modern Orissa), and he was assassinated by his brother-in-law, Vīrasena, hiding in his sister's bedroom. According to the *Harṣacarita*, Kārūṣa was the name of the kingdom, while the personal name of the king was Dadhra, whereas a commentary on this passage of *AŚ* contained in Kangle's manuscript D gives the name as Vajra. The reason for this parricide was Dadhra's decision to appoint another son as the crown prince. The *Harṣacarita* gives the name of the king of Kāśi as Mahāsena and his wife as Suprabhā. The reason for this murder is also succession; Mahāsena had appointed a son from a different wife as crown prince. Vairantya, that is, the king of Viranti, again according to the *Harṣacarita*, was named Rantideva (see *Buddhacarita* 1.52, where he is called Antideva); the Sauvīra king was named Vīrasena and his wife, Haṃsavatī; Jālūtha (or Jārūtha) was the king of Ayodhyā and his wife was Ratnavatī; and Vidūratha was the king of Vr̥ṣṇi and his murderous wife was Vindumatī.

1.20.18. *interaction*: The provisions here and in the subsequent statements apply to the wives of the king. Clearly, the women's quarters were viewed by the author as a source of constant danger to the king.

charlatans (kuhaka): This term is frequently associated with various kinds of ascetics and, in a context such as this (and at 4.4.3), refers to a particular ascetic group. However, at 4.1.66, it appears to refer in general to various insincere people including ascetics. The term generally refers to people who appear sincere but are actually cheats. At 5.4.9, the term along with *uddhata* (haughty or arrogant people) appears to refer more generally to people who are well-dressed and go about pretending to be important persons. The connection between *kuhaka* and *uddhata* occurs also at *MBh* 3.223.9.

1.21.5. *in the same manner* (tathaiva): The precise meaning is unclear. Perhaps he was to eat it straight from the chef's hand, or as soon as it was cooked. It is also likely that he should eat with the same kinds of precautions with which the food was cooked, that is, having it tasted repeatedly by his food tasters to make sure that the food is not poisoned. This clearly refers to the dangers of poison, as indicated in the next passage.

an offering to fire and birds: Here the offering (*bali*) may well be a religious oblation commonly made before a meal; but it is far more likely, in view of what is stated in the very next sentence, that throwing some of the food in the fire or to birds is meant to test whether the food contains poison.

1.21.7. *destruction... taste*: The probable meaning is that the poison alters the normal way the curry smells, feels, and tastes.

BOOK 2

2.1.1. *forcing people out*: The term *apavāhana* is translated by Kangle as "bringing in" and by Meyer as "Herbeiziehung." Scharfe (1993, 122) sees a stronger intent here and thinks that the foreign population was abducted to settle the countryside. I think Scharfe is correct, especially because this term and its verbal equivalent (*apavāhayet*) occur frequently within contexts that imply the forcible removal of a population, 7.1.33; 7.16.16; 8.2.8; 8.4.15; 9.4.8; 11.1.16, 53; 12.3.14; 13.5.18.

2.1.2. *families* (kula): This term may refer simply to families, perhaps joint or extended families. The term *kula* used in *MDh* 7.119, however, is interpreted differently by its commentators. Commenting on this verse, Medhātithi takes it to mean a segment of a village, known in some regions as *haṭṭa* and in others as *uṣṭa*. Nārāyaṇa cites a saying that a *kula* consists of two *halas*, a *hala* being an area of land that can be plowed by eight or six oxen. The latter view is adopted by Govinda, Kullūka, Rāghavānanda, and Rāmacandra. Nandana thinks it is the share of one cultivator. In any case, the commentators appear to take this term as referring to an area of cultivated land able to sustain a family rather than to a family as such. So also the commentary *Cāṇakyaṭīkā* on this passage.

2.1.3. *milk-tree*: This refers to trees that have milky sap. Four such trees are listed: banyan, Udumbara, Aśvattha, and Madhūka.

2.1.4. *In the middle... ten villages*: For these administrative centers, which also functioned as seats for law courts, see 3.1.1. As the name suggests, the collection center (*saṃgrahaṇa*) was probably intended to collect revenues and taxes at the local level. The expression *daśagrāmīsaṃgraheṇa* is somewhat unclear, but probably means that a collection center should correspond to ten village units.

2.1.6. *Caṇḍālas*: This term refers to outcaste people within the social structures described in the Dharmaśāstras. Here, however, it refers to some kind of tribal people living in remote locations, which was probably its original meaning.

2.1.7. *Brāhmaṇa land grants* (brahmadeya): This is a technical term referring to gifts of land given to Brāhmaṇas, lands that are free from taxes and meant to support their ritual and scholarly activities.

2.1.8–9. *cultivated* (kr̥ta), *uncultivated* (akr̥ta): By cultivated, I mean land that has been prepared for agriculture by clearing and tilling. Kangle's "arable" and "unarable," I think, miss the point, given that unarable land cannot be brought under cultivation. Unarable land is called *akr̥ṣya* in 2.2.1. For the meaning, see Wojtilla 2010, 1012.

2.1.9. *exempt from taxes*: Kangle's edition reads *kartr̥bhyo nādeyāni*, and he translates this as "should not be taken away from those who are making them arable." However, *kartr̥bhyaḥ* should be taken as a dative rather than an ablative, paralleling *karadebhyaḥ* of sentence 8. I have emended the text to read *kartr̥bhyo 'nādeyāni*, following Harihara Sastri (2011, 88). The term *ādeya* is used in the sense of taxes or duties taken by the state in many places: 2.6.2; 2.9.24; 2.22.8. For *anādeya* as land free from taxation, see 3.10.14.

2.1.11. *village servants* (grāmabhr̥taka): These appear to be individuals who worked in some official capacity for an entire village and, given that they are mentioned in the salary lists (5.3.23), who may have had official standing. They may have had independent means, just as the traders, and thus would have been able to have the work of cultivation carried out. At 3.11.29, they are excluded from acting as witnesses in a court of law, perhaps again because of their official capacity. It is unclear whether this term is used also in a more common sense to mean a lowly and poor servant carrying out menial tasks for the village. Thus, for example, at 5.2.11, remnants are left from heaps of harvested crop for use by mendicants/beggars and village servants.

2.1.12. *losses*: The losses are clearly sustained by the state. It is, however, unclear whether the losses are caused by the non-cultivation of state-owned land or because unproductive private land would not generate taxes.

2.1.15. *favors and exemptions* (anugrahaparihārau): These two words occur together frequently (7.1.32; 8.2.13; 9.5.11; 13.4.3; 13.5.4). Favors may comprehend various kinds of gifts and assistance, such as grain, animals, and money (2.1.13). Exemptions refer to immunity from taxes and other demands made by the state on the population.

2.1.20. *reservoirs... elsewhere*: The term *setu* refers directly to a dam or dike for containing water and secondarily to a reservoir or irrigation work so constructed. The water for it may come either from naturally occurring springs or some other direct source or from water channeled from far away, perhaps from a river or lake.

2.1.21. *routes* (mārga): As the commentary *Cāṇakyaṭīkā* clarifies, the routes are provided for canals to take water from the reservoirs to the fields.

2.1.22–23. *When someone... returns*: For the legal obligations incumbent upon each member of a joint enterprise, see 3.14.18–36.

2.1.24. *fish... vegetables*: The Sanskrit is ambiguous and can also mean fish, water fowl, and vegetables that are extracted as merchandise. In either case, this provision may exclude these items, or at least vegetables, if they are taken for personal use.

2.1.26. *helpless*: Kangle takes this term as an adjective qualifying all the categories of individuals listed. The reasoning is that otherwise the list would be overly extensive and include people who do not deserve state assistance. The syntax of the sentence argues against this, even though it is clearly assumed that these individuals need to be assisted only when they do not have other means of support; see the provisions of 2.1.28–29.

2.1.27. *legal age*: For the legal provision behind this statement, see 3.5.20. The legal age for females was 12 and for males 16 (see 3.3.1).

2.1.28. *except the mother*: That a son should look after his mother even if she has committed sins and fallen from her caste is a rule repeated frequently in the legal literature. *ĀpDh* (1.28.9): "[E]ven if (the mother) has fallen from her caste, he must always serve her"; *BDh* (2.3.42): "Even if she has become an outcaste, however, a man should support his own mother"; *VaDh* (13.47): "A father should be forsaken when he becomes an outcaste, whereas a mother is never an outcaste to her son."

2.1.29. *seizure fine*: The meaning and semantic history of *sāhasa* as a particular kind of fine with lowest, middle, and highest amounts are not altogether clear. It has been assumed that the standard crime whose punishment became a currency for other kinds of crime was *sāhasa*, the forcible seizure of property or violent robbery, defined at 3.17.1 as: "Forcible seizure is a violent act in the presence of the victim." However, Rocher (1975) has shown that the term may have Indo-European roots and that the reference may be to the seizure of the property (probably in the form of cattle) of the convicted man. Rocher refers to the law of *multa*. In view of Rocher's findings, I have translated *sāhasa* or *sāhasadaṇḍa* as "seizure fine." In the *MDh* (8.138), the three levels of fines for forcible seizure are lowest 250 Paṇas, middle 500 Paṇas, and highest 1,000 Paṇas. The *AŚ* (3.17.8–10), on the other hand, gives them as 48 to 96, 200 to 500, and 500 to 1,000. Sometimes the term *sāhasa* is left out, but the expressions "highest fine" etc. refer to the same scheme.

2.1.30. *potency*: The meaning of the Sanskrit term *vyāyāma* in this context is unclear. It probably refers to loss of vibrancy associated with old age, but may also refer in particular to lack of ability or interest to engage in sexual activity.

Justices (dharmastha): For the activities connected with these officials, see book 3. I have opted to translate *dharmastha* as "Justice" in preference to the normal "judge," because many civil matters, besides trying court cases, are part of his portfolio. For example, at 2.1.30, a man has to get his permission to become an ascetic; at 3.4.35, a widow needs his permission to remarry; at 3.12.14, a man holding a deposit needs his permission to sell it when the depositor cannot be found; and at 3.16.10, an owner discovering a lost or stolen property gets him to seize it. He was probably part of the second-tier bureaucracy (he is not listed in the salary list of 5.3), as opposed to his higher-level counterpart, the *pradeṣṭṛ* (Magistrate), who is listed as one of the *mahāmātras* (high official). I use the term "Justice" because we have in the justices of peace somewhat of a counterpart, and at least in the Anglo-American system, justices can also have judicial functions.

2.1.32. *kinsmen*: The meaning of the Sanskrit term *sajāta* in this context is uncertain. Kangle thinks that it may refer to people born in the same location, in which case the translation "countrymen" may be appropriate. In any case, the intent seems to be to prohibit associations with a broad membership from outside settling in the countryside, thus posing a danger to security.

group...task: The technical term *samayānubandha* occurs only one other time in the form *samayānubaddha* at 2.36.45. The technical term *samaya* in the legal literature refers to conventions and rules governing corporate entities, including professional guilds and monastic orders. Some such professional organization is probably intended here. Once again, such independent centers of power were viewed as a threat to security in the countryside and permitted only within strict limits, as when a group of people get together to perform a specific task (see 2.1.22).

2.1.33. *parks* (ārāma): At 2.1.21, *ārāmas* are permitted, but the connection to holy places there may indicate that those parks were for religious purposes. Here the prohibition pertains to parks for recreational activities.

2.1.35. *provide shelter*: This probably refers to entertainers mentioned in the previous sentence. The aim is to make the agricultural workforce in the countryside as productive as possible.

treasure (kośa): This term normally means the treasury of the king, and that is how it is interpreted by Meyer and Kangle. Given that the other items in this long compound are quantifiable things, I have chosen to take *kośa* to mean treasure or money, following Shamasastry.

2.2. *Covering…Land*: The expression *bhūmicchidrāpidhāna* has been subject to misunderstanding. It and the parallel expression *bhūmicchidranyāya* occur frequently in inscriptions. They are two versions of a common maxim often connected to the gift of land for religious purposes. The meaning appears to be that the use of land unsuitable for agriculture (hence the crevices or holes) for donative purposes is an act of healing of the otherwise broken land. Given that this is a maxim, it is impossible to translate it in a manner that would be immediately intelligible in English; hence the quotation marks around the expression. For a detailed study of these maxims, see Hinüber 2005. It is clear, however, that this topic deals with the disposal of non-agricultural land, which is how the commentators and Kangle understand the topic, while the disposal and settlement of agricultural land were covered in topic 19.

2.2.4. *where all…guests*: The meaning of the expression *sarvātithimṛgam* is far from clear. I take it to mean "where all are guest animals." Kangle thinks that this is some sort of a zoological garden, which may be an overstatement. However, this may be a park with tame animals that people were forbidden to hunt.

2.2.5. *forest produce*: The forest products coming to the central stores are listed at 2.17.4–16.

foresters: The term *aṭavī* ("forest") is often used metonymically with reference to tribal people living in remote forest areas. Here they appear to be at some level in the service of the state. It is unclear whether they are simply tribals recruited for this purpose or actually state employees who are forest wardens.

2.2.7. *Superintendent of Elephant Forests*: This official is referred to simply as Superintendent of Elephants (*hastyadhyakṣa*) at 2.31, although Kangle thinks that the two are different officials. At 2.31.1, however, the *hastyadhyakṣa* is charged with the protection of elephant forests. Although he has the overall authority over these preserves, the onsite protection is provided by elephant forest wardens (*nāgavanapāla*) and their subordinates (2.2.10). It is worth noting, however, that in this passage (2.2.6–10), the term *nāga* is used for elephant in the compound *nāgavana* (elephant forest), while outside this compound (except in sentence 6 where *hastivana* is used) the elephant is called *hastin*, which is the common term used throughout the *AŚ*.

2.3. *Construction of Forts*: For a comprehensive study of this chapter, see Schlingloff 1967; and for the city in the *AŚ*, see Laping 1982. Schlingloff makes a strong case for the accuracy of many of the provisions of the *AŚ* by comparing them to archeological evidence. For a comparison of the rules in the *AŚ* with those of the *Śilpaśāstra*, see Stein 1935–38.

2.3.1. *water fort…of shrubs*: These four kinds of forts are found in the set of six listed in other sources: *MDh* 7.70; *MBh* 12.87.5. The remaining two are an earthen fort and man fort. I see the latter as one protected by soldiers, while Schlingloff (1967) takes it to be manmade, in which case it is difficult to see how it differs from the preceding, which is also manmade. It appears that these four kinds of forts are located in the outlying areas of the kingdom (the countryside, *janapada*), which was the topic of discussion in the first two chapters, while the standard forts constructed with fortifications are located in the central areas and in the capital city.

2.3.2. *defenders of the countryside…tribals*: The commentaries *Cāṇakyaṭīkā* and the *Nītinirṇīti* identify the defenders as the commanders of the frontier (*antapāla*). Meyer and Scharfe (1993, 97) take the compound *janapadārakṣasthānam* as referring to the defense of the people in the countryside. Although *janapada* often does refer to the people too (Scharfe 1993, 120), I think it more likely that it refers here to the countryside as a whole, given its use in this sense in the very next sentence. The term *ārakṣa* may mean simply defense (so Scharfe), although this seems less likely in view of *aṭavī* (forest tribals) in the parallel compound, where the reference is to the people occupying these forts. The question with regard to the compound *aṭavīsthānam* is whether the tribals are the defenders or those being defended by these forts (so Gaṇapati Śāstrī, Meyer, and Scharfe). Throughout the *AŚ*, however, tribals and tribal chiefs are mentioned either as posing a threat or as part of the armed forces, rather than ordinary people needing protection. I follow the two commentaries and Kangle in assuming that all these forts were meant for the defense of the countryside, but that some were occupied by frontier commanders and others employed by the state, while some were occupied by forest tribes who were allied with the king.

2.3.3. *clockwise*: The water should be moving from the left to the right as one faces it from the city. This is, of course, the auspicious direction of movement.
market town (paṇyapuṭabhedana): The complex construction of this long sentence makes it unclear whether the provincial capital is constructed to serve several functions, including being a market town, or whether an existing market town is fortified to serve as the provincial capital. I think the use of the verb *niveśayet*, which everywhere indicates the creation of something new, favors the first interpretation. The compound *puṭabhedana* (Kölver 1985; Charpentier 1916, 237–242; Meyer 65) may mean simply a town or a town located by the bend or fork of a river. With the term *paṇya*, here it probably means simply a market town, but note that it is located by a river.

2.3.4. *Around it* (tasya): It has been assumed that the referent of this pronoun is the provincial capital (*sthānīya*) cum trading post mentioned in the previous passage. The fort described here and the layout of the fort described in the following chapter are too elaborate for a simple market town. It is assumed that the king's palace is also located within the fort. Thus, it appears that the referent of this pronoun (*tasya*) is found in the original source from which the description of the fort must have been taken by our author. It also appears that the previous passages dealing with forts at the frontiers and the provincial capital must have been taken from a source different from the latter. The first three passages of this chapter properly belong to the previous two chapters dealing with the countryside. From this passage onward, the discussion shifts to the city and the fort. This discussion actually concludes at the end of 2.4. At 2.4.31, the author says that the above discussion also explains the construction of the forts of the frontier commander, which again shows that 2.3.1–3 deals with precisely such frontier forts and was not part of the original discussion of the fort. The mention of a royal residence at 2.3.6 within a fort in a provincial town is explained by Scharfe (1993, 159–160), with the assumption that royal quarters may have been found in such forts, even though the main palace (*antaḥpura*) is in the capital. But Scharfe himself second-guesses this explanation, saying that a palace may be found in a provincial capital that doubled as a state capital. It is, however, easier to assume that the description of the fort is taken from a source that deals with the state capital, and it is used here by the author of the *AŚ* to describe both kinds of forts.

three moats: These form three concentric rings around the city, or at least around the areas of the city that do not face water. For an analysis of this description, see Schlingloff 1967, 46f.

14... Daṇḍas: The outer moats are broader than the inner ones. The width is calculated at the surface.

square: If the bottoms are narrower than the tops, then the sides would be slanting inward. If the top and the bottom are the same size, then the sides would meet the bottom at a rectangle.

lotuses and crocodiles: Regarding Meyer's interpretation, Schlingloff (1967, 47 n. 10) observes: "Meyer's assumption that *padma-grāha* does not refer to lotus blossoms and crocodiles but rather to 'lotus grabbers,' a locking mechanism which regulates the influx of water, is unlikely." He gives several sources for the presence of crocodiles in moats. Lotus leaves may have been useful in hiding the presence of crocodiles.

2.3.5. *from the moat*: We must assume that this distance is calculated from the innermost moat. This distance is important in order to stop any erosion of the rampart by the water of the moat (Schlingloff 1967, 48 n. 11).

well contained (avaruddha): The meaning is unclear. Kangle translates it as "made compact," but that is stated later when the use of bulls and elephants for this purpose is mentioned. Perhaps the meaning is that the earth should be held in place as it is being piled up, possibly with the use of wooden structures.

vaulted... pot-bellied: The terms are somewhat obscure, and I am here following the interpretation of Schlingloff (1967, fig. 5–8). He has given illustrations of these kinds of rampart constructions taken from the excavations at several ancient sites. The term *ūrdhvacaya* appears to mean a scalloped pattern with lower and higher elevations along the rampart. The top can be either flat or rounded.

2.3.6. *With the remainder... filled*: The idea is to level the inner area of the city before the construction of buildings can begin, using the leftover earth dug up from the moats to fill in craters and depressions. Although *rājabhavanaṃ* (royal residence) is found only in the fragmentary manuscript D and occurs nowhere else in the *AŚ*, it has been adopted by Kangle. The Malayalam commentary, as well as the *Cāṇakyaṭīkā* and *Nītinirnīti*, have the reading *rājavāstu* (the grounds of the royal residence, a term that occurs also at 10.1.2); this may be simply a gloss for *rājabhavana* (so Scharfe 1993, 159–160) or an alternate (original?) reading.

2.3.7. *foundation... trunks*: The Sanskrit expression *tālamūlam* has been explained by Schlingloff (1967, 49 n. 17) as referring to the reinforcement of the lower parts of the wall with wooden supports so that, in the event of damage caused by an enemy assault, the entire wall would not crumble and the damage could be easily repaired. Kangle, following the Malayalam commentator, thinks that the wall is shaped like the base of a palm tree, broad at the bottom and narrow at the top.

top... monkey heads: Schlingloff (1967, fig. 1) has explained this passage convincingly. The top of the rampart wall has merlons resembling drums or the heads of monkeys (as they sit along a wall).

2.3.10. *rectangular foundations*: The precise meaning of the pithy *viṣkambhacaturaśram* is unclear. Kangle thinks it is a square with each side measuring the same as the width of the wall. Schlingloff (1967, 59 n. 49), however, has demonstrated through archeological evidence that the towers are rectangular with their long sides running parallel to the wall and their short sides the same width as the wall.

at a distance... each other: The distance between towers is approximately 55 meters, which is the average range of an arrow shot, thus making it possible for archers at each end to strike anyone trying to climb the wall. See Schlingloff 1967, 61f.

drop-down ladders: The meaning appears to be (Schlingloff 1967, 60f) that these ladders could be controlled from the top of the tower. In normal times, they would remain down for ease of access to the tower; but when an attack is taking place, they could be retracted, thus preventing the attackers from climbing up to the towers.

2.3.11. *postern gate... a hall*: The term *pratolī* has been often misunderstood. As Schlingloff (1967, 62f) has shown, these gates were mainly pedestrian entrances. They, however, presented vulnerable points in the fortification, and the two-storied superstructure equipped with an upper hall was meant as a defense against attackers. Schlingloff takes *adhyardhāyāma* to mean that its height is one and a half times its width. Kangle takes it to mean that its length is one and a half times its width. I think here Kangle is correct; in every other place where *āyāma* is used (2.3.11, 16, 33; 2.11.76, 80, 84; 2.19.12, 17, 23; 2.20.35; 2.30.14; 2.31.2, 11; 10.1.2; 14.1 31), it means length, even though, as in the case of timber used as a post, when it is erected the length converts into height. In every other place where height is clearly intended, the author uses *utsedha* (2.7, 10) or *ucchrita* (2.3.5). The clearest place where *utsedha* is contrasted with both *āyāma* and *viṣkambha* (width) is 2.31.2; see also 2.30.14 and 2.31.11, where the length (*āyāma*) of a horse and elephant is differentiated from its height (*utsedha*). Finally, the term *harmya* appears to signify a large room for defensive purposes built on the upper floor of the postern gate. Illustrations of such gates with their two-storied defenses are given in Schlingloff 1967, fig 15.

2.3.13. *In the intervening... the side*: The meaning of this cryptic sentence is far from clear. Schlingloff (1967, 63 n. 65) comments: "Unfortunately, the statement of its [god's path] dimensions is extremely puzzling." He connects syntactically the width with the "intervening spaces" (*antareṣu*) and the length with the side. I follow Kangle in taking the intervening spaces to be the locations of this path, which is probably the same as the one called *indrapatha* ("Indra's path"), probably placed behind the embrasures.

2.3.14. *routes*: The meaning and the purpose of these passageways are unclear. Kangle thinks that these were steps going from the "god's path" to the "running pass," which is simply a guess.

passageway: The term *pradhāvanikā* is a hapax, and its meaning is thus obscure. The literal meaning indicates that it was a passageway though which soldiers could run from one location to another. Coming as it does next to the egress door, the two may have been connected. The commentary *Cāṇakyaṭīkā* takes it to be a place from which the soldiers could launch sallies.

egress door: The meaning of *niṣkiradvāra* is also unclear. As its name suggests, it was a door through which people could exit. The purpose of the exit is unclear, whether it was to flee or to confront an enemy at the rampart. The term is used again at 13.4.12, where the attackers drag out (perhaps soldiers) from these egresses and attack with horses. If this door was connected to the clandestine way, then it may have been an escape route from the fort in the case of a successful siege by an enemy (see book 13).

2.3.15. *outside*: The meaning appears to be that this secret passageway was to be constructed outside the fortifications, probably as a means of escape.

knee-breakers... water holes: The meanings of these technical terms are obscure. All clearly refer to various kinds of obstacles placed within this path, which was probably a tunnel (see Schlingloff 1967, 64 n. 70 for confirmation of such a tunnel in the excavations at Kauśāmbī), so as to make it difficult for pursuers to gain access. The commentary *Cāṇakyaṭīkā* takes "stumbler" to mean an area made slippery, and "shoe" to mean a hole with thorns covered with sand to form a trap.

2.3.16. *Having made...both sides*: I follow here the reading and interpretation of Schlingloff (1967, 67). Kangle has adopted the reading *meṇḍhaka* in place of the original *maṇḍalaka*. The object of the verb *kṛtvā* is the wall (*prākāra*), and *maṇḍalaka* (round, circular) is simply an adjective of *prākāra*. The builders have to make the wall circular or rounded (convex) on the two sides of the main gate that was set back from the wall. See an example of such a round wall discovered in the excavations at Śrāvastī given by Schlingloff (1967, fig. 20). The rounded wall around the recessed gate provided protection, because the invaders would have to come within the wall structure to access the gate, and defenders positioned on either side of the rounded wall could attack them from above.

large enough...postern gate: The expression *pratolīṣaṭtulāntaram* is quite obscure (Schlingloff 1967, 62 n. 61). In most other places where *antara* occurs in this chapter, it indicates the distance between two things rather than the dimensions of something (but see 2.4.3 and the note there). Here that meaning does not fit the context. One possible meaning is that the dimensions of the gate (probably the height, because the length and width are given later) should accommodate six beams. All this is, however, quite obscure.

with a minimum...its length: The construction is pithy, and the dimensions referred to remain unstated. As I have indicated above, *āyāma* generally refers to length, but in this particular case, it may refer to the "length along the wall," that is, to its width. The minimum of five Daṇḍas and the maximum of eight Daṇḍas probably refer to its width. Its depth measured from the wall should be one-sixth or one-eighth more (i.e., minimum of 5.83 or 5.62 Daṇḍas and a maximum of 9.33 or 9 Daṇḍas) than its width.

2.3.19–20. *The five...the area*: Kangle takes *pañcabhāga* as a compound to mean "one-fifth." I think Schlingloff (1967, 69) is correct in taking it to mean five sections. Kangle also divides the sentence into two, with the two platforms inserted into number 20.

2.3.20–21. *In between...edifice*: This should form a single sentence, even though Kangle has split it up into numbers 20 and 21. In the first edition, Kangle has the reading *āṇiharmyaṃ* as a compound and translates it as "small room." In the second edition, he has the reading *āṇī harmyaṃ* with the translation "two doors and a room." The latter is the reading given also in the commentary *Cāṇakyaṭīkā*, where the author explicitly states that *āṇī* is a dual. This term probably has the meaning of peg or linchpin (of an axle), and consequently may refer here to a small door locked only with a peg. The meaning of the phrase *ucchrayād ardhatale* is also uncertain;

if the meaning is that the ceiling of this floor was half the height of the ground floor, it would be between 7.5 and 9 Hastas. It would then be a sort of mezzanine floor supported by pillars. For the difficulty of this passage, see also Schlingloff 1967, 70.

2.3.24. *three-fifths wide*: The text does not explain the object relating to which the three-fifths are counted. Schlingloff (1967, 71 n. 98) thinks that the doors are three-fifths the width of the gatehouse; that is, the gates themselves are smaller than the interior of the gatehouse.

2.3.26. *threshold* (indrakīla): The meaning of this term is unclear. Kangle explains that it is "an iron stake or bolt to be fixed in the ground inside after the gate is closed." Meyer: "the wedge that is placed beneath the two mighty doors where they meet so that they are more robust." Rejecting these interpretations and basing his thinking on the use of the term in Buddhist texts, Schlingloff (1967) renders it "threshold." This meaning is more probable also because a stake of one Aratni (about 47 centimeters; see 2.20.10–12) is hardly long enough to secure such a large door. A threshold that runs the length of the gate under the doors with a width of 47 centimeters appears more reasonable.

2.3.28. *elephant bars* (hastiparigha): The meaning of this term is unclear. Kangle says that they were intended "to prevent the gate being broken down by elephants. They seem to be iron stakes fixed in the gates on the outside." Although such spikes on the outside of gates are attested from medieval times, Schlingloff (1967, 72 n. 103) is unsure whether the term has this precise meaning. He thinks that they are bars running across the door panels as reinforcement against an attack by elephants.

2.3.29–30. *to facilitate…with earth*: This is a very cryptic and difficult passage. First, the readings themselves are unclear: Kangle has *niveśārdham* ("half the width of the structure"), as also Gaṇapati Śāstrī, while Jolly has *niveśārtham*. I have followed the latter, both because it makes better sense in the context (the "elephant nail" makes the gate accessible) and because *niveśa* is never used in the *AŚ* in the sense of a building. The floor level of the gate was much higher than the ground level of the moat. Thus, an earthen ramp had to be built to make access to and from the gate possible. This ramp was called "elephant nail" probably because it looked like an elephant's nail jutting out of the rampart. I take *mukhasamaḥ* ("equal to the gate opening") as an adjective qualifying *saṃkramaḥ* ("concourse"), because in the passage all qualifications are placed before the nouns. I take the meaning of *saṃkrama* to be a bridge or causeway across water or a chasm. This meaning is attested frequently in the epics: *Rām* 6.3.15, 17, 28; *MBh* 3.16.15; 12.69.37; 12.99.31. The *AŚ*, however, appears to consider it not just a bridge but any concourse across such obstacles, because the final adjective takes it to be made of earth when the moat has no water. There is also a problem with the reading *saṃhāryaḥ*, with some manuscripts reading *asaṃhāryaḥ*. Schlingloff (1967, 73 n. 107) prefers the latter and thinks it means "indestructible by the waters of the moat." Whatever the reading, this is a hapax in the *AŚ*. Given the contrast between this term and *bhūmimaya* ("earthen"), I prefer the former reading in the sense that the concourse consists of a retractable bridge when it is over water. When there is no water, the passage went down into the moat and back up at the other end. The assumption is that when an attack is imminent, the moat along with the access road would be filled with water. Here I restore the contrastive *vā* ("or") after *saṃhāryo*, which is found in the manuscripts but deleted by Kangle. Here is my reconstructed reading: *niveśārthaṃ hastinakhaḥ | mukhasamaḥ saṃkramaḥ saṃhāryo vā bhūmimayo vā nirudake ||*

2.3.31. *equal in extent*: It is unclear whether this refers to the width or the height. Kangle takes it as the width, and Schlingloff (1967, 75) as the height. The only way the width can be said to be equal to the wall is if the width of the opening is the same as the width of the wall; that is, the opening forms a square.

"cow fort"... lizard: The meaning of *gopura* here is unclear, as also its shape. It probably refers to a particular type of gate different from the one described in the previous passage. Schlingloff (1967, 74f and fig. 19) thinks this is similar to the gate at Sisupalgarh with wide wings and a long entrance. This may be the reason the gate is compared to the snout or mouth of a monitor lizard, perhaps the wings resembling the front legs spread out. One-third here may refer to the middle third that comprises the "snout," while the two on either side would be the wings.

2.3.32. *pit* (vāpī): The meaning, as Schlingloff (1967, 76 n. 117) has pointed out, is to dig a pit between the brick facings on either side of the wall. The middle will consist of earth and rubble. Once this is done, a gate opening can be cut into the brickwork of the wall. The use of *vāpī* with the meaning of pit also occurs at *AŚ* 2.5.2.

"Lotus-pond" gate: The meaning is unclear. Kangle and Meyer think that it may have something to do with the defenses against an attack. Schlingloff (1967, 76 n. 117) thinks that the name may be derived from the fact that such pits had to be dug also in the construction of lotus ponds. This is the more probable interpretation.

four-halled... loopholes: Schlingloff (1969, 24f) has shown that here the gate imitates a farmhouse consisting of a long hall enclosing a courtyard. Four halls would thus enclose three courtyards, the central one proving the passageway. This may have been called "princess fort" because the quarters for the princesses may have been built in this manner. The meaning of *adhyardhāntaram* is obscure. Kangle thinks that this is the distance (one and a half Daṇḍas) between the four halls, which is probably incorrect. Schlingloff (1967, 76) translates "one and a half times the space" without further explanation. I have tentatively taken the one and a half to refer to the width of the courtyards: They have to be one and a half times the width of the halls themselves. Loopholes are probably for shooting arrows.

two-storied... upper hall: Once again, this is quite cryptic and unclear. The meaning of "bald" is obscure; Schlingloff (1967, 76 n. 120) takes it to mean a construction using bare or rough-hewn tree trunks.

2.3.34–35. *stones... forest produce*: The meanings of some of the Sanskrit technical terms for these instruments of war are unclear. "Camel-necks" is explained by one commentator as long-necked vessels for pouring hot oil upon attacking troops.

2.4.1. *division*: Assuming that the fort is a square or a rectangle, the three highways running east-west and three running north-south would intersect to create 16 divisions.

2.4.2. *twelve gates*: Each of the six highways would terminate at a gate along the rampart (north-south, east-west), thus creating 12 gates into the fort. As the commentary *Cāṇakyaṭīkā* notes, these are not the only gates into a fort; there are other smaller gates for pedestrian traffic and the like; see the postern gate above at 2.3.11 n.

water canals, drainage ditches: The commentary *Cāṇakyaṭīkā* notes that the first allows water into the fort and the second takes used water out of the fort. For the problems of drainage in ancient Indian cities, see Schlingloff 1969, 44.

2.4.3. *streets* (rathyā): These are probably city streets distinguished from the main thoroughfares referred to as royal highways. The streets are about 7.28 meters wide, whereas the royal highways, other major roads, and roads in the countryside and villages listed in the next sentence are twice as wide. Evidently, land was at a premium within the fort.

four Daṇḍas wide (caturdaṇḍāntarā): The meaning of width for *antara* is unusual; it generally means the distance between two things (see, e.g., 2.3.4, 10; but see 2.3.16 and the note there). The commentary *Cāṇakyaṭīkā* has the reading *caturdaṇḍottarāḥ*, with the meaning that the street is four Daṇḍas wide, and each of the roads mentioned after it, that is, the royal highway and roads to district municipalities etc. are four Daṇḍas wider than the previous. Although this solves the problem of *antara*, it gives an impossible width of 24 Daṇḍas or 175 meters for roads in pasture land. See 3.10.5 for fines for obstructing these roads.

2.4.6. *The king's... social classes*: This sentence appears to have been a gloss that found its way into the text. It is superfluous, given the precise wording of the next sentence. Further, in this book, *antaḥpura* is the term used for the royal residence and not *rājaniveśa,* a term not found in the *AŚ* outside of this sentence.

2.4.7. *one-ninth sector...sites*: This provision appears to assume a nine by nine grid giving rise to 81 sectors. The heart of this grid will be occupied by the sector intersected by the fifth N-S and E-W columns. Kangle says that this is called the *paramaśāyika* plan for a city. For a similar provision, in this case, the location of the king's quarters within a military camp, see 10.1.2.

2.4.8. *Its*: The referent is the king's residence, if these individuals were housed within the palace compound. However, since these directions are given for other buildings as well, the referent is probably the *vāstu* or the total building area of the fort. Kangle sees the distinction between the two words used, *āvaseyuḥ* for these individuals and *adhivaseyuḥ* for others (passage 9) as indicating the distinction between those who lived in the palace and those who lived in other areas of the fort. However, the clause in which the term *āvaseyuḥ* is used appears to be a gloss, and the same term, moreover, is used in passage 16 with regard to guilds and foreign traders who have nothing to do with the royal residence. For a plan of the city drawn from the *AŚ* evidence, see Ali 2004, 40.

east-northeast: As the commentary *Cāṇakyaṭīkā* explains, here we have eight subsidiary points, besides the four cardinal points. These are indicated in the Sanskrit by *pūrvottara* (east-northeast), *pūrvadakṣiṇa* (east-southeast), etc.

the dwelling...water: The compound *ācāryapurohitejyātoyasthānam* should literally mean the places for worship and water of the teacher and chaplain. This is the interpretation given by Harihara Sastri (2011, 86–87). Note also that the intermediate directions always house various public buildings, and the residential quarters are always located in the cardinal directions: east, south, west, and north. This sentence is probably corrupt.

and the counselors should reside there: Given the nominal syntax of all the statements relating to the location of various individuals and activities within the royal residence, this statement with a finite verb appears to be a gloss that found its way into the text.

2.4.10. *workshops* (karmaniṣadyāḥ): Kangle translates this compound as "workmen's quarters." Given that no residences are located in these intermediate directions, I have opted to take *niṣadyā* as a place where various artisan or commercial activities are carried out.

2.4.11. *City Manager...Factories*: In interpreting *nagaradhānyavyāvahārikakārmāntika,* I have followed the persuasive argument of Scharfe (1993, 175). We have here two high officials, *nagaravyāvahārika* (City Manager, equivalent to the *nāgarika* of 2.36 [and perhaps *nāgara* of 5.1.21] and *pauravyāvahārika* of 1.12.8; 5.3.7) and *kārmāntika* (5.3.7), with the grain dealers in between, perhaps because *vyāvahārika* goes with both City Manager and grain dealer. Scharfe has also drawn attention to the parallel officials called *nagala-viyohālaka* of the Aśokan bureaucracy recorded in his inscriptions.

2.4.12. *workshop* (karmagṛha): The reference is unclear, the compound being a hapax, but it may refer to a place where work for the royal household was carried out. The *Cāṇakyaṭīkā*'s gloss *yātanāgṛham* indicates that the author thought it to be a torture house, using *karman* with the meaning given to it at 4.8.

2.4.16. *In an area…site*: the expression *anusāla* or *anuśāla* means not "in enclosures" as Kangle has translated, but along the walls (see Schlingloff 1969, 43 n. 3). For *sālā* as wall, see 12.5.17; 13.4.9. The expression *vāstucchidra* here appears to indicate areas unsuitable as building sites, even though at 2.3.6, the same expression is used in a literal sense as crevices in building sites. See also, for a parallel use of *chidra,* 2.2 n.

2.4.17. *middle of the city*: As Kangle notes, the middle of the city, that is, the central 1/81st sector (see 2.4.7 n.), would be right in front of the royal palace. Regarding archeological evidence for temple structures at the center of cities, see Schlingloff 1969, 37f.

Madirā: Harihara Sastri (1956–57, 109), on the basis of passages in two architectural texts, *Mayamata* and Īśānaśiva's *Paddhati*, identifies Madirā with Jyeṣṭhā.

2.4.19. *presiding…Senāpati*: moving clockwise from the north, Brahmā is the presiding deity of the northern gate, Indra of the eastern, Yama of the southern, and Senāpati (Skanda) of the western.

2.4.20. *each quarter…deity*: The guardian deities of the quarters are from the north clockwise: Kubera, Indra, Yama, and Varuṇa. However, as the previous sentence shows, for the *AŚ*, Brahmā and Senāpati may have taken the place of Kubera and Varuṇa.

2.4.20–21. *or in the north-northeast…social class*: This passage is corrupt in the manucripts, the southern ones giving the reading *uttaraḥ pūrvo vā śmaśānavāṭo dakṣiṇena varṇottarāṇām,* while the Devanāgarī manuscript (D) has a longer version: *uttaraḥ pūrvo vā śmaśānabhāgo dakṣiṇena varṇottamanām dakṣiṇena śmaśānaṃ varṇāvarāṇām*. Kangle has adopted the latter, even though it is clearly the *lectio facilior* and includes an evident gloss attempting to interpret the difficult original, and translates: "The northern or the eastern part of the cremation ground should be for the best among the *varṇas,* to the south the cremation ground for the lowest *varṇas.*" Harihara Sastri (1956–1957, 109–110) notes the elaborate commentary in the *Cāṇakyaṭīkā,* which takes the reading *varṇottarāṇām* to mean each of the *varṇas* in the ascending order, providing a clue to the meaning of the original. This meaning of the term *uttara* is common in the *AŚ*; see 2.7.27, 2.19.11, 14. However, I think the provision here is not about the different sections of the cemetery reserved for various classes, but the transport of the corpse through the proper gate of a city. Otherwise, the infraction of this provision noted in the next sentence would not make much sense, because an individual would find it difficult to transgress the officially segregated divisions of a cemetery. At *MDh* 5.92, we have the explicit statement that a dead Śūdra should be taken out through the southern gate, a Vaiśya through the western, a Kṣatriya through the northern, and a Brāhmaṇa through the eastern. This is exactly what the *AŚ* states in using the compact term *varṇottarāṇām*. It is to the transgression of this rule that the next sentence refers; see the similar provision at 2.36.33. My reading requires two emendations. First, I think *śmaśānavāṭo* is an error for *śmaśānavāho*, "ṭ" and "h" in Malayalam being not very dissimilar. It is this strange *-vāṭa* that made the northern scribe correct it to the more familiar *-bhāga*. Second, I think the initial *uttaraḥ pūrvo vā* has migrated to this sentence from the previous, and the reading should have been *uttarapūrve vā*; the intermediate directions are given frequently in this passage, and the nominative probably replaced the locative once these words were viewed as qualifying *bhāgaḥ* or *vāṭaḥ*. Here is my reconstructed text of this passage: *yathādiśaṃ ca digdevatāḥ pūrvottare vā / śmaśānavāho varṇottarāṇāṃ dakṣiṇena /*

2.4.23. *religious orders* (pāṣaṇḍa): The provision here is contradicted by 2.36.14, which assumes that at least some of these ascetics lived within the city. I think that the passage 2.4.21–23 is an interpolation reflecting Brāhmaṇical viewpoints, including the denigration of *pāṣaṇḍas* not found elsewhere in the *AŚ*. When it is removed, we pass seamlessly from the distribution of city land to fixing the extent of a householder's property (2.4.24).

2.4.27. *strong timber* (*sāradāru*): That these two words form a compound is evident at 2.5.2.

2.4.28. *He should... stock*: For this provision, see 2.15.23.

2.5.1. *Treasurer* (saṃnidhātṛ): Scharfe (1993, 167) thinks that he is a provincial official in charge of treasuries located in the provinces, as he is not mentioned in the description of the royal capital (2.4). As Scharfe himself says, there may have been more than one such official, and one of them may have been in charge also of the treasury located in the capital. At least the description of the construction of the treasury and the underground vault indicates a major building. Another issue concerns the distinction, if any, between this official and the one named *kośādhyakṣa* (Superintendent of the Treasury), whose activities are very similar and are described in 2.11. I think one way to resolve this issue is to acknowledge the diverse provenance of sections of the *AŚ* with different technical terms, especially the sections where the officials bear the title *adhyakṣa*.

2.5.2. *underground chamber…statue of a deity*: This long and complex sentence has been long misunderstood, until the illuminating study of Schlingloff (1968). The major misunderstanding was to conceive the underground chamber (*bhūmigṛha*) as consisting of three stories based on the adjective *tritalam*. Schlingloff has shown that this compound means "having three floors"; that is, the floor is made up of three separate layers. The underground pit has a framework of joists as the ceiling. These joists probably rested on the stone slabs lining the sides of the pit. On this framework was laid the lowest of the three floors named *sthānatala*; this probably consisted of wooden planks that made the floor (if viewed from the ground level) or ceiling (if viewed from within the pit) stable and able to withstand people standing and walking on it. Over these planks was laid the second floor named *deśatala*. This is a curious term, and Schlingloff has given as good an explanation as possible, although the meaning remains uncertain. He thinks that *deśa* means the local soil. So a layer of local soil was laid on the planks. Over this soil was laid the third and uppermost layer of the floor called *kuṭṭimatala*. Both literature and archeology have shown a type of floor in ancient India made up of small stones or pebbles within a mixture of lime, a sort of a concrete floor. This floor is level with the ground floor of the treasury or the mansion built on top of the underground chamber. The entry to the chamber is hidden under a statue of a god (an expression found in all the manuscripts but eliminated by Kangle), and the staircase leading down to it is controlled by a mechanical device known only to the king or treasurer. All these precautions were taken to prevent burglaries. The large slabs of stone lining the walls and bottom would prevent access through an underground tunnel. The triple floor is meant to fool would-be burglars. After digging through the first layer of the floor (*kuṭṭimatala*) consisting of pebble and lime, they would encounter the local earth underneath. This would fool them into thinking that there was nothing underneath the floor. See also 1.20.2 and the note to it.

2.5.3. *sealed off on both sides*: The expression *ubhayatoniṣedham* is unclear. I take this to mean that on the two broad sides of the building, there are no entrances, or even that there were barricades on those sides. So everyone had to pass through the single entrance.

or a mansion: It is unclear to what other provision this is an alternative. Kangle takes this as an alternative to building an underground vault. However, the position of the term immediately after *kośagṛhaṃ kārayet* ("he should have the treasury constructed") makes that the prime candidate for the alternative. Why a *prāsāda* (a tall building with many floors) should be an alternative is unclear. See this provision at 1.20.2. The commentary *Cāṇakyaṭīkā* appears to connect this term syntactically with the following sentence: [H]e should get a mansion constructed at the border region (Harihara Sastri 2011, 82–83); but the reading I have followed agrees with 1.20.2.

2.5.4. *people condemned to death*: The strategy is to get these people to construct the secret location and then to kill them, so that its location will not be known to anyone. The use of men condemned to death in various state strategies is mentioned numerous times in the *AŚ*: 5.2.45, 55; 9.3.31, 38; 9.6.29; 12.4.4, 7; 12.5.29; 13.3.14, 39; 13.4.28; 14.1.33. In all likelihood, these people may have been given the assurance that if they carried out these tasks, they would be freed. But their deaths will be used by the state for a variety of uses, including accusing others of their murders.

2.5.5. *four halls*: For this kind of building construction, see the note to 2.3.33.

walls lined with courtyards: The compound *kakṣyāvṛtakuḍyam* is problematic. Literally it would mean that the walls are surrounded or enclosed by the courtyards, which would put the courtyards outside the walls. I think the meaning is that along the walls, there are many courtyards leading to the halls, each probably intended for different kinds of forest produce.

separate lockup...prevent escape: See 4.9.21 and the note there for the three kinds of jailhouses in the *AŚ*. The jail for high officials (*mahāmātrīya*) in all likelihood is the jail for the Magistrates (*pradeṣṭṛ*), who are here given the title *mahāmātra* (high official). I interpret the passage as showing three kinds of jails (*dhamasthīya, mahāmātrīya,* and *bandhanāgāra*) following 4.9.21. Meyer and Kangle, however, interpret the passage as containing of two kinds of prisons, taking *dharmasthīya* and *mahāmātrīya* as adjectives of *bandhanāgāra*.

2.5.6. *cats and mongooses for protection*: Mongooses are a defense against snakes (see 1.20.6). Both cats and mongooses exterminate mice and rats (see 4.3.21).

deity specific to each: The probable meaning is that these were shrines to the guardian deities of each structure. The commentary *Jayamaṅgalā* gives Vaiśravaṇa for the treasury, Sītā for the storehouse, Śrī for the depot for merchandise, Īśāna for the storage facility for forest produce, Skanda for the armory, and Yama and Varuṇa for the prison.

2.5.7. *rain gauge*: See 2.24.5 n. for the calculations of the various levels of rainfall. For the construction of the gauge, see Balkundi 1998.

2.5.8. *Guided by...commodity*: Kangle translates the compound *tajjātakaraṇādhiṣṭhitaḥ* as "Presiding over bureaus of experts for the different products." Such an active meaning, however, is unlikely, especially in view of the similar statement at 2.5.10. See also 2.11.1, where

Kangle thinks that the official is actually presiding over the committee of experts. See Scharfe 1993, 155, n. 61.

he: The subject of this sentence is unclear. These products would normally be accepted by the Superintendent of the Treasury as the nearly identical parallel passage at 2.11.1 indicates. That official, however, has not yet been introduced, and Kangle therefore thinks that the reference is to the Treasurer. Possibly, this and the subsequent statements should be understood in the sense that the Treasurer should oversee these transactions, even though the day-to-day operations are handled by the superintendents whose duties are to be discussed later. Or else, we have texts coming from different sources with different titles for the same office. Note that the term *kośādhyakṣa* occurs only once in the *AŚ* at 2.11.1.

2.5.13. *fully developed*: The meaning of the term *pūrṇa* (lit., full) in this context is not altogether clear. Kangle, as also the commentaries *Cāṇakyaṭīkā* and *Śrīmūla*, take it to mean that the grain should amount to a full measure. But surely the official will measure the grain, and the adjectives refer to the quality rather than to the quantity of the material. I thank Professor Wezler for suggesting the meaning of fully developed or ripe. The term "full" may also mean that the grain is unbroken and perfect. Broken grain is referred to at 2.29.43.

2.5.16. *one Paṇa ... than that*: Here I follow the reading of the northern manuscript D in Kangle's edition, a reading that is confirmed by the Malayalam commentary: *paṇadvipaṇacatuṣpaṇaparamāpahāreṣu*. The southern manuscripts have the reading *paṇādicatuṣpaṇaparamāpahāreṣu*, which is adopted by Kangle in his edition. Scharfe (1993, 5–7) has argued convincingly for the superiority of the reading here adopted.

2.5.17. *a manager of the treasury*: It is unclear whether the reference is to a particular official or to a group of officials working in the treasury. In the former case, it is likely that he is different from the Treasurer. It is unclear, however, whether this official is the same as the one identified as Superintendent of the Treasury (*kośādhyakṣa*) at 2.11.1 (see 2.5.8 n.) Given the seriousness of the crime and the severity of the punishment, he must be a high-ranking individual, as opposed to the ones listed in sentence 16.

2.5.18. *act as their agents*: The technical term *vaiyāvṛtyakara* refers to an agent through whom commercial transactions are carried out. This way of doing business is discussed at 3.12.25–31. In the present context, these are probably middlemen who facilitated the theft or embezzlement from the treasury.

half the fine: Probably the fines mentioned in 2.5.16, although this would be inapplicable in the case of the death penalty, unless, as Kangle suggests, the term *vadha* given there means corporal punishment rather than execution.

2.5.20. *vivid execution*: This is execution preceded by torture; see 4.11.

2.6.1. *fort...trade route*: All the items listed, as explained in the subsequent passages, indicate sources of revenue; see 2.6.9. This statement parallels the one at 2.6.13 and is meant to give topics that are elaborated in the following passages. This entire chapter and topic appear to reflect a period that saw the role of the Collector being transformed from a provincial governor to a major figure in the administration of the state (Scharfe 1993, 159–167); for a discussion of this official, see Introduction, p. 41.

2.6.2. *Duties...outsiders*: Duties are custom levies and tolls. For standardization of weights and measures, see 2.19; City Manager, see 2.36; director of the mint, see 2.12.24; of passports, see 2.34; of liquor, see 2.25; of abattoirs, see 2.26; of yarn, see 2.23; of goldsmiths, see 2.14; of commercial establishments, see 2.16; 4.2; of prostitutes, see 2.27; of gambling, see 3.20; of building compounds, see 3.8–9; temple superintendent, see 5.2.38–46; taxes at the gate, see 2.22.8; 2.4.32. These topics encompass most of the work of the superintendents discussed in the subsequent chapters of book 2, indicating the vast powers granted to this official. It appears that all these sources of revenue are located within the fort.

2.6.3. *Agriculture...thieves*: For agriculture, see 2.15.2; 2.24. Share (*bhāga*) appears to be the king's share, especially of the agricultural and farm produce (*MDh* 7.130; see Scharfe 1993, 160–161). Tribute (*bali*) appears to be distinct from share and tax, which are precisely determined; tribute seems to be extracted from the countryside according to the ability of the people (*MDh* 7.80; 8.307). The tax appears to be a monetary tax on various merchandise, as distinct from the state's share of agricultural produce. For road toll, see 2.21.24. Land survey: the meaning of the term *rajju* is obscure, and I follow Kangle in interpreting the term to mean the survey and measurement of land and implicitly the revenue from such activities.

province: See the definition at 2.15.3. These sources of income are concentrated in the countryside.

2.6.9. *corpus of revenue* (āyaśarīra): This term indicates the totality of the sources of revenue to the treasury; see the parallel corpus of expenditure at 2.6.11. The corpus of revenue is opposed to the "headings of revenue" given in the next sentence (see also 2.7.31) that relates to the categories under which revenue is classified.

2.6.10. *Price...penalty*: Price: This is derived from the sale of things produced by the state, such as products from mines; see 2.12.35. Share (2.6.3 n.) appears to be the state's share from the sale of products and from agricultural and farm produce, generally fixed at one-sixth (2.15.3). The surcharge is about a 5-percent surcharge or commission on items delivered to the treasury (2.12.26). Monopoly tax: The meaning of the term *parigha*, literally the bars that secure a gate, is unclear; it occurs only once elsewhere (2.12.35). Kangle, following Breloer, takes it to be a tax levied by the state for technical supervision. Meyer takes it as a tax collected at the gate of a fort. A fixed levy is a tax or levy paid by a community such as a village; see 2.28.2. Coinage fee: The meaning of *rūpika* is unclear, but it is related to the manufacture and distribution of coins; see 2.12.26. Penalty: This appears to be a kind of fine for violations of regulations, but distinct from *daṇḍa*, which is a legal fine; see 2.9.8 where penalties are assessed on officials for violations of official duties; see also 2.12.19, 26.

2.6.12. *accounting period* (vyuṣṭa): This term (lit., dawn or daybreak) is found once more in the *AŚ* in the passage 6.7.31–33. The meaning appears to be the period for which accounts are recorded.

the third... days: The meaning and the calendrical purpose of this provision are uncertain. Given that an Indian season consists of two lunar months, it is not possible to have a seventh fortnight within a season. Therefore, Kangle suggests that each of these three seasons actually lasts four months, thus including the other contiguous season: rainy season including autumn, winter including the cool season, and summer including spring. Normal fortnights have 15 days, while the shortened ones have 14. This reckoning appears to refer to the work or fiscal year, which is said to have only 354 days (2.6.6). Taking away the six days lost because of the subtraction of two days from three seasons, we arrive at 354 days.

intercalary month: Given the discrepancy between the lunar year and the solar year, Indians added an extra month every two and a half years; the *AŚ* follows this rule (2.20.65–66), although there are other ways of adding these months; see Kane 1962–1975, IV: 662–675.

2.6.13. *Estimated... balance*: This statement parallels the one at 2.6.1. Both give a list of topics, which are then further elaborated upon in the subsequent passages. These two sections are interrupted by 2.6.10–12, which deal with other subjects: revenue headings and recording, expenditures, and accounting periods. If the intervening section explaining the terms of 2.6.1 is a gloss that found its way into the text (or at least a parenthetical explanation), then we can see that this passage could be a clause that followed immediately after 2.6.1 and connected to the verb *avekṣeta* (oversee) in it (this is also the interpretation of the commentary *Cāṇakyaṭīkā*). To connect the two statements, we will have to change the nominative *nīvī* (balance) to the accusative *nīvīṃ*, which is not difficult given the frequent omission of the *anusvāra*.

2.6.14. *Canons... grand total*: The term *saṃsthāna* means elsewhere a canon or a rule promulgated by the king (Scharfe 1993, 197). This and procedures may be specific rules regarding taxes and other sources of revenue, and they could be used to arrive at an estimate of revenue. The corpus of revenue consists of the list given in 2.6.2–9. How the aggregate of all revenues and the grand total differ from the corpus of revenue is unclear. Kangle takes the former to mean the total of items listed in 2.6.2–8 and the latter to mean the total from all these sources. This list is far from clear.

2.6.15. *city outlay*: This is a curious entry in a list of revenue sources. The explanations of the commentators are unconvincing. The only way I can understand this is to take the compound *puravyaya* to mean payment by the city for a variety of services provided by the state.

2.6.16. *expended*: The meaning of the term *avamṛṣṭa* is unclear. The *Cāṇakyaṭīkā* takes it to mean what officers have used up without authorization and, therefore, what is recoverable from them. If this past participle is in any way related to the verbal root *mṛṣ*, it may mean something that has been disregarded or forgotten.

2.6.17–22. See the parallel passage at 2.15.1–11.

2.6.19. *someone else's operations*: The meaning is unclear, but it appears to refer to the transfer of funds from one superintendent's account to that of another. Perhaps such transfers were remitted to the treasury only after the lapse of some time. See 2.7.3 n.

2.6.20. *miscellaneous*: For another description of this category, see 2.15.9.

side income (pārśva): The meaning of this term, which also occurs at 2.15.3, is opaque. It certainly means some sort of subsidiary income. The meanings of impost, surcharge, levy, and bribe have been suggested.

gratuities (aupāyanika): Here also, the meaning is unclear, but it appears to refer to income in the form of presents and gratuities; see 1.18.4; 2.15.3.

2.6.21. This statement is repeated at 2.15.10.

demobilization (vikṣepa): This appears to be a technical term for the demobilization and dispersal of troops; see 7.9.22; 7.15.12; 8.5.1, 15; 9.2.11.

2.6.22. *Price increases…for purchase*: Kangle translates: "Accretion, viz. increase in the price of commodities at the time of sale, excess in weights and measures called surcharge or the increase in price because of competition for purchase." I think it is better to take *upajā* (increment; see 2.29.8, 11) and *vyājī* (surcharge; see 2.6.10 n.) as separate items; see 2.15.11. For the bidding process, see 2.21.7–9. The commentary *Cāṇakyaṭīkā* explains "special weights and measures" (*mānonmānaviśeṣa*) to refer to gains obtained by using specially altered weights and measures (cheating) in the weighing process.

these constitute income: This entire passage dealing with income appears to be somewhat disjointed, with both sentences 17 and 21 defining income. This confusion is found also in the next passage dealing with expenditure.

2.6.23. *periodic payments*: See 2.6.25 for the periods. The use of the term *lābha* (lit. "gain") for a payment or expenditure is curious. The term is used here from the perspective of the recipient of the funds. See also 2.7.32 for a similar use of the term.

2.6.26. *derived from these two*: It is unclear what expenses are derived from the regular and periodic expenses. Commentators think that these are the unforeseen expenses connected with the two basic and budgeted expenses. For example, one may have to cook twice as much food as normal on a particular day.

2.6.27. *received... carried forward*: The distinction seems to be that the former is actually received by and deposited in the treasury, whereas the latter is accounted for but not actually received. Its receipt is only anticipated.

2.7. *Bureau of Official Records*: With regard to this bureau and the activities of archiving and certifying records carried out by it, see Scharfe 1993, 193–195; Heesterman 1985, 133–138.

2.7.1. *Superintendent*: The identity of this official is unclear. The *AŚ* generally does not use the term *adhyakṣa* without a qualifier (e.g., superintendent of gold). Given the broad authority he exercises even over high officials (*mahāmātra*, 2.7.24), he must have been of very high rank. Perhaps the *samāhartṛ* (Collector) is here understood from 2.6. Shamasastry appears to read *akṣapaṭalam akṣapaṭalādhyakṣaḥ* in translating: "The superintendent of accounts shall have the accountants' hall constructed."

bureau... north: This office acted as both a records office, including financial records and information about various regions, and an audit office. At 2.4.10, this bureau is said to be located in the south-southeast sector of the fort. It is unclear why this bureau should bear the name *akṣa*. If it refers to dice in gambling, then perhaps the gambling hall may have become a prototype for other kinds of work areas. It is more likely that *akṣa* here refers to the axle and thus metonymically to a chariot. Such structures may have been built originally to house chariots. See, for example, the gold workshop at 2.13, which is called *akṣaśālā*.

books: The term *pustaka* occurs only in this chapter of the *AŚ*. This is a term that entered the Sanskrit vocabulary rather late. It appears that the first documented evidence for this term is found in the work of the sixth-century scholar Varāhamihira; see Jolly 1880, xxiii; Kane 1962–1975, I: 121.

2.7.2. *gain and loss*: In the manufacturing process, some substances, such as gold and silver, suffer loss (see 2.14.8), and others, such as yarn (see *MDh* 8.397), increase in weight.

additional weight (prayāma): The exact meaning of this term is unclear. From 2.19.24, it appears that an additional amount by weight was assessed when certain kinds of weighing implements were used.

admixture: The meaning appears to be the combining of different materials in the manufacturing process, such as the insertion of iron in the manufacture of gold to give it the right color (2.14.9).

precious stones... forest produce: For a detailed discussion of these four kinds, see 2.11 and 2.17.

sample (pratīvarṇaka): I agree with Meyer that this term refers to a sample, as it clearly does at 2.21.12 (where Kangle also translates it as such) and probably also at 2.13.57, where we have *prativarṇikā*. Kangle translates the term here as quality. The meaning appears to be that the value of a shipment is calculated on the basis of testing the quality of a sample.

Laws...canons: For the relative force of each, see 3.1.39. If the two passages are related, then canon (*saṃsthāna*) probably means rules set by the state and would equal *rājaśāsana* or royal edict (see Scharfe 1993, 197). But see 3.1.43, where *carita* is substituted with *saṃsthā*.

king's wives and sons: The Sanskrit could also mean "the king and his wives and children" (so Kangle). The placement of *ca* ("and") after king in *rājñaś ca* appeared anomalous to Kangle, but if we connect this to the preceding, we have the king's dependent *and* the king's wives and children.

2.7.3. *From that bureau* (tataḥ): The Sanskrit could also be taken to mean "from the registers" (so Shamasastry and *Cāṇakyaṭīkā*), but I think it refers to the bureau rather than to books; see the parallel *tatra* ("in that") at the beginning of the previous passage (2.7.2), which certainly refers to the place.

additional revenue (upasthāna): With Meyer, I take this term to have the same meaning here as it does in 2.15.1, 11. Kangle takes it to mean the time for interview, but this is attested nowhere else. Further, the time for audits is specified in 2.7.16.

procedures: For this meaning of the term *pracāra*, especially within the context of the two other terms *caritra* and *saṃsthāna*, see Scharfe 1993, 195–203. When it is not used within this specific context, however, I think it can have a broader meaning of activities or operations (2.1.19), or, as at 2.8.24, refer to an area (location or sphere) of an officer's activities. I have used both translations depending on the context.

2.7.4. *king...without regret*: The reading and the meaning of this phrase are problematic. As the commentary *Cāṇakyaṭīkā* notes, perhaps the intent is to appoint someone to this sensitive post who is not closely connected to the king so that, when he has to be punished, the king will not feel remorseful because of his affection for the official. For the appointment of officials to low, mid-level, and high posts, see also the parallel in the *MBh* 2.5.32f.

2.7.6. *work year...nights*: The work year seems to represent the fiscal year (Scharfe 1993, 194) that concludes the work of each government agency requiring the presentation of accounts. The year of 354 days is the lunar year of 12 lunar months with the subtraction of six days mentioned at 2.6.12 (see the note there). See also 2.20.48–49.

2.7.7. *full-moon...full*: The fiscal year ended on the full-moon day of Āṣāḍha (June–July), presumably just before the beginning of the monsoon season. For a primarily agrarian economy, this must have been the obvious time to take account of the past year (Scharfe 1993, 201). The expression *ūnaṃ pūrṇaṃ vā* ("short or full") has given rise to much perplexity, Scharfe (1993, 194 n. 337) commenting: "It is not quite clear what 'short or full' refer to." Kangle explains: "whether the work is spread over the full year or only a part of it." That would make sense if the accounting is done by a worker engaged in a specific task. But here the accounting is done by the superintendents in charge of various spheres of activity that would certainly spread across the whole year. The syntax of the sentence makes it clear that *ūnam* and *pūrṇam* must qualify the initial pronoun *tam*, which, as a masculine accusative, can refer only to *saṃvatsara* (year) and not to the work (*karman*), as Kangle would have it. What does it mean to say that the year is short or full? At 2.6.12, the fortnights are referred to as either short (14 days) or full (15 days); but that does not seem applicable here, because according to that reckoning of the seventh fortnight being short, the bright half of Āṣāḍha would always be short. One solution is to connect this statement to the presence or absence of the intercalary month. Generally, this month is added to Āṣāḍha or Śrāvaṇa. If added to Āṣāḍha, the intercalary month is called the second Āṣāḍha. In this case, the Āṣāḍha and the full year would be incomplete, hence short. In years without an intercalary month, the year would be full.

2.7.8. *bureau . . . intercalary month*: Given that the twelve lunar months account for about 354 solar days, 60 solar months will be equal to about 62 lunar months, necessitating the introduction of an additional month every second or third year. This additional month was inserted after Āṣāḍha or Śrāvaṇa (July–August). The author of the *AŚ* appears to assume the former. In such a year, the work year would be longer or, which seems less likely, the accounts for the intercalary month would be made separately. I think here also that the discussion is about the way to assess the fiscal year, rather than the accounts or the work done during the year, which is the interpretation of Kangle. For the expression *karaṇādhiṣṭhita* (overseen by bureau of experts), see 2.5.8; 2.11.1; 3.12.13; 8.4.31. I think the intent here is that the bureau would determine in which year the intercalary month would occur, and presumably the fiscal year would extend for another month. Kangle's assertion that the account books had only 12 sections, and thus the intercalary accounts had to be done separately, is mere conjecture.

2.7.9. *activities . . . spies*: The text does not make explicit whose activities should be overseen by spies, but the context points in the direction of the superintendents of various government agencies. I think the section from this passage until 2.7.15 is an interpolation. The transition is made nicely with *apasarpādhiṣṭhitam* paralleling the *karaṇādhiṣṭhitam* of the previous sentence. However, the parallel is deceptive. Generally, spies do not oversee the activities of others; they simply gather information and report back. Everywhere the term *adhiṣṭhita* is used in the *AŚ*, it refers to either physical control (mahout and elephant at 1.14.7; boatmen at 1.21.18) or bureaucratic control. The passage at 2.7.9–10 introduces the Kauṭilya dialogue of 2.7.11–15 (for the lateness of these dialogues, see Inroduction, p. 21f). See how the theme of the gathering of superintendents on the full-moon day of Āṣāḍha is picked up at 2.7.16.

2.7.10. *estimates* (tarka): On this term that occurs also at 2.21.15, see the analysis of Scharfe (1993, 263). The meaning here is that a calculation is made with regard to articles that cannot be or do not deserve to be measured accurately.

2.7.16. *They should... account*: All translators take *gāṇanikyāni* ("accounts") as the subject of the sentence "The accounts should come in" (Kangle). Besides the issue of how accounts could come in, Scharfe (1993, 194) has shown that the verb *āgaccheyuḥ* ("they should come") is picked up in the very first word of the next sentence, *āgatānām* ("of those who have come"); in both, the subject is the superintendents who have to present accounts from their respective agencies. There is, however, a syntactical problem with the nominative/accusative plural *gāṇanikyāni*; the best we can do is to treat it as the object or purpose for which the superintendents have come.

2.7.19. *When, with respect... that amount*: This is a very difficult sentence, and the reading is also uncertain, with some manuscripts reading *antaravarṇe* for *antaraparṇe*, and *nīvyāḥ* (genitive) for *nīvyām* (locative). The overall meaning, however, appears to be that upon closer inspection, certain expenditures claimed by the superintendent may be disallowed, and some incomes may be discovered that were not accounted for in the total. Thus the balance would increase by a certain amount. For such transgressions, the superintendent is fined eight times the increase in the balance. The review of the accounts, however, was not meant to be simply punitive; as the next statement points out, if the review finds that the recorded balance should be less, then the amount is paid back to the superintendent. A clearer description of the auditing procedure is given at 2.7.30–33, where incomes, expenditures, and balances are checked separately. It may be to this separate auditing of these items that the term *antaraparṇe* (in the inner folio) may refer. See 2.7.30, where reference is made to records for various periods of time, including daily; this term may refer to those other records against which the final account can be compared.

2.7.21. *one-tenth of the amount due* (deyadaśabandha): There are two issues relating to the compounds *pañcabandha* and *daśabanda*, or simply *bandha*, that occur frequently in the *AŚ*: 2.7.38; 2.8.6, 11; 3.1.20, 21; 3.3.4; 3.9.10; 3.11.7, 33, 41; 3.12.6, 16; 3.13.33, 34; 3.16.18. The first relates to the numeral: Is it one-fifth/one-tenth, or five times/ten times? As Wackernagel (III: 338) points out, the cardinal numbers in compounds often stand for ordinals, and in these compounds, *pañca* and *daśa* mean fifth and tenth (Sastri 1945–1946). The meaning of *bandha* in these contexts, however, is much less clear. A clue may be found in somewhat later usages of the term as a kind of pledge, often used alongside the more common term *ādhi*; see Kane 1962–1975, III: 419, n. 681. Kane notes that *ādhi* and *bandha* are treated as synonyms in the lexicon *Amarakośa* (3.3.97–98). Vijñāneśvara (commenting on *YDh* 3.89) speaks of two kinds of transactions: *sabandhaka* (with a collateral) and *abandhaka* (without a collateral). In all these usages, *bandha(ka)* parallels the etymologically related English "bond" in the legal sense of a sum of money paid as bail or surety. The meaning of bond was probably extended also to lawsuits where a claim is established against another person and the litigants are required to produce a surety that would assure the payment of the amount. A semantic extension appears to have occurred when the term was extended to mean any amount that is due or under dispute. At 3.9.20 and 3.12.16, the term means the value of a given property. How this value is different from the more common term *mūlya* is uncertain. Given that "bond" is unsuitable to translate the term in many contexts, I have used the more general term "amount."

2.7.22. *When…account*: The wording here is problematic, especially because of the two terms *kārmika* and *kāraṇika*. The first probably refers to field officers in charge of carrying out projects on the ground; see, for example, the use of this term at 2.1.38; 2.8.21; 2.28.27. The meaning of *kāraṇika* is more problematic. It is used only one other time in the *AŚ* at 2.7.34, which is a continuation of this passage. It probably refers to the officers who keep accounts relating to the work carried out by the works officers. The assumption then is that both these officials should present themselves at the bureau of official records. Kangle (note to 2.7.17) thinks that these two kinds of officials bring two kinds of items: the accounts officer the record books and the works officer the balance. That, however, is unclear from the text itself. The term *apratibadhnataḥ* is also unclear, its only other occurrence being at 2.7.34 within a similar context. Kangle takes it as "not ready for audit." I follow Scharfe (1993, 194) in taking the term to mean that the accounts officer is not ready with the accounts that correspond to the works officer's activities.

2.7.24. *All…procedures*: This is a very difficult sentence and has been subjected to diverse interpretations. Before Scharfe (1993, 194–203), all interpreters and commentators have assumed that the high officials (*mahāmātra*) also came to the bureau to give an account of their activities. Scharfe, however, thinks that it is the assembled high officials who act as the jury in rendering verdicts on the accuracy of the accounts brought to the bureau by various officers. This interpretation has been accepted by Heesterman (1985, 132–133), and I also have followed Scharfe in my translations. Scharfe (1989, 138–139) also speaks of this occasion as a "great gathering" and claims that the high officials did not give accounts but acted as "a body of sharers or coparceners with the king" in overseeing the audit. I am, however, not completely convinced that this is the correct interpretation. First, this is a rather odd sentence, being the only one in this entire chapter to have a third-person plural verb. All the others have third-person singular verbs, and the assumption has to be that they all refer back to the superintendent (*adhyakṣa*) of the very first sentence who built the bureau of official records (*akṣapaṭala*) and should be assumed to be in charge of this office. If we connect this chapter to the previous, then this superintendent would be the same as the Collector (*samāhartṛ*; see 2.7.1 n.). Moreover, if this is the final judgment on the audits, then this statement should have logically come after 2.7.40; the passages between this and that deal with how the audit is to be performed. Furthermore, if the high officials performed this central task of auditing, one would have expected a more explicit and more detailed statement about their activities rather than this cryptic and enigmatic statement. My suspicion is that this short piece, just like many others in this chapter, has been brought into this anthology from a different source and inserted without much editorial intervention to make it fit smoothly into the narrative.

2.7.25. *Anyone…fine*: This statement too has been subject to diverse interpretations. Kangle, assuming that the high officials are presenting their own accounts, translates: "And among these he who makes a divergent statement or speaks falsely shall pay the highest fine." Here also I follow Scharfe's interpretation. Scharfe, however, takes *pṛthagbhūta* to mean "abstain," presumably from voting on an audit. Although that may be true, I have kept other possibilities open with the translation "takes a separate stand," namely, does not go along with the rest of the high officials. The question, however, is why any official would abstain or not agree with the majority, if it meant that he would be fined! One possibility is that each high official recorded his opinion of the accounts received separately. The outliers would then surface only when their opinions are compared publicly.

2.7.26. *someone*: Although not specified, this probably refers to the accounts officer (*kāraṇika*).

2.7.28. *for five days*: It appears that here we are dealing with the works officer (*kārmika*), who would be the one bringing the balance. The provision in the very next sentence also seems to be directed at him.

2.7.30. *corroborate* (pratisamānayet): For the use of this term in the *AŚ*, see 4.6.12, 4.8.2, 10; 13.3.39. It implies that a statement or action is compared with other actions or statements that would either corroborate or disprove it.

them: The Sanskrit does not give the object of the verb. The most natural way to construct this sentence would be to connect it to 2.7.29, in which case, the corroboration would be directed at the daily accounts that had been delayed. However, I think Kangle is correct in taking 2.7.30–33 as having a broader application with reference to all accounts.

2.7.31, 33. *what is brought forward*: That is, the amount credited to the current accounting period from the previous period. See 2.6.15.

2.7.32. *periodic payment*: See 2.6.23–25 and 2.6.23 n. Kangle here takes *lābha* as "gain" even though he points out in a note the technical use of this term within the context of expenditures.

use: That is, the use to which articles or funds were put in the carrying out of their respective activities.

one who takes out ... receives: These appear to refer to an individual who takes out funds or articles for use in a project, who arranges the activities or delivery, and who actually receives the articles, that is, the end user.

2.7.33. *articles, their characteristics*: The term *rūpa* probably refers to the articles, including money, that are brought to the treasury as part of the balance or profit. For the articles to be deposited in the treasury and their proper characteristics, see 2.5.8–13.

2.7.34. *or offers ... written orders*: Kangle's edition reads *ājñāṃ* in the accusative, while the original Mysore edition and Jolly's edition read *ājñānibandhāt* as a compound. Kangle's translation, "or disregards an order," follows the former reading, although in the note, he comments on *ājñānibandha* as a compound: "the written statement handed out at the beginning concerning the head of income etc., as laid down in s. 3." It is quite unusual in the prose of this chapter for the object to come after the verb. It is also unusual for such a small fine to be imposed for violating an explicit royal command. I take *pratiṣedhayataḥ* to be an alternative to *apratibadhnataḥ* and to mean something like a denial of responsibility.

2.7.37. *consumes*: That is, puts the articles included in the balance to personal use.

2.7.38. *restitution*: This provision probably applies to both the destruction and the consumption of an article that was part of the balance.

2.7.39. *fine for theft*: Although the *AŚ* gives this penalty for numerous offenses, much like the parallel seizure fine (2.1.29 n.), nowhere does the *AŚ* actually lay down the punishment for theft; and yet the phrase *steyadaṇḍa* is repeatedly used (2.21.19; 3.9.19; 3.12.41, 44, 48; 3.16.6, 14, 16; 3.20.9; 4.1.27; 4.6.15). Indeed, there is no specific place within the *AŚ* where theft is dealt with (although many sections deal indirectly with theft, such as 4.6), whereas most Dharmaśāstras deal with theft under the grounds for litigation (*vyavahārapada*). The *MDh* 8.314–342 deals extensively with different kinds of punishment for different kinds of theft. It is also unclear whether the term *daṇḍa* here means a fine or punishment more broadly defined. Samozvantsev (in Vigasin and Samozvantsev 1985, 150) thinks that *steyadaṇḍa* had no fixed value and the size of the fine depended on the value of the articles stolen. But this does not resolve the issue, because in many instances, such as here, there is no direct relationship to a stolen article.

2.7.40. *fine is doubled*: The text is silent on the fine that is here doubled. The most obvious is the closest one, namely, the punishment for theft; but that would be strange, because an admission would entail a greater punishment than the crime itself. Meyer thinks it is the 12 Paṇas of 2.7.35, and I think this is reasonable, even though Kangle thinks that this is unlikely.

2.8.3. *procedures*: I think here the term *pracāra* (Scharfe 1993, 195–203) has the meaning of ways of doing things prevalent in various regions. As Scharfe has pointed out, *pracāra* often replaces *vyavahāra* (see 2.7.2, 29) in the sequence: *pracāra, caritra, saṃsthāna* (2.7.3 n.). In this passage, the first four items deal with creating the climate within a region for economic activities to flourish. The last five directly contribute to the treasury.

2.8.17. *under utilization*: The meaning appears to be that the punishment in the case of substitution is the same as those listed under utilization: for example, execution in the case of precious stones, etc.

2.8.20. *Their*: The referent of the pronoun is unclear. Meyer and Kangle take it to be the officials involved in the illicit activities listed in 2.8.5–19, while the *Cāṇakyaṭīkā* thinks that it refers to those involved in misappropriation (2.8.18).

are 40: A reference to these 40 ways of embezzlement is found in Daṇḍin's *Daśakumāracarita* (ed. Kale, ch. 8, 191).

2.8.21. *what was accrued... later*: Here and in the later pairings, we have opposite actions that create embezzlement. This is possible when, for example, what should be collected earlier is set down as collected later, perhaps for a bribe. In the alternative case, it may consist of payments made later being recorded as being made earlier, leaving the official to use the money in the meantime. Likewise, a small payment can be recorded as a large payment, the difference being pocketed by the officer. In the opposite case, a large payment received is presented as a small payment.

given, giving: The Sanskrit term *dattam* refers to anything that is given. It could be a gift or a payment. Kangle opts for the latter, and he may be right. I have kept the broader meaning of giving so as not to preclude other possibilities.

consolidation ... dispersion: These refer to the methods of selling goods; sometimes they are all sold in one location, while at other times they are sold at different locations; see 2.16.1–7.

a year ... the days: These statements apply to places of work. Here, a year's work may be counted without taking into account an intercalary month, or a month's work may not take into account all the days in that month; see 2.7.7–8 and notes to them.

weight, measuring: Although generally *māna* refers to measure or quantity, here, in contrast to *māpana*, the term appears to mean weight.

2.8.26. *convicted*: The technical term used here, *paroktaḥ*, indicates that we are dealing with a verdict in a judicial proceeding; see 3.1.19, 27.

2.8.29. *informant*: The status of *sūcaka* is unclear. He could have been part of the extensive surveillance system advocated by Kauṭilya or simply a whistleblower, a citizen, or a junior employee who informs the authorities about malfeasance by a senior official. Thus the *sūcaka* appears to be different from spies (*apasarpa*) employed to investigate the activities of officials mentioned at 2.9.30. Kātyāyana (*KSm* 33f), however, takes the *sūcaka* to be an appointed agent, as opposed to a *stobhaka*, who is a whistleblower; see Scharfe 1989, 165.

2.8.32. *When the accusation ... executed*: This statement is somewhat confused. If the case has been proven in a court, then the informant cannot withdraw the case. Besides, this verse appears to imply that the informant has brought a civil case against the officer, while the prose implies that the state is taking direct action.

2.9. *Officers*: The term *upayukta* is generally used in the *AŚ* for subordinate officers. Here in the title, it is evidently used with reference to senior officials, even though in the body of the chapter, that term is never used, once again highlighting the distinction between these titles and the text itself.

2.9.6. *If they ... destroy*: The meaning appears to be that the officers, conspiring with each other, will embezzle state resources and use it for their own purposes, or, quarreling with each other, will undermine the work of everyone. For the use of *bhakṣayati* (consume, eat up) with this meaning, see 1.19.3; 2.7.37. For officials conspiring and quarreling, see 1.15.37.

2.9.7. *master* (bhartṛ): Generally, this term, along with *svāmin*, refers to the king.

2.9.14. *ignorance and so forth*: For the list of these reasons beginning with ignorance, see 2.7.10.

right multiple of the amount (yathāguṇam): It is unclear what this multiple is. If the reference is to 2.7.10 and the opinion of the Mānavas regarding the punishment for shortfalls (2.7.11), then the fine is the amount lost in the case of ignorance, and it is increased onefold for each subsequent one in the list. If this is the case, then this passage follows the opinion of an opponent of Kauṭilya, whereas at 2.7.15, Kauṭilya himself gives the general principle that the fine should be proportionate to the offense, rather than following a rigid system. Meyer suggests substituting *yathāparādham* for *yathāguṇam* so as to conform to Kauṭilya's view; but this simply assumes logical consistency within the *AŚ* and an unwarranted readiness to emend the text.

2.9.17. *revenue as expenditure*: The succinct Sanskrit here is ambivalent. Meyer interprets the sentence to mean that the officer presents what was given to him for expenses as revenue, thus leaving the work undone. I think he is right. Kangle sees revenue as the direct object of the sentence. The officer does the work, but presents the revenue he received as a result of the work as expenditure, thus pocketing the revenue. The labor of the workers is thus wasted as far as the treasury is concerned. This is unlikely, as it is always the direct object of the verb *bhakṣayati* ("consume") that is harmed; see, for example, the countryside in 2.9.15. In the next sentence also, the people who are harmed appear to be the workers, whose salaries are not being paid.

2.9.19. *appointed...by his decree*: The expression *śāsanastha* is quite unusual and occurs only here within the *AŚ*. The actual meaning is also unclear, although it must mean that an officer holds the office through a royal edict; his authority is based (*stha*) on the edict.

2.9.20. *squander...miser*: For these three kinds of officials, see 7.13.13, although there, the discussion concerns kings rather than officials.

2.9.24. *he has a retinue*: The reference of the pronoun is unclear. In all likelihood, it refers to the miser, because in the case of the other two, confiscation of property would be meaningless. Kangle interprets the term "retinue" to mean a large group of people he has to maintain. However, in the only other place where the term *pakṣavān* occurs (5.6.8), this expression means an official who has a large following, that is, his own independent power base. The king is advised in that context also to treat such a man with kid gloves. This is also the interpretation of the commentary *Cāṇakyaṭīkā*. See also the way *pakṣa* is used in the very next sentence 2.9.25.

all his property should be confiscated: The word *paryādātavya* appears to be a technical term for a person whose property is to be confiscated. The term is used with this meaning also at 5.2.54 and 58.

2.9.27. *he should get him*: The referents of the pronouns are unclear. The subject is clearly the king. Regarding the object, even though the closest noun is the man traveling in enemy territory, the man to be killed is probably the miserly superintendent who is embezzling the state.

under the pretext...enemy: I follow Kangle in taking this to mean that a forged letter of the enemy is discovered with the official, and this is an excuse for executing him. Scharfe (1993, 224) explains that the man is killed "pretending that it is done on orders of the enemy." This seems unlikely, because it would not be a good-enough excuse, excuses being needed so that the people will think justice has been done. For planting fake messages from an enemy king to get rid of an officer, see 5.2.68; 9.3.31, 38; 9.6.29, 41, 47; 12.3.13; 13.3.14, 39.

2.9.28. *higher ranking supervisors* (uttarādhyakṣa): This term occurs only here in the *AŚ*. Its rarity may have been the reason for the gloss given in the next sentence. Kangle comments: "[T]hese are evidently trained in the army and work as supervisors ostensibly guarding the works and protecting royal property." Compounds ending with *sakha* generally include people who assist a person, rather than those who supervise him. It is thus more likely that the term refers to a higher ranking official whose job it was to supervise the work initiated by the superintendent, rather than someone who looks over his shoulder.

2.10. *Topic of Decrees*: For a discussion of this chapter with close attention to the Sanskrit grammatical literature, see Scharfe 1993, 60–66; Stein 1928a. Tieken (2006, 111–112) discusses its connection to the Kāyva tradition of poetics. Scharfe's investigation has shown that the author has taken over a small tract dealing with composition and inserted it within the discussion of royal decrees. The tract, according to Scharfe, consists of passages 6–37 and 57–62, in which there is no mention of a king and his decrees. These are referred to in the introductory section 1–5, in the long section in verse 38–46, and the section on strategies 47–58. Note that the discussion of grammar (13–20) here is embedded within a discussion of style and composition. If we take out that section, the verses along with their commentaries, and the section of strategies, the topic of writing a letter spans 6–12, 21–22, 57–62. This section forms a nice continuum, 6–22 dealing with the qualities to be expected in a document, and 57–62 pointing out the major defects that can mar a document. McClish (2009) has argued that the entire section on edicts is a later addition into the text, and the unusual number of verses within the prose text itself (rather than at the end of the chapter) confirms his view. See also 2.10.13 n.; Introduction, p. 23f.

2.10.3. *writes quickly*: This could mean that he writes fast or composes a message fast. Both may be intended, especially because according to the next sentence, he listens to the message that the king wants delivered and composes the decree himself.

2.10.9. *tiresome words*: The expression *aśrāntapadatā* is not altogether clear. I have translated it literally. Kangle and Scharfe (1993, 265) have "expressiveness of words," similar to the meaning "kräftig" given by Meyer to the term *aśrānta*. The commentary *Cāṇakyaṭīkā*, however, thinks that the expression means not to use many words to express something that can be said in one word. Gaṇapati Śāstrī basically follows this explanation, giving as an example the use of *sandhiṃ kuru* (make a peace pact) when the better way to say this is to use the finite verb *sandhatsva*. In any case, the expression relates to the elegance of the language.

2.10.13. *63 sounds*: These are the sounds of the Sanskrit alphabet. Different numbers are given by grammarians, depending on whether certain sounds are counted as separate. The number 63 is found only in rather late sources, indicating a late provenance for this chapter. See Scharfe 1993, 63–64.

2.10.16–17. *a noun... expresses action*: Similar definitions of nouns and verbs are found in Yāska's *Nirukta* (1.1) and in the Vedic Prātiśākhyas; see Stein 1928, 52–55; Scharfe 1977, 120; 1993, 65.

2.10.18. *beginning with* pra: This definition of preposition appears to be based on Pāṇini 1.4.58–59; see Scharfe 1993, 65–66. The preposition *pra* is the first in a list that provides 20 prepositions.

2.10.19. *beginning with* ca: This definition is based on Pāṇini 1.4.57.

2.10.20. *collection of words... sentence*: Scharfe (1993, 64) has pointed out that this definition of a sentence and the previous definition of a word (2.10.14) are related to the definitions of these terms given in the *Bṛhaddevatā* (1.117). This presents several problems, because this particular verse is relegated by Tokunaga to the longer version, which he assumes was created between the seventh century C.E. and 1187 C.E. (Tokunaga 1997, xliv). It is difficult to see how the *AŚ* definition could be based on such a late work. Possibly both definitions go back to a common ancient source.

2.10.21. *A cluster... to meaning*: This sentence has been subject to much analysis and debate among both translators and commentators (Stein 1928, 55–56). The reason for their perplexity is that they had assumed this sentence to be part of the text fragment (13–20) that dealt with grammatical definitions. This, I believe, is incorrect, as pointed out by Scharfe (1967). Sentence 21 resumes the topic of writing a good letter that was started at sentence 4 but was interrupted by the grammatical text fragment, which has all nominal sentences. At 21, we have the verbal sentence of instruction regarding composition ending in *kāryaḥ* ("it should be made"). Thus the term *varga* (cluster) is not a grammatical term, but rather a term that refers to the composition/writing of a letter. An opinion cited by the commentary *Pratipadapañcikā* points in the right direction. It says that *varga* means a stop or caesura (*virāma*); that is, after a cluster of words that should go together because they form a syntactic unit, there should be a stop. Without such stops, the flow of a sentence and the meaning of words would become unclear. Janert (1965) has perceptively noted precisely such clusters of words in Aśoka's Pillar Edicts, generally consisting of two or three words, which are separated from other words in the passage. Janert (1973, 142–143) observes: "In the versions of the edicts under discussion spaces within the lines are frequent and occur particularly after groups of two or more words. It is my conclusion that this spacing can scarcely be anything other than a form of notation for pauses made during recitation of the edicts and which the scribes each recorded in this fashion." See also Janert 1967–1968. Scharfe (1967) related this inscriptional practice of the Aśokan inscribers with this passage of the *Arthaśāstra,* demonstrating that *varga* actually means the grouping of words within a sentence. But a cluster should not contain words that would confuse the meaning of the rest of the sentence. Thus, in a passage such as *dhāvati mṛgaḥ pacati devadattaḥ* ("runs the deer cooks Devadatta"), for example, if a cluster is made so that *mṛgaḥ pacati* (the deer cooks) go together, the listener or reader would get confused. How this stop was marked is not indicated in our passage, but the examples of the Aśokan inscriptions indicate that a space was kept between such clusters and the other adjacent words. One must keep in mind here that in ancient Indian writing, both inscriptions and manuscripts, words were not separated, the letters running continuously along a line. The practice of *varga* would be the equivalent of "white spaces" between words in modern writing. I want to thank Madhav Deshpande for the above example and for helping me to clarify this passage. Why the author puts a maximum of three words in a cluster is unclear, given that a meaningful unit in Sanskrit often consists of more than three words. In Janert's examples, we find only two clusters of four or five words. One way to see this would be that a *varga* does not always have to contain a full syntactical unit, but a *varga* cannot contain words that do not go together syntactically. So stops should be made after one, two, or a maximum of three words, but those two or three words should be syntactically related to each other, even though the full syntactic unit may run beyond any single *varga*. See 2.10.62, where this term is used again. There it is clearly stated that making a *varga* when there should be no *varga* or not making a *varga* when there should be one are blemishes in a document. One place where *varga* is used within a grammatical context is in the *Taittirīya Prātiśākhya* (1.10), where the term refers to clusters of consonants. That cannot be the meaning in this passage.

2.10.22. *iti*: This Sanskrit term is used, among other things, to conclude direct speech, much like the quotation marks in modern languages. The full ending would be "This (*iti*) is the statement of his (the actual name would be given here)."

2.10.37. *Appeasement...so forth*: The first relates to appeasing someone to get something done for oneself. The second happens when someone is guilty of an infraction and is trying to mollify the other person. Regarding calamities affecting persons, see 8.3. At 8.1.5, there is a list of individuals and nonhuman entities that may be subject to a calamity.

2.10.39. *So-and-so... laid down*: The commentators understand the first three as elements of a letter sent to an officer in the field by an officer at the court. The first relates to someone telling the king about, for example, a treasure trove that the officer has found and not informed. The second refers to what the king said. The third is from the court official telling the other officer to give the treasure trove, if the report is true. The fourth is a simple statement that a good report has been given to the king about an officer. The use of the verb *vijñāpitam*, which is generally used when a subordinate is speaking to a superior (as opposed to *ājñā* in the reverse case), also suggests the above kind of scenario.

2.10.41. *two kinds of compliments*: This kind of document is called "gifts" (*paridāna*) in verse 38, while here it is called "compliments" (*upagraha*). The reason for this discrepancy is unclear; perhaps we have texts coming from different sources.

2.10.43. *The granting... contains authorization*: There is some dissonance between this verse and verse 38, where only authorization (*nisṛṣṭi*) is given. Here that category appears to be expanded to *vācika*, authorization to issue orders, and *naisṛṣṭika*, authorization to carry out tasks.

2.10.47. *strategies... force*: For further details about these, see 9.5.9f; 9.6.20f. The reason for placing this section here is because these strategies, especially the first, were used in the formulation of letters. Thus, for example, a letter would praise the other king's virtues, mention the long-standing relationships they have had, including matrimonial relationships, and the like.

2.10.50. *study... allies*: The kings may have studied together or participated in each other's sacrificial rites. The distinction between *hṛdaya* and *mitra* is unclear. I follow Kangle in taking the former as referring to the two kings' affection for each other, and the latter as referring to mutual friends and allies they have.

2.10.58. *dark paper*: The reference could be to palm leaves or birch bark used as writing material. Due to various causes, some of these leaves could turn dark and make the letters illegible.

faded: This indicates the use of some kind of ink in writing, as opposed to inscription on hard substances such as copper plate. In the case of palm leaves, in general they were scratched with a stylus, at least in southern India (although in northern areas, ink was used), and then rubbed with soot and oil to make the letters legible.

2.11.2. *Tāmraparṇi... Himavat*: Tāmraparṇi often refers to Sri Lanka, but Varāhamihira's *Bṛhatsaṃhitā* (81.1), in a very similar list, gives Tāmraparṇi and Siṃhalaka (Sri Lanka) separately. The editor takes the former to be a river in Tamil Nadu. Kālidāsa's (*Raghuvaṃśa* 4.50) reference to pearls from the area where the Tāmraparṇi flows into the sea also assumes a river. Trivedi (1934, 248) identifies the river as the modern Chittar, a river in Tinnevelly flowing into the Gulf of Mannar. Parpola (2002, 365) makes the same identification. Pāṇḍyakavāṭa is identified by commentators with Mount Malayakoṭi in the Pāṇḍya area of southern India. It is difficult to see how pearls could come from a mountain. A more likely identification is offered by Trivedi (1934, 248–250), who takes it to be Negapatam or Ramnad, a port of embarkation in the Pāṇḍya country for Sri Lanka. Parpola (2002, 365) identifies it as the port at the mouth of Tāmraparṇi. Pāśikā is identified in the commentary *Cāṇakyaṭīkā* as a river by that name in the Pāṇḍya country, and Trivedi (1934, 250) also thinks that it is a river in the extreme south of India. Commentators identify Kulā as a river in Sri Lanka and Cūrṇī as a river in Kerala, identified by Trivedi (1934, 250–251) as Muyirikkodu or Muyirikoṭṭa on the Malabar coast. Although the commentators locate Mahendra in the northeast, Trivedi (1934, 251) argues for locating it in the southernmost reaches of the Travancore hills, once again near the Gulf of Mannar. Thus, the first three kinds of pearls appear to come from the southern reaches of the subcontinent. Kardamā is also a river, and Trivedi (1934, 251) places it in the northwestern corner of the subcontinent, perhaps in Balkh in northern Afghanistan. Srotasī, according to the commentators, was located on the shore of Barbara or Parpara. If the connection made by the Malayalam commentary of this word with Ālakanda (see 2.11.42 n.; Scharfe 1993, 278) is correct, then the place should be somewhere along the eastern North African coast, if not near Alexandria itself. Hrāda also is identified as a pool in the sea off the coast of Barbara by commentators. Himavat is probably the same as the Himalaya, and likely refers to some river or pool located in or near those mountains.

2.11.4. *Tripuṭa lentil*: Kangle takes the term to mean simply triangular in shape.

2.11.6. *Śīrṣaka...Taralapratibaddha*: It is impossible to be certain about the meanings of these technical terms for various kinds of pearl necklaces. Commentators take Śīrṣaka to be a string with a large pearl at the center surrounded by smaller but even pearls. Upaśīrṣaka is viewed as a series of three pearls with the middle one larger than the other two. Prakāṇḍaka is viewed by Bhaṭṭasvāmin as having five prominent pearls at the center. Avaghāṭaka is viewed as a string with pearls gradually decreasing in size from the middle to the ends. Taralapratibaddha is a string with all the pearls of uniform size.

2.11.6–15. *Śīrṣaka...Maṇi-Sopānaka*: For a long and parallel list of names for different types of pearl strings, see Varāhamihira, *Bṛhatsaṃhitā* 81.31–36.

2.11.16. *Each...its type*: The meaning appears to be that when these necklaces of pearls have a gem at their center, they add the name Māṇavaka to their own original name. So an Indracchanda with a gem in the middle is called Indragaccha-Māṇavaka.

2.11.17–18. *A pure Hāra . . . same pattern*: The meaning appears to be that when there is a single pearl string of the Śīrṣaka type, it is called simply a Hāra. What the author means by "others" is unclear. If they refer to the other four kinds after Śīrṣaka, then a single string of Upaśīrṣaka would be Upaśīrṣaka-hāra and so forth. In the *Bṛhatsaṃhitā* (81.32), however, a Hāra is a necklace of 108 strings.

2.11.20. *Phalakahāra . . . five Phalakas*: A Phalaka is explained by commentators as a strip of gold on which pearls are set. This kind of necklace has three or five such strips.

2.11.28. *Koṭi*: This place has been variously identified as the region between the western Ghats (Malaya) of Malabar and the sea, as the mountain Koṭa, and as the modern Dhanuskoti at the tip of the subcontinent (so Narayanan 1993).

Mālā: In all likelihood, this refers to the Malaya or some areas of modern Kerala.

Pārasamudra: Kangle takes this in its literal sense to mean "from across the sea," and this is supported by Wojtilla (2009, 40) and Narayanan (1993, 23). Trautmann (1971, 178–183), however, in his detailed analysis of this passage and the connection of this term to the Greek Palaisimoundou has convincingly demonstrated that the term refers to the modern Sri Lanka, called Taprobane in other classical sources. This identification also fits the context better, because the author here is discussing not some generic source of gems but specific geographical locations. It is also worthy of note that all the regions specified are from the southern parts of the subcontinent.

2.11.29. *saffron flower*: The term *anavadya* (lit., "faultless") is problematic. Wojtilla (2009, 40) has taken issue with Kangle's rendering "colour of saffron," pointing out that rubies are not saffron-colored, meaning yellow. There are two other passages that use the compound *anavadyavarṇa*. At 2.11.51, it refers to the color of sandalwood (the other color mentioned there being red-black), and at 2.12.5, it refers to gold-bearing ores. It is difficult to see in these contexts what a "faultless color" may mean. In both contexts, the color is something close to red. The problem raised by Wojtilla can be solved if we take the color to be that of saffron stamens, which are the ones used in flavoring, rather than the flower or the yellow color normally referred to as saffron. The stamens of the saffron crocus (*Crocus sativus*) are dark red in color, and taking the color as related to a flower also fits the context in which numerous flowers are mentioned.

2.11.30. *Beryl*: The Sanskrit term *vaiḍūrya* may also include other gems, such as cat's eye; Wojtilla 2009, 41. The color of beryl varies from blue to green to gold. Some of the terms that I have translated according to their meanings may in fact be names of various kinds of beryl. Thus, for instance, Gomedhaka (colored like cow's fat) is given at 2.12.6 as the name of a gem.

Śirīṣa flower: This tree is *Accacia lebbeck*, and its blooms are white with a pufflike appearance and contain yellow filaments. There could be several varieties of related trees called by this name, some having a golden color and others with green tints, for example, pomelo (*Citrus decumana*). We find at 2.11.39 that diamonds also come in this color.

water: One would have to assume that this is the blue color of a large body of water.

bamboo: Given that this comes right before the parrot's wing (which is green), Meyer, Kangle, and Wojtilla (2009, 41) take the term to refer to a green bamboo. That is probably correct.

turmeric root: The Sanskrit *puṣya* is unclear. Kangle and Wojtilla (2009, 41) take it to mean simply yellow; but all the others refer to a real object and not simply to a color. I follow Meyer in taking the term to refer to turmeric root, which, of course, is yellow in color.

2.11.31. *"delighter" or a "flowing-middle"*: The meanings of these terms—*nandaka* and *sravanmadhya*—are totally obscure. Both may be simply gemological terms for certain kinds of stone. I wonder whether the second, with something falling or springing from the middle, may refer to a star sapphire.

2.11.32. *A clear... sunstone*: This sentence is quite problematic and possibly corrupt. The initial two words (*śuddhasphaṭika* and *mūlāṭīvarṇa*; Kangle reads *mūlāṭa* following Bhaṭṭasvāmin, although at 2.11.39, he has *mūlāṭī*) are missing in the manuscripts, although the very reliable northern manuscript D inserts these words at the beginning of the previous sentence. Based on Bhaṭṭasvāmin's commentary, Kangle has transposed these words to the beginning of this sentence, and I think, given the evidence, this is the best we can do. I have been unable to identify the plant Mūlāṭī. Once again, the term "cool shower" may be the name of a gem, in the same way as "sun-stone." Wojtilla (2009, 41) suggests the possibility that it is the same as *candrakānta*, moon-stone. As both Kangle and Wojtilla acknowledge, these terms may not be descriptions of clear crystal but specific names of various gems or crystal.

2.11.34. *improperly bored* (durviddha): Wojtilla (2009, 39) thinks this is an interpolation, because "it is hard to conceive technically that boring of gems might have been done in the age of the composition of the KA [Kauṭilīya Arthaśāstra]." But note that at 2.11.4, we do have a reference to the boring of pearls. The term, however, may also mean any defect in the cutting or otherwise shaping of the mined gems.

2.11.35. *Vimalaka... Śukrapulaka*: It is impossible to ascertain with any degree of certainty to what these words refer. Following the descriptions of authentic gems, Meyer, Kangle, and Wojtilla (2009, 42) have attempted to give translations, but with limited success. The words may well be technical terms for specific gems. I think Wojtilla (2009, 40) is right in thinking that this was originally a gloss that found its way into the text. I give here the translation offered by Wojtilla: "Spotless, blue, dark-blue, of the colour of cow's bile, white, copper(-coloured), always radiating, of flood of light, vermilion-coloured, of a faint red colour, with sand-grains inside, looking like bees' wax, of the colour of *mudga*-bean, milk-coloured, resembling the powder of pearl shell, coral-coloured, with a black interior, and with a white interior." Some of these terms, such as Māleyaka and Ahicchatraka, may refer to places of origin (Trivedi 1934, 252–255). This list appears to contain semiprecious stones in the mid-range.

2.11.36. *crystalline gems*: These are actually crystal or glass, forming the most inferior kinds of gems. The methods of coloring crystal or glass were known during this period (Wojtilla 2009, 40); see above 1.18.8 n.

2.11.37. *Sabhārāṣṭra… Indravāna*: It is impossible to identify these locations. The explanations offered by commentators are mere guesswork. The reading *tajjamārāṣṭrakam* is problematic. The Malayalam commentator and Bhaṭṭasvāmin have the reading *madhyamarāṣṭrakam*, while the *Cāṇakyaṭīkā* probably reads *tajjumārāṣṭrakam*, but places it at Kaliṅga. On the identification of this region with the city of Bhogavatī, see Harihara Sastri 2011, 66f.

2.11.39. *These are… of gems*: This passage looks extremely awkward. First, it repeats many of the colors associated with beryl and crystal at 2.11.29, 31, and ends with the statement that diamonds can have the color of any gem. That is simply not possible. I think this passage is an interpolation, following the pattern of gems where colors are specified (2.11.29–31).

2.11.42. *Alakanda*: Scharfe (1993, 276–278), following Sylvain Lévi (1936), has shown conclusively the identity of Alakanda with Alexandria in Egypt. This was the transshipment port for coral to India. This is supported by the Malayalam commentary that uses the form *ālasāndraka*. Kangle and Scharfe think that the term *praśastam* ("is superior") should be supplied here from sentence 40. I think this is unlikely; this is an introductory statement of the provenance of coral, rather than an evaluation of the quality of various corals.

Vivarṇa: This is identified in the commentary of Bhaṭṭasvāmin as a coastal region of what he calls *yavanadvīpa* (island of Greece?). This is also probably located somewhere in the Mediterranean or the Persian Gulf, where black coral was harvested. For these kinds of coral, see Introduction, p. 26f.

red and lotus-colored: I follow Scharfe (1993, 277) in taking these two colors as referring to corals from Alakanda and Vivarṇa rather than to two further kinds of coral. If the lotus color refers to a blue or dark lotus, then the identification of Vivarṇa with the Persian Gulf would be strengthened.

2.11.43–55. *Sandalwood from Sātana...is brown*: These place names are obscure, and the explanations given in the commentaries are probably educated guesses. Given that the major regions of sandalwood production are in South India, especially in Kerala, it is likely that these names refer to specific locations in the south. See Trivedi 1934, 258–260.

2.11.57, 58. *Joṅga, Doṅga:* Trivedi (1934, 260) places these in Assam. The commentary *Cāṇakyaṭīkā*, however, gives the reading *vāṅgakam,* from the Vaṅga region, that is, Bengal.

2.11.61–70. *Tailaparṇika...reddish yellow*: Even though these articles are not identified as incense, it is clear that we are dealing with substances that produce a pleasant smell either when burnt or when used in some other manner, for example, applied as an oil. The locations mentioned in this passage are difficult to identify. The commentator Bhaṭṭasvāmin locates all the places in Kāmarūpa in the northeastern corner of the subcontinent. Lauhityā probably refers to the Brahmaputra River, and Svarṇabhūmi probably refers to Myanmar (Burma). Kangle identifies Uttaraparvata with the Himalayas. The commentary *Cāṇakyaṭīkā* has the reading *āntaravantyam* (middle region of Avanti) in place of *āntaravatyam* (Antaravatī).

2.11.71. *Ability...combined*: The meaning appears to be that these substances are able to sustain these changes without losing their fragrance.

2.11.72. *That concludes...high value*: The manuscripts place this concluding statement (*iti sārāḥ*) after sentence 70. Following the suggestion of Kangle, I have moved it to the end of sentence 72, which concludes the discussion on incense. The other possibility is that 71–72 have been inserted here from a gloss and that the discussion of articles of high value indeed concluded at 70. The odd use of the term *teṣām* ("their")—*iti teṣāṃ guṇāḥ* (such are their qualities)—also points in this direction; see the very different expressions in the parallel passages at 33, 56, and 60 (e.g., *iti maṇiguṇāḥ*: such are the qualities of gems).

2.11.73. *Skins*: This section deals with valuable furs and not ordinary skins. The list begins with the furs of small animals and moves to those of large animals.

2.11.78. *shaggy*: The term *duhilitikā* is obscure and occurs nowhere else. Meyer suggests changing it to *dulihitikā* as a Prakrit form for *dvilikhhitikā*, but without much confidence. Unfortunately, this term and others like it appear to come from the leather industry (perhaps vernacular, *deśi*, words) and are thus not attested in other literature.

2.11.86. *dappled with "moons"*: The commentator Bhaṭṭasvāmin explains that the skin has small, round, white spots resembling the moon.

2.11.88. *Sāmūra...Bāhlava*: Scharfe (1993, 279) has identified conclusively that the term *Bāhlava* refers not to Bactria/Balkh but is an altered form of *pāhlava*, Parthian. Sāmūra would then be connected to the modern

Persian *sammur*, that is, skin of the Scythian weasel, marten, or sable. Sāmūlī would then be simply the skin of a light-brown variety of the sable. Scharfe was unable to identify Cīnasī.

2.11.94. *color of Nalatūla*: Both Meyer and Kangle take this to mean the color of the flower panicles of the Nala reed. The meaning is doubtful.

2.11.97. *undyed... partially dyed*: The Sanskrit is not altogether clear. Following the commentary *Cāṇakyaṭīkā*, I take *śuddha* to mean white or undyed; and *śuddharakta* to mean completely dyed.

cut-off threads: This probably refers to some form of lace or cut-work cloth.

2.11.98. *Kaucapaka... Samantabhadraka*: The meanings of these names are obscure. Commentators take Kaucapaka as some sort of head covering especially for animals; Kulamitikā and Saumitikā as coverings for elephants; Talicchaka as a bedspread; Paristoma also as a sort of a bedspread or a blanket; and Samantabhadraka as a hem at the bottom of the armor. The meanings given by them are less than certain.

2.11.100. *Bhiṅgisī... rain*: The names of the cloth and the numbers are unclear. I follow Kangle in assuming two kinds of cloth, with the other terms as descriptive of them.

2.11.101. *Saṃpuṭikā... Sattalikā*: Once again, the meanings of these names for textiles are obscure, commentators offering diverse explanations.

2.11.102. *Dukūla*: This appears to be the name of a particular kind of textile and a yarn. Here it appears to refer to a textile woven out of Dukūla yarn. At 2.22.6, it probably refers to yarn, while at 2.23.8 and 4.1.10, it definitely refers to yarn. Charpentier (1919, 144–145) thinks the term is a Prakritism for *dvikūla*, that is, a cloth with two borders. This is, however, unlikely, because of the use of the term for a kind of yarn. Like *kṣauma* with which it is often paired, the term Dukūla probably meant some kind of yarn produced from vegetable material.

2.11.104. *watery... mixed weave*: The meaning is unclear. Meyer offers the best explanation: a weave that produces the smoothness of a gem and the transparency of water.

2.11.107. *"Leaf-wool" silk*: According to Scharfe (1993, 290–92), this is uncultivated silk gathered from indigenous silkworms inhabiting various trees. The kind of tree the worms live on determines the color and quality of the silk. Evidently, this silk was produced in various regions.

2.11.114. *The above... Cīna*: For the Kauśeya and Cīna silk, see Scharfe 1993, 290–92. Evidently, Kauśeya silk was valued more than the "leaf-wool" silk, but the exact techniques of its production are unclear, although the silkworm for Kauśeya may have been cultivated. At 4.1.10, the wages for weaving these two types of yarn are given. The Chinese silk, on the other hand, appears to have been received as finished cloth, and no mention is made of its weaving.

2.12.1. *Mines*: For the distinction between mine (*ākara*) and *khani*, which I have translated as pit mine (2.12.27), see 1.10.15 n.; Olivelle 2012a.

strong color... taste: It is unclear whether the three qualities refer generically to earth, rock, and liquid or, as seems more likely, they refer respectively to earth, rock, and liquid. For the presence of ore-bearing soil, rock, and liquids, see also 2.6.4; 2.12.5, 12.

2.12.2. *Gold-bearing liquids*: The solubility of gold in certain kinds of liquids has been scientifically established; see R. W. Henley, "Solubility of Gold in Hydrothermal Chloride Solutions," *Chemical Geology* 11(1973), 73–87; I. Y. Nekrasov, *Geochemistry, Mineralogy and Genesis of Gold Deposits*. Rotterdam: Balkema, 1996 (131f).

recognized regions: The meaning appears to be that these mountains are in regions that are well known as containing metal ores.

2.12.3. *infusing... hundredfold*: The meaning of *veddhṛ* (found only here in the *AŚ*) is obscure. I think the term may refer to a process where this liquid is used in the smelting of copper and silver ore. We have a similar statement at the end of 2.12.5 with the term *vedhana*. Shamasastry translates as "amalgamate themselves more than cent per cent with copper or silver." Kangle (III, 71–72) dismisses the idea that this *rasa* in the *AŚ* refers to some kind of alchemy. Scharfe (1993, 275), however, supports Jolly's theory that the term *veddhṛ* in its current meaning is derived from Greek chemistry and alchemy. I do not think that as practical a text as this would be dealing with alchemy; and we do not find the mention of mercury anywhere in the text. The idea here appears to be the boiling of copper and silver with a liquid containing gold in solution. This process deposits gold ions on the surface of the other inferior metal, making it take on the appearance of gold. This is the kind of gold alloy that is referred to as *rasaviddha* at 2.13.3, where all the other terms also refer to sources of gold.

2.12.5. *admixture*: The term *pratīvāpa* indicates a chemical that is added to the smelting or boiling of something. This addition creates a coating, just as in 2.12.3. See the use of this term at 2.12.8, 11; 2.25.22; 14.2.6. It appears that here gold-bearing ore is heated with solid pieces of copper or silver. The gold is deposited on the surface of the other metal, creating a coating of gold similar to the one described in 2.12.3 n. I want to thank Gyula Wojtilla for his insights into these metallurgical processes. Much, however, remains obscure.

2.12.6. *Vimalaka, Sasyaka, Gomedaka*: For these varieties of gems, see 2.11.30 and 35. The last, Gomedhaka, appears to be a type of beryl that has the color of cow's fat.

2.12.9. *them*: I assume that *teṣām* of sutra 8 is understood here also. We are dealing here and in the following verse with ores that need processing before yielding metal.

2.12.10. *ferment*: This refers to the fermenting substance used in the manufacture of liquor; see 2.15.17; 2.25.26, 33.

Kandalī: It may well be that this is the same as *kadalī* (banana) listed in the previous sentence. The form *kandalī* may be because of metrical necessity. If *kandalī* is the correct form, it may refer to *Crinum defixum*.

2.12.11. *admixture... softening*: We are probably dealing with here a powder made out of these substances. It stops the chemical process that is used to soften metal.

2.12.12. *heavy, oily, and soft*: I follow Kangle's suggestion that these three qualities are common to all ores. The different metals are identified by the differences in the color, smell, and texture of the ores. Regarding the weight, see 2.12.7.

2.12.15. *orange* (khurumba): The meaning of this term is obscure. Kangle, following the commentary *Pratipadapañcikā*, takes it to mean ore consisting of smooth stones. I take it as a color because it is color that predominates in these descriptions. Variant spellings of this word include *kurumba*, which may connect it to *kuruba* and *kurabaka*, indicating a red-colored flower (*Barleria* or amaranth).

2.12.16. *Vaikṛntaka*: The meaning is unknown. Kangle guesses that it may be some sort of specialized iron. The term occurs with sufficient frequency (see 2.17.14; 4.1.35) in lists of metals for it to have been a well-known type of metal. Monier-Williams cites lexicons for the meaning of mercury, which is doubtful in this context.

Kākāṇḍa: Literally this means "crow's egg," but it is the tree *Diospyros tomentosa* (Macri 1988, 33) and identified as *mahānimba* in the *Śabdakalpadruma*.

2.12.17. *gem*: The term *maṇi* generally means a gem or a precious stone. Coming as it does at the end of a list of metal ores, it is certainly out of place. The term, however, does not occur anywhere else as a particular metal, even though Tokunaga (2005, 5) appears to indicate that it is the name of a metal.

with a very intense color: The reading here is probably corrupt. Kangle adopts *tīvras tanurāgaḥ* and translates: "hard and of a light colour." But nowhere in the *AŚ* do we find *tīvra* meaning hard. The Malayalam commentary and Bhaṭṭasvāmin connect the term with the preceding and read *śītatīvraḥ*, meaning quickly cooled. At 2.11.33, we have *tīvrarāga* (intense color) as a quality of good gems, and it is likely that here also *tīvra* should be connected with *rāga*. The commentary *Cāṇakyaṭīkā*, in fact, has the reading *tīvratararāgaḥ*, which I have adopted. The Malayalam characters for *ta* and *nu* can cause some confusion if written carelessly.

2.12.19. *penalty*: The amount of the penalty is not given. Within a similar context of violating provisions of state monopoly, the penalty is given as 25 Paṇas at 2.12.26, and as 600 Paṇas at 2.12.31 and 2.25.1.

2.12.20. *except in the case of gems*: For this offense, capital punishment is prescribed at 4.9.2.

2.12.21. *paying off...labor*: For such individuals, both men and women, see 2.23.2; 2.24.2; 3.13.18.

2.12.23. *brass*: The term *ārakūṭa* (found also at 2.17.14; 4.1.35), according to Tokunaga (2005, 6–7), refers to an alloy of copper and zinc called calamine brass. Tokunaga has also shown that this unusual term is derived from the Greek *oreichalkos* (mountain copper).

2.12.24. *strengthening alloy*: We must assume that *ājīva* here has the same meaning as *bīja* used in the context of the silver coins. As Kangle suggests, perhaps the original reading here also was *pādabīja*.

2.12.27. *alkali* (kṣāra): It is unclear what the reference is. Given that all other substances come from mining on land or from diving in the sea, this also must refer to some such substance, especially because salt (*lavana*) is listed in the parallel passage at 2.6.4. Citing the occurrence of this term at 2.12.34 and 2.15.14, and its association there with salt, the topic that immediately follows, Kangle suggests a sugarcane product (see the coupling of salt and sugar at 2.12.34). Meyer suggests mica or quartz.

2.12.30. *levies* (vibhāga): The meaning is unclear. The term must refer to something other than *bhāga* (share). Kangle takes it to mean dues, and takes the three kinds of dues listed as explicating this. The syntax does not support such an interpretation, especially because *vibhāga* occurs in a Dvandva compound.

2.12.31. *buyer*: That is, the buyer (probably a salt trader) of imported foreign salt. Such imports would undercut the state monopoly on salt.

2.12.35–36. *the 12 kinds*: The reference is unclear. Kangle, rejecting the interpretation of the commentators, follows Meyer in seeing the 12 kinds as referring to ores. Both refer to 2.12.23 for the varieties of ore; and Kangle thinks that the 12th kind is the gem ore. There are only nine ores listed in that passage; we must supply gold and silver to come up with eleven. Commentators take the 12 to consist of the ten kinds of taxes listed in this verse, plus the ore and products made from it. Given the likelihood that verses are derived from another source, only the original context, now irretrievably lost, can provide an adequate explanation.

2.13.1. *four halls*: See 2.3.32 and 2.5.5 and the notes to them.

2.13.2. *chief goldsmith*: He is an officer under the Superintendent of Gold. I translate *sauvarṇika* this way to distinguish this official, who handled day-to-day operations, from goldsmiths who were doing the actual work of manufacture. He is actually located in the gold market and oversees the day-to-day operations. His activities are spelled out in 2.14. As Scharfe (1993, 248–249) observes, there appears to be two different bureaucracies for work in gold and silver. The first is the government workshop called *akṣaśālā* under the direct control of the Superintendent of Gold. The second consists of independent operators (see 2.14.1 n.) whose workshops were located on the market street (*viśikhā*, could it be the gold dealers' street?), and they were under the supervision of the Chief Goldsmith.

2.13.5. *Among the best* (śreṣṭhānām): As Kangle notes, this word at the beginning of the sentence does not make much sense and perhaps migrated here from a gloss. The term also fits uneasily with the pale and white forms of gold that are not fully refined and cannot be counted among the best. Some commentators read it as the end of the previous sentence, which also makes little sense.

not fully refined: The meaning of the term *aprāptakam* (see also 2.13.6, 27) is unclear. Kangle translates it as "impure." I take it to mean that the refining process that would produce pure gold is still incomplete.

2.13.6. *four times... amount*: The expression *yenāprāptakaṃ taccaturguṇena* is unclear. The meaning should be that the amount of lead used should be four times that through which it is *aprāptaka*. But how would one know that amount? Perhaps this is a clumsy way of saying that he should use lead four times the quantity of the gold still needing refining.

2.13.16. *sequential substitution... standards*: These are instructions for establishing different varieties of gold, similar to the modern system of karats. The sentence is elliptical, with the upper limit of four left undefined; we suppose that it must refer to Māṣa, as at 2.13.50. At 2.12.24, a Kākaṇī is said to be one-quarter of a Māṣa, thus giving 16 types of gold: addition of 1, 2, 3, and so on up to 16 Kākaṇīs of copper to the gold. These along with the pure gold would give 17 standards.

2.13.21. *Tāpī-stones*: probably stones originating from the river Tāpī located in the area of Gujarat.

2.13.29. *he*: The subject of this sentence is probably the Superintendent of Gold.

2.13.33. *Artisans... ornamental work*: For these types of gold craftsmen, see below 4.13.41–48.

2.13.35–36. *He should assign... supervisor*: The context for these two statements is unclear. There is a distinction made between the two verbs: *dadyāt* ("he should give") of sentence 35 and *nidadhyāt* ("he should deposit") of sentence 36. I take the context to be the assignment of projects to individual artisans and the collection and deposit of their unfinished projects in the bureau for safekeeping. The subject of the third-person singular verbs is probably the Chief Goldsmith. Sentence 35 requires that the gold given by the client and the project to be completed should be assigned within the bureau and not elsewhere. The locative *karaṇamadhye* ("in the middle of the bureau") carries over into the next sentence that requires the Chief Goldsmith to deposit the unfinished product in the bureau with the seals of the artisan and his supervisor. It is unclear why the deposit is made both in the evening and in the morning; perhaps we have to assume implicitly that the unfinished product is locked up in the evening and taken out for inspection (to see that the seals are unbroken) and distribution in the morning.

2.13.38. *laying down the mounting* (kācārpaṇa): This seems to involve the preparation of the gold base on which the gem is set; see 2.13.41.

2.13.41. *In laying down . . . fastening*: I have emended the initial *arpayet* (he should lay down), which, as Kangle himself notes, is quite unusual (a verb normally does not occupy the initial position in the *AŚ*), to *arpaṇe* ("in laying down"); see 2.13.38 for the compound *kācārpaṇa* ("laying down the mounting"). Another possibility is to delete this term, which would restore the parallel statements regarding the first three kinds of gold work listed at 2.13.23: mounting at 41, beadmaking at 43, and gilding at 44; the last, ornamental work, has a different construction at 47. The meaning here appears to be that the setting that would take the gem has a strong base using 20 percent of the gold; the sides that hold the gem in place use up 10 percent. The remaining 70 percent of the gold, we must assume, is used to make the remaining parts of the piece of jewelry, for example, the construction of a ring.

2.13.42. *Silver alloyed . . . against this*: The meaning appears to be that goldsmiths may use alloyed silver or gold in the setting, because it is difficult to test. The smith is thus able to steal a certain amount of the original gold. The officers of the gold workshop should be on guard against this kind of pilfering.

2.13.43. *beadmaking*: I think Kangle is correct in thinking that this statement refers to the manufacture of gold and silver beads, rather than to their setting in an ornament. If that is the case, the word *kāca* in the compound *pṛṣatakācakarmaṇaḥ* seems superfluous. I think the three parallel sentences at 41, 43, and 44 make it certain that these statements simply describe the activities of goldsmiths enumerated at 33.

three parts, two parts, four parts, three parts: The meaning is that the gold to be used is divided into five parts, three parts being used for the border and two for the seat. In the alternative method, the gold is divided into seven parts, four parts being used for the seat and three parts for the border.

2.13.46. *by using . . . powder form*: The technique alluded to here is unclear, but it appears that the substance called "sand-vermilion" of unclear meaning is heated with the gold as it is applied on the article to be gilded; see 2.14.34.

2.13.47. *ornamental gold*: Harihara Sastri (2011, 80) thinks that sentences 47–57 are corrupt, and he has given a reconstruction based on the commentary

Cāṇakyaṭīkā and an explanation of the procedures for producing the different colors.

Sindhu-earth: The meaning of *saindhavikā* is uncertain, but it probably refers to soil from the Indus region, probably saline soil.

2.13.48. *iron*: The meaning of the term *tīkṣṇa* is unclear. Meyer takes it to mean "strong," that is, a strong form of gold. For iron producing various colors when alloyed with gold, see 2.14.9. The term is used for iron also at 2.12.24.

2.13.49. *Alternatively... purified*: Silver is here presented as an alternative to gold in the process of gilding.

2.13.50. *one Kākaṇī... Suvarṇa*: See 2.13.16 for another description of this process whereby one Kākaṇī of the original metal is replaced by an alloy. Given that there are four Kākaṇīs per Māṣa, the substitutions here would produce eight levels of alloy.

Suvarṇa: Here the term does not refer to gold but to a particular weight; see 2.19.8.

coloring material: probably iron described in 2.13.48.

2.13.51. *white-red*: It is possible that this refers to the kind of alloy produced by this process; note that the term *śveta* (white) is both the product and the kind of silver used (*śvetatāra*).

2.13.52. *This process*: The Sanskrit is ambiguous, the sentence having no subject. But the reference must be to the process outlined in the previous sentence, with the substitution of copper for silver.

2.13.53. *coloring*: The reference is to the iron used to give color to gold as stated in 2.13.48. One would then add one part of such iron to three parts of ornamental gold.

2.13.55. *half a part*: This refers to the one-third part mentioned in 2.13.53. Half of one-third would mean one-sixth part.

2.13.56. *covering liquid* (pratilepinā rasena): The meanings of both these words are extremely obscure, the term *pratilepin* occurring only here within the *AŚ*. Kangle thinks that the reference must be to iron, but we do not see iron referred to as liquid. Meyer thinks this may refer to the liquid gold ore of 2.12.2. Perhaps *pratilepin* refers to some kind of liquid used in the process of plating.

2.13.57. *he*: The reference must be to either the artisan or his supervisor (2.13.36).

particular touchstone: The term *prativarṇikā* is a hapax, but the related *varṇikā* occurs with the meaning of touchstone (2.13.17). I do not think that Kangle is right in thinking that the official should take a test regarding these colors before being entrusted with this work.

2.13.60–61. *without alloys* (asaṃpīta): This is another term that is a hapax. Kangle translates it as "not soaked (for a false glitter)." I follow Shamasastry and Meyer in taking it to mean that the gold has not been adulterated.

2.14.1. *workshop owners* (āveśanin): As Scharfe (1993, 248–249) has shown, *āveśanin* is not an assistant and probably not even a simple artisan (so Kangle), but a small businessman who owned and operated workshops (*āveśana*, 2.13.1; 2.36.14) for precious metals located on the market street (2.13.2). It is certainly likely that they were themselves trained in metalwork, but probably also employed others as well to do the work. Such businessmen would have the capacity to insure the work they are doing and accept deposits of gold and silver. That they were independent businessmen operating under government supervision is also indicated by the fact that they purchased their weighing equipment from the Superintendent of Standardization (2.14.15).

2.14.2–4. These three statements are repeated in a slightly different order at 4.1.4, 5, 7.

2.14.3–4. *twice that amount*: The amount is the wages. In both cases, the fine is twice the lost wages. Thus in the second case, the fine is twice the one-quarter of the lost wages, that is, one half of his original wage.

2.14.5. *quality*: The term *varṇa* literally means color, but in the context of gold, color (when rubbed on a touchstone) actually refers to the purity of the gold.

deposit: This refers to the raw gold or silver delivered to the artisans by the customers.

2.14.6. *they*: The reference is clearly to the customers who made the deposit of raw gold or silver.

2.14.7. *He*: The reference is certainly to the Chief Goldsmith.

2.14.8. *ornamental gold and silver*: The term *tapta* appears to be a synonym for *tāpanīya* (ornamental gold) used in the previous chapter. The second term *kaladhautaka* is a hapax, and the meaning is uncertain; the lexicon *Amarakośa* (3.3.74) takes the compound to mean gold and silver, and the commentator Bhaṭṭasvāmin takes it as referring to impure gold and silver. Given the context, however, I think Kangle is correct in taking it to mean silver. The commentary *Cāṇakyaṭīkā*, however, takes to it refer to smelting and purifying.

one Kākaṇī per Suvarṇa: There are 64 Kākaṇīs in a Suvarṇa. Thus a depletion of 1.56 percent is allowed in the manufacture of gold and silver articles.

2.14.9. *One Kākaṇī . . . silver*: The meaning appears to be that one Kākaṇī of iron is inserted into one Suvarṇa (= 64 Kākaṇīs) of gold as a coloring agent (2.13.48), while two Kākaṇīs are added to one Suvarṇa of silver. The calculation offered for the respective depletions by Kangle is as follows: For gold the loss allowed is one-sixty-fourth of gold and one-sixth of iron, thus leaving 63 five-sixths Kākaṇīs in the finished product while the raw material had 65; for silver the final product should have 64 two-thirds Kākaṇīs while the raw material has 66.

2.14.10. *reduction... weight*: The meaning is that the quality of the material has been reduced by substituting an inferior metal. If the amount so substituted amounts to one Māṣa, this provision comes into effect.

reduction in quantity: This is when the artisan simply takes away some of the gold or silver he had been given. We should understand the words "amounting to at least one Māṣa in weight" here also.

fraud with respect to a manufactured article:This probably refers to fraud in the inspection of or repairs to manufactured articles as described in 2.14.44.

2.14.13. *agency... thorns*: For this agency and its activities, see book 4.

2.14.14. *five fingers*: For this somewhat unusual meaning of *paṇa*, see also 4.10.1. Perhaps this meaning is derived from the use of five fingers to play at dice.

2.14.15. *They*: The reference is probably to the workshop owners referred to at 2.14.1.

2.14.17. *plating... gilding*: The difference between plating (*saṃyūhya*, 2.13.44) and overlaying (*avalepya*, 2.13.45) appears to be that in the first, a thick plate of gold is laid over a base metal article, and in the second, a thinner plate is placed over a silver article. Fastening (*saṃghātya*, 2.14.30–31) appears to be the fixing of different parts of an ornament together. Gilding (*vāsitaka*, 2.13.46) appears to be gilding with the use of vermilion liquid.

2.14.19. *ones that bend... magnetic*: The exact meanings of the terms and the ways in which they would give a false weight favorable to the goldsmiths are unclear. It is also unclear what kind of balance we are dealing with here; it is possible that at least some of these frauds pertain to the steelyard kind of balances (see 2.19.12 and the note there). The one that bends may be made of softer or thinner metal. Perforation and the insertion of lighter material would make sense in a steelyard balance. A cleft top apparently makes one side go down more easily. A secondary neck will make the balance uneven. In all cases, the amount weighed could be made to look heavier (if the trader is selling an item) or lighter (if the trader is buying an item).

2.14.21. *removed*: The fraud apparently is perpetrated by taking some of the gold out and using the substances mentioned to form an alloy with the remaining gold.

2.14.22. *Vellaka*: This is a hapax, and its meaning is obscure. Gaṇapati Śāstrī explains it as a compound of silver and iron in equal parts.

2.14.23. *Fake crucible... same gold*: A fake crucible probably had a false bottom into which some of the melting gold would seep. The artisan would recover that gold later. Stinking dross may be a place where gold could be hidden for later retrieval. "Crane's beak" is probably a pair of tongs with the ends hollowed out that can absorb molten gold. The term *joṅganī*, a hapax, is obscure. I have followed Kangle in translating it as a water vessel, but Kangle also proposes a sieve or strainer. The reference of "that same gold" (*tad eva suvarṇam*) is unclear. Kangle thinks that the very presence of the gold may give the opportunity to remove a small quantity from it. I wonder whether it refers to the false gold containing one-half copper mentioned in the previous sentence.

2.14.24. *sand lumps... broken*: It appears that lumps of sand (the commentary *Cāṇakyaṭīkā* says that these are lumps of copper) are placed in the fireplace while the crucible with gold is being heated. When the crucible breaks, the lumps now covered with gold would be taken out and presented as gold, while the rest of the gold would be removed from the fireplace later on. Perhaps this refers to the manufacture of small gold beads mentioned in the next sentence.

2.14.25. *Substitution... iron lumps*: The reference appears to be to ornaments with many parts, which are manufactured separately and then fastened together. It is at the time of this assembling of the parts that a silver part, probably with a gold gilding, is substituted for the gold part. Here "sand lump" probably refers to tiny gold beads, which are substituted with ones containing iron.

2.14.31. *copper article... "outside quality"*: The meaning of this sentence is quite obscure. The technical terms "fine-sided" (*supārśva*) and "outside-quality" (*uttaravarṇaka*) are opaque and must have belonged to the "inside" vocabulary of the gold trade of the time.

2.14.32. *both these*: The reference is to the two kinds of sheath: fixed and removable. The descriptions given in the preceding statements must refer not to the actual manufacture of these types, but to the ways in which fraud can be committed in their manufacture. The Chief Goldsmith must find ways of detecting these fraudulent practices, especially because in a crafted piece of jewelry with complicated parts, it is exceedingly difficult to know when a certain amount of gold or silver has been taken out.

2.14.34. *sand-vermilion*: As suggested by Kangle, I read here *vālukā* (as in 2.13.46) in place of *mālukā* in the manuscripts.

becomes deposited: This is one way of fraudulently increasing the weight of the ornament.

2.14.36. *dismantling* (avadhvaṃsana): The meaning is unclear. If it really means breaking, as Kangle thinks, then the very testing process would destroy the work, even if it turns out to be genuine! It must refer to some method whereby the parts of the ornament are taken apart.

2.14.37. *caustic gravel* (kaṭuśarkarā): The meaning is quite unclear. Meyer thinks that the reference may be to a kind of hard sugar.

2.14.40. *fraud*: The meaning of *kācaka* is unclear. Kangle translates it as "the fixing"; for this meaning, see 2.13.38, 41, etc. I think it is better to take it with the same meaning as *kāca* at 2.14.53 below.

pierced: The commentary *Cāṇakyaṭīkā* explains that when the mica is thus pierced, it breaks and one hears a sound when the object is shaken.

2.14.41. *Gems...hollow articles*: The meaning appears to be that gems, silver, or gold of inferior quality are embedded within the object, when superior quality ones are called for.

2.14.43. *he*: Once again, the reference is certainly to the Chief Goldsmith.

2.14.46. *cuts off...cutting off*: Kangle observes that snipping (*parikuṭṭana*) may indicate cutting something on the exterior, while cutting off may refer to cutting a piece from the interior.

2.14.50. *inference*: The estimate or inference is made with regard to possible loss of metal. All this is done by the Chief Goldsmith in order to estimate any loss incurred by the customers.

2.14.53. *He should know...brazier*: An unusual meaning of fraud is given to the term *kāca* here; the commentary *Cāṇakyaṭīkā* glosses it with *chala* (fraud). It appears that these objects or actions were used by the artisans to steal parts of the gold they were entrusted for the manufacture of ornaments. Exactly how the operations took place is unclear.

2.15.1. *purchase* (krayima): Scharfe (1993, 242) translates the term as "sale," but that would be *vikrayima*. However, the meaning may be the same depending on whose perspective we take. Since this is a source of revenue to the storehouse, the purchase is made by outsiders from the storehouse; so from the storehouse's perspective, it is a sale.

2.15.3. *Subsistence tax* (piṇḍakara): The meaning is unclear. Kangle suggests a tax given by a village as a whole, as opposed to individual cultivators. But Kölver (1982) has demonstrated clearly that this tax is different from the one-sixth share of the produce normally taken by the king. The subsistence tax was probably assessed on property as a fixed amount. The practice probably goes back to a time when the king was a local resident, and he had to be supported by the villages under his protection. An oblique reference to this tax may be found in *MDh* 7.118.

sixth-share: For this share of the king, especially of agricultural produce, see 1.13.6; 2.12.29; 2.22.4.

side income...gratuity: These three sources are listed under miscellaneous income at 2.6.20. See the notes there for these technical terms.

2.15.6. *Demanding*: For this meaning of *yācana*, see 5.1.12; 7.16.7. Here, asking someone for something amounts to demanding it, either as one's right or because of one's might.

2.15.8. *pounding...milling*: All these appear to be related to the work of processing grain. For grinding (*rocaka*), see 2.15.64, where a grinding machine is mentioned. Kangle takes *saktu* to mean frying without explaining how he came up with that meaning. In the *AŚ*, the term generally refers to barley meal or some kind of ground grain. Meyer takes it to mean making groats. For fermenting (*śukta*), see 2.15.17; 2.25.26, 33.

2.15.11. *Discrepancy in weights and measures*: The expression *tulāmānāntara* occurs also at 4.2.20, where it is explained as using sleight of hand to change the correct weight (using a balance, *tulā*) or measure and is considered a criminal offense subject to punishment. It appears that the practice was recommended in the case of state facilities to increase the intake! Kangle's explanation that there are different weights and measures used for receipts to the treasury (2.19.22, 29) ignores the use of the expression at 4.2.20.

filling the hand (hastapūraṇa): This expression occurs nowhere else. It must refer to a deceptive use of the hand in the act of measuring in order to take in a larger amount of grain. The Malayalam commentary explains it as holding the hand over the measure to heap the grain over its mouth (see 2.19.34), while Kangle thinks it refers to throwing a handful of grain over and above the amount measured out.

heap (utkara): The meaning is obscure, the word occurring only in one other place (4.6.16) in its normal meaning of a rubbish heap. The Malayalam commentary takes the term to refer to the heap of grain left over after the measuring has taken place. These leftovers would also go to the state.

earned income (prārjita): The term is a hapax and the meaning obscure. The Malayalam commentary takes it to mean gains from trading, and Gaṇapati Śāstrī, various plants grown by the storekeeper himself. All happen to be mere guesses.

2.15.13. *oil*: The term *taila* in the *AŚ* most often refers simply to oil rather than specifically to sesame oil; see 2.15.38–40.

2.15.15. *Biḍa salt* (biḍa or viḍa): This kind of salt is mentioned in the *Suśrutasaṃhitā* (Sūtrasthāna, 46.316), but it does not give a description of its manufacture. M-W gives several possibilities without, however, giving any sources: boiling earth impregnated with saline particles; black Āyurvedic salt prepared by "fusing fossil salt with a small portion of Emblic Myrobalan, the product being muriate of soda."

surface salt (udbhedaja): Bhaṭṭasvāmin takes this to mean salt derived from saline soil, while Meyer takes it to be from salt springs or salt wells. Perhaps this refers to salt that spontaneously erupts from the ground in certain areas along the Indus River and elsewhere especially after rains; see Slaje 2001, 30, 37.

2.15.17. *Cirbhita*: Jolly, Gaṇapati Śāstrī, and Kangle give the reading *cidbhita*. However, Shamasasty and Meyer have *cirbhita*, which is probably the correct reading.

2.15.21. *Dried…bulbous roots*: The reading *śuṣkamatsyamāṃsakanda* is extraordinary. All the manuscripts read *śulka* for *śuṣka*, but the commentaries vouch for the former. How fish and meat could fall under the category of vegetables is the main problem. The commentary *Cāṇakyaṭīkā* omits *matsya* and *māṃsa* and actually connects *śuṣka* with *kanda*, that is, dried bulbous roots. It gives ginger as an example of such a dried root. That would be an easy solution, but precisely because it is easy, it violates the editorial principle of *lectio difficilior*. The Malayalam commentary, however, has the reading of Kangle's edition. See, moreover, the list at 2.22.4 where *śuṣkamatsyamāṃsa* comes at the end of a list that also contains vegetables and fruits. What connects the items in that list is that they all pay a tax of one-sixth.

2.15.25. *Śāli-rice... one-third less*: The reading in the case of Śāli is uncertain. My translation follows the reading of the manuscripts: *ardhabhāgonaḥ*, implying that only one-quarter of the unhusked rice converts into edible kernel (see 2.15.42 n.). The Malayalam commentary and the *Cāṇakyaṭīkā* read *aṣṭabhāgonaḥ*, which would mean that three-eighths of the rice is converted into kernel. In the case of Varaka, the kernel would amount to two-thirds (or calculated differently one-sixth) of the unhusked grain.

2.15.26. *increase of one-ninth*: That is, the volume increases when the grain is pounded.

2.15.32. *Kulmāṣa-grain*: The meaning of *kulmāṣa* is obscure. It refers to both a particular grain preparation (a kind of gruel) and a kind of inferior grain.

2.15.33. *porridge* (pulāka): This term appears to refer to some kind of boiled or parboiled grains or beans given to livestock. So at 2.29.43 and 2.30.18, we hear of *pulāka* of Mudga- and Māṣa-beans.

2.15.35. *Inferior grains* (avarānna): The reading is uncertain, most manuscripts reading *aparānna*. I have followed the reading of two Malayalam manuscripts: *avarānna*. Kangle also seems to favor a reading with this meaning. Inferior grains are probably kinds of beans that are often sprouted.

2.15.39. *Kuśāmra*: The reading here is uncertain. Meyer and Kangle take *kuśa* and *āmra* as two words. The second is mango. The meaning of *kuśa* here is uncertain. Meyer, citing Shamasastry's translation of 14.2.24, takes it to be the *Ficus religiosa*. This is very doubtful. Shamasastry himself takes the term here to be Kuśāmra and offers no explanation. The same two words occur also at 14.2.24, 35, and there Kangle also takes it to be a single fruit, Kuśāmra. I think the reference in all three places is to a single species, although its identity is unknown.

2.15.42. *From five Droṇas... for kings*: This is quite a difficult passage to interpret. The whole section on rations, indeed, is out of place in this discussion and may be an interpolation. Another problem is the gradual diminution of the amount of rice, when we should have expected a rise; the king here receives the least amount! As Kangle notes, one way to understand the passage is to take the numbers as representing the amount of usable rice obtained from unhusked rice: the smaller the number, the higher the quality of the rice. Thus for the king, only one-fifth of the original amount of unhusked rice is used; that amount must represent the best, polished and unbroken kernels.

2.15.43. *A Prastha... kernels*: In Kangle's edition, this phrase, *akhaṇḍapariśuddhānāṃ vā taṇḍulānāṃ prasthaḥ*, is placed at the end of the previous passage. Kangle admits that at least part of this phrase is needed at the beginning of the next sentence and adds it, even though the manuscripts do not have it. I think that this entire phrase should form the beginning of this passage. This is also the interpretation of Shamasastry and Meyer. Given the confusion in the reading, I have chosen to delete the *vā* (or) in this phrase; it makes little sense within this passage (see 2.16.3 n.).

daily ration: The term *bhakta* probably refers to what a person eats during a day. See *ekabhakta* as eating once a day in *YDh* 3.318. See also *AŚ* 2.15.59 for this expression.

2.15.48. *higher quantities*: When using a larger quantity of meat, the recipe is proportionately increased.

2.15.60. *coal and chaff... plastered*: This seems to refer elliptically to the royal kitchen after they have finished their cooking. The coals and husks left over are taken to places where they could be put to use. It is unclear whether these provisions have migrated here from elsewhere, or whether the Superintendent of the Storehouse did oversee cooking activities as well.

2.15.61. *what is left over* (ato 'nyat): The phrase is clumsy, but the meaning appears to be what is other than the rations given above, that is, the leftovers. It is unclear whether this food is simply given to these dealers or, what is more likely, sold to them for resale to the public.

2.15.63. *bookkeepers*: The meaning of the compound *śalākāpratigrāhaka* is unclear. Both Kangle and Scharfe (1993, 13), following the Malayalam commentary, take it as referring to an officer keeping accounts. Given that this is a storehouse, I think a bookkeeper is probably a more accurate designation.

2.15.64. *Grain is stored... for salt*: For these three staple foods, see also 2.15.12. See Scharfe 1993, 58.

2.16.1. *dispersal and consolidation*: That is, the commodities are sold in a single location, thus increasing their price, or else distributed for sale in different locations, depending on supply and demand and on their popularity; see 2.16.2–8.

2.16.3. *and once the price... another price*: The meaning is not completely clear. Kangle thinks that the price may be reached because the commodity has ceased to be plentiful or the demand is greater. He thinks "another price" is a lower price. I think Meyer is correct in taking *prāpta* to mean proper, right, or natural. Both Bhaṭṭasvāmin and *Cāṇakyaṭīkā* gloss *prāpta* with *prasiddha,* that is, when the new price has become well known and accepted (Shamasastry: "becomes popular"). Then the superintendent can raise the price further. The *Cāṇakyaṭīkā* explicitly states that the new price should be reached through small and possibly unnoticeable increases (*stokastokāropaṇena*). Kangle's edition reads *vā* ("or"), but the *Cāṇakyaṭīkā* reads *ca* ("and"). As Kangle himself repeatedly observes (e.g., on 2.16.23), the *AŚ* uses *vā* often without much significance or simply to introduce a new or modified rule.

2.16.5. *favor to his subjects*: This is a theme that recurs in the *AŚ*, also in the context of granting favors and exemptions; see 2.16.11; 4.2.27, 35. In the present case, the king makes it possible for people to enjoy foreign commodities (2.16.11).

2.16.7. *evil of crowds* (saṃkuladoṣa): Kangle translates as "the evil of glut"; so also Meyer. But why would an excessive supply of essential foodstuffs be an evil—perhaps to the merchants? In every other place in the *AŚ* where *saṃkula* occurs, it means a tumult, a crowding or thronging of people; see 12.4.22, 24; 13.2.47; 13.4.43; 14.1.14. I take *saṃkula* here as referring to the crowding of people to buy essential commodities either because of restricted times of sale or because of artificial shortages created by merchants. Shamasastry has a similar understanding: "evils of centralization," which would create artificial scarcities.

2.16.9. *pay compensation . . . losses*: The idea appears to be that when traders sell royal monopolies, the state incurs some loss in revenue. Traders are required to compensate for this loss.

2.16.13. *members . . . bodies*: The meaning of the compound *sabhyopakāribhyaḥ* is unclear. I follow Kangle in taking this to mean that the foreign traders are in some way associated with local trader groups, in which case, legal action could be taken against them. The exemption is, of course, meant to assure foreign traders that they will not be subject to legal harassment when they bring their goods for sale.

2.16.18. *payments . . . ferries* (gulmataradeya): Although one would normally take *deya* as a separate category, I think it is connected to the previous two words, as seen also at 3.20.14.

rations (bhakta): Rations here include both food for the workers and fodder for the animals.

shares (bhāga): probably the amount of the merchandise taken by the foreign king. This entire statement is also found at 2.35.12.

2.16.19. *gain*: Kangle, rightly I think, sees a distinction between *lābha* (gain) and *udaya* (profit). The former may consist of not merely monetary profit but also other kinds of political and military advantages. Gain (*lābha*) is given as the reason for undertaking military expeditions (7.9; 9.4).

2.16.20. *with one-quarter...goods*: That is, one-quarter of the goods taken for export consists of goods of high value, such as gems, while the rest would be goods of low value.

2.16.23. *his own country* (ātmano bhūmim): Kangle translates this as "destination." But this expression is a variant of *svabhūmi*, which always means the home country. The meaning appears to be that the final settling of bills relating to the export of commodities is carried out after he returns home.

2.17.9. *Leaves*: This refers to writing material, which in India consisted largely of palm leaves. Thus here, even though writing material from the birch tree is its bark, it is still referred to as "leaf" (*pattra*). That there was a thriving trade in palm leaves is demonstrated by manuscripts in northern India, Nepal, and central Asia written in the local scripts on palm leaves imported from south India.

2.17.10. *crocus*: This is the crocus that produces saffron (*Crocus sativus*).

2.17.13. *river dolphins*: The term *śiṃśumāra* refers to the Ganges porpoise (*Delphinus gangeticus*). The term occurs also at 2.18.16, and there its skin and other parts are used to produce armor. In both these cases, a crocodile would make better sense, as crocodile skin would be a better material for armor. The final usage of the term is at 13.1.3, where it is coupled with crocodile (*nakra*) and probably refers to a river dolphin. It appears, however, that in early Europe the skin of a sturgeon was made into leather and used for such purposes as greaves for the shin and lower leg (Scharfe, personal communication; see Otto J. I. von Sadovszky, *The Fish and the Prop: A Study in Semantic Reconstruction*, Ph.D. dissertation, UCLA 1970, 25–36). So it is possible that porpoise skin was used to make leather.

2.17.16. *grass*: There is a concluding *iti* after this, indicating that the list of forest produce that began at 2.17.4 concludes at this point, which also explains the nominal sentence here.

2.17.17. *He who...produce*: The reference is probably to the Superintendent of Forest Produce.

both within and without: Kangle takes this to mean in the country and in the city. Meyer, rightly I think, takes it to mean within and outside the produce forests, which corresponds to the expression *dravyavanakarmāntāḥ* (2.17.2), which could mean both factories *for* and *in* produce forests.

2.18.1. *after he has...final product*: This is a formulaic statement repeated several times within the *AŚ* at 2.22.5; 2.23.7.

2.18.5. *Sarvatobhadra...Ardhabāhu*: The names of various weapons given in this chapter, coming no doubt from a specialized military vocabulary, are hard to identify. The meanings according to the commentators are as follows: Sarvatobhadra is a cartwheel-shaped device that, when spun, hurls stones. Jāmadagnya is a device for shooting arrows. Bahumukha appears to refer to a position or a device on a tower from which arrows are shot. Viśvāsaghātin consists of a beam placed outside the city walls that, when released, kills approaching soldiers. Saṃghāṭī is a machine for propelling incendiary devices to burn down turrets. Yānaka is a rod one Daṇḍa long mounted on wheels and meant to be hurled at oncoming soldiers. Parjanyaka is a kind of fire engine to put out fires. Bāhu consists of two pillars meant, when released, to crush those coming between them. Ūrdhvabāhu is a similar device, but it consists of only one pillar 50 Hastas long, and Ardhabāhu is a pillar half as high.

2.18.6. *Pāñcālika...discus*: The meanings according to the commentators are as follows: Pāñcālika is a large wooden plank studded with sharp nails to be placed under the water in the moat. Devadaṇḍa is a long pole to be released from the top of the defensive wall. Sūkarikā is a bag filled with cotton or wool to protect against stones hurled at the fortifications. Musalayaṣṭi is a pike made of hard Accacia wood. Hastivāraka is a pole with two or three prongs to ward off elephants. Tālavṛnta is a fan-like device to hurl up dust against the enemy. Hammer and mace are weapons discharged by a mechanical device. Spṛktalā is a club with sharp points. The function of a spade is left unexplained. Āsphāṭima is a sort of catapult to hurl weapons. Utpāṭima is a device for tearing down pillars. Udghāṭima is a hammer-type device. Śataghni is a large pillar studded with sharp nails with a cartwheel at one end and intended to be hurled down at the enemies.

2.18.7. *Śakti...Trāsikā*: The meanings according to the commentators are as follows: Śakti is a metal rod four Hastas long with a tip shaped like a Karavīra leaf or a cow's nipple. Prāsa is a rod 24 Aṅgulas long either all metal or with a wooden interior, probably a kind of dart. Kunta is a wooden rod five, six, or seven Hastas long used by cavalry. Hāṭaka is like a Kunta but has three prongs. Bhiṇḍipāla is similar to a Kunta but with a broad tip. Śūla is a single-pointed rod of unspecified length. Tomara is a rod between four and five Hastas long with an arrow-shaped tip. Varāhakarṇa is like a Prāsa with a tip shaped like a boar's ear, from which it gets its name. Kaṇaya is a metal rod 20, 22, or 24 Aṅgulas long with tridents at both ends and the handle in the middle. Karpaṇa is a javelin to be thrown by hand. Trāsikā is the size of a Prāsa with a tuft at one end.

2.18.8. *Kārmuka...Drūṇa*: The meanings of these names for bows are obscure and the commentators do not offer much explanation.

Cāpa: This appears to be a kind of reed or bamboo. The word itself is a common term for a bow.

2.18.9. *bamboo*: The strings are made using fine strips from the bark.

2.18.11. *their tips... wood*: It appears that the different kinds of tips are employed depending on the use to which the arrow is put, namely, cutting, piercing, and pounding.

2.18.12. *Nistriṃśa... Asiyaṣṭi*: The meanings according to the commentators are as follows: Nistriṃśa has a curved tip, and its name suggests that it was longer than 30 Aṅgulas. Maṇḍalāgra is straight with a round tip. Asiyaṣṭi is a thin and long sword.

2.18.14. *Paṭṭasa*: This is described as an ax with a trident at both ends.

Kāṇḍachedana: Literally a cutter of trunks, it is described as a large ax.

2.18.16. *Dhenuka*: This is identified as gayal (*Bos gaurus*) by Gaṇapati Śāstrī and as bison by Shamasastry. Since bison do not exist in India, it must be some kind of wild cattle or buffalo.

2.18.17. *Hastikarṇa... Balāhakānta*: The meanings according to the commentators are as follows: Hastikarṇa (lit., elephant ear) is a kind of board used as a shield to guard the body. Tālamūla (palm root) is probably a shield with a narrow handle and a large flat surface (see the same term in the architectural vocabulary at 2.3.7). Dhamanikā is a leather bag that could be inflated. Kapāṭa is a wooden board. Kiṭikā is a shield made of cane and leather. Apratihata is an instrument to drive back elephants. Balāhakānta is the same as the previous but with a metal strip at the end.

2.18.19. *Net... rites*: This statement refers to clandestine and esoteric practices connected with warfare. The esoteric practices are spelled out in book 14. The term *aindrajāla* (magic net) is found only here, but it also probably refers to magical rites or activities.

2.18.20. *intention*: Whose intention he should know is left unstated. Kangle thinks that it is the king's, but all the other items pertain to the factories and their operations. Perhaps this term refers to the purpose of any given factory.

2.19. *Balances and Measures*: The *AŚ* uses several technical terms with reference to weighing and measuring. The term *tulā* means a balance, and in an extended sense, especially when it is contrasted with *māna*, it means weighing (see 4.2.20). In contrast, *māna* refers to measures, especially to measures of volume used for measuring liquids and grains. It also refers to other kinds of measurements, such as length, area, and time (see 2.20). The term *pratimāna* (see 2.13.28; 2.19.28) refers to the actual weights used to weigh an item in a balance. All these kinds of equipment were standardized and regulated by the state.

2.19.2. *Ten... Māṣaka*: There is quite some confusion with respect to the term *māṣa* or *māṣaka*. As the name of a coin, it is one-sixteenth of a Paṇa (2.12.24), while as a weight, it refers to a normal weight and a weight with specific reference to gold and silver: The gold Māṣa is equal to ten normal Māṣas, while the silver Māṣa is about two-fifths the weight of a gold Māṣa.

2.19.8. *Half-Māṣaka...hundred-Suvarṇas*: While the previous discussion was more theoretical with respect to the various weights in use, this passage probably refers to actual weights manufactured in the factories under the authority of the Superintendent of Standardization.

2.19.11. *mechanical device...sides*: The meaning of the mechanical device is unclear. Kangle thinks that it may refer to the steelyard kind of scale. In any case, it appears that in this type of balance, only one side had the sling and scale pan for the object to be weighed. The second kind is the normal balance with slings at the two ends containing scale pans.

2.19.12. *Samavṛttā-balance*: The term indicates that the beam of this kind of balance is round. It is also heavier than the ones described earlier and was probably used to measure heavier loads. The description indicates that this is also a steelyard kind of device in which the beam is divided into two unequal parts and the article to be weighed is placed on the shorter side. The weight is measured by moving a poise along the predetermined markings.

2.19.16. *each fifth marking* (akṣeṣu): The commentators explain this as multiples of five. Thus, special marks are made to highlight five, ten, 15, etc.
Nāndī mark: For this special, auspicious mark containing a Svastika at the center that is often given within a list of eight auspicious things, see Hinüber 1972.

2.19.18. *On it...and 100*: This balance is used to weigh loads weighing more than 100 Palas, which was the maximum for the Samavṛttā-balance. Thus, the markings on this balance record weights in increments of 20, 50, and 100 beyond 100 Palas; so this balance is able to weigh articles weighing up to 200 Palas.

2.19.19–21. *A Bhāra...such Palas*: This passage is confusing, and I wonder whether it is either corrupt or some sections are missing. First, the definitions of Bhāra and Pala have nothing to do with each other, while in similar definitions elsewhere (2.19.2–5), there is a clear progression of weights. Second, it appears that the Pala here defined is different from the norm; Bhaṭṭasvāmin takes it to be larger than the standard Pala. Finally, the cryptic statement in 21 does not say how the 100 Palas is connected to the revenue balance. The translations of Meyer and Kangle do not clarify the issue. I think the 100 Palas mentioned here is the highest weight that can be measured with this scale, just as in the case of the Samavṛttā-balance. Kangle thinks that the revenue balance is the same as the Samavṛttā. This is probably correct, except that there must be a difference for it to be mentioned separately. I think the different weights used for measurements here would mean that the degree markings would be different. If this is used for revenue and if a Pala weight here is heavier, then the state would collect more revenue. See the parallel measure for revenue etc. at 2.19.29.

2.19.22. *Progressively...palace payments*: The reasons for such differential balances are unclear. The meaning of *bhājanī*, which, following Kangle, I have translated as payment, is also unclear. The commentary *Cāṇakyaṭīkā* takes it as the balance used for disbursing rations to servants. The trade balance weighs up to 95 Palas, the payment balance up to 90 Palas, and the palace balance up to 85 Palas. Given that the weights become progressively less in these balances, it appears likely that the payments referred to here are *from* the state and the palace, rather than *to* them.

2.19.23. *Of these...six Aṅgulas*: This is a complicated reckoning. The balance for trade is able to weigh up to 95 Palas (with 1 Pala = 9.5 Dharaṇas rather than 10); its metal beam is 33 Palas; and its length is 66 Aṅgulas. The balance for payments is able to weigh up to 90 Palas (with 1 Pala = 9 Dharaṇas); its metal beam is 31 Palas; and its length is 60 Aṅgulas. The balance for palace payments is able to weigh up to 85 Palas (with 1 Pala = 8.5 Dharaṇas); its metal beam is 29 Palas; and its length is 54 Aṅgulas.

2.19.24. *first two, the additional weight*: Commentators take these to be the Samavṛttā and the Parimāṇī balances. The provision appears to refer to revenue. Thus, the state gets up to an additional 5 percent when the former balance is used, and up to 2.5 percent when the latter is used. Kangle is incorrect in thinking that the additional weight (*prayāma*) is the same as surcharge (*vyājī*), because both are listed separately in the same passage at 2.7.2 (see note to it).

2.19.25. *with degrees...peacock's feet*: As Kangle observes, recording degrees implies a steelyard scale, while weights require a normal balance with two pans. These should be viewed as alternatives rather than features of every balance. This kind of balance had a framework with two vertical posts and one horizontal beam, from which the balance was hung. The whole contraption looked like the feet of a peacock; see *NSm* 2.273.

2.19.26–27. *Twenty-five...lower quantities*: This provision is quite out of place here and likely found its way into the text from a gloss or commentary.

2.19.30. *Of these...preceding*: "Of these" refers to the four types of Droṇa listed above. Each of these four kinds will have its own Āḍhaka, Prastha, and Kuḍuba measures, each being one-quarter less than the previous: Āḍhaka = one-fourth Droṇa; Prastha = one-fourth Āḍhaka; Kuḍuba = one-fourth Prastha. The quantities, however, in terms of the number of Māṣa-bean Palas will be different in each type of measure.

2.19.34–35. *even* (sama): Commentators explain that the measures are cylindrical in shape. Thus, the top and the bottom should have the same diameter.
with the heap...quarter of the measure: When measuring grain, one allows the top to form a heap above the mouth of the measure. According to this provision, that heap should amount to one-quarter of the total; thus, a one

Droṇa measure would actually contain only three-quarters of a Droṇa, the remaining quarter being above the measure.

For juice... within the measure: There is a problem with the reading here, *antaḥśikhaṃ vā rasasya tu*. All editions end the sentence 34 after *vā* and place *rasasya tu* in the next sentence. The awkward nature of this was recognized by Bhaṭṭasvāmin, who accepts the reading, but says that *antaḥśikhaṃ* is carried over to *rasasya tu*, while *vā* is not syntactically connected to the latter, *rasasya tv iti antaḥśikham iti vartate... na tatra vāśabdas sambaddhyate*. I think that this phrase was brought over from a verse, and that the original reading was *antaḥśikhaṃ rasasya tu* (which scans as the second pāda of a verse). Scribes, thinking that *antaḥśikham* was an alternative to the measures with the heap outside the mouth, probably added the *vā*, leaving *rasasya tu* dangling uncomfortably in the next sentence. Indeed, both Bhaṭṭasvāmin and Shamasastry take the latter to be a sentence separate from the last that deals with the doubling of the heap. The translators have thus seen two kinds of measures even for dry articles. I think the alternative here, possibly in a gloss, is that, since measures for liquids cannot have a heap, what would normally be the heap is contained within the measure itself.

heap... twofold: For the liquids in this list, we have to assume a measure that includes the heap within the measure. All these measures would have been larger than the standard one, hence the greater price charged for them as stated in 2.19.37. The grammar of this sentence is quite unclear, and the reading is possibly corrupt. The term *uttarā* at the end of a compound always means progressive increase, but taking it that way here (*dviguṇottarā*) would mean that an absurd amount would have to be added to these articles.

2.19.43. *heat surcharge*: The meaning appears to be that the customer should be given more of the ghee or oil when they are measured while hot, as explicitly stated in the commentary *Cāṇakyaṭīkā*. Kangle thinks that this is because a part of it may have been lost in the process of heating. But that would come into play only if the raw substance was given to the trader by the customer. I think it is better to assume that the surcharge is added because the hot liquids expand and thus measure more (so also Shamasastry).

2.19.44. *measure-flow*: The meaning appears to be that the trader has to give somewhat more to the customers when measuring liquids to compensate for the liquid that would stick to the sides of the measuring cup.

2.19.45. *He should... one-eighth Kuḍuba*: This provision is quite out of place. It probably migrated here from a gloss on liquid measures, possibly because of the mention of ghee and liquids in the previous sentence.

2.20.10. *Chāyāpauruṣa*: For this measurement relating to the sundial, see 1.19.7 and 2.20.39. Shamasastry observes that this is the shadow of 12 Aṅgulas cast by a gnomon 12 Aṅgulas high.

2.20.13. *measure for...pasture land*: The idea is that this measurement, that is, a measure of one Aratni plus one Dhanurgraha (= 28 Aṅgulas), is for use by the superintendents of standards and of pasture land (2.34.5–12). Meyer takes this to express a single idea, namely the standard measurement of pasture land. Kangle says that this measure is only 14 Aṅgulas, but that is incorrect, because it is the total of one Aratni (24 Aṅgulas) and one Dharnurgraha (4 Aṅgulas).

2.20.19. *one Pauruṣa...fire-altars*: This is the Vedic ritual of Agnicayana. The cord for measuring the altar is called Puruṣa and is the height of the sacrificer standing with raised arms on tiptoes (*Kātyāyana Śrautasūtra*, 15.32). In general, however, the Vedic texts take Puruṣa (the height of a man) to be 120 Aṅgulas (see *Kātyāyana Śrautasūtra*, 16.8.22), rather than the 108 given in this passage.

2.20.20. *measure...guests*: The reference must be to the measuring of land given to these people either as outright gifts or as dedicated land from whose harvest guests can be entertained.

2.20.23. *along one side*: This is probably a gloss that found its way into the text, because in later times, Nivartana is an area, rather than a linear, measurement. As Kangle observes, Nivartana initially was the distance a bullock walked before turning around during plowing.

2.20.29. *Ayana*: This is a half-year when the sun moves north (*uttarāyaṇa*) bringing spring and summer or when it moves south (*dakṣiṇāyana*) bringing autumn and winter. See 2.20.61–62.

2.20.37–38. *During the months...Muhūrtas*: The equinoxes fall in the months of Caitra (March–April) and Āśvayuja (September–October), during which days and nights are of equal duration in some parts of India (see Introduction, p. 37). In the following months, days increase and nights decrease, and vice versa. A Muhūrta is 48 minutes.

2.20.39. *Pauruṣas*: For this measurement, see 2.20.10; a Pauruṣa is 12 Aṅgulas long. For the description of the sundial, see 1.19.7.

three Pauruṣas: I follow Kangle's emendation of the reading in the manuscripts: *catuṣpauruṣyām*, in agreement with Jacobi's (1920, 252f) suggestion.

2.20.47. *work month*: I follow Kangle's emendation of the reading in the manuscripts: *prakarma* to *karma*, paralleling *karmasaṃvatsara*, "work year," of 2.7.6; see the note there. As that term means the fiscal year, so here also the term may mean the fiscal month. See also 2.6.12

2.20.52–53. *horses...40*: The significance of this separate calculation in the case of horses and elephants is unclear. Commentators think that this provision refers to the wages paid to attendants of these animals. Coming immediately after the army (*bala*), one could take these two provisions as referring to horse and elephant units of the army, in which case, the former (sentence 51) would refer to the infantry.

2.20.61–63. *Uttarāyaṇa, Dakṣīṇāyana, Ayana*: See note to 2.20.29.

2.20.65–66. *The sun...cycle*: The solar day is longer than the statutory day by one-sixtieth, thus making a day shorter by the same amount, creating a loss of one day in a two-month season. The lunar day is shorter by the same amount. Thus, together they cause a season to be short by two days, and a year by 12 days. Therefore, every two and a half years, an additional month (see 2.6.12 n.) has to be added to make the lunar and solar calendars coincide. This month is added in the summer of the third year and again at the end of the five-year cycle called Yuga.

2.21.5. *Ghaṭikāsthāna*: The meaning of the term is unclear. The only other place where the term *ghaṭikā* occurs in the *AŚ* (2.19.46), it refers to a measure of quantity. But more normally, it refers to a water jar and by extension a water clock. In later texts and inscriptions, *ghaṭikāsthāna* refers to a school. Kangle translates the term here as a warehouse, and it probably does refer to some kind of facility where the time was kept. It is unclear for how long the distraint lasted and what the traders needed to do to get their merchandise released. For a detailed examination of this term, see Scharfe 2002, 169–172.

2.21.8. *After it...bidders*: Clearly we are dealing with an auction here rather than a normal sale. Such auctions may have been carried out for imported goods, as well as for goods sold wholesale to retail traders.

2.21.9. *increase in price*: This must refer to the increase beyond the asking price that was initially announced. Such an increase caused by the bidding process appears to go to the state rather than to the trader (see also 2.21.13 n.).

2.21.13. *fearing competing buyers*: The meaning of *pratikretṛ*, being a hapax, is unclear. Kangle takes it to mean a rival purchaser and questions how this provision is different from the one given in 2.21.9. However, why would the trader fear purchasers who want to outbid each other? I think the fear must come from competing traders; they may sell their goods at a higher price than he. Scharfe (personal communication) suggests that *pratikretṛ* may be a retailer; he may turn a quick profit if he buys goods at bargain prices from wholesale importers. Another possibility is that the seller fears that bidders would increase the purchase price; the increase, according to 2.21.9 and 3.9.5, goes to the state. So it may be in the interest of a trader to set an artificially high price, from which it could only come down as a result of bidding. The whole situation, however, remains complex and unclear.

2.21.14. *conceals this*: The meaning appears to be that the Superintendent of Customs, perhaps because of a bribe, does not act when these infractions are disclosed.

2.21.18. *tonsure...observance*: These are rites of passage. For tonsure and initiation, see 1.5.7–8 n. For the first shaving called *godāna* (gift of a cow), see 1.5.10 n. The term *vratadīkṣaṇa* may refer to a consecration before commencing any kind of religious observance, but it may refer specifically to the consecration prior to a Vedic sacrifice.

2.21.21. *cow dung and straw as the standard* (gomayapalālaṃ pramāṇaṃ kṛtvā): The meaning is unclear, and the commentators and Kangle appear to be guessing (for this expression, see 1.11.3). They think that the merchant presents cow dung and/or straw on the basis of which the customs duty is assessed, while the actual merchandise is of far greater value. But it is difficult to see how this can be done, unless the real merchandise in a cart is covered by cow dung and straw. I wonder whether this is another example of a maxim (*nyāya*), whose true meaning may be eluding us (see 2.2 n.).

2.21.23. *outside*: probably outside the city gate. They are made duty-free to attract the import of such valuable goods.

2.21.24. *one-hoofed…small farm animals*: It is unclear whether the levy is imposed on each of these animals or, as seems more likely, on animals carrying loads on their backs, in the same way as the last mentioned, a man carrying a load on his shoulders, unless the animals themselves are for sale. One-hoofed animals are horses and mules; farm animals may be cattle; and small farm animals are goats and sheep.

2.21.26. *Superintendent*: probably the Superintendent of Customs discussed in this chapter.

2.22.1. *What is external…exchange* (bāhyābhyantaraṃ cātithyam): Following the commentators, Kangle takes this sentence as containing three categories: goods from the countryside (*bāhya*), goods from the city (*abhyantara*), and foreign goods (*ātithya*). This is the only place that the term *ātithya* is used with a meaning unconnected to guests or hospitality. The placement of *ca* ("and") after the compound, however, makes it more probable that the first two terms provide the classification of the third. This is confirmed by the very next sentence with an identical structure (*niṣkrāmyaṃ praveśyaṃ ca śulkam*). Meyer translates *ātithya* as *Austausch*, and I have followed him. The meaning of exchange or commerce probably became attached to this term from its usage within the Vedic Soma ritual. There the rite connected with the reception of Soma and its purchase for an outsider is referred to as *ātithya* (*ĀpŚr* 10.30.1–31).

2.22.6. *silk*: The term *kṛmitāna* (lit., worm fiber), as Scharfe (1993, 291) has pointed out, may refer to either the *kauśeya* silk or the *patrorṇa* silk (see 2.11.107–114).

2.22.8. *The customs duty…portion*: At 2.22.3 also, a duty of one-fifth share is mentioned. Commentators think that the provision here applies to imports and exports from the fortified city, given the mention of the gate. If that is true, a two-fifths share of goods would be paid as tax for goods to and from the city.

2.22.9. *Commodities...production*: The reason for this provision is unclear. Perhaps, as Breloer (III: 453–454) suggests, the state had an interest in the even distribution of goods across the country, and bringing them to the market allowed the state to collect duties and taxes.

2.22.10. *For taking...penalty*: This and the following infractions appear to be examples of sale at the point of production rather than theft. Indeed, the term *atyaya,* which refers to an administrative penalty for infraction of rules, is used here, rather than *daṇḍa* (fine), which would be called for in the case of theft. However, in the next three provisions, *daṇḍa* is used, indicating that theft may be involved there, while at 2.22.14, once again *atyaya* is used. Perhaps in these provisions the two terms are used indiscriminately. See Scharfe 1993, 165.

2.22.14. *The royal-land penalty...half Paṇas*: This penalty pertains to agricultural produce from royal lands (*sītātyaya*). The significance of this provision has been subject to dispute. Commentators say that the purchaser pays one Paṇa and the seller one and a half Paṇas. I think a distinction is made here between a fine (*daṇḍa*) and a penalty (*atyaya*); see previous note. This provision thus parallels sentence 10, which gives the penalty for purchasing goods directly from a mine. Here the penalty is for selling produce from a state-owned field (*sītā*). Scharfe (1993, 165) thinks that the penalty is light because the state does not suffer any real loss, the money being simply transferred from one state account to another. See 5.2.12–13, where the penalty is higher.

2.22.15. *region...custom* (deśajāticaritrataḥ): Kangle, following the commentators, translates this as a Tatpuruṣa compound: "in accordance with the customs of the country and the community." I think Meyer is correct in assuming this to be a Dvandva compound and in taking *jāti* as referring to the kind of commodity, rather than to a caste or community. This term may also refer to the point of production of a commodity, as indicated in 2.22.9. For custom, see 2.7.2 n.

2.23.1. *Superintendent*: For a study and translation of this chapter, see Thapar 2000, 411–421.

2.23.2. *spinsters* (kanyā): Given that we are dealing with mature and perhaps even older women, it is unlikely that the term *kanyā* here refers to young girls. Here and in sentence 11, the term probably refers to old, unmarried women. The commentary *Cāṇakyaṭīkā* also recognizes the problem and says that these are daughters of poor people (*daridraduhitaraḥ*).

prostitutes and madams: Kangle takes the compound to be a Tatpuruṣa and translates: "mothers of courtesans." I think *mātṛ* here, as elsewhere, has the technical meaning of the madam who runs an establishment of prostitutes, who may indeed be a former prostitute herself and the mother of a current prostitute; see 2.27.5.

female slaves of gods (devadāsī): The reference is probably to women who served in some capacity in temples. At least in later times, such women did engage in sexual activities pertaining to temple duties.

2.23.4–5. *After finding out…festive days*: It is probable that the women did their work in their own homes, as stated in sentence 11, even though some may have worked in the state factories, as stated in sentence 12. The gifts mentioned here and in sentence 8 are probably meant as bonuses to encourage them to work hard, especially because their work is unsupervised. The gifts are given when they produce an exceptional quantity of yarn. Regarding festive days (*tithi*), both Meyer and Kangle think that the Superintendent gets them to work on festive days by giving them gifts. I think this is incorrect; the intention is to get them to work harder all the time by giving them gifts and honors on festive days.

2.23.11. *secluded women*: These are probably upper-class women who are kept within the house. See 3.1.7; 4.13.32. In the *MDh* (8.376–378, 382), the term *guptā* (guarded) is used with a similar meaning.

women whose husbands have gone away: The term *proṣitā*, a judicious amendment by Kangle of the compound *proṣitavidhavā* of the manuscripts, probably stands for a Bahuvrīhi compound such as *proṣitabhartṛkā*, as pointed out by Scharfe (1993, 247; for a discussion of abbreviated compounds, see Gonda 1968). These are women who have to support themselves because their husbands have gone abroad without providing for their support; see *AŚ* 3.4.37. *MDh* 9.74–75 is explicit: "A man should provide for his wife before he goes away on business, for even a steadfast woman will go astray when starved for a livelihood. If he provides for her before going away, she should live a life of restraint; but if he leaves without providing for her, she may maintain herself by engaging in respectable crafts."

to carry out work…female slaves: The meaning is that these women remain in their own homes, and raw material for their work is sent by the Superintendent through his female slaves (perhaps the term *dāsī* here may simply refer to low-level indentured servants) to their homes. Kangle observes that this discussion should have come immediately after sentence 6 dealing with women textile workers. This is an indication that this section on women (2.23.11–15) may have its origin in another source.

2.23.15. *thumb-pinch*: The meaning of *aṅguṣṭhasaṃdaṃśa* is unclear. Both Meyer and Kangle take the expression to mean that the thumb and forefinger or middle finger are cut off. However, the term used for the cutting of limbs as punishment is *chedana* (e.g., 4.10.1–2), while here the verb *dāpayet* is used, which most frequently refers to the administering of a fine or penalty. Harihara Sastri (2011, 67) interprets the words of the commentary *Cāṇakyaṭīkā* to mean that she is pinched hard with the thumb and forefinger so as to cause intense pain. This seems more in keeping with the offense, cutting limbs being reserved for much more serious crimes. The word *saṃdaṃśa* refers to the act of pinching as with a pair of tongs, that is, with the thumb and forefinger; see *Mitākṣarā* on *YDh* 2.274.

accused of squander and theft: The compound *bhakṣitāpahṛtāvaskandita* is difficult to interpret. Meyer takes the three as separate situations: when anything is used up, stolen, or deliberately ruined. Kangle translates: "those who have misappropriated or stolen and then run away." I take *avaskandita* in the legal sense of being either accused or convicted.

2.24.1. *Agriculture*: The meaning of *sītā*, literally a furrow made by a plow, has been subject to dispute. At 2.15.2, it appears to refer to agricultural produce, while at 6.1.8, it clearly refers to land. Being a metonym, it probably had a wide semantic compass and stressed a particular aspect of agriculture in any given context. There has also been an argument among scholars whether the term referred specifically to agricultural land owned and operated by the state or to agricultural land in general. At least within the context of the Superintendent of Agriculture, the term probably had a restrictive meaning, referring to land owned by the king. For a detailed study of *sītā*, see Scharfe 1993, 240–246. For a translation and study of this chapter, see Wojtilla 2005.

geometry: The readings here is uncertain. Jolly reads *gulma* (shrub), and this reading is endorsed by Wojtilla (2005, 415), who comments that Kangle's reading of *śulba* has no manuscript support (in a personal communication, however, Wojtilla now supports Kangle's reading). This is, however, not the case; Kangle's manuscripts, as well as the Gaṇapati Śāstrī edition, have *śulba*, which is also the *lectio difficilior*. See the same word at 2.12.1 with regard to the Superintendent of Mines, who, like the Superintendent of Agriculture, needed to have some knowledge of how to survey the land (see 2.12.1 n.). The meaning of the term in these two contexts is likewise unclear. Given the work that these two officials have to undertake, it must refer both to the measuring and surveying of the land and to evaluations of land suitable for various kinds of agricultural and mining activities. In the context of mines, it may have the meaning of detecting hidden deposits of ores; we have an enumeration of such signs at 2.12.2–7. Kangle (III, 182) translates the term as geology, and the term probably encompasses some aspects of geology.

2.24.3. *hampered*: The idea is that the lack of any of the items listed would cause delays to the activities of agricultural workers. The Superintendent has to make sure that the infrastructure of agriculture is maintained.

hunters: The meaning of *medaka* is unknown; it is a hapax in the *AŚ*. The Malayalam commentary gives the meaning of "basketmaker," which is followed by Kangle. Meyer, taking a clue from *MDh* 10.48, where

Meda refers to a hunting caste, thinks that the term may refer to people employed to keep wild animals away from agricultural land, paralleling the snake catchers. Wojtilla (2005, 416) follows Meyer, and I think this is the best option, although the meaning is far from certain.

2.24.5. *dry regions, wet regions*: For a detailed discussion of the regions designated as *jāṅgala* (dry) and *ānūpa* (wet), see Zimmerman 1987, 25–30.

Droṇas: The rainfall measurements given here are according to volume. Kangle, calculating one Droṇa as being 511 cubic inches, gives the rainfall for dry regions (16 Droṇas) as 32 inches (81.28 cms) if the rain gauge is cylindrical, and 25 inches (63.5 cms) if the mouth is square. This is calculated on the basis of a rain gauge with an 18-inch (one Aratni) diameter; see 2.5.7 where this dimension of a rain gauge is given. Since the rain gauge there is called *kuṇḍa* (pot or urn), it is unlikely that the gauge was square. According to Balkundi (1998), on the other hand, the gauge was about 38 centimeters wide and 13 centimeters deep. When the gauge was full, it would contain one Āḍhaka of water. He calculates a rainfall of 83.2 centimeters for Aśmaka and 147.2 centimeters for Avantī.

Aśmaka: The commentator Bhaṭṭasvāmin identifies this region as Mahārāṣṭra, while Wojtilla (2005, 417) identifies it as the modern Marathwada, and Balkundi (1998) as northern inland Maharashtra. See Introduction, p. 37.

Avanti: the area of modern Madhya Pradesh.

Aparānta: Konkan and the coastal regions of Maharashtra.

unlimited amount: The idea appears to be that it rains so much in these regions that it is unnecessary to calculate the rainfall. Balkundi (1998) thinks it is beyond measurement, but that is probably incorrect. Water in irrigated areas also does not need to be measured, because a constant supply of water at the appropriate times would be available for the crops.

2.24.6. *first and the last month, middle two months*: The reference here is to the Indian monsoon season, which is defined as consisting of four months.

excellent year (suṣamā): Clearly, the reference is to agricultural productivity. Already in the *ŚB* (3.2.1.30), the term *suṣamā* is used with reference to cultivation and the abundance of the harvest in a good year.

2.24.7. *Its*: The referent is unclear, which is not unusual in Sanskrit. The prognostication probably refers to whether the coming year is going to be good, mediocre, or bad.

2.24.7–8. *position... will be rain*: These are astrological prognostications about the upcoming agricultural season. The term "impregnation" may be related to the belief that the clouds are seeded and produce an embryo, the birth of clouds and the resultant rain being compared to the gestation of a fetus. For a longer commentary on these astrological events, see Varāhamihira's *Bṛhatsaṃhitā*, 21–23; Wojtilla 2005, 417.

2.24.9. *Three periods... sixty days*: Literally, the numbers in this verse refer to the clouds, but it makes no sense to talk about three clouds or 80 clouds raining. None of the translators appear to note the anomaly of talking about the number of clouds. Generally, on a rainy day, one would not be able to count individual clouds. The meaning clearly is that clouds rain for that many days or periods. Kangle and Wojtilla (2005, 417) refer to the discrepancy between 2.24.6, where the rains last for four lunar months (112 days) and this statement, where rain lasts for 161 days. Perhaps, as the mention of three crops in the next verse hints at, the rains in this verse refer to the whole year. It is also probable that the verses derive from a source different from the prose.

2.24.10. *three periods for plowing*: Along with some manuscripts, as well as Meyer and Wojtilla (2005, 418), I adopt the reading *karṣakān* in place of Kangle's *karīṣān*, according to which the translation would be "proving three periods for preparing cow-dung patties." The verse makes clear that we are dealing with regions with sufficient rainfall throughout the year to allow three crops to be planted.

2.24.12–14. *first to be sowed... last to be sowed*: This refers to the three seasons for planting crops. The first is probably the monsoon crops, mostly wet agriculture such as rice, that are harvested in the autumn; the second is the autumn crop, harvested in the spring; and the third is the spring crop, harvested in the summer (2.24.19). See Medhātithi's commentary on *MDh* 7.182 for the two crops harvested in the autumn and the spring.

2.24.15. *Alternatively*: Kangle sees the insertion of *vā* ("or") as unnecessary, because the previous three statements recorded the sowing of various grains in accordance with the seasons. It is likely, however, that 2.24.12–14 was a gloss that found its way into the text. The alternative proposed in this sentence is made with reference to 2.24.11, where the sowing of different grains was proposed dependent on the region and the rainfall.

2.24.17. *They*: The reference here is to sharecroppers mentioned in the previous sentence and perhaps to other farmers to whom concessions had been given to bring virgin land under cultivation. The person to whom the shares are given, of course, is the king.

uncultivated (anavasita): This term refers to a field that has never been cultivated or left fallow for a while, or to a house or land that has been left unoccupied or unattended (see 3.16.31; 7.11.1). See 2.1 for settling new land.

time of adversity: It is unclear who is suffering from adversity. The king may suspend this concession when he is in financial trouble, or he may permit the farmers to keep the full harvest when they are in distress.

2.24.18. *They*: The reference here is to both the sharecroppers of 2.24.16 and farmers who have brought virgin land under cultivation. Here, I think, the author moves to another topic, the cultivation of irrigated land. The previous section (2.24.1–17) dealt with land that required rainfall, what is referred to as *devamātṛka* (land depending on the gods to bring rains); irrigated land is called *adevamātṛka* (land not so dependent; see 5.2.2; 6.1.8). I think much of the confusion in previous translations can be eliminated if we treat these two sections as dealing with different agricultural methods. Thus, the statement at 2.24.19 (which parallels 2.24.11–15) makes sense, because winter, summer, and rainy-season crops may be planted any time in irrigated fields, at least in most regions of India not subject to intense cold in the winter.

share: Given that we are dealing here also with sharecroppers and farmers working virgin land, these shares of the harvest must have been larger than what they would normally give if there was no irrigation. For public and private construction of irrigation projects, see 2.1.20–24; 3.9.32, 34. For constructing such irrigation works and for rehabilitating ones that have broken down, tax exemptions are extended: see 3.9.33. Meyer and Wojtilla (2005), however, think that the share given to the state is in water; the farmer would give the state, presumably for use on state farmland, a portion of the water he draws. I think this is unlikely, especially because this would imply that state farmland is always available within reach of every water source that farmers would tap for irrigation. If we take these provisions as not applying to all the farmers with irrigation facilities in general, but only to those who are either sharecroppers or have been given virgin land at concessional rates of taxation for farming, then many of the perceived difficulties with this passage disappear.

raised by hand operation... mechanical device: Although the Sanskrit is cryptic, the meaning appears to be that water is raised from an irrigation work through a device operated by hand, or by animals to whose shoulders (*skandha*) it is tied, or else through the power of a water current. The term *skandha* refers not just to the shoulders but to the front of the back below the neck and between the shoulders (front torso in the case of an animal). See Olivelle 1996.

one-fourth... well (caturthaṃ nadīsarastaṭākakūpodghāṭam): This is probably a gloss that found its way into the text. The wording of this phrase is quite different from the preceding, with the problematic word *udghāṭa* being used in place of the *prāvartima* of the previous phrase, and the amount (*caturtham*) coming at the beginning of the phrase, repeating the same amount given earlier, and breaking the gradual progression to higher levels of taxation.

2.24.19. *plant* (sthāpayet): Kangle's translation "he should decide on" is misplaced. Bhaṭṭasvāmin and Gaṇapati Śāstrī take the term to mean *vāpayet* ("he should sow"), and the same term is used in the sense of planting at 2.24.23 (Wojtilla 2005, 420). Perhaps the reference is to planting seedlings and cuttings.

irrigation water (karmodaka): Given that this section deals with irrigated fields (2.24.18 n.), I think the term *karma* in the compound refers to the mode of procuring water through labor (see also 3.10.1). Thus, the kind of crop to be planted is dependent less on the season than on the amount of irrigation water available. Kangle translates: "According to the amount of water (available) for the work," followed by Wojtilla (2005, 420); and Meyer, taking the compound as a Dvandva, translates: "Nach Maßgabe der Arbeitskraft und des Wasservorrates." For crops grown near irrigation works, see 2.6.5.

2.24.21. *beset with…expenditure*: For the disease called *mañjeṭṭhikā* (red rot), see Hinüber 1971, 98. Sugarcane cultivation was apparently expensive, requiring processing after the harvest. This passage indicates that the return on investment was less in the case of sugarcane than in the case of rice, grains, and vegetables. For a study of sugar in ancient India, see Gopal 1964; his conclusions on sugar and sugarcane in the *AŚ*, however, are not always accurate.

2.24.23. *herbs* (oṣadhī): Wojtilla (2005, 421) takes this term to refer specifically to medicinal plants. Although the term may include such plants, it appears to have a broader signification here, in contrast to grain crops (*sasya*) of sentence 19.

2.24.24. *the hole…proper time*: For the activities and rites relating to the planting and nurturing of fruit trees, see Das 1988, where Surapāla's *Vṛkṣāyurveda* has been edited and translated. Verse 67 of this text recommends that the hole dug for the tree be left for some time so that it can become dry, and then it is filled with cow's bones and dung and burnt. Fruit-bearing and flowering trees are compared to young women, and like them, trees also undergo pregnancy longings. Ceremonies are carried out to address such longings of trees (see Das 1988, 42, 248f). Das (1988, 466–471) has also edited a text called *Vṛkṣadohadaprakāra*, which gives details of how the pregnancy longings of trees can be satisfied.

2.24.25. *fresh acrid fish*: There is a problem with the accusative reading *aśuṣkakaṭumatsyān* and the placing of *ca* ("and") after it. As it stands, the verb *pāyayet* (lit., "he should make them drink") should govern both accusatives, the fish and the sprouts. I have followed the suggestion of Meyer and taken the compound to be instrumental: *aśuṣkakaṭumatsyaiḥ*. It is unclear whether this application is intended to be manure. As Wojtilla (2005, 422) suggests, it may have been some sort of chemical protection against parasites. See Gopal 1980, 99, who takes this passage as the earliest reference to manure.

2.24.26. *He should…smoke*: Although unstated, the cotton seeds and the slough are supposed to be burnt. Wojtilla (2005, 422) notes that cotton seeds contain oil that produces a quick and strong fire. Why snakes would run away from such a fire is unclear, and Wojtilla makes a good case for considering this verse as referring to a magical ritual against snakes. It appears that this passage and the next one on the rite of sowing have been imported into the text, which is generally oriented toward practical matters.

2.24.27. *Prajāpati... Deva*: I follow Wojtilla (2005, 422) in taking the three as three separate divinities. The *ca* ("and") after *devāya* makes this interpretation more likely. I also think that Wojtilla is right in considering *deva* here as referring to Indra (see 2.3.13 n.). The three appear to be the divine patrons of agriculture, with a text on agriculture being ascribed to Kāśyapa.

Sītā: This term, as we see in the very name of *sītādhyakṣa*, refers to the plow furrows and broadly to agriculture. Here she is personified as a goddess who would grow strong with the growth of the seeds.

2.24.28. *those who guard... cattle*: This phrase is cryptic, and the meaning is unclear. I take *vāṭa* as shorthand for *puṣpaphalavāṭa* (flower gardens and orchards), as seen at 2.4.25; 2.6.5; 2.28.27. It is unclear whether the cow (*go*) in the compound should be treated separately, as I have done, or whether *gopāla* should be taken simply as a watchman (as Meyer does). I have followed Kangle and Wojtilla (2005, 423).

2.24.29. *artisans* (kāru): Wojtilla (2005, 424) takes the term to mean laborer. I am not convinced, because generally *karmakara* is used with this meaning, as in the preceding sentence. Often (as at *AŚ* 5.3.16 and *MDh* 7.138), *kāru* is compounded with *śilpin*, meaning artisans and craftsmen.

2.24.30. *those who live by gleaning*: These are special kinds of ascetics whose name is derived from the manner in which they obtain their food; see Olivelle 1993, 162–170.

at the bottom of heaps: The meaning appears to be that, when harvested grain stalks are stacked up before they are taken to the threshing floor, some grains would fall to the bottom of the heaps and remain there when the stalks are transported.

2.24.32. *From the mounds... flimsy*: The verse is unclear. Kangle takes it as referring to a granary with walls and roofs. However, that is inappropriate given the context; we are still dealing with the transportation of grain stacks to the threshing floor. Kangle's reading *prākārāṇāṃ* should be changed to *prakarāṇāṃ*, as attested to in the next verse and by the commentators.

2.24.33. *circle*: This refers to the circle formed by the bulls or buffaloes going around the central pole and threshing the grain stalks on the floor with their hoofs. A threshing compound would therefore be a round structure.

2.25.1. *traders... ferment*: Kangle takes *tajjāta* to mean "born to that work." This expression, however, is used frequently in book 2 (5.8; 11.1; 12.1; 18.1; 22.5; 23.1, 10), and it refers to expertise in various occupations. I also think that the expression *tajjātasurākiṇvavyavahāribhiḥ* is corrupt; the repetition of *surā* and *kiṇva* is unnecessary and not found in parallel passages. I feel that these two terms may have been a gloss on *tajjāta* that found its way into the text.

2.25.6. *With the intention…source of income*: The insertion of this passage here is curious. Unless we assume that the man has used stolen property to pay for liquor, this passage has nothing to do with liquor.

2.25.10. *stimulating drink* (pratipāna): For such stimulating drinks given to animals, especially horses and elephants, see 2.29.43; 2.30.9, 18; 2.31.6, 13.

2.25.11. *many rooms…seats*: It appears that the taverns described here, like the inns and public houses of England, were both drinking houses and inns where people could spend a night.

advertise drinking: The compound *pānoddeśāni* must be a Bahuvrīhi qualifying the taverns, just like all the other terms in this sentence. I do not think Kangle is correct in taking it to be a separate noun and translating "(and) drinking bars." Perhaps *uddeśa* refers to a sign placed outside taverns advertising it as a drinking establishment; see *MDh* 9.237.

2.25.14. *traders*: Here and in the subsequent passages, this term refers to the people running the taverns.

2.25.16. *Medaka…Madhu*: The identity of these kinds of liquor is uncertain. From the descriptions given below, it appears that Medaka was a rice wine. Prasannā was also a grain liquor fermented with areca nut. Āsava was a sweet liquor made with wood apple, treacle, and honey, while Ariṣṭa of various kinds were decoctions used for medicinal purposes. Maireya was also a fruit liquor, while Madhu was grape wine. It does not appear that any of these liquors were distilled.

2.25.18. *mélange*: The term *saṃbhāra* is distinguished from *yoga*, which refers to the mixture of all the ingredients that is left to ferment into liquor. The former term, which I have translated as mélange to distinguish it from the latter, appears to be some form of mixture used as a fermenting agent that is specific to each kind of liquor. The manufacture of *saṃbhāra* is described in sentences 27–29.

2.25.22. *three fruits*: Meyer presents the options of three varieties of myrobalan, or nutmeg, arecanut, and clove. Sadhale (1996, 94), however, identifies the three fruits as the three kinds of myrobalan: *Terminalia chebula* (Harītakī), *Terminalia bellirica* (Bibhītaka), and *Phyllanthus emblica* or *Emblica officinalis* (Āmalaka, the Indian gooseberry). A mixture of these is used in Āyurvedic medicine.

2.25.25. *The explanation…origin*: This is a sentence with a strange syntax, although the meaning is clear. Kapiśa has been identified with an area around Kabul in Afghanistan, while Hārahūra may be a name of a people or region in the northwest of the subcontinent; see Kangle's note and

Scharfe 1993, 279. Its connection to the Hūnas has been disproven by Trautmann (1971, 183–184).

2.25.30. *seed* (bīja): The meaning is obscure. Kangle explains that this mixture is to be added as essence in the preparation of Āsava liquor as described in sentence 19. It appears to be some sort of seed for starting the fermenting process.

2.25.31. *Surā-liquor*: The author appears here to move to a discussion of a kind of liquor called Surā. It is, however, difficult to discern when Surā is used as a generic term for liquor and when it is used for a specific kind of liquor. The commentator of Manu, Kullūka (on *MDh* 11.96), cites a verse from Pulastya that lists 11 types of *madya*, and calls the 12th, *surā*, the worst kind of intoxicant.

2.25.33. *closed fistful* (antarnakho muṣṭiḥ): Literally, this means a closed fist where the nails of the fingers are invisible because they are pressed against the palm. This appears to contrast with an open fistful, which would hold a lot more of the substance.

2.25.36. *liquor license* (saurika): It is unclear what this license permitted: manufacture or sale or transportation. Manufacture appears to be certain, because it is mentioned in the previous sentence.

2.25.39–40. *Those dealing... customary*: There is a difference of opinion with regard to the syntax of this passage. Kangle takes the entire sentence 39 as forming a single syntactic whole; so the traders should pay 5 percent on the kinds of liquor enumerated. I follow Meyer and Shamasastry in taking the section "And with regard... Āmlasīdhu" as an introduction in prose to the verse. The commodities not controlled by the king must refer to various kinds of alcoholic beverages.

2.26.1. *householders... sanctuaries*: Why the householders are dealt with more leniently is unclear. Kangle thinks that it is because they kill the animals for their own use rather than for sale; but this is not indicated in the text. Perhaps the locative *parigraheṣu* is significant; this term generally signifies areas that are enclosed or fenced off. Bhaṭṭasvāmin takes *parigraha* to mean fields adjacent to the sanctuaries. If that is the case, then the householders may be killing these animals when they come onto their property. These enclosures may also be within the sanctuaries, and in that case, these householders may be living in designated and fenced-off areas of these animal preserves (see 2.6.6).

2.26.2. *not recognized* (apravr̥tta): The meaning is unclear. Perhaps it refers to animals whose killing is not generally recognized. Bhaṭṭasvāmin glosses *apravr̥tta* with *aprasiddha*, "not well known." Kangle and Scharfe (1993, 254) translate it as "not current." These animals are obviously outside the game sanctuaries. For a comparison between these provisions for animal protection and the prohibitions in the Aśokan inscriptions, see Scharfe 1993, 253–257.

2.26.3. *as also*: The particle *vā* in these clauses is problematic. Perhaps, as Kangle says, the original was *ca*. But quite often *vā* is interpreted by commentators as having the meaning of *ca*: *cārthe vā*.

duty: The amount of this duty is left unstated. On animals, the duty at 2.22.7 is one-twentieth or one-twenty-fifth.

2.26.4. *that are alive*: The assumption is that some of the animals collected by the state as its share are alive. Some of these are to be released into animal sanctuaries, possibly to replenish their animal populations. Fish and farm animals are excluded, perhaps because they would be generally dead by the time the state collects its due.

2.26.7. *They*: Although butchers and meat sellers have not been introduced in the discussion so far, it appears that the implicit subject of this sentence is precisely such traders.

2.26.8. *compensation* (pratipāta): See also 5.2.12 for the use of this same technical term. The compensation is for the loss suffered by the buyer, but it is not made clear to whom the compensation is paid—to the actual buyer or to the state or both? The provision in sentence 9, however, is more of a punishment and was collected probably by the Superintendent of Abattoirs.

2.26.12. *missing its head, feet, or bones*: The probable reason for their display is to confirm the identity of the meat being sold to the public.

2.26.14. *fish* (matsya): This category probably includes, besides fish, other aquatic creatures within animal sanctuaries.

2.27.1. *as a courtesan . . . establishment*: It appears that the 1,000 Paṇas are given to set up the home of the courtesan; thus, in sentence 11, we gather that her ornaments belonged to the state. The term used here, *gaṇikā*, appears to refer to high-class courtesans employed by the state, as opposed to common prostitutes, whom the *AŚ* calls *rūpājīvī* (1.20.20; 2.23.2; 2.27.27; 2.36.8) and twice *veśyā* (2.6.2; 5.3.47). The high position and education of courtesans are also indicated by the fact that in Sanskrit dramas, they often speak Sanskrit, while other women speak a variety of Prakrits. See Sternbach 1951. The alternate or deputy courtesan (*pratigaṇikā*) apparently substituted for the main courtesan when the latter was unable to perform her duties, as stated in the next sentence. She is given half the amount of the main courtesan, that is, 500 Paṇas, to set up her household.

2.27.2. *run away*: The term *niṣpatitā*, as noted by Meyer, most frequently means to flee (3.1.32; 3.4.1). Here, however, it may have a more general meaning of being absent for some reason (Meyer, p. 192, n. 2), although Sternbach's (1951, 28) understanding of going abroad for this term is nowhere attested. Yet, we have the two identical words used at 3.13.8 (*niṣpatitapreta*) in the sense of run away or dead, and the term is used with this meaning further down at sentence 14. Could it be that sometimes courtesans simply ran away to obtain better prospects, as suggested by Meyer? They could have also run away to escape their enslavement (see 2.27.6).

madam: The terms *mātṛ* or *mātṛkā*, meaning literally mother, refer to the older lady overseeing the running of the courtesan establishment or brothel. Often she may well have been the biological mother of the courtesan. However, she could also have been another retired courtesan, as indicated in sentences 5 and 11. That is the reason for my translation of the term as madam. Sternbach (1951, 48, n. 6) glosses the term with procures. In Śūdraka's play *Mṛcchakaṭika* (Act 2), we are also introduced to a *mātṛ* who sends orders to the courtesan Vasantasenā.

2.27.3. *it*: Probably the king takes away the courtesan establishment when those in charge are unable to continue its functions. These establishments were set up and in some way owned by the state.

2.27.4. *According to... chariot*: It is difficult to understand the point of this passage. It appears that certain courtesans were appointed to certain royal functions, for example, to carry the parasol or the fan. It is unclear whether the 1,000 is given to all, or whether the salary is lowered for the lower-ranking ladies. Passages of this chapter are somewhat confusing because they deal with both the courtesans in the service of the king and those who have establishments catering to the general public.

2.27.6. *ransom*: Apparently, a courtesan who enters the service of the state loses her freedom. She can free herself by paying the ransom. This also supports my interpretation of the next sentence, which also deals with a similar type of courtesan. See Sternbach 1951, 37.

2.27.7. *From the age... king*: The meaning is probably that these young boys, the sons of royal courtesans, are trained to become performers (*kuśīlava*). They are listed in the state payroll at 5.3.15. On these performers and entertainers, see Introduction, p. 13.

2.27.8. *courtesan who is a slave*: With Meyer, I take *gaṇikā dāsī* as two separate words in apposition; thus, the provision applies to a courtesan who is a female slave, as indicated in the previous sentence. Kangle, along with the commentators Bhaṭṭasvāmin and Gaṇapati Śāstrī, takes the two words as a Tatpuruṣa compound: "a female slave of a courtesan." This seems unlikely, as this chapter does not deal with such a slave anywhere else, and it seems odd that that topic is introduced here.

2.27.9. *If she refuses... Paṇas*: If the courtesan refuses to do these menial jobs, she is forced to pay a monthly wage. To whom it is paid is left unstated. Kangle is probably right in thinking that she has to pay another woman to carry out the work she was assigned to do, given that the amount is a wage, rather than a penalty or fine.

2.27.10. *profit* (āyati): See the use of this term, which often means income, in the sense of profit at 2.16.12. Here I follow Meyer (148, n. 1; 194, n. 2).

2.27.11–12. *ornaments, belongings*: As Sternbach (1951, 39) has pointed out, this provision does not refer to the personal property of a courtesan; her personal property was subject to inheritance, as seen in the case of Vasantasenā, in the drama *Mṛcchakaṭikā*, who is able to pawn her jewelry. According to Sternbach, the reference here is to ornaments and belongings given by the state to the courtesan.

2.27.12. *verbal abuse . . . half Paṇas*: In Kangle's edition, this passage is given as the continuation of the first half of sentence 12. Kangle thinks that these offenses are committed by the courtesan against her customers; this is also the interpretation of the commentators and Shamasastry. Meyer takes the opposite view, stating that these offenses were perpetrated on the courtesan by her clients. Sternbach (1951, 43) dismisses Meyer's interpretation, especially because the cutting of the courtesan's ear carries a low fine, while ruining the beauty of a courtesan at sentence 14 draws a fine of 1,000. However, such an argument can work both ways: Would such a low fine be tolerated if a client's ear was cut off by the courtesan? I think we should locate these three offenses within the context of sexual activities, maybe sometimes violent sex. Within that context, one can interpret *karṇacchedana* as not cutting off the ear but ripping the ear, perhaps by pulling on the earrings. Violence on the part of the courtesan is dealt with in sentence 22. I think with the current passage, the text turns to offenses committed against courtesans and prostitutes by their clients. This passage continues through sentences 13–17. Nevertheless, this passage sits uncomfortably within the text and was probably imported here from a gloss. Note that the fine is placed first and the offense last in this passage, whereas in the surrounding text, the reverse is true. The reasons for two separate fines in the case of cutting the ear (50 and one-quarter, and one and a half) are unclear. Kane thinks that the large fine goes to the state, while the smaller amount goes to the Superintendent. He also thinks that the smaller amount may be for medical expenses.

2.27.13. *unwilling woman or a young girl*: The presence of *vā* (or) after the second word (*akāmāyāḥ kumāryā vā*) makes it more likely that we are dealing with here two different individuals. Ignoring the *vā*, Kangle translates "a maiden who is unwilling." The situation probably involves young and sexually immature girls within a brothel, girls who may be daughters of the courtesans. Sex with them is an offense irrespective of consent (Sternbach 1951, 44).

2.27.16. *attained high rank* (prāptādhikārām): Kangle and Shamasastry take the expression to mean that the prostitute has been officially appointed. But as Sternbach (1951, 44) points out, all the courtesans dealt with in this chapter are so appointed. He follows Meyer in taking the expression to mean that the courtesan was murdered after she had reached her favorite place of rendezvous. I am not sure how one can get that meaning from *adhikāra*. Clearly, the murder here is not of any prostitute; if that were the case, the qualification is unnecessary. I have taken *adhikāra* here to mean high rank or status. That is the reason for the heavy fine.

2.27.17. *beauty-slave* (rūpadāsī): The meaning of this term is unclear. Kangle takes her to be a slave living by her beauty, thus identical to *rūpājīvā* (2.27.27). Meyer also takes her to be a lower form of prostitute who is, however, in the service of the king. Sternbach (1951, 45) takes her to be "a prostitute of lower degree, who was a maid of a *gaṇikā* and belonged to her retinue." Someone like that is probably what is meant.

2.27.18. *primary fine*: That is, the fines that were given in the above passages.

2.27.21. *residency*: The term *vasati* indicates a longer period of living together than a normal sexual encounter. Either the courtesan may have gone to the customer's house for an extended period of time, or the customer may have spent some time, perhaps overnight, in the brothel.

2.27.25. *dramatic storytellers*: For the meaning of the term *saubhika* (or *śaubhika*), see Lüders 1940a. These were professional storytellers who used various kinds of props, perhaps paintings, to illustrate their stories. For such entertainers, see Introduction, p. 13.

2.27.27. *twice their sex fee*: The probable meaning is that she pays the fee for a single sexual encounter as her monthly fee to the Superintendent of Courtesans.

2.27.30. *their*: The antecedent of this pronoun is left unstated. If the verse has been imported from a different context, then the antecedent is untraceable. Within the current context, the most obvious candidate would be the sons of courtesans who have become leaders among actors and dancers.

2.28.2. *villagers*: In the *AŚ* usage, the term *grāmāḥ* in the plural may refer to villages or to inhabitants of villages. It is often difficult to determine which of these is meant. I think here and in several other contexts that refer to actions by individuals, the reference is to villagers or village officials (4.4.4) rather than to villages (see 2.28.17, 24; 3.10.3; 4.3.3, 6).

2.28.3, 5. *boat fee*: The reading of the Sanskrit term for fee is unclear. Kangle's edition gives *bhāṭaka*, but Scharfe (1993, 7) has pointed out that Kangle depends on the Malayalam commentary for this reading. Yet that commentary on this chapter is missing, as Kangle himself admits. So he is depending on the text of the *AŚ* given in the printed version of this commentary, and that is simply a reprint of Gaṇapati Śāstrī's edition. So here Kangle is simply following Gaṇapati Sāstrī's conjecture. The term *hāṭaka* of the manuscripts is found elsewhere as a name of a place (2.13.3) and a kind of weapon (2.18.7; 9.2.26), neither of which fits the context here. It is plausible that it means some sort of fee or rent for boats owned by the state, because in sentence 5, using their own boats is given as an alternative to paying this fee. Professor Wezler (personal communication) has suggested that this may be a vernacular term used by boatsmen and that it may be connected to the Sanskrit *kṛtaka*, that is, "that which is taken" for the boat.

2.28.6. *What pertains... Mines*: This statement is problematic. The only passage to deal with the Superintendent of Pit Mines (*khanyadhyakṣa*) is a single sentence at 2.12.27. It is unlikely that the author is referring his reader here to that single statement. Perhaps this indicates that there are missing sections of the *AŚ*. There is also an issue of the two words *khani* and *ākara* used for mines (see Introduction, p. 12; Olivelle 2012a). The latter term is found infrequently (altogether 12 times), and seven of those occur just in 2.12–13. Perhaps there is here old and new nomenclature being used, creating confusion. The reference may well be to 2.12.

2.28.7. *customs of ports... Ports*: Both Shamasastry and Meyer see two provisions that the Superintendent of Shipping must uphold: customs of the port (*paṇyapattanacāritra*) and the orders of the Superintendent of Ports (*pattanādhyakṣanibaddha*). I think Kangle is correct in taking this as a single provision, the latter simply qualifying the former. However, I think he is incorrect in translating *nibaddha* as fixed, thus requiring him to translate *cāritra* as regulations. The terms *nibaddha* and *nibandha* are regularly used in the *AŚ* to mean writing down; see the requirement of writing down the customs of localities at 2.7.2. I think the Superintendent of Shipping is here instructed to make sure that the local customs (i.e., rules) of ports, as written down by the Superintendent of Ports, are not violated by boatsmen.

2.28.8. *he*: The antecedent of this pronoun is unclear, especially because two superintendents are mentioned in the previous sentence. The likely candidate, however, is the Superintendent of Shipping.

2.28.12. *approaching*: The manuscripts read *atigāḥ* ("going beyond, transgressing," found only at 3.4.3, 6; 14.3.25), which is probably an incorrect reading for *abhigāḥ* ("approaching"), which better fits the context.

2.28.13. *operator of cutters and ropes* (dātraraśmigrāhaka): First, it is unclear whether this compound refers to one or two people. Commentators think there are two in charge of cutters and ropes. Meyer takes this as referring to a hook and rope, that is, the anchor. What *dātra* or cutter refers to is unclear, and I think there is much to commend Meyer's interpretation, even though Kangle dismisses it.

2.28.20. *incendiary mixture* (agniyoga): For the use of such incendiary devices within military contexts, see 12.5.46; 13.4.14–21.

2.28.21. *Bhāra*: The weight is 20 Tulās. Taking a Tulā to be 100 Palas or about 37 kilograms, the load here would be about 740 kilograms.

a quarter: probably a quarter Paṇa, which would be 16 Māṣakas, or over twice the charge for a wagon.

2.28.22. *Bhāra of wares*: How the term *bhāṇḍa* used here differs from *paṇya* (commodities, merchandise) used in the previous sentence is unclear. Kangle thinks the *bhāṇḍa* refers to noncommercial goods, and that is plausible. The distinction also could be between *paṇya* as grain and other similar merchandise and *bhāṇḍa* as wares or manufactured products such as pots and pans. In any case, the charges for both kinds are identical.

2.28.24. *pay…wages*: Kangle thinks that the payment is made to the ferrymen. The fixed tax (*kḷpta*) that a community pays is recorded elsewhere as well (2.6.10; 2.28.2).

2.28.26. *shall be liable*: Kangle has emended the manuscript reading *abhyābhavet* to *abhyāvahet* here and at 2.29.14; 3.12.2, 4, 5, 19, 20, 23; 4.1.6; 4.13.23, saying that he is following the Malayalam commentary. Actually, this emendation was introduced by Gaṇapati Śāstrī. Kangle, however, maintains the manuscript reading of *abhyābhaveyuḥ* at 3.9.1. Harihara Sastri (1956–1957, 108) has shown that this emendation is unnecessary and is not based on the Malayalam commentary, and that this technical term corresponds to *ābhavet* in *NSm* 1.15; 6.20, 23. The meaning is that someone is responsible or liable for something, or that someone has a particular privilege, as at 3.9.1.

2.28.27. *A ferry…daily revenue*: This verse has a difficult syntax, and the translation is an approximation. The readings are also probably corrupt. I follow Kangle's emendation *kārmikaḥ pratyayaṃ* in place of *kārmikapratyayaṃ*.

2.29.1. *the impaired and discharged*: The expression *bhagnotsṛṣṭakam* (and *bhagnotsṛṣṭa*) refers to animals and facilities (e.g., irrigation works) that are no longer useful and have been abandoned. In the specific case of herd animals, the reference is to animals that cannot be kept with the normal herd and have been separated from it. As indicated in 2.29.6, such animals are given to herdsmen for a larger share of the proceeds. This expression occurs with reference to dikes (3.9.33; 3.10.2; 4.11.17) and a traveler who is robbed (3.12.19).

2.29.5. *Every year…skin with the brand*: Kangle estimates eight Vārakas to be about 19 gallons. According to the estimate of sentence 35 below, 19 gallons of ghee would require about 307 gallons of milk. Given that there are 20 milk cows in the herd, this would amount to about 15 and one-half gallons per cow, which Kangle estimates to be about two to three weeks' milk from each cow. Meyer thinks that this is too little and thinks the amount of ghee should be 800 Vārakas. Kangle counters that this would leave little or nothing for the cowherd. One must also remember that the herder gives one Paṇa per head totaling 100 Paṇas, which is a considerable amount of money. The statement about the skin with the brand must refer to animals that have died during the previous year while the cowherd was looking after them (2.29.25). A similar provision is given in the *MDh* 8.234: "When animals die, the herdsman should give their owners both ears, skin, tails, bladders, tendons, and yellow bile, and point out their distinguishing marks."

levy and counter-levy (karapratikara): As Kangle observes, these two terms appear to refer to the payment in cash and kind that the herdsman has to pay (levy) and the benefits that he gets from the herd in the form of milk and milk products (counter-levy).

2.29.8, 11. *additional*: The term *upaja*, as Kangle has noted, appears to indicate not just offspring but offspring born while the animals are within the herd. Thus, they constitute additions to the herd that the cowherd should record. For the use of this term in the context of revenue, see 2.6.22 n.

2.29.11. *features between its horns*: Kangle translates "the peculiarity of the horns," which is unlikely given that we are talking about young calves. Here the term *horn* may be used broadly to indicate the area of the head where the horns would be. Generally there would be peculiarities of color and hair formation in this area of the forehead.

2.29.13. *as a result of water or food*: The Malayalam commentary takes this to be defects in water or food, for example, poisonous water or food. It is less likely to mean the lack of water or food, because the cowherd is supposed to take care of such necessities.

2.29.14. *They*: The probable referents are the individuals listed in sentences 2–3 above.

2.29.17. *switches*: The idea seems to be that the cowherd passes off animals belonging to others as royal cattle by branding them with the royal brand. Kangle thinks that the other animals may be of inferior quality. This may be because of theft, or to escape the fines for losing a royal animal.

2.29.18–19. *A man...another country*: The exact meaning of these provisions is unclear. I take the first provision to refer to stolen cattle that are still within one's own territory. When the cattle have been taken outside one's own jurisdiction, a larger payment has to be made. I think Johnston (1936) is mistaken in thinking that the first provision refers to cattle taken outside one's jurisdiction, and the second to those that are stolen and brought into one's jurisdiction. If the cattle are within one's own state, one would not have to pay such a large amount to the rescuer.

2.29.27. *buttermilk*: This is the normal meaning of the term *udaśvit*, but it is unlikely that such a valuable drink would be given to animals. In this context, it must mean some kind of waste by-product of curd-making.

2.29.30. *One who sells...per animal*: The meaning is unclear. If it is the sale of an animal from the royal herd, the levy seems inappropriate. If it is a fine for unauthorized sale, it seems too low. As Kangle notes, this is either a levy on the private sale of animals (a sort of a sales tax) or a tax on the sale of a butchered animal.

2.29.31. *both times*: morning and evening.

2.29.34. *explains*: The meaning appears to be that a keeper of the herd who fails to do these things at their proper times is fined an amount equivalent to the loss that such a failure would cause.

2.29.38. *gets*: The Sanskrit causative here is ambiguous. It may mean that the herdsman deliberately gets the two bulls to fight (a sort of bullfight) or that through negligence he lets them fight, which appears more likely.

2.29.39. *according to class*: The meaning appears to be that the different animals—milk cows, pregnant cows, calves, etc.—are grouped separately so that they could be more effectively guarded.

2.29.41. *from goats and the like*: I have restored the reading of the manuscripts *ajādīnām*. Kangle has emended this to read *ajāvīnām*, "from goats and sheep."

2.29.43. *load* (bhāra): The normal weight of a *bhāra* is 20 Tulās, that is, about 91 kilograms; half of that would be around 45 kilograms. Given that this is clearly too much, Meyer suggests taking a load to be an armful. It is, however, unclear whether these are daily rations or for a longer period of time.

meat (māṃsa): Given the anomaly of meat in the diet of a bullock, Meyer reasonably suggests that the term *māṃsa* here refers to the "meat" or pulp of a fruit. See also B-R V: 687. Edgerton (1931, 26), however, objects to Meyer's interpretation and suggests that meat was actually fed to herbivorous animals, including elephants, in ancient India. But all his information comes from texts that simply use the term *māṃsa* and thus do not add any further support to his thesis.

liquor: For the practice of giving liquor to animals, including horses and elephants, in ancient India, see Bloomfield 1920, 336–339; Edgerton 1931, 26.

2.30.3. *collecting...storehouse*: A month in the case of caring for a horse is said to be 35 days (2.20.52). For the distribution of rations for animals by the Superintendent of the Storehouse, see 2.15.50,

2.30.4. *He*: Even though the horsekeeper is mentioned in the previous sentence, the likely subject of this sentence is the superintendent, given that construction of buildings in other chapters is undertaken by a superintendent and not by his subordinates.

monkeys...myna birds: These are for protection against snakes, rats, poisons, and the like; see 1.20.6–8; 2.5.6. Perhaps the intent is that these animals should be within the compound rather than within the stable itself.

2.30.14. *The finest...shank*: Thus, the height of the best horse would be about 1.6 meters or five feet, and its length about 3.2 meters or ten feet.

2.30.18. *ration*: See Scharfe 1989, 194 (note 217) regarding the bad diet fed to Indian horses.

2.30.29. *the best are...Vanāyu*: Scharfe (1989, 194–195) notes the difficulty of horse breeding in the subcontinent and the imperative to import horses from the northwestern territories.

2.30.31. *The military...comprehensive*: Here I follow Meyer. Kangle objects that "military" (*sāṃnāhya*) is predicative, and he translates: "The all-sided work of a horse is (work) connected with war." But the theme here is warfare, and the fact that it is all-encompassing is the comment that describes such activity of a horse. The meaning is that military activities of a horse include all the activities that a horse performs, for example, riding, transportation, pulling carriages and chariots, and the like, that are listed immediately after this sentence.

2.30.33. *upaveṇuka...tūpacālī*: Both the readings and the meanings of the technical terms here and in subsequent passages, clearly derived from an equestrian tradition, are unclear. The commentator Bhaṭṭasvāmin asks the reader to consult technical works on horse science (*śālihotra*), archery (*dharnurveda*), and the like for greater information about these. Without such information, any translation or explanation would be mere guesswork, including those offered by Bhaṭṭasvāmin. As Meyer notes (732f), Mallinātha's commentary on *Śiśupālavadha* (5.4) indicates that some of the gaits given here and in the subsequent sentences may not refer to the gaits of individual horses but of cavalry formations. Meyer's translations of the terms based on their etymologies are educated guesses. Given the uncertainties, I have left the terms untranslated. Kangle reads *aupaveṇuka* and *trikacālī* based, according to him, on the Malayalam commentary, which, however, is missing for this section. Kangle here has simply taken over the emendation of Gaṇapati Śāstrī, whose text is reproduced as the root text of the printed edition of the Malayalam commentary (Scharfe 1993, 7).

2.30.36. *one leap*: Kangle emends the manuscript reading *ekapluta* to *eṇapluta*, again based on the nonexistent Malayalam commentary. I have restored the original reading.

2.30.39. *journey*: This refers to the distance that a horse would travel within a single day. The different distances probably apply to the best, middling, and lowest kinds of horses.

2.30.46. *lustration* (nīrājana): This is a rite performed for war horses and elephants, as well as for warriors. The rite is described in Varāhamihira's *Bṛhatsaṃhitā*, ch. 44.

2.30.48. *unfortunate* (vailomya): That is, if the animal dies because of the negligence of its caretakers.

2.31.1. *retinue of…trainers*: The text as emended by Kangle reads: *cikitsakānīkasthaupasthāyikavargaḥ*, correcting a corrupt reading found in all the manuscripts. On the basis of 2.32.16, however, it appears that "attendant" is a generic term comprehending numerous categories of individuals needed to look after elephants. There the long list ending in *ādi* (and so forth) is headed by physicians and elephant trainers. I have thus emended the reading here also to reflect that list: *cikitsakānīkasthādyaupasthāyikavargaṃ*.

2.31.2. *"Princess" configuration* (kumārīsaṃgraha): The meaning of this expression is unclear. Kangle and Meyer think it is some sort of a structure built with beams. Why such a structure should be specified is unclear. Commentators take it to be a beam above the post to which the elephant is tied so as to make the tying of the elephant easier. These all seem like guesses. The closest parallel to this term is the *kumārīpura* (2.3.32), a particular kind of gate mentioned in the context of the construction of the defensive walls of a city; see above 2.3.32 n. If this is the meaning, then the stable for elephants would have two long parallel halls with a central courtyard.

2.31.7. *Two parts…getting up*: The meaning appears to be that the night is divided into three equal parts. Half of the first part and half of the last part are spent in getting the animals to lie down and to get up. The middle two-thirds of the night, about eight hours, are for sleeping.

2.31.10. *cubs…without tusks*: Here we have some technical terms from the vocabulary of those working with elephants: *vikka* (see 2.31.16), *moḍha*, and *makkaṇa*. The translation reflects the interpretation of the commentators.

2.31.11. *The best…length*: The best elephant at 40 years would be 10.5 feet or 3.3 meters tall and 13.5 feet or 4.23 meters long.*middling, lowest*: Sentence 15 below suggests that the middling one of 30 years would be six Aratnis tall (9 feet or 2.8 meters), and the lowest one of 25 years would be five Aratnis tall (7.5 feet or 2.35 meters).

2.31.13. *ration*: For the rations for different kinds of elephants, see 2.14.42.

2.31.15. *The remaining…Hastas*: These two types of elephants are the 30-year-old middling and the 25-year-old lowest (2.31.13). These elephants are six and five Aratnis, respectively. An Aratni is the same as a Hasta; so the principle of "ration per Aratni" (2.31.13) is still in force.

2.31.17. *appearances* (śobhā): The meaning is unclear. Gaṇapati Śāstrī takes these attributes as ways an elephant looks as it grows old. Meyer thinks that the term refers to different types of elephants, while the Malayalam commentary thinks it refers to different stages of recovery from an illness. I think this sentence is an interpolation to account for the same term (*śobhā*) that opens the concluding verse.

with even back muscles: I have followed the insightful suggestion of Kangle to change the reading from the convoluted *samatalpatalā* to *samatalpalā* (*talpala* being a known term for an elephant's back muscles).

2.32.1. *who are mainly devoted to work*: The curious compound *karmaskandhāḥ* has to be a Bahuvrīhi compound referring to elephants who are employed in various kinds of work. See the parallel compound *dharmaskandhāḥ* in the *Chāndogya Upaniṣad* 2.23.1 and my analysis of it in Olivelle 1996.

2.32.2. *five kinds*: These appear to be five different stages of training and development of a captured elephant. We see similar stages of development in the war elephant (2.32.4) and riding elephants (2.32.6). In these cases, however, some elephants may never go beyond a particular stage.

water: The meaning is unclear. Kangle, following the commentators, takes *vāri* to mean a place for capturing elephants and translates: "getting used to the place for catching elephants." It seems improbable, however, that an untrained elephant would be undergoing this kind of training to capture other wild elephants. The probable meaning is that the untrained elephant is being taken to a river to get him used to getting in and out of the water.

pits (avapāta): Again the meaning is unclear. Kangle thinks it is a trap. Probably the elephant is trained here to go into and come out of hollows and craters. It appears that elephants have a natural fear of holes and pits, and training would be directed at overcoming this natural fear (Scharfe, personal communication).

2.32.3. *preparatory...cub*: The term *upavicāra* appears to indicate a training regimen that precedes the training proper. The compound *vikkakarma* is taken by Kangle to mean the looking after of a cub; in other words, the untrained elephant is made to take care of a cub. This seems unlikely. Probably, the untrained elephant is initially given tasks that would normally be given to a cub during its training period.

2.32.4. *engaging in warfare* (sāṃgrāmikaṃ): For the kinds of activities elephants were used for during war, see 10.4.14 and 10.5.54.

2.32.6. *uses various gaits*: The meaning is uncertain. Meyer takes it to mean an elephant that goes forward under all circumstances.

2.32.7. *autumnal work, inferior work*: The meanings of *śāradakarma* and *hīnakarma* are uncertain. I have translated them literally. Kangle, following the Malayalam commentary, translates: "work of keeping fit, the work of recouping what is lacking." Meyer takes *śārada* to mean new or fresh. Like the preparatory regimen in the previous passage, here also these activities must be easy tasks given to the animal before a more complicated regimen of training is undertaken. The term *autumnal* here may refer to activities undertaken by a new and diffident animal.

2.32.8–9. *The vicious...inebriation diagnosed*: Kangle has emended the text so that the passage "It is one that is apprehensive...inebriation diagnosed" comes immediately after "one type of activity." But these qualities do not explain the one type of activity, which I think is here left unstated; its activity is vicious. I have restored the reading of the manuscripts. Perhaps all that comes after the statement on the preparatory regimen is interpolated to further explain the nature of a vicious elephant.

obstinate (avaruddha): I follow Shamasastry here. The normal meaning of being put under restraint does not fit the context, which deals with the attitudes and activities of an out-of-control elephant.

2.32.10. *simple...defects*: The meanings of these adjectives are totally obscure. The Malayalam commentary says that the "simple" has 18 defects; the "firmly resolved" has 15 defects; and the "erratic" has 33 defects. The last has all the above defects.

2.32.13. *mechanical device* (yantra): Bhaṭṭasvāmin takes this to be a device to trim the tusks, while he states the opinion of others according to which it is a device used in warfare. For the trimming of the tusks, see 2.32.22.

2.32.17. *meat*: It is unclear whether "meat" here should be understood as fruit pulp (see 2.29.43 n.) or simply as meat.

2.32.21. *junctures...seasons*: That is, on the full-moon days of Kārttika (October–November), Phālguna (February–March), and Āṣāḍha (June–July).

Senānī: the god Skanda or Kārttikeya.

2.33.3. *Ten-man*: The reference of *puruṣa* may be to the *pauruṣa* at 2.20.10, where the measurement is said to be one Vitasti. Thus "ten-man" would be approximately 2.3 meters; and "twelve-man" would be 2.8 meters. The term "interior" (*antara*) refers probably to the length of the chariot.

2.33.6. *servants and non-servants*: The technical term *bhṛtaka* (or *bhṛtya*) appears to indicate a long-term relationship between the servant and the master. Thus, an *abhṛtaka* may indicate a hired laborer who does not have such a lasting relationship (see *MBh* 12.83.2). See Vigasin and Samozvantsev 1985, 130–131.

2.33.8. *hereditary...troops*: For the different kinds of troops forming an army, see 7.8.27; 9.2.1. The use of enemy troops is somewhat puzzling, but alliances of convenience could be formed between natural enemies against a common enemy, but this category is absent in the other two places where this list is given; for alliances with the enemy, see 7.6.

deployment and non-deployment: The Sanskrit does not say who or what is to be deployed or not deployed, but the context makes it clear that we are dealing with the infantry here. The meaning appears to be that the superintendent should know the times and places for deploying infantry.

2.33.9. *four divisions of the army*: These are infantry, chariot corps, cavalry, and elephant corps.

2.33.10. *terrain suitable for his side* (svabhūmi): For the meaning of this expression in the context of warfare, see 7.16.1; 10.3.1, 3.

2.34.6. *between villages*: I follow Kangle's emendation of *bhayāntareṣu* (between dangers) to *grāmāntareṣu*, according to the parallel at 4.13.9.

2.34.10. *conveyance*: The term *vāhana* is difficult to translate because it includes vehicles (carts, carriages, chariots), as well as draught animals, beasts of burden, and riding horses. Given the nature of the terrain and the people engaged in the surveillance, a riding animal, such as a horse, is probably meant here (Meyer), rather than a vehicle (Kangle).

2.35.3. *according to their boundary limits* (sīmāvarodhena): Kangle translates: "by fixing their boundaries." I don't think that he fixed the boundaries as he was making a census, but followed the set boundaries. See 4.13.11, where this expression occurs again and where the boundaries are clearly fixed.

the boundaries and the fields: Given the loose syntactical connection between the words *sīmnāṃ kṣetrāṇāṃ ca* and the rest of the sentence, Meyer has suggested that they are glosses that found their way into the text. The two words, however, refer to the two broad categories of land surveyed by the Revenue Officers, that is, villages and fields, and here the villages are metonymically indicated by the word boundary.

2.35.6. *one-quarter of the countryside*: Thus, there would be four County Supervisors (*sthānika*) in charge of the four divisions into which the countryside was divided by the Collector (2.35.1). Perhaps they were located in the provincial capitals called *sthānīya*, even though in this passage, these capitals are not explicitly connected with the fourfold division of the countryside.

2.35.7. *Magistrates . . . tributes*: For Magistrates, see book 4, where these officers are in charge of the criminal division (*kaṇṭakaśodhana*) of the legal justice system. Here these officers appear to have additional functions, such as the collection of tributes. From this passage, it appears that the Magistrates did not have an office of their own, at least not in the countryside, but performed their duties there using the offices of the Revenue Officers and the County Supervisors.

2.35.8. *benefits and exemptions* (bhoga-parihāra): Kangle translates: "taxes and exemption," and notes the parallel to *karada* and *akarada* (tax-paying and tax- exempt) of sentence 3. See, however, the identical phrase at 2.7.2, where both *bhoga* and *parihāra* are viewed as benefits received by a person. We also see the use of *bhoga* as income or payment in the context of courtesans (2.27.10, 20).

2.35.12. *with respect to activities*: The strange syntax of *karmasu ca* has led Kangle to think that these words are spurious. It is, indeed, difficult to connect them syntactically to the rest of the sentence, unless we take them as a parenthetical comment referring to the activities and tasks of the traders who are importing goods from the foreign land.

2.35.15. *Exerting...of their own*: The verse is rather obscure, and the efforts of Meyer and Kangle, along with the commentators, have not yielded satisfactory conclusions. I think Scharfe (1993, 213) has the best explanation. The spy establishments under the control of the Collector given in this chapter are only three: householders, traders, and ascetics. The "other spy establishments" having their own distinct origin are the remaining two: the apostate renouncer and the crafty student (see 1.11.1).

2.36.4. *quarter section*: This corresponds to the County Supervisor of the countryside who supervised one-quarter of the countryside: 2.35.6. Both the County Supervisor and the Revenue Officer were in all probability originally associated with the countryside (*janapada*), confirming that this section is probably a later compilation that saw these officers as also exercising control over cities and forts.

2.36.5. *own assessment* (svapratyaya): The meaning is that the officers can judge the authenticity of these Brāhmaṇical recluses on their own and give them lodging. Non-Brāhmaṇical ascetics, on the other hand, have to be registered with the authorities. For the same expression in differing contexts, see 3.12.14; 3.14.34; 8.4.33. In all these places, an activity is undertaken on the basis of an evaluation or judgment made by the very person undertaking that activity, rather than relying on the assessment or testimony of others; see 3.8.1; 3.9.24; 3.11.43; 3.13.31.

2.36.11. *night offense*: The meaning is unclear, the expression appearing only in this chapter (see 2.36.42). Except for certain nights when free movement was permitted (2.36.39), there was generally a night curfew in the city (2.36.35; 3.12.46). Offenses committed during the night may have been subject to great punishment.

2.36.12. *secure nights*: The meaning is unclear, the expression *kṣemarātri* being found only in this passage. Perhaps the reference is to nights when free movement is permitted (2.36.39). Kangle interprets this to mean a night when no crimes are reported. This seems unlikely, because the term appears to indicate particular nights of the month or year.

2.36.16. *middle quarters*: Here the daytime appears to be divided into four equal parts of three hours each. So, if we assume the day to go from 6 A.M.

to 6 P.M., then the times when open fires are forbidden within the city would be 9 A.M. to 3 P.M.

2.36.18. *five jars*: One must assume that these are kept filled with water as fire extinguishers. Interestingly, the Buddhist *Milindapañho* (II.2.3; Trenckner, 42–43) says that among eastern regions (*puratthimesu janapadesu*), there is the custom of keeping five pots full of water beside each house in order to put out any fire that may break out there.

"hair-grabber": This appears to be a pole with hooks at the end to grab onto the hair of an enemy (see 9.2.27). Here, however, this must refer to an implement useful in putting out a fire.

2.36.19. *He*: The referent in all probability is the City Manager.

2.36.28. *successively increased*: That is, the fine is one Paṇa for voiding excrement in a holy site, two when it is done at a place of water, three in a temple, and so on. The expression *-uttara* is used frequently in the *AŚ* to indicate that the amount of the fine is progressively increased by a certain amount for each subsequent crime listed in the provision.

2.36.34. *watch* (yāma): This is a period of time that is generally about three hours; thus, there would be four watches during the night.

Nālikās: A Nālikā (or Nāḍikā) is 24 minutes. Thus, the instrument would sound two hours and 24 minutes after nightfall and before daybreak.

2.36.35. *outside* (bahiḥ): Kangle, following the Malayalam commentary, emends the clear reading of the manuscripts to *antaḥ*, and takes the provision to mean that the person is moving within the king's precinct during curfew. If we follow the reading of the manuscripts, the meaning is probably that the person goes outside the city limits during curfew hours.

2.36.38. *sounded the instrument*: This was perhaps to alert the citizens to an imminent danger, much like a siren in modern cities, or to summon them to a gathering.

2.36.39. *secretive or incongruous attire*: Secret attire probably means some form of disguise, while incongruous attire (*viparītaveśa*), also occurring at 3.9.11, is explained by commentators as men wearing women's clothes. Even though in this context, the expression may refer to transvestites, at 3.9.11, that meaning is inappropriate. Could it mean wearing clothes that are different or the opposite of the ones people of a particular class are expected to wear? In that case, at 3.9.11, it may refer to low-class people, such as farmers and herdsmen, wearing dignified clothing.

2.36.41. *woman kept confined* (avaruddhā): The reference probably is to a woman, possibly a slave, who is kept as a mistress by her master; see *YDh* 2.290.

2.36.42. *For not reporting... negligence*: Kangle says that "we should supply *rakṣiṇaḥ* and understand *nāgarikasya* in the sense of the dative" and translates: "For (a guard) not reporting to the City-superintendent an offense committed during the night whether by the animate or the inanimate, the punishment shall be in conformity with the offense; also in case of negligence." I doubt whether supplying such a word is necessary. The sense seems clear: The City Manager has to report night offenses to his superior, perhaps the Collector or the king. I follow here the understanding of Meyer and Shamasastry. The compound *cetanācetanikaṃ* is taken by both Kangle and Shamasastry as animate and inanimate. It is difficult to see how an inanimate thing can cause a night offense. I follow Meyer here in taking the two terms to mean deliberate or non-deliberate.

2.36.43. *clandestine passages*: For these kinds of hidden pathways within a fort, see 2.3.15 n. and 2.4.2.

run away: probably animals or slaves who have run away from their masters.

2.36.44. *birth constellation*: This must refer to the king.

2.36.45. *individuals belonging... by conventions* (samayānubaddha): This may refer to individuals who are connected to the accused by belonging to the same professional organization (see 2.1.32 n.); for example, the two may belong to the same guild. Others take this more strictly as referring to people who have come to an agreement with the accused to pay a ransom.

2.36.46. *bonded manual labor*: Kangle's edition following the manuscripts reads *karmaṇā kāyadaṇḍena*, which Kangle translates: "by (getting them to do) work, by (inflicting) corporal punishment." Jail is never given as a punishment for an offense; people are jailed because they are unable to pay fines. In this context, why corporal punishment would be a reason for releasing a prisoner is difficult to understand. Harihara Sastri (2011, 68) has suggested the plausible emendation of *kāyadaṇḍena* to *kāyabandhena* based on the reading of the commentary *Cāṇakyaṭīkā*, a reading that I have followed. Bonded labor as a substitute for fines is often mentioned in this and other texts.

BOOK 3

3.1.1. *Justices*: For a discussion of the translation of *dharmastha* as Justice, see note to 2.1.30. For a discussion of this sentence and the role of Justices, see Introduction, p. 16.

ministerial rank: For the qualities that are required of a minister (*amātya*), see 1.9.1. It appears that a large number of officials carried this rank. The specification here that the Justices who try cases should be of ministerial rank may imply that there were other *dharmasthas* who did not belong to this rank and were thus permitted to perform only non-judicial functions connected with this office (see 2.1.30 n.).

in groups of three: The repetition *trayas trayaḥ* has been taken distributively by all translators, the first referring to *dharmasthas* and the second to *amātyas*. Thus, Kangle translates: "Three judges, (all) three (of the rank of) ministers." We have, however, a nice parallel to this repetition in Pāṇini 1.4.101 that speaks of three triads (*tiṅas trīṇi trīṇi prathamamadhyamottamāḥ*), glossed by the Kāśikā commentary as *trayas trikāḥ*. A similar usage is found in the *Taittirīya Prātiśākhya* (1.3; 1.10), where we have the repetitions *dve dve* (in twos) and *pañca pañca* (in groups of five). The meaning in our passage also seems to be that benches consisting of three Justices each should try cases. This, of course, contradicts the provisions of the Dharmaśāstras, where a single learned Brāhmaṇa judge substitutes for the king in a court of law.

frontier posts... capitals: For these administrative centers, see 2.1.4.

arising from transactions (vyāvahārika): The reference is probably to the *vyavahārapada* or *vivādapada* (grounds for litigation, also called titles of law); see 3.1.17 n.

3.1.2. *carried out in absentia*: I have emended the reading of the text (*tirohitāntaragāranaktāraṇyopadhyupahvarakr̥tān*) here to read *tirohitān*, thus placing it outside the compound. Here I follow the suggestion of Rocher (1978, 20), with which Kangle also appears to agree ("*kr̥tān* is to be construed with *antaragāra* onwards"), even though he maintains the above reading. Indeed, at 3.1.6, we have the adjective *tirohitāḥ* outside a compound and qualifying *vyavahārāḥ* (implied [*anuvr̥tti*] from 3.1.2) while all the other words (3.1.7–11) compound with *kr̥ta*: for example, *antaragārakr̥tāḥ*. In all likelihood, a haplography has occurred here in the dropping of "*na*" in *tirohitānantaragāra-*.

3.1.5. *forfeit the object* (dravyavyapanaya): Kangle and the commentary *Cāṇakyaṭīkā* think that the transaction is declared null and void. The term *dravya*, however, appears to refer to the actual object (a piece of property or money) of the transaction. A person taking part in an invalid transaction in good faith simply forfeits that property and is not subject to an additional fine.

3.1.7. *consignments, deposits* (nikṣepa, upanidhi): These two technical terms have a broad range of meanings. In the current context, the former probably refers to the raw material a client may give to an artisan for manufacturing an article. Given the reference to secluded women, this appears to be the meaning; see the consignment of raw material for making yarn brought to the homes of such women at 2.23.11. These are dealt with in 3.12.33f. Deposits (*upanidhi*), on the other hand, refer to pledges or other items deposited in the care of someone. These pledges generally are used as collateral for loans; see 3.12.1f.

3.1.8. *trespass* (anupraveśa): For the use of this term to mean entry with criminal intent, see *AŚ* 3.19.17. See also parallels at *ĀpDh* 2.26.18; *VaDh* 19.38.

carrying out... night: Gaṇapati Śāstrī takes this as referring to people such as tavern keepers and prostitutes.

3.1.11. *secret association* (mithaḥsamavāya): The term *samavāya* (1.13.2; 3.1.25; 4.7.17; etc.) refers to any type of gathering, especially when there is an agreement to pursue a common goal. The most common secret association is consensual sex that constitutes the Gāndharva kind of marriage (3.2.6). But secret associations extended further than that (see 3.12.52).

3.1.12. *Transactions... valid*: The meaning is that the above are the only exceptions to the general rules enunciated in 3.1.2.

by a son living... husband or son: The context for all these provisions is a joint family where the property remains undivided. Generally, the authority for property transactions rests with the head of the family, that is, the father. If the father has retired, then the authority falls on his oldest son, and the father himself is regarded as a dependent. A brother excluded from the family probably refers to a brother who has either left or been cast out of the family. The commentary *Cāṇakyaṭīkā* gives the alternate reading *niṣkalena* (for *niṣkulena*), which is interpreted as an impotent brother. All such individuals are incompetent to conclude a valid transaction.

person given as a pledge (āhitaka): That is, someone given to a creditor as collateral. During the time the person is a pledge, he or she resembles a slave and cannot act independently; see 3.13.6, 16.

below or beyond the legal age: The age of majority in ancient India was 16 years for a male and 12 years for a female (3.3.1). Gaṇapati Śāstrī takes 70 years as the cut-off point; anyone older that that becomes incompetent to execute a transaction.

notorious criminal (abhiśasta): This term may refer to a wide variety of people guilty of serious crimes or sins, such as the five major sins that cause loss of caste (*mahāpātaka*); see *MDh* 9.235. A list of sins/crimes making someone an *abhiśasta* is given at *ĀpDh* 1.24.6–9.

3.1.13. *Even in such cases* (tatrāpi): The reference is not to what immediately preceded but to valid transactions noted above (3.1.6–11).

under someone else's control (avagṛhīta): Whether the man is physically constrained by the other or simply under the other's control, such an individual is unable to freely carry out a transaction; see 5.6.47; 7.5.41; 8.2.17.

3.1.15. *In each respective group*: This appears to be a rider to the conditions of a valid transaction listed above. Within each familial, social, or economic group (*varga*), the prevailing customs regarding valid transactions should be honored, within the limits set forth in the rest of this provision.

3.1.16. *the last document... pledge*: It is a general principle, well articulated in *YDh* 2.23, that the proof of a later transaction is stronger than that of an earlier one. Thus, if someone proves that he lent money to someone, such proof is thrown out if the borrower can prove that he returned the amount at a later date. The *YDh* gives three exceptions: pledge, gift, and purchase. In these three cases, the earlier document is more powerful than a later one, because once these transactions are made, the other person does not have the legal power to alienate the property. The term *ādeśa* (directive) is unclear. I have followed Kangle in taking this to mean a charge given to a person to perform a certain function at a distant location (see 3.12.18).

3.1.17. *Grounds for Litigation* (vivādapada): This term has the technical meaning of the various grounds on which a lawsuit may be filed (also called *vyavahārapada*). This meaning is clear in its use at 4.7.17. In other places, however (see 3.16.38; 11.1.4), a less technical meaning of legal disputes or filing lawsuits may be intended. Given that writing is involved here, I think the more technical meaning extending to the actual facts of the current case is intended. For their enumeration, see *MDh* 8.3–7; Kane 1962–75, III: 248–249. On this section, see Introduction, p. 16f.

He: The verb here is given in the singular, even though at the outset (3.1.1), there are three Justices in the court. Either the reference here is to a court recorder or clerk, or we are confronted with material from a different source that did not recognize a bench of three judges, such as the Dharmaśāstras.

Karaṇa: This is a division of a day. There are 11 such divisions, and they correspond roughly to one-half of a lunar day (*tithi*). Kangle and Meyer take the term to refer to some sort of government office, but why it should be repeated along with *adhikaraṇa*, which probably refers to the court hearing the case, is unclear. Coming after the day (*divasa*), I think it more likely that the term refers to a division of time.

3.1.18. *review*: This implies that the plaintiff and the defendant agree with regard to the accuracy of what has been recorded. If not, changes will be made to the official record. See *YDh* 2.6–7.

3.1.19. *produce a document... documentary evidence*: The meaning of *deśa* has been long misunderstood. Commentators take it as a reference to witnesses, and Shamasastry misses the point altogether, taking the term to mean a question. Kangle comes closest when he takes it to mean evidence. As I have shown elsewhere (Olivelle 2004; see also Samozvantsev 1980–1981, 355; Vigasin and Samozvantsev 1985, 137), in both Manu (8.53–56, see my notes there) and the *Arthaśāstra*, the term *deśa* refers to legally valid documentary evidence. The term was the earliest designation for what will later be termed *lekhya*. The plaintiff after first promising to produce a document, either does not do so or produces a faulty or defective document (*hīnadeśa*) or a non-document (*adeśa*), which probably means a document that is unacceptable in a court of law. For this term, see also 3.16.29.

secretly carries... discussed: For a discussion of this somewhat obscure statement, see Olivelle 2004. Others take *deśa* here to mean a place. Given the technical use of the term in this passage, I do not think this is likely.

3.1.20–21. *amount*: For the meaning of the technical term *bandha*, see 2.7.21 n. In the present case, *bandha* (amount) refers to the total amount under litigation.

3.1.22. *men*: The meaning of *puruṣa* in this context is unclear. It can refer either to an official or, more commonly, to subordinates and servants of such officials. The context here is a court that travels to places where sessions are held. The losing party is liable for the costs of such travel and other court costs.

one-eighth: The reading and the meaning are unclear. The manuscripts read *aṣṭāṅga*, whereas Kangle has adopted the reading *aṣṭāṃśa*, which, according to him, is the reading of the Malayalam commentary. Scharfe, however, in a personal communication, tells me that neither *aṃśa* nor *aṅga* is found in the Malayalam commentary, which gives this gloss: "The loser shall give the interrogating officer one-eighth of a Paṇa as expenditure." In either case, the meaning is opaque. Kangle, following Shamasastry, translates: "one-eighth part (of a *paṇa*)," while Meyer, adopting *aṣṭāṅga*, takes it to mean one and one-eighth Paṇas. This sort of expression, however, is never used with regard to a Paṇa. The text is probably corrupt, but, if *aṃśa* is the correct reading, it must refer to some sort of share given by the defeated party to these servants (see *dvyaṃśa* at 3.5.8).

3.1.25. *association*: I take *samavāya* as a separate and fourth exception. Kangle takes it together with the preceding and translates: "association in caravans." For *samavāya* as an association, often a secret association, see 3.1.11; 3.12.52; 4.7.17.

3.1.27. *response*: That is, the defendant has offered his response to the plaint of the plaintiff. After receiving this response, the plaintiff has to offer his own reply that very day.

3.1.32. *a defendant who absconds*: In light of the next statement, this would mean that the defendant is assessed the fine only when he does not show up after three fortnights.

3.1.34–35. *if he is dead... work done by him*: Following the suggestion of Meyer (Nachtrag, 746–757), I have departed from the sentence division of Kangle, moving *asāram* from the end of 34 to the beginning of 35. Kangle's translation of 34, "The statement of a witness who dies or suffers from a misfortune is without value" requires us to take the two genitives *pretasya vyasaninaḥ* as qualifying the word *sākṣi-* within the compound *sākṣivacanāt*, which, as Kangle himself admits, is quite irregular. Second, Kangle is forced to emend the text from the reading in the manuscripts *sākṣivacanāḥ* to *sākṣivacanam*. Further, the term *asāra* is regularly used in the *AŚ* as either a substance of little value or a poor person, but never in the sense of "invalid" (for the use of the term at 3.11.16, see note there). I interpret sentence 34 as continuous with 33, where the genitive *abhiyoktuḥ* occurs. The meaning, then, is that a plaintiff loses the case when he absconds; but if he dies or falls into misfortune, he loses the case upon the testimony of witnesses. My interpretation requires emending the reading *sākṣivacanāḥ* (a grammatically untenable masculine nominative plural) to *sākṣivacanād* (ablative singular). This is a plausible emendation, because the Malayalam "*d*" if written unclearly may resemble a *visarga*. Moving *asāram* to the following sentence also provides the missing object to the verb in that sentence. The provision in 35 is similar to others where a person may work in order to pay off a fine; see 3.13.18. Such a man is called *daṇḍopakārin* (2.12.21) and *daṇḍapratikartṛ* (2.23.2; 2.24.2). This emendation is also supported by the reading found in the commentary *Cāṇakyaṭīkā* (see Harihara Sastri 2011, 83).

3.1.36. *he*: The referent of the pronoun is unclear. In all likelihood, it is the defendant, who may provide a pledge so that he may pay the fine at a later time.

3.1.37. *guarded by... of a Brāhmaṇa*: This provision is completely obscure, especially the meaning of *rakṣoghna* ("demon-killing"), which apparently refers to some sort of ritual also mentioned with reference to Atharvaveda experts at 4.3.40. What that has to do with payment of a fine is unclear. Meyer suggests emending the text to *rakṣoparakṣitam*, "guarded by the police," which is plausible. The difference between this provision and the one in 3.1.35 is that there, the defendant works for the plaintiff, while here, the work is done for the state in lieu of a fine. The exception noted for a Brāhmaṇa from doing manual labor or even the entire passage, as Kangle thinks, was probably a marginal gloss that found its way into the text.

3.1.39–40. *Law, convention... king's command*: These two verses are found in *NSm* Mātṛkā 1.10–11. For this division of the sources of law, see *BṛSm* 1.18; Kane 1962–1975, III: 259f.; Lingat 1962. The first three of these terms occurs in a different context at *AŚ* 2.7.2, and that context, I think, provides us with useful insights into what these terms may have meant originally. Here, however, some terms, especially *vyavahāra*, have a different meaning; rather than convention or rules governing corporate bodies, here the term appears to refer to the judicial process based on proof, that is, predominantly witnesses. Lingat (1962), basing his arguments mostly on the rather late Dharmaśāstras of Nārada, Bṛhaspati, and Kātyāyana, and on medieval texts, takes these four factors as relating to the way in which a court arrives at a decision. Although it appears likely that he is right in the context of the literature he is examining, I think these Dharmaśāstras are engaged in interpreting a difficult text whose original meaning may have been lost to them. I think that *AŚ* 2.7.2 gives us some idea of what that original meaning may have been, namely, various kinds of "law" operating at different levels of society.

3.1.43. *renders verdicts*: For the technical use of *anu-śās* for a verdict or decision in a court case, see 4.9.15.

canon (saṃsthā): This term replaces *caritra* (custom) given in 3.1.39. For the use of both in a list, see 2.7.2.

3.1.44. *conventional treatise*: The meaning of the expression *śāstraṃ vyāvahārikam* is unclear. Kangle takes it to mean a matter based on a transaction, although he finds the use of *śāstra* in this sense strange. I think this expression probably refers to Arthaśāstra, which is here placed in opposition to and viewed as inferior to Dharmaśāstra. See the parallel verse at *YDh* 2.21, where this awkward expression is replaced by *arthaśāstra.*

according to Law: Here *dharma* is probably a shorthand for *dharmaśāstra.* So the meaning is that when provisions of various sources contradict each other, then the case must be judged according to the provisions of Dharmaśāstra.

3.1.45. *treatise*: The term *śāstra* here is probably a shorthand for Dharmaśāstra.

3.2.1. *Transactions presuppose marriage*: Regarding the connection of this to topic 57, see Introduction, p. 16.

3.2.2–9. *Brāhma... intoxicated girl*: For a longer and more detailed description of these eight forms of marriage, see *MDh* 3.20–35. In the Prājāpatya, the statement "jointly fulfilling the Law" is an abbreviated statement of a ritual formula uttered by the parents to the young couple: "May you jointly fulfill the Law" (*MDh* 3.30). Even though the same term *ādāna* is used in 4, 7, 8, and 9, it is clear that in the Ārṣa and Āsura, the pair of cattle and the bride price are received by the girl's parents, whereas in the other two cases, the seizure or rape of the girl is done by the man.

3.2.6. *secret union*: For the meaning of secret union or association of the expression *mithaḥsamavāya,* see 3.1.11; 3.12.50.

3.2.12. *second bride price*: The meaning is unclear. It may refer to a bride price paid at the second marriage of a woman. The Malayalam commentary thinks that it is a gift given out of affection.

3.2.13. *In all of them... affection*: In all eight forms of marriage, it is permitted to give gifts to the bride as a token of love.

3.2.14. *Woman's property*: I have used this somewhat awkward phrase to translate the technical term *stridhana,* that is, property or wealth that belongs to a woman or wife and that cannot be used or alienated by the husband.

3.2.17. *most righteous forms of marriage*: The most righteous forms of marriage (*dharmiṣṭha*) are the first four kinds (3.2.2–10).

he should not subject it to an inquiry: The technical term *anuyuñjīta* refers to a judicial inquiry conducted by a judge or state official. That is its meaning in all but two instances of its use in the *AŚ* (2.8.22; 2.36.26; 3.12.51; 3.13.32; 3.16.12; 4.5.11; 4.7.20, 22, 24; 4.8.1, 3). The only places where its meaning is somewhat ambiguous is here and at 3.16.31. Kangle thinks that the subject of this verb is the wife: "the (wife) shall not question," taking the verb in a non-technical sense. I think here, as in other places, the term retains its technical meaning and the questioning or inquiry is done by the Justice (*dharmastha*). The meaning, then, is that no judicial inquiry should be initiated with regard to property that has been used for three years or more.

3.2.18. *both*: The two types of woman's property noted above are livelihood (*vṛtti*) and ornaments (*ābandhya*).

penalty for theft: Given that such a marriage is consummated through forcible seizure and rape, the husband has no right to the wife's property. His use of that property amounts to theft. For the punishment for theft, see 2.7.39 n.

3.2.19. *remainder of the bride price*: The meaning, as Meyer points out, appears to be that the bride price may have often been paid in installments; see 3.4.15, 33. The payment is normally made to the bride's parents. In the event of the husband's death, the remainder of the bride price is paid to the widow probably from the husband's estate.

3.2.21. *If she desires… husband*: The reason for this provision is that the widow would normally bear a son for her deceased husband through his brother or other close relative (3.4.38–40). Thus, she remains within the deceased husband's family.

3.2.24. *When a woman… received*: The meaning of this obscure sentence is far from certain. Kangle interprets it to mean that upon remarriage, the new relatives (in-laws) should give back all the property she may have received from the relatives of her first husband. Meyer takes both sets of relatives to be the same, and thinks that the blood relatives of the widow, with whom she may be living after her husband's death, should give her entire property to her upon her new marriage.

3.2.26. *inheritance from her husband*: The compound *patidāya* literally means inheritance from her husband (so Meyer). Kangle objects to this because the widow is not listed as an heir in the list at 3.5.2–12. But see 3.5.1, where the sons are said to be without power over the property while the father *and* the mother are alive. It cannot mean simply a gift given by the husband, because that would be included within *strīdhana* (woman's property), and there is no reason to mention it here again (3.2.20, 28).

The other possibility is that this inheritance refers to the endowment the widow receives for her maintenance.

3.2.27. *dedicates herself to the Law*: The meaning is that she refuses to remarry and dedicates her life to religious and meritorious activities, while remaining celibate. This is the alternative to remarriage.

3.2.40. *give*: The first three items are given to the superseded first wife, while the fine is given to the state.

half the compensation for supersession (ardhaṃ cādhivedanikam): The meaning appears to be that if the husband had already given his wife the bride price and woman's property, then only half the standard amount of compensation for supersession is to be given. What the standard is appears to be hinted at in the next provision where the compensation is said to equal the total of the bride price and woman's property. At *YDh* 2.148, where this same provision is given, the commentator Vijñāneśvara takes the compensation to consist of an amount equal to what the husband spent on his new wedding. Kangle takes this provision to mean that the husband should pay half the woman's property as compensation, but that would require the reading *tadardhaṃ cādhivedanikam*.

3.2.42. *purpose of women is sons*: The compound *putrārthāḥ* can also mean that the women desire sons, especially in light of the similar use of *putrārthī* with regard to the man at 3.2.39. See also 3.2.47 below.

3.2.43. *according to... living sons*: Both Meyer and Kangle take *yathāvivāham* to mean according to the time of marriage and see it as qualifying in some way *pūrvoḍhām* (wife married earlier). But this would add nothing to what the latter term states and would be redundant. I think we have here three options: first, according to the marriage (either the eight forms given above or the social class of the wives; see *MDh* 9.85–87, where the seniority of wives is determined by their social class); second, the wife whom he married earlier; and third, the wife who has living sons. The context for this provision is the common rule that a husband should have sexual relations with his wife soon after the bath that signals the end of her menstrual period. A problem is created if several of his wives have their periods at the same time.

3.2.44. *For concealing... at the time of menstruation* (tīrthagūhanāgamane): I take both *gūhana* (concealment) and *agamana* (not going, i.e., not having sex) as connected with *tīrtha*. In the first case, it would be menstruation as such, and in the second, it would be the fertile period following menstruation (generally referred to as *ṛtu*, season). Commentators take both as faults of the wife, and Meyer as faults of the husband. Kangle, correctly I think, takes the first as the fault of the wife and the second as the fault of the husband.

3.2.47. *for the sake of a son* (putrārtham): If we take this compound adverbially, then the one who wants a son could be the wife, which is the more probable meaning. If we take it as a Bahuvrīhi compound qualifying *evaṃbhūtam* ("of that sort"), however, the person desiring a son is the husband, and the wife is obliged to accede to his desire even if he suffers from these sicknesses.

3.3.1. *reached the age for legal transactions* (prāptavyavahārā): The meaning is that she has reached the age of legal majority. But I think it is important to keep the notion of *vyavahāra*, transaction, in the foreground, because, as we can see from 3.1.1 and 3.2.1, the justices are entrusted with matters relating to social and commercial transactions and lawsuits arising from such transactions.

3.3.2. *obedience* (śuśrūṣā): Kangle translates this term as "marital duty." Although, within the context of the text as currently constituted, this meaning may be evident, I think that, within the original context of this discussion of the duties of Justices, the term probably had a broader meaning, as seen in the statement in the opening sentence about the legal age for concluding transactions. After reaching the majority, individuals of both sexes have to obey laws. See the use of *śuśrūṣā* in the sense of obeying rules at 1.5.5; 6.1.4.

3.3.3. *even more* (saviśeṣaṃ): This expression indicates that the person does more than he is required to do; see 1.8.13; 1.18.3; 2.9.9.

3.3.4. *security* (bandha): For the possible meanings of this difficult term, see 2.7.21 n. and 3.12.16 n. There is little support for Kangle's translation of the term to imply payment in installments. The context for all the provisions in this section is the failure of the husband to pay timely alimony to a wife who is divorced or separated from him. This is clearly evident in the last provision (3.3.6) regarding a lawsuit by the former wife. Thus, when the husband fails to pay the alimony at the appointed time, the amount payable has to be calculated, and the husband has to provide a security or a surety to guarantee future payment.

3.3.10. *a wife who is...jealous*: The reading of the manuscripts is obviously corrupt. I have accepted Kangle's emendation *prasiddhadoṣāyāḥ* (genitive qualifying the wife). Kangle, however, changes the genitive *īrṣyāyāḥ* of the manuscripts to the instrumental *īrṣyayā* and places it at the beginning of the next sentence. It makes better sense, however, to see jealousy as a motive for a wife attacking her husband, especially if he has several wives. Why she would take pleasure trips outside the house out of jealousy is less obvious. I take *īrṣya* here not as a substantive but as an adjective and accept the genitive reading of the manuscripts.

3.3.11. *(When it is done)...laid down*: This statement poses several difficulties in interpretation. Kangle translates: "On occasions of (her) enjoying herself outside (the home) out of jealousy, the penalty shall be as laid down," and refers to 3.3.20–22 and 3.4.1–23 as the places where the penalty is laid down. But why would a penalty for a wife going out without permission be listed under assault? As I mentioned in the previous note, the reading of this passage found in the manuscripts is probably corrupt. Yet, I think the occasions listed here (*bāhyavihāreṣu* and *dvāreṣu*) must be connected to the assault by the husband against the wife and by the wife against the husband listed earlier. The fines for such assaults were given as half the fines for verbal and physical assault (3.3.9). I think the provision here calls for the full fine for verbal or physical assault if the marital assaults are carried out while on a trip outside the home or at the door of the home where others can see the assault.

3.3.12. *does not adorn herself*: The reference is to the wife's refusal to prepare herself for sexual relations with her husband after her menstrual period (see 3.2.44 n.). Such an attitude demonstrates her hatred toward her husband and her unwillingness to perform her marital duties.

3.3.13. *guardian* (anvādhi): The term has the meaning of someone to whom a consignment has been made (3.12.18–19). See also the term *anvādheya* (property received on the occasion of marriage, 3.2.37). The Malayalam commentary takes this person to be the trustee of a woman's property. The term probably refers to an individual who acts in the interest of a married woman and can intervene on her behalf when marital problems arise.

3.3.14. *When he has cheated...social class*: We have here three locative compounds: *dṛṣṭaliṅge maithunāpahāre savarṇāpasarpopagame*. Kangle and Meyer take the three to be separate items about which the man lies. Kangle translates: "One who speaks a falsehood, when indications are clear, when there is a refusal of intercourse or when an approach is made to a person of the same *varṇa* through a secret emissary." I do not think this provision deals with extramarital affairs at all; the whole section deals with the mutual hatred of the couple and, therefore, must refer to refusal to have sex on the part of the husband (as 3.3.12 does with regard to the wife). I take *maithunāpahāre*, cheating with regard to sex, that is, withdrawal of sexual favors from the wife, as the real crime. The first compound gives the evidence for this crime. The meaning of *liṅga* here is not altogether clear, but it must refer to some kind of physical evidence from which the crime is inferred (*anumāna*); if the crime took place at the beginning of the marriage, it could refer to her continuing virginity. The third compound is also unclear; I read both *savarṇā* and *apasarā* as feminine. The meaning could be that the judge could find out the true state of affairs by sending to the woman a female spy of the same social standing or even a relative (see the use of *savarṇa* for a relative at 3.4.29).

3.3.17–18. *If the man . . . she has taken*: If we follow the reading of Kangle's edition, we will have a translation such as that of Kangle: "Or, if the husband seeks divorce because of the wife's offense, he shall give to her whatever he may have taken. Or, if the wife seeks divorce because of the husband's offense, he shall not give her whatever may have been received." Scharfe (personal communication) says that Kangle's translation is supported by the Malayalam commentary. Kangle himself admits, however, that this is a rather strange provision. Kangle thinks that the only criterion for the return of what has been given is the person who files for divorce; but if that was the intent, it could have been said much more simply. But who is the subject of *dadyāt* ("should give") in the two sentences? Kangle takes the man as the subject in both cases. I have taken the subject to be the wife, because generally it is the wife who receives the bride price and other gifts from the husband, not the other way around. Then, we have only to change *asyai* ("to her") of the manuscripts to *asmai* ("to him"). In both Grantha and Malayalam scripts, "*m*" and "*y*" in ligature with "*s*" (*sm* and *sy*) look similar. My tentative translation is based on this new reading. We can then assume that the return of the wife's property to the husband upon divorce is contingent on her being the guilty party.

3.3.26. *teeth . . . seizure fine*: Kangle and Meyer express surprise at the mention of teeth and nails, not the usual places for romantic fondling. Meyer suggests emending *danta* (teeth) to *hasta* (hand), and *nakhālambana* (caressing the nails) to *sakthyālambana* (caressing the thighs). Looking at the Malayalam ligatures, I can see how "*sta*" may be confused for "*nta*" (and then a scribe may have corrected "*ha*" to "*da*"). However, I cannot see how "*kthyā*" could be mistaken for "*khā*". Gaṇapati Śāstrī glosses *dantakṣatakaraṇe* and *nakhakṣatakaraṇe*, that is, in the case of breaking a tooth or a nail. I think this is unlikely, because the entire provision relates to various amorous activities. Although unstated, the fine mentioned is for the woman.

3.3.27. *lashes . . . Paṇas*: The meaning is that the offending parties are given one lash for each Paṇa prescribed as the fine.

3.3.30. *small articles . . . 54 Paṇas*: For these kinds of articles, see 3.17.6–8. Here again, the fines listed are for the woman; the man's is double that of the woman's.

3.3.31. *between two . . . each other*: That is, between a woman and a man who are close relatives and sex between whom would constitute incest. The fines are halved because the gifts may have been given innocently as expressions of affection without any sexual intentions.

transactions with forbidden men: This apparently refers to any dealings the wife may have with men with whom she has been forbidden to have dealings, for example, buying things from them. Here we are not dealing with the exchange of gifts.

3.4.3. *neighbor's* (prativeśa): At *MDh* 8.392, we have the technical use of the term *prātiveśya* to mean a neighbor in front of one's house, as opposed to *ānuveśya*, which refers to a neighbor behind one's house (see 3.20.14 n.). However, here the term is probably used in a more general sense to mean a neighbor; see also *YDh* 2.263.

3.4.17. *exclusion ... Law* (sarvadharmalopa): The probable meaning is that she is excluded from all religious and ritual activities of the family, and perhaps the loss of other rights and responsibilities attached to the position of wife and mother.

3.4.24. *period of one year ... in each case*: The Sanskrit is very concise. The meaning is that a Śūdra wife should wait for one year, a Vaiśya wife for two years, and so forth. The years are similarly extended for each class in the case of women who have children: Śūdra two years, Vaiśya three years, and so forth.

3.4.26. *custodians ... provided for*: The period of time the custodians should maintain the wives is not specified, but it is probably the periods listed in 3.4.24.

3.4.27. *they*: The referent is unclear, but they are probably the relatives of the husbands who were obliged to support the wives. However, at 3.4.30, the release is granted by her custodians.

release (pratimuñceyuḥ): This term, like the term *mokṣa* used at 2.3.15–17, refers to the granting of a divorce, after which the wife may remarry and the former in-laws are released from the burden of supporting her.

3.4.31. *the man who married her* (parigrahītāram): I think this word is used intentionally to show that we are dealing with a situation where the girl has been given in marriage before her puberty. This provision deals with the situation where the "husband" does not come to take her after she attains puberty.

3.4.38. *go to ... of her husband*: That is, have sex with the husband's brother, referring to the custom of levirate common in ancient India, especially when a husband dies without a son. For a discussion of levirate, see *MDh* 9.57–70.

3.4.42. *these heirs*: The reference is not altogether clear. If this verse was taken from a different source, then the original reference is lost. Alternatively, "heirs" (*dāyāda*) here may refer to the various close relatives (presumably also heirs in the absence of sons) of the deceased husband referred to in the preceding provisions.

3.5.1. *whose father ... still there*: As Kangle points out, this phrase is probably a gloss based on *MDh* 9.104, which refers to both parents, that found its way into the text, producing somewhat of a tautology. Note that in the next sentence, reference is made only to the death of the father.

3.5.5–6. *Until then...equal shares*: The balls of rice (*piṇḍa*) at a funerary offering are offered to the previous three generations of ancestors: father, paternal grandfather, and paternal great-grandfather. The offering is made by the son representing the fourth generation, mentioned in the previous statement. So, for four generations, the rice balls are offered to the same ancestors, and thus remain unbroken. With the fifth generation, this line becomes broken. Until then, all brothers receive equal shares, but their children only receive a portion of their father's share. Thus, if one brother has three children, they will inherit only one-third of a share, while if another brother has only one child, he will inherit a full share (3.5.13 n.). This kind of distinction is eliminated after the fourth generation; all after that receive equal shares.

3.5.7. *not received...through partition*: The first refers to those who are living in a joint family prior to partition, and the second refers to those who have received shares through partition but are now reunited, the so-called reunited coparceners.

3.5.8. *property was generated*: The reference is to a brother whose efforts have recovered ancestral property that has been lost or mortgaged or have acquired new property. See *VaDh* 17.51; *MDh* 9.204–209.

3.5.13. *Even if...their father*: This is an inelegantly constructed sentence. Kangle translates: "And a brother's sons, if without their father, shall receive only a single share of the father, even if they are many in number, along with the brothers." This does great violence to the syntax of the sentence, even though it probably brings out the intended meaning. When there is a partition of the paternal estate, each brother gets a single share. If one of the brothers has died, then his sons, even if they are many, receive only the single share that their father would have received had he been alive. This is the so-called *per stirpes* partition of inheritance.

3.5.15. *Among father...received wealth*: Meyer wants to emend the text to read *pūrve 'vidyamāne cāparam* (and when the one listed earlier is not present, they depend on the one listed afterwards); but the emendation is unsupported by the manuscripts and unnecessary. The reference is to the manager of a joint family estate. The older persons take precedence over the younger ones in the allocation of such responsibility.

3.5.20. *clearing any dues* (deyaviśuddha): See 2.16.23 for the same expression. Kangle translates: "clearing it of debts," but *deya* is broader than simply debts. It probably refers to all obligations that the estate has to satisfy.

3.5.24–25. *wordplay...nonexistent*: The term *chala* appears to be used in a logical sense to mean wordplay or sophistry (*Nyāyasūtra*, 1.2.10). If a man is utterly destitute (*niṣkiṃcana*), then he would not even have a water pot. The second sentence seems to confirm this; the poor man cannot partition wealth, not even a water pot, that he does not have.

3.5.26. *He*: The person overseeing the partition is not mentioned. Kangle thinks he is the Justice (*dharmastha*), which is probably right. This is the only place where the causative of the optative is used in the singular and the subject of the verb is left unstated (at 2.5.16, the father is clearly stated). If the person in charge is the Justice, then we have another indication of the broad civil functions of this officer. See Introduction, p. 17.

3.5.31. *have a wife*: The compound *bhāryārthe* is unusual to refer simply to the wife. Meyer compares this to *bhāryāvrata* at *MBh* 12.261.26.

their: Kangle, following Gaṇapati Śastrī, wants to restrict this provision to those who are idiots, etc., thus excluding the first three categories of people.

3.6.7. *single article*: How a single article can be equally divided is unclear. Other legal texts also speak to this issue: Manu (9.119), for example, exempts a single animal that is left after partition from being divided. The rule then is that such singular articles are shared equally by the heirs without subjecting them to physical division. Bṛhaspati (*BṛSm* in Jolly's ed. 25.80–84) supports such an interpretation. So here too, the probable meaning of "divided equally" may be that they are used equally by the heirs. For articles not subject to division, see also *GDh* 28.46–47.

3.6.8. *Sisters... inheritance*: The ability of women (wives, daughters, and other female relatives) to inherit property, especially immovable property, has been a matter of contention in the study of ancient Indian social customs. See above 3.5.10, where daughters are viewed as heirs. In many legal texts, daughters are given reduced shares (*MDh* 9.118; *YDh* 2.115, 117, 135–36; *ĀpDh* 2.14.4; *KSm* 921, 927; Olivelle 2004b).

3.6.17–18. *Among sons... two social classes*: This provision presupposes the norm of hypergamy articulated in the legal texts. A man may marry wives from his own and lower classes. Thus, a Brāhmaṇa may marry wives of all four social classes, a Kṣatriya may marry from three classes, Kṣatriya, Vaiśya, and Śūdra; while a Vaiśya may marry from two classes, Vaiśya and Śūdra. The ratios for partition in these cases are Brāhmaṇa = 4, 3, 2, 1; Kṣatriya = 3, 2, 1; and Vaiśya = 2, 1.

3.6.19–20. *son of a Brāhmaṇa... manly qualities*: These provisions appear to be an alternative to those given in the preceding statement. The meaning of sentence 20 is that the son of a Kṣatriya man from a Vaiśya woman, or the son of a Vaiśya man from a Śūdra woman, receives half a share.

3.7.1–3. *A seed deposited... to be found*: This is an abbreviated statement regarding a central controversy in Brāhmaṇical theology: To whom does a son belong? To the biological father or to the husband of the wife? See *MDh* 9.32–56. Two examples are often cited. Those who support the former position say that the seed determines which tree is produced (mango from a mango seed, etc.) irrespective of the field in which it is sowed. Those who support the latter position say that if a man plants a seed in someone else's field, then the fruit from that tree belongs to the owner of the field and not the owner of the seed. The connection between the example and the exemplified is made easy, because the term for wife and field is the same: *kṣetra*. The cryptic assertion of Kauṭilya is unclear. Kangle is probably correct in taking it to mean that the son may belong to either the one or the other, or even to both (see 3.7.7), depending on the context.

3.7.4. *When a man*: For a longer treatment of these 12 types of sons, see *MDh* 9.158–185, and Kane 1962–1975, III: 641–699.

3.7.19. *those*: The reference is to the other 11 kinds of sons listed above.

3.7.20. *very next class*: That is, a Kṣatriya woman in the case of a Brāhmaṇa, and a Vaiśya woman in the case of a Kṣatriya.

next but one class: That is, a Vaiśya woman in the case of a Brāhmaṇa, and a Śūdra woman in the case of a Kṣatriya.

3.7.24. *Among these*: That is, among the three upper classes, Brāhmaṇa, Kṣatriya, and Vaiśya.

3.7.25. *born in the natural order* (anuloma): According the principle of hypergamy, the natural order is when the husband belongs to the same or a higher class than the wife. The inverse order (3.7.30) is when the wife belongs to a class higher than the husband.

3.7.26–28. *From a Śūdra...the Sūta*: These are sons born from lower-class husbands and upper-class wives. Āyogava is from a Vaiśya wife, Kṣatta and Māgadha from Kṣatriya wives, and Caṇḍāla, Vaidehika, and Sūta from Brāhmaṇa wives.

3.7.29. *The Sūta... Kṣatriya*: This is probably a marginal gloss that found its way into the text. It tries to alert the reader that the Sūta and the Māgadha featured in the Purāṇas are different from the ones mentioned in the previous sentence. The meaning of the term *paurāṇika* is also not altogether clear (see Rocher 1968, 55). Along with Meyer and Kangle, I have taken it as an adjective qualifying Sūta. Yet, we come across the same term referring to a particular class of people; see 5.3.13; 13.1.7.

3.7.33. *Śvapāka*: Literally, a dog cooker, the term refers generally to a most despised and outcaste group of people.

Svayaṃguptā: Literally, "one guarded by oneself." The meaning is quite unclear. Meyer suggests several emendations with the meaning of a suicide.

3.7.36. *he should establish as the Law specific to them* (svadharmaṃ sthāpayet): This phrase is omitted from the critical edition by Kangle, even though it is found in all the manuscripts and the Malayalam commentary. I have restored it here, even though I agree with Kangle that it was probably inserted here from a gloss, in the same way as sentences 38–39. But see the verse, which also speaks of the king as administering the laws of inheritance.

3.7.37. *same qualities as Śūdras*: The term *sadharman* can mean that they have the same nature and/or qualities as Śūdras, and that they follow the same laws and duties of Śūdras. In other words, all these intermediate classes are basically the same as Śūdras.

3.7.38–39. *Only by acting... property*: It is apparent that these two sentences have found their way into the text from glosses, as Kangle has noted. The expression "Only by acting in this manner" (*kevalam evaṃ vartamānaḥ*) also can only be understood within the original context of this statement.

3.8.3. *Alongside... iron*: This passage is quite obscure and corrupt. Kangle's edition reads *karṇakīlāyasasaṃbandhaḥ*, and he translates: "fixed with iron wires in pillars at the corners." First, the meaning of *karṇa* is unclear. Kangle, following the Malayalam commentary, takes it to mean the corners of the property. Meyer takes it to be some kind of hook or protrusion to which possibly an iron wire could be attached. Second, the term *āyasa* means simply iron; Kangle sees an extended meaning and translates it as "iron wires." Harihara Sastri (2011, 89) has offered an emendation that I think is quite reasonable: *karṇakīlāyasasīmābandhaḥ*. We find the expression *sīmābandha* in later texts (see *MDh* 8.255; *BṛSm* 1.9.7) to indicate the erection of a boundary. The term *bandha* is clearly superior to *saṃbandha*, and the former has parallels in sentences 2 (*setubandha*) and 5 (*deśabandha*). I have taken Karṇa (see appendix 1), paralleling iron, as a name of particular trees or wood. This is clearly uncertain, but I think it fits the context better than the labored interpretation of Kangle.

3.8.4. *boundary line*: The expression *setubhoga* occurs only in three places of the *AŚ*, all in the third book (3.8.4; 3.9.3, 14). I have not found it in any other Sanskrit text, including the epics and the Dharmaśāstras. Kangle follows Gaṇapati Śāstrī's commentary in taking *bhoga* to mean "expanse, extent." It is unclear how they arrive at this meaning of the term or whether they derive the term from √*bhuj* (*bhunakti*, to enjoy) or √*bhuj* (*bhujati*, to curve). Meyer translates the expression as "Grenzzeichen" (boundary mark), without showing how that would defer from the simple *setu*. The compound *pranaṣṭasetubhogaṃ sīmānam* at 3.9.14 offers us a clue. Here the boundary (*sīman*) has lost its *setubhoga*. Kangle translates this passage as "the boundary, the extent of the marks of which is lost." But how could the "extent" be lost? I think here *bhoga* indicates the visible line of the *setu*, which, consisting, for example, of a tree or a shrine, may often be located at specific locations along the boundary (e.g., at the corners of a field), rather than all along the boundary. I think *bhoga* means a winding line (from *bhoga* as curve, coil of a snake) of a boundary, perhaps marked either with a wire/rope or with a raised mound of earth. Thus, although *setu* could have and often does have the identical meaning, in the current context, *bhoga* adds the meaning of the continuous and visible borderline between two fields or compounds.

3.8.5. *foundation wall*: Kangle's edition reads *deśabandham*, and he translates it as "fixing of the boundary." The readings of the manuscripts here, however, are very uncertain, some having *vāde* or *pāde* (*va* and *pa* are very similar in southern scripts). I have followed Harihara Sastri's (2011, 89) emendation of *pādabandham*, a technical term in architectural manuals referring to the foundation walls of a house.

3.8.6. *The latrine... tenth day*: The reading of this passage is not altogether clear. The manuscripts appear to read *vānāgṛhocitam*. Kangle emends this to read *vā na gṛhocitād anyatra*. I think the reading *vā na* is justified, but not the other parts of Kangle's emendation. He says that *anyatra* is taken from the Malayalam commentary, but there it was probably part of the gloss rather than the reading of the text. I have looked at all the occurrences of *anyatra* (62 in all) with an ablative in the whole of the *AŚ*. In all these occurrences, *anyatra* comes *before* the word in the ablative. In only three instances (2.27.11; 2.36.33; 3.14.5) does *anyatra* come after the word in the ablative, and in all these cases, *anyatra* forms either a compound or is in close syntactic relationship with a verbal equivalent governing it (*anyatrābharaṇanyāse, anyatra nyāse, anyatra gṛhītavetanaḥ*). It is, therefore, unlikely that *anyatra* would have come in this passage after the ablative *gṛhocitāt*. The reading *gṛhocitam* as qualifying the latrine and the like is problematic, but it probably refers in an indirect way to the fact that they should not be in or adjacent to a place suitable for a house. The meaning of the passage, however, is clear: Water and waste from one house should not go into or near the neighbor's house, except in such emergencies as childbirth, when a lot more water than normal would be used.

3.8.13. *halls*: The reading here is *śālā*, which can mean any room, shed, or other kind of enclosed area. I wonder, however, whether *śālā* should be read as *sālā*, which means a wall. See 2.4.16, where we have a similar error. It is easier to imagine why a protruding wall, which is distinct from the building itself, would be mentioned separately than a room, which would be part of the building itself, unless the reference is to an outside shed for storage and other purposes.

passageway: The term *antarikā* occurs only here and two sentences later at 3.8.15. The meaning is unclear, but it must refer to a space left open between two houses. I take *antarikā* to be derived either from *antar* √*i*, "go between," or from *antara*, "between," and thus a passageway, perhaps to the backyards without having to go through the house itself. From the measurements given, it is clear that the houses were built very close to each other, so much so that the eaves of the roofs could overlap. Also at 3.8.15, *anatarikā* appears to refer to a specific place or path rather than to an unspecified open space. Schlingloff (1969, 27) comments: "The firewalls of adjacent houses never jibe together and a narrow alley lies between them." Such a pathway between houses is also mentioned in the *VaDh* 16.8.

3.8.15. *side door…passageway*: This sentence is quite obscure in both syntax and meaning. Kangle translates: "He should cause to be made a side-door in the intervening lane, measuring one *kiṣku*, for making repairs to what is damaged, not (allowing) crowding." It is difficult to see how this meaning could be derived from the Sanskrit except by forcing a meaning into *khaṇḍaphulla*. I think Meyer is correct in taking *khaṇḍa* to mean the panel(s) of the door and *phulla* to mean their wide opening. I would see the syntax this way: *kiṣkumātram āṇidvāram asaṃpātaṃ khaṇḍaphullārtham antarikāyām*. The meaning is that the side doors of two houses should not face each other so that they would not collide when both are opened.

3.8.17. *covered*: It is unclear how this was done. If it was completely blocked, then its purpose of giving light would be thwarted. It is possible that the window was covered with a curtain, but, of course, we do not know whether curtains were used for windows in ancient India. Another way of covering windows was with a latticework.

3.8.19. *Over the verandah…from rain*: The reading and the meaning of this passage are quite obscure, Kangle and Meyer giving quite different translations. The meaning of *vānalāṭyāḥ* is unknown; "verandah" given by Kangle is an educated guess. From the fact that the violation of this provision carries a fine, it appears that the construction of these covers or walls is viewed as important for the public good. Perhaps the damage from rain concerned not just the private residence of the homeowner but also other buildings nearby and/or the road.

3.8.20. *against the normal procedure*: The expression *pratiloma* (see 3.7.25 n.) implies something done against the normal rules, customs, or conventions. It is unclear what the expression may mean in the present context, but something like "against the normal customs" may be meant.

except…road: The reason and context for this exception are unclear. Kangle finds this provision strange and thinks that instead of avoiding this fine, the provision may be intended to impose a larger fine. In that case, however, one would have expected a specification regarding the enhanced fine. Perhaps obstructing a window that opens onto a road may have been permitted within the rules governing construction in an urban setting. Given the provisions at 3.8.26, however, we may be here dealing with a dwelling used by several families or a large joint family. If that is the case, then we can understand the prohibition of obstructing windows and doors. In any case, I do not think we possess a full grasp of the building practices and codes presupposed by this passage.

3.8.24. *assault*: This is generally viewed as consisting of verbal and physical assault, 3.18–19.

wrongful use: The exact meaning is unclear, but it must refer to the use of the house by the tenant in ways other than those agreed upon or permitted by law.

3.8.25. *annual rent*: The assumption is that the tenant had signed a lease for a full year.

3.8.26. *obstructing…to its use*: The manuscripts have the reading *bhoganigrahe* (as in 3.8.21), which has been emended by Kangle to read *bhogaṃ ca gṛhe*, taking this to be the reading of the Malayalam commentary. Scharfe informs me (personal communication), however, that this reading is found only in Gaṇapati Śāstrī's edition and not in the Malayalam commentary, which supports the reading *nigrahe*. I find this reading quite awkward syntactically. The reading of the manuscripts probably came from a gloss; *bhoganigrahe* (for causing a hindrance to its use) simply elucidates what was stated in *sāmānyam uparundhataḥ* (for someone obstructing a common property). Perhaps the insertion of *bhoga* to qualify *sāmānya* was influenced by its use in the following verse.

3.9.3. *40 neighboring families*: The meaning probably is that there must be representatives from 40 neighboring families. For the division of a city into groups of 40 houses, see 2.36.2. It is possible that such a section constituted a neighborhood, and individuals within that neighborhood had obligations toward each other (3.8.18). This is also indicated by the severity of the punishment for harming members of such a neighborhood: 3.20.15.

borders (maryādā): The distinction between *maryādā* and *sīman* (which I have translated as boundary) is not altogether clear. I think Kangle (notes to 3.9.21 and 5.1.43) is correct in taking the first as referring to the property lines between fields, houses, and the like, and the second as referring to the boundaries between villages. We can make a more general distinction in taking *maryādā* as borders between private property and *sīman* as boundaries between societal or public entities, such as villages, towns, and states; the term is also used for the boundary limit of a Buddhist monastery. Thus, we can see how *maryādā* can be used metaphorically with reference to moral or legal bounds for individuals (1.3.17; 1.7.8; 2.25.3). For an exception, see 3.8.3 n.

In conformity…at this price: For a parallel passage regarding the auctioning of merchandise, see 2.21.7. Meyer and Kangle take the expression *yathāsetubhogam* (see 3.8.4 n. for its meaning) to be outside the proclamation of the auctioneer. I think it is part of the announcement, showing the boundary lines of the piece of property to be auctioned. This corresponds to the announcement of the quantity and quality of the merchandise to be auctioned at 2.21.7–9.

3.9.5. *If the price increases*: It appears that the house could be sold at a set price, or it could be auctioned to the highest bidder, perhaps above the set price (see 2.21.13 n.). As Professor Wezler has pointed out (personal communication), the provisions 3–4 deal with the former, and provisions 5–9 with the latter.

3.9.7. *not an owner*: The meaning of *asvāmin* in this context is not altogether clear. The probable meaning, as Meyer has pointed out, is someone who is not a property owner and thus has no right to bid; perhaps he is an agent or a broker acting on someone else's behalf.

3.9.9. *transgression*: The meaning appears to be that the owner of the property that has been auctioned refuses to hand over the property to the successful bidder.

3.9.11. *incongruous attire* (viparītaveśa): See 2.36.39 n. for this expression. Why in this context witnesses should use such attire is unclear. Perhaps the meaning here is not that they wear female or other incongruous attire, but that they wear unusual clothes. At *MDh* 8.256 and *YDh* 2.152, it is said that the witnesses should wear red clothes and garlands and smear earth on their heads.

3.9.13. *He*: Here as at 3.5.26 (see note to that), the subject is probably the Justice (*dharmastha*).

3.9.14. *apportion the boundary* (sīmānaṃ vibhajet): The underlying meaning is that the king should consider the usefulness of the land or the irrigation works and fix a boundary in such a way that the lands allotted to the two parties yield maximum benefit to them. It is, of course, not the boundary but the land demarcated by the boundary that is apportioned with the creation of a new boundary line. See the identical expression at 3.9.18.

3.9.16. *they*: The subject of this sentence is left unstated. As in the case of the singular verbs (3.5.26; 3.9.7), in spite of the change in number, those making decisions are the Justices (*dharmastha*), 3.1.1.

endorsed: The meaning appears to be the witnesses who initially had the backing of both parties. Their testimony is superior to that of other witnesses. For this entire passage, see the parallel at 2.11.26, 39.

middle course: The meaning appears to be that the Justices should simply divide the land in dispute equally between the two litigating parties.

3.9.20. *If it is seized... for profit*: A good reason may be a loan for which a creditor may have taken a pledge legitimately. The payment is probably made to the owner of the property. The term *bandha* ("amount," see 3.3.4 n., 2.7.21 n.) here probably means the value of the property after making the appropriate deductions.

3.9.25. *each previous...encroachment*: The meaning is that in this list, each preceding one may have to tolerate encroachment by the ones listed later. Thus, dry land brought under cultivation may legitimately encroach on grazing land.

3.9.26. *exclude*: The intent of this exception to the previous rule is to exclude these four kinds of holy places from encroachment. Thus, if there is a temple within dry land, that property cannot be encroached on by others listed later. As Kangle observes, this must have been a gloss that found its way into the text.

shrines, sacrificial grounds: I have taken *devayajana* as two separate items in the list. In the parallel passage at 3.9.23, we have the reading *devakulayajana*. I think *deva* in this sentence stands for *devakula*. Perhaps both these statements are later glosses; the expressions *devakula, devayajana,* and *yajana* with this kind of meaning are not found elsewhere in the *AŚ*.

3.9.33. *newly constructed*: The expression *navapravartana* (turning out something anew) is construed with all the clauses of this sentence with slightly different meanings: new construction, renovation/restoration, and cleaning up. In the case of dry land, we have the most extended meaning of this expression: turning virgin/barren tracts into newly cultivated land.

3.9.34. *That person*: That is, the owner of the reservoir or dike to whom an exemption has been granted by the state. In spite of this concession, he is free to mortgage or sell it. Perhaps it is implied that the mortgagee or the new owner also continues to enjoy the same concession.

3.9.35. *They should give...produced from them*: The long compound that takes up much of this sentence has an impossible syntax (*khātaprāvṛttimanadīnibandhāyatanataṭākakedārārāmaṣaṇḍavāpānām*). The reading must be corrupt, but there is no easy emendation without doing violence to the text. This compound also has unique words and expressions not encountered elsewhere: *prāvṛttima, nadīnibandhāyatana*. I follow Meyer and Kangle in taking the first half to refer to sources of water and the second half to the fields that are irrigated and from which the owners of the water sources receive a share.

3.10.1. *canal for irrigation water* (karmodakamārga): The meaning of *karmodaka* is not apparent. Kangle translates "water-course in use," taking *karma* to mean in use. However, at 2.24.19 (see my note there), where also the compound *karmodaka* occurs, the meaning clearly is water that is provided through labor, that is, irrigation water (so also Meyer).

3.10.6. *reducing their size*: The meaning of the term *atikarṣaṇa* is unclear. It is juxtaposed to *karṣaṇa* (plowing) of the next sentence. I follow the lead of Kangle, who thinks that the original reading may have been *atikarśane*.

3.10.13. *Even...to him*: A new settler in a village may be given the freedom to buy a house or land in the community. It is unclear who has the power to give this right. Kangle thinks it is the village headman. Given that the unstated subject of verbs in this book is generally the Justice (*dharmastha*), it is also likely that this authority may have rested in the Justices.

3.10.15. *Persons exempt ... revenue*: The fields exempt from taxes are in a tax-exempt village. If a person from such a village lives in a taxable area, he may yet use the tax-exempt yield from his fields.

3.10.21. *They should live ... grazing*: The subject of this sentence appears to be grass cutters, both here and in the next sentence. Perhaps these were individuals who took care of the pasture land and charged fees and fines on those who used the land for grazing. The transition, however, is abrupt, perhaps indicating that this passage is taken from another source.

3.10.24. *Bulls belonging to a god or a village*: The Sanskrit compound *grāmadevavṛṣāḥ* could also be translated as "Bulls belonging to a village god (i.e., village temple)." Meyer and Kangle follow the latter interpretation. I follow Gaṇapati Śāstrī's interpretation, taken from the Malayalam commentary: *grāmavṛṣabhāḥ devavṛṣabhāś ca*, especially because we do not encounter a village god or temple in the *AŚ*. For the property of gods, see 1.19.29 n.
old bulls and stud bulls: I follow the Malayalam commentary and Gaṇapati Śāstrī in taking *ukṣāṇo govṛṣāś ca* as referring to two classes of animals. Meyer and Kangle take both terms as referring to the same class, namely stud bulls.

3.10.35. *after entering into an agreement*: The expression *abhyupetya* is a technical term within the context of contracts. We find in the *YDh* (2.182) and the *NSm* (5.1) the expression *abhyupetyāśuśrūṣā*, which is one of the grounds for litigation (*vyavahārapada*). In the present case, a farmer takes up residence in a village that imposes contractual obligations on him as a member of the village.

3.10.36. *not paying the money*: The probable context is a common activity for which each villager is assessed a share of the cost.

3.10.39. *They*: The subject of this sentence is not specified. Given that the discussion focuses on conventions that must be upheld by those who have entered into agreements, the reference must be to villagers and others who belong to communities governed by conventions. The person issuing orders is probably the one elected or appointed to act on behalf of the community, for example, the village elder or headman.

3.10.40. *concourses*: For the meaning of *saṃkrama*, see my note to 2.3.29–30. These concourses were either bridges or causeways across rivers and streams.

3.11.1. *righteous*: The Sanskrit *dharmyā* in this context is ambiguous. It means "in keeping with *dharma*," but the meaning of *dharma* here is uncertain. I think it refers to righteousness and piety (see 3.10.2) and also to interest rates between individuals, as opposed to the commercial (*vyāvahārika*) rates, which are higher. These rates are also only for monetary debts. The distinction between *dharmya* and *vyāvahārika* may also relate to the four areas of law enunciated at *AŚ* 2.7.2; 3.3.1.39.

3.11.4. *it is monetized... that capital*: The compound *mūlyakr̥tā* (feminine) must qualify interest (*vr̥ddhi*). So, if the interest is not paid in grain at the end of the harvest, then the grain given on loan and the interest due on it are monetized and converted into capital to which the normal interest rate would apply.

3.11.6. *remains obstinate*: The reference is to a person who has taken the investment loan but refuses to pay the interest. In this and the preceding example, the debtor has defaulted on the interest payment for quite some time. The payment of twice the capital follows the normal rule of Indian commercial law, according to which interest can only amount to twice the loan, after which it ceases to bear interest (this rule is called *dāmdupaṭ* in modern times); see *MDh* 8.151.

3.11.7. *amount*: For the meaning of the difficult term *bandha*, see the note to 2.7.38. Kangle takes the term to mean one-fifth (*pañcabandha*) or one-tenth (*daśabandha*) that a person losing a lawsuit has to pay as a fine. If that was the intent, it is unclear why the author did not use those expressions, as, for example, at 3.12.6. It appears to me that the meaning here is that the person committing this fraud before the court is assessed four times the full amount he has claimed. See the similar expression at 3.11.41.

3.11.8. *trifling amount*: Kangle takes this to mean that a small amount that was never lent is claimed through witnesses. Gaṇapati Śāstrī thinks that a small amount was lent, but a greater amount is claimed through witnesses. In either case, the amount of the fraud is small.

3.11.9. *three-quarters*: The meaning of *tribhāga* is not altogether clear. Kangle takes it to mean one-third; but then the witness would be paying more than the claimant! We see that *bhāga* often refers to a quarter, *dvitīyam āyuṣo bhāgam* in *MDh* 4.1. The B-R Dictionary cites the *Pañcatantra* for the meaning of *tribhāga* as three-quarters.

3.11.14. *A money-lender's... co-responsibility*: In the interpretation of this and the following sentences, I have departed from the ones offered by Meyer and Kangle. These three sentences deal with liabilities of a dead person in decreasing importance. The first is *kusīda*, which I have taken as a loan given by a professional money lender. The obligation to pay this back in the event of the borrower's death falls on three groups of individuals related in various ways to the borrower: his sons, other heirs who have inherited his estate, and finally sureties who guaranteed the loan's repayment. To interpret this passage adequately, we have to understand the technical meaning of *kusīda*. This appears to have been an old term meaning someone who is lazy or indolent, and it appears with that meaning in both the Vedic literature and the Buddhist Pāli literature (*kusīta*). Its technical meaning of a loan carrying interest probably developed later, being first attested to in a significant verse cited in the Śrautasūtras (*ĀpŚr* 13.24.15; *BauŚr* 4.11). But its most frequent use in this sense is in the Dharma literature (*GDh* 10.6, 49; 11.21; 12.29, 36; 15.18; *MDh* 1.90; 8.151, 152; 8.410; 10.116; *YDh* 1.119; 3.42; *VaDh* 2.19; *NSm* 1.42, 86; *BṛSm* 1.1.8, 11, 74; 1.2.11; 1.7.4; 1.9.29; 1.10.6, 69, 102, 122; 1.26.147). In general, the term refers to professional money lending. It is looked down upon as usury (*vārddhuṣya*) in the Dharma texts and sanctioned mostly for Vaiśyas. *Kusīda* is a special kind of debt (*ṛṇa*) surrounded by special rules (*BṛSm* 1.10.102), especially the requirement of a pledge or surety (*BṛSm* 1.10.5–6). Further, *kusīda* is a monetary debt as opposed to other kinds of borrowing (e.g., grain), which were probably carried out among private individuals rather than through money lenders. Thus, the borrower and all related to him have a special obligation to pay back a *kusīda* (we can compare this kind of loan to a modern bank loan). Another problem in interpreting this sentence relates to the meaning of *sahagrāhiṇaḥ* that precedes *pratibhuvaḥ*. Kangle takes the two as separate entries in the list and translates the former as "co-debtors," that is, individuals who took the loan along with the deceased person. Both the syntax of the sentence and the occurrence of these two terms together at 2.7.5 indicate, however, that the former is an adjective qualifying the latter. After stating that the loan of a dead man should be paid by his sons, the author gives alternatives in pairs: *dāyādā vā rikthaharāḥ* (or by the heirs who inherited his estate) and *sahagrāhiṇaḥ pratibhuvo vā* (or the sureties who assumed co-responsibility); for the use of *vā* after the second member of a noun phrase, see 1.20.21; 3.13.11–12; 3.18.6). The latter expression occurs also at 2.7.5 in the context of a state official who fails to carry out his assigned task, thereby incurring a loss to the treasury. Here the sureties are placed first in the list of those responsible for repairing the loss. It is apparent that within the context of an appointed official, *sahagrāhin* cannot be "co-receivers" (as Kangle translates the term there). Who could be the people who undertook a task along with an appointed official? It is more likely that officials in charge of carrying out work projects involving the outlay of expenditure were required to post a bond in the form of a surety who would assume responsibility for the official's malfeasance. I think the term *sahagrāhin* refers to a particular kind of surety who assumes financial responsibility for a loan or an official appointment, quite similar to the category of *dānapratibhū* of later texts I discuss in the next note.

3.11.15. *and not any other liability of a surety* (na prātibhāvyam anyat): It is in the context of the explanation of the previous sentence that we can understand the provision of this phrase, which provides an exception regarding the liability of a surety. He is obliged to pay only a *kusīda* and not other kinds of obligations assumed by a surety. In later texts, the former kind of a surety is called *dānapratibhū*, a surety responsible for the payment of a debt (and I think *kusīda* specifically refers to such a debt). Other kinds of sureties include *darśanapratibhū*, a surety for appearance (i.e., that the man will appear either at the time stipulated to pay the debt or in court), and *pratyayapratibhū*, a surety who is a guarantor of the debtor's trustworthiness (*YDh* 2.53; *MDh* 8.158–162). In this and the following sentences, I understand the term *prātibhāvyam* as referring to the liabilities assumed by or connected with a surety (see 3.16.9, where this meaning is clear), rather than simply to the state of being a surety (suretyship, according to Kangle). In this way, we can understand the connection of this and the following sentences to the main provision of sentence 14.

3.11.16–17. *A surety's liability... take the estate*: All editors and translators take 16 and 17 as separate sentences containing different provisions. Kangle's edition reads: 16—*asāraṃ bālaprātibhāvyam* ("The suretyship of a minor is void in law"); 17—*asaṃkhyātadeśakālaṃ tu putrāḥ pautrā dāyādā vā rikthaṃ haramāṇā dadyuḥ* ("But sons, grandsons or heirs inheriting the property shall (be liable to) pay a (debt about the repayment) of which the place and the time are not fixed"). I think this is incorrect; these two statements form a single syntactic unit. My emended version reads *asārabālaprātibhāvyam asaṃkhyātadeśakālaṃ tu putrāḥ pautrā dāyādā vā rikthaṃ haramāṇā dadyuḥ*. My emendation makes 16 a single compound *asārabālaprātibhāvyam* that nicely parallels the compound in 18, *jīvitavivāhabhūmiprātibhāvyam*, with both being qualified by the identical compound, *asaṃkhyātadeśakālaṃ*. The editors have been misled by the *anusvāra* occurring at the end of *asāraṃ*, thus taking it as qualifying *prātibhāvyam*. As I have shown in the note to 3.1.34–35, the term *asāra* in the *AŚ* never means a statement or an act that is invalid or null and void. It always refers to articles of little value or to a poor person. Further, it is quite extraordinary to have a provision about the invalidity of a suretyship entered into by a boy within this context! My reading requires simply the deletion of the *anusvāra* at the end of *asāraṃ* (which is not a major change given the frequency with which these diacritics are inserted and omitted in manuscripts) and taking the term as part of the compound. This compound parallels the one in the next sentence and, as in that compound, here also the first two words do not indicate the subject of the suretyship, but the persons/things pertaining to which the suretyship is assumed. Note that in this provision as I have interpreted it, the obligation to pay the liability incurred as a surety by a deceased person falls on only three categories of people: sons, grandsons and heirs (sureties of the previous provision are omitted). In the next provision, such obligations fall only on sons and grandsons. The issue, however, is what a liability relating to a pauper or a child would be. Given that a child would not be able to enter into a legal contract (3.3.1), it cannot refer to a surety in such a transaction. The likely scenario then, is that a legitimate transaction, to which the deceased individual was a surety, at the current time involves a pauper or a child. That is, the money owed as a result of the transaction will go to such a person. We may assume that the original lender has now fallen on hard times and is in need of the money, or that the lender has died leaving the estate to his minor children, who are now the beneficiaries. In such cases, there is a stronger obligation on the part of the sons and heirs to pay back the loan of their dead kinsman. This obligation, however, is effective only if the surety had not specified a place and time of repayment (so also in the next provision). Thus, the obligation is open-ended. If such a specification had been made and that time and place had passed, then there is no obligation. See 3.16.9, which makes the general rule that sons and heirs, if unwilling, do not have to pay the monetary liabilities derived from their father's suretyship. Clearly, the current provision is an exception to that general rule when the recipient is a pauper or a minor.

3.11.18. *A surety's liability…grandsons*: This kind of suretyship appears to carry the least weight; the obligation to fulfill it falls only on the deceased man's sons and grandsons. The surety for life guarantees the life of someone, that is, a guarantee that the man will not be harmed (see an example at 3.18.11). A surety for marriage probably refers to the guardian (*sukhāvastha*; see 3.3.13 n.; 3.4.9, 26), while a surety for land may refer to a person who guarantees that a piece of land will be returned by a tenant. Note the change of verb from *dadyuḥ* (they should give) of the first two provisions to *vaheyuḥ* (they should bear) here. The latter is also the verb used at 2.7.5 (see 3.11.14 n.) with respect to the sureties. Here there is no loan to be paid back, but other responsibilities that must be carried out. Later literature, however, exempts descendants from obligations derived from their deceased father's suretyship, except when the surety guaranteed payment (*dānapratibhū*); see Kane 1962–1975, III: 437.

3.11.19. *two…single individual*: That is, two creditors should not file lawsuits against the same debtor simultaneously. This principle is articulated more generally in *YDh* 2.9.

3.11.23. *herdsmen and sharecroppers*: The relationship between wives and husbands of certain communities and professions was viewed as different from the general norms. See, for example, *AŚ* 3.4.22; *MDh* 8.362. For specific rules regarding debts, see *YDh* 2.48; *NSm* 1.15–16.

3.11.25. *It is best…made*: If the party being sued admits the claim made by the plaintiff, that would be the best outcome. This may be the course intended when the *MDh* 8.49 speaks of *dharma* as the first course in settling a lawsuit. When an admission is not forthcoming, then a trial with witnesses ensues, which is called *vyavahāra* by Manu.

3.11.27. *never one with regard to a debt*: Other sources, including the *YDh*, which depends heavily on the *AŚ*, permit a single witness within specific contexts; *MDh* 8.77; *YDh* 2.72. The intent here may be to preclude a single witness specifically in litigations regarding debts.

3.11.29. *a man with sores*: The term *vraṇin* could also mean a man with a wound (so Meyer and Kangle). Coming immediately after a leper, however, it probably makes more sense to take the term to mean a man who has a long-term skin affliction with sores, rather than a man who simply happens to be wounded.

self-appointed (svayaṃvādin): That is, a man who presents himself as a witness on his own, without being formally nominated or appointed by either of the parties to the dispute. See *NSm* 1.143.

3.11.37. *your*: Note that, even though the words are supposed to be addressed to a Śūdra in the singular, they contain pronouns in the plural (*vaḥ, yuṣmān*).

if an untruth is spoken: I think this statement and what follows are general provisions that apply to Kṣatriyas, Vaiśyas, and Śūdras, thus making 37–38 a single syntactical unit.

3.11.38. *fined 12 Paṇas*: According to the Malayalam commentary, followed by Gaṇapati Śāstrī, this is for each day after the seventh day.

3.11.39. *they*: The reference is probably to the three Justices (*dharmastha;* 3.1.1).

3.11.41. *excess amount as penalty* (atiriktasya bandham): For the meaning of *bandha*, see 2.7.21 n. Kangle assumes that *bandha* here is a shorthand for *pañcabandha* (one-fifth of the amount; see 3.11.33 n.). I doubt that *bandha* is used in this sense in the *AŚ*, especially because such a usage would create confusion, because we have both *pañcabandha* and *daśabandha*. I think *bandha* is used within the context of litigation to indicate that the amount paid to the state is a penalty but not a fine (for which *daṇḍa* is used; 3.11.45). It is also difficult to understand why the full amount of the excess is taken by the king when the witnesses testify to an amount larger than the claim and not when it is less.

3.11.43. *poorly witnessed* (duḥśrutam): Kangle translates "badly heard," thus connecting both this and bad writing to a document. But the verb √*śru* and its derivatives are used frequently for witnesses (e.g., *śrotṛ* at *AŚ* 3.1.4, 14; 3.10.2; 3.11.48–49; 3.13.2). Scharfe (personal communication) informs me that my interpretation is supported by the Malayalam commentary.

3.11.45. *that*: That is, the amount under litigation. See 4.9.20.

3.11.46. *break their trust*: The expression *visaṃvādayatām* is unclear. Because of the causative, Kangle takes it to mean testimony that leads to a wrong judgment. The term, however, never has the meaning of a judgment in its various usages within the *AŚ*. Most frequently, it refers to people who break their word or trust. In the present context, the reference is to bearing false witness.

3.11.48–49. *for witnesses . . . do not speak*: This passage is somewhat unclear. I think the author is using the verb √*śru* in a pregnant sense of testifying truthfully. Thus, in the last sentence, those who fail to testify truthfully (*aśṛṇvatām*) are distinguished from those who simply will not speak in the court when questioned (*abruvāṇānām*; see *MDh* 8.13). The intent of the entire passage, however, is obscure.

3.12.1. *The discussion . . . deposits*: Note that only the special rules applying to deposits are given here; other issues pertaining to deposits are implicitly explained under debt. Thus the topic of debt becomes the *prakṛti* or the archetype for litigation. That is the reason why aspects of judicial procedure, such as witnesses, are dealt with under debt in the legal literature.

3.12.2. *when one is besieged . . . salvaged*: The manuscript reading here is probably corrupt: *grāmamadhyāgnyudakābādhe vā kiṃcid amokṣayamāṇe kupyam anirhāryavarjam ekadeśamuktadravye vā jvālāvegoparuddhe vā*. Kangle emends this radically by deleting *vā kiṃcid . . . -muktadravye vā*, taking these words to be derived from a marginal gloss. I think some changes have been made to the text by a scribe who did not fully understand the original and wanted to insert a comment. The likely candidate for such an insertion is *kupyam anirhāyavarjam* (forest produce, with the exception of what cannot be exported; see *VaDh* 19.14–16; *MDh* 8.399), which stands out in a statement with words in the locative. They were probably inserted to account for the term *dravye*. I have deleted just these words, as well as the final *vā* following *jvālāvegoparuddhe*; clearly, with so many *vā* in the text, a scribe may have inserted one here thinking that the compound was independent of the preceding. I think this compound should be taken within the context of the previous three: During a major fire or flood in a village, either all the good of the village could have perished or only a small portion was saved, but the man holding the pledge suffered a total loss. The overall meaning of the passage, however, is clear. A person holding a deposit is not liable for its loss in the event of a natural or other form of catastrophe over which he had no control. However, he himself must have been subject to such an event, and the deposit should have been destroyed or plundered in the process.

3.12.4. *flees under other conditions*: This implies that the deposit consists of a living being, animal or human. See also the death of a deposit mentioned in the following sentence. The statement "under other conditions" (*anyathā*) probably means circumstances other than its use. Kangle thinks it refers to the ill treatment of the pledge (see 3.12.7).

3.12.6. *four times one-fifth the amount* (caturguṇapañcabandha): For the meaning of *bandha*, see 2.7.21 n. The payment of four times one-fifth is somewhat strange; see 3.11.7, where it is *bandhacaturguṇaḥ* (four times the *bandha*). The amount refers to the value of the deposit.

3.12.8. *pledge* (ādhi): A pledge is like a collateral for a mortgage to guarantee repayment. It is different from a deposit (*upanidhi*), which is given for safekeeping and is not supposed to be used by the one taking the deposit.

3.12.13. *facility for . . . destruction*: The meaning of the compound *anāśavināśakaraṇa* is unclear. Kangle thinks it may refer to "a lost property office." It is more likely, however, that the reference is to a common depository or bank where property could be held for safekeeping. Generally in ancient India, property for safekeeping was deposited with prominent individuals (see, for example, the story of the iron-eating mice in the first book of the *Pañcatantra*). This provision may indicate that there may have been also collective depositories for such items. We see that property of minors could be deposited with village elders, 2.1.27; 3.5.19; but this is the only place where this kind of depository or office is mentioned. At 3.16.21, the customs house acts as a place for lost-and-found property. See also the guardian of pledges mentioned in the next sentence. This official is mentioned nowhere else in the text.

3.12.16. *security*: The meaning of the term *bandha* here is unclear. Kangle takes it as the equivalent of *pañcabandha* (one-fifth) or *daśabandha* (one-tenth). See my note to 3.3.4 (also 3.11.7), which parallels this passage. Here also the reference probably is to a security that is provided to forestall any future abuse of the pledge.

3.12.18. *directives and assignments*: The term *ādeśa*, occurring also at 3.1.16, appears to mean a directive given to someone to carry out a task at some other place. An assignment (*anvādhi*), on the other hand, is an actual item that is handed over to another person to be delivered to a distant location.

3.12.25. *original price* (mūlya): This refers to the actual value of the goods given to the agent. It appears that the understanding is that the agent would sell the goods to realize at least the original value. If they are sold above that value, then a profit is realized.

3.12.30. *intended for distant places and times* (deśakālāntaritānām): The meaning appears to be that the goods are to be sold either at a distant location or after a long lapse of time.

3.12.33. *consignments*: The term *nikṣepa* refers especially to raw material, such as gold and yarn, given to artisans for conversion into finished products (see 2.14.5), but the term also refers to other kinds of deposits given for safekeeping.

3.12.34. *he forfeits it* (hīyeta): This probably refers to a situation where an artisan is given some raw material by one person, and the artisan hands over the finished product to a different person. The artisan loses his right to the article and has to compensate the original owner for the loss. See 3.16.30 for *hīyeta* with a genitive, meaning that the man loses his right to something.

3.12.37. *written receipt*: The term *karaṇa* refers to any kind of legal evidence, but often specifically refers to documentary evidence; see 3.1.15–16. In the present context, the term probably refers to a receipt given to the depositor that would prove that the consignment was actually handed over to the artisan. In the absence of this practice, judges will have to use other criteria.

3.12.39. *An old*: The provisions in this paragraph appear to involve the authorities. They are the ones who will use these ruses to test the honesty of artisans who take consignments. The previous paragraph deals with the person who was cheated and ways he may prove to a court that the artisan is lying.

3.12.45. *Or else…marked article*: The meaning of this provision is unclear, and it is also difficult to see how it is connected to the rest of this section, given that it says nothing different from the other provisions. Perhaps we are dealing again with a marginal comment that has found its way into the text.

3.12.46–50. *Alternatively…stated above*: This section is somewhat convoluted, and there is a good likelihood that these provisions have found their way into the text from a commentary. The natural sequence of the text appears to be as follows: sentence 38, where the man cheated of his consignment attempts to gather evidence against the artisan. Then section 3.12.39–44 instructs the official, probably the Justice (*dharmastha*), to initiate clandestine operations to find out the honesty of the artisan. This should be followed by 3.12.51 that deals with the actual investigation undertaken by the official, probably connected to a trial. In sentence 45, the meaning of the verb *pratyānayet* (draw in, recover; see 3.16.26–27) is unclear. I take it to mean some form of entrapment. Kangle thinks that the difference between this and passage 42–44 is that here, the cheated man himself takes the initiative. In the passage 3.12.49–50, it is unclear what "both" refers to; the reference may be to the raw material and the finished product (see 4.1.2 n.). The statement is probably derived from a different context. The Malayalam commentary, however, takes the two to be a deposit (*nikṣepa*) and an article given for use (*prayogadravya*). Meyer thinks that two items should have been mentioned, and one of them has dropped out of the text.

3.12.51. *circumstantial evidence* (upaliṅgana): The meaning appears to be that the judge should look at various marks and indicators, that is, circumstantial or corroborative evidence, that would prove the connection of the article to the claimant. This term appears to refer to subsidiary kinds of evidence that may be used to prove a case when the major sources of evidence are lacking. See the similar use of the term *upaliṅgana* in judicial settings at 3.13.37; 3.19.21; 4.6.12–13; 4.12.35.

3.12.52. *secret associations*: The meaning is that transactions of such associations also need to be investigated clandestinely, just like those of artisans (see 3.1.11).

3.13. *Topic 65*: This topic is subdivided into two sub-topics (65a and 65b). The second sub-topic is further subdivided into two, dealing with employers and employees. The first part of 65b constitutes the second half of chapter 13, while the second spills over into chapter 14. Regarding this rather problematic division of topic 65, see Scharfe 1993, 30–31.

3.13.1. *subsistence slave* (udaradāsa): This is an individual who becomes a slave in order to obtain maintenance. Thus, no sale takes place. The *MDh* 8.415 and *NSm* 5.26 call this kind of slave a *bhaktadāsa*. For a detailed account of the textual sources for slavery, see Kane 1965–1972, II: 180–187; Chanana 1960.

3.13.1–2. *his own people, different group of people* (svajana, parajana): The man who makes the sale or pledge of some person either belongs to the same group as that person or to some other group. Kangle takes the terms to mean kinsman and stranger. I follow Meyer in taking the terms more broadly to refer to particular social groups not necessarily based on kinship. At *AŚ* 2.36.6 and 3.10.37, *svajana* means people belonging to one's own profession.

3.13.4. *Ārya*: Here, as in the preceding passage, the reference is to a child who is still a minor.

3.13.5. *when the family has become bonded* (kulabandhane): Kangle explains that the whole family has pledged itself to another, more wealthy family. It appears that the entire family has placed itself in some form of bondage in order to survive a time of adversity. Within that context, a young member of the family (referred to here as Ārya) has been given as a pledge to another family.

3.13.6. *succumbs*: I think Kangle is right in taking the verb *sīdet* to indicate that the person is reduced to slavery. Here we are dealing, of course, with a human pledge. A pledge has more rights than a slave (see 3.13.9), and this threat would have kept a pledge from fleeing his master.

or have stolen money: All the editions read *vittāpahāriṇo vā* and place this at the beginning of the next sentence. This qualification of *dāsasya* in that sentence has caused a lot of problems in understanding the provision. I have emended the reading to *vittāpahāriṇau*. It is easy to confuse *-hāriṇo* (gen. sing.) and *-hāriṇau* (mas. dual) both in Devanāgarī and in southern scripts. Translators also have had trouble explaining *vā* ("or"), because coming at the beginning of the sentence, it would have to be an alternative to the previous sentence. That, however, is unlikely. The alternative given by *vā* is, I think, to the immediate reduction to slavery, which happens when the pledge runs away to a foreign country *or* runs away after stealing money. Thus, 3.13.7 deals with such a pledge turned into a slave.

3.13.7. *Someone... half the fine*: See the previous note for the emendation of the reading. I think this sentence deals with a pledge who has been converted into a slave, which answers Kangle's puzzlement over this sentence dealing with a slave in the middle of a discussion of pledges. If that pledge was an Ārya individual, then even after being converted into a slave, he maintains his Ārya status, and the master cannot deprive him of that. What this amounts to in practice is difficult to say, but it probably refers to exemption from menial jobs such as carrying filth (3.13.9). Half the fine probably refers to the fines listed in the very first sentence.

3.13.10. *servant who has had a child*: The gender of *upacārakasya* is masculine, which has caused some problems in the interpretation of this provision. Kangle thinks that in spite of the gender, a female attendant is intended, and indeed the surrounding provisions deal with female pledges and servants. The term *abhiprajāta* occurs only here and at 3.15.13. In the latter passage, the term is given in the dual and the reference is clearly to the birth of a child to parents. Thus, it is possible to use the term with reference also to the father. I think this is the meaning in the current passage. If a male attendant given to a creditor as a pledge receives news that he has had a child, namely, that his wife has given birth, then it is not an offense for him to leave the creditor and go home. Note also that the term for going away here is *apakramaṇa* (see 3.3.32; 3.14.23–24), while for fleeing or running away, the term used is *niṣ* √*pat*.

3.13.11. *female nurse given as a pledge*: The position of *vā* ("or") after the second word is unusual, and one is tempted to translate "female nurse or pledge"; but see the very next sentence where *vā* also occurs after the second word (*kanyām āhitakāṃ vā*), but the second clearly qualifies the first.

under his control... someone else: If a man rapes a woman given as a pledge, and he is the creditor to whom the woman was given, then the fine is lower than if the rape was done by another man.

3.13.15. *Ārya status*: Here the term *āryatva*, which occurs only here, probably means freedom from slavery, rather than the condition of being an Ārya.

3.13.19. *An Ārya individual... half the price*: The syntax is rather problematic, and the exact meaning is unclear. We must assume that this refers to the redemption of an enslaved prisoner of war. The specific time period or who fixes that period is left unstated (see 3.13.27 for the same expression and *MBh* 12.97.4, where a period of one year is specified). It is also unclear what "price" (*mūlya*) means in this context. Kangle takes it to mean the usual or the going price for a slave, but such a price is never discussed in this text. One other possibility is that a man captured in battle is then sold, and the price here may refer to that sale price.

3.13.20. *born in... purchased*: Other legal texts make explicit classifications of slaves. The most elaborate is given in the *NSm* (5.24–26), where 15 kinds of slaves are listed.

3.13.23. *non-slave*: The exact meaning of *adāsa* here and elsewhere (see 2.36.41; 3.13.24; 4.12.27) is not altogether clear. The woman (or man) is no longer to be considered a slave. However, what sorts of rights of a free person that he or she is granted remain uncertain. In other places, where a slave pays a fee for his redemption, the term *ārya* is used with reference to such a freed person; see 3.13.21. The question is whether there is a difference between *ārya* and *adāsa*.

3.13.24. *her brother and sister*: That is, if they also have been slaves of the same master.

3.13.33–34. *one-tenth... one-fifth*: The intent appears to be that the fine should be either one-tenth or six Paṇas, or one-fifth or twelve Paṇas, whichever is higher.

3.14.6. *he*: Here and in the following passages, the Sanskrit does not identify the subject of any of the verbs. It is clear, however, that when the reference is to the work being carried out, the pronouns refer to the employee, whereas when the question is about payment of wages or evaluating the completion of a task, the reference is to the employer.

come to him: The situation seems to be that a contract had been made with this particular worker. When he comes to do the work, the employer is obliged to give him the work and the wages.

3.14.8–9. *Wages are... as done*: It is unclear whether these statements constitute a part of Kauṭilya's view, because there is no *iti* at the end that would signify the completion of a quotation. Yet, I think it is reasonable to assume that these qualifiers are intended to support the initial "no" of Kauṭilya.

3.14.13. *theirs*: The plural here must refer to the workers within a sodality. One of their members is sent as a pledge, that is, to perform the work contracted by the sodality. The worker is similar to a pledge in that he is sent by a third party and is obliged to work for the employer for a set period of time. It appears that after seven days, he is replaced by a new worker.

3.14.24. *no one... quit*: It is unclear whether we have a general rule here: Once the work of a partnership has commenced, a partner is not free to quit whenever he feels like it. That is how I have interpreted it. Kangle takes this provision as an extension of the previous one: "Nor shall he have the freedom to keep away." But the word *apakramaṇe* here (interpreted by Kangle as "keep away") and the word *apakrāmataḥ* of the previous sentence must have the same meaning, that is, quitting or going away. For the obligations of partners, see also 2.1.22–23.

3.14.25. *A swindler...ensnared*: The term *grāhayet*, which I have translated as "ensnare," is problematic, and its meaning is unclear. The provision, I think, refers to the case when one of the workers in a partnership is suspected of swindling the company, but there is no clear proof. He should be caught by setting a trap. The subject of the verb here is also unclear. Kangle translates as "he." I think the subject is probably the sodality (*saṅgha*), but I have left the subject open by using the passive.

3.14.26. *goes elsewhere* (anyatra): The meaning is unclear. Kangle takes this to mean that the man has abandoned the work and gone away for good. But see the use of *anyatra* at 3.14.5, where the meaning is clearly another employer. Thus, the term here may mean that the man has joined another partnership or sodality.

3.14.27. *traitor* (dūṣya): The term is used in 5.1–2 with reference to traitors to the state. That cannot be the meaning here, except that the man has become a traitor to his sodality or partnership. It is unclear whether the sodality is supposed to inflict secret punishment on such a man, as the state does to a traitor.

3.14.28. *except for...activities of each*: The *MDh* (8.209) gives examples of such special fees: "At the establishment of the sacred fires, the Adhvaryu priest should take the chariot, the Brahman priest the steed, the Hotṛ priest the horse, and the Udgātṛ priest the cart used for the purchase of Soma."

3.14.29. *Agniṣṭoma...the full share*: The Agniṣṭoma is the principal Soma sacrifice. The consecration of the sacrificer takes place on the first day. The Upasad is a set of rites that takes place twice a day before the pressing of the Soma and after the heating of the Pravargya vessel. The first of these takes place on the second day, so the middle Upasad takes place on the third day of the Soma sacrifice. The heating of the Pravargya vessel takes place before each Upasad rite. The day of the pressing is the fifth day of the rite. So, given that the entire rite is almost complete, a priest who falls ill on this day receives almost the entire share of the sacrificial fee.

3.14.31. *pressing for Bṛhaspati*: This is a one-day Soma sacrifice that follows the major *Vājapeya* sacrifice; see *ĀpŚr* 22.7.5f.

3.14.37–38. *three sacred fires*: These are the three major Vedic fires required for Vedic sacrifices: offertorial fire (*āhavanīya*) in the east, householder's fire (*gārhapatya*) in the west, and southern fire (*dakṣiṇāgni*). For these provisions regarding the obligation to offer sacrifices, see *MDh* 11.7–15.

3.15.1. *defect, a disaster, or unacceptability*: This expression is repeated at 3.10.8 and 3.15.9. We have a similar expression "decay or disaster" (*bhreṣopanipāta*) at 3.12.23, 29; 4.1.6. These set down conditions under which a transaction may be annulled by the seller. The defect in the merchandise probably refers to a defect that the seller discovered after the sale. See 3.15.14–16 for the seller's obligation to disclose defects. The last condition, namely unacceptability (*aviṣahya*), is the most unclear, and I deal with it in the next note.

3.15.4. *Unacceptability... distress*: The meaning of *aviṣahya* is not altogether clear. I take "it" (the absent noun of the Sanskrit adjectives) to be the transaction itself, rather than the merchandise. The author's explanation has two parts. The second, that the transaction was made under duress or when one of the parties was under stress, clearly refers to the validity of the transaction. The first, *bahuguṇahīnam* ("lacking in many qualities"), is taken by Meyer, Kangle, and Vigasin and Samozvantsev (1985, 178–180) as referring to serious deficiencies in the article sold or purchased. But such deficiencies of the product were included in the very first condition (3.15.2). Moreover, interpreting the compound this way makes it necessary to take it as an adjective qualifying the sold or purchased article, while the second compound (*ārtakṛtam*) would have to refer to the transaction itself. This results in a very untidy syntax. I take the first compound also as referring to the transaction. When some required attributes of a legitimate transaction are lacking, then it should be considered null and void. For the attributes of a valid transaction, see 3.1.

3.15.6. *for people... seven days*: This provision, tagged at the end, appears to be an interpolation or a part of the later redaction of the *AŚ* that laid emphasis on Brāhmaṇical notions such as caste. The term *vyāmiśra* to indicate mixed social classes is found only here in the entire text.

3.15.11. *joining of hands*: This is a central act of the Brāhmaṇical marriage ceremony.

3.15.15. *For a suitor... groom*: There is a lack of clarity regarding the identity of the suitor (*varayitṛ*) and the groom (*vara*). I think Kangle is right in taking the two to be identical, because the verb *vindataḥ* (marry) qualifies the suitor. So the situation in the case of the man appears to be different from the woman, where the penalty falls on the father or the elder giving her in marriage.

3.15.16–18. *ill-disposed, well-disposed*: The terms *śuci/śauca* and *aśuci/aśauca* often refer to purity and impurity. In the *AŚ*, however, the most common meanings of these terms are honest and dishonest (1.20.21; 2.35.13; see Olivelle 1998). In this passage, however, neither meaning works: Honesty does not work with animals, and it does not take a year to find out whether someone is clean. I think Gaṇapati Śāstrī is right in glossing the two terms as *duṣṭāduṣṭa*. Basically, the requirement is that the animal or the slave sold has an even temper and is not wicked or ill-tempered.

3.15.19. *In the case... harmed*: This is clearly a versification of 3.16.5 intended to establish a link between the two chapters.

3.16.2. *In the event... transaction*: The meaning of this provision is unclear. The context appears to be a cancellation of a gift by the donor. In that event, the object of the gift should be kept securely in a single location, and it cannot be subject to a transaction, that is, it cannot be sold or given as a gift, possibly until the Justices have made a ruling regarding the validity of the cancellation.

3.16.4. *as also... unworthy people*: This is a reference to the Triple Set (*trivarga*). Gifts, generally, may be given in pursuit of any one of these three aims; see 1.7.

3.16.7. *as also someone giving*: The phrase *prayacchataś ca* is placed by Kangle at the end of sentence 3.16.6, and sentence 7 is given there without a verbal equivalent. I have moved the above phrase to the beginning of phrase 7, where it fits more naturally. It seems odd that a man making a gift out of fear of reprisal or bodily harm is also assessed the same fine as the man who caused him to give the gift under duress.

3.16.8. *in this case... highest*: The case when the highest fine is assessed is left unclear. In all likelihood, this provision pertains to the last kind of gift when the donor is trying to outdo the gifts given by the king. For the highest fine, see 2.1.29 n.

3.16.11. *urgency* (atipatti): The only other occurrence of this term is at 7.18.11, where it clearly refers to an urgent matter with regard to either time or place, something that has to be attended to then and there.

3.16.12. *owner*: That is, the man who is the current owner of the article from whom it has been impounded by the original owner.

3.16.14. *pay the price*: That is, he has to pay the man who bought the article from him the price he paid for it, given that the article would be returned to its original owner.

3.16.15–16. *If he were... for theft*: The meaning appears to be as follows: Seller A points to seller B as the man from whom he purchased the article; that exonerates him. Seller B may, in turn, point to seller C, and so on, until the chain ends. The last person in this chain becomes liable for the sale without ownership and has to pay a fine and indemnify the people in that chain.

3.16.18. *one-fifth the amount* (pañcabandha): For this technical term, see 2.7.21 n. The meaning here is that the claimant pays a fine equal to one-fifth the value of the property he claimed. For the necessity of proof of ownership to conclude a valid transaction, see 3.1.15.

3.16.27. *individual plunder* (svayaṃgrāha): This appears to be a kind of warfare in which each individual soldier is given the right to plunder and take whatever he wants from the regions devastated by the war. In *MDh* 7.96, we have the statement: "Whatever a man wins—chariot, horse, elephant, parasol, money, grain, livestock, women, all goods, and base metal—all that belongs to him." This technical term is used frequently in the *AŚ*: 8.1.44; 8.4.23, 24; 9.3.17; 9.6.24; 10.3.45. At 9.2.9, we have the description of an army called *autsāhika*, translated there by Kangle as "the volunteer army." The term may more properly mean energetic or enterprising. This kind of soldier is not given any food or salary and is totally dependent on looting from the people with whom they fight.

3.16.29. *documentary evidence*: For the meaning of *deśa* as documentary evidence, see 3.1.19 n.

3.16.31. *He should not subject to an inquiry* (nānuyuñjīta): For the meaning of the technical term *anuyuñjīta*, see the note to 3.2.17. As in that passage, here also the subject of the verb is the Justice (*dharmastha*) and not the previous owner of the property, even though he may be the one who would move to court to initiate a judicial inquiry. The meaning is that no legal challenge can be initiated with regard to an abandoned property to which no claim had been made for over 20 years.

3.16.32. *outside the presence of kings*: The meaning of this expression is obscure, and Kangle translates the phrase *rājñām asaṃnidhau* as "in the absence of kings." Perhaps the text is corrupt here or a marginal gloss has been inserted into the text.

nor over a deposit... Vedic scholar: The syntax is rather loose. The meaning is that someone cannot claim ownership of these items through possession.

3.16.35. *lodging in turn*: The expression *vāsaparyāya* is unclear. The meaning appears to be that a person arriving early in the season is obliged to allocate lodging in turn to those who come later. The context is probably the four-month rainy season when ascetics were forced to abandon their itinerant lifestyle and take up residence in one location.

3.16.38. *Mahākacca*: The meaning is unclear. The same term occurs at 4.3.12 in a list along with lord of Śacī (Indra), Ganges, and mountain (perhaps the Himalaya) and at 4.3.15. The reference may be to the ocean or to the god Varuṇa.

3.17.1. *Forcible seizure... victim*: For this definition and for an explanation of the curious term *anvayavat*, see my note to *MDh* 8.332. Forcible seizure is robbery perpetrated in the presence of the owner of the property stolen. This is distinguished from theft, which is done when the owner is absent or is unable to observe the theft, for example, while asleep. For a study of the term *sāhasa* used also as a particular kind of punishment (2.1.29 n.), see Rocher 1975.

3.17.2. *in the case of denial*: The meaning appears to be that when an article has been taken by someone, perhaps on loan, a denial would amount to theft.

3.17.15. *impost* (rūpa): This must be some sort of fee related to the inspection of the coins used to pay the fine. See the use of the term with reference to the examiner of coins at 2.12.26, and with reference to the sale of salt at 2.12.28.

3.17.16. *Impost... legitimate*: This verse undercuts the entire argument presented in the previous verse. The two verses in their original context may have been part of a prolonged argument between two opposing viewpoints regarding the assessment of additional levies beyond the basic fines.

3.18.1. *Insult, abuse, and threat*: Insult appears to be a lesser offense than abuse. The former is dealt with in 3.18.2–3, while the latter is discussed in 3.18.4–6. Threat, of course, is the most serious, even though the threat may not be carried out (3.18.9–11).

3.18.6. *froth... in water*: The absence of froth when a man urinates on the ground is a sign that he is impotent or infertile, as also feces that float in water. Opposites of these are indicators of virility and fertility. See *NSm* 12.10.

3.18.7. *fine is three Paṇas... by two Paṇas*: When, for example, a lowest-born insults a Śūdra, the fine is three Paṇas; it increases to six Paṇas for insulting a Vaiśya, and so on, up to 12 Paṇas for insulting a Brāhmaṇa. In the reverse case, for a Brāhmaṇa insulting a Kṣatriya, the fine is eight Paṇas; it decreases to six Paṇas for a Vaiśya, and to four Paṇas for a Śūdra, and two Paṇas for a lowest-born.

3.19.8–10. *When a Śūdra... impure persons*: As both Meyer and Kangle have argued, this section is probably an interpolation based on Dharmaśāstric provisions, see *MDh* 8.279–284; *YDh* 2.215.

compensation: This may refer to the monetary fines that could be paid to redeem a man from having various parts of his body cut off. The exact monetary equivalencies are given in 4.10.

3.19.12. *infected blood* (duṣṭaśoṇita): The meaning appears to be that the blood has come from an ulcer or a preexisting wound, in which case, the blood may not be due solely to the blows received. See the reference to an infected wound in the very next sentence. It is also possible that this is a reference to the medical practice of bleeding.

3.19.22. *convicted*: The term *paścātkāra* refers to the decision of the court declaring that one party has won the lawsuit. In the current case, a preemptive decision is made when the accused fails to respond. In the *KSm* (264), this term is used with reference to the written document given to the victor by the court.

3.20.1–2. *The Superintendent... secret occupations*: These provisions are summarized in one half-verse at *YDh* 2.203a–b. It becomes clear that the medieval commentators Vijñāneśvara and Aparāditya did not understand the expression *ekamukha*, located in one place; they understood it as referring to the single official who should oversee gambling. Of the commentators of *YDh*, only Viśvarūpa, who predates the other two by several centuries, correctly understood this expression. The last statement regarding the purpose of this rule relates to forcing people to gamble in only one officially approved location.

3.20.3. *winner receives... middle fine*: The winner/loser here refers to gambling and not to the lawsuit. It is assumed that the man being fined has lost the lawsuit between him and the man against whom he played. According to this view, if the loser of the lawsuit happens to be the winner at the gambling match, then he is assessed a lower fine than if he were loser.

3.20.9. *fraud*: It appears that this kind of fraud pertains not to cheating while gambling, but to other kinds of fraud within the context of gambling, such as in making payments for gambling losses.

3.20.10. *shells... ivory cubes*: All these are items used in gambling. Cowrie-shells (*kākaṇī*) and dice (*akṣa*) are well known as what the players threw in the gambling area. Gaṇapati Śāstrī, following the Malayalam commentary, takes *arāla* to be a leather strip, although it could be any other kind of strip. Falk (personal communication) notes that *arāla* occurs occasionally elsewhere but in contexts that make the interpretation difficult. The last term *śalāka* can mean a peg, but it is taken within the context of gambling as a cube of ivory or bone. The terms *akṣa* and *arāla* also occur in Pāṇini 2.1.10.

3.20.13. *betting*: The distinction between gambling and betting is given in *MDh* 9.223: "When it is done with inanimate things, people call it gambling; when it is done with living beings, on the other hand, it is known as betting."

3.20.14. *neighbors to the front and back*: This provision is a brief allusion to a rule expressed more fully in the Dharmaśāstras (3.4.3 n.). See, for example, *MDh* 8.392: "When a Brāhmaṇa fails to feed his two worthy neighbors—the one living in front of his house and the one behind—at a festival attended by 20 Brāhmaṇas, he ought to be fined one Māṣaka." See also *YDh* 2.263.

3.20.15. *as directed*: The reference is to a directive given to a person to deliver something to a particular individual. See 3.12.18–19.

buys: As Kangle remarks, it should be the seller and not the buyer who should be at fault for selling a piece of merchandise that has been reserved by another buyer. Perhaps the term *krīṇānasya* ("for one who buys") of the edition should read *vikrīṇānasya* ("for one who sells"). The latter reading appears to be followed by the Malayalam commentary.

3.20.16. *Śākyas and Ājīvikas*: The former are Buddhist monks, and the latter belonged to a community of ascetics founded around the same time as the Buddhist order. The use of these terms, clearly with a derogatory intention, indicates that this passage is a rather late interpolation. The term Śākya is not found in any ancient Brāhmaṇical text, including the Dharmaśāstras and the two Sanskrit epics. See also the use of the term *tīrthakara* (head of a religious order) at 3.20.21.

3.20.22. *helpless* (anāthānām): Along with Meyer, I take this term also as part of the list, even though it is placed outside the long compound containing the other items. Kangle appears to take it as an adjective qualifying either sick persons or all those listed. However, this term often concludes lists such as this elsewhere (1.19.29; 2.1.26; 2.36.44; 13.5.11). There may even be a scribal error here in replicating the many similar sounds at the end (*vyādhitānāmanāthānām*).

BOOK 4

4.1.2. *deposits*: These consist of the raw material (e.g., gold, silver, or yarn) given by a client to an artisan for the manufacture of an article. See 2.13–14 for further information and notes. Evidently, any freelance artisan was not allowed to accept these deposits; only businessmen of a higher rank, supported and guaranteed by their respective guilds, were permitted to accept deposits.

4.1.3. *death*: For this meaning of the term *vipatti*, see 3.19.15; 4.1.56. The guild assumes responsibility for the deposit in the event that the artisan or the man who received the deposit dies.

4.1.4–7. *They should perform . . . twice that amount*: The statements 4–5 and 7 are derived from 2.14.2–4 (see note there). The provisions given there with reference to goldsmiths are here extended to all artisans.

4.1.8–9. *Weavers . . . the reduction*: The weight of the yarn increases in the process of making the cloth with the addition of starch (see *MDh* 8.397). If the weight increase of the manufactured cloth is less than 10 percent, then the weaver must have used less yarn; hence the fine.

4.1.10. *Pay*: Here and elsewhere in this chapter, the pay (or wages) for various workers (weavers, washermen, goldsmiths) is specified, something that is anomalous in a section dealing with crimes and punishments. The reason may be that some of the fines are calculated as fractions of the workers' pay. Notice that the pay for washermen comes immediately after the provision for deducting the pay when the work is not done in time (4.1.20–22). Nevertheless, I think that the passages dealing with pay in this chapter were probably glosses that found their way into the text. I have used the term "pay" here for *vetana*, because these are not really wages for workers in the normal sense of the term, but payments for services rendered. The term "charges" may also be a close approximation of what is intended here.

4.1.11. *reduction in size*: The meaning appears to be that the woven cloth is of a lesser length or breadth than stipulated (so also Gaṇapati Śastrī). Thus, if the length is stipulated to be eight meters and the final product is seven, then one-eighth of the pay is subtracted.

fine: One must assume that the fines are in addition to the reduction in the pay mentioned in the first provision.

4.1.14. *Washermen* (rajakāḥ): This term refers to both washermen and to dyers of clothes, both tasks being performed by the same profession (see 4.1.19 n.).

4.1.16. *marked with a club sign*: This may have been a common sign marking ownership by a washerman; a wooden club was used to beat the clothes during the washing process. Perhaps washermen were required to have this mark on the outside of their clothes so that others could see that they were not wearing the clothes of their clients.

4.1.18. *They should return…four days*: It appears that the four processes of washing produce four levels of whiteness, from "bud white," which is probably a slightly yellow color, to the burnished white. Each of these levels of whiteness takes one day longer than the preceding. The Sanskrit uses the pithy *ekarātrottaram* (after one night, increased subsequently by one). Given that this is irreproducible in English, I have given the actual days to produce each kind of whiteness.

4.1.19. *dyed light red…seven days*: In contrast to the washing that was the subject of the preceding statement, here we are dealing with dying raw-white garments in a variety of colors.

4.1.20. *loss of pay* (vetanahāni): It is unclear whether this means that the washerman forfeits all his pay or there is a reduction in the pay, which is more likely. Nowhere else is the term *hāni* ("loss") used with reference to pay or wages.

4.1.22. *For garments…double*: The issue here is whether the pay is for washing the clothes or for dyeing. Meyer considers the amounts too large for simply washing. Gaṇapati Śāstrī takes the first three as referring to dyeing, and the last two as referring to simple washing. Given that the amounts of pay are given in the context of loss of pay for taking too long to dye a garment, all probably refer to dyeing. The last in the list is a garment that is already dyed. This could mean that it is being dyed again or dyed another color. That could be the reason for the double payment. If that is the case, dyed garments of the highest quality require a payment of two Paṇas, those of mid-value, one Paṇa, and so forth.

4.1.23. *At the first wash…one-fifth*: This provision is related to the three levels of value stated in the previous sentence. After each wash, the value of a garment diminishes, so that a garment that was initially of high quality may, after a few washes, become one of low quality. The loss of one-fifth at the second wash may be calculated either from the initial value or, what is more likely, from its diminished value after the first wash. For a different reckoning, see *NSm* 9.8–9.

4.1.26. *silver or gold in its original form*: The reference is to silver and gold ornaments. The reading here probably should be *rūpyasuvarṇam* (as at 2.14.1), rather than *rūpyaṃ suvarṇam*. The original form is the form the ornament had when it left the hand of the original owner (either through sale or theft). If the form was altered deliberately to avoid detection, then the fine is increased.

4.1.30. *enhancement of the color...removal*: The reading here is corrupt. The manuscripts read *apasārāṇāṃ yogaṃ*, while Gaṇapati Śāstrī reads *asārāṇām*, glossing it with *hīnavarṇānām*, referring to color enhancements and alloys made with base metals. Kangle takes this to be the reading also of the Malayalam commentary, but Professor Scharfe informs me that it has no such reading. Kangle, following a suggestion by Meyer, emends the text to *apasāraṇaṃ yogaṃ* and translates it as "practising removal or mixture (with base metals)." According to Kangle, therefore, there are three offenses. The reference to two in the very next sentence (see the next note) and the fact that *yoga* is not used in 2.12–14 (dealing with metals) with the meaning of an alloy make Kangle's interpretation less likely. I think the commentaries are correct in detecting only two offenses here. I think, however, that *apasāraṇa* is used here in the technical sense in which it was used at 2.14.18–24, namely, the removal of gold or silver through a variety of strategies. Thus, I have emended the text to read *apasāraṇayogaṃ* as a compound.

4.1.31. *deceit...extraction of color*: There is some uncertainty regarding the referent of the dual pronoun *tayoḥ* (of/with regard to those two). Kangle takes the two as articles of gold and silver (4.1.26), but this is very doubtful, especially because of the distance between the two statements. If we take 4.1.30 as referring to two kinds of offenses, then the two would refer to those two offenses: enhancement of color and removal. The expression "extraction of color" (*rāgasyāpaharaṇam*) refers to what is also mentioned at 4.4.22 as a serious offense. It appears, then, that the term *apacaraṇa* (which I have translated as deceit; it could also mean wrongdoing or crime) points to an offense more serious than the one listed in the previous provision. Kangle thinks that, here, the precious metal is completely substituted with an inferior metal. The exact meaning of extraction of color is also unclear. It must mean that the original color of a base metal is enhanced with the additional of other compounds (see 2.13–14 for techniques of color enhancement). Meyer takes *rāga* to mean metal, but that meaning is not encountered elsewhere in the *AŚ*. However, the extraction of color clearly refers to the extraction of the precious metal and its substitution with base metals.

4.1.32. *one-eighth*: Gaṇapati Śāstrī and Meyer take this to be one-eighth of a Māṣa, although Gaṇapati Śāstrī (following the Malayalam commentary) takes this to be a gold Māṣa. Kangle notes, however, that no such coin is known in the text. I think Kangle is correct in taking "one-eighth" as one-eighth of a Paṇa. See the similar use at 2.12.24; 2.36.16, 26.

4.1.35. *five per 100:* That is, five Paṇas per 100 Palas of metal.

4.1.37. *loss of one Pala*: This must mean that the metal has suffered the loss of one Pala in weight beyond the amount (i.e., one-tenth) permitted during the process of manufacture.

4.1.46. *earning* (upajīvataḥ): This term appears to indicate that the official makes a living out of what he gets from passing coins into circulation, rather than collecting fees for the treasury. This may imply that he waves the official fees for the payment of a bribe.

4.1.52–53. *treasure trove... one-sixth*: Kangle's translation appears to indicate that when a treasure trove is valued above 100,000 Paṇas, the entire amount is taken by the king. This is probably incorrect. It is the amount above that limit that goes to the king. One-sixth of anything below that is probably given by the king to the finder, as implied in sentence 51. The assumption here is that treasure troves belong to the king, and he gives a finder's fee. At *MDh* 8.35 and *YDh* 2.35, the assumption is that the finder owns the treasure but has to give a portion to the king.

4.1.57. *an injury... impairment*: The compound *marmavadhavaiguṇyakaraṇe* can also be translated as "a physical impairment through an injury to a vital part."

4.1.59. *avoid... one person*: I take *kāmadāna* in a metaphorical sense of bestowing love on someone. This should be understood within the context of a stage play or mime, where members of the audience or well-known people of the area could be targets for satire. Kangle and Meyer take *dāna* here to be actual monetary gifts. I think this provision stands in contrast to that of 61, where actors are permitted to poke fun at others; but here they are forbidden to single out one individual. For *ativāda* as insult, see its use at 7.16.22. Kangle takes it to mean praise here, but as reproach at 7.16.22. I think the *EDS* is wrong in citing both these passages with the meaning of praise.

4.1.60. *schools* (caraṇa): These were hereditary Vedic traditions within which members studied and followed a particular recension of the Veda (*śākhā*) and claimed descent from a particular Vedic seer.

4.1.63. *For them... with a whip*: There are several points that are unclear in this statement: *teṣām ayaḥśūlena yāvataḥ paṇān abhivadeyus tāvantaḥ śiphāprahārā daṇḍāḥ*. The initial "For them" (*teṣām*) I take as referring only to the mendicants, who in this case are probably religious mendicants. I also take the subject of the verb *abhivadeyuḥ* ("they should declare") as the same mendicants, while Kangle and Meyer take it to be the judges; when reference is made to the Magistrate (*pradeṣṭṛ*) elsewhere, the singular is used (4.2.11), while the plural is used with reference to the those under surveillance. Their interpretation makes it difficult to understand the term *ayaḥśūlena* ("with an iron spike"); given its location in the subordinate clause, I think it should be connected to the verb "they should declare." Further, we do not have another example of a plural verb in this chapter referring to the magistrates. I think that the reference here is to an offense committed by religious mendicants when they brandish their iron spikes (e.g., the trident or *triśūla* of Śaiva ascetics) and demand money. The iron spike is mentioned by Pāṇini (5.2.76) with reference to a class of ascetics called *āyaḥśūlika.* Patañjali (Agrawala 1963, 383) comments that the reference is to "the practice of violent methods to recruit followers." Agrawala says that "the *āyaḥśūlika* Śaivas pierced their tongues or arms or other parts of the body with iron prongs and extracted forced sympathy." Perhaps, beyond sympathy, they extracted money as well. The perceived lack of money among such mendicants necessitated another form of punishment than fines.

4.2.3. *Parimāṇī…an offense*: For the Parimāṇī balance, see 2.19.17–18, and for the Droṇa measure, see 2.19.29. Each amounts to 200 Palas. Thus, a deviation of one-four hundredth was allowed in these weights and measures.

4.2.6. *Tulā…an offense*: One hundred Palas make a Tulā, and a Karṣa is one-quarter of a Pala. Thus, the deviation permitted is the same as for Parimāṇī, that is, one-four hundredth.

4.2.9. *Āḍhaka…offense*: An Āḍhaka is one-quarter of a Droṇa, that is, 200 Palas (2.19.30). So the permitted deviation of one-four hundredth remains the same.

4.2.12. *inference*: The meaning is probably that the superintendent should use the same fraction, that is, one-four hundredth, of the weight or measure in question as a permissible deviation. Anything above that is subject to a fine, taking the above ones as benchmarks.

4.2.13. *after buying…smaller than the standard*: Here the trader uses a weight heavier than the permitted deviation of one-four hundredth to buy an item and then uses a weight lighter than the permitted deviation to sell it. So the resultant transaction deviates at least double the permitted deviation, to the benefit of the trader.

4.2.14. *pilfering…commodities*: First, the term *apaharataḥ*, which generally refers to stealing, must here refer to the salesman who somehow undercounts the articles sold by number, for example, ten mangoes sold for ten Paṇas. If the undercount amounts to one-eighth of the cost of the articles sold to that buyer, then the seller is fined 96 Paṇas.

4.2.15. *causes a diminution*: Here I follow the reading *avacarataḥ*, proposed by Harihara Sastri (2011, 90), in place of *ācarataḥ*.

For a weigher...200 Paṇas: I follow here and in the subsequent passages the new arrangement of sentences proposed by Harihara Sastri (2011, 90–92); I have departed from his sequence in keeping 13 and 14 together and placing [20] after these two. (The numbers of the sentences in Kangle's edition that were moved to new positions are given within brackets in the translation.) I think this arrangement makes the best sense. First (4.2.13–16), we have offenses pertaining to shortchanges in weights, measures, and amounts; the consumer is defrauded by being given a lesser amount than promised. And the gravity of the offenses increases with fines from double the fraud to 200 Paṇas, with the final statement for those exceeding 200. Next (4.2.17–20), we have offenses consisting of adulteration of the commodities or passing off merchandise of lesser value for ones of higher value. Here also, we have a progression from 12 Paṇas to 200, with the final sentences providing for fines over 200. Finally (4.2.21–22), we have the offense of collusion among traders to artificially raise the price of goods, the fines (1,000) for these acts being the highest in this passage. After this section dealing with offenses committed by traders, we have from 4.2.23 onward the allowances that the state may grant to traders and the control of their activities. As Harihara Satri has pointed out, this new sequence corresponds nicely to the parallel passage in the *YDh* 2.244–251. The new arrangement of the text reads:

tulāmānābhyām atiriktābhyāṃ krītvā hīnābhyāṃ vikrīṇānasya ta eva dviguṇā daṇḍāḥ ||13|| *gaṇyapaṇyeṣv aṣṭabhāgaṃ paṇyamūlyeṣv apaharataḥ ṣaṇṇavatir daṇḍaḥ* ||14|| *dharakasya māyakasya vā paṇamūlyād aṣṭabhāgaṃ hastadoṣeṇāvacarato dviśato daṇḍaḥ* ||15 [20]|| *tena dviśatottarā daṇḍavṛddhir vyākhyātā* ||16 [21]|| *dhānyasnehakṣāralavaṇagandhabhaiṣajyadravyāṇāṃ samavarṇopadhāne dvādaśapaṇo daṇḍaḥ* ||17 [22]|| *kāṣṭhalohamaṇimayaṃ rajjucarmamṛṇmayaṃ sūtravalkaromamayaṃ vā jātyam ity ajātyaṃ vikrayādhānaṃ nayato mūlyāṣṭaguṇo daṇḍaḥ* ||18 [15]|| *sārabhāṇḍam ity asārabhāṇḍaṃ tajjātam ity atajjātaṃ rādhāyuktam upadhiyuktaṃ samudgaparivartimaṃ vā vikrayādhānaṃ nayato hīnamūlyaṃ catuṣpañcāśatpaṇo daṇḍaḥ, paṇamūlyaṃ dviguṇo, dvipaṇamūlyaṃ dviśataḥ* ||19 [16]|| *tenārghavṛddhau daṇḍavṛddhir vyākhyātā* ||20 [17]||

kāruśilpināṃ karmaguṇāpakarṣam ājīvaṃ vikrayakrayopaghātaṃ vā saṃbhūya samutthāpayatāṃ sahasraṃ daṇḍaḥ ||21 [18]|| *vaidehakānāṃ vā saṃbhūya paṇyam avarundhatām anargheṇa vikrīṇatāṃ vā sahasraṃ daṇḍaḥ* ||22 [19]||

tulāmānāntaram arghavarṇāntaraṃ vā yanniṣṛṣṭam upajīveyus tad eṣāṃ divasasaṃjātaṃ saṃkhyāya vaṇik sthāpayet ||23 [20, 23]||

4.2.19. *container is switched*: Vijñāneśvara, commenting on *YDh* 2.247 where this provision is reproduced, takes the switching of the container to be a sleight of hand: The trader shows the container full of gems, but the buyer gets a different container with glass pieces.

4.2.21. *For artisans...purchases*: The phrase *karmaguṇāpakarṣam ājīvaṃ vikrayakrayopaghātaṃ vā* is problematic. It has been interpreted as containing three items done in collusion. Kangle translates: "bring about a deterioration in the quality of the work or (increase in) profit or a hindrance to purchase or sale." As one can see, the second item, *ājīva* (profit; for this meaning, see 4.2.28), creates a problem, and Kangle is forced to add a parenthetical qualifier. I take the phrase as containing two ideas: the generating of profit illegitimately by lowering the standards of craftsmanship or controlling and suppressing the free market in sales and purchases. Grammatically, I take both compounds before and after *ājīvam* as Bahuvrīhis qualifying it. Both Meyer and the commentators of *YDh* 2.249, which is based on this passage, think that the provision is addressed to traders who collude to take advantage of artisans and craftsmen.

4.2.23. *After adding up*: For the new arrangement of the sentences, see the note to 4.2.15. The new arrangement also removes the difficulty of the referent of the pronoun *eṣām* (of/for them); now it clearly refers to the traders in the preceding sentence. It appears that from here onward we have an interpolation or excursus dealing with the Superintendent of Commodities (see 2.16) and not with the Superintendent of the Marketplace or the Magistrates. The person referred to as "Trader is actually the Superintendent of Commodities mentioned also at 4.2.26, 33.

distinct from...kind: The meaning of the phrase *tulāmānāntaram arghavarṇāntaraṃ vā* is not altogether clear. At its original location in the edition, Kangle translates: "As to difference in weight or measure or difference in price or quality." Harihara Sastri (2011, 90), within its current context, translates: "on sale of goods by weighing and measuring and also on profits over purchase price." The first compound occurs at 2.15.11 and the second at 2.16.1, 3. However, here I think *antara* has the meaning of different or distinct. I think the terms *tulā, māna* (4.2.13), *argha* (4.2.22), and *varṇa* (4.2.17) refer to the deceitful practices of traders using these methods mentioned earlier. The allowance comes from honest profits distinct from anything derived from such malpractice.

4.2.24–25. *Whatever...commodities*: The text in Kangle's edition here reads *kretṛvikretror antarapatitam ādāyād anyad* (mss. read *anyaṃ*) *bhavati* | *tena dhānyapaṇyanicayāṃś cānujñātāḥ kuryuḥ* || The reading of the first half here is possibly corrupt, and there is no easy way to amend it. The suggestion of Kangle that the two phrases make a single sentence is reasonable, but I am not convinced by his emendation *antarapatitam ādāya yad bhavati*. It is unclear how such a straightforward text could have been corrupted into the present difficult reading. I have also accepted the reading *ādāyād anyad bhavati* as the basis for my translation, taking *ādāya* as "taking or what was taken in," namely the original outlay of items for sale received from the superintendent. If an emendation is to be offered, I would propose *ādāyād anyad yad bhavati* with the correlative pronoun corresponding to *tena* of the main clause. Given the unusual form of *ādāya* (a term not found elsewhere in the *AŚ*), we may take it as a corruption of *ādāna* (as suggested by Wezler in a personal communication). The expression *kretṛvikretror antarapatitam* is also an awkward expression, and I think Kangle's interpretation that the reference is to what remains of the merchandise or grain after the buyers and sellers have concluded business, that is, unsold goods, is reasonable. However, it may well be that these sales agents of the state may have been engaged in both buying (see 4.2.31) and selling grain and goods, beyond the initial outlay from the superintendent, thus making a profit for the state. If the sales agents buy more than they sell, that may cause a surplus that they are allowed to store for sale at a different time. The meaning of the sentence appears to be that the salesmen can create stockpiles of unsold goods as long as they were not originally taken from the Superintendent of Commodities and they have his permission.

4.2.33. *have ... sold*: The simple verb *vikrīnīta* here may carry a causal meaning, a phenomenon attested in epic Sanskrit (Professor Wezler, personal communication).

4.2.35. *for a daily wage* (divasavetanena): As Meyer suggests, the meaning appears to be that the traders sell these goods without a profit for a fixed daily wage. For the expression *divasavetana*, see 2.9.8; 2.30.45.

4.2.36. *he*: That is, the Superintendent of Commodities.

4.3.2. *He*: The subject of this sentence and of several other provisions in this chapter (e.g., 5, 10, 12, 15, etc.) is unclear. Given that the countryside is overseen by the Collector (*samāhartṛ*), he may be understood here, especially given that he is mentioned in the very first sentence of the next chapter (4.4.1). The king is mentioned at 17, and it is possible that different officials may be carrying out these instructions.

4.3.3. *overseen ... households*: The reading and meaning of the expression *daśamūlīsaṃgraheṇa* are uncertain. The Malayalam commentary, followed by Gaṇapati Śāstrī, has the reading *daśakulī* ("ten families"), which is the *lectio facilior*. The term *mūlī* may be derived from *mūla*, often referring to people (*maula*) who are long-time residents of a place. I have taken it to mean households. See the division of a city into ten households at 2.36.2. The meaning probably is that anyone cooking indoors must follow rules agreed to by the neighborhood association. It is unlikely that this is a reference to fire-fighting equipment (so Kangle; see 2.36.18), because the term *adhiṣṭhita* in the *AŚ* always refers to supervision by individuals. On lighting fires during the hot season, see 2.36.15–20.

4.3.5. *days of the moon's change* (parvan): These are the new moon, the eighth day after the new moon, the full moon, and the 14th day after the full moon. See *MDh* 4.128. Note that within the *AŚ*, the term *parvan* occurs only in this chapter.

4.3.13. *They should counteract*: The subject of the verb in the plural is uncertain, probably the magical practitioners and Vedic specialists mentioned in 4.3.11.

4.3.15. *headless trunk* (kabandha): This is probably a headless trunk of a human in some sort of a magical rite. Kangle translates the term as "effigies," but see the same term at 4.8.28; 4.13.34.

gods' night (devarātrī): The meaning is unclear, but it must refer to some sort of divine rites carried out at night.

4.3.17. *hand over the region*: The meaning is that the king would entrust the famished region to another king who would be better able to look after its population. The use of the technical term *nikṣepa* (deposit) indicates that the transfer was temporary and that the original king could reclaim the territory at a later time.

4.3.18. *reduction* (karśana) *or a transfer* (vamana) *of population*: See 2.1.1 for the forcible transfer of people from one region to another. It appears that reduction is done by the migration of people to another kingdom and by moving people to other parts of the kingdom.

4.3.24. *rat tax*: The probable meaning is that each household is assessed a "tax" in rats, that is, each household must bring so many dead rats per day or week. See the very similar *manuṣyakara* demanded by an evil spirit at 5.2.41.

4.3.28. *mixed with... Kodrava-grain*: The term *madanarasa* may mean either a coma-inducing liquid or the sap of the Madana plant. In all likelihood *madanarasa* is the same as *madanayoga*, the preparation of which is described at 14.1.16–17. We have *madanayoga* at 4.4.19; 4.7.10; and 7.17.44. We have the expression *madanarasayoga* (*-yukta*) at 1.18.9; 4.3.28; 4.5.16; 11.1.24; 12.4.4; 13.3.54, 56; and *madanarasaviddha* at 13.3.52; and simply *madanarasa* at 13.3.53. I do not think there is a great variation in meaning among these. They all appear to refer to a liquid preparation that induces coma and/or death. The expression *madanakodrava* also poses a problem. Kangle is inconsistent, taking it to be a single plant here and as separate plants at 14.1.9, 13, 16, 22. Meyer (640, n. 6) also thinks it is a single plant. Yet, we find *madana* used clearly as a separate category of plant at 14.4.4, and the fruit of *madana* is mentioned at 14.1.6. Although there is still some doubt, I have translated the compound *madanakodrava* as a Dvandva referring to two distinct plants. It is not altogether clear whether the *madanarasa* mixture only put people to sleep or actually killed them. The statement at 4.7.10 indicates that it killed (with vomiting and purging), while at 13.3.52–54, it appears that the mixture only induced a coma.

4.4.3. *traveling holy men* (cakracara): Kangle translates the term as "cart drivers," and Meyer as a kind of wandering ascetic ("Wanderheilige"). The term is found in *Rām* 5.45.38 and 5.46.21, where *cakracara* is associated with great seers (*maharṣayaḥ*), and Goldman translates: "who follow the orbits of the heavenly bodies," as an adjective to the great seers. The term is found in *MBh* 3.83.67, 73, where it is given as a distinct category of holy and divine beings, and van Buitenen leaves the term untranslated as a proper name. Also at *MBh* 12.235.24 and 13.129.43, 47, the term refers to celestial beings. In the *ŚB*, we have moving about in wagons (*cakra*) associated with gods. In *BDh* 3.1.5, *cakracara* is listed after *śālīna* and *yāyāvara* as three kinds of holy householders, where the term *cakracara* is explained as going (*caraṇa*) in sequence or regular order (*anukrameṇa*). Given the context of the *AŚ* occurrence, the term must refer to actual groups of humans, and we may not be far wrong in taking them to be some kind of holy persons who traveled about in carts, as the connection to carts is explicitly made in the only other place of the *AŚ* where the term occurs (7.17.55). See Scharfe 1987.

entertainers (pracchandaka): This is a hapax, and its meaning is unclear. Kangle has "tramp," and Meyer "Wunscherbötige."

4.4.6. *Justice or Magistrate*: The manuscripts, as well as the Malayalam commentary, have the reading *dharmasthaṃ pradeṣṭāraṃ vā*, and Kangle (followed by Scharfe 1993, 227) emends the text by dropping *pradeṣṭāraṃ vā*. His reason is that 4.4.8 makes these words superfluous. I have restored the text; there may be many reasons for the provision in 4.4.8, and one could argue with equal justification that this may have been simply a marginal gloss.

Remedy…this money: The author is playing with the multiple meanings of *artha* and *anartha*. The former can mean lawsuit, fortune, or money, and the latter can mean both misfortune and a wrongful lawsuit. The Justice thus removes *anartha* by being offered *artha*.

4.4.7. *sent into exile* (pravāsyeta): This term in the *AŚ* has the meaning of both exile and execution. Often, as in this chapter, it is unclear which meaning is applicable. Kangle says that the term means exile in this chapter without offering any proof. He is probably right, but it is important to remember that the other meaning is also possible. See the same term at sentences 10, 12, 15, 18, 21, and 23.

4.4.9. *village official or corrupt superintendent*: The manuscripts read *grāmakūṭam adhyakṣaṃ vā*. Kangle and Meyer interpret *grāmakūṭam* as the head of a village. This usage is recorded in both texts (Yaśodhara on *Kāmasūtra* 5.5.5) and inscriptions (Sircar 1966, 120). Nevertheless, the term *kūṭa* is never used with the meaning of chief in the *AŚ*, and it is used within this very chapter frequently with the normal meaning of false (e.g., false witness). It is a simple emendation to place an *anusvāra* at the end of *grāma* and to take *kūṭa* as an adjective qualifying *adhyakṣa* ("superintendent"); it is also possible to take it as also qualifying *grāma*. The simple term *grāma* is used above in 4.4.4 to mean a village chief.

misfortune: The term *anartha* here also may hint at a lawsuit as at 4.4.6, and that may be the reason for the extortion. See also the context of a lawsuit in the very next sentence.

4.4.14. *root witchcraft*: The meaning of the expression *mūlakarma* is quite unclear. The commentators on *MDh* 11.64, where this term also occurs, are unanimous in taking it to mean some kind of witchcraft by which another person is brought under one's power (*vaśīkaraṇa*); see *MDh* 9.290, where the meaning is clearly some form of witchcraft. In the *Kāma Sūtra* (4.1.9), a class of women is designated as *mūlakārikā*, and at 6.2.56, a reference is made to *mūlakarma*. The reference appears to be to some form of magic potion made with roots to win the love of a woman; this is the interpretation of the commentator Yaśodhara. See also *AV* 4.28.6, where *mūlakr̥t* ("root cutter") is in apposition to *kr̥tyākr̥t* ("witchcraft maker"). This is also the meaning ascribed to the expression in B-R.

4.4.23. *The 13*: We get 13 in the previous passages if we take the extractor of color and the dealer in counterfeit gold as a single person; and, indeed, the past participle *vyākhyātaḥ* used there is in the singular.

4.5.1. *After…secret agents*: This initial phrase appears to refer to the sequence of topics, as clearly indicated at the beginning of 4.6.1. This phrase refers to the activities of the Collector, while the rest of the sentence deals with the activities of the ascetics working as secret agents.

4.5.6. *disguised as wives* (bhāryāvyañjanāḥ): These women were probably prostitutes who have been recruited to pose as wives. Given that the technical term *vyañjana* (used for undercover agents) is used here, it may well be that these women were also in the employ of the secret service.

4.5.7. *mark of identity*: The term *abhijñāna* is used in three other places (2.21.2, 26; 3.12.49) with the meaning of an identity card or a mark of identification. Perhaps the initiation rite required some kind of mark or brand to be made on the bodies of the initiates. This may have been the way to identify and convict criminals. This may also explain the other methods outlined in the following provisions that are given as alternatives.

4.5.9. *won their confidence* (anupraviṣṭa): For this meaning of the term, see the related term *anupraviśya* (at 1.17.39; 1.18.9; 2.9.26; 4.4.20), which, beyond the literal meaning of entering, has the extended meaning of winning someone's trust and confidence in these contexts. Scharfe (1993, 209–210) translates this term occurring at 4.5.12, 15 as "mingling." Although that meaning is also possible, I think in all these places that winning of trust is the more probable meaning.

4.5.11. *he*: We have here a sudden change to a verb in the singular. The referent is unclear, but the likely candidate is the Collector (4.4.1), who is mentioned explicitly in a similar context at 4.5.13.

4.5.12. *Alternatively*: The following passage with secret agents posing as old thieves is probably given as an alternative to enticing criminals with agents posing as thaumaturgic ascetics.

4.6.2. *family fortune* (kuṭumba): See 2.27.1 for this meaning of the term. Meyer takes the term *kṣīṇadāyakuṭumbam* to express a single idea: one whose family has depleted its inheritance. I think Kangle is correct in taking *dāya* and *kuṭumba* as two kinds of wealth a person may have, the latter possibly referring to the property and money his wife may have brought into the family. At 2.27.1 also, the term refers to money of a woman, in that case of a courtesan. The Malayalam commentary takes *kuṭumba* to mean wealth earned by oneself, while Gaṇapati Śāstrī equates it with agriculture. Further, if only the inheritance was meant, it would have been simpler to say *kṣīṇadāyam*.

food, delicacies (bhakṣyabhojana): Although both terms, as also the related *bhojya*, can refer simply to food, as Yagi (1994) has shown, when the two are used together or contrasted, *bhakṣya* refers to food that needs mastication, while *bhojya* (*bhojana*) refers to less dense food, perhaps delicacies that are soft and melt in the mouth. See also Olivelle 2002.

with merchandise…transported to: The manuscripts have the reading *avijñātasthānagamanapaṇyam*, which Kangle has emended to *avijñātasthānagamanam*, following the reading of the Malayalam commentary and Gaṇapati Śāstrī. Kangle thinks that *paṇya* does not go well with *sthāna* and *gamana*. Precisely because of this, the manuscript reading is the *lectio difficilior*, and I have adopted it. I follow the lead of Meyer in his note to this sentence in my interpretation of the compound. The man is unable to give an account of the location of his merchandise and/or where he is transporting it.

going here and there (abhyadhigantāram): The meaning is unclear. Kangle translates: "proceeding (stealthily?)." The use of two prepositions *abhi* and *adhi* is unusual and must affect its meaning. I take the first as movement toward and the second as movement away. The expression may also have sexual overtones, because both *abhi* and *adhi* with the verb *-gam* have sexual connotations.

wild tracts: The manuscripts and editions have the reading *kāntāparam*, translated by Kangle as "one devoted to a beloved." But clearly such a meaning is inappropriate within the context that deals with people doing odd things. I follow here the suggestion of Harihara Sastri (2011, 90) that *kāntā* was originally *kāntāra*, a wild tract. This emendation is supported by the fact that *kāntā* as woman is found nowhere else in the *AŚ*.

possessions...houses: It is unclear whether "other people's possessions" (*paraparigrahāṇām*) and "other people's wives, assets, and/or houses" (*parastrīdravyaveśmanām*) are to be taken separately, or whether the second expands on the first (so Kangle). It may well be that the second was a gloss explaining the first that found its way into the text, especially because we do not have either a copula (*ca*) or the usual *-ādi* at the end of the second compound.

night's end (virātra): Both Meyer and Kangle, following Gaṇapati Śāstrī (glossed as *ardharātre*), take the term here and at 4.13.6 to mean the middle of the night or midnight. But I think B-R is correct in taking the term to mean end of the night, that is, daybreak or possibly just before dawn. It makes little sense to think that someone can walk in the shadows of a wall in the middle of the night. The term is found in *MBh* 3.282.28, 32; 10.3.33; 13.91.8; *Rām* 5.16.2. Johnson (1998; *MBh* 10.3.33) translates it as the darkness before dawn, and Goldman (1984–2009; *Rām* 5.16.2) translates it as daybreak; these translations fit the contexts well. I think they are correct in their interpretation; van Buitenen's (1973–1978) rendering "dead of night" (*MBh* 3.282.28, 32) is incorrect.

high official (mahāmātra): This term is used in the *AŚ* to refer to the highest level of officials (see 1.13.1 n.). However, in the present context, the term may refer to the Magistrate (*pradeṣṭṛ*). See 2.5.5, where the term *mahāmātrīya* is used with reference to the jail of the Magistrate. Scharfe (1993, 173) and Harihara Sastri (2011, 73) take the term as qualifying *nāgarika*, that is, "the high official city manager." If that were the case, this would be the only place where the title is used to qualify some particular official.

remains seated without voiding excrement (anucchvāsopaveśinam): I take *ucchvāsa* with the technical meaning it appears to have in the *AŚ*. The meaning then is that the man sits down pretending that he is defecating, which was often done out in an open field. This is the meaning given to the expression by the Malayalam commentary (see Harihara Sastri 2011, 83). See the parallel *ucchvāsamṛttikā* at 14.3.67–68, referring to the earth usually used by ancient Indians to clean up after voiding excrement. Commenting on the word *varcagṛha* (latrine, 2.5.6), the *Cāṇakyaṭīkā* gives the gloss *ucchvāsabhūmiḥ* (place for evacuating urine or excrement).

4.6.3. *lost or stolen*: For another discussion of lost and stolen property, see 3.16.10–28.

4.6.7. *legal title* (āgama): I take this term in its technical meaning of legal title; see *MDh* 8.200; *YDh* 2.27, and the repeated use of the term at the end of this sentence, and the use of the technical term *deśa* at 4.6.9. Both Meyer and Kangle, however, take the term to mean the origin or acquisition of the article.

4.6.9. *document of title* (deśa): For the meaning of this technical term, see 3.1.19 n.

4.6.11. *If he were to say*: This passage is an alternative to the passage 4.6.8–10 and provides a different answer to the question posed to the man arrested with the article.

4.6.16. *joint or the hinge*: The terms *saṃdhi* and *bīja* here appear to have technical meanings within the context of burglary, which was turned into an art and a science. The term *saṃdhi* is used in Śūdraka's play *Mṛcchakaṭikā* (Act 3) with reference to breaching of a wall by making holes. Perhaps *saṃdhi* (joint) in that context means the chiseling of the mortar that joins one brick to another. In the context of a door, it may refer to the joints of the planks that form the door. The term *bīja* (germ) is more difficult. A clue is found in the expression *yantraghaṭṭanabījaṃ lohakīlam* found in the play *Mudrārākṣasa* (Act 2, between verses 15 and 16), which expression probably refers to the iron bolt that acted as a linchpin (*bīja*) in the working of the mechanism. Thus, here also, *bīja* may refer to the hinge that attaches the door to the frame or the wall.

it could have been found out: That is, the thief could have found out that the articles he was after were in the house only if the information was supplied by a person living in the house.

4.6.17. *both of them*: That is, by both an insider and an outsider working in collaboration.

4.6.18. *close by* (āsanna): Kangle translates this term as "closely related." However, in other places this term refers to proximity in space rather than in kinship (1.15.53; 1.17.1; 1.19.27; 1.21.9; 3.4.40; 3.13.26; 4.7.19).

4.7.1. *He*: Even though the Collector was the official implied in the previous chapters, it appears that here we transition to the Magistrate (*pradeṣṭṛ*), as signaled by the verse 4.6.20. Yet the Magistrate is nowhere named in this chapter, and the official conducting these investigations within the original context of these provisions remains unclear.

4.7.4. *taken down* (avaropita): The word used for impaling is *āropita*. Here *avaropita* probably has the opposite meaning: taking someone down from the stake. So the original cause of death is now unknown and can be determined only by the signs.

4.7.9. *insect* (kīṭa): The reference may be to a scorpion. The term *kīṭa* is regularly associated with snakes (*sarpa*) in Varāhamihira's *Bṛhatsaṃhitā*, and there, *kīṭa* may be a generic term for all poisonous creepy-crawly things.

4.7.11. *his neck was lacerated by hanging*: Both Meyer and Kangle think there are two acts here, hanging and cutting the throat. Kangle thus emends the manuscript reading *udbandhanikṛttakaṇṭham* to *udbaddhanikṛttakaṇṭham*. If, as Kangle suggests, this was a ruse to make the forensic experts believe that the death was a suicide, it is difficult to see how cutting the throat would lead to such a conclusion. I take the term *nikṛtta* to mean not cut in the sense of cutting through, but lacerated by the hanging (*udbandhanikṛtta* as a Tatpuruṣa compound). The lacerated neck would lead to a verdict of suicide. See 4.7.15–16. In this case, the hanging was to camouflage death by poison.

4.7.28. *When someone ... such people*: Variants of this well-known verse are found in *VaDh* 1.22; *MDh* 11.181; *ViDh* 35.3–5. For an analysis, see my note to *MDh* 11.181 in my edition and translation of this text.

4.8.1. *external and internal*: The meaning is unclear, and neither Gaṇapati Śāstrī nor Kangle offers an explanation. Professor Scharfe informs me that the Malayalam commentary offers an interpretation that is difficult to understand. The reference is probably to witnesses drawn from those within the household of the victim and from the outside.

4.8.2. *depositions*: For this meaning of the technical term *apadeśa*, see 4.6.7; 15.1.21. The intent seems to be that the statements of the accused man are checked against other depositions from witnesses.

4.8.5. *questioning becomes infeasible* (pṛcchābhāvāt): The meaning is unclear. Kangle translates: "because of the inadmissibility of interrogation (after that interval)," meaning that such interrogations are inadmissible as evidence in court. Gaṇapati Śāstrī thinks that questioning after three days is impossible because he may not remember what happened that far back. Indeed, both may be meant, because when memories fade, their use as evidence becomes problematic.

4.8.12. *stolen goods ... found*: The manuscripts read *gṛhyamāṇo dṛṣṭaś corabhāṇḍasyopavāsena*. Kangle has emended the text by deleting *dṛṣṭaḥ* as unnecessary and duplicative of *dṛśyate* found at the very beginning of the sentence. Not wanting to mutilate the received text so drastically, I have simply deleted the palatal 'ś' of *dṛṣṭaś* and taken the term as part of the following compound: *dṛṣṭacorabhāṇḍasya*. See the use of *darśana* in 4.8.5, with the meaning of finding the tools of the trade of a thief.

Māṇḍavya-of-the-Stake: The story of the sage Māṇḍavya is narrated in the *MBh* 1.101. Once some thieves, with soldiers in hot pursuit, came to the sage's hermitage while he was observing a vow of silence and hid there with their loot. When the sage would not reply to the soldiers' questions upon finding the thieves in his hermitage, they impaled him. Learning the truth, the king removed him from the stake, but he could not entirely pull the stake out of him. A part of the stake (*aṇi*) remained embedded in his anus, and thus he came to be called Aṇi-Māṇḍavya. The *AŚ* version of the story is somewhat different in that here the sage does not remain silent but confesses to a crime he did not commit, fearing torture. For a study of the legal significance of this story, see Wezler 1997.

4.8.19. *for a Brāhmaṇa... recluses*: Kangle and Scharfe (1993, 226) take *śrutavataḥ* ("learned") as an adjective qualifying the Brāhmaṇa, while Meyer thinks it likely that it qualifies the ascetic. I prefer to see these as three separate categories of individuals not subject to torture, especially in light of the word sequence and the placement of *ca* (and) at the end after the ascetic: *śrutavatas tapasvinaś ca*.

4.8.21. *two suspensions, and the water tube*: It appears that the suspect was hung from an elevated place twice, rather than two kinds of hanging, given that all numbers in the passage refer to the number of times the punishment was to be carried out. The meaning of the water tube is unclear. The Malayalam commentary says that the tube was inserted into the nostril and saltwater was poured into it, a kind of waterboarding.

4.8.22. *thigh bindings... Balbaja-grass*: One can only guess at the meanings of several of these kinds of torture. Thigh binding must have involved the tying of the feet to the thighs and keeping the person in that position. Naktamāla is the tree *Pongamia glabra* (Indian Beech, in Hindi Karanj). Perhaps the thin branches were used as a cane. Commentators explain hanging either by the hands or upside down. Needle in the hand is explained as pricking under the fingernails with a needle.

4.8.23. *the 18 types*: It is difficult to come up with this number based on the text and the readings we have. There are 11 kinds in sentence 22 and four in 21. One possible way to arrive at 18 is to regard the two thigh bindings, two scorpion bindings, and two hangings as six kinds of torture, which is the solution offered by Gaṇapati Śāstrī. Professor Wezler (personal communication) thinks that a line in sentence 22 may have been lost due to haplography. This is possible, especially because one fails to see how drinking gruel would make a difference in burning a man's finger.

4.8.24. *its diagnosis, and its restriction*: Both Sanskrit terms are unclear. The first, *pradhāraṇa*, perhaps refers to the diagnosis as to whether a particular kind of torture is suitable for a particular individual. The second, *avadhāraṇa*, appears to indicate the limits as to time and severity. All four terms, with the last three beginning with *pra-*, probably come from a technical vocabulary of a text dealing with torture.

Kharapaṭṭa: Literally meaning something like "hard/rough tablet," the reference is unclear. It may be the title of a treatise or a chapter dealing with the mechanics of torture.

4.9.1. *The Collector and the Magistrates* (samāhartṛpradeṣṭāraḥ): On the use of the plural in this compound, see Scharfe 1993, 157. Even though these officials are most frequently mentioned in the singular, there may have been more than one such official within a state.

4.9.2. *For someone*: All the provisions in this chapter concern officials and their assistants. See 2.5.16 for an abbreviated statement about punishments for theft by officials.

clean execution (śuddhavadha): This expression occurs in the *AŚ* at 4.9.2; 4.10.16; 4.11.2, 15, 26. At *AŚ* 4.9.7 and 4.11.1, we have the expression *citro ghātaḥ*, "vivid execution," that is, killing that involves various forms of torture. The very next sentence, 4.11.2, has the expression *śuddhavadha*, which must, therefore, be contrasted with *citravadha*. A neat and clean execution is probably what is meant. Several commentators of Manu (*MDh* 9.279) interpret the expression to mean decapitation, which is quite probable. At *AŚ* 4.11.26, *śuddhavadha* is contrasted with *kleśadaṇḍa*, "painful punishment," which must mean something close to *citravadha* (see *MDh* 9.291, where we have the expression *vikṛtavadha*, execution with bodily mutilation).

4.9.4. *sites for commodities* (paṇyabhūmi): Both Meyer and Kangle take these sites to be the factories where the commodities are manufactured. Although the term *bhūmi* could also mean the places where these commodities are stored, given that such storehouses are mentioned in the next sentence, that is the likely interpretation.

4.9.6. *warehouse* (bhāṇḍāgāra): It appears that a distinction is made in the *AŚ* between *bhāṇḍāgāra* and *koṣṭhāgāra* (which I have translated as storehouse). The former is found only here and at 2.4.10. It probably housed expensive items. At 2.4.10, it is associated with the bureau of official records, an important office, while at 2.4.8, the storehouse is associated with more humble buildings, such as kitchens and stables.

4.9.9. *with a brickbat* (iṣṭakāśakala): I think Gaṇapati Śāstrī is correct in taking this to mean that the man is driven out of the city or village by throwing brickbats at him. The Malayalam commentary interprets the term to mean a stick.

36 Paṇas: Gaṇapati Śāstrī thinks that, for this and the following crimes, exile is also implied along with the fine.

4.9.10. *periods of curfew* (antaryāmikam): This term is a hapax in the *AŚ*. However, the use of *yāmikam* with this sense at 2.36.35 makes it clear that the term must refer to periods when the population of a city was expected to remain indoors.

4.9.13. *threatens…suppresses*: These are obviously various ways in which a Justice may become partial to one party in a lawsuit by making it difficult or impossible for the other party to bring the matter to court. The first three acts all involve some kind of verbal threat. For the final item, we have the verb *abhigrasate*. It is a hapax in the *AŚ* and is not recorded in any dictionary either. Its literal meaning should be something like "swallow up." Gaṇapati Śāstrī thinks that it refers to bribery, which is unlikely because the justice is trying to prevent the man from filing a lawsuit. I think the meaning here is that the justice "swallows up," that is, makes the lawsuit disappear by suppressing it in some way. We have the related word *graseta* in *MDh* 8.43, where it clearly refers to the suppression of a lawsuit brought by a private individual.

he: The person imposing penalties on the Justices for malfeasance appears to be the Collector (see 4.9.18, where Magistrates also are the targets of punishment), while both the Collector and the Magistrates exercise control over superintendents (4.9.1).

4.9.14. *questions someone*: As the previous provision dealt with the person filing a lawsuit, this provision appears to deal with witnesses and how they should be dealt with. The next provision, significantly, deals with the other type of evidence, written documents.

4.9.20. *eight times that*: This means eight times the amount under litigation. For this provision with regard to false witnesses, see 3.11.45.

4.9.21. *a court lockup, a jail, or a prison*: Here we have three levels of jailhouses, perhaps in increasing levels of importance. The first (*dharmasthīya*) is connected to the courts of the Justices (*dhamastha*), and they were probably used to hold people in connection with civil lawsuits. The second (*cāraka*) is probably the same as the *mahāmātrīya* mentioned at 2.5.5 and connected with the criminal courts of the Magistrate (*pradeṣṭṛ*). However, 2.9.22 appears to indicate that people who were accused in civil lawsuits were also kept in this kind of jail, because someone releasing such a man has to pay the amount under litigation. The fourth (*bandhanāgāra*, the most common term for prison in Sanskrit literature) is probably the highest level of prison (possibly under the king's direct control), where major criminals and political prisoners were kept (2.5.1, 5; see *MDh* 9.288) as indicated by the more severe punishment at 4.9.22, 27, although the term also appears to be used more generally for a jail (2.36.44; 3.12.44). It is managed by its own superintendent (4.9.23). See Scharfe 1993, 172.

4.9.23. *different station* (sthānānyatvam): The meaning is unclear. It could mean the transfer to another location or to a different class or level within the prison.

4.10.1. *someone striking at…raised hand*: The meaning of the second in the list, namely cutpurse (*granthibheda*), is clear; it refers to a thief who manages to cut the knot of a garment that contains valuables. The other two are less so. Given the context of finger cutting and the progressive severity for repeated offenses, all three probably refer to kinds of petty theft (see the parallel at *MDh* 9.277 and *YDh* 2.274). The first (*tīrthaghāta*) may refer to theft at river crossings (or sacred fords); the Malayalam commentary takes it to be the theft of a bundle of goods at a crossing. The last (*ūrdhvakara*) is unclear; the term could also simply mean "raising up" (the same as *ūrdhvakarman*, suggested by Professor Wezler in a personal communication). It does have some resemblance to *utkṣepaka*, a term that is compounded with *grantibheda* in *YDh* 2.174. The *Aparārka* commentary on this verse explains *utkṣepaka* as someone who picks up a man's property using the thumb and finger, in other words, a pickpocket. According to the editor of the Malayalam commentary, it is breaking into a house through an upper floor.

in any way desired (yathākāmī): The meaning appears to be that the method of execution is left to the discretion of the Magistrate. He could order a clean or a vivid execution (4.9.2 n.).

4.10.3. *carrying off*: The offense here is the theft of these animals from traps set by other hunters and fowlers. The restitution is made to the owner of the trap.

4.10.6. *implements*: The term *dravya* can mean simply an article. However, the expression *kr̥ṣidravya* means not "agricultural goods" (Kane), but agricultural implements or tools; Gaṇapati Śāstrī correctly gives the example of a plow. Given that context and the heavy fines, the term *dravya* in this provision must refer to tools of the trade, rather than simply any article.

4.10.7. *tendon*: The meaning of *kāṇḍarā* in this context is unclear, as is the reading itself. Generally *kaṇḍarā* is a tendon or sinew, and *kāṇḍarā* is probably a variant of that. The Malayalam commentator speaks of the two tendons at the back of the feet, and he is probably on the right track. At *MDh* 8.325 (see my note there), we have the reading *sthūrikā* (Achilles tendon), which is cut as a punishment for the theft of certain animals, and, as I have shown in my note to this verse, the meaning is that the Achilles tendon is severed. That is probably also the meaning here. It is a less severe punishment than cutting off the feet, but still leaves the criminal unable to walk unaided.

4.10.9. *cheating*: The reference is to gambling (see 3.20.1–13).

4.10.10. *for providing...double that* (stenapāradārikayoḥ sācivyakarmaṇi striyāḥ saṃgr̥hītāyāś ca karṇanāsācchedanaṃ pañcaśato vā daṇḍaḥ puṃso dviguṇaḥ): The syntax of this sentence is ambiguous. Kangle's translation takes the genitive *striyāh saṃgr̥hītāyāś ca* as separate and unconnected to the locative *sācivyakarmaṇi*, and translates: "In the case of aiding a thief or an adulterer, and for a woman caught in adultery." But see 4.12.30–31, where the term *saṃgr̥hīta* is used for keeping an adulteress under lock and key while her husband is away. So the entire provision deals with a person who renders help to various kinds of offenders: thief, male adulterer, and adulteress kept under guard. The final "to the man," I think, refers to the lover of the adulteress who, according to 4.12.33, is also assumed to be similarly kept under restraint. The punishments for these individuals are given there; here the provision relates only to persons rendering assistance to them.

4.10.17–18. *standing... subjects*: Here I follow the interpretation of Scharfe (1993, 170–71). The magistrate stands between the king and the subjects as the king's representative. Others have interpreted the statement *rājñaś ca prakṛtīnāṃ ca antarā sthitaḥ* as either asserting the independence of the judge from the king or even his authority to impose punishments on the king, a very unlikely scenario. I have followed Scharfe in taking *antarā sthitaḥ* as uncompounded.

proclivity (anubandha): For the meaning of this term, see Rocher (1954), who has demonstrated that *anubandha* refers to the criminal propensities of the accused individual, that is, the likelihood that he will be a repeat offender in the future because of his past behavior patterns. See *MDh* 8.126.

4.11.7. *kill*: Kangle takes the term *ghātaka* to mean simply "beat," rather than the more serious "kill," because the other terms in the list indicate different forms of assault. I follow Meyer, the Malayalam commentary, and Gaṇapati Śāstrī in taking the term to mean killing, although a physical attack short of death is also possible.

4.11.12. *consign him to darkness*: The meaning is ambiguous. We have a similar provision at *ĀpDh* 2.27.17, where the expression *cakṣunirodha* with a similar ambiguity is used. These expressions may mean that the Brāhmaṇa is made blind or simply blindfolded or kept in a dark cellar. There is a general prohibition in the Dharmaśāstras against corporal punishment for Brāhmaṇas. This rider for a Brāhmaṇa is probably a later interpolation based on the general prohibition against killing a Brāhmaṇa. In a passage in Daṇḍin's *Daśakumāracarita* (Kale ed., 2.4, 131) that appears to be based on this provision, however, a Brāhmaṇa who coveted the kingdom enters blind darkness (*andhatamasapraveśa*) by having his eyes pulled out (*akṣyuddharaṇa*).

4.11.15. *involuntary*: The term *yadṛcchā* can mean accidental, and that is how Meyer and Kangle have taken it. But it is difficult to understand how an accidental death could merit such a severe punishment. I have taken it to mean a killing that happened without forethought or premeditation. The Malayalam commentary takes it to be killing "without knowing," which could be either accidental or unpremeditated.

4.11.18. *man*: The term *puruṣa* may also refer to her husband. But, given that the husband is mentioned in the very next provision, here it probably means any man.

4.12.4. *he should pay...the loss*: The way this provision is phrased, it is unclear whether it applies only to deflowering a girl who has attained puberty or also to a pre-pubertal girl. It appears to make no sense to restrict this to the former, given that the father would incur a loss in bride price in either case.

4.12.5. *right to have her* (prākāmya): That is, if the girl did not consent to the sexual encounter, the rapist does not get the right to marry her and thus avoid paying compensation for her loss of virginity. If she did consent, it would constitute what was called the Gāndharva form of marriage (3.2.6). Kangle appears to think that the term *akāmāyām* refers to her unwillingness to marry the man, rather than to her unwillingness to have sex. If that were the case, the next provision that imposes a fine on her if she is willing makes no sense. See also the parallel use of *sakāmā* at 4.12.20.

4.12.14. *equal status* (tulya): That is, if the substitute girl is of the same status as the original girl (see 4.12.10). The meaning of *tulya* is not certain, Kangle taking it to mean the social class (*varṇa*). The term, however, can have a broader meaning, including social class, age, attractiveness, intelligence, and the like.

4.12.16. *A woman...the surety* (avasthāya tajjātaṃ paścātkṛtā dviguṇaṃ dadyāt): This is a difficult sentence that is probably corrupt. Kangle takes *avasthāya* as a gerund and translates: "If after maintaining that kind (of condition) [*tajjātam*] she fails, she shall pay double." Then, the issue is to whom this payment must be made. I think *avasthāya* is the dative of the noun *avastha*, a surety or trustee (see 2.8.29; 3.1.17; 3.18.11; 8.4.33); and this is the understanding of Gaṇapati Śāstrī, who glosses it with *pratibhuve*. A surety or trustee of a girl at marriage is called *sukhāvastha* (3.4.9, 26, 30). He is, among other things, the guarantor to the groom that the bride is what she has been represented to be. In the event of a cover-up of her virginity, he has to be compensated. I have slightly emended the text from *tajjātaṃ paścātkṛtā* to the compound *tajjātapaścātkṛtā*. The expression *tajjāta* is frequently used with reference to experts in a particular area; see, for example, 4.6.3; 4.12.35. I take *paścātkṛtā* as a technical term to refer to a person who has been found guilty of a charge; for the related term *paścātkāra*, see 3.19.22.

4.12.21. *for satisfying her passion* (ātmarāgārtham): The meaning of this compound is quite obscure. What her passion has to do with the payment of the fine and the bride price is also unclear. Kangle thinks that the payments are for the satisfaction of her passion, that is, the penalty for letting her passions rule her. This is attractive as an interpretation, but one wonders why this could have not been stated more simply and clearly. For similar provisions, see *MDh* 8.369–370.

4.12.32. *both*: That is, both the woman and her lover, who, we must assume, was also kept under guard.

4.12.34. *For someone... thief*: The meaning is that an accomplice would claim that the lover is a thief and take him away from his confinement to the Magistrate. As a thief he would receive a lighter sentence. For a parallel, see *YDh* 2.301.

4.13.1–2. *For someone... into exile*: This passage looks very much like an interpolation stemming from the influence of Dharmaśāstras. It sits quite awkwardly within this chapter, which itself appears to contain sundry rules and was possibly an insertion into the *AŚ*. But this provision is cited almost verbatim in *YDh* 2.296.

4.13.6. *For someone... middle fine*: The reason why climbing on the perimeter wall or fence is an offense is unclear. A clue may be found in the clause "after the end of night" (*virātra;* see 6.4.2 n.), that is, early dawn. Could it be that standing on the wall would give a person a clear view of the neighbors' yard and house at a time when people may be going to the latrine?

4.13.8. *anything stolen... headman*: For this provision, see *YDh* 2.271. The term *pravāsita* (see 4.4.7 n.) here probably refers to killing (see also *AŚ* 4.13.20), given that the parallel in the *YDh* has the unambiguous *ghātita*.

4.13.11–12. *For areas... ten villages*: This is a difficult sentence and subject to varying interpretations. The first issue is the meaning of *tathāpy aguptānām*. Kangle's translation, "If they are unprotected even then," leaves unresolved what are left unprotected. I have followed Samasastry's and Meyer's interpretation in taking *aguptānām* as referring to regions or areas of the country that are not protected by the officials referred to in the previous provisions. The subject of the sentence is left unstated, but since the boundary limits, which refer to villages (see 2.35.3), are mentioned, we must assume it is the villagers. This is confirmed by *YDh* 2.272 (which is a paraphrase of this passage), where we have *svasīmni dadyād grāmas tu*, "within its boundary, however, the village should give." The difference is that the officials providing protection have to compensate for the losses, whereas the villagers have to simply permit a search within the village and perhaps also within their homes (for the expression *vicayaṃ dadyuḥ*, see also 5.1.24). In areas outside such boundaries, a group of neighboring five or ten villages (see 2.35.2) should permit such a search, a provision found also in *YDh* 2.272.

4.13.15–17. *A man... mahout*: This passage is quite out of place in this chapter and is perhaps an interpolation. This is also the only place where reference is made to the horse sacrifice.

4.13.19. *restitution*: Payment of compensation implies that the man who permitted the fight is not the owner of the animals.

4.13.22. *when it skids...slides back*: The expression *tiryakpratimukhāgata* is found also at *MDh* 8.291, where commentators and translators have taken *tiryak* and *pratimukha* as two separate directions: sideways and backward. Within that context, this may be a reasonable interpretation, given that Manu does not give the alternative of sliding backward separately. However, *pratimukha* generally means facing (see 3.9.3), just the opposite of backward. Further, we have in the *AŚ* passage the other statement, *pratyāsarat,* which, even though this form is not found in dictionaries, must mean going backward or in reverse. I have, therefore taken the compound *tiryakpratimukha* as expressing a single idea, namely that the direction of forward movement (*pratimukha*) is now toward one side (*tiryak*); the cart is skidding to one side and is beyond the control of the driver. In the second situation, perhaps while climbing a hill, the cart begins to slide backward, once again out of the driver's control.

4.13.26. *without a man*: The term *apuruṣa* is ambiguous. At 3.4.9, it is used with reference to a woman traveling without a male companion. Here also, it may have a similar meaning or, more likely, *puruṣa* here may be used in the sense of an official or supervisor. In that case, the reference would be to a vehicle without a qualified driver.

4.13.32. *unguarded* (aguptā): This refers to women who go outside the home and who are not under, or not always under, male control (see 2.23.11). A guarded woman (*guptā*), on the other hand, would be under strict control and would not go out of the house without an escort (see 3.1.7). For a longer discussion of these two classes of women, see *MDh* 8.374–385.

BOOK 5

5.1.3. *equally partial to the enemy* (śatrusādhāraṇa): Kangle translates: "in league with the enemy," which is also the understanding of Meyer. Gaṇapati Śāstrī glosses: *ubhayavetanāḥ*, that is, in the pay of both parties. I think, however, that these officials have equal loyalty to both the king and his enemy, or at least they are not strong partisans of the king. Traitors are dealt with in 5.1.4. See 7.9.44, 46, where this expression is defined. This meaning is also found in other places (7.18.36; 8.1.27; 9.2.5).

section on capturing an enemy town: For the title *pāragrāmika*, see 1.18.10 n. The rules for instigating sedition are found in 13.1 and for espionage in 13.3. There is no distinct chapter in the *AŚ* with this title, although at 13.1.1, we have the expression *paragrāmam avāptukāmaḥ* ("desirous of capturing an enemy town").

5.1.4. *he*: Here and in the rest of the chapter, the person carrying out the punishments is the king himself.

finding delight in his duty (dharmaruci): This expression is found only here in the *AŚ*, although in the third book, we have numerous instances of the parallel *dharmakāma*, which appears to have a deeper religious meaning. Why this expression is used here when assassination is recommended is unclear, perhaps to imply that such assassinations are not unrighteous, are part of the king's duty, and are undertaken not out of passion or anger but out of a sense of duty.

5.1.6. *by granting*: That is, the king promises to hand over the property to him once he has killed his traitorous brother.

5.1.8. *Pāraśava...attendant*: A Pāraśava is the son of a Brāhmaṇa from a Śūdra woman (see 3.7.21), but here the term may indicate a son from a lower-class woman, or simply a bastard (so Meyer). The meaning appears to be that the king can use such a son or a son the traitorous official has fathered on his female servant using the same technique as in the case of his brother.

5.1.9. *inheritance*: The assumption is that the official and his brother are living in an extended family with their paternal estate undivided. The brother is here asking for his portion of the inheritance so he can live separately, and the implication is that the official would want to maintain the integrity of the entire estate.

5.1.10. *lying down...house*: This is a reference to a common practice in ancient India of a creditor fasting until death (*prāyopavāsa*) outside the house of a debtor until he pays up. This seems to be a similar situation. See *MDh* 8.49, where most commentators talk about this custom, and Scharfe 1993, 151, n. 34.

or staying elsewhere: This added phrase appears to be a gloss that found its way into the text. If the man is murdered elsewhere, it would not be clear that the murder was committed by the traitor. Also, the general practice of fasting at the door of a creditor noted in the previous note supports the first and not the second alternative. See the parallel at 5.2.57.

5.1.21. *caravan escort*: The term *sārthātivāhya* (2.34.12) refers to escorts provided by the state to commercial caravans, and the term *ātivāhika* (2.16.18; 2.28.25; 2.35.12) refers to the charges for such escorts. I follow Meyer in taking this to be the meaning here also; Kangle takes it to mean a caravan route. The meaning, however, is not that different; under both interpretations, the official is sent to provide protection for caravans.

area subject to recapture: The term *pratyādeya* refers to an area of land that is easy for the enemy to recapture and thus difficult to defend; see 7.11.43; 9.4.4.

5.1.24. *middle courtyard*: For the plan of the king's residence and the circles of protection surrounding the king, see 1.21.1.

5.1.30. *chef, baker*: For chef (*sūda*), see my note to 1.12.9. The term *bhakṣyakāra* is a hapax in the *AŚ*. Its meaning could be simply a kind of cook, but I have followed its listing in the *Amarakośa*, where it is one of three terms for those who make bread or cakes.

5.1.31–32. *both:* The references of the two duals are unclear. Gaṇapati Śāstri is probably correct in taking the two who must taste the poisoned food in sentence 31 to be the cooks, and the two who are executed as poisoners to be the two traitorous officials.

5.1.55. *brooding* (anukṣipatsu): The meaning of this unusual verb appears to be the mourning and brooding produced by the death of a father along with thoughts of revenge. See 13.5.17 for this meaning. Kangle takes it to mean "surviving."

5.2.2. *one-third or one-fourth part*: This requisition by the state is different from the normal tax (*bhāga*) on agricultural produce. It appears that this special tax (called here *aṃśa*) was assessed on the stocks of grain held by the farmers. See Scharfe 1993, 162.

not dependent on rain (adevamātṛka): That is, land that is cultivated through irrigation (2.24.18 n.).

5.2.4–7. *He should give grain... as a favor*: This passage stands awkwardly within a chapter that deals with raising new revenue for the treasury. Scharfe (1993, 162) explains that buying a quarter of the crop enables the king to corner the market and thus raise new funds by selling the crop at a profit. Although an attractive explanation, it does not explain why the king is asked to exempt forest produce and the property of Vedic scholars and then given the option to purchase these also "as a favor." As a favor to whom? If it is a favor to the people involved, then it has little to do with the emergency measures with which we are dealing. Perhaps this passage crept into the text from a gloss dealing with settling virgin land mentioned in 5.2.2. If we eliminate this passage, the remark "if that does not work" (*tasyākaraṇe*) of 5.2.8 (see also 5.2.31) connects naturally to the provisions in 5.2.2–3.

5.2.8. *officers... in the summer*: As Scharfe (1993, 163–66) has clearly pointed out, the term *udvāpa* does not mean sowing (so Shamasastry, Meyer, Kangle) or preparation of the soil (so Johnston 1929, 99). The evidence of Vedic texts (*ŚB* 6.7.4.14; *KātŚr* 16.6.1, 3; 25.2.6) shows that the term refers to throwing away or out. And the genitive *karṣakāṇām* cannot be construed as the agent of the causative verb in this sentence, *kārayeyuḥ*. The meaning, then, is that in emergency situations, farmers who would normally farm royal fields (*sītā*) as sharecroppers would be ejected from those properties and rehired as farm laborers. For further reflection on this term and other Vedic usages, see Wojtilla 2010, 1022–23. His new information from the use of the term in the *Atharva Veda* (Śaunaka) 3.17.3 as "turn up," in a metaphorical sense to mean finding wealth, does not contradict Scharfe's interpretation.

5.2.9. *document regarding seeds*: That is, a document that would record the amount of seed corn distributed to the farmers.

5.2.17. *tax of one-fiftieth* (pañcāśatkarāḥ): I follow the persuasive argument of Scharfe (1993, 98) that this expression is an example of what he calls an "internal abbreviation" here and in the following passages (see Gonda 1968). A word is often dropped, even though it is assumed. Here the full compound should have been *pañcāśadbhāgakarāḥ*, as we find in *MDh* 7.130. The traders are subject to an additional tax of one-fiftieth on their profits. Kangle interprets the compound to mean 50 Paṇas, but in the *AŚ*, only amounts above 100 are given without Paṇa, while those below always have Paṇa attached. See Note to Translation.

5.2.24. *not upright in their work* (akarmaṇyān): I follow the Malayalam manuscript and commentary in restoring the reading to the negative *hiraṇyakaram akarmaṇyān.* Kangle offers a conjectural emendation, *hiraṇyakaraṃ karmaṇyān,* saying "the reading proposed alone yields a reasonable sense" and thinks that those who are skilled in their work are more likely to cheat (this is also the translation of Meyer). I find this assumption dubious. But the major reason for keeping the negative is the use of the positive in a very similar context at 5.3.6, where state officials are said to become *karmaṇya* when they are provided with a reasonable salary. It is difficult to see how the same word is used with negative and positive connotations in these two contexts. Here Kangle translates the term as "efficient," but it is more likely that they become honest in their work when they receive good remuneration. We do find the term *karmaṇya* used with the meaning of proper or fit (*MBh* 12.323.41), and the meaning here seems to be an extension of it.

5.2.28. *Using royal maids...the treasury*: The meaning is that the brothel keepers would use young women working for the royal household as prostitutes and hand the earnings back to the treasury.

5.2.30. *This should...not twice*: The reference is probably to the demands made above on various categories of people. It appears that this sort of emergency taxation and fund-raising cannot be done more than once.

5.2.37. *Executive officers* (kṛtyakarāḥ): The meaning of this term, also found at 9.1.4, where it is used adjectivally, is unclear. Although *kṛtya* is regularly used in the *AŚ* to mean people who are seducible, here it probably has a more general meaning of what must be accomplished. These were officers who performed tasks (perhaps unpleasant) that had to be carried out for the good of the state. See also 1.18.9 for plundering religious establishments.
stating that...burnt down: The intent appears to be to pretend that the property was not plundered by the king. The officers let it be known that the property of the religious orders or temples was actually deposited (for safekeeping?) with a person who has since died or whose house has burnt down, perhaps destroying the property.

5.2.42. *a snake...underground tunnel*: First, the meaning of *aniyataśiraska* ("with undetermined head") is unclear. I follow the traditional interpretation that it means a snake with many heads, although, if this was what the author wanted to convey, he could have simply said *bahuśiraska* or *anekaśiraska*. Second, the presence of an underground passage connected to the well is probably intended for operatives who would manipulate the artificial snake and its heads.

5.2.43. *He should show... anthill*: This is a very difficult and possibly corrupt sentence. Kangle changes the manuscript reading *antaśchidrāyām* ("containing a cavity within") to *antaśchannāyām* ("hidden within") without much justification; we must then think that the statue is hidden in a hole of a sanctuary or anthill, and the snake is shown in that statue. I take the three locatives as the three cavities within which the snake is shown. For a cavity within a statue, see 12.5.43; 13.1.3.

5.2.44. *administering poison... stung*: As Gaṇapati Śāstrī observes, one must assume that the poison administered to the unbelievers only induces a coma (see 14.1.16–17). If they were actually killed, the final option becomes irrelevant. The alternative is to get a condemned man (see 2.5.4 n. for the use of such men) to be bitten by a real snake and claim that he was bitten by the snake that was being exhibited.

5.2.45. *he should... appearances*: This is probably similar to the provision in 5.2.39–41. The agent would provide remedies to a manufactured occult appearance foretelling disaster. This sentence is repeated at 13.2.38.

5.2.48. *Examiner of Coins and the Goldsmith*: In both cases, these officers are robbed at night when they are holding deposits given to them by the citizens.

5.2.50. *at a fair... merchandise*: The agent acting as the trader displays his wares in one place to impress the people with his wealth and borrows money using his wares as collateral. He also sells his products to the people with the promise that the merchandise will be delivered the following day. That night, however, all the money is stolen.

5.2.52. *guise of holy women* (sādhvīvyañjana): This is the only place in the entire *AŚ* where we have the term *sādhvī* for a holy or ascetic woman. In all other places, the term is *bhikṣukī* without the use of *vyañjana* (see Note to the Translation, p. xv).

5.2.55. *the principal of a loan* (ṛṇaprayoga): Kangle translates "a loan given," and Scharfe (1993, 232) "interest on a debt." In the *MDh* 10.115, *prayoga* is used in the sense of an investment, and in *GDh* 12.31, *prayoga* is used with the meaning of the principal of a loan.

5.2.56. *servant woman*: The usual meaning of the term *bhāryā* is wife, and that is how it has been translated by Meyer and Kangle. But why would calling these women "wife" be an insult in the same way as "slave"? I think the term *bhāryā* is used here as the feminine of the adjective *bhārya*, one who has to be supported, that is, a servant. Thus, we have three insults: slave (*dāsa*) for the man, and slave woman and servant woman for the women of the household.

5.2.57. *lying down...traitor's door*: For this custom, see 5.1.10 n. It is probable that the condemned man may have been promised a pardon if he did these things. He, of course, had no idea that he himself would be killed in the pursuit of the king's broader goal of destroying the traitorous men and confiscating their property.

as he was pursuing a just desire (itthaṃkāmukaḥ): Kangle, following the suggestion of Meyer, has emended the unanimous reading of the manuscripts to *arthakāmukaḥ*. However, he keeps this reading in the other place where the phrase occurs, 11.1.35. I think Meyer and Kangle were misled by taking *itthaṃ* ("thus") to be a separate adverb qualifying *hataḥ* ("he was killed thus"); indeed, in his critical apparatus, he separates the two words: *itthaṃ kāmukaḥ*. I take *itthaṃkāmukaḥ* as a compound, in the same way as a similar compound in a similar context at 5.1.10, *dāyakāmukaḥ* ("longing for his inheritance"). See the parallel compounds *itthaṃbhāva* and *itthaṃvidha*. I think *itthaṃ* in this compound has a meaning similar to the old *itthā*, which, in *Ṛgveda* 8.4.20, has the meaning of just right, or in exactly the right way. I thank my colleague Joel Brereton for pointing out this parallel. Thus, in the passage at 11.1.35, the men are killed as they pursue a legitimate claim or goal, their killing being thus unjustified.

5.2.58. *Others* (itare): The plural is out of place here, given that the guilt can only be assigned to the traitorous man at whose doorstep the man was killed. Perhaps this phrase has been brought over here from 5.2.54, where the plural is appropriate (see also 5.1.42, 44, 46, 49, where *itare* is used). It is also possible that using the same strategy of false accusation, other traitorous officials could also have their property confiscated.

5.2.59. *or strike...a son*: I think that the ascetic does not say to the man that his magic can do all or any of these things. The list is given so that the ascetic will choose the one appropriate for the man with whom he is dealing. If he is after money, then the magic can obtain wealth; if he wants to get rid of an enemy, then the magic can strike him with a disease, and so on. For similar alternatives, see 4.4.14; 5.1.39.

5.2.61. *single coin* (ekarūpam): The meaning of this compound is unclear. Meyer thinks that it refers to a counterfeit coin, suggesting an alternate reading, *kūṭarūpam*. If that is the case, then the later arrest is due to his use of a false coin. I follow Kangle in taking the meaning to be "a single coin," which permits the ascetic to claim that it was too little. See the next note for the reason for the man's arrest.

limb of a corpse or a dead child: The reason for placing these at the location of the find is unclear. Kangle thinks that it is simply to mark the place where the coin was buried. But surely there were easier and less gruesome ways of marking such a spot. It appears that the reason for this burial was a magical rite involving either the sacrifice of a child or the use of a corpse. The connection of the coin to the uncovered remains may be the reason why the man was arrested while trying to purchase material for the new rite using that coin. Note that sentences 53 to 65 consist of falsely claiming that these men committed murder. It is in sentences 66–67 that the accusation involves counterfeit coins.

5.2.64. *a secret agent... remain in great anguish*: The reading and meaning of this phrase are uncertain. The manuscripts read *mātṛvyañjanāyā* (genitive) and *avarūpitā*. These readings have been emended by Kangle to *mātṛvyañjanayā* (instrumental) and *avarūpitaḥ* on the basis of the Malayalam commentary; but as Scharfe (1993, 233, n. 201) has shown, this reading is purely a conjecture of Gaṇapati Śāstrī and not supported by the Malayalam commentary. I think both emendations are unjustified. Although a bit awkward, I take the first to be *mātṛvyañjanā yā* (as two words in the nominative). Thus, the manuscript reading of *avarūpitā* would go nicely with the feminine nominative. The problem is the meaning of *avarūpita*, and both Meyer and Kangle have been groping for a meaning that would fit the context. Taking *avarūpitaḥ* (masculine) as referring to the traitorous man, Kangle translates: "should be charged." I think that the original may have been the uncommon term *avarupitā*, from the verb *-rup*, to suffer violent pain, changed to the easier reading *avarūpita* by a scribe. My conjecture is supported by the reading *avakupitā* ("enraged") of the manuscript G2. It is the female agent pretending to be the mother of the slain son who remains grieving.

5.2.65. *As his... forest sacrifice*: The person doing these rites is the traitorous official. Kangle is probably correct in taking *vanayāge* (forest sacrifice) to be a scribal error introduced by dittography: *yāge* from the previous *rātriyāge* and *vana* from the following *vanakrīḍāyāṃ*.

who has been well prepared (saṃsiddha): This term, coming at the very beginning of the sentence, is unclear in syntax and meaning. Kangle thinks that it refers to a condemned man who is now ready to be executed; so also Scharfe (1993, 233). But why would that information be so important to be placed at the beginning of the sentence? I think that it may refer to the preparation (clothing, etc.) of the condemned man to look like the son of the woman who is accusing the traitor. For uses of *saṃsiddha* as well prepared or successful, see 1.16.29; 3.14.21.

5.2.68. *send word*: The communication is made to the authorities. The articles for coronation and the false papers from the enemy are to be planted in the house of the traitor by the agent. Their discovery would enable the state to confiscate the man's property after his execution and thus to replenish the treasury.

communicated the reason: Namely, that the traitor is planning to usurp the throne at the instigation of an enemy king and to have himself anointed as king (Scharfe 1993, 205).

5.3.1. *According to... of the work*: This opening statement is unclear and possibly corrupt. Kangle has changed the manuscript reading *samudāyavādena* to *samudayapādena*, which is reasonable. The term *samudāya* occurs nowhere else, whereas *samudaya* (revenue) is common; and the characters for *pa* and *va* are very similar in both Grantha and Malayalam scripts. Kangle takes *bhṛtyakarma* as the object of the verb, but he has to understand wages as a missing element: "fix (wages for) the work of servants." I think the problem can be solved if we take *karma* here to be the *lectio facilior* and a scribal "correction" of an original *bharman* ("wages"). According to this option, the total wages of government servants cannot exceed one-quarter of the total revenue. In the second half of the sentence, an alternative is given: The salary should be such that it would assure the completion of the tasks assigned to an official.

5.3.2. *corpus (of revenue)*: The term *śarīra* is used for the corpus or totality of the revenues (2.6.9) or of expenditure (2.9.11).

5.3.13. *chroniclers* (paurāṇika): The meaning of this term is not altogether clear. It probably refers to some kind of reciter of past events; see his connection to *sūta* and *māgadha* at 3.7.29. See also 13.1.7, where we have a list similar to this.

5.3.17. *Servants…bipeds*: The long compound *catuṣpadadvipadaparicāraka-pārikarmikaupasthāyikapālakaviṣṭibandhakāḥ* is difficult to parse. Kangle takes all up to *pālaka* as referring to *catuṣpadadvipada* (quadrupeds and bipeds), and takes *viṣṭibandhaka* (which is a hapax) to be a separate Tatpuruṣa compound meaning foremen of laborers. Both Gaṇapati Śāstrī and Meyer take the latter also to be part of the long Dvandva compound and to contain two categories of individuals. I have followed Kangle, especially because *bandhaka* is usually preceded by what they catch or procure (2.28.3; 2.30.44; 3.4.22).

climbers, manikins, and hill diggers (ārohakamāṇavakaśailakhanakāḥ): The meanings of these terms are unclear. Kangle takes *ārohaka* to mean a rider and *māṇavaka* to mean a bandit. I have taken a clue from the last term *śailakhanaka*, which refers to quarrying on hillsides. All these terms may thus refer to activities connected with mines and quarries. Thus, *māṇavaka* here may be used in its literal sense of "little man," perhaps employed to work in mines.

5.3.20. *"king"*: The reference here is not to the king as such but to the Adhvaryu priest, who acts in place of the king in long and complicated sacrifices. This substitution is explicitly mentioned in the *BauŚr* 15.4 and the *ĀpŚr* 20.2.12.3. See also Kane 1962–1975, III: 28.

5.3.25. *units*: The meaning of *varga* in this context is unclear, but the following statements make it clear that the reference is to military units.

disbandment: For *vikṣepa* as the disbandment of an army unit after mobilization, see 2.6.21; 2.15.10.

5.3.29–30. *children…honors*: It is most likely that the provisions in these two statements also pertain to the families of those who die while performing official duties, especially soldiers who die in battle, and not to all state employees.

5.3.32. *conventions pertaining to the total revenue from the villages* (grāmasaṃjātavyavahāra): For the meaning of *saṃjāta* as the total revenue coming to the treasury or the totality of the produce, see 2.6.27; 2.7.2; 2.29.1. For *vyavahāra* as convention, that is, the general rules applicable to commercial transactions, see 2.7.2, 29.

5.3.33. *With that*: The instrumental *etena* at the beginning of the sentence is unusual. It occurs most frequently with reference to the preceding passage, which is said to explain also something else (*etena vyākhyātam*; see 1.21.15; 2.4.31). It is quite unlikely that the term would have the same meaning as *evam*, as assumed by Kangle ("In this manner"), unless we imply *vidhinā* (this would be the only such instance in the *AŚ*; see 10.5.57) or the meaning of "Danach" given by Meyer. I take "with that" as referring to the money (perhaps also the forest produce, farm animals, and fields) of the previous statement. The meaning appears to be that with these gifts, he should supplement (make special: *viśeṣa*) the normal rations and wages of specially gifted employees.

5.3.34. *Taking one... monetary wages*: This provision is connected to the statement in 5.3.31 regarding the practice of a king with a small treasury. When he is unable to pay his employees in cash, he should pay them in kind, giving them one Āḍhaka of grain for each 60 Paṇas owed in wages.

5.3.35. *liminal days* (saṃdhidivasa): This expression probably refers to days at the juncture of two calendrical periods, such as the new-moon and full-moon days that divide the dark and bright halves of a month, or the day between two seasons. It may further refer to days that are more commonly called *parvan*, which includes, besides the new moon and full moon, the eighth and 14th days of each fortnight.

5.3.39. *he*: The antecedent of the pronoun is unclear. The closest noun is the king, but it is unlikely that the provision refers to the king. The reference is either to the Superintendent of the Armory, because an inventory of lost or destroyed items is to be maintained, or the man who was responsible for the loss. The last portion of this chapter deals with quite disparate material probably derived from diverse sources.

5.3.42. *Or*: This option makes no sense within the current context, making it likely that these provisions were taken without editorial intervention from another source.

5.3.43–44. *at the time of... salaries*: The strategy appears to be this: Just before the expedition, king's agents disguised as traders give provisions to them, probably for use by their families while they are gone. The deal requires the soldiers to pay double the cost of the merchandise when they return. If they die, their families would assume the liability. If they return, they will receive wages, but most of it will be taken back by the king because of the double payment for the merchandise. This provision returns to the topic of the previous chapter, perhaps indicating that the salary list is a later addition.

5.4.4. *subject himself... science*: The expression *śāstrānuyogaṃ dadyāt* is ambiguous, but it is quite unlikely that the prospective official would have the temerity to question the king. He subjects himself to such questioning regarding the "science" (*śāstra*), which here means the discipline of political science.

5.4.7. *in connection... the moment*: The phrase *matsaṃyoge tadātve ca* is not altogether clear. Kangle translates: "on the instant on those associated with me," a translation that is also somewhat vague, and which he clarifies in the note: "no punishment for my people at once," that is, without due process. I think the particle *ca* coming after *tadātve* makes it likely that we are dealing with two occasions when punishment should not be inflicted. Further, *matsaṃyoge*, in the singular with the noun *saṃyoga* is quite different from the preceding *balavatsaṃyukteṣu* ("on people associated with powerful individuals") and likely does not refer to people associated "with me" (for the use of *saṃyukta*, see also 5.4.10). I interpret this to mean that the king should not punish people when the punishment can be associated with the official or in a rash manner without due process (*tadātve:* instantaneously).

5.4.8. *sit on one side... at a distance*: The reading and meaning of this sentence are unclear. Kangle emends the unanimous reading of the manuscripts from *saṃnikṛṣṭaḥ viprakṛṣṭaḥ* to the compound *saṃnikṛṣṭaviprakṛṣṭaḥ*, and translates: "sit at the (king's) side neither very near nor far, on another seat," while admitting in a note that "the sense requires *asaṃnikṛṣṭaḥ aviprakṛṣṭaḥ*." It is difficult to obtain Kangle's meaning from either the manuscript reading or his emended reading. I have restored the manuscript reading and take *saṃnikṛṣṭaḥ* and *viprakṛṣṭaḥ* as two conditions of his seating; he could be assigned a seat near the king (*saṃnikṛṣṭa*) or far from the king (*viprakṛṣṭa*). In the former case, he would sit on one side of the king (*pārśvataḥ*), and in the latter case, on what is called *parāsana*, whose meaning is unclear given the wide range of meanings for the term *para*. I take *para* in this context to indicate distance. Thus, if the new official is asked to sit far away from the king, he should take a seat far away, thereby showing his humility. I think this whole provision deals with rules of court etiquette.

5.4.9. *combative speech* (vigṛhya kathanam): For the spectrum of meanings for the term *vigṛhya*, see 7.4.4 n.; Olivelle 2011.

indistinct (apratyakṣa): The meaning is not altogether clear. Kangle takes the term to mean a statement not based on personal knowledge, and the Malayalam commentary takes it to be hearsay. I think the term refers to the manner of speech, just like combative speech, within the context of court etiquette. It could refer to speaking too softly or secretively or in a manner that is difficult to follow.

5.4.12. *pleasing and beneficial* (priyahita): The author plays with the two meanings of the terms; *priya* is both someone who is dear and something that is pleasing, and *hita* is a close friend and something that is beneficial. When applied to individuals (as at 5.4.1, 11; 5.6.2) the first meaning is at the forefront, while when applied to advice and activities, the second meaning is prominent (see 2.9.36; 3.10.46; 7.6.20; 7.14.10; 13.5.4).

5.4.13–14. *Or else…laughter*: For a parallel passage, presented as a citation of Cāṇakya, see Daṇḍin's *Dasakumāracarita*, ch. 8 (Kale ed., 195).

5.4.17. *Fire…prosper*: Variants of this proverb are found elsewhere as well; see *MDh* 7.9.

5.5.1. *he*: The antecedent is unclear, but it appears that the discussion is still about the man who has taken service as a high official under a king, which was the subject of the previous chapter.

5.5.5, 7. *his, he*: All these pronouns refer to the king.

5.5.9. *goading another person*: The meaning seems to be that the king incites someone else to act against the official.

similar faults as he (samadoṣa): For a similar comment on the king's behavior toward an official out of favor, see Daṇḍin's *Daśakumāracarita*, ch. 8 (Kale ed., 195), which reads *matsamānadoṣān vigarhayati*, "he scorns people with faults (or offenses) similar to mine."

paying attention to the back (pr̥ṣṭhāvadhānam): The meaning of this expression is obscure. Kangle translates: "paying attention at the back" and explains in a note: "paying attention at the back (and not in front where the minister is)." I think this is probably correct; the king focuses his attention on the back of the room and not the front where the minister is sitting, thus deliberately ignoring him. Gaṇapati Śāstrī in his *Śrīmūla* commentary glosses: *pratigacchatas tasya pr̥ṣṭhato vilokanam*, "looking at the back when he is going away." But the term is *avadhāna*, which means paying heed or attention and not simply looking (*avalokana*).

speaking falsely (mithyābhibhāṣaṇam): This could mean that the king tells falsehoods to him (so Kangle), or that the king speaks to him in an unbecoming manner (Meyer: "ungebührlich," but *mithyā* is used regularly in the *AŚ* to mean a falsehood), or that the king speaks falsely about the minister or spreads false rumors (the term *abhibhāṣaṇa*, however, generally refers to someone addressing another person, but this is the only occurrence of the term in the *AŚ*).

5.5.11. *This one…high above*: The referent of the pronoun *ayam* ("this," masculine) is unclear. It must refer to someone near, and not the clouds or something high up in the sky, which would be referred to as *asau* ("that one"). The explanation of the Malayalam commentary that the gardener was watering the plants from above rather than at the bottom (which was customary) indicated to the minister that the king was acting against him. This is probably a guess, especially because the introduction in the previous statement refers to nonhuman beings. Given the mention of a flying bird in the very next omen, this one may refer to a bird dropping on the official, portending danger at the hand of the king.

Grass: This single word appears to be an exclamation. Kangle may be right that the exclamation is directed at grass growing in a spot where it should not be growing.

The garment is cold: The context and meaning are obscure.

sprayed outward (pratyaukṣīt): I take this to mean that the elephant has sprayed water in the direction of the official, which is taken as a bad omen here.

Chariot and horse have cried out (rathāśvaṃ prāśaṃśīt): Both Meyer and Kangle take the subject of the verb to be some other person, perhaps the king: "He has praised the chariot and horse." Given that all the surrounding omens deal with activities initiated by animals (elephant spraying, dog barking), I think it appropriate to take the subject of *prāśaṃsīt* to be *rathāśva* (a Samāhāra Dvandva compound; see *MDh* 7.96). The meaning of the verb, however, causes a problem, because it usually means to praise. I have taken it to refer to the squeaking of the chariot and the simultaneous neighing of the horse.

5.5.14. *his*: That is, a close ally of the king, presumably so that the ally can put him back in the good graces of his master, as pointed out in the verse.

5.5.15. *there*: That is, with the ally of the king.

5.6.1. *calamity* (vyasana): Here and in the following provisions, calamity probably refers to the death of the king. The procedure appears to be that the king's death should not be publicly announced until the succession plans have been duly put in place, for fear of a power vacuum.

minister (amātya): This term refers in general to any high-ranking officer of the kingdom. Here it is unclear who this minister is. Likely candidates are the Counselor (*mantrin*), the Chaplain (*purohita*)—if these two officers are considered separate individuals (see 1.9 n.)—or one of the high officials (*mahāmātra*); see 1.13.1 n.; 2.7.24 n.

5.6.7. *He*: It appears that the discussion from this point on deals with the death of the king and the problems arising out of succession. The minister is advised to make preparations for a smooth transfer of power, making sure that powerful individuals are neutralized.

5.6.11. *inviolable* (adūṣyam): For the use of this term with reference to the violation of a pact or alliance, see 7.14.7.

5.6.17. *remedial measures against calamities*: The whole of book 8 is devoted to the topic of calamities. For conspiracies originating within the capital and in the outlying districts, see 9.5.

5.6.20. *one of these…so forth*: The expression *sāmantādīnām* refers to the standard list of individuals who may succeed a king given repeatedly in the *AŚ*: neighboring lord, tribal chief, a man from the king's family, and prince in disfavor (see 1.13.18; 7.15.12; 7.16.7; 9.3.24; 9.6.71; 12.4.1). Kangle ignores the final *ādi* of the compound when he translates: "one of the vassals." See 7.2.6 n.

5.6.25. *get the members…chief officers*: The meaning could be that the three groups attack other chief officers, or that the first two groups (family members and princes) would attack the chief officers.

5.6.34. *princess, or a pregnant queen*: In all likelihood, these royal women are appointed to produce a son, who would become the king. In the case of the pregnant queen (i.e., a wife of the deceased king), this is very clear. In the case of a princess, who would technically be a *putrikā* (see *MDh* 9.127 and my note to it), the fathering of a son by her through the leviratic procedure (3.4.38 n.) is given later at 5.6.40.

his (ātmanaḥ): Kangle and Meyer think that the reference is to the character and high birth of the officials. I think Scharfe (1993, 191) is right in taking this as referring to the young prince. The term *ātmanaḥ*, furthermore, may refer back to the *ātmasaṃpanna* ("endowed with the entire set of exemplary qualities of self") of 5.4.2–3.

5.6.41. *fear that…agitated*: The reference is to the princess from whom the next king is to be born. The reason for the agitation is not given, but it is likely that the guardians want to keep her pure and not attracted by temptations.

family member…auspicious marks: The family member is to make sure that she is kept under surveillance. That he does not have spirit and energy makes it less likely that he will conspire with the princess. The meaning of *chāttra* ("pupil") is unclear. Kangle takes this to be a young boy.

BOOK 6

6.1.3. *Coming from a noble family…eager to be trained*: These qualities are enumerated as belonging to the ideal king at *YDh* 1.309–311.

6.1.8. *strongholds*: The term *sthāna* here probably refers to forts or fortified towns able to withstand enemy attacks. See the term *sthānīya* used for such places at 2.1.4; 2.3.2–3.

criminals (kaṇṭa): This term may refer simply to thorns (so Kangle), but coming right before *śreṇī*, which here probably refers to nefarious gangs, it probably has the metaphorical meaning of social parasites dealt with in book 5.

landlords who are prudent (abāliśasvāmī): Kangle in his note to this passage thinks that *svāmin* in this compound refers to the king himself. This, I think, is unlikely, given that all the qualities refer to things and people who are actually within the countryside. If not the landlords, then the term at least refers to masters as distinguished from the agricultural workers.

6.1.13. *without a refuge* (agati): For this meaning of *gati*, see 7.2.24–25.

not following up (ananubandha): This is also an unclear compound. Kangle translates: "without a following." For the meaning of *anubandha* as a proclivity to do certain acts, or as repetition/continuation (as in 1.16.29), see 4.10.17–18 and the note to it. The Malayalam commentary explains that he has no one to help him when he has been defeated.

exemplary qualities... of an enemy: It must be remembered that the term *sampad*, which means all that goes to make an ideal enemy (or minister, etc.), is viewed always from the perspective of the seeker after conquests (*vijigīṣu*), the king to whom these instructions are given (see 1.9.1 n.). Thus, the essential qualities of an enemy do not make him a good king but rather a good enemy to have, because these qualities make it easy to overpower him, as stated in the very next sentence (Bodewitz 2003, 233).

6.2.1. *Rest... security*: The translation of the compound *yogakṣema* poses several problems. As a single concept, it often refers to security or security measures. Thus, at *MDh* 9.219, *yogakṣema* is one of the items that cannot be divided during the partitioning of an inheritance, and there it clearly refers to security measures, such as fences for fields and houses. In the Vedic usage, *yoga* referred to the trek, when the people were on the move in search of wealth, while *kṣema* referred to a time of encampment and rest in a defensive position. I think this dual meaning of the compound is prominent in the *AŚ*. In this passage, rest (*śama*) is connected to *kṣema*, and exertion (*vyāyāma*) to *yoga*. I have regularly translated the compound as a dual, unless the context dictates otherwise (e.g., 1.13.7, 8; 3.11.3).

6.2.16. *vulnerable* (yātavya): For the definition of this kind of enemy, see 7.5.1–18. The gerundive in this and the following terms indicates both the state of affairs in the enemy kingdom and the fact that it is beneficial or imperative for the king who desires conquest to attack, oppress, or weaken that opponent.

vanquishable (ucchedanīya), *oppressable* (pīḍanīya), *enfeebleable* (karśanīya): For these kinds of king, see 7.7.13; 7.10.26–27; 7.18.14–16; 9.7.58.

6.2.20. *life*: The term *jīvita* is used for livelihood at 3.4.30, but most frequently it refers to a man's life (3.11.18; 10.3.57; 12.1.7).

6.2.21. *when they are united... intermediate*: I take the past participle *saṃhata* as connected to *saṃdhi*, the formal peace pacts contracted between both enemies and allies. The intermediate king is one who is probably stronger than either of the other two parties, and who is thus able to render assistance to either. But he is able to defeat them only if they are not united. For the peace pact (*saṃdhi*), see Olivelle 2011.

6.2.22. *constituents*: both Meyer and Kangle take these to be the constituent elements (*prakṛti*) of the three listed kings (see 6.1.1). However, as the mention of *prakṛti* at 6.2.23–24 indicates, the meaning of the term here appears to be the 12 constituents of the circle of kings (*maṇḍala*) listed in 6.2.13–22. The neutral king (*udāsīna*) is thus the most powerful king among the kings that constitute the circle.

6.2.24. *its*: As indicated in the previous note, the antecedent of the pronoun is implicitly the circle of kings (*maṇḍala*).

6.2.24–27. *constituents are three... 18-fold circle*: In the previous passage, we have one theory of the circle consisting of 12 kings in various relationships to each other. In this passage, an alternative theory is given, where the circle has only three constituents: seeker after conquest, ally, and ally's ally. Each of these has five constituent elements internal to each kingdom, for a total of 15. These 15 together with the three kings constitute the 18 constituent elements of the circle.

6.2.28. *There are 12 royal... 72*: The 12 kings constituting the circle are given in 6.2.13–22. The material constituents are the five given in 6.2.25. When multiplied by the 12 kings, they add up to 60. Together with the 12 kings they constitute 72.

6.2.33–34. *might* (prabhu): This term is found only here in the *AŚ*, and its exact meaning within this context is unclear. The term as an adjective means mighty and as a noun means lord or king. It appears that here it is used with a somewhat abstract meaning, equivalent to *prabhāva* in other sections (7.6.33; 7.15.3).

6.2.35. *When he is... coequal*: It appears that the comparison is with the other kings of the circle. Superiority, inferiority, and equality among them are determined by the relative amount of power and success each has.

6.2.36. *if he is similar* (sādhāraṇa): The meaning of this term within this context is unclear. Meyer takes it as a synonym of *sama* ("coequal") of the previous sentence. If that is the case, then a king whose power and success place him at the same level as the other kings should seek to increase these in his material constituents.

6.2.39. *leader* (netṛ): The reference is to the seeker after conquests, at whom the instructions in the *AŚ* are directed. This term is used for the seeker after conquests (*vijigīṣu*) only in books 6 and 7 and always in verses, except at 7.18.29.

BOOK 7

7.1.1. *sixfold strategy* (ṣāḍguṇya): See Rocher 1981 for a detailed discussion of this technical term, which is found only in book 7, with the exception of 6.2.4. As Rocher has demonstrated, the sixfold strategy qualifies policy (*naya*), which is explained as constituting human endeavor at 6.2.6–12. This explains the use of the term *guṇa* (literally, quality or attribute), because these are the six attributes of good policy. The connection is brought into focus in *YDh* 1.346–47. For a study of the circle and strategies, see Scharfe 1989, 206–210.

7.1.2. *peace pact, initiating hostilities* (saṃdhi, vigraha): For a study of these two strategies, see Olivelle 2011.

7.1.11. *double stratagem... at the same time*: At 7.1.37 and 7.3.19, this strategy is explained as entering into a peace pact with one king, while initiating hostilities against another king (Scharfe 1989, 208). Yet, as Botto (1972) concludes, it may have originally meant concluding a peace pact while preparing for war at the same time and with the same enemy. However, the term *dvaidhībhāva* (in spite of the fact that its literal meaning is clear: "becoming divided into two parts") appears to have been subjected to diverse interpretations at a very early date. At *MDh* 7.160 (see my note to this) and 167, it is implied that the strategy consists of separating the army from the king, whereas some commentators take it to be the division of the army into two. For a study of this term and its various interpretations, see Botto 1972.

7.1.31. *alternative* (vibhāṣitam): The meaning of this term here is unclear. I follow Meyer ("Entweder-oder") in taking the term to mean an option or alternative, which is its meaning within grammar. The objection appears to be to the "*vā*" (or) in the opinion. Kangle translates: "This is not disputed."

7.1.32. *both*: As Kangle notes, the king has started his commercial operations away from his enemy and close to another king. In this situation, he will enter into peace pacts with both his enemy and this other king.

7.1.34. *between a dog and a boar*: This proverb is repeated at 9.2.6, where a Caṇḍāla is said to be the winner in the battle between a dog and a boar. If both or either of the two combatants die in the battle, the Caṇḍāla, who would eat the flesh of either, would gain the meat. The moral of the story is that a smart king could get two enemies to fight with each other, leaving both either dead or weakened, of which he would be the beneficiary.

7.2.1–5. *When equal prosperity... and not his own*: This passage looks very much like an introduction or an interpolation. The topic of this chapter starts at sentence 6.

7.2.2. *losses, expenses*: For the definitions of these two, see 9.4.1–2.

7.2.6. *neighbor*: Even though the term *sāmanta* may refer to a neighboring and subordinate vassal, in the *AŚ*, it usually refers to his natural enemy whose territory is adjacent to his. Gopal (1963) attempts to restrict the term to neighboring cultivators, but this is clearly erroneous, especially in view of the technical term *śakya-sāmanta*, a weak or pliant neighboring ruler (*AŚ* 6.1.3, 8; 7.10.9). See also Ali 2004, 35.

7.2.18. *occupy himself... hostilities*: The sentence is somewhat unclear, but the reasons or motives for undertaking either of these strategies are spelled out in 7.1.32–33.

7.3.8–9. *heat is the cause... metal*: Here we have an interesting play on the double meaning of the verb *saṃ -dhā*, which means to unite, to join, and within political strategy, to join with another king in a peace pact (*saṃdhi*). So here the strategy for joining metal is used for the strategy for uniting kings: the use of heat for the former and the use of force for the latter, both indicated by the Sanskrit term *tejas*. See also the same term in 7.3.11, where it is applied to forest fire and to internal rancor and grief.

7.3.25. *unseen person*: That is, the weaker king or the commander of his army is unseen by the stronger king with whom the pact has been negotiated. The army or the weaker king is expected to go to a different region from where he would render assistance to the stronger king.

7.3.26. *marriage alliance for the chief*: The meaning appears to be that the one sent to serve the stronger king, either the chief of armed forces or the prince, is to contract a matrimonial alliance with royal women of the stronger king.

7.3.30. *administered poison*: The manuscripts read *vāgurānvitam* ("equipped with snares"), which Kangle has emended to *vā garānvitam* based on the Malayalam commentary and the parallel at 12.1.25. The meaning appears to be that the poison would take effect after some time (perhaps making them sickly rather than killing them outright), thus preventing the use of the animals to augment the king's power. This is done in the first two kinds of pacts given in verses 27–28.

7.4.1. *Remaining... have not yet been explained:* The reading of the edition is *saṃdhivigrahayor āsanaṃ yānaṃ ca vyākhyātam*, which literally should mean "has been explained." First, the participle should have been in the dual to agree with *āsanaṃ yānaṃ ca*, but one can see how the singular is used by attraction to the nearest substantive. But these topics have not yet been explained and are actually the subject of this chapter. The sense of this particular past participle could be that of a gerundive (*vyākhyātavyam*), as assumed by Kangle, although such a gerundive is not found anywhere in the *AŚ*. Another solution offered by Professor Wezler (personal communication) is to emend the reading from *ca vyākhyātam* to *cāvyākhyātam*, making it a negative with the meaning of not yet been explained. This is attractive, even though the negative *avyākhyāta* is nowhere used in the *AŚ*. I have adopted this emendation.

7.4.5. *needful*: The meaning appears to be that he takes precautionary measures to defend the outer and inner regions of his own kingdom in anticipation of an attack by the enemy or his allies.

7.4.8–12. *Having turned around…remain stationary:* This little dialogue pertains only to the last of the several conditions under which the king decides to initiate hostilities and then remain stationary. That is when the enemy has mobilized his entire army but, ignoring him, the enemy attacks his other enemy, who would then be the king's ally. The teachers think that this is a bad idea, because the enemy may well turn his troops around and destroy him. Kauṭilya defends the stated position. He thinks that, unless the king is facing a calamity himself, the most the enemy can do is to weaken him. But the man's other enemy will become stronger due to this and then cause his destruction and, being grateful, will render assistance to the weakened king. It is unclear, here and at 7.5.4, where exactly the Kauṭilya quotation ends. Kangle takes it to end at the initial "No." I think that it more likely includes also the reasons for the negative answer.

7.4.16. *rear ally*: For this and other allies and enemies around a king, see 6.2.18 and the Note to the Translation, Table 0.3.

7.4.19. *in one place…more than one place*: The meaning appears to be that, if the joint operation is conducted at a specific location and with a specific aim, then the shares of the spoils taken by the partners will be specified beforehand. If the operation takes place in different locations and has different aims, then the shares will be left undetermined. Perhaps the shares received by each partner in that case will be proportionate to the effort of each in the various battles.

7.5.14. *In loyalty is every strategy* (anurāge sārvaguṇyam): This appears to be an adage, occurring also at 8.2.24. Both Meyer and Kangle take *guṇa* here as virtue or good quality, which is certainly possible. Given the use of the term as strategy within the title of this book, *ṣāḍguṇya,* I have chosen to translate it as strategy. The meaning appears to be that every political strategy ultimately rests on the loyalty of the subjects.

7.5.19–28. *For, by casting…redress them*: This topic begins quite unusually with a long verse passage detailing the causes of poverty, greed, and disloyalty of the subjects. This section appears to be a redactoral insertion; see the initial "For" (*hi*), which does not make much sense within the context. Sentence 29 and the following correspond somewhat to the style of the preceding topic, although the responses are not as clear-cut as in the preceding sections. In the second half, furthermore, the impoverished, the greedy, and the disloyal are taken as three different categories of people, whereas in the first half (see 7.5.27), the three are taken as causally connected: impoverishment causes greed, and greed causes disloyalty.

7.5.29. *Is it…disaffected*: These are curious nominal sentences ending in *iti* presenting a question in the form of a series of options: *kṣīṇā lubdhā viraktā vā prakṛtaya iti*. These kinds of questions are found only, and frequently, in books 7, 8, and 9, and indicate a kind of informal oral style; see, for example, 7.9.9, 13, 18, 22, 26, 31, 50; 8.2.2, 9, 13, 21; 9.3.1; 9.7.64. Clearly the question pertains to which of the options is better or worse, clearly seen at 7.9.9.

7.5.30–32. *The impoverished…enemy attack*: The Malayalam commentary makes clear that each subsequent one is more serious than the one preceding.

7.6.1. *second constituent*: That is, the second member of the circle of kings, who is one's natural enemy occupying the territory adjacent to that of the seeker after conquest.

7.6.2. *neighboring ruler*: This is the same as the second constituent, namely the enemy. The attacks are always launched against the *yātavya*, the vulnerable king.

7.6.3. *If the spoils…attack*: The meaning appears to be that if both get equal spoils after their joint operation, then the seeker after conquest should enter into a peace pact with the enemy. If the spoils are unequal and he gets a smaller amount, then he should launch a preemptive attack. It could also be that he attacks if he gets the larger share, because then he would be more powerful than the enemy (see 7.6.12); this is the explanation of Gaṇapati Śāstrī and the Malayalam commentary.

7.6.11. *task from which…recover*: This refers to the conquest of land that can be easily taken back by the opponent, land that is called *pratyādeya*, see 7.10.24; 7.11.43.

7.6.11. *seven types*: That is, the four listed here, plus pacts related just to region, time, and objective.

7.6.14–15. *On this…completely*: As Kangle observes, this passage is out of place here and has nothing to do with peace pacts. This sort of verse with the introductory prose, so frequent in the Dharmasūtras, is foreign to the *AŚ*. The meaning appears to be that the seeker after conquest gets two of his neighbors to wage war against each other, which enables him to seize the land of one of them who is his natural enemy. The last phrase is somewhat unclear. Perhaps the meaning is that he cuts off the enemy, who may be far away with his troops, from his supporters.

7.6.21. *by outwitting…traitorous persons*: The seeker after conquest gets traitorous persons within his kingdom to establish contacts with the king whose peace pact he wants to violate. If the latter accepts the overtures of the traitors, then he has a good excuse to abrogate the peace treaty.

7.6.25. *both*: That is, both the king under whom he served and the enemy to whom he went.

7.6.26. *he fears…his foe*: The meaning is somewhat unclear. Kangle explains that the enemy to whom he has gone punishes his foes severely. Knowing that he himself is at fault, which was the reason for leaving his own master in the first place, he fears that the man may turn around and destroy him.

7.6.30. *commodifying learning* (vidyāpaṇyatvam): The meaning appears to be an official who offers his services to the highest bidder, thus making his knowledge and expertise a commodity.

7.6.32. *caused harm here* (ihāpakārī): Kangle appears to take *iha* as a separate particle uncompounded with *apakārī*, and translates: "Among these." I think this is a compound (albeit a clumsy one) paralleling *parāpakārī* ("caused harm to the enemy") and *ubhayāpakārī* ("caused harm to both"). The term *iha* probably refers to the kingdom of the seeker after conquest.

7.6.36. *if he is not... his enemy*: This is a rather convoluted verse, but the meaning appears to be that a deserter from the enemy side who is seen to be disloyal should be sold back to the enemy for a price. The same can be done to a loyal deserter, by accusing him of the crimes associated with the disloyal deserter, in case such a bargain is necessary to conclude a peace pact with the enemy.

7.6.39. *like a pigeon... Śālmali tree*: The simile concerns the propagation of the Plakṣa (*Ficus lacor* or *infectoria*) tree. Its fruits are sticky, and a pigeon eating one will rub its beak on a branch of a Śālmali or silk-cotton tree. The seed germinates on the branch, sending down roots to the ground. When it grows, it uses the mother tree as a support, but will ultimately take over and strangle it.

7.7.6. *"outwitting" pact* (atisaṃdhi): That is, through such a peace pact, the king manages to outwit the other king in the partnership and eventually to defeat him. As we have seen (Introduction, p. 50), the whole purpose of a *saṃdhi* is not to have lasting peace, but to obtain a temporary advantage and ultimately vanquish the partner (Olivelle 2011).

7.7.7. *facing dangers* (anarthinam): For the definition of *anartha* as danger (*bhaya*), see 9.7.7.

7.7.8. *one with whom the bargain is made*: That is, the superior or stronger king, who is placed in a difficult position through this offer.

7.7.9. *same situation*: That is, the weaker ruler is beset with all the problems listed in the previous passage with reference to the stronger ruler.

7.7.22. *Someone may demand... vulnerable ruler*: This provision envisages a demand subsequent to the initial pact, when one of the signatories demands more than the stipulated amount due to changed circumstances. Regarding the vulnerable ruler (*yātavya*), see 7.5.1–18. This is the ruler against whom one party to the pact is waging a war. Here, one of the parties thinks he can get more from the vulnerable ruler than the amount stipulated in the pact. The threat is that he can supply troops in exchange for a lot more from the latter ruler, thus posing a threat to the one who is waging a war against him.

7.7.24. *making a gift* (tyāga): The meaning is not altogether clear, but the intent appears to be that the superior king gives a larger portion of the spoils to the weaker king, with the intention of recovering it at a later time by attacking him.

7.7.26. *remain after...tribal chiefs*: The vulnerable king is the one against whom the weaker king is waging war. This is another way of defeating the weaker king with whom he has entered into a peace pact. The person to whom the troops are given is unclear, but the probability is that this is an alternative to a pact with the vulnerable king. Thus, these troops, which would ultimately further weaken the weak king, are given as spoils to the latter.

7.8.1. *if he wants...for the pact*: The reason or the basis for the pact is the spoils to be gained. The ways he may get these back are spelled out in the following statements.

7.8.4. *provoke...from them*: That is, the vulnerable king gets his partner to become hostile toward the other confederate rulers. This would obviously cause his downfall, so that the vulnerable king could seize all the gains for himself.

7.8.9. *sequence* (kramam): The meaning appears to be that the king should reflect on what would be the best for the present and for the future, that is, what sequence in the sharing of gains (first small and later large, or vice versa) would be best for him.

7.8.10. *earlier cases*: These are probably the ones mentioned in sentences 5–7. This entire passage has little to do with the topic at hand, namely the vulnerable king, and appears to have been either an interpolation or a parenthetical remark.

7.8.17. *an ally or a stronger ally*: That is, the man receiving assistance is a true ally of king A or a stronger ally to him than to king B, from whom he is also receiving assistance.

7.8.19. *foe*: That is, the supposed ally that king B had helped. Once he has attained his goal, he will turn against king B. Given that the latter is also the enemy of king A, this will prove to be useful to him.

7.8.23. *intermediate's enemy*: That is, king A, who is the seeker after conquest and the one to whom the text is addressed. In this case, king A has expended his efforts on the intermediate, who has now spurned him. He is thus forced to make an alliance with king B, presumably under conditions favorable to king B, and thus the latter has outwitted king A within this scenario.

7.8.27. *deployed*: The manuscripts read *pratihataḥ*, and Kangle (in his second edition) has suggested the emendation to *prahitaḥ*. I have opted for *praṇihitaḥ*, first because *prahita* is found only once in the *AŚ*, in the verse 1.12.29, where the choice may have been determined by meter, while *praṇihita* is widely used (2.23.8; 5.1.36; 5.2.53; 7.17.34, 61; 9.3.30, 33; 9.5.14, etc.). Second, *ti* and *ṇi* in the Malayalam script can look very similar, although not in Grantha.
give: These troops are given to another ruler as part of a pact.

7.9.3. *or else...two*: According to this alternative, any one of the three that permits the ruler to secure at least one of the other two should be preferred, acknowledging that land cannot be preferred over the other two under all circumstances.

7.9.5. *You acquire an ally*: This statement implies a second part, namely, "I will obtain money *or* land." That is what makes the pact unequal.

7.9.22. *one whose troops... non-submissive*: Given that this entire passage deals with allies, I take the two compounds *vikṣiptasainyam* and *avaśyasainyam* as Bahuvrīhi compounds, rather than Karmadhārayas, as assumed by Kangle. It is true that the following sentences deal with the troops as such, but the discussion implicitly revolves around the allies who are expected to supply troops.

7.9.25. *engaged in diverse tasks*: Here we are dealing with a citizen army, whose soldiers, when not mobilized, would be engaged in a variety of occupations. This appears to be the meaning of dispersed troops.

7.9.38. *six qualities* (ṣaḍguṇa): This is clearly a play on the topic of book 7, *ṣāḍguṇya*, the sixfold strategy. For a parallel, see 6.1.12.

7.9.43. *connected by... disadvantages*: All the manuscripts have the reading *ekārthenārthasaṃbaddham,* which is clearly corrupt. Kangle has emended the reading to *ekārthenātha saṃbaddham,* but this reading introduces a style with *atha* that is foreign to this verse passage. I have followed the reading *ekārthānārthasaṃbaddham* found in the commentaries *Nayacandrikā* and *Śrīmūla.* For the compound *ekārthānartha* (common advantages and disadvantages) in the context of foreign policy, see 9.7.

7.9.44. *disposition of both... the two*: The expression *ubhayabhāvin* (also at 7.9.48) is somewhat unclear. Kangle translates: "with feeling for both," namely for the king and his enemy. I think this expression parallels *mitrabhāvin* and *mitrabhāva* (disposition of an ally; 7.9.43–44) and *amitrabhāvin* (disposition of an enemy; 7.10.6; 7.18.29). Thus, *ubhaya* does not refer to both the seeker after conquest and his enemy, but to the condition of an ally and an enemy. A ruler who has the dispositions of both an ally and an enemy simultaneously is an *ubhayabhāvin*. Thus, he is distinguished from an *udāsīna* (neutral), who lacks the disposition of either an ally or an enemy.

7.9.45. *become an interposed king*: For the meaning of the term *antardhi,* see 7.13.25. Here the so-called ally is actually the enemy, who has been placed between two other powerful kings (see 7.13.25).

7.9.53. *blossoming of strategy* (guṇodaya): I take *guṇa* here as referring to the topic of the book, the sixfold strategy (*ṣāḍguṇya*). The term, however, could also mean simply excellence, quality, or distinction.

7.10.2. *quality land* (sampannāṃ bhūmim): For *sampanna* and *sampad,* see 1.9.1 n. I agree with Bodewitz (2003, 236) that here the term *sampanna* refers to growth and fertility (see *sasyasampad,* "success of crops" at 2.8.3), but it need not be restricted to that. What makes for a quality piece of land may also include good forests with game, elephants, and produce, as well as mines and rivers.

7.10.6. *neighboring king...enemy*: This presupposes the circle theory. The neighbor of the weak king from whom he seized land would have been his natural ally. But by seizing that land, the weak king's neighbor now becomes his own neighbor, and thus his natural enemy.

7.10.7. *entrenched enemy* (sthitaśatru): This expression clearly refers to a king who has taken refuge in a fort, as the mention of a fort in the very next sentence confirms (see also 7.13.8–9, 22; 9.6.53).

7.10.9. *mobile enemy* (calāmitra): That is, an enemy king who has not taken refuge in a fort and is marching across open land; see 7.13.7–8.

7.10.16. *frontiers have many forts*: The reference apparently is to forts along but outside the frontiers of the kingdom; they are within the enemy territories. If they were within the conquered territory, then it would enhance its security. *barbarians and forest tribes* (mlecchāṭavībhiḥ): Kangle notes that "*mleccha* is an adjective of *aṭavī*, not an independent substantive." See, however, the parallel compound *coragaṇāṭavikamleccha* at 7.14.27 (and a similar one at 12.4.28), where Kangle himself takes *mleccha* as a separate category.

7.11.26. *someone seeks...to settle*: The intent seems to be that a king may want to take by force or through diplomacy a tract of land that requires enormous expenditure to develop. He does so with the intent of selling it to someone else who is ignorant of this problem. People listed here are kings who would become weak or destroyed in the process, thus enabling the original seller to regain the land at no cost.

7.11.27. *constituents with close family ties*: For the meaning of the expression *sagandha* ("having a common smell"), see 1.8.17 n. I take the term *prakṛti* here to refer to the constituents of a kingdom (6.1.1), especially the chief officials. Meyer and Kangle take it as referring to the subjects, but it is difficult to see how all the people within a state could have such close connections to the king.

7.11.30. *does not get...and expenses*: This is a somewhat unclear expression. The idea appears to be that without a following, the king who has purchased the land is unable to make his losses and expenditures bear fruit by investing in the land. Thus, he gets no produce from the land that would make up the losses and expenses incurred in obtaining it.

7.11.40. *solicited pact* (abhihitasaṃdhi): The meaning of *abhihita* here is unclear (Kangle: "pact for fixing;" Meyer: "beredetes Abkommen"). Kangle notes that it "seems rather to have reference to 'fixing' or fastening the land on someone through the treaty." The term *abhihita* can also have the meaning of requesting or soliciting (see 10.3.27), and here may mean that the seeker after conquest has solicited the pact by offering the vacant land to another king who, he believes, will fail in the effort and bring ruin upon himself in the process.

7.11.45. *treatise*: This is probably an equivalent of Arthaśāstra, found in similar verses elsewhere: 5.6.47; 7.10.38; 7.18.42.

7.12.8. *causes distress to the adjoining enemy*: The meaning and the reading here are uncertain. The manuscripts read *anantāvakleśi*, and this reading is adopted by Kangle. Meyer emends the text to read *avakledi*, meaning "containing a lot of moisture." I have adopted the reading *avakleśi* (see the same term at 8.4.44). Yet, I think the first term of the compound, *ananta*, is probably incorrect; following the parallel of *prativeśa* (neighbor on the side or flank; see 7.13.24) in the previous compound, I think the reading here should be *anantara*, referring to the immediate neighbor in the front (that is, without an intervening territory; see 6.2.18, 19, 39). Thus, having an elephant forest at the edge of one's territory is a cause of concern and distress to the enemy whose territory abuts the elephant forest.

7.12.25. *extensive scope for their sale*: The compound *prabhūtaviṣaya* (having extensive scope) is certainly an abbreviated form of the similar compound (Gonda 1968) *mahāviṣayavikraya* (having a large scope for their sale) at 7.11.12. I have translated it accordingly.

7.13.6. *home territory empty*: The king has taken his entire army with him as he attacks the enemy in the front, thus leaving his home territory behind him empty and unguarded. The attacker from the rear can thus easily take over the man's home territory. The king would normally make sure that it is protected when he is away (9.3.10 n.).

7.13.10. *mentioned earlier*: These appear to be the powerless man, the man with few operations, and the man who has marched with only a portion of the army (7.13.2, 4, 6).

7.13.21. *the one whose…hostilities*: This sentence has a rather complicated syntax. According to Kangle's interpretation, which seems reasonable, the enemy is the king whom he attacks from the rear. That enemy is in the process of attacking another king, called *yātavya* ("vulnerable king") here, who is able to cause serious damage to the enemy, thus helping the king attacking from the rear.

7.13.26. *The enemy…outwits*: This is another complicated sentence. Kangle again presents a reasonable interpretation. Both king A, the seeker after conquest, and his enemy king B attempt to attack the intermediate ruler, king C, while the latter is attacking a fourth, king D. Now, it is assumed that king B is an ally of king C, while king A is the latter's enemy. If king C defeats king D and returns after securing what he was after, the question is who will come out ahead, king A or king B? The answer is that king C will excuse king A for attacking him, because he was, after all, his enemy. He will be much more incensed at king B, who, in spite of being an ally, attacked him. So, king A outwits king B by making king C his enemy and by obtaining king C, who was previously his enemy, as an ally.

7.13.38. *The leader…in the rear*: This scenario goes like this: The leader is king A. In front of him is his natural enemy, king B, who is attacking his own enemy in the front, king C, who is the natural ally of king A. So, king A attacks king B from the latter's rear. Before doing that, however, he should take care not to let the king to his rear, king B1, attack him. King B1 is king B's ally and technically called *ākranda,* who is supposed to attack the rear enemy, in this case king A. The latter prevents an attack by king B1 by getting the help of king A1, who is his own natural ally, and will attack king B1 from his own rear, thus preventing him from attacking king A.

7.14.1. *in this manner*: This statement might indicate that this discussion may have been taken from a source that contains the description of an attack by confederated troops.

7.15.2. *presence...dependents*: The dependents (*āyatta*) are probably the ministers, but may include other senior officials; see 9.6.7 for this same term, which is there distinguished from *pradhāna,* the chief, namely the king. For the exemplary qualities of a minister, see 1.9.1.

7.15.12. *I will entangle...by myself*: The meaning appears to be that the enemy would have to spend a lot of money and suffer enormous losses in order to counteract the secret measures employed by the king. For some of these secret measures, see 12.5.

right here: That is, remaining within the fort.

7.15.13. *absence of any reason*: The reference is probably to the reasons enumerated in the previous passage, if this dialogue did not belong originally to a different context.

7.15.22. *secure locations*: The meaning of the term *sattra* is not always clear. It is most frequently used with the meaning of a secure location that is also good as a hideout or escape from danger (perhaps also fortified) and as a place of ambush at 7.5.46; 7.17.56–57; 8.4.41 (where it probably means ambush); 8.5.11, 19; 10.2.15, etc., and a rest house at 2.35.3. Kangle interprets the term here within the terminology of the Vedic sacrifice: "holding a sacrificial session," whereas elsewhere, he translates it as hiding place. For a list of locations that can be considered *sattra,* see 10.3.24, where even the night and fog are viewed as *sattra*; clearly, here the reference is to a place or time where one is safe from being detected or, at 8.4.41, from where robbers can attack unsuspecting travellers. See Scharfe 1993, 217.

7.15.27. *Counselor, Chaplain* (mantripurohita): Regarding this compound, see 1.9 n. In the second half of the *AŚ*, this appears to be a Dvandva compound referring to the Counselor and the Chaplain as two distinct officials (8.4.26; 10.1.6; 10.3.32; 13.5.16). This same list appears also at 9.3.12, and the explanation at 9.2.19 clearly indicates that the authors of this section consider the Counselor and the Chaplain as two distinct individuals.

7.16. *Behavior...with Troops*: The exact meaning of the title *daṇḍopanāyivṛttam* is unclear. Kangle translates: "Conduct (Proper) for the King Subjugating (Other Kings) by Force." However, as 7.16.29 makes clear, the reference is to a king who has forced another king to surrender with his troops. The compound *daṇḍopanāyin* (as opposed to *daṇḍopanata*, which was a topic of the previous chapter) may mean someone who forces another to come to him along with his troops.

7.16.1. *no help...backup*: The reference is to the lack of a *pārṣṇigrāha* (the ally who would attack the enemy from behind) and an *āsāra* (the ally who would attack his own *pārṣṇigrāha*), who would attack anyone attacking the latter from his rear.

7.16.10. *Among them*: The reference is probably to his allies or to enemies whom he has subjugated and turned into allies. The neuter adjectives of this and the following passages can only be correct if they refer to *mitram*, the neuter noun for ally.

7.16.16. *cut off*: Whether the reading is *avachinnayā* (as suggested by Meyer and Kangle, which is also the reading of the commentary *Nayacandrikā*) or *upacchinnayā* (as in the manuscripts), the meaning appears to be land that had been previously taken from the same enemy.

gathered together: For this meaning of the term *saṃhata*, see 6.2.38.

both characteristics: That is, with land that has been cut off and with strong neighbors.

lured away: That is, a person who has been lured away from the enemy's side and has come over to his. For this meaning of *apavāhita*, see 12.3.14.

7.16.31. *Those ministers...to him*: These are the ministers of the ruler who had been killed after surrendering. They are living in their respective territories but are subject to the conquering king. The location of *asya* just before *amātyāḥ* is unusual, and commentators take these ministers to be those of the seeker after conquest. But the pronoun should be, as Kangle observes, connected with *āyattāḥ* (are subject).

7.17.1–3. *hostage*: In sentences 1 and 2, as also in 15, the term *samādhi* is used for hostage, but in the rest of the discussion, 3–31, the term *pratigraha* is used. Then in topic 123 on the liberation of a hostage (7.17.32), *samādhi* is used once again. It is unclear whether there is a difference or a nuance between the two terms. The semantic difference could be from the perspective of giving and receiving a hostage, *samādhi* indicating the giving of a hostage and *pratigraha* the taking of one (I thank Professor Wezler for this observation).

7.17.20. *erase the abundance of targets to strike* (prahartavyasampallopāt): This compound is difficult to interpret. The obvious meaning of *prahartavya* is something that must be or can be struck or attacked. I think it refers to targets within the enemy formations. When a man skilled in the use of weapons is given as a hostage, the targets that can be attacked become fewer. For the multiple meanings of *sampad*, see 1.9.1 n.

7.17.29. *When both... to procreate*: Two kings each have the same number of offspring from their sons when they give one of them as a hostage. In this case, the king who still has the capacity to produce more sons has the advantage.

7.17.31. *has that ability*: That is, the single son has the ability to procreate while, presumably, the father, who is the king, does not. In this case, the king should give himself up as a hostage.

7.17.41. *carrying a nightly offering*: The meaning of *niśopahāreṇa* is unclear. Commentators explain that the prince gets rid of the guards and servants under the pretext that he has to make a night offering. Then he is able to exit through the tunnel. Kangle thinks the night offering may be a pretext for leaving his residence, thus being able to find the tunnel and leave.

7.17.42. *Varuṇa ruse*: The meaning appears to be that the prince would hold his breath and swim underwater to a place far away from his entry point. In this way, he will be able to escape the notice of his guards. Commentators refer to 13.1.3–4.

7.17.47. *he*: The subject here is the hostage prince himself. The houses set on fire in this passage are all meant to facilitate the prince's escape, as guards and other officials are busy putting out the fires.

7.17.54–55. *Agents operating... from that*: This refers to a pursuit by guards after the prince has escaped. The agents should point them in the wrong direction, and the prince, as a further precaution, should take still another route.

7.17.60. *he*: That is, the king who is the father of the hostage.

7.18.1–2. *With respect... hostile constituents:* The initial *madhyamasya* (literally, "of the intermediate") is anomalous within the context. Thus, I have put it outside the syntax of the sentence. The friendly constituents are with reference to the seeker after conquest (*vijigīṣu*) and not the intermediate king. If the word is original, then it must be an introductory statement regarding the entire topic. The third in the circle is the ally, and the fifth is the ally of the ally. The second is the enemy, the fourth the ally of the enemy, and the sixth the ally of the enemy's ally.

7.18.3. *both those*: That is, the seeker after conquest's ally and the ally's ally.

7.18.11. *traitorous officials*: In all likelihood, these officials belong to the intermediate king. The pact is made so that in the long run, he could assist these officials in overthrowing the intermediate king.

7.18.16. *If the allies... another person*: Gaṇapati Śāstrī takes the two who need to be weakened or vanquished to be allies of the seeker after conquest, while Kangle takes them to be allies of the latter's ally. For a pact using another person, such as the commander in chief of the army, see 7.3.24. The pact here and in the following sentence is concluded with the intermediate king.

7.18.18–27. *his, he*: The referent of all these pronouns in this section is the seeker after conquest to whom these instructions are addressed.

7.18.21. *have some regard* (sāpekṣam): The meaning of this expression, occurring only here, is unclear. Meyer takes it adverbially as "rücksichtsvoll," while Kangle thinks that the intermediate king cares for the seeker after conquest and thus would listen to his advice.

7.18.29. *Even though... omnipresent* (saty apy amitrabhāve): This is a very terse expression. The meaning appears to be that an inimical disposition is a universal characteristic of all the kings forming the circle. In spite of this, one can in fact determine those who are enemies and those who are allies.

7.18.39. *there*: That is, in the territory of the weak king, who is being removed from his own territory.

BOOK 8

8.1.1. *When calamities arise simultaneously*: That is, when a calamity strikes a particular constituent element of the king and his enemy at the same time. Generally, when such a calamity strikes the enemy, it is an opportunity for the king to attack him. But when both are affected, then a more nuanced approach is required, and that is spelled out in this chapter. For an examination of this book on calamities, see Kangle 1964a.

8.1.3. *The inverse... calamity*: Each of these five constitutes a calamity affecting a constituent element of the kingdom. The inverse of qualities means the opposite attributes to those enumerated for each of the constituents at 6.1.2–14. Absence happens when the king lacks one of the seven constituent elements (6.1.1). The meaning of *pradoṣa* ("great defect") is unclear, the term occurring only here in the *AŚ*. It probably refers to an extreme deficiency in a constituent element. Afflictions (*pīḍā*) are listed in 8.4.

8.1.16. *When the lord... exemplary qualities*: For the interpretation of this sentence, see Bodewitz 2003, 236. For a parallel, see 6.1.16.

8.1.34. *commercial transactions of army troops* (daṇḍabalavyavahāra): The compound is unclear and has been interpreted variously in its four occurrences (8.1.34, 38; 9.2.4; 13.3.15). Kangle translates: "the use of armed forces." The compound *daṇḍabala* is found at 6.2.33, where it is a Tatpuruṣa compound meaning "strength of the army." In the longer compound, however, *bala* probably refers to the troops or soldiers. The term *vyavahāra* in the second half of the *AŚ* regularly refers to commercial transactions involving buying and selling. It is most likely that this expression refers to occasions for the buying and selling of soldiers. At 7.17.43, *vyavahāra* is clearly used with the meaning of selling. See the several places where reference is made to soldiers who have been purchased or hired for a fee (7.18.29; 9.1.7, 9; 10.2.13; 13.4.8). At 9.2.11, furthermore, the king is advised to keep the troops belonging to a foe, troops obviously under his command now, away from an enemy who is in the process of raising an army. The raising of an army would have required the purchase of soldiers from other or inactive armies.

8.1.38. *rear reinforcements* (āsārapratigraha): The term *pratigraha* is used extensively in the second half of the *AŚ* to refer to reinforcement of troops, and this is accentuated in the current compound with the use of *āsāra,* who is the king supporting the seeker after conquest from behind his rear enemy. For this usage, see 8.1.42; 10.2.20; 10.5.58; 10.6.1, 2; 12.4.19; 13.3.46. At 10.2.7, *āsāra* is defined as troops of an ally (*mitrabala*), but in all likelihood, there also the ally is located in the rear.

8.2.7. *A dual reign...endure*: Kangle, correctly I think, held the reading of the manuscript *tulyayogakṣemamatyāvagrahaṃ* to be corrupt and followed the emendation of Gaṇapati Śāstrī, *tulyayogakṣemam amātyāvagrahaṃ,* and translated: "with well-being and security equally shared and with ministers held in check." Raghavan (1951, 103–04) rightly points out that the control of ministers is out of place here, given that in the rejection of dual reign in the previous sentence, its two deficiencies mentioned are, first, mutual hatred and loyalty of each faction and, second, jealousy toward each other. Kauṭilya's rebuttal should relate to these two. Raghavan has cited verse 5.14 of Kālidāsa's drama *Mālavikāgnimitra,* which follows this *AŚ* passage and reads *parasparāvagrahanirvikārau.* Raghavan rightly takes *parasparāvagraha* to be parallel to the original reading here of the *AŚ* and suggests *mitho'vagraha* as the original reading. I have thus emended the reading to *tulyayogakṣemaṃ mitho'vagrahaṃ,* taking the compounds as Bahuvrīhis qualifying *dvairājyam.* The second problematic reading is the verb *vartayateti* (*vartayata* + *iti*), which was emended by Gaṇapati Śāstrī to *vartayeteti* and by Kangle to *vartayati.* I think the final *iti* is unnecessary, as the conclusion of the quotation is marked by *iti* in sentence 8. Thus, I propose to emend the manuscript reading to *vartayate* (Ātmanepada), taking the verb to mean something like to continue to exist, to endure.

8.2.9. *science*: Here *śāstra* probably refers to Arthaśāstra, the science of government, or perhaps more specifically to the treatise on government.

8.2.19. *evil disease*: The term *pāparoga,* which occurs frequently in the *MDh* but only here in the *AŚ,* does not refer simply to a serious sickness. The disease is regarded as the consequence of sins committed in previous lives (see *MDh* 11.48–53). Evil diseases are generally viewed as skin diseases of various types.

8.3.1. *vices*: The term *vyasana* is used in this book with two related meanings: (1) calamities and evils affecting various constituents of a kingdom, and (2) the vices and personal failings of the king, which can also have calamitous consequences for the kingdom.

8.3.4. *There is...pleasure*: The three stemming from wrath are enumerated in sentences 23 and 37 (which form a single syntactical unit if we delete the intervening dialogue), and the four stemming from lust in sentence 38. It appears clear from this that the Kauṭilya dialogues given between these main sentences are later additions, possibly influenced by the long passage on these vices in the *MDh* 7.45–53. See Introduction, pp. 21f.

8.3.7. *wrathful revolts*: The author is here playing with the double meaning of *kopa:* wrath/anger and revolt. People rebel because they are angry at the king, and such rebellions are also called *kopa.* I have used the extended translation "wrathful revolts" to make this connection.

8.3.16. *Of the two*: The explanation takes two of the defining characteristics at a time, one from hatred and one from pleasure, for comparison.

8.3.30–32. *Between injury...joined to property*: Here we have the transition of the meaning of *artha* as property or money (in 24–30) to its meaning within the Triple Set (*trivarga*), or *artha, dharma,* and *kāma.* Sentence 31 is found verbatim at 1.7.7.

8.3.40, 44. *Jayatsena and Duryodana, Nala and Yudhiṣṭhira*: The name Jayatsena is associated with several kings in the *Mahābhārata,* even though I have not been able to find any association with gambling. Given the pairing, however, it may well be that Jayatsena is the one who defeated Nala, although in the *MBh* (3.56.5), the name of Nala's opponent is given as Puṣkara. Duryodhana, of course, is the cousin of the Pāṇḍavas, who initiated the fateful game of dice, which he won against Yudhiṣṭhira and which led to the great war. The story of king Nala is also recorded in the *Mahābhārata.* After his marriage to Damayantī, he too was possessed by the muse of gambling and gambled away everything he possessed.

8.3.45. *Aversion...illegitimate wealth:* The terms *sataḥ* and *asataḥ* have been taken as existent and nonexistent. Kangle thus translates: "Uncertainty as to existing wealth and obtaining nonexisting wealth." However, why would obtaining wealth one does not have constitute something harmful, especially when kings are supposed to conquer land and wealth? I take the two terms to have a moral meaning in this context. See 8.3.64, where *asat* is used with this meaning.

8.3.60. *Both these*: That is, evils associated with women outside the home (no children and threat to personal safety) and with women with whom sex is forbidden (destruction of everything).

8.3.61. *aftermath of drinking* (pānasampad): For the multiple meanings of *sampad,* see 1.9.1 n. Here the term refers to the effects of drinking; see

Bodewitz 2003, 232–233, 239. If we want to stick closely to the more common meaning of *sampad*, we could see these as inherent qualities of drink and drinking.

8.3.65. *calamity*: In these verses, the meaning of calamity returns to the term *vyasana*, which has the meaning of vice in the prose section (8.3.1 n.).

8.4.5. *afflicted*: The meaning of *upasṛṣṭa*, which occurs only here in the *AŚ*, is unclear. Gaṇapati Śāstrī glosses with *rogi* (suffering from a disease), but that would not say anything different from the previous word *vyādhita* (sick). Perhaps the term refers to afflictions more generally, as when family members of workers succumb to the sickness, which here must mean some kind of contagious disease short of an epidemic mentioned in 8.4.8.

8.4.12. *and because common…on him*: This clause is absent in the commentary *Nayacandrikā*. It was probably a gloss that found its way into the text, because it does not give the reason why chiefs are extremely rare and it is difficult to find replacements for them.

8.4.15. *abduction* (apavāhana): This is the forced evacuation of people from one region and their settlement in another. In this case, people are taken from the enemy's territory into one's own; see 2.1.1.

8.4.21. *three times*: past, present, and future. With respect to agriculturalists, the *Nayacandrikā* says, this involves not taking care of crops that have already been planted, not planting the current crops, and not preparing the soil for future plantations.

8.4.37–40. *Is it a land…sowing of crops*: This passage is quite obscure. The term *uparuddha* must mean "obstructed," rather than occupied or seized, as in Kangle. See the use of the same term in sentence 40 for obstructing the sowing of crops. The situation seems to be that some land has been taken over by either a nobleman or a herd station. The question is not really whether the king *can* recover these lands, but whether it is the right or wise thing to do. The whole reason for this dialogue, however, remains unclear.

8.4.41. *under the cover of night* (rātrisattracarāḥ): For night as a secure place (*sattra*), see 10.3.24. Here *rātri* and *sattra* are not two separate items (see 7.15.22 n.).

8.4.49. *these two*: That is, the two hindrances noted in the previous passage. *obstructed among the chiefs* (sakto mukhyeṣu): The meaning of *sakta* here is that revenues do not flow freely into the treasury but become attached to various people along the way. Here the revenues get attached to the chiefs, that is, they pilfer them.

8.5.1. *not honored*: This long list contains past participles and adjectival compounds in the neuter singular. All are syntactically connected to the implied *balam*, "army."

8.5.12. *in unison with the enemy*: This is because an "absorbed" army appears to be one that has been given over to the enemy as part of a pact and is under the unified command of the enemy.

8.5.22. *weakness, greed, or affection*: The weakness of the ally is the cause for abandoning him. Greed is on the part of the king, who would get money from an enemy for abandoning the ally. Affection toward an enemy may cause him to abandon the ally.

BOOK 9

9.1.1. *power, place...dangers*: This is actually a list of most of the topics (*prakaraṇa*) covered in this book. This list is somewhat different from the actual topics within the book: power 9.1.2–16; place 9.1.17–21; time 9.1.22–33; proper times for military expeditions 9.1.34–52; proper times for mustering troops 9.2.1–30; revolt in the rear 9.3.1–42; losses, expenses, and gains 9.4.1–27; dangers 9.5–7. It is unclear whether this discrepancy indicates that new topics may have been added to the original list. In any case, the first topic and the first chapter should probably have begun after this statement, which is a general introduction to the entire book.

9.1.2. *energy*: The structure of the book appears to be a commentary on the items listed in 9.1.1, where power is listed first. In this discussion, power is said to be derived from three sources: energy (*utsāha*), might (*prabhāva*, which, among other things, probably refers to the richness of a kingdom), and counsel (*mantra*); see 9.1.16. The discussion of place (*deśa*), next on the list, is in 9.1.17–21; time in 9.1.22–25, followed by a comparison among these three in 9.1.22–33. The other items in the list are discussed in their respective topics.

9.1.17. *one thousand Yojanas*: Taking a Yojana as nine miles, the distance would be 9,000 miles or 14,484 kilometers, which is much too large as a measurement of the Indian subcontinent. "One thousand" here is probably given as a large round number and not intended to be taken literally.

9.1.18. *universal sovereign* (cakravartin): This term, common in ancient Indian literature, is never used in the *AŚ* outside of this sentence. Such a monarch is supposed not to have any opponents, which is diametrically opposed to the basic conception of the *AŚ*, with its circle of kings divided into allies and enemies.

9.1.31. *during the day...crow*: For the innate enmity between owls and crows, see the story in book 3 of the *Pañcatantra*.

9.1.40. *calamity*: This must refer to a calamity affecting the enemy, when he could march in order to burn down the enemy's territory at any time.

9.2.5. *tribal troops... reinforcements*: All these belong to the enemy. After using the troops supplied by the ally to attack these places and forces, he will use his own forces to attack the enemy himself.

9.2.6. *My enemy troops... by my foe*: First, the king uses the troops supplied by his natural enemy, with whom he has made a peace pact. The king uses the troops thus supplied to wage war against a third king, who is also his enemy. It is this third king's capital and tribal troops that he is attacking.

Now, he should... of his foe: This passage is somewhat out of place here. It does not indicate the thinking process of the king, as other provisions do. This passage may be a gloss, but it is an early one because it is cited in 15.1.50.

9.2.8. *Let a wood apple... wood apple*: This appears to be a common proverb. Wood apple has a very hard outer covering that can only be split by hitting it with a very hard substance or with another wood apple. Here the king uses tribal troops against similar kinds of forces. This same proverb is given at *MBh* 12.106.10.

9.2.11. *when the time... the foe*: the troops of the foe are now under the king's command. He is using these strategies to keep these troops from being recruited by his enemy as he is beginning to raise an army. See 8.1.34 n.

9.2.13. *among these*: Even though these kinds of troops are given in the following statements, it is clear that this is a reference to the opening sentence of this chapter, 9.2.1.

9.3.2. *revolt of the constituents* (prakṛtikopa): The term *prakṛti* may also refer to the subjects in general, but the references to revolts by senior officials later (12, 15, 20, 22) make it likely that here, and in the title of topic 141, the reference is to revolts by officials.

9.3.5. *Misfortunes... a needle*: The term *sūcīmukha* is used with reference to a particular type of battle formation (*MBh* 6.19.5; 6.73.55) where the front of the formation is very narrow. It is also used with regard to certain malevolent spirits with tiny mouths and large bellies. The proverb probably refers to the fact that misfortunes rarely seem big when they first appear, but subsequently become very large.

9.3.9. *their*: These are the sons of wives of the officials in the outer districts under suspicion. The assumption is that these officials still keep their families in the city.

9.3.10. *Regent* (śūnyapāla): This is an official, perhaps a prince, who is appointed to guard and administer the home territory of the kingdom while the king is absent, especially when the king is away on a military expedition.

9.3.11. *revolt in the interior... outlying regions*: For the definitions of these two kinds of revolts, see 9.3.12, 20, 22. For this statement, see 8.2.3.

9.3.20. *interior ministers*: These are ministers operating within the palace, such as the head of the palace guard and the chief gate guard.

9.3.31. *secret agent... to death:* The compound *abhityaktaśāsana* ("decree of a condemned man") appears to be an abbreviated compound (found also at 9.3.38; 13.3.14, 39; see Gonda 1968) standing for the longer descriptions of this strategy given at 9.6.29 and 13.4.28–33. See also 2.5.4 n.

9.3.33. *secret agent... by him*: After the warriors have returned to their old master, a secret agent should tell the enemy king that those men were agents of that king, implying that the high official who had defected may also be such an agent.

9.3.38. *If he kills... condemned to death*: This reasoning on the part of the officer in the outer region is very condensed and difficult to follow. The commentary *Nayacandrikā* gives the most reasonable explanation. The "enemy" here is the seeker after conquest. If the interior official kills the king and installs the external official as king, that is the best outcome. If the king gets wind of the plot and kills the interior officer, then his relatives and friends, afraid of a similar punishment, will flock to the external official and strengthen his following. When the king begins to suspect all his other chiefs of sedition, the external official will use the ploy of sending misleading decrees and get them all killed.

9.3.39. *empty home territory*: The home territory will remain empty and vulnerable if the king gathers all his troops (*sarvasaṃdoha*) to attack an enemy, without leaving some to guard the homefront; see 6.2.38; 7.4.7.

9.4.4. *attributes of a successful gain* (lābhasampad): Bodewitz (2003, 235), commenting on this compound, emphasizes that here *sampad* refers to the preconditions required for success in the sphere of economic profit or gain. Here, as in many other places in the *AŚ*, however, gain refers primarily to the gain of land. The list gives the attributes that make a gain profitable and good, for some gains of land, such as those that involve immense expenditure, can be catastrophic. The attributes listed are a bit confusing, because they are stated from the perspective of the seeker after conquest and involve attributes of land that may be won by an opponent. Thus, "fit to be recovered" and "causes revolt" refer to land seized by the opponent; such gains are useless for him because the land will be recaptured or lost because of an internal revolt.

forerunner (puroga): Kangle translates this as "foremost." As an attribute of a successful gain, that does not make much sense. I take the term *puroga* to mean that it is the first of many other gains, a gain that leads to further gains.

9.5.1. *what is prescribed*: The six strategies of foreign policy are dealt with in book 7.

9.5.18–19. *for once treachery... to treason*: The author plays on the multiple meanings of the etymologically related terms *doṣa* (which I have translated as treachery; it also means simply a flaw or fault), *dūṣya* (which I have translated as traitor), and *dūṣayati* (which I have translated as incite to treason). Here *doṣa* is, in fact, more than mere treachery; it indicates the basic flawed conditions of the kingdom that lead to treason. The commentary *Nayacandrikā* explains that *doṣa* resides with the instigator to sedition and that the term means simply instigation (*doṣaś cātropajāpa eveti bhāvaḥ*). Thus, when guile is only with those instigating sedition, the very basis for treason is eliminated by getting rid of the instigators. But simply getting rid of traitors when treachery is widespread does not get rid of treachery; it will only raise its head elsewhere.

9.6.1. *danger*: The term *āpad* (danger) is not given even a single time in this chapter. The feminine adjectives presuppose that term. Given the impossibility of translating without the use of that term, and my avoidance, for the sake of the general English reader, of words in parentheses, I have added this term whenever it is needed for comprehension.

9.6.16. *confederacy of allies*: The rest of the chapter deals mostly with dangers posed by kings who have formed a confederacy, even when no explicit reference is made to the confederacy. The strategy is to break the confederacy by exposing one of the kings as a traitor to the group.

9.6.26. *one of them:* That is, using either their mutual hatred or enmity or the fear of having his land seized.

9.6.29. *or*: I have placed this in italics because, as in several other places, two items are given for use in the speech, only one of which is to be actually used.

9.6.35. *to defect*: The defection of the minister to the enemy is merely a ploy. He is really a trusted minister, who goes over to the enemy in order to outwit him. His family is hidden by the king, who publicizes that they have been killed in order to make the defection seem real. For a similar strategy, see 13.3.11–14.

9.6.44. *They*: The probable antecedent is the secret agents mentioned in the previous sentence.

9.6.46. *one of them* (paraspara): Literally, it means by each other, but the meaning probably is that the killing is attributed to a conspiracy among the confederate kings.

9.6.50. *explains*: That is, the sowing of dissension among these individuals should be carried out in ways similar to those described in the case of confederate kings.

9.6.56. *Those are . . . strategy*: Peace pact or conciliation is given in 6.6.21–22; gifts in 6.6.23–25; dissension in 6.6.26–52; and military force in 6.6.53–55.

9.6.59–61. *preceded by*: That is, one resorts to each later strategy when the previous ones have been tried and failed.

9.6.72. *Castes and confederacies . . . each other*: Kangle here translates *jātisaṅgha* as guilds of castes, whereas in other places where the two occur together, he takes the compound to be a Dvandva. I think that here also we are dealing with two entities, castes and confederacies, both of which may transcend the territorial limits of the confederate kings. The seeker after conquest can use these cross-regional allegiances to instigate sedition.

9.7.1. *constituents* (prakṛti): Here the term is used first with reference to the constituent elements of his realm (6.1.1) and then with reference to the kings that constitute the circle (6.2.13–22).

9.7.8. *these two*: That is, an advantage coupled with danger and a disadvantage.

9.7.13. *relating to an advantage*: This would clearly include the first: whether something is an advantage or not, and perhaps also the third: whether something that looks like an advantage is actually a disadvantage. He should opt to act in these cases, and refrain from acting in the others.

9.7.22. *laid down the tasks*: This chapter is divided into three sections that establish task, place, and time. These three are listed in the discussion of calamities in 8.1.50. In this chapter, the dangers that present themselves are likewise classified according to the task with which the danger is associated, the places from which danger comes (9.7.53), and the times when danger occurs (6.7.66).

9.7.34. *lesser importance*: The meaning is that he should sacrifice a constituent of lesser importance while preserving one of greater importance. Thus, he should give up the army before he gives up the treasury; he should give up the treasury before he gives up the fort, and so on (6.1.1).

by means of the home territory: That is, by surrendering the kingdom.

9.7.36. *Suyātra and Udayana*: Suyātra is another name for Nala (see 8.3.40, 44 n.), whose loss of his kingdom through gambling and subsequent recovery of it are narrated in *MBh* 3.50–78. The story of the hero Udayana is well known in Sanskrit literature, with repeated retellings in the epic and story literature. He was taken prisoner but managed to escape and marry his love, Padmāvatī.

9.7.39. *for, otherwise... the kingdom*: The significance of this clause is unclear. With the particle *hi* (for), it appears to be related to the previous phrase, giving a reason for that provision. Yet, the thwarting of an attack on the kingdom is something that should be done. Kangle ignores the particle and takes this as a lesser alternative to the previous, translating: "Otherwise, he should ward off the attack on the kingdom." This is possible, but I think the author believes that taking this alternative would simply eliminate the disadvantage while not securing the advantage. The former provision permits him to kill two birds with one stone.

9.7.44. *both sides*: As Meyer has pointed out, a sentence appears to be missing after this, a sentence that would parallel 6.7.42. Such a statement, as Kangle rightly points out, should have instructed the king to deal with the uncertainty concerning the disadvantage, and then with the advantage.

9.7.50. *the opposites*: These would be initiating hostilities (*vigraha*), marching into battle (*yāna*), and seeking refuge (*saṃśraya*); 7.1.1.

9.7.60. *Advantage...relating to advantage*: The section 9.7.60–65, I feel, is a later redactoral insertion, having little to do with actual dangers faced by a king on the march, but in structural imitation of the previous passages. Note also that the term *śoka* (sorrow, grief) is found only in this section, except for the verse 13.2.46. Here the term *artha*, used throughout the chapter to indicate an advantage, is given a new nuance taking it back to the Triple Set given at 1.7.4–7. Then at 9.7.62, we have an unusual Triple Set with reference to disadvantage (*anartha*), and at 9.7.64, the Triple Set of uncertainty. Note, however, that, just as in the opinion of Kauṭilya at 1.7.6–7, here also *artha* (success, power, wealth) is said to be better than *dharma*. See the similar connection to the Triple Set made at 9.7.81.

9.7.69. *normal ways...abnormal*: The three pairs given above are the ordinary or normal (*anuloma*). Their opposites would be the abnormal or extraordinary (*pratiloma*)—instead of conciliation and gifts, we have force and dissension; instead of gifts and dissension, we have force and conciliation; and instead of dissension and military force, we have conciliation and gifts.

9.7.73. *restriction, option, combination* (niyoga, vikalpa, samuccaya): These technical terms and concepts are drawn from the exegetical tradition of Mīmāṃsā and clearly show the influence of the Dharmaśāstric tradition on the Śāstric Redaction of the *AŚ*; see Introduction, pp. 14f.

9.7.77. *four operations...in fours*: When each of the four strategies is used singly, there are four possible uses. When used in threes, we also have four: ABC, ACD, BCD, and ABD. When used in twos, we have six: AB, AC, AD, BC, BD, and CD.

9.7.81. *achievement, objectives*: Within this possibly interpolated passage (see 9.7.60 n.), these two words are given different nuances than the ones they had in the rest of the passage. Thus, *siddhi*, which had meant overcoming or suppressing a danger or an enemy, is here given the meaning of success or achievement. The term *artha*, used frequently in the rest of the passage as "advantage," is here given the meaning of either political ambition or objective.

9.7.82. *demonic creation* (āsurī sṛṣṭiḥ): This is explained by the commentators as rats, snakes, and the like. For these dangers, see 8.4.1; 4.3.1

BOOK 10

10.1.1. *On a site...turrets*: The construction of a military camp (*skandhāvāra*) broadly follows the construction of a fort and a fortified city given in 2.3–4. Many of the technical terms occurring in this chapter are explained there.

10.1.5. *four enclosures...parapet*: The long compound *śakaṭamethīpratatistambhasālaparikṣepāḥ* is unclear. Kangle, following the commentators, translates: "with carts, stretches of thorny branches, pillars, and the parapet." The compound must refer to defensive fortifications around the royal compound. I doubt that carts were used for such fortifications. I take cart and creeper (*pratati*) to be particular arrangements of the fortifications. The term cart, for example, is used for a particular battle formation (see *AŚ* 10.2.4, where the term *cakra*, wheel, is used; and *AŚ* 10.2.9; 10.6.26; *MDh* 7.187, where *śakaṭa*, cart/wagon is used). For an explanation of the formations, see 10.6.

10.1.11. *Fowlers...fire*: Fowlers and hunters would be familiar with the wild terrain and would be able to move about without attracting notice. According to Gaṇapati Śāstrī, these individuals would send signals to the camp about the movement and approach of the enemy army by sounding drums or setting up fires.

10.1.13. *the 18 groups*: The reference is unclear. Kangle plausibly argues that the reference is to the groups mentioned in sentences 6–9, taking horses and chariots as a single group: counselor, chaplain, storehouse, kitchen, depot, armory, hereditary troops, hired troops, horses and chariots, chief of armed forces, elephants, corporate troops, camp administrator, laborers, commander, ally's troops, enemy's troops, and tribal troops.

10.2.4. *expansive foraging raids* (prasāravṛddhi): See 10.4.13 for this term. It probably refers to cavalry regiments specializing in foraging raids thrust outward from the battle formation. These would be used on the flanks when elephants are unavailable. According to the explanation of the commentary *Nayacandrikā*, however, the deployment of foraging raids occurs only when there is no danger of an attack to the army on the march. If such a danger is foreseen, then the defensive formations of elephants and the like are deployed.

10.2.5–8. *Obtaining... hideaway*: This section looks very much like an explanatory gloss giving definitions of several technical terms, a gloss that found its way into the text.

10.2.12. *lowest speed*: The commentaries *Nayacandrikā* and *Śrīmūla* take the speed to be the distance traveled during one day. Taking a Yojana to be approximately 14.5 kilometers, the highest speed would cover a little less than 30 kilometers in a single day.

10.3.22. *elephant and horse...turns back*: The idea seems to be that the bags with pebbles will make a noise that would frighten the animals. When they run around in fright, the elephants and horses will be confused and alarmed and run away. The pebbles may also have been intended to fall on the ground and hurt the feet of the advancing elephants and horses.

10.3.24. *cattle*: The commentary *Nayacandrikā* explains that the ambush takes place from a herd of cattle that would hide the attackers.

10.3.28. *In the Vedas too*: The section 28–31 appears to be a later interpolation, possibly from a commentary. The king's speech ends with the concluding *iti* after sentence 27, and the speechs of the Counselor and Chaplain do not begin until sentence 32. Also note the fact that verse 31 is found in Bhāsa's play. And, as Kangle notes, it is quite unlikely that someone rousing troops would say in effect, "And by the way, there are two verses in support of this!"

10.3.31. *A new cup...his master*: This verse is found in Bhāsa's play *Pratijñāyaugandharāyaṇa*, Act 4, verse 2.

10.3.46. *The leaders...to them*: For these leaders, see 10.6.45. The meaning appears to be that these leaders should certify that a particular soldier under their command has actually killed certain individuals of the opposing army.

10.3.48. *sun at the back...favorable direction* (anulomavātam): The meaning is that they should not face the sun, so that the blinding glare would affect the enemy soldiers. Likewise, the wind should be at their back, so that it would blow at the faces of the enemy and make their arrows and missiles less effective (10.3.23).

10.3.57. *The vehemence...crushed*: For a parallel verse, see *MBh* 12.10.13.

10.4.3. *even and an uneven battle formation*: The two terms *same* and *viṣame* are taken by Kangle to mean normal and difficult situations. Meyer takes them to refer to the terrain; but in that case, we should have had the feminine *samāyām* and *viṣamāyām* (see 10.3.53) to agree with *bhūmi*. I have taken the two terms to refer to the two basic kinds of battle formations recorded in 10.5.14–17 and also alluded to at 10.3.53.

10.4.13. *destroying or guarding*: The cavalry would guard one's own supplies while destroying those of the enemy.

clearing and stabilizing: Clearing (*viśuddhi*) may refer to the evacuation of the wounded from the front lines (see 10.4.17 and the reference to doctors at 10.3.47), while stabilizing (*sthāpanā*) may refer to plugging any breaches or weaknesses in the battle formation.

gathering; dispatching (grahaṇa, mokṣaṇa): The commentators and translators take these two terms to mean capturing and releasing, that is, taking enemy soldiers as prisoners or releasing them. It is, however, unclear why this task should be singled out in the midst of activities aimed at one's own army. The term *mokṣayitvā* at 10.5.2 provides a clue to a possible meaning. There the term refers to the release or dispatching of the army from its confines within the army camp into the field to assume battle formations. I think that a similar meaning may be present here in the sense of dispatching army units to various areas of the battle formation. If that is the case, then *grahaṇa* may mean the opposite, that is, the gathering of dispersed troops into a single location.

10.4.16. *carrying... times*: The commentators and translators take this to mean that the infantrymen should carry weapons at all times and in all places. But this seems obvious. Another meaning may be that they should carry all the different weapons suitable for different terrains and different seasons.

10.5.2. *out of sight*: This probably means unseen by the enemy or his spies.

10.5.6. *five Aratnis*: A normal Dhanus is said to be four Aratnis at 2.20.18. This particular computation may be confined to the military. The commentary *Nayacandrikā* thinks that the spacing given in the previous sentences is for soldiers fighting with swords, while the larger distances given here are for archers.

10.5.12. *breast* (urasya), *flank* (kakṣa), *wing* (pakṣa): It is clear that the battle formation of an army is visualized as a bird, perhaps an eagle, in the same way as a fire altar (*agnicayana*). We find frequent comparisons between sacrifice and battle. Given this image, I have chosen to maintain in the translation the terms for the three parts of a bird's body: breast or chest, the flanks, and the wings. Sometimes we see mention of the rear or hind (tail?) and the front or tip (head or beak).

10.5.17. *with respect to each other*: That is, center, flanks, and wings have different numbers of chariots, for example, nine in the center, 15 in each flank, and 17 in each wing.

10.5.20. *insertion unit* (āvāpa): This is probably a reserve military unit that was sent in as reinforcement when a particular part of the army was weak, threatened, or depleted.

10.5.22. *one-third less*: That is, an insertion unit is two-thirds of a normal unit, namely 30 chariots into a 45-chariot unit.

10.5.28. *over-insertion unit*: The technical term *atyāvāpa* occurs in two other places: 9.2.2, 5. This term is not commented on by the commentators or the translators. The use of the prefix *ati* in the *AŚ* often has a strategic meaning; that is, the one using *ati* places himself at a strategic advantage over his adversary. Thus, we see the term *atisaṃdhi* for outwitting or overreaching an enemy through trickery (7.7.6; 7.9.6). Here also, therefore, *atyāvāpa* may refer to the king overreaching the enemy by the use of these traitorous troops, who are expendable; see 10.3.15.

10.5.53. *techniques of fighting*: We have here a list of technical terms derived from usage in cavalry. Some of them are self-explanatory, while others are obscure. The explanations of commentators appear to be educated guesses.

zigzag movement (gomūtrikā): Literally, the "cow's urine," the meaning is that the movement of the military formation resembles the urination of a cow while it is walking, namely going from side to side as it moves forward. For this formation, see also 10.6.25.

10.6.31. *"propitious-on-all-sides"* (sarvatobhadra): The pattern was probably a square, thus facing and able to repel an attack from any of the four directions.

10.6.35. *"harpoon"... their form*: It appears that this particular formation has five *anīkas,* that is, arrays or faces, perhaps in addition to the center or breast (*uras*). These would correspond to the snout and the four legs of a lizard, or the head and the four hooked sides of the ancient *vajra* that is similar to the front end of a harpoon. Indeed, several Vedic texts use the term *anīka* to refer to the front point of a *vajra* (*TS* 6.2.3.1; *AitBr* 1.25.2–5; *ŚB* 3.4.4.14). For the form of the *vajra,* see Rau 1974.

10.6.45. *The single commander...commander*: This passage provides a very distinct nomenclature of senior army commanders: *patika, senāpati, nāyaka.* Generally, the chief of armed forces is called *senāpati,* and he is probably the brother or close relative of the king (Scharfe 1993, 139). He is listed next to the chaplain at 1.12.6 and in the top category within the salary list (5.3.3). The *nāyaka,* who is regarded here as commanding ten *senāpatis,* is generally a lower-ranking official (Scharfe 1993, 173); see 1.12.6; 10.2.4. This may indicate a different source for this chapter.

10.6.48–50. *carts... elephants*: The meaning of carts is unclear. Perhaps the reference is to the military formation called a cart at 10.6.26. I follow Kangle's emendation of *hastibhūṣaṇaiḥ* ("with decorations of elephants") to *hastibhīṣaṇaiḥ* ("frightful [demonstrations] with elephants"); see 10.4.14, where causing fright is given as one activity of elephant regiments.

BOOK 11

11.1.1. *best among... ally*: The expression *daṇḍamitralābhānām uttamaḥ* is problematic; see Wezler 2000a. One would have expected *saṅgha* to also be included in the compound. Wezler thinks that this is a case of an abbreviated compound, with *lābha* standing for *saṅghalābha.* Even though it is true, as Wezler notes, that the compounds *daṇḍalābha* and *mitralābha* are not found in the *AŚ,* we do have a parallel compound at 7.9.1: *mitrahiraṇyabhūmilābhānām uttarottaro lābhaḥ śreyān.* I have refrained from introducing *saṅgha* into the compound, even though the meaning is clear: Gaining a confederacy is the best of all gains one can expect from a war, although such gains also include treasures and land. Perhaps there is an implied *ādi* (etc.) before *lābha* in the compound.

11.1.4–5. *The Kāmbojas... title "king"*: These two sentences present several problems in interpretation. In the first, some take *kṣatriya* and *śreṇi* to refer to

Kṣatriyas and guilds. I think Kangle is correct in taking the entire compound as a Dvandva, especially in view of the concluding *ādi* at the end, and the parallel compound in the next sentence. Kṣatriya and Śreṇi (or some local names translated into Sanskrit with these terms) must refer to some peoples or polities. In both sentences, the reference to their livelihood probably concerns not all the people but the leaders of these confederate communities. The use of the title "king" may simply mean that these leaders called themselves *rāja*, a common enough practice even in later India, and lived by the privileges conferred by that title, such as levying taxes (Wezler 2000a). It is also likely that these two sentences have migrated into the text via a gloss. The initial word of sentence 6, *sarveṣām* ("in the case of all") probably refers to the two kinds of confederacies mentioned in sentence 3.

11.1.7. *agents posing...sports*: The syntax of this sentence is murky, and the compound *bālakalahān* is unclear. Kangle takes *bāla* ("children") to be the confederates themselves, but that would be a strange use of the term *bāla* simply to mean a pupil. I take the disputes to be among the children of the confederates who are being taught by the agents in the guise of teachers. The teachers talk about the excellence of the one or the other confederate with regard to the various skills listed. These would lead to quarrels among the boys with respect to the relative excellences of their fathers, news of which would, of course, reach the ears of their fathers.

11.1.9. *They*: The referent here and in the following sentences is unclear. Three groups have been mentioned: secret agents, agents posing as teachers, and assassins. Given that, in this and the following passages, these people convince portions of the population to change their behavior, norms, and aspirations, it is more likely that we are dealing here with agents posing as teachers.

inferior (hīna), *superior* (viśiṣṭa): Note the way the author plays with these two words with their multiple nuances in the following sentences. Further, the two compounds may also be understood as Tatpuruṣas: *hīnacchandika* as one enjoying luxuries of inferiors (lower-level people), and *viśiṣṭacchandika* as one enjoying luxuries of superiors.

11.1.13. *convention* (vyavahāra): Kangle takes the term to mean a transaction. But it appears that here we are talking about something more serious than a single commercial transaction. Here *vyavahāra* probably has the meaning of a norm or convention found in 2.7.3, 29.

11.1.27. *he*: Here the author reverts to the singular, and the subject from now on is the king who wishes to undermine a confederacy.

11.1.28. *periodic interest*: The term *kālika* has been subject to diverse interpretations. Kangle translates: "temporary use of vehicles or money." Wezler (2000a) is correct in thinking that the context calls for some form of interest. He focuses on the term *prakhyāta*, which I have translated as "specified," that is, the interest that was publicly fixed at the time the articles or money were taken on loan. The term *kālika*, however, gives a stronger backing to this interpretation. In the *Nārada Smṛti* (1.87–89), four kinds of interest are mentioned, the second of which is *kālikā*. This is periodic interest that is payable every month. The stipulated interest is to be paid periodically (perhaps monthly), and it is this interest, perhaps in the form of goods (the term *dravya* is used in Sanskrit), that is paid to a single chief in order to cause dissension. For *kālika* as giving on credit, see also 12.4.8.

11.1.35. *confidence... abduction*: The agents assure one of the chiefs that the woman is madly in love with him and then get her to go to another chief, or have the woman abducted, creating the impression that she has been abducted by another chief.

11.1.39. *by that man*: That is, by another chief of the confederacy. Such an accusation will lead to a quarrel and create disharmony within the confederacy.

11.1.42. *or wives... singers*: This phrase coming after the previous completed sentence may simply be a gloss. Kangle, following the reading of the commentary *Nayacandrikā*, gives the reading *unmādayeyuḥ aditikauśikastriyo*, whereas the unanimous reading of the manuscripts is *unmādayeyur iti kauśikastriyo*. As Raghavan (1945–1946) has pointed out, the commentator was probably thinking of *AŚ* 1.17.19, where the term *aditikauśika* occurs, when he corrected the reading here. I think Raghavan is correct in thinking that the reference here is only to wives of a group called Kauśika. He has demonstrated that this term, along with the parallel *kaiśika*, refers to communities of entertainers. As such, I have taken *nartakīgāyanāḥ* to be in apposition to the wives of Kauśikas, namely such women who are professional actresses and singers. The placement of *vā* after this compound also supports my interpretation. It is only these kinds of attractive and available women who could tempt the chiefs to meet them at a secret location, not the wives of snake charmers. Kangle translates this phrase as "or Aditikauśika women or dancers or songstresses (should do so)."

11.1.52. *I will carry on* (pratipatsyāmi): The meaning is unclear. Kangle explains that the woman will carry on as if she is doing the bidding of the rival until a meeting can be arranged and the rival is killed by the chief. But given that the rival had not sent the mendicant as a go-between, such a clandestine meeting would have been difficult to arrange. Perhaps she wants the chief to think that she is carrying out the commands of the rival, until he has a chance to deal with him in secret.

11.1.54. *sovereign king* (ekarāja): On the term and concept of *ekarāja*, see Wezler 2000a, 494–495. It appears that the grammarian Kātyāyana uses the term to distinguish a king who has sovereignty (*ekarāja*) from those within confederacies (*saṅgha*) who may also bear the title of king (*rāja*); Kātyāyana on Pāṇini 4.1.168 (in Patañjali's *Mahābhāṣya* II: 268).

BOOK 12

12.1. *Envoy*: Even though envoy (*dūta*) appears in the title of this topic, the very term or any substantive treatment of the work of an envoy is absent in the discussion, except perhaps the mention of peace pacts toward the end. This shows that sometimes the "topics" are artificial and divorced from the substance of the section; see Introduction, pp. 9f.

12.1.7. *herd ram*: The meaning of *kulaiḍaka*, which also occurs at 13.1.16, is unclear. It is probably a proverbial saying and, like similar sayings in the *Pañcatantra*, there was probably a story underlying the proverb. Kangle explains that the ram has been separated from his herd and is, therefore, despondent. The context of 13.1.16, however, where the comparison is with people who are alarmed or agitated (*udvigna*), is somewhat different. If the general perception of donkeys and goats as oversexed can be applied to a ram as well, *kula* here may refer to a human house rather than a herd. If the ram is kept at a house alone, he may pine for his herd and female companionship. See the description of a ram (*meṣa*) kept in an inner courtyard of Vasantasenā's house and massaged with oil (*Mr̥cchakaṭikā* 4.27–28).

12.1.24. *by successively…nights*: The meaning here is unclear. I take it to mean that the weaker king, as part of the bargain for a pact, allows the stronger king to use his treasury or troops for a longer period of time, increasing that period by one day each time his offer is refused.

12.1.24–31. *peace pact*: For the various kinds of peace pacts, see 7.3.21–36.

12.1.27. *both*: That is, both the traitorous troops, etc., that he has supplied and the enemy to whom they were supplied.

12.2.1. *he*: That is, the stronger king who was the subject of discussion in the previous chapter.

12.2.3. *righteous* (dharma) *and profitable* (artha): Clearly, here *dharma* and *artha* refer to the Triple Set (1.7.4).

12.2.4. *to fight…to profit*: This looks very much like a gloss explaining the three central terms of the previous sentence, a gloss that found its way into the text proper.

12.2.14. *agents…the chiefs*: The wording of this statement is problematic, especially because it leaves the persons who would be administering the poison unspecified. Kangle thinks that the chiefs administered the poison to themselves so as to make the women love him. In the two other places where this trick is used, it is the woman who is tricked into giving the man the poison at 5.1.19, and at 11.1.40, the poisoned love potion is given to the man. Clearly in all cases, it is the man who is the target for assassination. We do not know the cultural practice behind administering love potions. We take for granted that it is the one in whom love is to be induced who takes the potion. It may well be, however, that either the target or the other person, or both, may be required to take the potion.

12.2.21. *a female agent... wandering ascetic*: The problem with this statement is how an agent can pretend to be the wife of a high official. Kangle thinks that this refers to a long-term plan whereby an agent has made a high official fall in love with and marry her. This appears far-fetched. I interpret this statement in the following way: The agent is pretending to be one of the king's wives in love with the high official. The king has got wind of this and is at the point of putting her under guard. The issue for this interpretation is the meaning of the word *brūyāt*, "should say." I think we should interpret this broadly: She has sent a letter and ornaments (perhaps as a token) through a female ascetic. It is probably in this letter that she communicates her love and her impending imprisonment.

12.2.23. *success of the undertaking* (kāryasiddhi): The meaning is unclear. Perhaps the trader tells the high official that he had actually sold the poison to the king for use in this plot.

12.2.33. *them, him*: The people the assassins kill are probably the officers of the Regent. The cryptic *brūyur asya* probably means that the assassins should proclaim that all this mayhem was perpetrated by the Regent or, perhaps, by the Collector.

12.3.2. *after taking... at night*: This probably means after obtaining official passes to go about at night within the military camp.

12.3.14. *army chiefs or ranking officials*: Kangle sees a single category of persons in the compound *senāmukhyaprakṛtipuruṣān* and translates: "the principal officers among the chiefs of the army." I follow the commentary *Nayacandrikā* and take the compound to refer to two categories. For *prakṛtipuruṣa*, see 8.4.15.

12.4. *Destroying... Raids*: This topic is somewhat artificial, given that it is dealt with in just a section of sentence 20. The entire chapter is actually devoted to topic 166.

12.4.4. *death of a son or wife:* This expression is probably taken from 11.1.24. The editor/author clearly forgot to delete "wife," which is out of place within this context, because the man killed was supposed to be his son. The wife does not enter into the picture.

12.4.5. *or liquor...poison* (pādyaṃ vā madyam): This is a curious expression, and the meaning is unclear. Kangle is probably right in thinking that this may have come into the text because of a scribal error.

12.4.11. *Agents...same products*: The ruse is meant to sell poisoned products to unsuspecting troops within a fort or military camp. This sentence is, however, incomplete.

12.4.24. *fight by candestine operatives* (gūḍhayuddha): Kangle remarks that this is different from the *kūṭayuddha* (10.3) and calls it simply murder. Yet, these agents in the guise of hunters were expected to use methods of fighting connected with this form of battle. I take *gūḍha* as a noun referring to clandestine operatives of the king, a term that is frequently used with this meaning, either alone or compounded with *puruṣa* (1.11.1, 18; 7.5.45; 7.13.43).

12.4.27. *occult fire or smoke* (yogāgnidhūma): Recipes for producing lethal kinds of fire and smoke are given in 13.4 and 14.1.

12.4.29. *secret strategies, secret means*: The author appears to be playing here with the multiple nuances of the term *yoga*. Within the *AŚ*, it has the meanings of occult or secret practices (see the previous note), secret or even occult methods, and simply trickery and fraud. The last of these meanings is predominant in the next chapter and in topic 168.

12.5. *Topics 168–170*: As in the previous chapter, there are no clear demarcations of the three topics within this chapter, suggesting once again that the topic division was superimposed over an existing text. Topic 170 appears to begin at sentence 43, and "lone" refers to a king who is left alone after his fort has been captured by the enemy.

12.5.10. *an area of the enemy's territory*: That is, an area of his own territory that has now been seized by the advancing enemy. He hopes that the influx of these people into that territory would both cause the enemy some problems and that subsequently, that territory, now with a large influx of his own people, would be easily recaptured.

12.5.12. *in the section . . . his troops*: This section is topic 120 (7.15.21–29). The reasons for barricading oneself in a fort, however, are given in 7.15.12, which falls under topic 119. Here also, we see that perhaps topic 120 covered this whole chapter at one point, as reflected in this cross-reference and the verse 7.15.30.

12.5.18. *pots with water or brass vessels*: The vibrations from the digging would manifest itself in the waves created within the water pot or a sound in the brass pot. The manuscripts read *atoyakumbhān*, pots without water. I think Kangle's emendation to eliminate the negative is correct.

12.5.42. *he should rush . . . slay him*: As Kangle explains, the scenario appears to be this: The enemy has been advised through secret instigations that the troops of his adversary are disloyal to him and traitorous. So, when he comes out of the fort to fight, he expects his opponent's troops to turn around and kill him. As the enemy is careless due to this expectation, he is overwhelmed by the troops who are, in fact, loyal to the king.

12.5.43. *hollow within . . . statue of a god*: For the underground chamber, the entrance to which is closed by a statue, and for the false wall, see 1.20.2. It appears that one of the precautions a king would take was to equip a sanctuary (*caitya*) with hiding places for an emergency.

BOOK 13

13.1.3. *intimacy with gods*: In this context, we can compare the boast of King Aśoka in his Minor Rock Edict that because of his work, gods have mingled with the people. See Strong 2012.

Nāga and Varuṇa: Nāga is a serpent, here probably a divine serpent emerging from the water. The worship of snakes was widespread in India. All the manuscripts read *hariṇa* for *varuṇa*, which is a conjectural emendation of Kangle following Gaṇapati Śāstrī (see the use of Varuṇa in sentence 6). If we keep *hariṇa*, the reference could be to some kind of divine being; the term is used for a variety of deities, including Viṣṇu and Śiva, as well as for a serpent demon in the *MBh* 1.52.10.

circle of fire... sea sand: This is clearly some sort of spectacle within water that gives the illusion of fire in the water. It is unclear to what sea sand (*samudravālukā*) refers, but it must have been some device or substance that gave the illusion of fire. See 14.2 for a variety of recipes for creating illusions or realities of fire on the body and in water. There is a reference to columns or balls of fire (*aggikhandha*) that Aśoka in his Fourth Rock Edict says he displayed to the people. On this and other displays of Aśoka, see Strong 2012, where he suggests a modern parallel in the mysterious fireballs that rise out of the Mekhong River at Nongkhai, Thailand.

13.1.10. *constellation of the enemy*: That is, when the moon has entered the constellation under which the enemy was born.

13.1.16. *skilled individuals... donkey's milk*: These proverbs must be based on well-known stories (see 12.1.7 n.). Without access to these stories, we can only guess at the meaning of the proverbs. I give here the explanations of Kangle, along with some comments of my own. A communal donkey works for everyone without being adequately compensated by anyone. One could also see how according to this proverb, a skilled man can find good work with anyone, given that he is not bound to a single individual. A stick tires itself out by beating a branch, but someone else enjoys the fruits that fall to the ground. Likewise, army officers risk their lives so that the king can live in opulence. For the opaque "herd ram" proverb, see 12.1.7 n. The proverb of the shower of thunderbolts is also opaque; it may mean that an insult is as damaging as thunderbolts. A barren reed shows promise of bearing fruit but leads to frustration. A ball of rice given to a crow indicates that the offering is meager and shows contempt for the recipient. A magic cloud cannot produce rain, just as the king who does not follow through on his promises. Giving ornaments to an ugly wife, like rewards that consist only of empty honors, is useless and even insulting. Regarding the tiger skin (*vyāghracarman*), Kangle thinks that this suggests the ferociousness of the king. That, however, makes little sense, especially in juxtaposition to the next one, death trap, which indicates an unforeseen danger. I think the compound is not a Tatpuruṣa (skin of a tiger) as Kangle assumes, but a Dvandva (tiger and skin) that recalls a story. A similar story is found in the *Pañcatantra* (book 3, story 1), where a donkey wears the skin of a leopard. Here we probably have an opposite story where a tiger wears the skin of a domestic animal and pretends to be harmless (a wolf in sheep's clothing!). The king appears harmless and loving, but he is actually a death trap. Regarding people who always render assistance, there are four proverbs listed. The compound *pīluvikhādana* is taken by Gaṇapati Śāstrī and Kangle as eating Pīlu fruit. Kangle thinks that this fruit has no nutritious value, and Gaṇapati thinks that it tastes bitter. Pīlu is *Salvadora persica* or the toothbrush tree. It makes better sense to take Pīlu to refer to the twigs of this tree used as a toothbrush by chewing the end. The term *vikhādana* probably refers to either this chewing or to the brushing or both. This "eating" does not benefit the eater, just like a king who is served so faithfully. Gaṇapati takes *karakā* to be a bitter plant, while Kangle thinks it is hail. Both are mere guesses. I see that every one of the proverbs listed has at least two words either separately or in compound. So it would be natural to take *karakayā uṣṭryā* as referring to a single situation. Given that both *karakā* and *uṣṭrī* have the meaning of a water vessel (see *Amarakośa*, 3.3.23 [359]; see *uṣṭrikā* at 14.1.33; 14.2.44), I think it is possible to take the one as qualifying the other: camel-shaped water vessel (possibly one with a long neck). Why such a vessel would be a waste of time is unclear, unless its use did not benefit the user in the long run. Note also how camel and donkey are constantly associated in the *AŚ*. Regarding the churning of donkey milk, this is also a fruitless action, either because it will not yield butter (so Kangle) or because, being a single-hoofed (*ekaśapha*) animal, its milk is forbidden (*MDh* 5.8).

13.1.19. *They should…fail to agree*: I take the verb *abhihareyuḥ* to mean carry off or abduct (10.4.13). Note also the change of number from singular in 17–18 to the plural here, referring to secret agents. Kangle, following Meyer, translates: "they should bring ornaments to the women and children." But it is difficult to see how we can get this meaning from the single compound *strīkumārālaṃkārān*, although the use of *abhihareyuḥ* at 13.3.45 favors "they should bring."

13.1.20. *king*: This is the enemy king. The request to the king is meant to divide the people from him, when he is unable or unwilling to offer assistance.

13.2.5. *he*: The subject is probably the king who is the seeker after conquest. Generally in these passages, the singular verbs refer to the king and the plural verbs to his secret agents.

13.2.11. *fire…substance* (tejanāgniyukta): The term *tejanāgni* is probably an abbreviated compound (Gonda 1968) standing for *tejanatailāgni* or *tejanacūrṇāgni*. We have *tejanataila* (glowing oil) at 13.2.23, 25 and *tejanacūrṇa* (glowing powder) at 14.2.19. Substances that make a person smeared with it glow as if on fire are described in 14.2.18–26. If these secret recipes were effective, the person may have appeared to glow or, perhaps, glow when a light was directed at his body.

13.2.19. *making an image ... foe*: All this pertains to a magic rite whereby the enemy would be captured within an image and then eliminated. The king is invited to this rite so he can witness the enemy brought into the image.

13.2.29. *with men eaten up while erect* (ūrdhvabhakṣitair manuṣyaiḥ): The meaning is unclear, with Gaṇapati Śāstrī taking it to mean that the upper parts of their bodies have been eaten. Clearly, the image is of half-eaten corpses (presumably by demons) kept erect within a sanctuary in a cemetery. See the parallel in the Vetāla stories of later times, where a corpse is hanging from a tree. It is possible that *caitya* (sanctuary) in this passage may be an abbreviation for *caityavṛkṣa* (sanctuary tree); see *MDh* 9.264; 10.50; *MBh* 6.3.37; 12.69.39.

13.2.34. *On these occasions*: That is, the occasions mentioned in 13.2.21–31.

13.2.36. *when these tricks ... his enemies*: He would get his secret agents to perform these same tricks on him, and he would successfully counteract the evil omens. Of course, he would not be assassinated during his nighttime rituals. His enemies watching this would be persuaded to perform the same remedial actions, during which, of course, they would be killed.

13.2.42. *an inheritance or a deposit*: Here, as in 11.1.42, these women are probably brought to the king to settle disputes regarding an inheritance or a deposit. The legal situation makes them vulnerable.

13.2.44. *Stūpas*: That is, the typically Buddhist sacred structures often containing the relics of the Buddha. It is, of course, not clear whether the reference is specifically to a Buddhist *stūpa*. This is the only place where the term occurs in the *AŚ*.

13.3.12. *disaffected ... weak*: These are spies planted by the king in the enemy's territory. Kangle takes *yogāpasarpa* to be treacherous spies, but that would be merely a repetition of *dūṣya* given in the same compound. The term *yoga* within the context of spies and secret agents indicates someone operating clandestinely. Thus, *yogapuruṣa* is a clandestine operative. The term must have the same meaning here. Some of these spies operating in the enemy territory may become traitorous or disloyal. The minister who seemingly defected to the enemy will disclose the names of such spies, thus getting rid of them. The mention of their being powerless is probably because, if they were independently powerful, they may end up rendering assistance to the enemy.

13.3.15. *his foe*: That is, the enemy of the enemy whom the king wants killed.

13.3.16. *after getting...that king*: The syntax is somewhat complicated. King A has an enemy, king B, who also has an enemy king C, who by definition should be an ally of king A. But king A supports seducible factions of king C, thus prompting king C to perpetrate injuries on king A. This is an excuse for king A to attack king C and to ask king B to join him in vanquishing his own enemy, king C.

13.3.21. *him* (tam): The pronoun is ambiguous in Sanskrit. Kangle takes it as referring to the army. But *ghātayet* ("he should kill") in this passage always has the enemy as the object, as seen in the very next sentence. However, the pronoun refers to the army at 13.3.32.

13.3.25. *ally, foe*: As is evident from 13.3.33, this is the foe (*śatru*) of the seeker after conquest, while the ally is the ally of that foe. The aim is to break their alliance and get them to turn on each other. Here king A has a foe, king B, who has an ally, king C. The bargain for king C's land is made by king A with king B. Then king A gets king C to attack him. When this happens, king B, who normally would have helped king C, would turn against him, and together the two vanquish king C (the ally) and share his land. The scenario can be repeated with king A and king C joining forces to attack king B.

13.3.46. *disguised as them*: The meaning of *tadvyañjanāḥ* is unclear. The probable meaning from the context is that the soldiers now disguise themselves as soldiers of the enemy. They are the ones who raise the alarm that the enemy has arrived within the fort, evidenced by the mayhem that they themselves have created. The syntax of the sentence is somewhat murky, but the general outline of the strategy appears clear.

13.3.51–53. *Spies should...juices*: The syntax of these sentences is problematic. This is the probable scenario: The spies infiltrate the forest tribe and get them to raid a herd station or a caravan located nearby. The robbers mentioned are actually members of the tribe, as we see explicitly in 13.3.58. The herdsmen and traders are also part of the plot. When they are attacked, they flee leaving behind food and drink that have been adulterated. The tribesmen/robbers eat and drink that, and when they are unconscious, the herdsmen or traders get the king's troops to launch an attack.

13.3.54. *Saṃkarṣaṇa*: This is a deity subsumed within the broader theology of Vaiṣṇavism and often identified with Bala-Rāma. For his association with palm wine and liquor in both literature and iconography, see Parpola 2002 and especially Parpola and Janhunen 2011, 87.

13.4.1. *laying siege*: The enemy is assumed to be entrenched within his fort. This section of the discussion deals with laying siege to the fort until the enemy surrenders.

13.4.3–4. *He should get anyone...one location*: Jolly's and Kangle's editions place the phrase *anyatra apasarataḥ* as the conclusion of sentence 3, syntactically connected to the rest of that sentence. This interpretation is found also in Gaṇapati Śāstrī and Meyer. It poses several problems, however, with regard to both meaning and grammar. Taking it as part of sentence 3 leaves sentence 4 without an object, except for an implied "them." Connecting the phrase with sentence 3 makes little sense either; it simply says that he should let the people who are leaving go and not give them any favors. Given the need for an ablative after *anyatra* ("except"), one is also forced to take *apasarataḥ* as an ablative singular of the present participle. It makes much better sense, I think, to unite it with sentence 4, where *apasarataḥ* would be an accusative plural and *anyatra* will have its normal meaning of elsewhere, while also providing a good object to the verb *niveśayet* ("he should settle").

13.4.9. *cave room* (valakuṭikā): The meaning of this compound is quite obscure. No one has really understood it. If the reading is correct, I propose to read *vala* in place of *bala* in the editions. The term *vala* ("cave") gives us some idea that this was also a way of getting inside the fort by digging underground. I think it must refer to something like this (rather than storming by troops as suggested by Kangle), especially because we find *suruṅgā* ("tunnel") associated with *bhūmigṛha* ("underground chamber") in the *AŚ* (12.5.47; 13.2.16, 44). It is, of course, unclear how the two were different; the meaning of this compound remains uncertain.

gate with an armored elephant (dāraṃ ca guḍena): The reading and meaning of this phrase are opaque. The first word *dāraṃ* means some kind of cleft, which is unusual after moat and rampart; one would have expected another part of the fortifications. I think Meyer is correct in emending the word to *dvāram* ("gate"). The confusion may have been caused by the Malayalam character for *dvā*, which can be mistaken for *dā*, or by the term *nimna* ("a hollow or cavity") that begins the next sentence. In fact, in some editions, the *dāraṃ* phrase is placed in that sentence. The word(s) following *dāraṃ* are *ca guḍena* (or *guṛena, hulena*), or in another reading, *bahulena*. Clearly, there is a lot of confusion here. Lexicons give a meaning of *guḍa* as the armor of an elephant. I have, very hesitantly, taken it as a metonym for an elephant wearing armor.

13.4.10. *wetlands…dirt*: Although the term *nimna* literally means a hollow or a low-lying area, it is used frequently in the *AŚ* to refer to marshes and waterways; see 7.10.34, where *nimna* is opposed to *sthala* (dry land) and 7.10.35, which refers to *nimnayodhinaḥ*, soldiers specializing in fighting in water. The compound *pāṃsumālā* (lit., garland of dust) is unclear. It appears that the wetlands and waterways were in some way covered with a layer of something that would make enemies mistake them for dry land. How one could cover them with dust or dirt is unclear. The term *pāṃsu*, however, also refers to some forms of vegetation. Thus, *pāṃsucāmara* (M-W) is said to be a bank covered with grass. If that is the meaning, the wetlands could be covered with layers of grass or leaves.

13.4.20–21. *Either the power... mixture*: This passage is very difficult to understand, and the syntax is opaque; it is not even certain that the readings we have are correct. I have departed from both Meyer and Kangle in taking sentences 20–21 as a syntactic unit somewhat clumsily put together. The reason for this is that I believe this passage parallels sentence 19, which gives one kind of incendiary mixture, one that can be hurled (*kṣepya*). I think 20–21 gives a different kind of mixture, one that can be attached to or used to coat various devices, *yukta*. I have slightly emended the text by changing *pāribhadraka... śrīveṣṭakayukto 'gniyogo* to *pāribhadraka... śrīveṣṭakaṃ yukto 'gniyogo*, taking the long compound as a Bahuvrīhi. The term *yukta* here parallels *kṣepya* in sentence 19; two kinds of incendiary mixtures are given here, one to be attached to various devices (these are the ones that were probably attached to birds) and another that is to be hurled by hand. The mixture to be attached is optionally called Viśvāsaghātin (a mechanical device; see 2.18.5) when an arrow is coated with it. This device launches an arrow with the incendiary mixture at the fort, I assume, from a longer distance than the hurled mixture (for a mechanical device that has a string, see 14.3.66). The meaning of Keśa is unclear; Gaṇapati Śāstrī takes it as a particular kind of plant (Monier-Williams identifies it as the Indigo plant), but it could also simply mean hair. The final *ity agniyogaḥ* I take to be simply the conclusion of the discussion of incendiary mixtures.

Kumbhī: The meaning is unclear. Gaṇapati Śāstrī takes it to be the plant Śrīparṇī (*Gmelina arborea*), while Meyer takes it to be a kind a metal.

13.4.25. *taking by storm*: Here and in the subsequent discussion, the enemy is still assumed to be entrenched in a fort, but now instead of laying siege, the king storms the fort either with the use of force or by drawing the enemy out of the fort with some trick (13.4.12).

13.4.44. *an ally or a tribal chief*: These are allies or partners of the man who is under siege.

13.4.45. *He achieves... his ally*: That is, he puts the blame for the killing of the ally on the man who is under siege.

13.4.50. *after getting harm... surprise attack*: The scenario is that the seeker after conquest manages to get some treasonable people or tribal chiefs associated with the enemy to cause him harm. When the enemy sends part of his army to deal with that and the fort is thus left with fewer troops, the seeker after conquest attacks it.

13.4.56. *enemy constituents... beyond that*: The enemy constituents are the kings within the circle who are his enemy and the enemy's allies (6.2.14). The constituents of the circle beyond that are his natural allies (6.2.15). I take the compound *guṇātiśaya* (strategic preeminence) to refer to the six strategies (*ṣāḍguṇya*) given in book 7.

13.5.12. *constellations of the king and the region*: That is, when the moon enters the constellation under which the king was born or the constellation with which the region is associated.

BOOK 14

14.1.2. *Well-liked* (abhipreta): That is, well-liked or held in good regard by the enemy.

14.1.3. *insert fire*: On the face of this, the insertion of fire clandestinely makes no sense. It would be impossible to keep the presence of the fire a secret. As in the first case where weapons were smuggled in, the reason appears to be to help operatives working inside the palace. If that is so, the fire here probably stands for the incendiary mixtures (13.4.19–21) given in other places. So, here also, we may have an abbreviated compound: *agninidhāna* standing for *agniyoganidhāna* (13.2.11 n.).

14.1.5. *Or, after…death*: This verse has a loose construction, whether it is interpreted the way I have (following Kangle) or according to Gaṇapati Śāstrī. According to him, the insect boiled alone will cause a person to dry up, and when boiled with a black snake and panic grain, it will cause instant death. This interpretation does violence to the natural sequence of the feet in the verse.

14.1.8. *grain*: The term used is *kalā*, which generally refers to a tiny part of anything or one-sixteenth. This measure is not mentioned in 2.19. For a parallel formula, see 4.4.10.

14.1.18. *together*: I follow Meyer and disagree with Kangle (who takes it to mean each singly and not mixed together) regarding the meaning of *samasta*. Regularly in the *AŚ* (see 14.1.37), this term is contrasted with *vyasta*, the former indicating a combination of items in a list and the latter their separation or individual use.

14.1.29. *boiled*: I take the term *siddha* to mean boiled or cooked, as this is the prevalent meaning in 14.2. Kangle translates: "prepared."

14.1.35. *from a brothel*: The readings of the manuscripts here are all corrupt: *bhāgaṃyognim*, *bhāgaḥyosim*. Kangle has conjecturally emended it to *mārgato 'gnim* ("fire from the roads"); but this is problematic because "bh" and "m" in Malayalam and Grantha scripts are quite dissimilar, and because the fires are fetched from places or people associated with professions. I have very tentatively followed Meyer's suggestion *bhāgato 'gnim* ("fire from a brothel"), deriving *bhāga* from *bhaga* (vagina). This is also a long shot, but it is the closest one can come. The change of "y" in the manuscripts to "t" is not too problematic, because the Malayalam character "y" looks like an inverted "t." The connection of ghee with a brothel is also possible, as ghee is often connected with semen.

14.1.37. *fig wood*: The meaning of *dhruva* is uncertain. It is also uncertain whether it is connected with *mānuṣeṇa* ("with human"). I have taken the latter to stand by itself with some connection to *māṃsena* ("with flesh") of the previous verse. The term *dhruva* has the meaning of fig (Vaṭa), which is how Gaṇapati Śāstrī interprets it.

14.2.6. *these two*: That is, the white goat and the white donkey listed in the previous two sentences.

14.2.10. *The insect known as Alojunā*: I follow the conjectural reading of Kangle, *alojuneti yaḥ kīṭaḥ*. The word *yaḥ* is missing in the manuscripts and is supplied based on Jolly's edition. Jolly himself has the reading *alābuneti* for the first word, which is borrowed from Shamasastry's edition where he gives it as a conjecture. This reading is followed also by Meyer who adopts the reading *alābunā pūtikīṭaḥ*, the second word once again borrowed from Shamasastry's translation, which reads: "A bitter gourd, a stinking insect (pūtikīṭa)." Gaṇapati Śāstrī gives the reading *arkatūlo 'rjune kīṭaḥ* (some kind of panicle or wool growing on Arka; two kinds of Arjuna, given in his commentary as Kakubha and Yavasa; and an insect). Unfortunately, Gaṇapati Śāstrī does not give the grounds for this reading. Because no commentary, including the Malayalam one, extends to book 14, it is probably his own conjecture. Clearly, the reading here is corrupt, but Kangle is correct in adopting the *lectio difficilior* of *alojuneti*. However, an insect by this name is unknown in Sanskrit literature, while *pūtikīṭa* (stinkbug) is found at 14.1.4, 10.

14.2.25. *May you be kingdomless* (ārājyāya): The meaning and significance of this dative are unclear. I take the compound to be a Vṛddhi derivative of the Bahuvrīhi *a-rājya*, "one without a kingdom" (see the parallel *ābalīyasam* as the title of book 12). The magic ritual alluded to may be aimed at reducing the enemy to a man without a kingdom.

14.3.9. *any one of them*: The reference appears to be to the animals listed in the preceding recipes.

14.3.21. *Camūkhalas:* The reading and the meaning of this word are uncertain. It probably refers to some kind of animal who is prone to long periods of deep sleep.

14.3.27. *its*: That is, the ritual formula given in the verses 14.3.19–26. It appears that these formulas and rites are meant for robbing houses, perhaps taken from a manual for thieves.

14.3.28. *scrapings of a Bilakhā*: According to Gaṇapati Śāstrī's reasonable explanation, Bilakhā (derived from "digging a hole") refers to some kind of rat. It is usual for some tribals in India even today to be experts at catching and eating field rats. Scrapings are probably the earth that is pushed out as a rat digs a hole. We must assume that when the beans are buried in a basket along with this soil, they will begin to germinate.

14.3.44. *Ghaṭodbala:* The reading is unclear. In the first edition Kangle uses Ghaṭodbala, and gives Ghaṭobala as the reading in the manuscripts G1 and M. In the second edition, Kangle adopts Ghaṭobala, and gives only a single variant, Ghaṭodbala in manuscript T, but keeps the reading Ghaṭodbala in the second edition of his translation. I have adopted the latter reading, which is also found in Meyer and Jolly.

14.3.49. *four mealtimes*: Standard mealtimes for an average human being are twice a day, in the morning and in the evening. Thus, fasting for four mealtimes means fasting for two full days.

14.3.61. *akin:* For the meaning of the term *sagandha,* see 1.8.17 n.

14.3.73–6. *Kāmamadhu*: Literally, this means the sweet of love/pleasure; Meyer reads it as "Liebsüßchen." Perhaps this is not the name of a plant but rather a euphemism for semen or sexual juices.

14.4.2. *Cleansing water*: The meaning of *nejanodaka* is unclear (see also 14.1.14). It may refer to a particular kind of cleansing water (perhaps ritually purified) that is mixed with the stated substances, or it may be simply a term for water when it is mixed with these substances.

Śvetā, and Vāraṇa: I follow Gaṇapati Śāstrī and Meyer in taking these as two different plants. Kangle, without comment, takes it as one, Śvetāvaraṇa. But see Śvetā used alone at 1.20.5; 14.4.12.

14.4.8. *Kaṭa fruit*: Kangle and Meyer take *kaṭaphala* to be the name of a particular plant or tree. Given that Kaṭa (*Strychnos potatorum*) is a well-known tree the fruits of which are used for medicinal purposes and to purify water, I take *phala* here as simply fruit.

14.4.10. *Akṣa*: Gaṇapati Śāstrī says that this is equal to 16 Māṣakas. See 14.1.8 for a parallel formulation.

14.4.13. *Aśvattha... drumstick tree*: For this recipe, see 1.20.5 and the notes given there.

BOOK 15

15. *Organization of a Scientific Treatise*: For a discussion of the expression *tantrayukti*, see Dikshitar 1930; Wezler 1975; Scharfe 1993, 263–274; Chevillard 2009.

15.1.52. *the first constituent... the third*: It is quite remarkable that this particular quotation is not found in the text, although there are similar expressions. Given that all the other citations correspond verbatim to passages in the text, one must suppose that either this passage has been corrupted or that the author of book 15 had a somewhat different text before him. This passage also makes it clear that, at least in the eyes of the author of book 15, the use of the term *prakṛti* to refer to kings in the circle was a peculiar usage of the *AŚ*.

[*Noticing... commentary*]: This verse coming at the very end was probably inserted into the text during the time when the ascription of the text to a definite author was still under review. See Introduction, pp. 35f.

Bibliography

EDITIONS AND COMMENTARIES

Bhāṣāvyākhyāna, a Malayalam commentary on Kauṭilya's *Arthaśāstra*. Part I and II (Adhikaraṇas 1–2), ed. K. Sambasiva Sastri. Trivandrum: Government of Travancore, 1930, 1938. Part III (Adhikaraṇa 3), ed. V. A. Ramaswami Sastri. Trivandrum: University of Travancore, 1945. Part IV (Adhikaraṇas 4–7), ed. K. N. Ezhuthachan. Madras: University of Madras, 1960.

Dātāra, Śrī Viśvanātha Śāstrī. 1991. *Kauṭalīyam Arthaśāstram of Ācārya Viṣṇugupta*, with the commentaries *Śrīmūla, Jayamaṃgalā, Cāṇakyaṭīkā, Pratipadapañcikā, Nītinirṇīti*, and *Nayacandrikā*. Sarasvatībhavana Granthamālā, 130. Two volumes in four parts. Varanasi: Sampurnanand Sanskrit University.

Gairola, Srī Vācaspati. 1977. *The Artha Śāstra of Kauṭilya and the Cāṇakya-Sūtra*, edited with a Hindi translation. 2nd ed. The Vidyabhawan Sanskrit Ganthamala, 75. Varanasi: Chowkhamba Vidyabhawan.

Gaṇapati Śāstrī, T. 1924–1925. *The Arthaśāstra of Kauṭalya*, with the commentary *Śrīmūla*. 3 Parts. Trivandrum. Reprint: Delhi: Bharatiya Vidya Prakashan, 1984.

Harihara Sastri, G. 1958. *Arthaśāstra-vyākhyā Jayamaṅgalā* (First Adhikaraṇa). Madras.

———. 1956–1971. *Arthaśāstra-vyākhyā Cāṇakyaṭīkā* of Bhikṣu Prabhamati, with an introduction. *Journal of Oriental Research*, published serially in Vols. 26–37.

———. 2011. *Two Commentaries on the Arthaśāstra: Jayamaṅgalā & Cāṇakyaṭīkā. Critically re-edited from Harihara Sastri's Fascicle Editions*, ed. Andreas Pohlus. Halle: Universittäsverlag Halle-Wittenberg.

Jina Vijaya, Muni. 1959. *A Fragment of the Koutalya's Arthaśāstra alias Rajāsiddānta With the Fragment of the Commentary named Nitinirṇīti of Ācārya Yogghama alias Mugdhavilāsa*. Bombay: Bhāratīya Vidyā Bhavana.

Jolly, J., and R. Schmidt. 1923–1924. *Arthaśāstra of Kauṭilya: A New Edition*. Vol. I: Edition; Vol II: Notes, with the commentary *Naya Candrikā* by Mādhava Yajva. Lahore: Motilal Banarsidass.

Kangle, R. P. 1969. *The Kauṭilīya Arthaśāstra*. Part I: A Critical Edition and Glossary. 2nd ed. (1st ed. 1960). Bombay: University of Bombay.

Jayaswal, K. P., and A. Banerji-Sastri. 1925–1926. *Pratipadapañcikā* of Bhaṭṭasvāmin (fragment 2.8.5–2.36.47). *Journal of the Bihar and Orissa Research Society* (Patna), Vols.11–12.

Shama Sastri, R. 1909. *Arthaśāstra of Kauṭilya*. 4th revised ed. by N. S. Vekatanathacharya. Mysore, 1960.

TRANSLATIONS

Jolly, J. 1920. *Das Erste Buch des Kauṭilīya Arthaśāstra*. *ZDMG* 74: 321–355.

Kangle, R. P. 1972. *The Kauṭilīya Arthaśāstra*. Part II: An English Translation with Critical and Explanatory Notes. 2nd ed. (1st ed. 1963). Bombay: University of Bombay.

Meyer, J. J. 1926. *Das altindische Buch von Welt und Staatsleben: Das Arthaśāstra des Kauṭilya*. Wiesbaden: Harrassowitz. Reprint: Graz (Austria): Akademische Druck-u. Verlangsanstalt, 1977.

Rangarajan, L. N. 1992. *The Arthashastra*. New Delhi: Penguin. (Care must be taken with this translation, which rearranges the text.)

Ray, Kumudranjan (or Kumar Ranjan). 1966. *An Introductory Study of Kautilya's Arthashastra* (English and Bengali translations with notes of book 1, ch. 1–21). Calcutta: K. Ray.

Shamasastry, R. 1961 (1915). *The Arthaśāstra of Kauṭilya*. 7th ed. Mysore: Mysore Printing and Publishing House.

OTHER PRIMARY TEXTS

Āpastamba-Dharmasūtra. Ed. and tr. in Olivelle 2000.

Aśvaghoṣa, *Buddhacarita*. Ed. and tr. by P. Olivelle as *Life of the Buddha: Buddhacarita by Aśvaghoṣa*. The Clay Sanskrit Library. New York: New York University Press, 2008.

Bāṇa, *Harṣacarita*. Tr. E. B. Cowell and F. W. Thomas. Reprint. Delhi: Motilal Banarsidass, 1961.

Bāṇa. *Kādambarī*. Ed. and tr. M. R. Kale. 4th ed. Delhi: Motilal Banarsidass, 1968.

Baudhāyana-Dharmasūtra. Ed. and tr. in Olivelle 2000.

Bṛhaspati-Smṛti (reconstructed). Ed. K. V. Rangaswami Aiyangar. Gaekwad's Oriental Series, 85. Baroda: Oriental Institute, 1941. Tr. in Jolly 1889.

Carakasaṃhitā. Ed. Jādavji Trikamji Ācārya. 4th ed. New Delhi: Munshiram Manoharlal, 1981.

Gautama-Dharmasūtra. Ed. and tr. in Olivelle 2000.

Gautama, *Nyāyasūtras with Vātsyāyana's Commentary*. 2nd ed. Delhi: Sri Satguru Publications.

Kāmandaka. *Nītisāra* with Śaṅkarārya's commentary. Ed. T. Gaṇapati Śāstrī. Trivandrum Sanskrit Series, 14. Trivandrum, 1912.

Kātyāyana-Smṛti. Ed. P. V. Kane. Poona: Oriental Book Agency, n.d.

Lakṣmīdhara, *Kṛtyakalpataru*. Ed. by K. V. Rangaswami Aiyangar. Gaekwad's Oriental Series. 14 vols. Baroda: Oriental Institute, 1942–1979.

Mahābhārata. Critically edited by V. S. Sukthankar et al. 19 vols. Poona: Bhandarkar Oriental Research Instite, 1933–1959. Translated in van Buitenen 1973–1978; Fitzgerald 2004; Johnson 1998.

Nārada-Smṛti. Ed. and tr. in Lariviere 2003.

Pañcatantra. Ed. and tr. by F. Edgerton. American Oriental Series 2–3. New Haven: American Oriental Society. Tr. in Olivelle 1997.

Pāṇini, *Aṣṭādhyāyī*. Ed. and tr. S. C. Vasu. 2 vols. Reprint. Delhi: Motilal Banarsidass, 1962.

Patañjali, *Mahābhāṣya* on Pāṇini's *Aṣṭadhyāyī*. Ed. F. Kielhorn. 3rd revised ed. by K. V. Abhyankar. Pune: Bhandarkar Oriental Research Institute, 1962–1972.

Rāmāyaṇa. Critically edited by G. H. Bhatt et al. 7 vols. Baroda: Oriental Institute, 1958–1975. Tr. in Goldman et al. 1984–2009.

Śabdakalpadruma. 5 vols. Vārāṇasī: Caukhamba, 1961.

Somadeva, *Nītivākyāmṛta*. Ed. M. L. Sharma. Delhi: Bhāratīya Jñānapīṭha Prakāśana, 1971.

Śūdraka, *Mṛcchakaṭika*. Ed. and tr. M.R. Kale. Reprint of 1924. Delhi: Motilal Banarsidass, 1994.

Suśrutasaṃhitā. Ed. Jādavji Trikamji Ācārya. 5th ed. Vārāṇasī: Caukhambha Orienṭālīyā, 1992.

Taittirīya Prātiśākhya with the commentary *Padakramasadana* by Māhiṣeya. Critically edited by V. Venkatarama Sharma. New Delhi: Panini, 1982.

Tantrākhyāyika: Die älteste Fassung des Pañcatantra. Ed. J. Hertel. Leipzig: Teubner, 1906.

Vaiṣṇava Dharmaśāstra. Ed. and tr. in Olivelle 2009; tr. in Jolly, 1880.

Varāhamihira, *Bṛhatsaṃhitā*. Ed. and tr. M. Ramakrishna Bhat. Revised ed., 2 vols. Delhi: Motilal Banarsidass, 1987.

Vasiṣṭha-Dharmasūtra. Ed. and tr. in Olivelle, 2000.

Vijñāneśvara, *Mitākṣarā*. Commentary on *YDh*. Ed. U. C. Pandey. Kashi Sanskrit Series, 178. Varanasi: Chowkhamba Sanskrit Series, 1967. Translated with Mitramiśra's *Vīramitrodaya* and Śūlapāṇi's *Dīpakalikā* by J. R. Gharpure. 3 vols. Bombay: 1936–1938.

SECONDARY LITERATURE

Agrawala, V. S. 1963. *India as Known to Pāṇini: A Study of the Cultural Material in the Ashṭādhyāyī*. 2nd ed. Varanasi: Prithvi Prakashan.

Ali, Daud. 2004. *Courtly Culture and Political Life in Early Medieval India*. Cambridge: Cambridge University Press.

Ayyar, K. Balasubrahmanya. 1924. "A Study of Kālidāsa in Relation to Political Science." *Proceedings of the Third All-India Oriental Conference*, 1–16. Madras.

Bagchi, Satish Chandra. 1933. *Juristic Personality of Hindu Deities*. Calcutta: University of Calcutta.

Balkundi, H. V. 1998. "Measurement of Rainfall in Ancient India." *Asian Agri-History* 2: 37–48.

Banerjee, N. C. 1925. "Politics and Political History in the Mahābhārata." *Indian Historical Quarterly* 1: 94–99.

Begley, Vimala. 1991. "Ceramic Evidence for Pre-*Periplus* Trade on the Indian Coasts." In Begley and De Puma 1991, 157–196.

Begley, Vimala, and Richard Daniel De Puma. 1991. *Rome and India: The Ancient Sea Trade*. Madison: University of Wisconsin Press.

Betai, R. S. 1963. "Widowhood and Niyoga in the Arthaśāstra and the Manusmṛti." *Our Heritage* 11: 1–11.

Bloomfield, Maurice. 1920. "Notes on the Dviyāvadāna." *JAOS* 40: 336–352.

Bodewitz, H. W. 2003. "The Concept of *sampad* in the Arthaśāstra, the Vedic Prose Texts and the Gītā." *Indo-Iranian Journal* 46: 231–259.

Boesche, Roger. 2003. *The First Great Political Realist: Kautilya and His Arthashastra*. Lanham: Lexington Books.

Botto, Oscar. 1972. "*Dvaidhībhāva* in the Kauṭilīyārthaśāstra and in other Texts." In *India Maior: Congratulatory Volume Presented to J. Gonda*, ed. J. Ensink and P. Gaeffke, 46–56. Leiden: Brill.

Breloer. Bernhardt. (1927–34). *Kautilya-Studien*. 3 vols. Bonn/Leipzig: Schroeder.

Bronkhorst, Johannes. 2011. *Buddhism in the Shadow of Brahmanism*. Leiden: Brill.

Bronner, Yigal. 2012. "A Question of Priority: Revisiting the Bhāmaha-Daṇḍin Debate." *Journal of Indian Philosophy* 40: 67–118.

Burrow, Thomas. 1968. "Cāṇakya and Kauṭalya." *Annals of the Bhandarkar Oriental Research Institute* 48–49: 17–31.

Chakraborty, Kedareswar. 2002. *Art of Spying in Ancient India*. Calcutta: Sanskrit Book Depot.

Chanana, Dev Raj. 1960. *Slavery in Ancient India as Depicted in Pāli and Sanskrit Texts*. New Delhi: People's Publishing House.

Charpentier, Jarl. 1919. "Beiträge zur alt- und mittelindischen Wortkunde." *ZDMG* 70: 129–158.

Chevillard, Jean-Luc. 2009. "The Metagrammatical Vocabulary inside the Lists of 32 *Tantrayukti*-s and its Adaptation to Tamil: Towards a Sanskrit-Tamil Dictionary." In *Between Preservation and Recreation: Tamil Tradition of Commentary*, ed. Eva Wilden, 71–132. Collection Indologie, 109. Pondichéry: École Française D'Extrème-Orient.

Dallapiccola, Anna Libera, ed. 1989. *The Sastric Tradition in the Indian Arts*. Beiträge zur Südasienforschung. Wiesbaden: Steiner.

Daniel, J. C. 2002. *The Book of Indian Reptiles and Amphibians*. Mumbai: Bombay Natural History Society and Oxford University Press.

Das, Rahul Peter. 1988. *Das Wissen von der Lebensspanne der Bäume: Surapāla's Vṛkṣāyurveda*. Stuttgart: Franz Steiner.

Dave, K. N. 2005. *Birds in Sanskrit Literature.* Revised ed. of 1985. Delhi: Motilal Banarsidass.

De Romanis, Federico. 2000. "Esportazioni di corallo mediterraneo in India nell'età ellenistico-romana." In *Corallo di ieri corallo di oggi.* Ed. Jean-Paul Morel, Cecilia Rondi-Costanzo, and Danela Ugolini, 211–216. Centro Universitario Europeo Per i Beni Culturali, Scienze e materiali del patrimonio culturale, 5. Bari: Edipuglia.

Derrett, J. Duncan M. 1976. "Rājadharma." *Journal of Asian Studies* 35, 597–609.

———. 1965. "A Newly-discovered Contact between Arthaśāstra and Dharmaśāstra". *ZDMG* 115: 134–152.

———. 1975. Ed. and tr. *Bhāruci's Commentary on the Manusmṛti* (The Manu-Śāstra-Vivaraṇa, books 6–12). 2 vols. Wiesbaden: Steiner, 1975.

Dikshitar, Ramachandra. 1926. "The Religious Data in Kauṭalya's Arthaśāstra." *Zeitschrift für Indologie und Iranistik* 7: 251–258.

———. 1930. "Tantrayukti." *Journal of Oriental Research* IV: 82–89.

Dwivedi, G. 1969. "Geographical Data in the *Kauṭilīya Arthaśāstra.*" *Proceedings of the Twenty-Sixth International Congress of Orientalists.* III.1, 222–226. Poona: Bhandarkar Oriental Research Institute.

Edgerton, Franklin. 1931. *The Elephant-Lore of the Hindus.* Reprint. Delhi: Motilal Banarsidass, 1985.

Falk, Harry. 1986. *Bruderschaft und Würfelspiel: Untersuchungen zur Entwicklungsgeschiche des vedischen Opfers.* Freiburg: Hedwig Falk.

———. 1986b. "Die Prüfung der Beamten im Arthaśāstra." *Wiener Zeitschrift für die Kunde Südasiens* 30: 57–72.

Fitzgerald James L. 1998. "Some Storks Eat Carrion; Herons and Ospreys Do Not: Kaṅkas and Kuraras (and Baḍas) in the Mahābhārata." *JAOS* 118: 257–261.

———. 2004. *Mahābhārata,* books 11–12. Chicago: University of Chicago Press.

Ghoshal, Upendra Nath. 1959. *A History of Indian Political Ideas: The Ancient Period and the Period of Transition to the Middle Ages.* Bombay: Oxford University Press.

Goldman, Robert P., et al. 1984–2009. *The Rāmāyaṇa of Vālmiki.* 6 vols. Princeton: Princeton University Press.

Gonda, Jan. 1968. "Abbreviated and Inverted Nominal Compounds in Sanskrit." In *Pratidānam: Indian, Iranian and Indo-European Studies Presented to F. B. J. Kuiper on his Sixtieth Birthday,* ed. J.C. Heesterman et al., 221–246. The Hague: Mouton.

Gopal, Lallanji. 1961. "Ownership of Agricultural Land in Ancient India." *Journal of the Economic and Social History of the Orient* 4: 240–263.

———. 1963. "Sāmanta—Its Varying Significance in Ancient India." *Journal of the Royal Asiatic Society of Great Britain and Ireland,* Nos. 1–2: 21–37.

———. 1964. "Sugar-Making in Ancient India." *Journal of the Economic and Social History of the Orient* 7: 57–72.

———. 1980. *Aspects of History of Agriculture in Ancient India.* Varanasi: Bharati Prakashan.

———. 1989 (1965). *The Economic Life of Northern India c. A.D. 700–1200*. Delhi: Motilal Banarsidass.

Gupta, P. L. 1960. "Numismatic Data in the Arthashastra of Kautalya." *Journal of the Numismatic Society of India* 22: 13–37.

———. 1969. *Coins*. New Delhi: National Book Trust.

Gupta, V. K. 2004. *Kauṭilīya Arthaśāstra: A Legal, Critical and Analytical Study*. Delhi: Bharatiya Kala Prakashan.

Hacker, Paul. 1958. "Ānvīkṣikī." *Wiener Zeitschrift für die Kunde Südasiens* 2: 54–83.

Halbfass, Wilhelm. 1988. *India and Europe: An Essay in Understanding*. Albany: State University of New York Press.

Hara, Minoru. 1973. "The King as Husband of the Earth (*mahī-pati*)." *Asiatische Studien/Études Asiatiques* 27: 97–114.

———. 1980. "Hindu Concepts of Teacher. Sanskrit *guru* and *ācārya*." In *Sanskrit and Indian Studies*, ed. M. Nagatomi, B. K. Matilal, J. M. Masson, and E. Dimock, 93–118. Dordrecht: Reidel.

———. 1994–95. "*Bhartṛ-piṇḍa-niṣkraya*—The Hindu Concept of Loyalty to the Kings." *Bulletin of the Deccan College Post-Graduate and Research Institute* 54–55: 299–311.

Harihara Sastri, G. 1956–1957. "Notes on the Arthaśāstra of Kauṭalya." *Journal of Oriental Research* 26: 107–113.

———. 1945–1946. "Some Terms of Kauṭalīya Arthaśāstra in the Light of Commentaries." *Journal of Oriental Research* 8: 352–357.

———. 2011. *Two Commentaries on the Arthaśāstra: Jayamaṅgalā & Cāṇakyaṭīkā*. see under Editions and Translations.

Heesterman, Jan. 1985. "Kauṭilya and the Ancient Indian State." In *The Inner Conflict of Tradition*, 128–140. Chicago: Chicago University Press.

Hinüber, Oskar von. 1971. "Zur Technologie der Zuckerherstellung im alten Indien." *ZDMG* 121: 94–109.

———. 1972. "Das Nandyāvarta-Symbol." *ZDMG*, Supplement II: 356–365.

———. 1978. "Probleme der Technikgeschiche im alten Indien." *Saeculum* 29: 215–230.

———. 2005. "Der *bhūmicchidranyāya*." *ZDMG* 155: 483–495.

Hultzsch, E. 1919. "Zu Aśvaghoṣa's Saudarananda." *ZDMG* 73: 229–232.

Jacobi, Hermann. 1920. "Einteilung des Tages und Zeitmessung im alten Indien." *ZDMG* 74: 247–263.

Jamison, Stephanie W. 1997. "Sanskrit pāriṇāhya 'household goods': Semantic Evolution in Cultural Context." In *Festschrift Eric Hamp*, ed. D. Q. Adams. Vol. I. *Journal of Indo-European Studies Monograph* 23: 139–45.

Janert, Von Klaus L. 1965. "Studien zur den Aśoka-Inschriften." *ZDMG* 115: 88–119.

———. 1967–1968. "Recitations of Imperial Messengers of Ancient India." *Adyar Library Bulletin* 31/32: 511–518.

———. 1973. "About the Scribes and their Achievements in Aśoka's India." In *German Scholars on India: Contributions to Indian Studies*. Vol. 1, 141–145. Varanasi: Chowkhamba.

Jayaswal, K. P. 1924. *Hindu Polity.* 2 vols. in one. Calcutta: Butterworth.

Johnson, W. J. 1998. *The Sauptikaparvan of the Mahābhārata: The Massacre at Night.* Oxford: Oxford University Press.

Johnston, E. H. 1929. "Two Studies in the Arthaśāstra of Kauṭilya." *Journal of the Royal Asiatic Society of Great Britain and Ireland* 1: 77–102.

———. 1936. "Cattle Theft in the *Arthaśāstra.*" *Journal of the Royal Asiatic Society,* No. 1: 79–83.

Jolly, Julius. 1880. *The Institutes of Vishnu.* Oxford: Clarendon Press.

———. 1885. *Outlines of an History of the Hindu Law of Partition, Inheritance, and Adoption.* Tagore Law Lectures 1883. Calcutta: Thacker, Spink, and Co.

———. 1889. *The Minor Law-Books: Nārada, Brihaspati.* Sacred Books of the East 33. Oxford: Clarendon Press.

———. 1913. "Arthaśāstra und Dharmaśāstra," *ZDMG* 67: 49–96.

———. 1914–15. "Kollektaneen zum Kauṭilīya Arthaśāstra." *ZDMG* 68: 345–359; 69: 369–378.

———. 1916–18. "Textkritische Bemerkungen zum Kauṭilīya Arthaśāstra." *ZDMG* 70: 547–554; 71: 227–239, 414–428; 72: 209–223.

———. 1920. "Das erste Buch des Kauṭilīya Arthaśāstra." *ZDMG* 74: 321–355.

———. 1927. "Kauṭilya oder Kauṭalya." *Zeitschrift für Indologie und Iranistik* 5: 216–221.

Kane, P. V. 1926. "The Arthaśāstra of Kauṭilya." *Annals of the Bhandarkar Oriental Research Institute* 8: 83–100.

———. 1962–1975. *History of Dharmaśāstra.* 5 vols. Poona: Bhandarkar Oriental Research Institute.

Kangle, R. P. 1964a. "The Vyasanas according to Kauṭilya." *Indian Antiquary* (3rd Series) I: 145–153.

———. 1964b. "Manu and Kauṭilya." *Indian Antiquary* (3rd series) I: 48–54.

———. 1965. *The Kauṭilīya Arthaśāstra.* Part III: A Study. Bombay: University of Bombay.

Kirtikar, K. R., and B. D. Basu. 2001. *Indian Medicinal Plants with Illustrations.* 2nd ed.; 1st ed. 1918. Dehra Dun (India): Oriental Enterprises.

Kölver, Bernhard. 1982. "Kauṭalya's *piṇḍakara*—Reconsidered." In *Indology and Law: Studies in Honor of Professor J. Duncan M. Derrett,* ed. Günter-Dietz Sontheimer and Parameswara Kota Aithal, 168–184. Wiesbaden: Steiner.

———. 1985. "Kauṭalyas Stadt als Handelszentrum: der Terminus *puṭabhedana-.*" *ZDMG* 135: 299–311.

Konow, Sten. 1945. *Kauṭilya Studies.* Oslo: Dybwad. Reprint: Delhi: Oriental Publishers, 1975.

Kosambi, D. D. 1965. *The Culture and Civilization of Ancient India in Historical Outline.* London: Routledge and Kegan Paul.

Laping, Johannes. 1982. "Aspekte der Stadt im altindischen Staatslerhrbuch des Kauṭilya." In *Städte in Südasiens: Geschichte Gesellschaft Gestalt,* ed. Hermann Kulke, Hans Christoph Rieger, and Lothar Lutze. Wiesbaden: Steiner.

Lariviere, Richard W. (ed. and tr.). 2003. *The Nāradasmṛti.* 2nd ed. Delhi: Motilal Banarsidass.

Lévi, Sylvain. 1936. "Alexander and Alexandria in Indian Literature." *Indian Historical Quarterly* 12: 121–133.

Lienhard, Siegfried. 1978. "On the Meaning and Use of the Word *Indragopa.*" *Indologica Taurinensia* 6: 177–188.

Lingat, Robert. 1962. "Les quatre pieds du procés." *Journal Asiatique* 250: 489–503.

———. 1973. *The Classical Law of India.* Tr. J. D. M Derrett. Berkeley: University of California Press.

Lüders, Heinrich. 1940a. "Die Śaubhikas." In *Philologica Indica,* 391–428. Göttingen: Vandenhoeck & Ruprecht.

———. 1940b. "Sanskrit *ālāna.*" Ibid., 77–78.

Machiavelli. 1988. *The Prince.* Tr. by Quentin Skinner and Russell Price. Cambridge: Cambridge University Press.

Macri, Maria Vittoria. 1988. *Lexicon Phytonimicum (Therapeutica ex Suśrutasaṃhitā).* Torino: Pubblicazioni del CESMEO.

McClish, Mark. 2009. *Political Brahmanism and the State: A Compositional History of the* Arthaśāstra. Ph.D. dissertation, University of Texas at Austin.

———. 2012. "Is the *Arthaśāstra* a Mauryan Document?" In Olivelle et al. 2012, 280–303.

McGee, Mary. 2000. "State Responsibility for Environmental Management: Perspectives from Hindu Texts on Polity." In *Hinduism and Ecology,* ed. C. K. Chapple and M.E. Tucker, 59–101. Cambridge: Harvard Center for the Study of World Religions.

Meyer, J. J. 1927. *Über das Wesen der Altindischen Rechtsschriften und ihr Verhältnis zu einander und zu Kauṭilya.* Leipzig: Harrassowitz.

Mital, Surendra Nath. 1976. "The Relation Between the Social System and the State in Kauṭilya's Arthaśāstra." *Annals of the Bhandarkar Oriental Research Institute* 57: 77–91.

Modelski, George. 1964. "Kautilya: Foreign Policy and International System in the Ancient Hindu World." *The American Political Science Review* 58, No. 3: 549–560.

Nadkarni, K. M. 1976. *Indian Materia Medica.* Revised ed., 2 vols. Bombay: Popular Prakashan.

Narayanan, M. G. S. 1993. "Product-associated Place-names in the Arthasastra." *Studies in Indian Place Names* 14: 21–35.

Ojha, K. C. 1952. "On the Controversy about the *Arthaśāstra.*" *Indian Historical Quarterly* 28: 265–272.

Olivelle, P. 1987. "King and Ascetic: State Control of Asceticism in the Arthaśāstra." *Adyar Library Bulletin* 50: 39–59.

———. 1993. *The Āśrama System: The History and Hermeneutics of a Religious Institution.* New York: Oxford University Press.

———. 1996. "*Dharmaskandhāḥ* and *brahmasaṃsthaḥ:* A Study of *Chāndogya Upaniṣad* 2.23.1." *JAOS* 116: 205–219.

———. 1997. *The Pañcatantra*. Oxford: Oxford University Press.

———. 1998. "Caste and Purity: A Study in the Language of the Dharma Literature." *Contributions to Indian Sociology* 32: 190–216.

———. 2002. "*Abhakṣya* and *abhojya:* An Exploration in Dietary Language." *JAOS* 122: 345–354.

———. 2004a. "Manu and the Arthaśāstra." *Journal of Indian Philosophy* 32: 281–291.

———. 2004b. "Rhetoric and Reality: Women's Agency in the *Dharmaśāstras*." In *Encounters with the Word: Essays to Honour Aloysius Pieris.*, ed. R. Crusz, M. Fernando, and A. Tilakaratne, 489–505. Colombo: Ecumenical Institute for Study and Dialogue.

———. 2009. "The Temple in Sanskrit Legal Literature." In *Temple in South Asia*, ed. H. P. Ray. Delhi: Oxford University Press.

———. 2010. "Dharmaśāstra: A Literary History." In *Hinduism and Law: An Introduction*. Ed. Timothy Lubin, Donald R. Davis Jr., and Jayanth K. Krishnan, 28–57. Cambridge: Cambridge University Press.

———. 2011. "War and Peace: Semantics of *saṃdhi* and *vigraha* in the *Arthaśāstra*." *Pūrvāparaprajñābhinandanam: East and West, Past and Present, Indological and Other Essays in Honour of Klaus Karttunen*, 131–139. Studia Orientalia 10. Helsinki: Finnish Oriental Society.

———. 2012a. "Material Culture and Philology: Semantics of Mining in Ancient India." *JAOS* 132: 23–30..

———. 2012b. "Patañjali and the Beginnings of Dharmaśāstra: An Alternate Social History of Early Dharmasūtra Production." In *Aux dabords de la clairière*. Ed. Caterina Guenzi and Silvia d'Intino, 117–133. Paris: Brepolis..

———. 2012c. "Differing Roles of Judge in the Arthaśāstra and Dharmaśāstras." Paper presented at the 15th World Sanskrit Conference, New Delhi, Jan. 5–10, 2012.

Olivelle, P., and H. P. Ray and J. Leoshko (ed.). 2012. *Reimagining Aśoka: Memory and History*. Delhi: Oxford University Press.

Pandey, V. C. 1979. "Some Corroborative Evidences from the Arthaśāstra of Kauṭilya." In *Indologica Taurinensia* 7: 339–344.

Paramhans, S. A. 1984. "Units of Measure in Medieval India and their Modern Equivalents." *Indian Journal of History of Science* 19(1): 27–36.

Parpola, Asko. 2002. "Πανδαίη and Sītā: On the Historical Background of the Sanskrit Epics." *JAOS* 122: 361–373.

Parpola, Asko, and Juha Janhunen. 2011. "On the Asiatic Wild Asses (Equus hemionus & Equus kiang) and their Vernacular Names." Revised version. In *Linguistics, Archaeology, and the Human Past*, Occasional Papers 12, ed. Toshiki Osada and Hitoshi Endo, 59–124. Kyoto: Indus Project, Research Institute for Humanity and Nature.

Pollock, Sheldon. 1985. "The Theory of Practice and the Practice of Theory in Indian Intellectual History." *JAOS* 105: 499–519.

———. 1989a. "The Idea of Śāstra in Traditional India." In Dallapiccola 1989, 17–26.

———. 1989b. "Playing by the Rules: Śāstra and Sanskrit Literature." In Dallapiccola 1989, 301–312.

———. 1990. "From Discourse of Ritual to Discourse of Power in Sanskrit Culture." *Journal of Ritual Studies* 4: 316–45.

———. 2005. *The Ends of Man at the End of Premodernity*. Amsterdam: Royal Netherlands Academy of Arts and Sciences (Gonda Lecture).

———. 2006 *The Language of the Gods in the World of Men: Sanskrit, Culture, and Power in Premodern India*. Berkeley: University of California Press.

Prater, S. H. 1997. *The Book of Indian Animals*. Bombay Natural History Society. Reprint. Delhi: Oxford University Press.

Raghavan, V. 1951. "Kālidāsa and Kauṭilya." *Proceedings and Transactions of the All-India Oriental Conference, Thirteenth Session, Nagpur University, October 1946*, 102–108.

———. 1945–1946. "On a Meaning of the Word kauśika." *Journal of Oriental Research* 15: 110–116.

Rau, Wilhelm. 1974. *Metalle und Metallgeräte im vedischen Indien*. Mainz: Akademie der Wissenschaften und der Literatur.

Ray, Kumar Ranjan. 1966. *An Introductory Study of Kautilya's Arthashastra*. Calcutta: K. Ray.

Renou, Louis. 1961. "Sur la forme de quelques textes sanskrits: Le Kauṭilīya." *Journal Asiatique* 249: 183–197.

———. 1963. "Sur le genre du sūtra dans la littérature Sanskrite." *Journal Asiatique* 281: 163–216.

Ritschl, Eva. 1997. "Überlegungen zu aṭavi und anderen Gruppen der Anārya-Bevölkerung im alten Indian nach Sanskritquellen." In *Recht, Staat und Verwaltung im klassischen Indien*, ed. Bernard Kölver, 245–253. München: Oldenbourg.

Ritschl, Eva, and Maria Schetelich. 1973. *Studien zum Kauṭilīya Arthaśāstra*. Berlin: Akademie-Verlag.

Rocher, Ludo. 1954. "The Technical Term '*anubandha*' in Sanskrit Legal Literature." *Annals of the Bhandarkar Oriental Research Institute* 35: 221–228.

———. 1958. "The Ambassador in Ancient India." *The Indian Yearbook of International Affairs* 7: 344–360.

———. 1968. *The Purāṇas*. History of Indian Literature, ed. Jan Gonda, Vol. II, Fasc. 3. Wiesbaden: Harrassowitz.

———. 1975. "Notes on the Technical Term *sāhasa* 'Fine, Pecuniary Penalty.' " In *Sanskrit and Indological Studies: Dr. V. Raghavan Felicitation Volume*, ed. R. N. Dandekar et al., 515–531. Delhi: Motilal Banarsidass.

———. 1978. "Avyāvahārika Debts and Kauṭilya 3.1.1–11." *Journal of the Oriental Institute* (Baroda) 28: 17–20.

———. 1981. "A Note on *ṣāḍguṇya*." In *Ācārya-Vandanā: D. R. Bhandarkar Birth Centenary Volume*. Ed. Samaresh Bandyopadhyay, 319–325. Calcutta: University of Calcutta.

———. 1985. "The *Kāmasūtra:* Vātsyāyana's Attitude toward Dharma and Dharmaśāstra." *JAOS* 105: 521–529.

Sadhale, Nalini. 1996. *Surapala's Vrikshayurveda*. Secunderabad: Asian Agri-History Foundation.

Salles, Jean-François. 2007. "Travelling to India without Alexander's Log-Books." In *Memory as History: The Legacy of Alexander in Asia*, ed. Himanshu Prabha Ray and Daniel T. Potts, 157–169. New Delhi: Aryan Books.

Samozvantsev, A. M. 1980–1981. "Arthaśāstra and Dharmaśāstra: Two Traditions." *Indologica Taurinensia* 8–9: 353–363.

———. 1983. "The Dharmaśāstra: Ritual and Juridical Terminology (Concerning One Trend in Its Functional Evolution)." *Archív Orientální* 51: 116–128.

Scharfe, Hartmut. 1967. "Satzphrasen (*varga*) in einigen Inschriften Aśokas." *ZDMG* 117: 146–147.

———. 1968. *Untersuchungen zur Staatsrechtslehre des Kauṭalya*. Wiesbaden: Harrassowitz.

———. 1977. *Grammatical Literature*. A History of Indian Literature, ed. Jan Gonda. Vol. V.2. Wiesbaden: Harrassowitz.

———. 1979 "Kauṭalya on Conflicts within the Ruling Class." In *Indologica Taurinensia* 7: 387–391.

———. 1987. "Nomadisches Ergut in der indischen Tradition." In *Hinduismus und Buddhismus: Festschrift für Ulrich Schneider*, ed. Harry Falk, 300–308. Freiburg: Hedwig Falk.

———. 1989. *The State in Indian Tradition*. Leiden: Brill.

———. 1993. *Investigations in Kautilya's Manual of Political Science* (revised English version of Scharfe 1968). Wiesbaden: Harrassowitz.

———. 2002. *Education in Ancient India*. Handbook of Oriental Studies, II: 16. Leiden: Brill.

Schetelich, Maria. 1997. "Die maṇḍala-Theorie in Artha- und Nītiśāstra." In *Recht, Staat und Verwaltung im klassischen Indien*, ed. Bernard Kölver, 211–237. München: Oldenbourg.

Schlingloff, D. 1965. "Arthaśāstra-Studien, I. Kauṭilya und Medhātithi." *Wiener Zeitschrift für die Kunde Südasiens* 9: 1–38.

———. 1967. "Arthaśāstra-Studien II. Die Anlage einer Festung (*durgavidhāna*)." *Wiener Zeitschrift für die Kunde Südasiens* 11: 44–85.

———. 1968. "Bhūmigṛha." *Journal of the Oriental Institute* (Baroda), XVII: 345–352.

———. 1969. *Die altindsche Stadt: Eine vergleichende Untersuchung*. Abhandlungen der geistes- und sozialwissenschaftliches Klasse, Nr. 5. Wiesbaden: Steiner.

———. 2012. *Fortified Cities of Ancient India: A Comparative Study*. London: Anthem. Contains English translations of Schlingloff 1967 and 1969.

Shah, H. A. 1919–1920. "Kautilya and Kalidasa." *Journal of the Mythic Society of Bangalore* 10: 303–317.

Shah, K. J. 1981. "Of artha and the Arthasastra." *Contributions to Indian Sociology* (n.s.), 15, 1–2: 55–73.

Sharma, J. P. 1968. *Republics in Ancient India c. 1500 B.C.—500 B.C.* Leiden: Brill.

Sharma, P. V. 1979. *Fruits and Vegetables in Ancient India.* Jaikrishnadas Ayurveda Series, 28. Varanasi: Chaukhamba.

Sharma, Y. D. 1950–1951. "Building Laws in the Arthaśāstra." *Journal of Oriental Research* 20: 5–10.

Sil, N. P. 1989. *Kauṭalya's Arthaśāstra: A Comparative Study.* New York: Peter Lang.

Sinha, B. P. 1954. "The King in the Kauṭilian State." *The Journal of the Bihar Research Society* 40: 277–308.

Sircar, D. C. 1964. "Dharmādhikaraṇa and Dharmādhikārin." *Purāṇa* 6.2: 445–450.

———. 1966. *Indian Epigraphical Glossary.* Delhi: Motilal Banarsidass.

Slaje, Walter. 2001. "Water and Salt (I): Yājñavalkya's *saindhava dṛṣṭānta* (BĀU II 4, 12)." *Indo-Iranian Journal* 44: 25–57.

Sontheimer, Günther-Dietz. 2004. "Religious Endowments in India: the Juristic Personality of Hindu Deities." In *Essays on Religion, Literature and Law,* ed. H. Brückner, A. Feldhaus, and A. Malik, 15–68. New Delhi: Manohar.

Spellman, John W. 1964: *Political Theory of Ancient India. A Study of Kingship from the Earliest Times to circa A.D. 300.* Oxford: Oxford University Press.

Stein, Otto. 1921. *Megasthenes und Kauṭilya.* Wien: Hölder.

———. 1925. "Ευριγξ und *suruṅgā.*" *Zeitschrift für Indologie und Iranistik* 3: 280–347. Reprint in *Kleine Schriften.* Stuttgart: Steiner, 1985, 1–42.

———. 1928a. "Versuch einer Analyse des *śāsanādhikāra.*" *Zeitschrift für Indologie und Iranistik* 6: 45–71.

———. 1928b. "Pāṇḍyakavāṭa." *Indian Historical Quarterly* 4: 778–782.

———. 1935–1938. "Arthaśāstra and Śilpaśāstra." *Archív Orientální* 7 (1935): 473–478; 8 (1936): 69–90; 10 (1938): 163–209.

Sternbach, Ludwik. 1951. "Legal Position of Prostitutes According to Kauṭilya's *Arthaśāstra.*" *JAOS* 71: 25–60.

———. 1953. *Gaṇikā-vṛtta-saṃgraha: Or Texts on Courtezans in Classical Sanskrit.* Hoshiarpur: Vishveshvarananda Vedic Research Institute.

———. 1963. *Cāṇakya-Rāja-Nīti.* Adyar Library Series, 92. Adyar: Adyar Library.

———. 1972. "Place and Time of King's Counsel with Ministers according to the Dharmaśāstra-s, Arthaśāstra-s and Subhāṣita-saṃgraha-s." In *India Maior: Congratulatory Volume Presented to J. Gonda,* ed. J. Ensink and P. Gaeffke, 200–207. Leiden: Brill.

———. 1973. *Bibliography of Kauṭilīya Arthaśåstra.* Hoshiarpur: Vishveshvaranand Institute.

Strong, John. 2012. "The Commingling of Gods and Humans, the Unveiling of the World, and the Descent from Trayastriṃśa Heaven: An Exegetical Exploration of the Connections of Minor Rock Edict I to Buddhist Legendary Literature." In Olivelle et al., 2012, pp. 342–355.

Sullivan, Bruce M. 1999 (1990). *Seer of the Fifth Veda: Kṛṣṇa Dvaipāyana Vyāsa in the Mahābhārata*. Delhi: Motilal Banarsidass.

Thapar, Romila. 2000. *Cultural Pasts: Essays in Early Indian History*. Delhi: Oxford University Press.

Thite, G. U. 1982. *Medicine: Its Magico-Religious Aspects according to the Vedic and Later Literature*. Poona: Continental.

Tieken, Herman. 2006. "Aśoka's Fourteenth Rock Edict and the Guṇa *mādhurya* of the Kāvya Poetical Tradition." *ZDMG* 156: 95–115.

Tokunaga, Muneo. 1993. "Structure of the *Rājadharma* Section in the Yājñavalkyasmṛti (i. 309–368)." Kyoto: Kyoto University Research Information Repository (http://hdl.handle.net/2433/73058).

———. 1997. *The Bṛhaddevatā: Text Reconstructed from the Manuscripts of the Shorter Recension with Introduction, Explanatory Notes, and Indices*. Kyoto: Rinsen Book Co.

———. 2005 "On the Origin of the *Leśyās*." *The Journal of Philosophical Studies* (University of Kyoto), No. 580: 1–11.

Trautmann, Thomas. 2012. *Arthaśāstra: The Science of Wealth*. New Delhi: Allen Lane/Penguin.

———. 1971. *Kauṭilya and the Arthaśāstra: A Statistical Investigation of the Authorship and Evolution of the Text*. Leiden: Brill.

———. 1968. "A Metrical Original for the *Kauṭilīya Arthaśāstra*?" *JAOS* 88: 347–349.

Trivedi, Harihar V. 1934. "The Geography of Kauṭilya." *Indian Culture* 1: 247–261.

van Buitenen, J. A. B. 1973–1978. *Mahābhārata*. 3 vols (books 1–5). Chicago: University of Chicago Press.

Vigasin, A. A., and A. M. Samozvantsev. 1985. *Society, State and Law in Ancient India*. New Delhi: Sterling.

Wackernagel, Jakob von. 1957–1975. *Altindische Grammatik*. 3 vols. Göttingen: Vandenhoeck & Ruprecht.

Waldauer, Charles, William J. Zahka, and Surendra Pal. 1996. "Kautilya's Arthashastra: A Neglected Precursor to Classical Economics." *Indian Economic Review* 31.1: 101–108.

Wezler, Albrecht. 2000a. "Some Remarks on the 135th *Adhikaraṇa* of the 'Kauṭilīya' *Artha-śāstra* Entitled 'Policy towards *Sa? gha*.' " In *On the Understanding of Other Cultures*. Special issue of *Studia Indologiczne* 7: 489–503.

———. 2000b. "*Sampad* of Bhagavadgītā XVI Reconsidered." In *Harānandalaharī: Volume in Honour of Professor Minoru Hara on His Seventieth Birthday*, ed. Ryutaro Tsuchida and Albrecht Wezler, 433–455. Reinbek: Verlag für Orientalistische Fachpublikationen.

———. 1997. "The Story of Aṇī-Māṇḍavya as Told in the Mahābhārata: Its Significance for Indian Legal and Religious History." In *Beyond Orientalism: The Work of Wilhelm Halbfass and its Impact on Indian and Cross-Cultural Studies*, ed. Eli Franco and Karin Preisendanz, 533–555. Amsterdam: Rodopi.

———. 1993. "Über Form und Charakter der sogenannten 'Polemiken im Staatslehrbuch des Kauṭalya': Untersuchungen zum *'Kauṭilīya' Arthaśāstra* II." *ZDMG* 143: 106–134.

———. 1977. *Die wahren "Speiseresteesser" (Skt. vighasāśin)*. Beiträge zur Kenntnis der indischen Kultur- und Religionsgeschichte I. Akademie der Wissenschaften und der Literatur. Abhandlungen der Geistes- und Sozialwissenschaftlichen Klasse, Jahrgang 1978. Nr. 5. Wiesbaden: Franz Steiner.

———. 1975. "Some Observations on the *Yuktidīpikā*." *ZDMG*, Supplement III.1: XIX: 434–455.

Wilhelm, Friedrich. 1960. *Politische Polemiken im Staatslehrbuch Kauṭilyas*. Münchener Indologische Studien, Bd. 2. Wiesbaden: Harrassowitz.

———. 1967–1968. "The Eighteen Dignitaries (*tīrthas*)." *Adyar Library Bulletin* 31–32: 152–157.

Will, Elizabeth Lyding. 1991. "The Mediterranean Shipping Amphoras from Arikamedu." In Begley and De Puma 1991, 151–156.

Willis, Michael. 2009. *The Archaeology of Hindu Ritual: Temples and the Establishment of the Gods*. Cambridge: Cambridge University Press.

Winternitz, Moritz. 1926–1928. "Dharmaśāstra and Arthaśāstra." *Sir Asutosh Memorial Volume*, 26–48. Patna: J. N. Samaddar.

Wojtilla, Gyula. 2006. *History of Kṛṣiśāstra: A History of Indian Literature on Traditional Agriculture*. Beiträge zur Kenntnis südasiatischer Sprachen und Literaturen, 14. Wiesbaden: Harrassowitz.

———. 2005. "The Sītādhyakṣaprakaraṇa of the Arthaśāstra." In *Indische Kultur im Kontext: Rituale, Texte und Ideen aus Indien und der Welt*. Festschrift für Klaus Mylius, ed. Lars Göhler, 413–425. Wiesbaden: Harrassowitz.

———. 2009. "Ratnaśāstra in Kauṭilya's Arthaśāstra (KA)." *Acta Orientalia Academiae Scientiarum Hung.* 62: 37–44.

———. 2010. "Some Remarks on the Agricultural Terminology of the Arthaśāstra." In *From Turfan to Ajanta: Festschrift for Dieter Schlingloff on the Occasion of his Eightieth Birthday*, ed. Eli Franco and Monika Zin, 1001–1027. Lumbini, Nepal: Lumbini International Research Institute.

———. 2011. "Glossary: A Collection of Words Pertaining to Sanskrit Agricultural Vocabulary." *Acta Antiqua et Archaeologica*, 31. Szeged: Acta Universitatis Szegediensis.

Wujastyk, Dominik. 2003. *The Roots of Ayurveda: Selections from Sanskrit Medical Writings*. Revised ed. London: Penguin.

Yagi, Toru. 1994. "A Note on *bhojya-* and *bhakṣya*." In *A Study of the Nīlamata: Aspects of Hinduism in Ancient Kashmir*, ed. Yasuke Ikari, 377–397. Kyoto: Kyoto University.

Zimmerman, Francis. 1987. *The Jungle and the Aroma of Meats: An Ecological Theme in Hindu Medicine*. Berkeley: University of California Press.

Index